ISBN 978-0-266-15140-1
PIBN 10923538

English
Français
Deutsche
Italiano
Español
Português

www.forgottenbooks.com

Mythology Photography **Fiction**
Fishing Christianity **Art** Cooking
Essays Buddhism Freemasonry
Medicine **Biology** Music **Ancient**
Egypt Evolution Carpentry Physics
Dance Geology **Mathematics** Fitness
Shakespeare **Folklore** Yoga Marketing
Confidence Immortality Biographies
Poetry **Psychology** Witchcraft
Electronics Chemistry History **Law**
Accounting **Philosophy** Anthropology
Alchemy Drama Quantum Mechanics
Atheism Sexual Health **Ancient History**
Entrepreneurship Languages Sport
Paleontology Needlework Islam
Metaphysics Investment Archaeology
Parenting Statistics Criminology
Motivational

REPORTS

OF

CASES AT LAW AND IN EQUITY

DETERMINED BY THE

SUPREME COURT

OF THE

STATE OF IOWA.

DECEMBER 15, 1897—APRIL 6, 1898.

BY

BENJ. I. SALINGER.

VOLUME XV,

BEING VOLUME CIV OF THE SERIES.

DES MOINES, IOWA:
GEO. H. RAGSDALE, PUBLISHER.
1898.

JUDGES OF THE SUPREME COURT

DURING THE TIME OF THESE REPORTS.

L. G. KINNE, Des Moines, *Chief Justice.*

H. E. DEEMER, Red Oak.*

GIFFORD S. ROBINSON, Sioux City.

CHAS. T. GRANGER, Waukon.

JOSIAH GIVEN, Des Moines.

SCOTT M. LADD, Sheldon.

CHARLES M. WATERMAN, Davenport.

OFFICERS OF THE COURT.

MILTON REMLEY, Iowa City, *Attorney General.*

C. T. JONES, Washington, *Clerk.*

BENJ. I. SALINGER, Carroll, *Reporter.*

---

*The term of Chief Justice Kinne expired December 31, 1897, being succeeded by Mr. Justice Waterman, and, thereupon, Mr. Justice Deemer became Chief Justice by order of rotation.

JUDGES OF THE COURTS

FROM WHICH APPEALS MAY BE TAKEN TO THE SUPREME COURT.

DISTRICT COURTS.

First District—HENRY BANK, JR., Keokuk.

Second District—M. A. ROBERTS, Ottumwa; T. M. FEE, Centerville; F. W. EICHELBERGER, Bloomfield; ROBERT SLOAN, Keosauqua.

Third District—H. M. TOWNER, Corning; W. H. TEDFORD, Corydon.

Fourth District—WM. HUTCHINSON, Orange City; GEO. W. WAKEFIELD, Sioux City; F. R. GAYNOR, Le Mars; JOHN F. OLIVER, Onawa.

Fifth District—J. H. APPLEGATE, Guthrie Center; J. H. HENDERSON, Indianola; A. W. WILKINSON, Winterset; JAMES D. GAMBLE, Knoxville.

Sixth District—DAVID RYAN, Newton; BEN MCCOY, Oskaloosa; A. R. DEWEY, Washington.

Seventh District—C. M. WATERMAN, Davenport; W. F BRANNAN, Muscatine; P. B. WOLFE, Clinton; A. J. HOUSE, Maquoketa.

Eighth District—MARTIN J. WADE, Iowa City.

Ninth District—W. F. CONRAD, CALVIN P. HOLMES, THOMAS F. STEVENSON, W. A. SPURRIER, Des Moines.

Tenth District—J. J. TOLERTON, Cedar Falls; A. S. BLAIR, Manchester.

Eleventh District—D. R. HINDMAN, Boone; S. M. WEAVER, Iowa Falls; BENJAMIN P. BIRDSALL, Clarion.

Twelfth District—JOHN C. SHERWIN, Mason City; J. F. CLYDE, Osage.

Thirteenth District—L. E. FELLOWS, Lansing; A. N. HOBSON, West Union.

Fourteenth District—LOT THOMAS, Storm Lake; WILLIAM B. QUARTON, Algona.

Fifteenth District—A. B. THORNELL, Sidney; WALTER I. SMITH, Council Bluffs; N. W. MACY, Harlan; W. R. GREEN, Audubon.

Sixteenth District—S. M. ELWOOD, Sac City; Z. A. CHURCH, Jefferson.

Seventeenth District—GEORGE W. BURNHAM, Vinton; OBED CASWELL, Marshalltown.

Eighteenth District—H. M. REMLEY, Anamosa; WILLIAM G. THOMPSON, Marion.

Nineteenth District—FRED O'DONNELL, Dubuque; JAMES L. HUSTED, Dubuque.

Twentieth District—JAMES D. SMYTH, Burlington; WINFIELD S. WITHROW, Mt. Pleasant.

SUPERIOR COURTS.

Cedar Rapids—THOMAS M. GIBERSON.

Council Bluffs—J. E. F. MCGEE.

Keokuk—JOSEPH C. BURK.

IN MEMORIAM.

JOHN C. BILLS.

On the twenty-third day of August, 1897, John C. Bills, a leading member of the bar of the state and of this court, departed this life at his home in Davenport.

On October 12, 1897, E. E. Cook presented memorial proceedings of the Scott county bar on his death, and after appropriate remarks by E. E. Cook, Fred Heinz, Nathaniel French, L. A. Ellis and N. M. Hubbard on behalf of the bar, and by Justice Robinson and Chief Justice Kinne on the part of the court, it was ordered that the proceedings of the Scott county bar be entered of record in this court. It was accordingly done, and they follow:

MEMORIAL ON THE DEATH OF HON. JOHN C. BILLS.

It is customary when a member of this bar dies, to spread upon the records of the court a memorial, that those who come after us may know the manner of man he was—how his associates regarded him When the greatest among us dies, a plain recital of the record he has made, is the most fitting tribute to his memory

John C. Bills came to Davenport in 1856, and spent his professional life a member of this bar.

He represented the county for four years in the state senate, and was recognized as the leader of his party He made a creditable record as the advocate of good laws, but a better one as the eloquent denouncer of bad ones.

He was for ten years a member and president of the school board of this city. He gave to the discharge of the duties of the position the same fidelity and devotion and hard work as to his most lucrative employment. He gave to our schools an efficiency and comprehensiveness of scope unequaled by any schools of the state. He was for three terms mayor of Davenport, and there made a record equal to the best. His administration was judicious, liberal, and able. He was energetic and fearless in enforcing law and maintaining order. As in all his public positions, he was utterly regardless of public opinion, in the sense that he did not cater to it, nor was he influenced by its surface manifestations. He formed his own ideas of duty, his own measure of the public's rights; solved for himself public problems. His judgments formed, he frankly stated them and fearlessly carried them into execution. He never posed for effect nor adopted the low artifices of the demagogue. In all his relations with the public or with society, he abhorred hypocrisy, detested sham. It is sufficient tribute to the honesty of his purpose and the wisdom of his judgment, that he commanded the commendation of the best public opinion.

It is as a lawyer that we can best measure his greatness. He was content to be only a lawyer. He never sought honors or distinction or success outside his profession. Public honors were thrust upon him.

His sturdy, strong, physical build; forceful, keen, rugged and retentive mental faculties; natural combativeness; intense strength of feeling, and command of forceful language, made a magnificent foundation upon which to develop the world's greatest example of human development—a great lawyer.

The aids he used were energetic continued application, the acquisition of a large store of general knowledge, complete mastery of the facts and law of every case he tried in court. No case was trivial with him, after he accepted a retainer. It was then a case to be studied—understood—to be won. No lawyer at this bar went into court with a better knowledge of all the evidence obtainable in the case, and of all the law bearing upon the questions at issue.

Having been enlisted in a client's cause, no oath-bound soldier was ever more devoted or loyal or true to the cause he fought for. He made the cause his own. He never doubted its justness or its merit of success. If he was merciless to opposing witnesses and parties and attorneys, it was because they threatened the sacred rights of his client.

In the trial of causes he was fair and honorable. He sought no secret, underhand advantages, but all the time he was vigilant, ingenious, persistent, relentless, and resourceful in pressing on court and jury the claims of his client. After such a trial, he went before a jury so seemingly sincere and honest, and sure of his position and the sacred justness of his cause, that by the overmastering influence of his aggressive intensity he wrung a verdict from them.

He was a trained mental athlete, who always kept himself in training, ever ready for the most severe contest.

The contest over, professional duties put aside, Mr. Bills was the most companionable of men. Those only who knew him well, knew that he was kind-hearted, sociable, witty, and interesting. His mind was more than a store-house of legal propositions; reminiscence, anecdote, repartee, all flowed in a broad stream of enjoyment for his companions He was toastmaster of our first bar banquet—pressed into the service at a moment's notice; he filled the position as no other could; he sparkled and scintillated with a brilliancy of humor that we will never forget.

It is a satisfaction to us to recall that when John C. Bills lived, we conceded him the foremost place; that we made him the first president of this bar association, and freely acknowledged him a great lawyer, a leader of men, a sincere friend. At his death, while we mourn our loss, we can do no more

TABLE OF CASES REPORTED

IN THIS VOLUME.

A

Agne v Seitsinger........... 482
Allamakee County, et al,
  Broderick v.............. 750
Allison's Estate, In re 130
Anchor Mut. Fire Ins. Co.,
  Medearis et al. v 88

B

Bailey et al , Sloss v........... 696
Bailor, State v. 1
Bankers' Alliance Ins. Co. of
  California, Schoep v....... 354
Barrett, Muecke v......... ... 418
Bauernfiend et al. v. Jonas et
  al. 56
Beach, Hoyt v.............. 257
Bebber et al., Sigmond et al.v. 431
Beem v Tama & Toledo Elec-
  tric R'y & Light Co........ 563
Beeman v. Farmers' Pioneer
  Mut Ins Assn............ 83
Behren's Estate, In re........ 29
Bernstein et al., Carrier v.... 572
Berry et al., Hays v. 455
Binford et al , Wescott et al. v. 645
Board of Sup'rs of Harrison
  County et al., Noyes et al. v. 174
Boston Inv. Co. v. Pacific
  Short-Line Bridge Co..... 311
Bourrett v Palo Alto County 850
Bracken, Miller Co v........ 648
Broderick v. Allamakee
  County et al 750
Brooke v. King............. 718
Brown et al., Floete v........ 154
Brown et al , Wood et al. v.. 124
Burlington, C R & N. R'y Co.
  v. City of Columbus Junc-
  tion et al 110
Burlington, C. R. & N. R'y
  Co., Fisher v.............. 588
Burroughs et al , Watson v.. 745

C

Callanan v Votruba........ 672
Cameron v Tucker et al ... 211
Carrier v Bernstein et al ... 572

Cathcart v. Grieve et al....... 330
Chambers v. Illinois Cent R'y
  Co....... 238
Chambers v. Oehler et al 278
Chancy Park Land Co. v.
  Hart 592
Charleton, Robinson et al. v . 296
Cheney et al. v. McColloch et al 249
Chicago, B & Q. R'y Co. Sar-
  ver v...................... 59
Chicago & N-W. R'y Co,
  Faust v.............. ... 241
Chicago & N-W. R'y Co.,
  McLeod v............ 189
Chicago & N-W. R'y Co.,
  Smith v 147
Chicago M & St. P. R'y Co ,
  Kingsbury v............ 68
Chicago, M. & St P. R'y Co.,
  Riley v................ 285
Chicago, M. & St P. R'y Co ,
  Waterbury v............. 82
Chicago, R. I. & P. R'y Co ,
  Christie v................ 707
Chicago. R I & P. R'y Co ,
  Dalton v 26
Chown et al., Marsh v....... 556
Christie v. Chicago, R I. & P.
  R'y Co 707
City of Cedar Falls v. Hansen 189
City of Columbus Junct et
  al., Burlington, C. R & N.
  R'y Co v....... 110
City of Davenport, Peters v.. 625
City of Lyons et al , Osburn
  et al v 160
City of Muscatine, Reed v... 188
Clark v Ellsworth 442
Clark, McCoy v 491
Clark, Reizenstein v....... 287
Clay et al v Maynard Savings
  Bank et al...... 748
Clever et al., Hyatt v 338
Close et al , Davis v 261
Cole v. Edwards et al....... 373
Commercial State Bank, Met-
  ropolitan National Bank et
  al v...................... 683

(ix)

Cone, McGregor v........... 465
Cooper v. Mohler 801
Council Bluffs Ins. Co., Weigen v............. 410
Crawford, McWhirter v...... 550
Cresap, Payne v............. 749

D

Dalton v. Chicago, R. I. & P.
R'y Co..................... 26
Davenport v. Olerich 194
David et al. v Hardin County 204
Davis v. Close et al......... 261
Day v. Goodwin et al........ 374
Debolt et al., State v......... 105
Dee & Sons Co. v. Key City
Fire Ins Co........... 187
De Kalb v. Hingston........ 28
Dennis et al., Higgins v...... 605
Des Moines Marble & Mantel
Co., Vorse v............... 541
Dixon, State v. 741
Doolittle v. Smith ..... _ 408
Douglas, Fidelity Loan &
Trust Co. v................ 532
Dunham, Pierce v........... 749

E

Edwards et al., Cole v....... 873
Ellsworth, Clark v........... 442
Engelthaler & Hasek v. Linn
County.................... 293
Ewell, Sherod v............. 253
Exchange Bank of Leon et
al v. Gardner et al......... 176

F

Farmers' Pioneer Mut. Ins.
Assn., Beeman v.... 88
Farrer v. Farrer............. 621
Faust y. Chicago & N. W. R'y
Co 241
Fidelity Loan & Trust Co. v.
Douglas................... 532
Fielding v. La Grange et al.. 580
Fisher v. Burlington, C. R. &
N. R'y Co................. 588
Floete v. Brown et al........ 154
Fred Miller Brewing Co. v.
Hansen et al............... 307
Frey-Sheckler Co. v. Iowa
Brick Co.................. 494
Fry et al., Garner et al. v.... 515

G

Gardner et al., Exchange
Bank of Leon et al. v..... 176

Garner et al. v. Fry et al 515
Garretson et al., Valley Nat.
Bank v 655
Gensburgh v. Marshall Field
& Co..................... 599
German State Bank v. Northwestern Water & Light Co.
et al...................... 717
Giddings et al. v. Iowa Sav.
Bank of Ruthven.......... 676
Gifford et al., Phillip v. 458
Goodwin et al., Day v 374
Greenlee et al. v. Hanover
Ins. Co................... 481
Grieve et al., Cathcart v. ... 880
Grieve v. Illinois Cent R'y
Co........................ 659

H

Hamilton et al, Williams v.. 423
Hanover Ins Co., Greenlee et
al. v..................... 481
Hansen, City of Cedar Falls v 189
Hansen's Empire Fur Factory
v. Teabout et al 360
Hansen et al, Fred Miller
Brewing Co. v............ 307
Hansen et al, Security Fire
Ins. Co. v................ 264
Hardin County, David et al v. 204
Harrison v Stebbins et al.... 462
Harrison v. Palo Alto County 388
Hart, Chancy Park Land Co.
v......................... 592
Hartman Steel Co. v. Hoag &
Son....................... 269
Hays v. Berry et al.......... 455
Hazen, State v.............. 16
Hersey, Wilenburg v........ 699
Higgins v. Dennis et al...... 605
Hingston, DeKalb v 28
Hipsley v. Price et al....... 282
Hoag & Son, Hartman Steel
Co. v..................... 269
Holmes v. Redhead... 399
Hoyt v. Beach 257
Hubbell, Stout et al, v....... 499
Hyatt v. Clever et al........ 838

I

Illinois Cent. R'y Co., Chambers v.................... 238
Illinois Cent. R'y Co., Grieve
v......................... 659
In re Assignment of Shoukwiler..................... 67
In re Allison's Estate 130
In re Behren's Estate........ 29
In re Doolittle...... 403

In re David et al............ 204
In re Kauffman's Estate..... 639
In re Smith et al............ 199
Iowa Brick Co., Frey-Sheckler
    Co. v.................... 494
Iowa Cent. R'y Co., McFall v. 47
Iowa Sav. Bank of Ruthven,
    Giddings et al. v.......... 676

J

Jacobs, Kiburz v............ 580
Jamison State v 343
Johnston et al. v. Robuck et
    al......................... 523
Jonas et al , Bauernfiend et
    al. v.................. ... 56
Jones et al , Van Vechten v.. 436

K

Kauffman's Estate, In re..... 639
Keller v. S rong 585
Kent, Metcalfe v 487
Key City Fire Ins Co., Dee &
    Son's Co v............... 167
Kiburz v. Jacobs............ 580
Kimble, State v............. 19
King, Brooke v............. 713
King, State v 727
Kingsbury v. Chicago, M. &
    St. P. R'y Co.......... 63
Kinney v. Kinney 703
Kleppish et al., Moore v..... 319

L

La Grange et al., Fielding v. 530
Ledbetter, White v......... 71
Lewis et al , Odden v........ 747
Life Indemnity & Security
    Co , Pray v 114
Linn County, Engelthaler &
    Hasek v............. 203
Long et al., Steel v 89
Lucas County, Twinam v.... 231

M

Mahoney et al. v. McCrea.... 785
Marsh v. Chown et al........ 556
Marshall Field & Co., Gens-
    burgh v.. 599
Maynard Sav. Bank et all.,
    Clay et al. v.............. 748
McCartney et al , Polk v..... 567
McClintock et al., Spurrier v. 79
McCollock et all , Cheney et
    al. v 249
McCoy v. Clark.............. 491

McCrea, Mahoney et al. v.... 785
McDonough, State v......... 6
McFall v. Iowa Cent. Ry. Co. 47
McGregor v. Cone........... 465
McLeod v. Chicago & N. W.
    Ry. Co.................. 189
McWhirter v. Crawford...... 550
Medearis et al , v. Anchor
    Mut. Fire Ins Co.. 88
Metcalfe v. Kent 487
Metropolitan Nat. Bank et al.,
    v. Commercial State Bank. 682
Miller v. Miller............. 186
Mill Co v. Braken........... 643
Mohler, Cooper v........... 361
Monroe et al , Salyers v 74
Moore v. Kleppish et al 319
Moore et al., Tower v 345
Moran v. Moran et al........ 216
Muecke v. Barrett........... 418

N

Names v. Union Ins. Co..... 612
Northwestern Water & Light
    Co et al., German State
    Bank v.................... 717
Northern Inv. Co. et al., Stet-
    son v..................... 398
Noyes et al. v. Board of
    Sup'rs of Harrison County
    et al...................... 174

O

Odden v. Lewis et al........ 747
Oehler et al., Chambers v.... 278
Olerich, Davenport v. 194
Osburn et al. v. City of Lyons
    et al...................... 160

P

Pacific Short-Line Bridge Co.,
    Boston Inv. Co. v......... 311
Palo Alto County, Bourrett v. 850
Palo Alto County, Harrison v. 883
Payne v. Cresap 749
Peters v. City of Davenport.. 625
Phillips v. Gifford et al...... 458
Pierce v. Dunham. 749
Polk v. McCartney et al..... 567
Polk County v. Kauffman.... 639
Pratt v. Prouty 419
Pray v. Life Idemnity &
    Security Co............... 114
Price et al , Hipsley v........ 282
Prouty, Pratt v.............. 419

R

Redhead, Holmes v.......... 399
Reed v. City of Muscatine... 188

Reilly, State v........ 18
Reisenstein v. Clark......... 287
Repp, State v...... 305
Riley v. Chicago, M. & St. P.
   R'y Co...... 285
Risser et al , Sutton v. 631
Robinson et al. v. Charleton. 296
Robuck et al , Johnston et al.
   v....................... 523
Rowe, State v 328

S

Salyers v. Monroe et al....... 74
Sarver v. Chicago, B. & Q. R'y
   Co....................... 59
Schoep v. Bankers Alliance
   Ins. Co. of California...... 354
Security Fire Ins. Co. v. Han-
   sen et al................. 264
Seitsinger, Agne v... 482
Shea, State v................ 724
Sherod v Ewell............. 253
Shonkwiller et al. v. Stewart
   et al. 67
Sigmond et al. v. Bebber et al. 481
Skillicorn, State v........... 97
Sloss v. Bailey et al......... 696
Smith v. Chicago & N.-W. R'y
   Co....................... 147
Smith, Doolittle v........... 403
Smith et al , In re 199
Spurrier v McClintock et al. 79
State v. Bailor..... 1
State v. Debolt et al 105
State v. Dixon.............. 741
State v. Hazen. 16
State v. Jamison............. 348
State v. Kimble. 19
State v. King................ 727
State v. McDonough. 6
State v. Reilly.............. 18
State v. Repp............ ... 305
State v. Rowe.............. 328
State v. Shea 724
State v. Skillicorn.... 97
State v. Stevenson, Judge ... 50
State v. Young 730
Stebbins et al., Harrison v... 462
Steel v. Long et al 89
Stetson v. Northern Inv. Co.
   et al..................... 893

Stevenson, Judge, State v ... 50
Stewart et al v. Shonkwiller v 67
Stout et al v Hubbell....... 499
Strong, Keller v............. 585
Stuart, Young v............. 597
Sutton v. Risser et al...... . 631

T

Tama & Toledo Electric R y
   & Light Co , Beem v...... 563
Tantlinger, Trimble v....... 665
Teabout et al., Hansen's Em-
   pire Fur Factory v........ 360
Tower v. Moore et al....... 345
Trimble v. Tantlinger....... 665
Tucker et al. Cameron v..... 211
Twinam v. Lucas County.... 281

U

Union Ins. Co., Names v..... 612

V

Valley Nat. Bank v. Garret-
   son et al..... 255
Van Vechten v. Jones et al.. 436
Vorse v. Des Moines Marble
   & Mantel Co 541
Votruba, Callanan v......... 672

W

Walker v. Walker............ 505
Walrod, Younie et al., v ... 475
Waterbury v. Chicago, M &
   St. P. Ry Co.... 32
Watson v. Burroughs et al... 745
Weigen v. Council Bluffs Ins.
   Co....................... 410
Wescott et al , Binford et al. 645
White v. Ledbetter.......... 71
Wilenburg v. Hersey.... ... 699
Williams v. Hamilton et al... 423
Wood et al., v. Brown et al. . 124

Y

Young, State v.............. 730
Young v Stuart............. 595
Younie et al., v. Walrod 475

REPORTS

OF

CASES AT LAW AND IN EQUITY

DETERMINED BY THE

SUPREME COURT

OF

THE STATE OF IOWA

AT

DES MOINES, OCTOBER TERM, A. D. 1897,

AND IN THE FIFTY-SECOND YEAR OF THE STATE.

State of Iowa v. Ed. Bailor, Appellant.[*]

Rape: AGE OF CONSENT. In a prosecution for rape upon a female child under the age of fifteen years, under Code 1873, section
1 3861, as amended by Laws Twenty-sixth General Assembly, chapter 70, fixing the age of consent at fifteen years, it is immaterial that the prosecutrix is large of her age, physically strong, and of a romping disposition, as the defendant was guilty of rape whether the sexual intercourse was against her will or not.

INSTRUCTIONS: *Conflict.* An instruction that, in determining whether or not a rape had been committed, the jury should consider the prosecutrix's demeanor, condition, and declarations, immediately after the alleged commission, does not conflict with an instruction
2 that in case they found the crime had been committed, they should not consider the prosecutrix's conduct, declarations, nor condition, in determining whether or not she was corroborated in charging the defendant with it.

*The figures on the left of the syllabi refer to corresponding figures placed on the margin of the case at the place where the point of the syllabus is decided.

Newly Discovered Evidence. Two witnesses, in affidavits filed in support of a motion for a new trial on the ground of newly discovered evidence, after defendant was convicted of rape, testified that the prosecutrix told them the defendant "had never done
4   anything to her," but upon being cited before the court, and examined orally, with the prosecutrix, it appeared that her statements referred to her being pregnant only. *Held*, not ground for a new trial.

Venue: PROOF OF. An allegation in an indictment that a crime was committed within the county is sufficiently established by evidence as to the places where certain persons reside, and as
8   to where the defendant went, from which the alleged fact may be inferred.

Appeal from Mills District Court.—HON. W. R. GREEN, Judge.

WEDNESDAY, DECEMBER 15, 1897.

THE defendant was indicted, tried, and convicted of the crime of rape, upon a female under the age of fifteen years, alleged to have been committed in Mills county, Iowa, on the twenty-fourth day of December, 1896. His motion for a new trial was overruled, and judgment of imprisonment in the penitentiary for the period of five years rendered against him, from which he appeals.—*Affirmed.*

W. S. Lewis, L. T. Genung, and *Henry J. Baird* for appellant.

Milton Remley and *Jesse A. Miller* for the state.

GIVEN, J.—I. Defendant offered to prove that the prosecutrix was of a romping disposition, that she had wrestled with boys of the neighborhood, and was physically strong, for the purpose, as was said at the time,
       "to show the improbability of the story she tells
1   on the witness stand." The state objected, on the ground of immateriality, which objection was sustained. The prosecutrix had testified that she

would be fourteen years old on the second day of April, 1897; that on the night of the twenty-fourth day of December, 1896, while defendant was taking her to her home in his top buggy, and when they were alone, he had sexual intercourse with her; that she tried to get out of the buggy; that he held her in; that he had one arm around her neck; and that she called for her mother. It is contended that this evidence offered was material, as tending to show her physical ability to resist the defendant, and to prevent the intercourse. The argument ignores the distinction made in our statute between this crime when committed upon a female of the age of fifteen years or more and one under that age. Section 3861 of the Code of 1873, as amended by chapter 70 of the Laws of the Twenty-sixth General Assembly, and then in force, is as follows: "Sec. 3861. Rape. If any person ravish and carnally know any female of the age of fifteen years or more, by force and against her will, or carnally know and abuse any female child under the age of fifteen years, he shall be punished by imprisonment," etc. The evidence is undisputed that the prosecutrix was under the age of fifteen years. Therefore it was immaterial whether the sexual intercourse was by force and against her will, or not, so far as the question of guilt was concerned.

II. The defendant complains of the sixth and seventh paragraphs of the charge, as being contradictory. The prosecutrix testified, in addition to what has already been stated, that she was crying when she got home, and that she then told her father that "Ed Bailor had tried to get ahead of me." Her father and mother testified to substantially the same. Her father stated that he heard an outcry about fifteen minutes before she came in, and her mother stated that she examined the girl's clothing, and found a wet slime spot on her skirt. A physician testified as to the result of an examination made by him of the prosecutrix on the twenty-ninth day of December, 1896, and other physicians gave their opinion based upon what was observed on that examination, as to whether sexual intercourse had taken place. In the sixth para-

2   graph the court instructed that, in determining whether the offense had been committed by some person, this evidence should be considered. It is not questioned but that it may be found that the crime was committed, upon the testimony of the prosecutrix alone, and that the corroboration required is as to the defendant's connection therewith. That it may be found on the testimony of the prosecutrix alone does not exclude from consideration evidence tending to corroborate her as to the fact that the crime was committed by some person. The evidence showed that these persons were alone in the buggy at a late hour in the night, while driving, three-quarters of a mile to her home. There was also evidence as to the conduct of the defendant when arrested, claimed to be inconsistent with his innocence. In the seventh paragraph the court instructed that, if they found that some person did in fact have intercourse with the prosecutrix, they should consider this evidence in determining whether she is corroborated in charging that it was the defendant. Surely, this evidence tended to connect the defendant with the commission of the crime, and to corroborate the prosecutrix in her testimony that he did commit it. If the crime was committed when and where it is claimed, it must have been by the defendant. The court further instructed that, in determining whether the prosecutrix was corroborated in charging that it was the defendant who committed the crime, they should not consider her evidence, nor the evidence as to her conduct, declarations, or condition when she arrived at home. She could not corroborate herself by her own

acts or declarations, and her condition does not necessarily point to the defendant. While this evidence was
competent to show that the crime was committed, it
does not tend to connect the defendant therewith. These
instructions are not contradictory, but a plain and con-
cise statement of the law, and as favorable to the
defendant as he could ask.

III.   The defendant moved for a verdict at the
close of the evidence for the state, and for a new trial
after the verdict, upon the ground that the evidence was
insufficient to sustain a verdict. We will not set out
nor discuss the evidence in detail. Much of the argument in support of this contention ignores the distinction arising from the age of the prosecutrix. This girl
being under fifteen years of age, the real contention is
whether the defendant did carnally know and abuse
her at the time and place charged. We have examined
the evidence with care, and are of the opinion that
under it the jury was warranted in finding as it
3   did. It is insisted that the state failed to prove
that the crime was committed in Mills county.
It is true that no witness so said in direct terms, but,
taking the evidence as to the places where certain persons resided and the direction the defendant and prosecutrix drove, there can be no doubt on this subject.

Another ground of the motion for a new trial is
newly discovered evidence, which the defendant was
unable to ascertain and procure before the trial. This
motion is supported by the affidavits of two wit-
4   nesses, to the effect that the prosecutrix said
that defendant had never done anything to her,
but only tried to, and by the affidavits of defendant and
his counsel showing diligence. The court ordered that
said two witnesses appear for oral examination, and
they and the prosecutrix were examined as to said
statements. Their evidence shows that the statements
of the prosecutrix were with reference to her not being

pregnant, and not that the defendant had not had sexual intercourse with her.

Question is made whether a new trial may be granted in a criminal case because of newly discovered evidence. It is not so expressed in the Code, as it is with respect to civil cases. It is provided that a new trial in criminal cases may be granted "when from any cause the defendant has not received a fair and impartial trial." Defendant's counsel insist that, if it appears from newly discovered evidence that the trial has not been fair or impartial, a new trial should be granted. Let this be conceded; yet we think the newly discovered evidence is not such as to show that the trial had was not a fair and impartial one. Our conclusion is that there was no error in either of the respects complained of, and the judgment is therefore AFFIRMED.

STATE OF IOWA v. JAMES McDONOUGH, Appellant.

6}
9

Rape: MENTAL CAPACITY: *Evidence.* It was competent to show
  the appearance, condition, and actions of the prosecutrix at
6 and for some time prior to the time of the commission of the
  offense, to prove mental capacity, by non-expert witnesses.

SAME: *Plea and proof.* Evidence of the mental weakness of the
  prosecutrix was admissible as bearing on the question of consent,
7 though it was not alleged in the indictment that she was feeble
  minded.

INCLUDED OFFENSES. Assault with the intent to inflict great bodily
9 injury is not necessarily included in a charge of rape, and the
  court need not instruct respecting it.

Same. It was not necessary to instruct respecting a simple assault,
  where the evidence showed that, if defendant was guilty of an
9 assault, he also committed a battery.

SAME. The court in a trial for rape need not instruct, the defendant
  may be found guilty of a simple assault, although evidence of
10 such an assault, made by the defendant upon the prosecutrix
  after he was placed under arrest, was given, where he was not

tried for that offense, but for an assault included in the crime charged.

Evidence: TIMELY OBJECTION. A motion to strike out certain evidence as irrelevant and immaterial, was correctly overruled, where no objection was lodged against such evidence until after
4   it was fully adduced, and where it constituted a part of the history of the crime charged.

EVIDENCE: *Reputation.* In a prosecution for rape the character of
2   the prosecutrix may be proved by evidence of general reputation,
8   but testimony as to particular acts or specific facts is not admissible.

Same. In a trial for rape, testimony offered to show certain acts of the prosecutrix in wrestling with persons other than the defend-
8   ant in an unbecoming manner, is inadmissible when it is not shown that such improper conduct occurred before the commission of the alleged offense, and as being evidence of specific acts.

HARMLESS ERROR. In a trial for rape where the prosecutrix was enticed from a dance hall by one of the defendants and taken to a stone quarry, where drunken men were carousing, by several of
5   whom she was ravished, evidence of the presence of such defendant and the complaining witness at the dance hall and as to what occurred at the quarry prior to their arrival there, is not prejudicial to the defendant on the trial, when the jury were instructed not to consider any acts or statements of other defendants not made in the presence and hearing of the accused.

Change of Venue. A change of venue need not be granted in a trial for rape, by reason of sensational newspaper articles in reference
8   to the crime, which allege that the organization of a vigilance committee is seriously contemplated. and that it might take a hand in the proceedings if the preliminary trial is unduly prolonged, when no feeling against the defendant pervades the county, although some exists in the vicinity where the crime was committed.

Continuance. A motion made by defendant, in a trial for rape, for a continuance, based upon the absence of two witnesses, will not be granted where no excuse is made for the delay in making the
1   application, nor any facts constituting diligence in endeavoring to procure the attendance of the witnesses set forth, and when most of the facts expected to be proved by them are immaterial and irrelevant.

Appeal from Johnson District Court.—HON. P. B. WOLFE, Judge.

WEDNESDAY, DECEMBER 15, 1897.

The defendant, with four other persons, was indicted for the crime of rape. He demanded and was granted a separate trial, resulting in a verdict of guilty of an assault with intent to commit rape, and from the sentence imposed appeals.—*Affirmed.*

Cash & Coldren for appellant.

Milton Remley, attorney general, for the state.

Deemer, J.—In the early evening of August 25, 1896, Emma Gromas, a feeble-minded unmarried woman, was induced by one McGuan to leave a dance hall in Iowa City, and go with him to an old stone quarry, across the Iowa river, and west from Iowa City, where they met some men who had been there all the previous night, indulging their thirst for beer, and making night hideous with their ribaldry and song. The woman claims that she was ravished while there by at least four of these men, and in this she is corroborated by other witnesses. The state introduced evidence to show that the defendant was one of the men who committed the crime.

When the case came on for trial, the defendant filed a motion for a continuance, based upon the absence of two witnesses, who, it was claimed, would testify to certain acts of unchastity on the part of the pros-
1   ecutrix prior to the time the offense is said to have been committed. The motion was not filed until the day the case was reached for trial, and it did not state any facts excusing the delay in making the application; nor did it set forth any facts constituting diligence in endeavoring to procure the attendance of

these witnesses. Moreover, most of the facts that
defendant expected to prove by these witnesses
2 were immaterial and irrelevant. In prosecutions for rape, the character of the prosecutrix
must be proven by evidence of general reputation.
Particular acts or specific facts are not admissible.
See cases cited in 5 Am. & Eng. Enc. Law (2d ed.) p. 878;
1 McClain, Criminal Law, section 460. For these reasons
the motion was properly overruled.

II. The men were discovered in their bestiality
early in the morning, and a posse was organized in
Iowa City to accomplish their arrest. This posse went
to the scene of the disorder, and, after some difficulty,
succeeded in arresting all but two of the crowd. In
endeavoring to land them in jail, one of the prisoners
was killed by the deputy sheriff. The discovery
3 of the crime and the killing of one of the prisoners necessarily led to considerable newspaper
comment and quite a little excitement among the people of Iowa City. When the case was called for trial,
the defendant filed a motion for change of place of
trial. This motion was supported by affidavits of three
disinterested persons, and to it were attached some of
the newspaper articles written near the time of the
commission of the offense. The state also filed affidavits in resistance. The affiants to the motion were
cross-examined upon their affidavits, and, after fully
considering the matter, the trial court overruled the
motion, remarking at the time: "The order asking for
a production of witnesses, and the affidavit filed by the
county attorney in resistance to the motion for a change
of venue, is by the court refused, for the reason that it
is apparent to the court from the trial of same issues in
the case tried agai1st one of these defendants, and from
the examination made of these defendants, that no
such prejudice exists in this county as would justify

the court in granting the change of venue, as the court takes notice of the fact of a case involving this same question, in this same indictment, and one of the same parties defendant, was tried in the court, and the jury examined in that case. That coupled with the affidavits filed in resistance to the motion and the affidavit filed for the change of venue, and the examination of these parties who made the affidavit for the change of venue, satisfies the court that there is no ground which would warrant him in granting a change of venue in this case, or wasting time in examining all those who are required on the examination. Therefore the motion for change of venue is refused." Consideration of the cross-examination of the affiants who made oath to the motion for a change of venue convinces us that there was no such prejudice against this defendant in Johnson county as interfered with his having a fair trial. There was some feeling against all the defendants in and around Iowa City, but it did not pervade any other part of the county. Generally speaking the newspaper articles contained nothing more than a somewhat sensational statement of the facts as the reporter gleaned them at the time. In one of the articles it is said that the organization of a vigilance committee is seriously contemplated by the decent element of both town and county, with a view to dissipating a reign of crime, which the writer said prevailed in the county at the time. The article further said that threats were made that, if pettifogging were adopted to prolong the preliminary trial, this committee might take a hand in the proceedings, and make a final disposition of the matter. The showing is not nearly as strong as in the cases of *State v. Weems,* 96 Iowa, 426, and *State v. Hamil,* 96 Iowa, 728, wherein like motions were overruled; and we are fully satisfied that the trial court did not abuse its discretion in overruling the motion.

III. The court permitted the state to show what was done at the stone quarry on the day and night before the crime is said to have been committed, and also allowed in evidence certain statements 4   with reference to the presence of McGuan and the prosecuting witness at the dance hall in Iowa City on the evening of August 24. After the evidence was adduced, defendant's counsel moved to strike it out, because of irrelevancy and immateriality. The motion was overruled, and we think the ruling was correct. No objection was lodged against the evidence until it was fully adduced. Defendant appeared to be willing to take his chances on the evidence being against him, and he cannot, after it is admitted without objection, be heard to complain. Again, the 5   court said, in its instructions to the jury, that they should not consider any statements or actions of the other defendants not in the immediate presence and hearing of this defendant. Moreover, it does not appear with certainty when the defendant joined the crowd at the stone quarry. Nearly all of them had gone there on the twenty-fourth, with beer and provisions, evidently to make a night of it; and the preparations made by them immediately preceding the commission of the offense were a part of the history of the crime. The same may be said with reference to the evidence as to the presence of McGuan and the prosecuting witness at the dance hall on the evening of the twenty-fourth.

IV. Witnesses were allowed to testify as to the appearance, condition, and actions of the prosecutrix at the time of the crime, and for some time prior to the commission of the offense, for the purpose of showing that a crime had been committed upon her, and 6   that she was in fact feeble-minded. Two objections were lodged against this evidence: *First,* it is said it is incompetent, because it came from non-

expert witnesses; and, *second*, because it is not alleged
in the indictment that the prosecutrix was feeble-
minded.   There is no merit in either objection.

7   Evidence as to the conduct and condition of the
prosecutrix, when material, may be shown by
non-expert witnesses.   *State v. Shelton,* 64 Iowa, 333;
Pelamourges v. Clark, 9 Iowa, 1; *Parsons v. Parsons,*
66 Iowa, 754; Rogers, Expert Testimony (2d ed.), section 4.   Proof of the prosecutrix's strength or condition of mind is admissible without an allegation in
the indictment that she was feeble-minded.   Evidence
of mental capacity is admissible as bearing upon the
question of consent, although the indictment was not
framed under the provisions of section 3863 of the
Code of 1873.   *State v. Philpot,* 97 Iowa, 365; *State v.
Tarr,* 28 Iowa, 397; *State v. Atherton,* 50 Iowa, 189.

V.   Defendant offered to show certain acts of the
prosecutrix in wrestling with persons other than
defendant in an unbecoming manner.   The evidence
was properly rejected, because specific acts are
8   not admissible (see authorities heretofore cited),
and for the further reason that it does not appear
that it was before the commission of the alleged offense.

VI.   The court did not instruct that the defendant might be found guilty of an assault with intent to
inflict a great bodily injury, or of a simple assault.
The former offense is not necessarily included in
9   a charge of rape, and the court need not instruct
with reference to it.   *State v. McDevitt,* 69 Iowa,
549.   While both an assault and an assault and battery are included in the charge, yet the evidence in this
case shows that, if defendant was guilty of an assault,
he also committed a battery, and there was therefore

no error in the charge.   *State v. Sigg*, 86 Iowa, 746;
10   *State v. Beabout*, 100 Iowa, 155.   There was,
it is true, some evidence which tended to show
a simple assault made by the defendant upon the
prosecutrix after he was placed under arrest; but he
was not on trial for this offense.   It was for an assault
included in the crime charged that he was upon trial.
The state asked for no conviction for the subsequent
assault, and the evidence was brought out as an incident of the arrest, and not as substantive proof of the
commission of a crime.

We have gone over this entire record with care,
and discover no prejudicial errors.   There is no question in our minds of the defendant's guilt, and the judgment is AFFIRMED.

STATE OF IOWA V. PATRICK REILLY, Appellant.

Seduction: LAW OF THE CASE.   A conviction of the crime of seduction will not be sustained, when the court instructed the jury
that the case rested entirely on an alleged promise of marriage,
and that if the prosecutrix assented to the intercourse upon the
5   defendant's promise to marry her should pregnancy result therefrom, they should find for the defendant, where the testimony of
the prosecutrix was that the promise of marriage was conditioned
upon her getting in a family way.

Evidence: RESERVED RULING: *Appeal.*   Where defendant moved to
strike out an answer of a witness, and the trial court reserved its
1   ruling, and the matter was not again called to its attention,
defendant cannot complain, as there was neither a ruling nor an
exception.

STRIKING OUT: *Curing error.*   In a prosecution for seduction, a certain witness testified that the neighbors, three strange ladies,
prosecutrix and a lady named O, had told her that prosecutrix
and defendant were engaged to be married.   Thereafter the court
4   struck out the evidence of said witness as to what the neighbors said,
and charged that all evidence of other witnesses as to talk among
neighbors about such engagement was withdrawn.   *Held*, that the
statements of the three strange ladies, the prosecutrix, and O, were
not withdrawn, and the error of their admission was not cured.

HARMLESS ERROR. A defendant accused of seduction cannot complain of a refusal to permit the prosecutrix to answer, on cross
examination, whether she ever thought, from his words and
2   conduct prior to her alleged seduction, that he desired to have
connection with her, where he was permitted to inquire of her
what his object and purpose were in going with her.

Same. In a prosecution for seduction, the error of permitting prose-
3   cutrix's doctor to testify that the prosecutrix had stated that she
was unmarried was cured by prosecutrix's testimony to that effect.

Appeal from Dubuque District Court.—HON. FRED
O'DONNELL, Judge.

WEDNESDAY, DECEMBER 15, 1897.

DEFENDANT was indicted, tried, and convicted of
the crime of seduction, and from the sentence imposed
appeals.—*Reversed.*

Horatio B. Smith and *George T. Lyon* for appellant.

Milton Remley, attorney general, and *Jesse A.
Miller* for the state.

DEEMER, J.—The prosecuting witness testified that
she was induced to surrender her virtue by reason of a
promise of marriage, and, in response to a question,
said that she had told her friends that she
1   intended to marry defendant. Defendant moved
to strike out this answer. The trial court reserved
its ruling, and it does not appear that the matter was
again called to its attention. As there was neither
ruling nor exception, the defendant cannot complain.
II.   Counsel, upon cross-examination, asked the
prosecuting witness whether she had ever thought,
from the conduct of defendant, and from what he had

said to her prior to her alleged seduction, that he
desired to have connection with her. Objection
2   to this question was sustained, but the court said
that counsel might show, if they could, what
defendant's object and purpose was in going with her.
This they attempted to do by further interrogatories,
and we see no ground for complaint.

III. A doctor who made an examination of the
prosecutrix was permitted to testify that she (the prosecutrix) said to her (the doctor) that she was
3   unmarried. The error, if any, in this, was cured
by subsequent evidence from the woman herself
that she was unmarried.

IV. A witness was permitted to state, over the
defendant's objection, that the neighbors and three
certain strange young ladies told her that they had
.   heard that the prosecutrix was engaged to marry
4   the defendant. This same witness testified, over
defendant's objection, that the prosecutrix and
a lady by the name of Oster had both told her that
defendant and the prosecutrix were to be married.
These rulings were clearly erroneous. Thereafter the
court struck out the evidence as to what the neighbors said, and also instructed the jury that the evidence
of this witness as to what neighbors had said, and all
the evidence of other witnesses as to reputation, or talk
or absence of talk, among neighbors of the parties, as
to their being engaged, was withdrawn from their consideration, and should not be considered for any purpose. It will be noticed that the statements made by the
witness as to what the three strange ladies, the prosecutrix, and Miss Oster said about the matter were not
withdrawn; and the error in allowing this evidence
to stand was not cured by instructions or otherwise.
Some other rulings on the admission and rejection of
evidence are questioned. None of them are of sufficient

importance to demand separate consideration, and we dismiss them with the statement that we see no error.

V. Certain of the instructions are assailed. Without setting them out, it is sufficient to say that we discover no error prejudicial to the defendant.

VI. The court instructed that the case rested entirely upon an alleged promise of marriage, and that, if the prosecutrix assented to the intercourse upon the promise of the defendant to marry her should 5   pregnancy result therefrom, then the verdict should be, Not guilty. These instructions constituted the law of the case, and, whether right or wrong, it was the duty of the jury to follow them. We find, on looking to the evidence, that while the prosecutrix testified that she yielded her virtue because of a promise of marriage, yet she said that this promise was a conditional one, to the ‘effect that he (defendant) would marry her if she would let him have intercourse with her and he got her in a family way. The condition was a part of the promise, according to her own evidence; and the jury should have found the defendant not guilty, under the instructions referred to. For the errors pointed out, the judgment is REVERSED.

STATE OF IOWA v. W. W. HAZEN, Appellant.

False Pretenses: INDICTMENT   An indictment for "obtaining property under false pretenses" charged that defendant did designedly, and with intent to defraud, feloniously and falsely represent to L that he was solvent, and worth ten thousand dollars, whereas he was not worth that sum, or any other; that L believed and relied on such representations, which were made knowingly, designedly, and feloniously, to obtain L's signature as security for defendant to a note; that the note so obtained was signed by L, and delivered to the payee; and that the facts that the defendant was not worth ten thousand dollars, nor any other sum, and that he was insolvent, were at the time unknown to L. *Held,* sufficient, under Code 1873, section 4073, providing that if one designedly, and by false pretense, and with intent to defraud, obtains the signature of any person to any writing, the false making of which would be punished as forgery, he shall be punished, though the intent to defraud L was not specifically alleged.

Appeal: VERDICT. A verdict in a criminal case is sustained by the evidence, although the proof on the part of the state is not entirely satisfactory, where it is so materially strengthened by the testimony of the defendant, given in his own behalf, as to authorize the verdict.

Appeal from Jasper District Court.—HON. A. R. DEWEY, Judge.

THURSDAY, DECEMBER 16, 1897.

THE defendant was convicted of the crime of obtaining property by false pretenses, and adjudged to be imprisoned in the state penitentiary at Fort Madison for the period of six months. From that judgment he appeals.—*Affirmed.*

No argument for either party.

ROBINSON, J.—I. The indictment in this case was found under the provisions of section 4073 of the Code of 1873, which contains the following: "If any person designedly and by false pretense, or by any privy or false token, and with intent to defraud, obtains from another any money, goods or other property; or so obtains the signature of any person to any written instrument, the false making of which would be punished as forgery, he shall be punished by imprisonment in the penitentiary. * * *" The indictment accuses the defendant of "the crime of obtaining property under false pretenses," committed by obtaining, by means of false and fraudulent representations, the signature of one H. M. Little to a promissory note. It was claimed by the defendant during the trial, and in a motion filed by him in arrest of judgment, that the indictment was fatally defective in not charging that the note was

obtained by the defendant with intent to cheat and
defraud Little; that it did not sufficiently charge that
the signature of Little was obtained by means of the
false representations alleged; that it did not aver in
express terms, nor in effect, that the defendant
obtained the signature to the note by means of the
alleged false pretenses; and that it fails to show that
the signature was obtained with intent to defraud.
We do not find that any of these claims, so far as they
are material, are well grounded. The indictment
charges explicitly that the defendant did designedly,
feloniously, falsely, and with intent to defraud, feloniously and falsely represent to Little that he, the defendant, was then and there in solvent circumstances, and
worth ten thousand dollars, whereas the truth was he
was not worth that sum, nor any other; that Little
believed and relied upon and was deceived by those
representations, which were made knowingly, designedly, and feloniously, to induce and obtain the signature
of Little as security for the defendant to a promissory
note, a copy of which is set out in the indictment; that
the note so obtained was signed by Little, and delivered
to the payee of the note; and that the fact that the
defendant was not worth the sum of ten thousand dollars, nor any other sum, and that he was wholly
insolvent, were, at the time, wholly unknown to Little.
We think this was sufficient to charge an offense under
the statute. It is true the indictment does not charge
that the representations set out were made with the
specific intent to defraud Little, but the averment of
the indictment in that respect follows the statute, and
is sufficient. If it were true that the indictment should
show a specific intent to defraud Little, we think it must
be sustained; for the language used, fairly construed,
states that the false representations were made to him
to obtain his signature, and that he relied upon and

believed the representations, and in consequence affixed his signature to the note, which was then delivered. That he was defrauded is clear, if the statements are true, and the intent to do just what was done is sufficiently stated. See *State v. McConkey*, 49 Iowa, 499; *State v. Neimeier*, 66 Iowa, 634; *State v. Jamison*, 74 Iowa, 613. We conclude that the indictment is sufficient.

II. A ground of the motion for a new trial is that the verdict was not supported by the evidence. The evidence on the part of the state was not entirely satisfactory, but the defendant testified in his own behalf, and thereby materially strengthened the showing made by the state. We think the evidence was ample to authorize the verdict. We have examined the rulings made on the admission of evidence, and the objections made by the appellant, but without finding any error which was of a character to prejudice the defendant. We are of the opinion that his trial was fair, and according to law, and that his conviction must be sustained. The judgment of the district court is AFFIRMED.

STATE OF IOWA, Appellant, v. J. R. KIMBLE.

Incest: INDICTMENT. Indictment for incest, charging carnal knowl-
1 edge on part of accused only, is sufficient.

Criminal Practice: DEFECTIVE INDICTMENT. Upon the discharge of
  a jury. and the termination of a criminal trial by reason of a
2 defective indictment, the court may in its discretion re-submit
  the case to the grand jury, under Code 1873, section 4450, when
  it will tend to prevent the failure of justice.

SAME. The court may in a criminal trial, when by an objection to the
2 offering of testimony it is pointed out that the indictment does
  not charge a crime punishable by law, discharge the jury and end
  the trial, under Code 1873, section 4444.

DEMURRER. Defendant should demur to indictment on the ground
  that it does not charge a crime (Code 1873, sections 4345, 4352),
3 this not being one of the grounds for which section 4337 authorized the indictment to be set aside on motion.

Appeal from Washington District Court.—HON. A. R. DEWEY, Judge.

THURSDAY, DECEMBER 16, 1897.

THE defendant was charged by indictment with the crime of incest. The case coming on for trial, objection to the introduction of evidence was sustained. A motion to direct a verdict for the defendant was overruled. A motion to re-commit the case to the grand jury, and to hold the defendant as provided in preliminary examinations, was overruled. The jury was discharged from the further consideration of the case, and the defendant was discharged from custody. The state appeals.—*Reversed.*

Milton Remley, attorney general, for the state.

No appearance for appellee.

ROBINSON, J.—The case was called for trial; a jury was impaneled; and a witness sworn in behalf of the state. The defendant at that time objected to the offering of testimony, on the alleged ground that the indictment did not charge the crime of incest, nor any other crime, under the statutes of this state. The objection was sustained, and we infer that subsequent rulings of the court were also based upon the theory that the indictment did not charge a crime.

I.   Section 4337 of the Code of 1873 authorized the setting aside of an indictment upon motion when any one of several grounds specified was shown to exist. That section did not, however, authorize the set-

1   ting aside of an indictment on the ground that it did not charge a crime. That defect could have been presented by demurrer. Code 1873, sections 4345,

4352. In case a demurrer to an indictment were sustained, the court could, on being shown that the defect might be remedied or avoided in another indictment, re-submit the case to another grand jury.   Code 1873, section 4357. The usual and better course for the defendant to pursue when the indictment is believed to be defective is to demur to it. But that was not the 2 only means of defeating a defective indictment.

Section 4444 of the Code of 1873 provided that "the court may also discharge the jury when it appears * * * that the facts as charged in the indictment do not constitute an offense punishable by law;" and section 4450 provided that, "if the jury be discharged because the facts set forth do not constitute an offense punishable by law, the court must order that the defendant, if in custody, be discharged therefrom, or if admitted to bail, that his bail be exonerated, or if he has deposited money instead of bail, that the money deposited be refunded, unless in its opinion, a new indictment can be framed upon which the defendant can be legally convicted, in which case the court may direct that the case be submitted to the same or another grand jury." These sections apply to a case in which the court is convinced after the jury has been impaneled, that the indictment is defective. The method of invoking the action of the court in such a case is not pointed out, and we are of the opinion that the court may act on its own motion without a request from either party. Certainly the court would not be required to permit a useless trial to be continued merely because neither party objected to it. A further reason for not permitting the trial in such a case to proceed is the fact that a conviction or acquittal by a judgment upon a verdict would have barred another prosecution for the same offense. Code 1873, section 4364. In this case the alleged defect was pointed out

by an objection to evidence, and we think that, if
the indictment was defective as claimed, the court was
authorized to refuse to receive evidence, and to end the
trial.   It was within the discretion of the court, if it
believed that a new indictment could be framed upon
which the defendant could be convicted, to re-submit
the case to the same or another grand jury; but the
statute does not require the court to do so, although that
should always be done when it will tend to prevent the
failure of justice.

Numerous authorities have been cited which are
claimed to support the theory that the court erred in
sustaining the objection to the introduction of evidence, but they are from other states, and our decision
in this case rests upon the statutes of this state.   The
objection made by the defendant has been spoken of as
a demurrer to evidence, but, while intended to exclude
evidence, the ruling which sustained it was based upon
the conclusion of the court that, whatever the evidence
might be, it could not authorize a conviction, because
no crime for which a conviction could be had was
charged by the indictment.   The effect of what was
done was to adjudge that the indictment was insufficient in that it did not charge the commission of a
crime.

II.   It is claimed that the indictment was sufficient in law to sustain a conviction for the crime of
incest, and we are told that the defect claimed in the
district court to exist is the omission of the indictment
to aver that the parties to the alleged crime had carnal
knowledge of each other.   The indictment
3   charges that the defendant "did unlawfully and
feloniously carnally know and have sexual intercourse with" the daughter of his wife, but it does not
allege that the daughter had carnal knowledge of him.
The precise question thus presented was determined in

State v. Hurd, 101 Iowa, 391, where we held that an indictment which charged carnal knowledge on the part of the accused only was sufficient. We are of the opinion that the indictment in this case was sufficient, and that the court erred in refusing to receive evidence, and in dismissing the jury, and in discharging the defendant. The judgment of the district court is, for the reasons shown, REVERSED.

B. D. DE KALB v. S. O. HINGSTON, Appellant.

Breach of Contract: CONVEYANCE OF HOMESTEAD. Where a husband agrees to convey a homestead, and received the full consideration therefor, without his wife's concurrence, and failed to make such conveyance, such consideration may be recoveres back, though such contract was void because not concurred in and signed by the wife, as a judgment therefor is for the return of the money obtained by a false pretense, rather than for damages for the breach of a contract to convey a homestead.

Appeal from Clarke District Court.—HON. W. H. TED-FORD, Judge.

THURSDAY, DECEMBER 16, 1897.

THE facts of this case, because of the concessions of counsel that but a single question is to be considered in this court, may be much simplified from those stated in the record or argument. The defendant is the head of a family, and was the owner of one hundred and seven acres of land. The land is designated as two tracts, one containing one hundred acres, and the other seven acres. The east two acres of the seven-acre tract contained the buildings, and was the homestead of the defendant. The transactions between plaintiff and Hingston were such that there was an agreement that Hingston should convey to plaintiff the two tracts, including the homestead. Mrs. Hingston was not a

party to the agreement. A deed was made, signed by
Mr. and Mrs. Hingston, and delivered, but it omitted
the two-acre tract that was the homestead, but was
accepted by plaintiff in the understanding that it was
included. The homestead was afterwards sold to one
Ruffcorn, who is a defendant in the suit, and who sets
up the fact of the purchase of the homestead, and asks
that the title thereto be quieted in him. The petition
asks as a relief that the sale to Ruffcorn be set aside,
and the defendants be required to specifically perform
the agreement to convey, or that, in case such relief
cannot be granted, judgment be rendered against
defendant S. O. Hingston for the sum of one thousand,
five hundred dollars and costs. The district court
denied the relief for specific performance asked by
plaintiff, and quieted the title to the homestead tract
in Ruffcorn, and gave to plaintiff a judgment for one
thousand, two hundred dollars against S. O. Hingston,
and for costs. Defendant S. O. Hingston appealed.—
Affirmed.

Earle & Prouty for appellant.

Harvey & Parrish for appellee.

Granger, J.—Counsel for appellant frankly concede the questions of fact in a way to present a single
legal proposition, and as to what that proposition is
there is but slight controversy. The legal proposition
is entirely controlled by the homestead question
involved. It may be stated that the situation, as
between De Kalb and Hingston, is such that, were
there no homestead rights in the land, plaintiff would
be entitled to a decree for specific performance, which
means that plaintiff bought and paid for the land,
including the homestead, and was deceived by its being
omitted from the conveyance. The district court

denied relief by way of specific performance because of
the homestead character of the land. It is now contended by appellant that, inasmuch as the contract as
to the homestead was void and unenforceable, S. O.
Hingston cannot be held in damages for the failure to
perform such a contract. Appellant states the legal
proposition to be considered, in this way: "Where a
husband agrees to convey a homestead without his
wife concurring, and fails to do so, can he be made to
respond in damages?" Appellee presents the proposition like this: "Where a husband agrees to convey a
homestead, *and receives the full consideration therefor*, without his wife concurring, and fails to do so, can
he be made to refund the money received?" The latter
statement brings the proposition directly in line with
the conceded facts, and has the merit of avoiding the
somewhat uncertain meaning of the term "damages"
in appellant's statement, for there might be a view of
appellant's proposition decidedly favorable to his
claim, for there might be damages, under such a contract, other than a return of money wrongfully received.
Hence we think the latter statement the better, one of
the propositions to be considered. Appellant relies on,
and cities, our holding to the effect that such a contract
as to a homestead, is void, because the wife concurred
therein, and signed the same joint instrument. Appellee
concedes all this, and concedes that he has no claim,
by virtue of the contract, on the homestead, or against
Mrs. Hingston, but maintains that, because S. O. Hingston represented to him that the deed signed by himself
and wife was to, and did, contain the homestead, and
that because of such representation he paid for the
homestead and did not receive it, Hingston should not
be permitted to retain the homestead and the money so
wrongfully taken. To permit appellant to retain the
money is so abhorrent to natural justice that a court

could not and should not give its assent thereto except
in obedience to an undoubted and unyielding rule of
law, and we are not favored with a reference to such a
rule, and have no knowledge of any such. Such a rule
would be a violation of that universal one that denies
to a party a legal right to take advantage of his own
wrong, a rule that has graced the jurisprudence of civ-
ilization throughout its history. The judgment is not,
in the sense contended by appellant, damage for a
breach of the contract to convey a homestead, but
nearer, if not clearly, for a return of money obtained by
a false pretense. We are not in doubt as to the proposition, and the judgment will be AFFIRMED.

MARY E. DALTON, Administratrix of the Estate of
   JAMES DALTON, Deceased, Appellant, v. THE CHI-
   CAGO, ROCK ISLAND & PACIFIC RAILWAY COMPANY.

Evidence: INJURY BY TRAIN. In an action against a railway company to
   recover damages for the death of the plaintiff s intestate, evidence
2 as to the value of a farm of which the deceased was a co-tenant,
   offered as bearing upon the question of damages, is immaterial.

SAME: *Jury question.* It is a question of fact for the jury whether
   the circumstances attending the death of one killed at a railway
   crossing are such as to overcome the presumption that the
1 deceased, prompted by the instinct of self-preservation, exercised
   the care required of him, when no one witnessed the accident nor
   the manner in which the deceased approached and went upon the
   track.

Appeal from Louisa District Court.—HON. D. RYAN,
                  Judge.

THURSDAY, DECEMBER 16, 1897.

ACTION to recover damages for the death of plaintiff's
intestate, alleged to have been caused by the negligence
of defendant. At the close of the evidence on behalf of
the plaintiff, the court, on motion of the defendant,

directed a verdict for the defendant, and rendered
judgment thereon. Plaintiff appeals.—*Reversed.*

Earle & Prouty for appellant.

J. Carskaddan and *L. A. Reiley* for appellee.

GIVEN, J.—I. The accident which resulted in the
death of James E. Dalton occurred about 3:50 o'clock
A. M., December 26, 1894, at the crossing of Linn street
and the defendant's track in the incorporated town of
Lettsville. The night was dark and cold, and the roads
rough. Deceased, seated alone in a somewhat worn,
sidebar, covered buggy, drawn by two horses, when
passing north over said crossing was struck by defendant's fast passenger train going east, and he and the
horses were killed. The negligence charged against
the defendant is that the train was run at a high and
unlawful rate of speed, and without the required signals being given. The grounds of defendant's motion
for a verdict were that the evidence failed to show that
the deceased was free from contributory negligence,
and did show affirmatively that he was guilty of negligence contributing to the accident that resulted
in his death. Appellant contends that the court
erred in sustaining said motion, and, in considering this complaint, we may treat the charges of negligence made against the defendant as established. No
one witnessed the accident, nor the manner in which
the deceased approached and went upon the crossing.
Therefore the question as to whether or not he exercised care must be determined from the known circumstances as shown by the evidence. In view of the
conclusion we reach, we will not set out or discuss these
circumstances. It cannot be questioned that, in going
upon that crossing when he did, the exercise of ordinary care required that the deceased should have

stopped and looked and listened, to know if a train was approaching. It is a recognized rule of human conduct that persons in their sober senses naturally and instinctively seek to avoid danger. Therefore it must be presumed, until the contrary appears, that the deceased, prompted by this natural instinct, did exercise care in approaching and going upon that crossing. It is urged by the appellee that, because of deceased's opportunities to see and hear the approach of the train, if he had stopped and looked or listened, it is evident that he did not do so. It is urged by appellant that because of the absence of required signals, and the unlawful speed of the train, deceased would not have known of its approach by stopping and listening, nor by looking, at the points from which the train could be seen by him. Whether the circumstances are such as to overcome the presumption that deceased, prompted by the instinct of self-preservation, did exercise the care required of him, was a question for the jury. Therefore we think the court erred in sustaining defendant's motion for a verdict. This view finds support in *Hopkinson v. Knapp & Spaulding Co.*, 92 Iowa, 328, and cases therein cited.

II.   Plaintiff offered evidence as to the value of a farm of which her intestate was a co-tenant, as bearing upon the question of damages, which was excluded on defendant's objection. We do not see wherein 2   the value of the farm was material, and we think there was no error in the ruling. For the reason given in the first paragraph of this opinion, the judgment of the district court is REVERSED.

IN THE MATTER OF THE ESTATE OF PHILIPHENE BEHRENS, Deceased.

New Trial. An order entered in a proceeding by an administrator to recover property alleged to belong to the estate which directs the
2 return of a sum of money with interest, will be vacated where the administrator's petition asked for the return of a note.

Appeal. An appeal will lie from a decision which overrules a
1 demurrer to a petition for re-hearing in a proceeding by an
2 administrator to obtain property alleged to belong to the estate.

SAME. The granting of a new trial in a proceeding instituted by an administrator to recover property alleged to belong to the estate,
4 rests in the discretion of the court, and its decision will not be reversed on appeal, in the absence of abuse of such discretion.

RULE APPLIED Defendant was cited under Code 1873, section 2379, to be examined with reference to a writing in his hands which it
1 is claimed belonged to the estate of which petitioner was the administrator. After the close of the term at which the examination was held, the court made an order directing the defendant to pay the administrator three hundred dollars. Defendant petitioned for a re-trial, on the ground that the original petition did
3 not ask a personal judgment against him; that he had no notice thereof until the order was served upon him: that the order was entered in vacation, and without his consent; that he was misled by statements of counsel for the petitioner into believing that no personal claim was made against him; that he never had any money belonging to the estate; that the writing referred to was merely a memorandum made by him as priest at the time the deceased made a gift to the church; that the court in the examination, which was conducted partly in German and partly in English, misunderstood the effect of the memorandum. *Held,* that the grant of a new trial was in the sound discretion of the trial court.

Appeal from Lee District Court.--HON. HENRY BANK, Judge.

THURSDAY, DECEMBER 16, 1897.

APPEAL from an order granting to one Peter Kern a new trial upon a petition presented by the administrator of the estate of Philiphene Behrens for the examination of said Kern with reference to property, in his hands, belonging to the estate.—*Affirmed.*

J. M. Hamilton and *J. L. Benbow* for appellant.

Craig & Harrington and *Bernard Dolan* for appellee.

DEEMER, J.—Section 2379 of the Code of 1873 provides, in substance, that the court may require any one having the effects of one deceased under his control to appear and submit to an examination under oath touching the matter, and, if it appears that he has the wrongful possession of any such property, may order the delivery of the same to the executor of the estate. The administrator filed his petition under this section, and Kern was examined before the court with reference to an instrument in writing in his hands, which it was claimed belonged to the estate. After the examination was concluded, and after the term at which the examination was held closed, the court made an order directing Kern to turn over to the administrator the sum of three hundred dollars in money within thirty days from date. At the beginning of the first

1　　　term of court after the order was made, Kern filed what he denominated a "petition for re-hearing," in which he recited, in substance, that no personal claim was made against him in the original petition, and that he did not learn any such claim was made until after the order was entered and served upon him; that the order was entered in vacation, and without his consent or agreement, and that he was misled by statements and promises of counsel for the executor into believing that no personal claim would be made against him; that he never had any money belonging to the estate of Behrens, and that the note referred to in the original petition was nothing more than an undelivered memorandum made by him as priest, at the time deceased made a gift to the church of which he was in charge; that the court, in his examination, which was conducted partly in German and partly in English, misunderstood the effect of the memorandum. On these allegations, Kern asked for a re-trial of the case.

2   The administrator demurred to the petition, on the ground that it constituted no defense to the order. This demurrer was overruled and the appeal is from the ruling.

Appellee contends that the ruling is not appealable. In the case of *In re Pyle*, 82 Iowa, 146, we held that an appeal might be taken from an order made under section 2379 of the Code of 1873. If an appeal will lie from such an order, it will, *a fortiori*, lie from an order granting a re-trial of the proceedings. After making certain admissions in his amended abstract, appellee "denies that his abstract and that of appellant and the two together are true or correct or contain the record." The admissions relate to the mat-

3   ters of record above recited. Every other statement in appellant's abstract is eliminated by the denial, and the sole question left for our consideration is whether the court erred in sustaining the demurrer to the petition for a re-trial. A court has power, after the term at which an order is made, to vacate or modify such order for irregularity in obtaining the same, or for fraud practiced by the successful party. The allegations of the petition for re-hearing clearly show that the order made by the court was irregular, in that it was, in effect, a judgment against Kern for the sum of three hundred dollars with interest, whereas the petition or affidavit filed as a basis for

the proceedings simply asked that Kern be ordered to turn over a note held by him to the administrator; and this was all the citation required him to meet. He was not aware that any claim for personal judgment was made until served with a copy of the order made by the court.

Again, the petition for re-trial recites that the alleged note was a mere memorandum, which was never delivered, and that the trial court was misled, because of the fact that the proceedings were conducted in two languages, into believing that the instrument was a note signed by Kern, or that Kern had received a certain sum of money from the deceased. The petition also recites that the memorandum, when properly translated, shows on its face that the money obtained was given to the church of which Kern was a priest, or to the bishop of that church, and that he never had any interest in the same. The granting of a new trial
4   in such a proceeding as this rests peculiarly within the sound discretion of the court. From the facts above recited, we think it clearly appears that there was no such abuse of discretion as will justify us in interfering. The demurrer was properly overruled, and the order is AFFIRMED.

J. W. WATERBURY v. THE CHICAGO, MILWAUKEE & ST. PAUL RAILWAY COMPANY, Appellant.

Negligence: RAILROADS. It is negligence on the part of a railway company to allow an accumulation of ice upon the platform of
8   its passenger station, caused by the dropping of water from the roof, to remain without any effort to remove it, or cover it with some substance that would be less dangerous.

CONTRIBUTORY NEGLIGENCE. One who, in entering a railway depot,
1   passed over a place made unsafe by an accumulation of ice, and
8   knew of its dangerous condition, yet who soon thereafter, while
4   watching upon the platform for the incoming train, stepped backward upon the ice without looking or taking any precaution for

his safety, whereby he fell to his injury,—is guilty of contributory negligence.

Evidence: CROSS-EXAMINATION. A question asked on cross-examina-
2 tion which has already been answered may be properly objected to on that account.

Appeal: REVIEW OF FINDINGS. Special findings by a jury will not be sustained if contrary to the evidence, and when material and
5 determinative in their character, the party found against will not be presumed to have had a fair trial.

LADD, J., taking no part.

Appeal from Plymouth District Court.—HON. SCOTT **M.** LADD, Judge.

THURSDAY, DECEMBER 16, 1897.

ACTION to recover damages for a personal injury. Verdict and judgment for plaintiff. Defendant appeals. —*Reversed.*

Shull & Farnsworth for appellant.

Argo, McDuffie & Argo for appellee.

KINNE, C. J.—I. Plaintiff, a merchant in the town of Hudson, S. D., on December 30, 1893, went to the depot of the defendant in said town with his mother, she intending to take passage to Akron, Iowa. The negligence charged is "that for a long time prior to the 30th day of December, 1893, the said defendant rail-road company, carelessly, negligently, and unlawfully suffered and permitted ice to accumulate on the platform adjacent to its passenger depot in said town of Hudson, and on a place on said platform necessarily used by the public in going to and from the passenger trains stopping at said station; that said accumulation of ice on said platform was by said defendant negligently permitted to remain in an unsafe and dangerous condition, without any guards around the same, or without any sand, ashes, or other material covering the same, and in such a manner that it was dangerous and unsafe for persons to pass over and cross the same; that on the thirtieth day of December, 1893, the plaintiff accompanied his mother, an old lady of the age of sixty-one years, to said depot for the purpose of assisting her to get aboard of a passenger train which would be due in about five or ten minutes, she intending to return to her home where she resides at Akron, Iowa; that while the plaintiff was standing on said platform, at a place where he had a lawful right to stand, and at a place used by the public, without any knowledge on his part of the dangerous condition of the said platform, and without any knowledge of the fact that the defendant had carelessly and negligently let the ice as aforesaid accumulate and remain on said platform, and without any negligence or fault whatever on his part, he stepped upon said ice, causing his feet to slip, violently throwing him down upon said platform, striking upon the corner of an elevated portion thereof, whereby plaintiff was greatly injured, his left collar bone was broken, his left shoulder and side badly bruised and injured, causing him to be made sick, sore, and lame, and suffering great pain and anguish, and being permanently injured." In response to certain special interrogatories submitted to them by the court, the jury found that the ice on the platform was not caused by a general storm which continued at the time of the accident; that plaintiff could not, by the exercise of ordinary care, have seen the ice where he slipped, and have avoided the injury by the exercise of such care; that plaintiff did not fall because of the mere slipperiness of the ice on the platform; that plaintiff's fall was not caused by stepping back, and his foot striking the incline of the platform, while he was looking in another

direction; that the platform was not in a reasonably
safe condition at the time plaintiff received his injury,
and that defendant was negligent in permitting the
platform to be in the condition in which it was; that
plaintiff did not contribute to his injury by his own
negligence. The errors assigned arise on the introduction of evidence; the refusal to direct a verdict; the
refusal to submit interrogatories asked; the refusal to
give certain instructions; and in overruling the motion
for a new trial.

II. It will be necessary to briefly describe the situation surrounding the accident in order that what we
may say may be correctly understood and applied. The
defendant's depot building at Hudson is erected
1   so that the side of the building is opposite the
track. A platform runs along the east side of
the building, between it and the track. There is a door
opening into the waiting room. The platform on the
west side of the building is higher than the east side,
and level with the bottom of the doors of the freight
cars. At the north or back end of the depot there is a
platform built with an incline from the platform on the
west side of the building to the platform on the east
side. Previous to the day of the accident it had rained
and sleeted, and some snow had fallen, and the entire
surface of the ground and platform was covered with
ice, and at places with patches of snow. At about 2
o'clock P. M. plaintiff, with his mother, an elderly lady,
came to the depot, she intending to take passage on a
train which was soon due. They came upon the high
part of the platform by means of steps at the north end
of the building, passed down over the incline to the
level part of the platform on the east side of the building, and proceeded south on the platform to the south
end of the building, into the waiting room. After seat-
ing his mother, the plaintiff passed out onto the level

part of the platform on the east side of the building, and
walked along until he came to the incline at the north
end of the building. He stopped at a point a few feet
north of the north end of the building, and a few feet
east of the bottom of the incline, and was looking north
and east in the direction of the incoming train. His
back was towards this incline. Without turning
around, he steeped backwards a few steps, when his
feet struck this incline, and he slipped and fell, breaking his collar bone and otherwise injuring him. The
defendant's claim is that his own negligence produced
the fall and injury.

III. The plaintiff, on cross-examination, was
asked if in going down the incline with his mother he
had not come over the ice upon which he claimed to
have slipped. The objection was that the ques-
2   tion had already been answered. There can be
no question from this record that the objection
was well taken, and there was no error in the ruling.

IV. At the close of the evidence for the plaintiff,
defendant moved for a verdict because the evidence was
not sufficient to sustain a verdict for plaintiff, because
plaintiff was guilty of such negligence as to prevent his
recovering, and no negligence had been shown on part
of the defendant. Two questions were presented by
this motion: *First*, was the defendant negligent? and,
second, if it was, did plaintiff by his own negligence
directly contribute to produce the injury of which he
complains?

As to the defendant's negligence. The evidence for
the plaintiff tended strongly to show these, among
other, facts: That about December 24th it rained; that
the weather turned cold, and the rain was frozen
3   until the entire surface of the depot platform and
of the streets and sidewalks of the village was
covered with a thin sheet of sleet and ice; that at the

northeast corner of the depot the water from the roof
accumulated, and dropped upon the platform, freezing
there, and forming an accumulation of ice upon and
near to the foot of the incline where the plaintiff fell;
that this ice was much thicker than it was on other
parts of the depot platform by reason of this dropping
of the water from the roof, and was in size from three
to five feet wide by from four to six feet long. There
was evidence also tending to show that this ice was
covered with some snow. It is clear that this extra
accumulation of ice at the place where plaintiff fell was
not the result of natural causes. It was to a great
extent an unnecessary accumulation, due to the manner in which the roof of the depot was constructed,
and by the exercise of ordinary care could have been
avoided. It was the duty of the defendant to have
removed it, or, if that could not be done, to have taken
precautions to prevent injury to persons passing over it
by covering it with salt, ashes, or some substance which
would render it less dangerous. This extra accumulation of ice had taken place several days before the
plaintiff fell thereon. We have no doubt, then, under
the evidence, that defendant was negligent.

Did plaintiff, by his own negligence, contribute
directly to produce the injury of which he complains?
It may be conceded that he was at the depot for a lawful purpose; that he had a right to go out upon the
platform to look for the train, but in so doing he was
bound to exercise ordinary care. He testifies
4   that when he took his mother to the waiting
room they came down over this same incline
upon which he afterwards fell; that it was covered
with ice, and there was some snow at the bottom of it,
and it was very slippery; that he was familiar with this
incline,—knew how it was built; that it was so slippery
everywhere that one walking had to keep watch. It

clearly appears that he had as full knowledge of the
condition of the depot platform at the point where he
fell as the defendant could have had.   Knowing its
dangerous condition at that place, he walked out to or
near the foot of this incline, and when about three feet
from it, and while standing with his back to it, he began
stepping backwards without looking or taking any precautions whatever for his own safety.   In view of these
circumstances, it seems to us it cannot be said that he
exercised ordinary care.   Having full knowledge as to
the dangerous condition of this incline, and the point
near it,—having passed over it a few minutes before
with his mother, when he says he was especially careful,
—he proceeds to step backwards upon it without exercising any care whatsoever.   From the undisputed
facts,—from his own evidence,—but one conclusion can
be drawn, and that is that he was guilty of negligence
which resulted in his injury.   It does not appear that
there was any necessity for stepping backwards onto
this incline, which he knew was especially dangerous,
save to escape the wind, and that would not justify his
so doing without exercising any care for his safety.   We
have given the evidence careful consideration, and
reach the conclusion that the plaintiff was, as a matter
of law, guilty of contributory negligence which will
preclude a recovery.

V.   After the evidence was all in, the defendant
renewed its motion to direct a verdict.   This motion
should have been sustained, as no further evidence was
introduced in any way tending to show that plaintiff
was in the exercise of ordinary care when he fell.

VI.   In view of our conclusion as to these motions,
we need not consider all of the other questions discussed.   The jury found specially that plaintiff could
not, by the exercise of ordinary care, have seen the ice

where he slipped and fell, and by such care have avoided
the injury. This finding, as well as the seventh,
5   that plaintiff did not directly contribute to his
injury by his own negligence, was clearly contrary to the evidence, and cannot be sustained. These
facts were material and determinative in character, and
it cannot be presumed, in view of the answers of the
jury, that the defendant had a fair trial.

VII. The instructions given were correct, and
fully and clearly presented the law of the case, and
those asked, so far as correct, were substantially embodied in the court's charge. As we have indicated, the
error of the court consisted in refusing to sustain the
motion to direct a verdict for the defendant and in
overruling the motion for a new trial. As for the error
pointed out the case must be reversed, we shall not
discuss the question as to the verdict being excessive,
nor the complaint made as to misconduct of plaintiff's
counsel.—REVERSED.

LADD, J., taking no part.

JOHN STEEL v. H. E. LONG, MARY A. LONG, and T. J. · 104
FOSTER, Appellants.   122

Forfeiture: LAND CONTRACT. A failure to make a payment at the
time agreed does not of itself work a forfeiture of contract, but
forfeiture for such cause is optional with the payee, the contract
having, after reciting the agreement of S to sell to J certain land,
1   and, after receipt of full payment, to make a deed to J, and of J
to make the payments in certain installments, provided that, till
said payments are fully and promptly paid, no title shall pass;
that time is of the essence of the contract, and, if there be any
default in any of the payments, then all rights of J, except as
hereinafter provided, shall, because thereof and thereby, be immediately forfeited without notice from S; and that, unless S shall,
in writing, expressly waive such forfeiture, J shall thereafter simply be a tenant in common at sufferance, and shall surrender

possession on demand; and that, in case of forfeiture, all improvements may be retained by S as liquidated damages for breach of
the contract and for rent; or S, waiving such forfeiture, may at
any time before such surrender proceed to require the fulfill-
ments of J's obligations, or may treat any amount unpaid as
overdue.

Quieting Title: PARTIES.   One in possession of land under an agreement of another to sell it to him, and to convey it to him on pay-
 2 ment of the purchase price, is not bound by decree in suit to
   which he is not a party, against such other, to quiet title.

Appeal from Dallas District Court.—HON. J. H. APPLE-
GATE, Judge.

THURSDAY, DECEMBER 16, 1897.

PLAINTIFF states as his cause of action that he is the
owner of the southeast quarter of section 26-81-27,
Dallas county; that he derives his title through Pliny
T. Sexton by virtue of a purchase under a contract in
writing set out; that upon the execution of said contract he went, and has ever since remained, in possession of said land thereunder; that he has performed all
the conditions thereof, and has been ready and willing
to perform the same, and that no forfeiture of said contract has been made or declared by said Sexton; that
defendants claim some right, title, or interest in and to
said land, but have none therein.   Plaintiff prays to be
established and confirmed in his title and estate as
against the defendants, and that they be barred from
claiming any right in said land, and for costs.   The
contract set out, dated October 6, 1891, shows: That
for the consideration named Sexton agreed to sell to
plaintiff said land.   That plaintiff agreed to pay therefor four thousand dollars, as follows: "$200.00 cash
down; $200.00 on March 1, 1892; and the balance in
installments of $100.00, or multiples thereof to amount
of $500.00, on March 1 in each succeeding year, as per
second party's note to said first party; and agrees to pay

on March 1, 1893, and annually thereafter, interest
thereon at the rate of eight per cent. per annum until
the same be fully paid." Plaintiff also agreed to pay all
taxes before delinquent, and to pay the expenses of
insurance; all taxes, expenses of insurance paid by Sexton, and all interest to be treated as additional and
overdue principal. Sexton agreed, upon receiving full
payment of purchase money, taxes, expenses of insurance, and interest, to make to plaintiff a warranty deed
of said land. Following these recitals, said contract
provides as follows: "It is expressly agreed, however,
that until and unless the aforesaid payments shall be
fully and promptly made, no title whatever to said
premises shall pass to said second party, but the latter
may occupy the same, while faithfully and promptly
fulfilling all the obligations of this instrument, as the
tenant of the first party, without charge, except as hereinafter provided, and shall neither commit nor permit
any waste thereon. And it is expressly further agreed
that time is the essence of this contract, and, if there
shall be any default in any of the aforesaid payments, or
any breach of the provisions of this instrument by the
second party, then all rights of said second party here-
under, except as hereinafter provided, shall, because
thereof and thereby, be immediately forfeited, without
notice from the first party; and that, unless the first
party shall, in writing, expressly waive such forfeiture,
said second party shall thereafter be simply a tenant at
will and sufferance, and shall surrender the possession
of said premises to said first party on demand, without
further notice. In case of such forfeiture the latter
shall not be chargeable with any improvements that
shall have been made on said premises, and may retain
same, and all insurance thereon, together with all growing crops, and said one-half of the purchase money, and
all interest; taxes, and expenses of insurance paid

thereon, as liquidated damages for the breach of this contract, and for rent of said premises. Or the first party, waiving such forfeiture, may at any time thereafter before the surrender of the premises as stipulated, take proper legal proceedings to require the fulfillment of the second party's obligations under this contract, or may treat all or any portion of any amount unpaid hereon as overdue." Defendants Long answered, admitting that plaintiff had possession of said land; that H. E. Long makes some claim of title and right thereto, and denying the other allegations of the petition. H. E. Long, as further defense and cross bill, alleges, in substance, as follows: That he is the owner of said land, and that his title and ownership are based upon the following grounds: That Sexton sold said land to William Torpey, and that Torpey thereafter, and prior to September 27, 1882, went into possession; that about March 1, 1882, William Dickerson obtained a judgment against William Torpey in the circuit court of Polk county for four hundred and twenty-eight dollars and forty-two dollars attorney's fees, a transcript of which was filed about March 16, 1882, in the office of the clerk of the court of Dallas county; that said Torpey was then in possession, and claiming to be the owner of said land; that execution was issued on said judgment April 21, 1892, and levied upon said land as the property of William Torpey, and sold under said execution on May 21, 1892, to H. E. Long, to whom a certificate was issued which he thereafter assigned to Mary A. Long; that on May 23, 1893, a sheriff's deed was executed to Mary A. Long, and she thereafter, on September 25, 1893, conveyed said land to H. E. Long. It is upon these alleged facts that H. E. Long based his claim of title. He further alleges that prior to the bringing of this action plaintiff had failed to pay the installments of purchase money and the taxes as agreed in said written contract,

by reason of which he had lost all rights in said land.
He further alleges that on July 10, 1893, Mary A. Long
commenced an action against William Torpey, Martin
Torpey, and Pliny T. Sexton to quiet her title to said
land; that said defendants failed to appear, and that
on September 12, 1893, decree was rendered quieting
the title in said plaintiff; that said decree was in full
force when this action was brought; and that prior to
the time Mary A. Long brought her said action the
plaintiff had forfeited all rights under said contract,
and that he is wrongfully in possession of said land.
Defendant H. E. Long prays to be quieted in his title,
and for possession. Defendant T. J. Foster answered,
denying that plaintiff is the owner of said land, and
adopting the answer of defendants Long. He alleges
as cross bill that H. E. Long, being the owner of said
land, and indebted to him in the sum of three thousand
dollars, evidenced by his promissory notes, did, with
his wife, Mary A. Long, execute to him a mortgage
dated March 1, 1894, on said land, to secure said indebtedness, which mortgage is a lien prior to any claim of
plaintiff. He prays that plaintiff's petition be dismissed, and that his mortgage be established as a superior lien to any right of the plaintiff. Plaintiff, in separate replies to the cross bills, denies H. E. Long's
claim of title. The questions to be considered were
raised by motion and demurrers, and on the final hearing decree was rendered in favor of the plaintiff.
Defendants appeal.—*Affirmed.*

E. W. Gifford for appellants.

White & Clark for appellee.

GIVEN, J.—I. We first inquire as to plaintiff's
claim of ownership or interest in the land. His rights,

if he has any, rest upon the admitted written contract
with Sexton, under which the plaintiff took and
1   held possession of the land, and made certain
payments thereon. There is a dispute as to the
amount of the payments, and whether they covered the
payment due March 1, 1893; but this is immaterial, as
it does appear that plaintiff failed to make later payments of purchase money when due, and pay taxes
before delinquent. There is also a dispute as to whether
plaintiff withheld payment because of Mr. Long's claim
to the land and to possession thereof. This, too, is
immaterial to the question now being considered, which
is whether this written contract, by its terms, became
immediately forfeited by plaintiff's failure to pay, or
whether the forfeiture rests upon the election of Mr.
Sexton to so treat the contract because of such failure.
Appellants contend that, because of the failure to pay
at the time provided in the contract, plaintiff forfeited
all rights under it, and that thereby he became a tenant
at will, and has no right, title, or interest in the land,
and, therefore, no right to maintain this action. Appellee contends that by the terms of the contract the
option is given to Mr. Sexton alone whether to treat it
as forfeited or not, and that he has not so treated it;
therefore the contract is in full force and effect.

.   We have examined the many cases cited by counsel,
and reach the conclusion that there is no dispute
between them as to these propositions; that parties contracting for the sale and purchase of real estate on
payments may provide that a failure to make any of the
payments at the time agreed shall of itself work a forfeiture of the contract (*Barrett v. Dean*, 21 Iowa, 425);
that parties making such contract may make a forfeiture thereof for failure to pay at the time agreed optional
with the payee. The contention is as to which of these
classes this contract belongs. The first is an unusual

contract, and it is said in *Barrett v. Dean, supra:* "But
to give a contract such a construction, it should be plain
and clear beyond question from the terms used that
such was the intention of the parties." Taking parts of
this contract as quoted above alone, a forfeiture would
clearly follow from the mere fact of failure to pay at
the time agreed, but, taking the whole instrument
together, we think it is clear that the right is reserved
to Mr. Sexton alone to say whether or not a forfeiture
will follow such failure. The provision that the waiver
of a forfeiture shall be in writing recognizes the right to
waive it. The concluding provision that Sexton waiving such forfeiture may at any time thereafter take
proper legal proceedings to enforce the contract seems
to us to clearly show that the right to waive the forfeiture was reserved to Sexton. When defendants
asserted claim to this land, the plaintiff declined to
make further payments until their rights were determined, and brought this action for that purpose. Mr.
Sexton was informed, by letters written to him by his
agent, of the defendants' claims, and of the plaintiff's
refusal to pay because thereof. To this Sexton made
no reply either claiming or waiving forfeiture, and,
while it is true that his mere silence might not be construed as a waiver, it warrants the inference that, notwithstanding the plaintiff's failure, he stands upon
the contract. The contract, as we view it, being one
which Mr. Sexton may treat as forfeited or not, and
which he has thus far treated as in force, it is a binding,
enforceable contract between the parties to it. It does
not appear that Mr. Sexton had done anything to prevent him from insisting upon the enforcement of the
contract, and, as the option is reserved to him alone,
we think the defendants have no right to insist upon a
forfeiture. If nothing further appeared, we would say
that the contract is an existing and enforceable contract, and that the plaintiff has such rights and interest

in the land under it as entitles him to maintain this
action.

II. We now inquire as to the title of the defendant H. E. Long, which is derived through Mrs. Long
from the sheriff's sale. The judgment upon which the
sale was made, being more than ten years old, was not
a lien on Torpey's land until made so by levy, which was
on April 21, 1892. Torpey previously held this land
under a contract with Sexton, which they had both
treated as at an end long prior to the levy. The plaintiff occupied the land as tenant under Sexton for a time
prior to October 6, 1891, after which he held it under
said written contract. The evidence leaves no doubt
but that at the time of the levy, April 21, 1892, Torpey
was not in possession of the land, and neither had nor
was making any claim thereto. It is clear, therefore,
we think, that Long took nothing by his purchase at the
sheriff's sale. It is true that in 1882 William Torpey,
who had no record title, made a quit-claim deed to this
land to his father, who thereafter quit-claimed to plaintiff, who was then in possession under his contract with
Sexton. Thereafter plaintiff, for the purpose of removing that cloud from Sexton's title, quit-claimed to him.
Thus explained, there is nothing in this transaction at
variance with the conclusion we have reached that
Torpey had no interest in the land at the time of the
levy and sale. Appellants insist that, as the contract
provides that forfeiture shall take place without notice
unless Sexton shall, in writing, expressly waive such
forfeiture, and that, as Sexton has not so waived it, the
contract stands forfeited. It is a sufficient answer to
this to say that even now Mr. Sexton has the right to
expressly waive a forfeiture in writing, and to have a
performance of the contract, notwithstanding the
decree in favor of Mrs. Long, as in that case plaintiff
might waive his right to defend because of that decree.

III.   Defendants insisted that by the decree quieting title in Mrs. Long she became seized of any interest that Sexton then had in the land.   If this be true as between Mrs. Long, her grantee, and Sexton, it is certainly not true as to this plaintiff, who, though in possession under said written contract, was not made a party to that action.   As we view the facts, there was no foundation whatever for that decree, as Torpey had no interest in the land at the time of the levy and sale.   The plaintiff, not being a party to that action, is not concluded thereby, and may therefore now question defendants' title under the sale and decree.   As we view the case, the equities are manifestly with the plaintiff, and most of the authorities cited are inapplicable to the questions presented.   Our conclusions that the plaintiff has such an interest in the land as entitles him to maintain this action, and that neither the defendant Long nor the defendant Foster, his mortgagee, has any right, title, or interest therein, are so manifestly correct that we do not cite any authorities in support thereof.   The judgment of the district court is AFFIRMED.

CHARLES McFALL, Appellant, v. THE IOWA CENTRAL
RAILWAY COMPANY.

Negligence: JURY QUESTION.   An action against a railway company for injury to a brakeman through defendant's negligence in permitting its water tank to become out of repair, in consequence whereof the water was permitted to run on and over the tracks, which rendered it dangerous for brakemen to perform their duty of coupling cars, was clearly one for the jury, where there was evidence to show negligence on the part of the defendant, and that plaintiff was not guilty of negligence.

Appeal: LAW OF CASE.   A ruling on a prior appeal in the same cause must control on a subsequent trial, where the situation is not changed by the issues or evidence.

Appeal from Mahaska District Court.—Hon. A. R. Dewey, Judge.

Thursday, December 16, 1897.

Action to recover damages for a personal injury. Jury trial. Verdict for defendant. Plaintiff appeals.— *Reversed.*

J. F. & W. R. Lacey and *J. B. Bolton* for appellant.

Anthony C. Daly, L. C. Blanchard, and *Theo. F. Bradford* for appellee.

Kinne, C. J.—I. It is without dispute that plaintiff was employed by the defendant company as a brakeman on its line of railway extending from Peoria, Ill., to Oskaloosa, Iowa; that on January 8, 1893, at Keithsburg, Ill., and while in the performance of his duty in coupling cars, his hand was so mangled and crushed between the bumpers of some cars that it became necessary to amputate it. The negligence charged is in not furnishing a reasonably safe place for the plaintiff to work, and in negligently permitting its water tank to become out of repair, whereby the water was permitted to run on and over its tracks, forming a sheet of ice thereon, which rendered it dangerous for brakemen to perform their duty of coupling cars passing on its tracks, and over said ice. After plaintiff had introduced his evidence, the court, on motion of the defendant, directed the jury to return a verdict for it, which was done. Plaintiff appeals.

II. This is the second appeal in this case. See 96 Iowa, 723. On the former appeal the case was reversed for the error of the trial judge in not submitting it to

the jury. It was then held that there was evidence tending to establish plaintiff's cause of action, and that he
was not negligent. On the first trial below, the answer
of the defendant was a general denial, only. On the
last trial, an amendment to the answer was filed, pleading the knowledge of the plaintiff of the dangers complained of, and his assumption of the risk, as incident
to his employment, and his waiver of want of repair of
the water tank. Plaintiff, in a reply, denied all of the
allegations of this amended answer. It appears that
all of the evidence on the first trial was presented in
the form of depositions. On the last trial the same
depositions were used, except that plaintiff was orally
examined as a witness on the trial. The grounds of the
motion to direct a verdict were, in substance, the same
on both trials. Appellant contends that the trial court
erred in its action in refusing to submit the case to the
jury. It is a doctrine always adhered to by this
1   court, that a ruling made on a prior appeal in
the same case is controlling upon a second
appeal. Therefore, if the issues and evidence were substantially the same on the last trial as on the first, the
cause should have been submitted to the jury. While
the amendment pleaded that the plaintiff had knowledge of the risk, and assumed it, as an incident of his
employment, and while evidence was introduced which,
it is claimed, tends to sustain this plea, it seems that
the same evidence was introduced on the first trial
under the pleadings as they then stood. In this respect,
therefore, the case presented is substantially the same
as in the first trial and appeal. The only difference in
the evidence upon the two trials seems to be that on the
last trial the plaintiff was examined touching a written
statement that he made about three weeks after the
injury, as to its cause. Without entering into a discussion of this evidence, it may be said that the most

that can be claimed from it is that it may tend to show that the defendant was not negligent. It presented facts to be considered, in connection with other facts, in determining whether or not the defendant was guilty of negligence. In view of this entire record, and of the evidence before us in the prior appeal, it is evident that what was then said as to the duty of the court to submit the case to the jury was applicable and controlling on the last trial. As we have indicated, there was no such change in the issues, in view of the evidence introduced on each trial, or in the evidence, as to warrant the trial court in ignoring the direction of this court upon the second trial. There was evidence on the last trial which tended strongly to show negligence on the part of the defendant. There was evidence, likewise, tending to show that plaintiff was not guilty of negligence. Such being the situation, the case was clearly one for the jury. The court is not authorized to weigh the evidence as to negligence, and to decide as to its preponderance. It having been held by this court on the former appeal that under the holding in *Meyer v. Houck*, 85 Iowa, 319, the case should have been submitted to the jury, that holding was controlling on the last trial, inasmuch as the situation was not changed by the issues or evidence. For the error of the court in refusing to submit the case to the jury, the judgment must be REVERSED.

STATE OF IOWA v. T. F. STEVENSON, Judge.

Contempt: NEW TRIAL. While a proceeding to punish for contempt
1 is in its nature criminal, the provisions of Code 1873 as to new trials in criminal cases do not apply, but such new trials may be
2 granted under the statutes governing new trials in civil actions.

SAME: *Newly discovered evidence.* In a proceeding to punish for contempt, in violating an injunction against the maintaining of a liquor nuisance, defendant applied for a new trial for newly dis-
4 covered evidence, and because that he had been advised by an

attorney that such injunction had been dissolved.　The alleged
ne w ly discovered evidence consisted of a package of applications
5　for the purchase of intoxicating liquor, which had been used by
an employe, who was a registered pharmacist, but whose certificate did not authorize him to do business at the place kept by
defendant; and it appeared that they might have been produced
on the trial with little effort　It also appeared that defendant
had been informed by another attorney that the injunction was in
force as against him, though not as against the building, and
knew that he was carrying on such business in violation of law.
H ld, that such application was without merit, and should have
been denied, and that had he acted in good faith, and upon the
advice of counsel, it would constitute no defense to the contempt
charged.

Appeal: OBJECTION BELOW.　That one who applied for a new trial in
a contempt proceeding did so by a paper entitled "motion for
3　re-hearing and new trial," which was filed ten days after judgment, instead of by petition, cannot be first raised on appeal.

From Polk District Court.—HON. T. F. STEVENSON,
Judge.

THURSDAY, DECEMBER 16, 1897.

THIS is a proceeding in *certiorari* to review an
order of the district court of Polk county, which granted
a new trial to a person adjudged to be in contempt for
violating an injunction against the maintaining of a
liquor nuisance.　Order *annulled.*

James Howe, county attorney, and *Jesse A. Miller*
for the state.

McVey & McVey for defendant.

ROBINSON, J.—In July, 1894, in a case then pending
in the district court of Polk county, Iowa, in which the
state of Iowa was plaintiff and Joseph Lehner was
defendant, a decree was rendered which in terms perpetually enjoined Lehner from selling or keeping for
sale, and from permitting others to sell or keep for sale,
in violation of law, intoxicating liquors at No. 213 Wal-

nut street, in the city of Des Moines, on a portion of a
lot which was particularly described. In October,
1895, a petition was filed, in which Lehner was charged
with having violated that injunction. He was required
to appear and show cause why he should not be punished for contempt of court, and appeared and filed an
answer. Evidence was offered in behalf of the state
and for Lehner; and on the nineteenth day of November,
1895, he was found to have violated the injunction, and
was adjudged to be guilty of contempt of court, and
required to pay a fine of five hundred dollars and costs.
On the twenty-ninth day of the same month, he filed a
paper entitled a "motion for re-hearing and new trial,"
supported by an affidavit, in which he asked for a
re-hearing and a new trial in the contempt proceedings.
At the next term of the court, in January, 1896, the
attorneys for the plaintiff were orally notified of the
application for a new trial, and appeared thereto. The
affidavit of Lehner, and some applications to one of his
clerks for the purchase of intoxicating liquors, were
introduced in evidence, and the motion was sustained.

I. The plaintiff contends that the court acted
illegally and exceeded its jurisdiction in granting the
relief asked by the motion; that a re-hearing or new
            trial in contempt proceedings is unauthorized;
1   that, if authorized, it is governed by the
            statute which regulates new trials in criminal
cases; and if that is not the law, and a new trial
was authorized, as the application in question was
made ten days after the judgment in the contempt
proceeding was rendered, it should have been by
petition, and, as it was by motion, it should not,
for that reason, have been granted. It has been said
that a proceeding to punish a contempt of court is in
its nature criminal. *First Congregational Church v.
City of Muscatine*, 2 Iowa, 71; *Fisher v. District Court*,
75 Iowa, 234; *Grier v. Johnson*, 88 Iowa, 102. In *New*

Orleans v. New York Mail S. S. Co., 20 Wall. 392, it was said: "Contempt of court is a specific criminal offense."
See, also, 4 Enc. Pl. & Prac. 766. While it is
2   undoubtedly true that proceedings for the punishment of a contempt of court are designed to punish wrongful acts, and are to that extent criminal in their nature, yet they are not governed by the general provisions of the law which provide for the punishment of crimes, but by special statutes. *Jordan v. Circuit Court*, 69 Iowa, 180. They are usually brought in the name of the state. *Fisher v. District Court, supra.* But they may also be entitled as in the case in which the contempt is alleged to have been committed. *Manderscheid v. District Court*, 69 Iowa, 240. The charges in such proceedings are not triable by jury (*McDonnell v. Henderson*, 74 Iowa, 619), although it may be that the court can submit to a jury a disputed question of fact (4 Enc. Pl. & Prac. 789). The punishment for a contempt does not constitute a bar to an indictment for the same offense. Code 1873, section 3500; Code, section 4469. And the general statute which defines contempts and provides for their punishment is found in that portion of the Code of 1873 which was devoted to civil, and not to criminal, procedure. The provisions of the law under which Lehner was punished as for contempt are of the same character as is the general statute in regard to contempt. We conclude that the provision of the Code of 1873 which authorized new trials in criminal cases did not apply in proceedings to punish for contempt.

The power of a court to grant a new trial in contempt proceedings is questioned. We do not know on what legal principle the denial of the power in proper cases can be based. The statutes which authorize new trials in civil cases are sufficiently comprehensive to include within their scope new trials in contempt proceedings, and, in our opinion, apply to them.

II.   It is said that, as more than three days from
the rendition of the judgment in the contempt proceedings had elapsed when the application for a new trial
was filed, it should have been by petition, and not by
motion.   Section 2838 of the Code of 1873 required an
application for a new trial in civil cases to be made "at
the term and within three days after the verdict, report
or decision is rendered, except for the cause of newly-
discovered evidence," and that the application must be
by motion upon written grounds.   Sections 3154 and
3155 of the Code of 1873 authorized new trials to be
granted for specified purposes upon petition, not more
than one year after a final judgment had been rendered,
upon the making of a proper showing, which need not

3   be specified.   It may be conceded that, under
these statutory provisions, the application for a
new trial in this case should have been made by
petition.   We do not find, however, that any objection
to the form of the application, nor to the notice thereof
which was given, was made in the district court.   The
application may as well have been entitled a "petition"
as a "motion;" and since it was considered in the district court on its merits, without objection, it will be so
considered by this court.

III.   The chief ground of the application for a
new trial is the alleged discovery of new and material
evidence.   On the trial had in the contempt proceed-

4   ings it was shown that one Beidenkopf was
employed by Lehner as clerk in the place of
business in question, and that, as such clerk, he
sold intoxicating liquors in violation of law. Beidenkopf
was a registered pharmacist, but his certificate authorized him to do business as a pharmacist at No. 123 West
Fourth street, and not in the establishment of Lehner.
The alleged newly-discovered evidence consisted in a
package of applications for the purchase of intoxicating

liquors, addressed to Beidenkopf, and signed by various persons. The only excuse Lehner gave for not having discovered the applications before the trial in the contempt proceedings was that his health was in such a precarious condition at that time that he was unable to give personal attention to the carrying on of his business. But he testified on the trial that Beidenkopf had such blank applications, and was told by Lehner to have all purchasers sign them, and that Beidenkopf used them. It is manifest that with little effort the applications in question could have been had and produced on the trial, and that Lehner failed to use any diligence whatever to obtain them. Moreover, it is clear that they did not have the effect to make valid the sales which they represented.

The remaining grounds of the application for a new trial are, in effect, claims that Lehner had been advised by Attorney Sickmon that the injunction which he violated had been dissolved; that he under-

5   stood and believed that it had been dissolved; that he did not intend to violate any order of the court; and that, without such an intent, his acts should not be treated as a contempt of court. All of these claims were made and the alleged advice of counsel shown on the trial for contempt. It was also shown on the trial that, after Sickmon is claimed to have given the advice stated, Lehner was informed by another attorney that the injunction was in force as against Lehner, but not against the building. It was thus shown by his own testimony that he knew that he was not authorized to sell intoxicating liquor, and that the business he carried on was in violation of law. But, had he acted in good faith upon the advice of counsel, that fact would not have constituted a defense in the contempt proceedings.

Lindsay v. Hatch, 85 Iowa, 332. See, also, *State v. Bowman*, 79 Iowa, 566. The application for a new trial was without merit, and should have been denied. The order of the district court in granting it is therefore ANNULLED.

BAUERNFIEND, *et al.*, v. WILLIAM JONAS, *et al.*, Appellants.

Appeal: TRIAL DE NOVO: *Judge's certificate.* The failure to file in the district court the certificate of the judge, attached to the testimony taken before a commissioner, renders the presence of such testimony in the abstract improper, and precludes a trial *de novo*, on appeal.

CLERK'S CERTIFICATE. Bringing up the evidence certified by the clerk, as provided by Code 1873, section 3184, is not sufficient for a trial *de novo*. It is the office of the judge's certificate to identify the evidence, and make it of record when filed, while the purpose of the clerk's certificate is to identify and authenticate the record.

DISMISSAL. A defect in preserving evidence in an equitable action is not ground for dismissing a properly perfected appeal, but it goes to the disposition of the cause on the merits.

LADD, J., took no part.

Appeal from Plymouth District Court.—HON. S. M. LADD, Judge.

FRIDAY, DECEMBER 17, 1897.

ACTION for the possession and right of occupancy of certain church property, and to restrain the defendants from interfering therewith. Decree for defendants, and the plaintiffs appealed.—*Affirmed.*

E. P. Smith, Patrick Farrell, and *Read & Read* for appellants.

Argo, McDuffie & Reichman for appellees.

GRANGER, J.—This is an equitable action, triable *de novo* in this court. There is a controversy as to the sufficiency of the record for that purpose. The certificate of the trial judge to the evidence was never filed in the district court. The original abstract by appellants contains a statement that it is one of all the evidence offered or introduced on the trial, and is, in form, sufficient, for the purpose of an abstract, to justify a trial anew in this court. Appellees present an abstract denying the correctness of appellants' abstract in the following particular: "The certificate of Hon. Scott M. Ladd, attached to the testimony taken before L. Emma Jones, as commissioner, has never been filed in said cause in the office of said clerk." The abstract

1   then shows a statement of the different papers and documents in the district court. There is no claim that the certificate was ever filed. It appears that the certificate was attached to the evidence, but that the certificate was not filed. We are at a loss to know precisely the situation; that is, just what was done. We must, however, act upon the conceded fact that the certificate was not filed, in a legal sense. It is probably true that the evidence, after being certified, was not

filed. A motion is made by appellees to dismiss

2   the appeal because of this; but, as the appeal was properly perfected, a defect in the manner of preserving evidence would not justify a dismissal. The defect goes to the disposition of the case on its merits, or whether, because of the condition of the record, the merits can be considered. That the evidence, to justify a trial anew in this court, must be certified and filed within six months (the time allowed for taking the appeal), see *Kavalier v. Machula*, 77 Iowa, 121. In that case it is said: "We conclude that the translation and certificate in question were not filed within the time required by statute, and that the evidence which it was

intended to identify thereby must be disregarded." The rule in this respect is not open to question. Many cases have announced it. It is the certified evidence that is to be filed.

It is suggested that there is no claim that any of the testimony is left out. That is true. The complaint is not of that. It is of the fact that testimony is in that should not be there, because not properly identified, and which is essential to a trial in this court. It is also said that appellees do not supply the omitted testimony. The complaint is not that the abstract is not one of all the evidence of record, but that the record has not been preserved in a way that all the needed evidence can be brought to this court. By the failure to file, a part of the evidence is lost for the purpose of a further trial, and without it there can be no trial anew, and none other is sought. Since the filing of appellees' 3   abstract, appellants have brought to this court the evidence, certified by the clerk as provided by section 3184 of the Code of 1873, and urge that that is sufficient for the purposes of a trial. This contention is set at rest by *Teague v. Fortsch*, 98 Iowa, 92. That with other cases cited, fixes the rule that it is the office of the certificate of the judge to identify the evidence, and make it of record when filed, while it is the office of the certificate of the clerk to identify and authenticate the record. As we have said, the complaint here is that the evidence is not in the record, and, if not, it is not the province of the clerk to certify it to this court. There seems to be no escape from the conclusion that the evidence is not here for consideration. With this conclusion there is no pretense that the cause can be tried on its merits, and the judgment must be AFFIRMED.

LADD, J., took no part.

S. D. SARVER v. THE CHICAGO, BURLINGTON & QUINCY RAILROAD COMPANY, Appellant.

Railroads: KILLING STOCK. The mere fact that a portion of a right of way of a railroad company adjacent to a highway is outside
4   the cattle guard and fences, does not justify a presumption that such land was used for highway purposes.

DEDICATION AND ACCEPTANCE. The fact that a railway company
2   has left a portion of its right of way adjacent to a highway
8   unfenced is not a dedication thereof, unless there has been an acceptance; and it is held that the facts at bar show an acceptance by travel.

Same. A railway company failing to fence a portion of its right of way adjacent to a highway, which portion has not been used for
8   highway purposes, and which it had a right to fence, is, under Code 1873, section 1289, liable for the value, and, in case of failure to pay the actual value within thirty days after notice given, for double the value, of stock killed on such portion.

Appeal: CERTIFICATE. On a motion to dismiss appeal, submitted on certificate, the certificate may be somewhat liberally construed to
1   avoid dismissal.

*Appeal from Monroe District Court.—*HON. F. W. EICHELBERGER, Judge.

FRIDAY, DECEMBER 17, 1897.

ACTION at law to recover double the value of four pigs alleged to have been killed by a train of the defendant at a point on its railway where it had the right to fence, but had failed to do so. There was a trial by jury, and a verdict and judgment for the plaintiff. The defendant appeals.—*Affirmed.*

T. B. Perry for appellant.

D. M. Anderson and *J. T. Clarkson* for appellee.

ROBINSON, J.—This action was commenced in justice's court, and an appeal from the judgment rendered by that court was taken to the district court. The amount in controversy is but twenty-four dollars, and the cause is submitted in this court on a certificate of the trial judge.

I. The appellee has filed a motion to dismiss the cause on the ground that the judge's certificate is not sufficient to give this court jurisdiction to determine the case on its merits. The certificate is certainly
1   not a model one. The appellant has made two attempts to state the question of law certified, and each time has stated a mixed question of law and fact, and the appellee states a third question as the one contained in the certificate. Moreover, the argument of the appellant is largely devoted to alleged facts not set out in the certificate. We are of the opinion, however, notwithstanding this confusion of theories, that the certificate, if somewhat liberally construed, may be said to set out a question of law which this court should determine, and the motion to dismiss is therefore overruled.

II. The certificate shows the following facts: A public highway, at the place of the accident in question, is sixty-six feet in width, and was located before the year 1854, and has been traveled by the public since that time. In the year 1867 the defendant constructed its road southwestward across, and at right angles with,
2   the highway, and at the time of the accident it had double tracks at the place in question, and cattle guards which extended across both tracks. The cattle guards were at right angles with the track, and extended nine feet along the line of the railroad. Wing fences from the right of way fences connected with the cattle guards. The distance between the cattle guards on the opposite sides of the highway, measur-

ing along the north railway track, was seventy-three
feet, and the distance between the corresponding wing
fences, where they connected with the cattle guards,
was eighty-four feet. The east cattle guard was originally located about eighteen feet northeast of the
northeast line of the highway, and it is not shown that
any objection was made by any road supervisor, or other
official or person, to the location of the cattle guard as
made. Two of the four pigs in question were killed in
the space between the northeast line of the highway
and the northeast cattle guard, and the question we are
required to determine is, was the defendant liable for
stock killed in the space described? The certifi-
3   cate does not show that the space was ever used
for highway purposes, and the mere fact that it
was outside the cattle guards and fences does not justify the presumption that it was so used, and that it
was not is shown by evidence. We thus have a case
where a railway company has, by mistake or design,
failed for nearly thirty years to inclose all of its right of
way which it was entitled to fence, and has so left it
that a dedication thereof to the use of the public may
be inferred. But a dedication of land for a public use,
to be effectual, must be accepted, and an acceptance is
not shown by the certificate nor by the record. Section
1289 of the Code of 1873, which was in force when the
accident in question occurred, contains the following:
"Any corporation operating a railway that fails
4   to fence the same against live stock running at
large at all points where such right to fence
exists, shall be liable to the owners of any stock injured
or killed by reason of the want of such fence, for the
value of the property or damage caused, unless the same
was occasioned by the willful act of the owner or his
agent." It also contains a provision for the recovery of
double the value of the stock killed or damages caused

thereto in case of the failure of the corporation to pay
the actual value of the stock killed, or damages caused
thereto, within thirty days after the statutory notice
has been given it. The statute made the defendant liable for the stock killed under the facts stated in the
certificate. See *Andre v. Railroad Co.*, 30 Iowa, 107;
Mundhenk v. Railroad Co., 57 Iowa, 718. In the case of
Soward v. Railroad Co., 33 Iowa, 386, relied upon by
appellant, it appeared that the railway company had
constructed a fence across a legally established highway, and had made a crossing from one hundred and
fifty to two hundred and fifty feet west of the legally
established highway. It appears that before the railway was constructed, at certain seasons of the year
and when the ground was wet, the travel was not on
the highway at the point where the railroad afterwards
crossed it, but at the point where the crossing was made,
and the public had used that crossing more than two
years when the animals in controversy in that case were
killed. Therefore there was evidence of a dedication
of the crossing by the railway company and an acceptance by the public. *State v. Birmingham*, 74 Iowa, 410.
It is true the crossing made in the Soward Case was
more than sixty-six feet in width, but that fact does not
appear to have had any effect in the decision of the case.
The case of *Knowles v. City of Muscatine*, 20 Iowa, 248,
also cited by the appellant, did not involve the question
which is controlling in this case, and is not in point. We
conclude that the question involved in the certificate
must be answered in the affirmative, and the judgment
of the district is AFFIRMED.

R. J. KINGSBURY v. THE CHICAGO, MILWAUKEE & ST. ¹⁰⁴
PAUL RAILWAY COMPANY, Appellant, and C. W.
KINGSBURY v. THE SAME DEFENDANT, Appellant.

Pleading. In an action to recover damages for the killing of a horse
    which entered on the right of way at a point where the company
1 had a right to fence, a general denial presents the issue whether
    the railroad had a right to fence at the point in question, and not
    whether it had legal excuse for failing to do so. The last is mat-
    ter in estoppel which must be specially pleaded.

SAME. If the fact that a duty required by law involves difficulty or
1 expense would be a legal excuse for failure to meet the require-
    ment, it must be pleaded as a matter of affirmative defense, to be
    available.

SAME: *Instructions.* In an action against a railroad company for the
    killing of live stock, resulting from the failure of said road to
    build a fence along a portion of its right of way, acts of plaintiff
2 excusing such neglect are not available under a general denial,
    and under such issues, an instruction allowing a recovery if a
    horse was killed through neglect of defendant to fence, is proper.

Fences. A fence built along his holding by a tenant of lands leased
3 from a railway company is not a right of way fence, in the absence
    of some agreement, express or implied.

Evidence: RAILROADS. A finding that horses killed on a railroad
    right of way entered at a point where there was no fence, will be
4 supported by evidence that the hoofprints of the animals indi-
    cated such to be the fact.

Appeal from Appanoose District Court.—HON. T. M.
FEE, Judge.

FRIDAY, DECEMBER 17, 1897.

THE two cases are so nearly identical in facts that
they were tried together below, and are so submitted in
this court. Our consideration will have especial reference to the first-entitled case. The defendant's line of
road crosses plaintiff's land. On plaintiff's land, and
adjacent to defendant's right of way, is a coal mine,

which in 1888 was leased to the Enterprise Coal Company for a term of fifty years.   For the use of the coal
company in shipping its coal, the defendant company
run a spur track from its main line to and past the mine.
The area occupied by the coal company was from one
and one-half to two acres, on which were its shaft,
machinery, dumping ground, and other conveniences
for the operation of the mine, and across this the spur
track was built and operated.   Before the construction
of the spur track, the right of way fence had extended
along the main line of defendant's road.   The mine is on
the north side of the main line, and around the area we
have mentioned is a fence, built by plaintiff, which con-
nects on the east of the coal mine, and also on the west
of it, with the right of way fence along the main line.
Between these points of connection there is no right of
way fence, as the one once there had been taken away
or broken down, and the track is open to the space
around which is the fence of plaintiff's above described.
We should state here that we may be mistaken as to
some of the facts, for the testimony designates lines and
locations by letters, figures, and a dotted line on a plat,
and all of the figures, most of the letters, and the dotted
line are omitted from the plat, so that some of the evidence is absolutely unintelligible.   As we understand,
plaintiff's horse and one belonging to his son (who is
plaintiff in the other suit) passed through a gate in the
fence made by plaintiff, that we have described, and
then across the coal land, onto the right of way, and
were killed by a passing train.   These actions are to
recover, under the statute, for double their value. There
were verdict and judgment in each case for the plaintiff, and the defendant appealed.—*Affirmed.*

Mabry & Payne for appellant.

C. F. Howell for appellees.

GRANGER, J.—I.   The petition alleged a failure to
fence the right of way at a point where defendant had
a right to fence, and also negligence in the operation of
defendant's train, as the cause of the injury. The
answer is a denial. The court gave the case to
the jury only on the question of the neglect to
fence the right of way. We do not understand appellant to claim but that defendant had the right to fence
its right of way at the point where the horses came onto
it,—that is, between the points east and west of the coal
land; but its claim is that, because of the mutual interests of the parties, the defendant was excused from
keeping a fence on that part of its right of way. It is
not claimed that plaintiff ever made any agreement to
that effect. If he has no right now to insist that the
company should maintain a fence at the place in controversy, or be liable for a neglect to do so, it must be
because of his acts in leasing the land for mining purposes, and fencing around it as he did. The legal effects
of the acts, if sufficient as a defense, would be an estoppel, which is not pleaded, and it must be before advantage could be taken of it. *Glenn v. Jeffrey*, 75 Iowa, 20.
The rule is familiar. The issues under a general denial,
presented simply the question, had the company the
right to fence its right of way at the point in question?
not, has it a legal excuse for not so doing? The latter,
if it should be that, because of the acts of plaintiff, or
the relationship of the parties arising from plaintiff's
acts, or the mutual interests of the parties growing out
of the coal-mining interests, it was not bound to fence,
would be an affirmative defense, to be pleaded as such,
and does not arise on a denial, as in this case. We take
it that the court below took this view of the issues, for it
denied the admission of evidence on the theory of an
affirmative defense, and submitted the case on the
theory alone of the defendant's liability if it had

neglected to build or maintain a fence along its right of
way at the point in question, and the horses went onto
the right of way, and were killed in consequence of it.
It told the jury that if there had been such neglect, and
the horses were so killed, there should be a recovery.
We think the rule thus stated is the correct one under
the issues. Thus understood, the facts to warrant a
recovery were without dispute so far as the acts of the
defendant were involved concerning the fence. It was
simply a question if the horses were killed in consequence of the failure to maintain the fence, and the
amount of damage. It is said in argument that the
company could not keep a fence along the right of way
at this place without making a cattle guard on the spur
track. That, of course, would involve expense,
2   but it would not change the right of defendant to
maintain the fence. The case turns on the right
to maintain the fence and the failure to do so. If diffi-
culties or costs in so doing would be an excuse in law,
it would, as before stated, be a matter of affirmative
defense to be pleaded. Some assignments are argued
on the ruling as to the admission of evidence. Such
rulings were in line with the court's theory that the
claim of mutual interests or understandings, as a
defense, was not involved, which we hold to be correct.
The court said to the jury that the fence built by plaintiff around the leased land was not a right of way fence,
and the court was clearly right. The undisputed facts
show it to be a fence built by plaintiff from the
3   right of way line, on the east of the coal land to
the same line on the west, inclosing a piece of
plaintiff's land that he had leased. It could only be
treated as a right of way fence by virtue of some agreement, expressed or implied, to that effect; and, as we
have said, no such issue is presented. The court, however, offered defendant the right to show that the fence

built by the plaintiff was, by arrangement, to be taken
and adopted in lieu of a right of way fence; but the
offer was disregarded. *Bond v. Railroad Co.*, 100 Ind.
301, and some other cases are cited. None of them are
against our conclusion here. This case turns on a question of pleadings. Those deal with issues presented.

II.   A question is made as to the sufficiency of the
evidence to show that the horses went onto the right of
way where there was no fence. In this respect we
experience a difficulty because of what we have
4   said as to the defective plat to which the testimony refers, and, without the reference letter,
figure, or mark, the evidence is in some respects obscure.
A witness refers to a dotted line on the plat as indicating the point at which it is thought the horses went onto
the right of way. There is no such dotted line on the
plat before us. The only dotted line is that indicating
the railway track. It does, however, appear that there
were indications that the horses went from the coal
land onto the right of way, because of tracks to show
that fact. Some cases cited, holding the evidence insufficient to show that stock went onto the track at the
point where no fence was kept, are not like this in their
facts, and do not control it. We think the evidence in
this respect is such that the question was one for the
jury. The judgment in each case will stand AFFIRMED.

IN THE MATTER OF THE ASSIGNMENT, ETC., OF O. M.
SHONKWILER, I. N. DRAKE, and O. M. WHITMAN v.
D. T. STEWART AND GEORGE ATKINSON.

Mulct Law: PHARMACIST'S PERMIT. Under Acts Twenty-fifth General Assembly, chapter 62, section 1, which provide for the assessing of a tax for the selling of liquors against persons, other than
registered pharmacists holding permits, such a pharmacist is not
liable for the tax although selling liquor in violation of his permit. A statute which is clearly expressed must be given the effect
of the legislative intent as thus expressed.

Appeal from O'Brien District Court.—HON. GEORGE W. WAKEFIELD, Judge.

FRIDAY, DECEMBER 17, 1897.

W. P. Briggs for appellants.

Milt H. Allen for appellees.

KINNE, C. J.—I. Defendant Stewart was the owner of certain real estate in the town of Hartley, O'Brien county, Iowa. He was conducting, in 1895, upon said premises, a drug store and pharmacy. Defendant Atkinson was employed by Stewart as a clerk in said pharmacy, and both appellees were registered pharmacists, and their certificates as such were in force. The district court of O'Brien county, in May, 1890, issued a permit to defendant Stewart, under the laws of this state, authorizing him to keep and sell intoxicating liquors in his pharmacy for certain purposes, which permit was in full force in the year 1895, and at the time of the assessing of the tax hereinafter mentioned. In June, 1895, the assessor of the town of Hartley assessed against the defendant and against the premises a tax of six hundred dollars for selling intoxicating liquors in and upon said premises during said year, said assessment being made under the provisions of chapter 62, Acts Twenty-fifth General Assembly, known as the "mulct law." Under said assessment, the board of supervisors of said county levied a tax of six hundred dollars against the defendant and against said premises. Thereafter defendant presented a petition to said board of supervisors for the abatement of said assessment and tax, and, upon a hearing thereon, said board, finding that said tax was wrongfully assessed and levied, did abate and cancel the same. Plaintiffs appealed from the decision of said board to the district

court of said county. Upon a trial and hearing had
before said court, the action of the board of supervisors
in abating said tax was approved, and a judgment was
entered against said plaintiffs for costs. They appeal.—
Affirmed.

II.   This record presents a single question for our
determination. If a registered pharmacist, who has a
permit for the keeping and selling of intoxicating
liquors under the laws of this state, keeps for sale or
sells intoxicating liquors in violation of his permit, is
he liable to the payment of the tax imposed under the
provisions of the mulct law? Section 1, chapter 62,
Acts Twenty-fifth General Assembly, provides: "There
shall be assessed against every person, partnership or
corporation, other than registered pharmacists holding
permits, engaged in selling or keeping with intent to
sell, any intoxicating liquors, and upon any real property and the owner thereof, within or whereon intoxicating liquors are sold, or kept with intent to sell in
this state, a tax of six hundred dollars per annum."
Section 2 provides that it shall be the duty of the assessor to return to the county auditor of each county "a
list of places, with name of occupant or tenant, and
owner or agent, where intoxicating liquors are sold, or
kept for sale as herein contemplated, with a description
of the real property wherein or whereon such traffic is
conducted." It is not necessary to refer to other sections of the act. By section 1 of the act, "registered
pharmacists holding permits" are expressly exempted
from this tax. The argument of appellant is that the
legislature must have intended that the exemption
should not apply to such registered pharmacists holding permits who sell intoxicating liquors in violation of
said permits. The statute makes no such provision, and
we cannot assume the prerogatives of the legislature,
and add to its plain provisions. If the statute was
ambiguous or uncertain as to the persons or property

who should be subject to this tax burden, we might well
follow appellants' suggestion, and seek for the intent
of the legislature in the enactment of the act. Indeed,
if the language of the act was such as that it was subject to two constructions, one of which would effectuate
the manifest intent of the law-making power, it might
be our duty to give effect to that intent. But such is
not the case. Section 45 of the Code of 1873 provides:
"In the construction of the statutes, the following rules
shall be observed, unless such construction would be
inconsistent with the manifest intent of the general
assembly or repugnant to the context of the statue."
And in paragraph 2 of said section it is provided:
"Words and phrases shall be construed according to
the context and the approved usage of the language."
Here is a statute plainly exempting certain persons
from the tax imposed. There is no other provision in
the act which even tends to show that the legislature
did not intend just what the plain provisions of this
exception, construed according to the approved usage
of the language, mean. This is the only statute which
undertakes to impose a tax upon the business of keeping for sale or selling intoxicating liquors. This court
is committed to the rule that, when the legislative
intent is clearly expressed, it is our duty to so construe
the statute as to give force and effect to such intent.
French v. French, 84 Iowa, 655. Many rules might be
referred to touching the construction of statutes, but it
is not necessary that we do so, in view of the plain provisions of the section under consideration. Indeed, it is
a case where the language used is too plain to require
construction. The action of the district court was
proper.—AFFIRMED.

C. C. WHITE, Appellant, v. L. LEDBETTER.

Costs. Under Code 1873, sections 2938, 2934, making the costs of different issues taxable against the party who fails to succeed on such issue, costs are properly divided between plaintiff and defendant in an action on a contract for the sale of live stock, where plaintiff succeeds on the issues raised by the pleadings that the matters in controversy had been settled, and that the defendant accepted the stock under the contract, although as not in full performance thereof, and defendant succeeds on the issue raised by a counter-claim asking for a reduction from the amount due, on account of plaintiff's non-performance of the contract.

Appeal from Appanoose District Court.—HON. T. M. FEE, Judge.

FRIDAY, DECEMBER 17, 1897.

APPEAL from an order and judgment taxing certain costs to plaintiff, White.—*Modified and affirmed.*

C. F. Howell for appellant.

Mabry & Payne for appellee.

DEEMER, J.—Appellant sued upon a written contract for the sale of certain live stock to the defendant, alleging that he had delivered the stock to defendant pursuant to the terms of the written instrument, and that there was due him thereunder the sum of four hundred and seventy-five dollars, with twenty-five dollars additional as damages for its non-performance. Defendant admitted the execution of the contract, but denied performance on the part of the plaintiff. He also pleaded a settlement. Defendant further pleaded a counter-claim, based upon plaintiff's non-performance of the contract, and asked for a deduction from the amount due on account thereof in the sum of one hundred

and thirteen dollars. The plaintiff, in reply, denied the
allegations of the counter-claim, and pleaded a waiver
on the part of the defendant of any failure on his (plaintiff's) part by acceptance of the stock and a promise to pay
the contract price. In an amendment to his petition,
filed after the case was called for trial, plaintiff
admitted that the stock delivered by him did not meet
the obligations of his contract, but pleaded waiver on
the part of the defendant, and a parol agreement to
accept the stock so delivered as a full performance.
Evidence was adduced on all of these issues, and the
court submitted the various questions of fact to a jury.
The jury returned a verdict for the plaintiff in the sum
of five hundred and thirteen dollars. Thereafter defendant filed a motion for a new trial. While this motion
was pending, the parties entered into an agreement to
the effect that in consideration of the defendant's withdrawing his motion plaintiff would relinquish one hundred dollars from the amount of the verdict returned;
that judgment should be rendered as if the verdict had
been for four hundred and thirteen dollars; and that the
court should dispose of the question of costs as if the
verdict had been for this last-named amount; the exact
language of the stipulation with relation to costs being
as follows: "It being the intention that this stipulation
shall leave open the question of costs to be disposed of
and adjudicated according to law, and shall be no
waiver by either party of their right to have the court
dispose of the question of costs to all intents and purposes the same as if said verdict had been rendered by
the jury for four hundred and thirteen dollars, that the
defendant shall have the same right to file and submit
his motion as to the costs, and have the same passed
upon by the court according to law, to all intents and
purposes the same as if said verdict had been for four
hundred and thirteen dollars originally." Thereupon

defendant filed a motion to tax all costs to plaintiff.
This motion was sustained, and it is from the ruling
upon this motion that the appeal is taken.

In the bill of exceptions filed in the case we find
this statement of the trial judge: "In addition, and
explanatory of the stipulations of the parties for remission of one hundred dollars from the verdict of the jury,
signed and filed by them in writing, as above set out, at
the time of the submission of defendant's motion to tax
the costs to plaintiff, it was orally agreed by both parties in open court, and the motion was so argued in that
view, that the remission of the one hundred dollars by
the plaintiff, in order to avoid the probability of a new
trial, should have the same force and effect, and the
court should so treat it in considering said motion, as if
the jury had specifically found for the defendant one
hundred dollars on his counter-claim." The counter-
claim to which we have referred was filed after the jury
was sworn and some of the evidence adduced. Turning
now to the issues, we see that, briefly stated, they were
three: (1) That plaintiff did not comply with the contract on his part; (2) that there was a settlement of the
matters in controversy; and (3) the counter-claim of
defendant. Plaintiff had the affirmative on one, and
the defendant on two of them. Under the stipulations
and agreements of the parties it is apparent that defendant must have recovered on his counter-claim, and it is
likewise apparent from the verdict returned that
defendant failed on his issue as to settlement, and that
plaintiff succeeded in convincing the jury that
defendant accepted the stock under the contract,
although not as in full performance thereof. Under
the statute (Code 1873, sections 2933, 2934), all costs
made on the issue presented by the counter-claim were
properly taxable to the plaintiff, and all other costs
should be taxed to the defendant. As nearly as we are

able to judge from an examination of the record, about
one-half the time was occupied, and perhaps one-half
the witnesses were examined, with reference to the
counter-claim upon which the parties now agree the
defendant was successful, and in equity each party
should pay one-half the costs. The court was in error
in taxing all the costs of witnesses and expense made
necessary in securing them, to the plaintiff. We think
the costs should have been equally apportioned. The
parties will each pay one-half the costs of this appeal.—
MODIFIED AND AFFIRMED.

D. W. SALYERS v. D. M. MONROE, *et al.*, Appellants.

Negligence: INSTRUCTIONS. In an action for personal injuries, where
there is a conflict in the evidence in regard to the circumstances
under which the accident occurred, and there is direct evidence of
2   proper care on the part of plaintiff, it is prejudicial error to instruct
that the jury are to take into consideration the natural instinct of
man to guard himself from danger and preserve himself from
injury.

Witness: PERSONAL TRANSACTION. Under Code 1873, section 3639,
providing that no party to any action shall be examined as
a witness in regard to any communication between him and a
1   person who is dead at the commencement of the examination,
against the survivor of such deceased person, the plaintiff in an
action for personal injuries against the members of a partnership
is incompetent to testify to a conversation with one of the partners who dies before the trial, although his personal representative is not substituted as a party to the action.

Appeal from Appanoose District Court.—HON. M. A.
ROBERTS, Judge.

FRIDAY, DECEMBER 17, 1897.

ACTION at law to recover damages for personal injuries sustained by the plaintiff, for which the defendants
are alleged to be liable. There was a trial by jury, and a

verdict and judgment for the plaintiff. The defendants appeal—*Reversed.*

George D. Porter and *J. A. Elliott* for appellants.

C. F. Howell and *L. T. Richmond* for appellee.

DEEMER, J.—In the latter part of the year 1893, the defendants, D. M. Monroe, H. P. Richardson, and John Benefiel (now deceased), constructed a coal shaft for the purpose of opening a mine on land which belonged to Monroe. Richardson was in charge of the work, although Monroe assisted, and the plaintiff was an employe. Coal was reached at a depth of about fifty feet. The shaft was divided by partitions into three subdivisions or compartments, one of which was for air, and two for hoisting purposes. The middle shaft was in use at the time plaintiff was injured; and the men and materials were lowered to and raised from the bottom by means of a pulley fastened to a timber, suspended above the mouth of the shaft. A rope passed over the pulley, and a horse was hitched to one end of the rope. A bucket was provided to be fastened to the other end. Whatever was to be raised from the shaft was attached to the lower or shaft end of the rope, and was drawn up by the horse. When men were raised and lowered, they sometimes sat upon a stick which was fastened to the rope in a horizontal position. In the latter part of September, of the year named, when the shaft was nearly completed, the plaintiff, who was at the bottom of the shaft, was directed by Richardson to come out, and bring his shovel. In obedience to that order, plaintiff fastened the stick to the rope, placed himself in the proper position, and, with his shovel in one hand and the rope in the other, was drawn towards the top of the shaft. When within five or six

feet of the top, his head came in contact with a board
which had been placed across one side of the shaft for
use in completing the woodwork. He was thereby
thrown from the stick, and fell to the bottom, and
received the injuries for which he seeks to recover. He
alleges that the defendants were co-partners in sinking
and completing the shaft and in opening the mine, and
were responsible for Richardson's undertakings and
acts connected therewith; that he had agreed, and it
was his duty, to so manage the rope, when plaintiff was
being drawn from the shaft, as to prevent his coming in
contact with the board, but that at the time of the accident he neglected to attend to his duty with respect to
the rope, and that his failure to do so, or to cause the
speed of the horse to slacken as the plaintiff approached
the board, was the cause of the accident. The defendants
deny that they were co-partners when the accident
occurred; deny that the plaintiff was employed by them;
and aver that he knew of the existence of the board in
question, but made no objection thereto, and continued
to work without protest, thereby waiving liability on
the part of the defendants on account of its proximity
to the shaft. The death of Benefiel was shown at the
trial, but his administrator was not substituted as a
party, and the trial proceeded, and judgment was
rendered against Monroe and Richardson.

I. The appellants complain because the plaintiff
was permitted to testify in regard to a conversation he
had with Benefiel, upon the ground that, at the time
of the trial Benefiel was deceased, and for
1   that reason the testimony was incompetent,
under section 3639 of the Code of 1873. That
section contains the following: "No party to any
action or proceeding, nor any person interested in the
event thereof, * * * shall be examined as a witness in regard to any personal transaction or communi-

cation between such witness and a person at the commencement of such examination deceased, * * *
against the * * * survivor of such deceased person." It was said in *Reynolds v. Insurance Co.*, 80
Iowa, 565, that "the word 'survivor' is usually applied
to the longest liver of two or more partners or trustees,
and has been applied in some cases to the longest liver
of joint tenants, legatees, and to others having a joint
interest in anything." See, also, *Brown v. Allen*, 35
Iowa, 311, and 17 Am. & Eng. Enc. Law, 1154, and notes.
A surviving partner is within both the letter and the
spirit of the statute. As he cannot have the benefit of
the testimony of his deceased partner as to what the
conversation really was, he should not be made liable
on the testimony of his adversary respecting it. Since
the mouth of one of the parties to the conversation is
closed by death, the law compels the other to remain
silent. The fact that the representative of the deceased
partner was not a party to the action is immaterial. It
may be said that the defendants denied they were partners, but the testimony in question was admissible only
on the theory that a partnership existed, and was subject to the statute applicable to the survivor of a
deceased partner. It was held in *Brown v. Allen, supra,*
that the defendant was competent to testify to an agreement made between himself and the deceased partner
of the plaintiff; but that action arose under section
3982 of the Revision of 1860, which did not contain the
provision which is controlling in this case. It follows
from what we have said that the testimony in question
was improperly received.

II. On the trial of the case, plaintiff submitted
evidence which tended to show that he was free from
negligence which contributed to the accident, and that
Richardson, who was at the top of the shaft, had
2   agreed to so manage the rope as to prevent the
plaintiff from coming in contact with the board,
but had negligently failed to attend to that duty. The

evidence on part of the defendants tended to show that
Richardson had not agreed to manage the rope as
claimed; that it was not his duty to do so; and that he
was not guilty of any negligence which caused or contributed to the accident. The court charged the jury
that the plaintiff, in order to recover, must show that,
at the time of the accident, he was in the exercise of
ordinary care and caution, and that his own negligence
or want of ordinary care did not contribute to the
injury. The eleventh paragraph of the charge contained
the following: "In considering the question of whether
the plaintiff was negligent, you will take into consideration his situation, and all the facts and circumstances
surrounding him at the time, his condition, as to
whether he was incumbered with a shovel, or any other
incumbrance, his knowledge of the dangerous position
of said board, if you find it was so dangerous and he
knew it, the natural instinct of man to guard himself
against danger and preserve himself from injury. * *
* All these matters should be inquired into by you,
and you should consider all other facts bearing upon
the question as shown by the evidence, and then say
whether, under all the circumstances, he acted negligently or otherwise." The jury was thus instructed to
consider "the natural instinct of man to guard himself
against danger, and preserve himself from injury," in
determining whether plaintiff was guilty of contributory negligence. It is settled that such an instruction may be given where the care exercised by a person
at the time of an accident which caused his death is in
question, and direct evidence as to such care used cannot be had. *Way v. Railroad Co.*, 40 Iowa, 342. But,
when there is such evidence, the instinct of self-preservation cannot be given any weight. *Dunlavy v. Railway
Co.*, 66 Iowa, 439; *Whitsett v. Railway Co.*, 67 Iowa, 157;
Reynolds v. City of Keokuk, 72 Iowa, 372. The eleventh

paragraph of the charge was therefore erroneous, for
the reason that the plaintiff gave direct testimony
respecting the care he used at the time of the accident.
But it is said that the error was without prejudice, as
he alone knew and testified as to such care. But there
was a conflict in the evidence in regard to the circumstances under which the accident occurred, and the
jury was told that it should consider the natural instinct
of man to preserve himself from injury; and we must
presume that it did so, and cannot say that it did not
give any weight to the instruction.

III. Questions we have not discussed are suggested by the appellants, but some of them are not presented by proper assignment of error, some are not
argued, and others are not likely to arise on another
trial. Therefore we need not consider them. For the
errors pointed, the judgment of the district court is
REVERSED.

ZANE SPURRIER v. WILLIAM McCLINTOCK, Defendant,
Appellant, MABEL H. BAKER, Intervener,
Appellant.

Fraud: SETTING DEED ASIDE. A widow made deed to F. Part of
the land belonged to a minor and a bond was given that the minor
should deed upon attaining majority. The land passed to M and
the bond was acquired by plaintiff. When the minor attained
majority she desired not only to relieve the makers of the bond
from liability, but, as well, to perfect the title of M, to whom the
land had passed Plaintiff fraudulently induced her to make
deed to him, representing that by so doing she would quiet the
title of M. *Held*, the deed should be set aside.

Appeal from Taylor District Court.—HON. W. H. TED-
FORD, Judge.

FRIDAY, DECEMBER 17, 1897.

ACTION of partition. Decree for plaintiff. All parties appeal.— *Reversed*.

Charles Thomas and *Maxwell & Winter* for appellants McClintock and Baker.

Crum & Haddock and *W. M. Jackson* for plaintiff.

KINNE, C. J.—I. Prior to January 21, 1888, Sarah
S. Sargent (widow) was the owner of the northeast
quarter of section 5, township 69, range 32, in Taylor
county, Iowa, except an undivided one-eleventh of the
same, which her minor daughter, Mabel H. Sargent,
owned by inheritance from her father. On January 21,
1888, Mrs. Sargent conveyed the whole of said land to
George H. Finley, by warranty deed containing full
covenants, except as to a certain mortgage incumbrance
thereon. When this deed was made, all of the parties
to the transaction understood that said daughter was
the owner of the legal title to an undivided one-eleventh
interest in said land, and that, as soon as she arrived of
age, it was expected she would fulfill her mother's contract. So believing, Mrs. Sargent, as principal, and
John Knox, as surety, at the time of making the deed,
executed and delivered to Finley a bond by which they
bound themselves unto "George H. Finley, his heirs,
executors, legal representatives, or grantees, in the
penal sum of two hundred and fifty dollars." The condition of said bond was as follows: "Whereas, the
above-bounden Sarah S. Sargent has this day made warranty deed to the said George H. Finley, conveying the
northeast quarter of section five. township sixty-nine,
range thirty-two, in Taylor county, Iowa; and whereas,
the above-bounden Sarah S. Sargent has one child, viz.
Mabel H. Sargent, who at this date has not arrived at
her majority: Now, if, at the time the said Mabel H.
Sargent shall arrive at her majority, she will, for the

consideration of one dollar, quit-claim her interest in above-described land to said George H. Finley, his heirs, executors, legal representatives, or grantees, then and in that case this bond to be null and void, and otherwise to be and remain in full force and effect." On the same day, and after the execution and delivery of the deed and bond by Mrs. Sargent to Finley, the latter executed a mortgage upon the whole tract, for two thousand dollars, to Monmouth College. Said mortgage contained full covenants as to warranty, title, etc. Afterwards Finley became insolvent. Still later the college foreclosed its said mortgage, and procured a decree, upon which an execution issued; and the premises were sold thereunder, on June 25, 1890, to the appellant McClintock. Thereafter McClintock purchased Finley's equity of redemption in said land. June 27, 1891, the sheriff of the county executed and delivered to McClintock a sheriff's deed for said land. McClintock took possession of the land, and has ever since held it. In September, 1895, the daughter, Mabel, attained her majority, by her intermarriage with one Frank D. Baker. Mabel desired to fulfill her mother's contract, and to release her and her surety from liability upon the bond, or on the covenants of the deed. Knox, the surety, was an uncle of Mabel. Plaintiff induced Mabel and her husband to believe that a deed to him would, in effect, be the same as to Finley; and it was so executed and delivered to plaintiff, without any consideration paid, except the nominal sum of one dollar, though the deed contained an expressed consideration of two hundred and fifty dollars. Under this deed, plaintiff claimed to own an undivided one-eleventh of the land, and began this action for partition thereof. McClintock answered, claiming all of the land; that the deed to plaintiff was procured by fraud, connivance, and deception of both Finley and plaintiff, and for the purpose of cheating and defrauding McClintock, and of casting a cloud upon his title. Mabel II. Baker, intervened, alleging the execution of the deed by her and her husband in fulfillment of the provisions of the bond, and that, by the fraud and misrepresentations of plaintiff and Finley, she was induced to make the deed without any consideration, other than one dollar and the delivery of the bond. She offered to return the one dollar, and asked that the deed be set aside, and that McClintock's title be quieted. A decree was entered awarding plaintiff one-eleventh of the land, subject to a lien of two hundred and fifty dollars against the same in favor of McClintock. Referees were appointed to divide or sell the land, and other orders were made. From the decree, all parties appeal.

II. We first consider the appeal of McClintock and of the intervener. It is clear that the object of giving the bond was to make good to Finley, or to his grantees, the title to the land heretofore described. True it is, that, on arriving at her majority, Mabel might refuse to convey her interest in the land to either Finley or his grantee, in which event the penalty of the bond would be the measure of the liability of the makers of it. But what are the facts? Mabel and her husband, as the evidence shows, intended, by the conveyance which they made, to not only take up the bond, and thus release the obligors therein from any liability thereon, but likewise, by the same act, to perfect the title to the land to McClintock, who had acquired Finley's interest in the land. She supposed that she was accomplishing this, in executing the deed to plaintiff. Representations to that effect were made to her, on the faith of which she executed and delivered the deed. We think it is clear that she would never have executed the deed to plaintiff, had she not supposed that the result would be as we have stated. She was, then, induced to make title to plaintiff by reasons of representations which were false, and, no doubt, made with the intent to deceive her. The plaintiff was fully advised of the situation. He knew, when he purchased the bond, of its object, and purposely and fraudulently induced the execution of the deed to himself. Whether he could, under any circumstances, claim any right under the bond, by assignment or otherwise, we need not determine. Certain it is that he could not—at least, as against his grantor—acquire title by reason of fraudulent representations. The deed should be set aside, and, as both Mabel and McClintock ask that the title be quieted in the latter, we think that the decree should have so ordered. The intervener and the defendant may, if they so elect, have a decree in this court setting aside and canceling said deed, and quieting title to the land in controversy in the defendant, and the plaintiff will pay the costs, or the case will be remanded for an entry of such a decree in the lower court. We do not find it necessary to consider other questions discussed.

III. As to plaintiff's appeal: The parties stipulated that, in case plaintiff was entitled to recover, he should receive the undivided one-eleventh of the land. The trial court apparently overlooked this stipulation, and made a charge of two hundred and fifty dollars against the one-eleventh interest, title to which was found to be in the plaintiff. From this decree, plaintiff appealed. As we find that plaintiff is not entitled to any relief, the decree below was erroneous. As to both appeals, therefore, the cause must be REVERSED.

S. P. BEEMAN, Appellant, v. THE FARMERS PIONEER MUTUAL INSURANCE ASSOCIATION.

Insurance: ASSESSMENT: *Waiver*. The reception by a mutual insurance company, after a loss of part of the property insured, of an 1 assessment which had become payable before the loss occurred, does not waive a forfeiture of the policy for non-payment of such

2 assessment, under a provision of the policy that it shall be null
and void in case of non-payment within a specified time "until"
the assessment is paid; as the insured had the right to make the
payment at any time, and the company was bound to accept it,
to revive the policy for the remaining time as to the other property.

SAME A second assessment by a mutual insurance company after a
failure of a member to pay a prior assessment within the time
1 required by a provision of the policy, that if any member fails to
pay his assessment within a specified time after receiving notice
2 thereof his insurance shall be null and void until such assessments are paid, does not estop it to claim that it is not liable on
the policy because of the failure to pay the prior assessment.

NOTICE OF ASSESSMENT. A mutual insurance company organized
under Acts Sixteenth General Assembly, chapter 103, expressly
prohibiting such companies from receiving premiums or making
8 dividends is not within Acts Eighteenth General Assembly, chapter 210, section 1, providing that in every instance where a fire
insurance company takes a note for the "premium" of any policy,
such company shall not declare the policy forfeited or suspended
for non-payment of the note, without first giving a prescribed
notice. Hence, the failure on part of such mutual company to
give notice which conforms to such statutes, is not material.

Appeal from Keokuk District Court.—HON. A. R.
DEWEY, Judge.

FRIDAY, DECEMBER 17, 1897.

THE defendant is a mutual insurance company, and
on the thirtieth day of October, 1893, it issued its policy
to the plaintiff, for the term of five years, on certain
property, including a frame dwelling house, which was.
on the eleventh day of March, 1896, entirely destroyed
by fire and this action is to recover therefor. The answer
admits the insurance and loss alleged, and shows that
the defendant company is a mutual insurance company
that can insure no person not a member of the association; that plaintiff became a member thereof at the
time he received his policy of insurance in the way provided by its laws; that by article 12 of the constitution
of the association it is provided: "Should any member

fail to pay his assessment within thirty days from the
date of notice of his assessment, his insurance in this
association shall be null and void until such assessments are paid; but this provision shall not affect the
liability of said member for such delinquent assessments, and also for any dues and assessments which
may be levied for his share of any loss which may occur
while such delinquent assessment is due and unpaid, or
in course of collection." It then appears from the
answer that an assessment was made on plaintiff's policy, payable October 1, 1895, which became delinquent
November 1, 1895; that he was notified of such assessment the twenty-seventh of September, 1895, by the
same being sent to his postoffice address; that February
10, 1896, another assessment was made, and notice
thereof given, which assessment became delinquent
about March 15, 1896; and that the first of said assessments was delinquent when the loss occurred, because
of which the policy was void. It is admitted that on
the twenty-seventh of March, 1896, both of the assessments were paid. In a reply, plaintiff pleads an estoppel because of the making of the second assessment,
and because of the acceptance of payment of the two
assessments. The cause was tried to the court without
a jury, and at the conclusion it dismissed plaintiff's
petition, and he appealed.— *Affirmed.*

Woodin & Son for appellant.

C. H. Mackey for appellee.

GRANGER, J.—I. There was no estoppel because of
the second assessment, for the reason that it was the
right, if not the duty, of the association to make it. The
building burned was but a part of the property
1   insured, and by the terms of the contract the
plaintiff could at any time within the life of the
policy on its face pay delinquent assessments, and

restore the policy. The language of the article of the
constitution of the association above quoted is: "Should
any member fail to pay his assessment within thirty
days from the date of the notice of his assessment, his
insurance shall be null and void until such assessments
are paid." The only way of making assessments delinquent was to give notice, so that the thirty days might
run in which payment could be made, and avoid delinquency. The same article provides that a delinquent
member shall be liable for assessments levied while he
is delinquent because of a prior assessment. Thus it
will be seen that the liability of the plaintiff continued
as to other assessments, and the only way to escape
such liability is by payment of assessments due, when,
under article 14 of the constitution, he may withdraw
from membership. Under such conditions there could
be no estoppel because of making the assessment. There
is nothing in *McGowan v. Northwestern Legion of
Honor*, 98 Iowa, 118, to sustain such a claim.

II. Both assessments were paid on the twenty-
seventh of March, 1896, which was sixteen days after
the loss occurred, and it is said that the acceptance of
payment was a waiver of forfeiture of the policy.
2   Numerous cases are cited to support the claim of
waiver, but none of them are based on facts the
same, in substance, as in this case. The payment of
these assessments was necessary to restore the insurance provided for in the policy for the remainder of the
period of five years. The plaintiff had the right to make
the payments, and the association was bound to accept
them, in order to revive the policy for the remaining
time it had to run. There is not a word of testimony
that the plaintiff paid under a misapprehension as to
his rights because of it; not a word that he was misled
by the acts or statements of the officers of the association. The record simply shows that he paid what was

due from him, and the law fixed his rights because of
it under the terms of his contract with the association.
By the very letter of his contract, he had no insurance
when the loss occurred, because of his delinquency.

III. It is said that the notices of the assessments
are not sufficient, as not being in conformity to chapter
210, Acts Eighteenth General Assembly, for which reason the policy did not become void as to the insurance.

It is a matter of fact that the notices did not
3   conform to such requirements, either as to matter
or form of service; but appellee contends that the
chapter has no application to associations organized on
the mutual plan. The following is section 1 of the chapter referred to: "Section 1. That in every instance where
a fire insurance company or association, doing business
in this state, shall hereafter take a note or contract for
the premium on any insurance policy, or shall hereafter
take a premium note or contract which, by its terms, or
by any agreement or rule of the company or association,
is assessable for the premium due on the policy for
which it was given, such insurance company or association shall not declare such policy forfeited, or suspended
for non-payment of such note or contract except as hereinafter provided, anything in the policy or application
to the contrary notwithstanding." The other sections
provide for a notice to be given before a forfeiture can
be declared for unpaid premiums, and what the notice
shall contain. The section quoted contains all the
language as to what companies or associations are
within the provisions of the act. The defendant association is organized under the provisions of an act of
the Sixteenth General Assembly (chapter 103) and
amendatory acts. It is organized on the plan of making
mutual pledges and giving valid obligations to each
other for their own insurance from loss by fire. Such
associations are expressly prohibited by the act from

receiving premiums or making dividends. Referring to
the section quoted from the act of the Eighteenth General Assembly, it will be seen that the act applies to
companies or associations having a note or contract for
a premium on an insurance policy, or a premium note
or contract, which, by its terms, or by an agreement or
rule of the company or association, is assessable for a
premium due on a policy. The act has to do only with
associations or companies allowed to receive premiums,
and this association is not, and does not do it. The
obligations of the members are for assessments made
on the mutual plan, which the act under which it was
organized does not recognize as a premium, for it provides for such obligations, but prohibits receiving premiums. The several provisions of the statute are conclusive of the question. Neither the policy nor the laws
of the association provide for a premium, so that, as is
thought by appellant, the policy is not the contract contemplated by the act. The judgment is AFFIRMED.

MEDEARIS & BOWEN v. THE ANCHOR MUTUAL FIRE
INSURANCE COMPANY, Appellant.

In-urance. An insurance company is liable upon a policy of fire
insurance forwarded to it by its agent to be indorsed with its con-
1 sent to a transfer of the policy, when an additional premium was
demanded and paid to the agent, although the following day the
4 property was destroyed by fire, and before an indorsement by the
company.

ESTOPPEL. Where an insurer had written its agent that it could not
approve an assignment of a policy to the purchaser of the insured
1 property, unless he agreed to an advanced rate, and instructed him
2 to secure a new note for the rate as advanced, return same, together
3 with policy, when, if found satisfactory, consent to the assignment
4 of the policy would be indorsed thereon, and the agent had procured
the advanced rate and followed such instructions, it is estopped
to take advantage of the provisions of a policy rendering it void
where the legal title to the property was changed, and that an
agent could not waive any of the conditions of the policy.

EVIDENCE: *Principal and agent.* Letters in reference to the transfer
of a policy of fire insurance written by an agent to the company,
8 which notify it of the facts and form the basis of its communications to him, are admissible in evidence.

Same. Testimony given by the insured in an action brought upon a
fire insurance policy, that after a conversation with the com-
7 pany's agent he believed that he was insured in defendant company, is harmless error where the liability is fixed by an estoppel,
resting upon undisputed testimony.

Same. Evidence of a conversation between the insured and an
agent who acted as the medium of communication between the
6 insurance company and the insured, is admissible, although he was
only a soliciting agent with authority to organize certain counties
and look after local agents.

Instructions. An instruction is not objectionable for collating the
8 facts instead of charging separately on each point and stating
5 the rule of law applicable thereto, when the method adopted is
calculated to better bring the case within the comprehension of
the jury.

Appeal from Wapello District Court.—HON. F. W.
EICHELBERGER, Judge.

FRIDAY, DECEMBER 17, 1897.

ACTION on a policy of fire insurance. Judgment for
plaintiffs, and the defendant appealed.— *Affirmed.*

A. W. Enoch and *Sullivan & Sullivan* for appellant.

McNett & Tisdale for appellee.

GRANGER, J.—I. On the sixth day of August, 1893,
the defendant company issued to Medearis & Myers a
policy of insurance for the sum of eight hundred dollars, on what is known as "Cascade Laundry." While
the policy was in force, and about May 18, 1894, the
personnel of the firm was changed by the substitution
of Bowen for Myers, and the ownership of the property
correspondingly changed. At this time the company

held the note of Medearis & Myers for the insurance
      held by the firm. On the nineteenth of May,
1   1894, Medearis, in the interest of the firm of
      Medearis & Bowen, went to one T. H. Corrick,
who was a special agent of the company, to obtain the
consent of the company to change the ownership of
the property to the new firm, and presented to Corrick
the policy for that purpose. On the back of the policy
were forms, in blank, for the indorsement of the company, and for the assignment of the policy from one
firm or person to another. Corrick filled in, in writing,
the blank for the assignment by Medearis & Myers to
Medearis & Bowen, and Medearis signed the name of
Medearis & Myers thereto, so as to complete the transaction between the firms. Corrick also filled in the
blank for the consent of the company, and inclosed the
policy, with a new note from Medearis & Bowen, to
the company at Creston, Iowa, with the following letter, omitting unimportant parts: (1) "Herewith I hand
you policy No. 6,478, Medearis & Myers, asking for
transfer of same to parties whose names appear on the
new note inclosed. The risk is all right, but I think I
would suggest to you that the rate on this was too low,
and you would have to ask for a raise of fifty cents, and
I think I can secure it." (2) "I told the assured this
morning I thought you would ask for 2 per cent. or
cancel policy. You use your own judgment in this
matter, and I will act accordingly." Under date of May
31, 1894, Corrick received the following letter in answer
to his of May nineteenth: "Creston, Iowa, May 31st,
1894. T. H. Corrick, S. A., Ottumwa, Iowa—Dear Sir:
Inclosed herein we hand you policy 6,478, Medearis &
Myers, and would advise you that we cannot consent
to assignment of this policy unless parties will agree to
an advance in rate of 1-2 per cent. per annum. You
will please secure new note made on the basis of

advanced rate, return same, together with the policy, when, if found satisfactory, consent to the assignment of said policy will be endorsed thereon, and the original note executed by Medearis & Myers canceled and returned to them. Yours, truly, Geo. J. Delmege, Secy." On receipt of this letter Corrick went to Medearis with the policy and surrendered the note before given, for some seventy-two or seventy-six dollars, and took a new one for ninety-six dollars to meet the requirement for additional premium, and collected in cash two dollars and seventy cents, which was indorsed on the note. The policy and new note were then sent to the company at Creston the same day, June 2, 1894, by Corrick, with the following letter: "Ottumwa, Iowa, 6-2-1894. Geo. J. Delmege, Secy., Creston, Iowa—Dear Sir: Herewith I hand you policy No. 6,478, with rate increased to two per cent., as per your instructions of recent date. I thought I could get the raise. Please charge me with $2.70, balance due on present year's payment. Please send me some more large envelopes, unaddressed. With best wishes, I am, very respectfully, T. H. Corrick." On the next day, Sunday, a fire swept away a part of the city of Ottumwa, including the laundry in question. On the same day Corrick wrote the company of the fire and that the laundry was burned, and advising the company to give the loss attention. On the next day, Monday, June 4, 1894, the company canceled the policy by a writing on the face thereof, and on the same day returned the policy and note, and the note given originally by Medearis & Myers, to Corrick, with information that the attention of the president of the company had been called to the matter, and that, as steam laundries were prohibited by the company, it would not consent to the assignment, and Corrick was directed to return the notes to the parties with a check for two dollars, in payment of pro rata cash premium paid by them. This action is to recover on the policy

II. The following is a provision of the policy: "It is hereby agreed that no agent or employe, or any other person or persons, other than the regular manag-
2   ing officer or officers of this corporation, can in any manner waive, alter, or change any or either of the conditions of this contract. This contract is made and accepted sub- ject to the above conditions." It contained the further provision that if the property be sold, or any change made in the legal title or possession, the policy should be void. In view of the facts of the case, and these provisions of the policy, the right of recovery is made to depend on a waiver of such provisions, or that the company was estopped to assert them. The court instructed the jury that the secretary of the company had power to waive the conditions of the policy, and also to consent in writing to the change of title to the property. It then gave the case to the jury on he ques-
3   tion of waiver or estoppel, in the following instruction: "If you find from the evidence that on or about May 19, 1894, Medearis, a member of the plaintiff firm, took the policy in question to Cor- rick, the special agent of defendant, at Ottumwa, Iowa, and informed him that the plaintiffs had become the owners of the insured property, and requested a trans- fer of the policy from the firm of Medearis & Myers over to the plaintiffs; that Corrick then filled out the blank form of transfer printed on the back of the policy from the firm of Medearis & Myers to the plaintiff, and that Medearis signed the name of the plaintiffs thereto, and left the policy with said Corrick, to be by him sent to the defendant's home office at Creston for considera- tion and indorsement, if the transfer was approved; that a premium note was also made out and signed for the

plaintiffs and left with said Corrick; that said Corrick either on said day, or on or about the twenty-sixth
day of May, 1894, mailed to the defendant said policy
and note, and with it the letter of Corrick dated May
19, 1894 (Exhibit I), in evidence, and that the letter,
policy, and note reached the defendant, and its secretary, Delmege, by due course of mail, at Creston; that
said secretary wrote and sent to the said Corrick his
letter of date May 31, 1894 (Exhibit X), in evidence,
inclosing the policy, and that they were received by
Corrick on June 1 or 2, 1894; that the said Corrick then
went to the plaintiffs and took from them the new note
for ninety-six dollars, in evidence, and collected from
them two dollars and seventy cents as cash premium,
and credited the same upon said new note; that on the
same day, to-wit, June 2, 1894, Corrick mailed said
policy and new note at the postoffice at Ottumwa,
addressed to the defendant at Creston, together with his
letter dated June 2, 1894 (Exhibit V), in evidence;
that the fire and destruction of plaintiffs' property took
place on June 3, 1894; that plaintiffs from May 19, 1894,
until after the fire received no notice from defendant,
or any of its agents, that defendant would not accept
the risk, or would not carry the insurance for them,
or would or had canceled the policy, or would treat it
as forfeited by reason of the transfer or change of possession of the insured property, or that, notwithstanding the new note given and the cash paid, the policy
would not be considered in force until the defendant or
its secretary had actually made and signed the written
consent upon the policy,—then you would be justified
in finding a waiver or estoppel, and in holding defendant upon the policy." This instruction is made the
basis of an assignment, and its consideration first will
set at rest some of the points argued, as they are essentially involved therein.

It is appellant's idea that on the nineteenth of May, when the change in the firm was made, the condition of the policy was violated and the contract of insurance at an end. Not necessarily so. It is to be borne in 4 mind that the negotiations between the new firm and the company were not with a view to new insurance, but with a view to such a consent on the part of the company as would continue the old policy. The policy, with the assignment on the back of it, was in the hands of the secretary, and also a note of the transferee, to take the place of the note of the old firm, and continue the insurance for the new firm; and it is clearly manifest that the company did not at that time intend to cancel the policy or treat it as void, until further negotiations were attempted, with a view to a higher rate of premium; and the secretary, in his letter of May 31, 1894, directed the agent, Corrick, to secure a new note on the basis of the advanced rate, and return the same, together with the policy, when, if found satisfactory, consent to the assignment of the policy would be endorsed thereon, and the original note executed by Medearis & Myers canceled and returned to them. Importance is attached by appellant to the words in the letter, "if found satisfactory," and it is thought that they save to the company a right, for any reason, to refuse its consent. The letter, in the light of facts that may be noticed, will not bear that construction. The company then knew all the facts to govern its conduct, so far as the policy was concerned, except as to whether it could get the increased rate; and a fair construction of the letter is that, if a satisfactory note was returned, it would indorse its assent on that policy, for which purpose it was to be returned. It is not to be doubted that had the note first made by Medearis & Bowen, that accompanied the policy, been for the amount of the last note, the consent would have been at once indorsed.

The delay was only for the added premium of twenty dollars. The company, when it did conclude to treat the policy as void, left no doubt of its purpose, and leaves to us unmistakable evidence of its method of procedure. With the policy at hand, it indorsed the fact thereon, and returned what it had received, barring, perhaps, as is claimed by appellee, the two dollars and seventy cents. Before that it was keeping what it had and seeking the added premium, for no other purpose than the continuation of the policy. We can construe the letter of the secretary to Corrick in no other way than that it authorized him to secure another note, which if given, and was satisfactory, the policy should be indorsed with the consent of the company. If so, the company is now estopped to take advantage of the provisions of the policy as to the indorsement thereon. No question whatever is made as to the sufficiency of the note. The only reason given for the cancellation is that the property insured was a laundry, which fact was, at all times known. With this view, we think there is no reason for complaint as to the legal proposition involved in the instruction. There is a criticism that the court should have instructed on each point in a way asked by appellant, instead of collating the facts as they appear in the instruction, and stating the rule of law applicable. We think the method adopted by the court the better one, and well calculated to bring the case to the comprehension of the jury.

5

.

III There is a complaint that the court erred in admitting in evidence the conversation between Medearis and Corrick, because Corrick was only a soliciting agent, with authority to look after local agents, and organize certain counties, etc. As to this particular question, we do not think it important to determine the scope of his authority as agent. That he was an agent there is no doubt, and

6

in this particular transaction he reported to and
received instructions from, the company, and his authority, in so far as he acted, was fully understood and
recognized by the company. He was the company's
medium of communication with the assured, so that his
acts became those of the company, as much as if he
were a general officer. The facts showing this situation
appear in the former divisions of the opinion.

IV. The court permitted Medearis and Bowen to
testify that, after the talk with Corrick on May 19, they
believed they were insured in the defendant company.

7
The ruling is thought to be error. If so, it is
without prejudice. The really essential facts to
justify a recovery on the basis of estoppel are so
few, and appear so conclusively, that a right of recovery
was not a doubtful question under the law as we have
determined it. The verdict really has support on the
documentary proof and the testimony of defendant's
witnesses.

V. It is thought that the letter of Corrick to the
company, under date of May 19, 1894, being the first
letter on the subject, was incompetent, and should not
have been admitted. Nothing more need be said
than that it was what notified the company of
what was wanted, and was the basis of its communication and authority to Corrick to act, and,
together with the company's letter in answer, shows its
understanding and purpose in the negotiation. The
same claim is made as to the final letter of Corrick to
the company, in which he inclosed the policy and the
note, with the added premium, which completed the
agreement. There can be no doubt of the admissibility
of such evidence. At the close of the testimony there
was a motion by defendant for a verdict in its favor,
which the court denied, and error is assigned on the

8

ruling. The assignment presents only such questions as we have considered, and the ruling was without error. The judgment is AFFIRMED.

STATE OF IOWA V. WILLIAM SKILLICORN, Appellant.

Intoxicating Liquors: INSTRUCTIONS Where the jury were instructed in a prosecution for maintaining a liquor nuisance, that if they found that a person commonly, or frequently, or whenever the
3 opportunity offers, uses intoxicating liquors as a beverage, they would have the right to infer that he was in the habit of so doing, and the evidence showed that several persons purchasing were in the habit of using intoxicating liquors as a beverage, the jury were warranted in so finding, though it did not appear that any of them made such use thereof "whenever the opportunity offers "

SAME: *Applicability.* In a trial for the illegal sale of intoxicating liquors, a reference in the charge to sales to minors is not preju-
2 dicial, although there is no evidence that any of the purchasers were minors, when such reference was necessary to a full statement of the law, and the question was plainly stated to the jury to be whether purchasers habitually used liquor as a beverage.

SAME. An instruction in a trial for the illegal sale of intoxicating liquors, which, without purporting to enumerate all, enumerates
4 certain facts to be taken into consideration in determining whether any of the sales were unlawful, to which is added, "and all other matters throwing light thereon," is not objectionable as authorizing the jury to go outside of the testimony.

SAME: *Construction.* The expression "to use as a beverage is to use as a drink," followed by the statement, "It will be seen, therefore,
6 that, when liquor is not used with intent to either treat, cure, or alleviate some bodily disorder or disease, it is not used for medical purposes," could not have been understood to mean that such liquor was used as a beverage merely because it was taken into the system through the process of "drinking "

Same. In a trial for the illegal sale of intoxicating liquors an instruction to the jury that whoever uses any building as a place for selling, or keeping for sale, intoxicating liquors in violation
7 of law, is guilty of the crime of nuisance, and proof of a single sale in a building so used, will warrant a conviction, is not objectionable as a charge that a single sale, whether lawful or unlawful, will warrant conviction. The words "single sale" have reference to a sale "in violation of law."

Same. An instruction to the jury in a trial for the illegal sale of intoxicating liquors that they should so construe the law as to prevent its evasion, and that no devise, art, or contrivance can
9 avail the defendant if they find there was a substantial violation of the law, is in harmony with Code, section 1554, and not objectionable as leaving the jury to place their own construction upon the law as given in the instructions, and allowing them to hold the law to be other than that given in the instruction.

Medicinal use. An instruction given to the jury in a trial for the illegal sale of intoxicating liquors, that "to use as a medicine is to use as a remedy for some disease, or as a medical agent in the treatment thereof" is not objectionable as a charge that if an ailment does not in fact exist, a purchase is unlawful however honest the belief and purchase of the purchaser. It merely requires that purchases should be in good faith, for medical purposes.

SAME: *Liquor applications.* An instruction to the jury in a trial for the illegal sale of intoxicating liquors, which directs it to take into consideration the applications for the sale of liquor, the hab-
8 its of the purchaser with reference to the use of ardent spirits, the frequency of the applications, and the amount purchased, in determining whether the law had been violated, sufficiently gives the defendant the full benefit of the proposition that applications made to him are evidence tending to show that the sales were legal.

EVIDENCE: *Sufficiency.* In a prosecution for maintaining a liquor nuisance, the evidence was sufficient to sustain the verdict, where
1 it warranted the jury to find that several of the purchasers were
10 persons in the habit of using intoxicating liquors as a beverage, and that their purchases were for such purposes, and that, as to some of them, defendant had reason for so believing, though they represented in each instance that they wanted the liquor for medical purposes.

Appeal from Mills District Court.—HON. W. R. GREEN, Judge.

FRIDAY, DECEMBER 17, 1897.

DEFENDANT was indicted, tried, and convicted of the crime of nuisance, and judgment rendered against him, from which he appeals.—*Affirmed.*

John Y. Stone, P. P. Kelley, W. S. Lewis, and *L. T. Genung* for appellant.

Milton Remley, attorney general, *Jesse A. Miller,* and *Shirley Gilliland* for the state.

GIVEN, J.—I. The charge is of maintaining a liquor nuisance. It was admitted by the state that the defendant was a registered pharmacist, and that he held a permit to sell intoxicating liquors, as authorized by law. The state called fourteen witnesses, each of whom testified to having purchased intoxicating liquors from the defendant at his store at different times between July 1 and the finding of the indictment, December 14, 1895. Each of said witnesses identified "requests of purchase," made and signed by them, respectively, to the defendant for each of said purchases. The number of purchases by each thus shown range from four to ten. The state also introduced these requests in evidence, each of which states the amount and kind of liquor desired to be purchased; that it was for medical use; the name and address of the purchaser; and that he was not a minor, and did not habitually use intoxicating liquors as a beverage. Said witnesses were examined as to the purposes for which the liquors were in fact purchased, and the use made of them, and as to whether they were in the habit of using intoxicating liquors as a beverage. The defendant having offered to prove that he was a regular registered pharmacist, and held a permit, these facts were admitted, as we have already stated. It was also admitted that he had filed his bi-monthly statements of purchases, sales, and use of intoxicating liquors for said period, verified as required by law. We have stated sufficient of the evidence to show that the controlling issue was whether any of these purchasers did habitually use intoxicating liquors as a beverage.

II. The court instructed as follows: "(6) While the law does not allow a permit holder to sell intoxicating liquors when he knows or has reason to believe that the same are purchased to be used as a beverage, yet, if he should in fact have reason to believe the statements contained in the application, the mere fact that the purchaser afterwards used the same as a beverage, or for a different purpose from that stated in the application, would not create any liability on the part of the seller. On the other hand, it is not sufficient to protect the permit holder that he has no knowledge in relation to the statements contained in the application. If he sells intoxicating liquors without having reason to believe that the statements of the applicant are true, he has violated the law.

(7) With respect to sales to persons who are in the habit of using intoxicating liquors as a beverage and minors, the law goes further. The holder of a permit must personally know that the person applying for liquors is not a minor nor in the habit of using intoxicating liquors as a beverage, before he has the right to sell the same; and, if he sells to a person who is in the habit of using intoxicating liquors as a beverage, then, so far as this case is concerned, it will be immaterial whether the permit holder knew of that fact or not, and he will be liable in the same manner as if he held no permit." Appellant complains of the reference here made to minors. It is true, as stated elsewhere in the instructions, that there is no evidence that any of these purchasers were minors; but this reference to minors was necessary to a full statement of the law, and was without prejudice to the appellant, as the question submitted was plainly stated to be whether any of said purchasers habitually used intoxicating liquors as a beverage.

III. The court, after defining "habit" as meaning the customary conduct of a person, to pursue which he has acquired a tendency from frequent repetitions of the same act," added: "If you find that a person commonly, or frequently, or whenever the opportunity offers, uses intoxicating liquors as a beverage, you would have the right to infer that he was in the habit of so doing." Appellant contends that there is no 3 evidence that any of these purchasers used intoxicating liquors as a beverage "whenever the opportunity offers. The evidence, as set out in appellee's amendment to the abstract, tends strongly to show that several of these purchasers were in the habit of using intoxicating liquors as a beverage, and the jury was warranted in so finding. In the fif- 4 teenth instruction the court enumerated certain facts to be taken into consideration in determining whether any of the sales were unlawful, and added, "and all other matters throwing light thereon." It is insisted that by this the jury was authorized to believe that it might go outside of the testimony; but not so, we think, as all matters appearing in the evidence were not enumerated, and the other matters referred to must have been understood as matters proven in addition to those enumerated.

IV. In the eighth instruction the court said: "To use as a medicine is to use as a remedy for some disease, or as a medical agent in the treatment thereof. To use for medical purposes is to use for the cure or alleviation of some bodily disorder." Appellant insists that 5 under this instruction liquors can only be lawfully purchased for medical use when the one for whose use it is purchased has in fact an ailment for the alleviation or cure of which it is purchased, and that if an ailment does not in fact exist the purchase is unlawful, however honest the belief and purpose of the purchaser. We do not think the instruction

is susceptible of this construction. It does not say that
an ailment must actually exist, but that the purchase
must be made to use as a remedy for disease. The
jury was not required to find that, in the case of each of
said purchases, the purchaser was in fact suffering from
a disease or ailment, but simply that he, in good faith,
made the purchase for medical purposes. Following what we have quoted above, it is said in this
instruction: "To use as a beverage is to use as a
drink." Appellant objects to this definition of the term
"beverage," and insists that the term "drink" is swal-
lowing or imbibing of the liquid for any purpose, and
that liquor taken as a medicine may be taken by drinking, the same as if taken as a beverage. The instruction taken in its connections could not have been understood as meaning that the liquor was used as a beverage
merely because it was taken into the system by drinking the same. Following what we have quoted it is
said: "It will be seen, therefore, that when liquor is
not used with intent to either, cure, treat, or alleviate
some bodily disorder or disease, it is not used for medical purposes." The jury must have understood that to
use as a drink, as distinguished from use as a medicine,
was to use as a beverage.

V. The second paragraph of the charge is as follows: "Under the laws of this state, whoever establishes or uses any building as a place for selling or
keeping for sale intoxicating liquor in violation
of law is guilty of the crime of nuisance, and
proof of a single sale in a building so used for
that purpose by the party making the sale will
warrant a conviction of this crime." Appellant
7   contends that under this instruction proof of a
single sale, whether it be lawful or unlawful,
will warrant a conviction; but not so, as the single sale
referred to in the instruction has reference to a sale

"in violation of law." If any doubt might arise upon the language of this instruction taken alone, it is made entirely clear, by all the instructions taken together, that to convict there must have been one or more sales in violation of law.

VI.   Section 8, chapter 66, Acts Twenty-first General Assembly, in force when this case was tried, provided that "proof of actual sale shall be presumptive evidence of illegal sale," and the court so instructed. This presumption is changed by section 2427 of the present Code.   Appellant insists that it being conceded that he held a permit, and that he took requests in form and substance as prescribed, and made the reports required, the presumption of illegal sale was thereby overcome, and the presumption that the sales
8   were legal thereby arose. The complaint is that the court did not instruct as to the presumption arising from the permit, requests, and returns. The permit showed authority to sell as authorized by law, and the requests tend to prove that these sales were legal. To rebut this evidence the state introduced proofs tending to show that certain of these purchasers were in the habit of using intoxicating liquors as a beverage, and it was upon this evidence, and the frequency and amount of the sales to these individuals, that the state relied. This being the state of the evidence the court instructed as follows: "(15) In determining whether the law has been violated by the defendant in selling intoxicating liquors, you may take into consideration the applications indorsed by him and offered in evidence; the habits of the purchaser with reference to the use of intoxicating liquors; the frequency of such applications; the amount of liquor purchased by any one person; whether or not the applications for liquors were accompanied with a physician's prescription therefor; and from these matters,

so far as they appear in the evidence, and all other
matters, throwing light thereon, determine whether
the defendant violated the law by selling intoxicating
liquors in a building used by him for that purpose."
By this instruction appellant was given the full benefit
of the requests as evidence tending to show that the
sales were legal.

VII. The court told the jury that "the statutes
of the state especially direct that you should so construe the law as to prevent its evasion, and no device,
art, or contrivance can avail the defendant, if you find
there was a substantial violation of the law."
9   Appellant contends that this left the jury to
place its own construction upon the law as given
in the instructions. Section 1554 of the Code is as follows: "Courts and jurors shall construe this chapter
so as to prevent evasion and so as to cover the act of
giving as well as selling by persons not authorized."
Neither this statute nor the instruction authorized the
jury to hold the law to be other than as given in the
instructions, and the effect of both is to require the
jury to apply the law as thus given so as to prevent
evasions. The instruction is in harmony with the
statute.

VIII. Appellant's last contention is that the evidence is insufficient to sustain the verdict. It is insisted
that the evidence is undisputed that in each instance
the purchaser wanted the liquors for medicine, and
that there is no evidence that the seller acted in bad
faith in making any of said sales. We will not
10   set out nor discuss the evidence upon this subject
at length. It is sufficient to say, as already inti-
mated, that, in our opinion, the jury was fully warranted in finding that several of said purchasers were
persons in the habit of using intoxicating liquors as a
beverage, and that the purchases were for that purpose. As we have seen in the seventh instruction, the

jury was told that "the holder of a permit must personally know that the person applying for liquors is not a minor, nor in the habit of using intoxicating liquors as a beverage, before he has a right to sell the same." The correctness of this statement of the law is not questioned, but, if it were not so required, we think that under the evidence the jury might well have found that as to some of these purchasers the defendant had reason to believe that they were in the habit of using intoxicating liquors as a beverage, and that their purchases were for that purpose. In examining this case we have kept in view the right of permit holders to the protection which the law contemplates, but upon the entire record we are led to the conclusion that the judgment of the district court should be AFFIRMED.

STATE OF IOWA V. GEORGE DEBOLT, *et al.*, Appellants.

Extortion by Accusation: INDICTMENT. An indictment under Code,
1   section 8871, providing for the punishment of one who "maliciously threatens to accuse another of crime," with intent to extort money, need not allege that the person threatened was not guilty of the crime; and his guilt or innocence is immaterial.

Evidence: *Intent.* In the case of malicious threats to accuse another
2   of an offense with intent thereby to extort money or pecuniary
3   advantage, the intent to extort is of the essence of the crime, and
4   proof of the threats, even though conclusive, is not proof of the specific intent or that it accompanied the act.

Instructions: CHARACTER AND DEGREE OF EVIDENCE. It is improper
2   to charge the jury that the intent with which an act was com-
4   mitted "must be strictly proven." It is misleading, since circumstantial evidence is often sufficient for the purpose.

Appeal: INSTRUCTIONS. In the absence of evidence, it will not be
5   presumed to have been such as to sustain a charge which is clearly erroneous upon any imaginable state of facts.

Appeal from Guthrie District Court.—HON. J. H. APPLE-
GATE, Judge.

FRIDAY, DECEMBER 17, 1897.

THE defendants, George Debolt and Walter Smith, were convicted of the offense of maliciously threatening to accuse another of the crime of sodomy with the intent thereby to extort money; and from the judgment, which required that they be imprisoned in the penitentiary at Ft. Madison for the term of one year, they appeal.— *Reversed.*

F. O. Hinkson and *Carr & Parker* for appellants.

Milton Remley, attorney general, and *Jesse A. Miller* for the state.

ROBINSON, J.—The indictment charges that the offense in question was committed as follows: "The said George Debolt and Walter Smith on or about the tenth day of October, A. D. 1894, in the county of Guthrie and state of Iowa, as aforesaid, the said George Debolt and Walter Smith acting together and in concert, did then and there, with malicious intent to extort money from one T. J. Simcoke, did then and there, maliciously and feloniously, verbally threaten to accuse the said T. J. Simcoke of the crime of sodomy," (describing the particular act of which the defendants threatened to accuse Simcoke). The indictment does

1   not charge that Simcoke was not guilty of the act thus described, and the appellants insist that in that respect the indictment is defective. The statute upon which this prosecution was founded is section 3871 of the Code of 1873, which contains the following: "If any person, either verbally or by any written or printed communication, maliciously threatens to accuse another of any crime or offense, * * * with intent thereby to extort any money or pecuniary advantage whatever, * * * he shall be punished by imprisonment in the penitentiary not more than two years, or by a fine not exceeding five hundred dollars." Nothing in

this statute makes it necessary, in order to constitute
the offense defined, that the person threatened shall be
innocent of the crime of which he is threatened to be
accused. It is said that the threat to accuse, in order
to constitute an offense, must be made maliciously;
that the court charged the jury that " 'malice,' in a
legal sense, denotes a wrongful act done intentionally,
without just cause or excuse," and that, if Simcoke was
guilty of the act of which the defendants threatened to
accuse him, the threat could not have been without just
cause or excuse. It is further urged that it is the duty
of every citizen to accuse the perpetrators of a crime,
before the proper tribunal, and that to declare an intention to do an act which it is the duty of the declarant to
perform cannot be a crime. All that may be conceded
without admitting that the indictment is defective in
the respect claimed. The crime for which the statute
provides is not the declaration by a person of an intent
to bring an offender against the law to justice, but the
malicious threatening to accuse a person of a crime or
offense, "with intent thereby to extort any money or
pecuniary advantage whatever." Whether the person
against whom the threat is directed be guilty or innocent of the crime or offense specified in the threat is
wholly immaterial to the commission of the crime by
the making of the threat. *State v. Waite*, 101 Iowa, 377.
The threat may be to accuse by instituting judicial proceedings. 1 McClain, Criminal Law, section.737. But
it may also refer to accusation by newspaper publication, or other means. *State v. Lewis*, 96 Iowa, 286. It
follows from what we have said that in our opinion the
indictment is not defective in the respect claimed by the
appellants.

II. The defendants asked the court to instruct the
jury as follows: "(8) You are instructed that intent to
extort money is a material part of the crime charged.

This intent cannot be presumed, but must be established by the evidence to the exclusion of all reasonable doubt. The intent to extort money is the gist of the crime charged, and, before you can convict the defendants, you must be satisfied that such intent existed and was in the minds of the defendants at the time of making the alleged threats, if you find that such threats were in fact made. Such intent cannot be presumed, but must be strictly proven." The court refused to give that instruction, and charged the jury as follows: "(8½) 'Malice,' in a legal sense, denotes a wrongful act done intentionally, without just cause or excuse; and intention is an inference of law resulting from the doing of the act, except where the circumstances rebut the presumption of its existence. And in this case, if you should find from the evidence, beyond a reasonable doubt, that the defendants committed the acts charged in the indictment in this case, and you shall further find that said acts were intentionally done by them, without just cause or excuse, the acts so done by them would warrant the conclusion that the alleged threats were maliciously made. And if you shall find from the evidence, beyond a reasonable doubt, that the defendants committed the acts charged in the indictment, then such acts would warrant the inference of the intent charged in the indictment, unless the facts and circumstances, as developed by the proof, rebut the presumption of the existence of such intent." The acts charged in the indictment were that the defendants, acting in concert, on a day specified, did maliciously and feloniously threaten to accuse one T. J. Simcoke of the crime of sodomy. It will be observed that the paragraph of the charge quoted did not require proof that the threat was made with the intent thereby to extort any money or pecuniary advantage, but instructed the jury, in effect, that proof which satisfied it beyond a reasonable doubt that the defendants,

without just cause or excuse, maliciously and feloniously threatened to accuse Simcoke of the crime of
sodomy, would warrant the inference that the threat
was made with the intent thereby to extort money from
him, unless the facts and circumstances, as developed
by the proof, showed that such intent did not exist. We
do not think that is the law. It is a general rule that a
person intends the natural and ordinary consequences
of his premeditated act. If a man intentionally assault
another with a deadly weapon, and take his life, in the
absence of justifying or extenuating circumstances, it
will be presumed that the act was done with intent to
commit murder. In that case the thing done would be
unlawful, and the criminal intent would be inferred
from the nature of the act, and the premeditation with
which it was done; and specific proof of the intent would
not be required, to convict. But it is the general rule
that, when an act becomes criminal only by reason of
the specific intent with which it is done, proof of the
intent is as necessary to a conviction as is proof of the
act. See *State v. Malcolm*, 8 Iowa, 415; *State v. Jarvis*,
21 Iowa, 46; *Roberts v. People*, 19 Mich. 401; 4 Am. &
Eng. Enc. Law, 674; 11 Am. & Eng. Enc. Law, 378;
Lawson, Presumptive Evidence, Rule 66. In the
4   case of malicious threats to accuse another of an
offense, with intent thereby to extort money or
pecuniary advantage, the intent to extort is of the
essence of the crime. Threats, however wrongful and
malicious, would not constitute the statutory crime, if
the intent to extort money or pecuniary advantage be
lacking. Therefore, proof of the threats, even though
conclusive, would not be proof of the specific intent
required by the statute, or justify a presumption that it
had accompanied the act. The paragraph of the charge
we have set out was therefore erroneous. We do not
think the court erred in refusing the eighth instruction

asked by the defendants, although, with some modification, it would have been correct. The intent to extort
money was of the gist of the crime charged, and cannot
be presumed, but must be proven, but to say that it
"must be strictly proven" might be misleading. Direct
proof of the intent with which an act was committed is
not to be had in many cases, and, when that is true,
circumstantial evidence may be sufficient. What would
be required to "strictly prove" an intent might not be
understood by a jury.

III. The evidence submitted on the trial in the
district court has not been abstracted, and it is said we
must presume that it justified the charge given. It is
true that we must indulge in every reasonable
5   presumption to sustain the charge, but we are
unable to imagine any evidence which could have
justified the erroneous statement of law contained in
the charge. For the error in the charge given, the judgment of the district court must be, and is, REVERSED.

The Burlington, Cedar Rapids & Northern Railway Company, Appellant, v. The City of
Columbus Junction, et al.

Highways: DEDICATION: *Cities and towns.* Land uninclosed by a
railroad company and made use of for over twenty years with
1   adjacent land for a public highway upon which a town has
expended money and labor, will be held to have been dedicated
to, and accepted by it, unless a formal acceptance of the strip is
required by law.

CONSTRUCTION OF STATUTE. The provision of Code 1873, section
1   527, which requires that a dedication of land to public use can be
2   acquired and confirmed only by special ordinances passed for the
purpose, does not apply to towns, but to cities, only.

SAME. Such statutes, being intended to protect cities from liability
being imposed upon them from land owners in dedicating streets
irrespective of necessity therefor, does not prohibit the city from
2   acquiring title to streets in some other way than by a dedication,
and an acceptance by ordinance, as by purchase or prescription.

PRESCRIPTION AND ADVERSE POSSESSION. A town will acquire title
by prescription and adverse possession to a strip of land forming
1 part of the right of way of a railroad company, but left uninclosed
for many years, and which has been taken into a public highway
8 and used and improved as such, where the property was originally
entered upon under an agreement with one purporting to represent
the company, that it would dedicate the strip for road purposes.

Appeal from Louisa District Court.—HON. BEN McCoy,
Judge.

FRIDAY, DECEMBER 17, 1897.

ACTION in equity to restrain the defendants from
tearing down and removing a fence. There was a hearing on the merits, and a decree in favor of the defendants. The plaintiff appeals.—*Affirmed.*

Gray & Tucker and *S. K. Tracy* for appellant.

B. F. Van Dyke for appellees.

ROBINSON, J.—The plaintiff owns a right of way for
its railway track which extends through a portion of
the town of Columbus Junction, from the southern limit
of the town, in a northwesterly direction. The right of
way appears to have been acquired by condemnation
proceedings in the year 1868, and it seems that a public
highway was established along the west or southwest
side of the right of way, although the evidence in regard
to the time of acquiring the right of way and of establishing the highway is not definite. But we do not understand that there is any controversy in regard to those
matters. The right of way was fifty feet in width on
each side of the center of the railway track. In the year
1875, if not earlier, the railway company constructed a
fence twenty-eight feet southwest of the center of its
track, leaving outside the fence a strip of its right of way
twenty-two feet wide, next to the highway. That fence

was of boards, and in time was replaced with a wire
fence. In September, 1895, the wire fence was moved
out to a line parallel to, and fifty feet from, the center
of the track. Later in the same year the town ordered
the plaintiff to remove the fence, and directed that, in
case of its failure to do so for ten days, the removal
should be made by the street commissioner. This action
was brought to restrain the enforcement of that order.

The defendants, the town and its street commissioner, claim that the strip of ground outside the line on
which the first fences were built (the strip being about
one hundred and twenty rods in length) was dedicated to the town as a public street, and accepted
by the town; also, that title thereto has been
acquired by prescription. It is shown that the portion
of the highway or street used, and the strip of land in
question, were, together, about forty feet in width; and
it is admitted that the strip was used with the highway
as a street for twenty years before the fence in controversy was built, and that during that time the town
used and improved it, expending money and labor upon
it. It is clear, unless a formal acceptance of the dedication is required by the town that there was a dedication of the strip which was accepted by the town. Had
land outside a city or town been treated as was that in
question, there would have been an actual dedication
to the use of, and an acceptance for, the public. *State v.
Birmingham*, 74 Iowa, 407; *Sherman v. Hastings*, 81
Iowa, 372, and cases therein cited. But it is said that a
dedication by the railway company would not have been
effectual, unless formally accepted by ordinance, and in
support of that claim section 527 of the Code of 1873 is
cited. That section provided that "no street or alley
which shall hereafter be dedicated to public use by the
proprietor of the ground in any city, shall be deemed a
public street or alley, or to be under the use or control

of the city council, unless the dedication shall be accepted and confirmed by an ordinance especially passed for such purpose." It is not shown that the town ever accepted the dedication of the land in question by ordinance, but the provision quoted applies to cities only, and not to towns. The defendant municipality is described in the title of this cause as a city, but in the body of the pleadings as a town, and that we understand to be the class to which it belongs.

2 But, if we are in error in this respect, we should be compelled to reach the same conclusion as to the final disposition of the case. It was said in *Byerly v. City of Anamosa*, 79 Iowa, 206, that the section referred to was "clearly intended to protect cities from liability and responsibility thrown upon them by landowners in dedicating streets to public use without giving the city an opportunity to determine whether such streets are demanded by the public good, and the wants of the citizens. In the absence of the statute the city would be powerless to resist the designs of landowners to make it liable for all streets they might dedicate, without regard to the public good, or the wants of the people." But the right of a city to assume the use and control of streets dedicated by landowners without an acceptance by ordinance, and its liability for not keeping such streets in good condition, was recognized in the case. The statute only refers to streets and alleys which are dedicated to public use by the landowner, and not to streets and alleys, the title to which has been acquired by the city by purchase or by prescription. The evidence in this case shows that the town acquired the right to use the land in controversy as a street by prescription, if not by dedication. It is true that title by prescription could not have been acquired by mere use for the required time, and that adverse pos-

session must be proven by evidence distinct from, and independent of, the use. Code 1873, section 2031.

3   But there is sufficient evidence of that character in this case to sustain the right claimed by the town. Before the first fence was built by the railway company, a person who claimed to represent the company talked with the owner of the land from which the right of way was taken, and it was agreed between them that the company should give land for one-half the road at the place in question. The rough character of the land at that place made it desirable to use a part of the right of way for road purposes. It is not shown that the person who represented the company was authorized to act for it, but the company carried out the agreement, by so building its fence as to leave the strip of land in controversy as a part of the street. It certainly knew of the use made of it by the town, and that improvements were made by the owners of property adjacent to the road as thus made with a view to its continued use for road purposes. We conclude that the judgment of the district court is right. That denied the plaintiff relief, and gave to the town the strip of land in question for highway purposes, and it is AFFIRMED.

SARAH PRAY v. THE LIFE INDEMNITY AND SECURITY COMPANY AND C. E. MABIE, Secretary, Appellant.

Assessment Insurance: PAYMENT OF INTEREST. A life insurance company will not be required to collect and pay over interest in a death claim where the contract of insurance entitles the bene-
4   ficiary to "the net proceeds of one full assessment at schedule rates" and there is no provision in the schedule for assessment for the payment of interest, but simply for a specific sum for each death, according to the age of the person assessed.

ASSIGNMENT: *Practice.* A life insurance association against which a beneficiary has recovered judgment cannot ask to be protected
6   against an assignment of a portion of the claim made by the

plaintiff when the assignee, although testifying as a witness, did not claim an interest in the case and it does not appear that the company is liable to him, though it is notified by the beneficiary that she has borrowed of the assignee and is directed by her to charge the amount against the policy and retain it for the lender.

SET-OFF. Upon the granting of a decree directing an assessment to be ordered by a life insurance association for the payment of the
5 plaintiff's claim, a judgment held by the defendant against the plaintiff will be allowed as a set-off against the amount realized from the assessment ordered.

NOTICE: *New contract.* Notice of assessments not having been mailed within the time after their date required by by-laws, and not having allowed the insured the full time he was entitled to in which to make payment, and the payment made after the time
8 they were due having been retained, the provision in the receipts that they were given and accepted on condition that assured was in as good health as when received as a member of the association (which conditional receipt was not authorized by the by-laws or otherwise, except that it was examined and approved by the board of directors, but without record of their action), cannot be asserted to defeat recovery on the certificate of insurance.

WAIVER OF PROOF OF LOSS   An action upon a life insurance certificate is not barred for failure to furnish proofs of death of a pre-
1 scribed form, where the beneficiary applied to the company for blank forms to be filled out, and which were refused on the sole ground that the certificate had been forfeited.

Actions: DISMISSAL WITHOUT PREJUDICE. An action agreed to be argued and submitted in vacation, but dismissed by the plaintiff
2 before a hearing, is not a bar to a subsequent action for the same cause, although the defendant's answer in the first suit set up a counter-claim as set-off, where the defendant sets up the same defense in the subsequent action

PARTIES. In an action against an assessment insurance company on
7 a certificate entitling the beneficiary to the amount of an assessment, it is not necessary to make the secretary a party.

Appeal from Black Hawk District Court.—HON. J. J.
TOLERTON, Judge.

FRIDAY, DECEMBER 17, 1897.

PLAINTIFF, the beneficiary named in a certificate of life insurance issued by the defendant on the life of Ira Christie, now deceased, brings this action for judgment, and for an order requiring the defendant to make an assessment to pay the amount alleged to be due under said certificate. The defendant answered, pleading as defense, in substance, as follows: That this action is barre 1, for the reason that proofs of loss were not made within sixty days from the date of the death, as required by section 3, chapter 211, Laws Eighteenth General Assembly; that there was another action pending between these parties, involving these same issues; that said certificate was forfeited by reason of failure to pay benefit assessments Nos. 34, 35. 38, and 40. The defendant also pleads two unsatisfied judgments, which it holds against the plaintiff, and asks that the amount thereof be set off against any amount found due the plaintiff. The plaintiff, in reply, denies that said assessments were legally made, and denies that Ira Christie was legally notified thereof, or that, by reason of non-payment of said assessments said certificate was forfeited. The issues will more fully appear in the opinion. Decree was rendered in favor of the plaintiff. Defendant appeals.—*Modified and affirmed.*

Alford & Gates for appellant.

Boies, Couch & Boies for appellee.

GIVEN, J.—I. Appellant's first contention is that this action is barred, for the reason that proofs of loss were not furnished within sixty days from the date of Mr. Christie's death. There is nothing contained in the defendant's by-laws, nor in this certificate, fixing the time within which proof of death must be made; but appellant's contention is that the case comes within chapter 211, Laws Eighteenth General Assembly, and that proof of death must be made within sixty days from the date of the death. Whether this statute

applies we will not stop to consider, as, in the view we
take of the case it is immaterial. Mr. Christie
1 died September 7, 1886, at Pasadena, Cal., and
on that day plaintiff sent "an order of notice"
to the defendant, which was received, "reciting the
death of her son, Ira Christie," also stating that
she had been compelled to borrow two hundred and
fifty dollars of M. W. McGee, and directing the defendant to charge that sum against the policy, and to retain
it for Mr. McGee. Mr. McGee wrote the defendant on
the same day, inclosing the notices of the death and
of the loan to Mrs. Christie, which notices were also
received by the defendant. The certificate provides
that "upon the receipt at the Waterloo office of satisfactory proofs, on blanks furnished by the association
of the death of Ira Christie, this association will pay to
his mother, Sarah Christie," etc. On September 17,
1886, plaintiff wrote to defendant, from Rock Falls, Ill.,
as follows: "Send blanks to me to be filled out for the
death of Ira Christie, certificate No. 6,699, and give me
such other information as I shall require." Defendant
did not send the blanks, but answered September 20,
1886, returning money sent in payment of assessment
No. 44, for the reason that "the certificate expired on
the evening of the 5th of September." The defendant
further says: "The death, as you said, occurred on the
7th of September. Therefore, the association is not
liable, and we cannot accept the money." It is manifest from this and other correspondence that the
defendant, as is alleged by the plaintiff, at all times
denied its liability, solely upon the ground that the
certificate had been forfeited. It did not furnish
blanks, as required by the certificate, because it did not
desire other proofs of the death than those which had
already been furnished. Under these circumstances, it
was not required, even under said act of the Eighteenth
General Assembly, that plaintiff should do more in the

way of furnishing proof of the death. It is true that the plaintiff did, a long time after the death, furnish formal proofs thereof, but this act cannot affect the rights of the parties. This action is not barred for want of poofs of the death, for the reason that the defendant waived any right it had to other or different proofs of the death than those which were furnished by failing to furnish the blanks when required, and by basing its denial of liability solely upon the claim of the forfeiture of the certificate.

II. Appellant's next contention is that this action is barred by the pendency of the other action between these parties, upon these same issues. That action was heard at the March term, 1894, and, "by agreement, case to be argued and submitted in vacation, and decision to be rendered in vacation." This case was commenced July 27, 1894, and was heard in June, and decided July 26, 1895. On April 12, 1894, plaintiff filed a written dismissal of the other action, but, at the time of this hearing, that case had not been taken from the docket. Appellant contends that the written dismissal did not dismiss that case, because it was after submission, and because the defendant's answer contained a counter-claim. That case was to be submitted in vacation, and it does not appear that it had been submitted before the dismissal was filed. The alleged counter-claim was the same two judgments set up in this case, and the relief asked was not for judgment on these judgments, but that the amount thereof might be set off against any amount found in the plaintiff's favor. As, by the dismissal, the plaintiff waived any right to recover in that case, there was no ground for granting the relief asked by the defendant, and the dismissal was an end of the case, and therefore it is not a bar to this action.

III. Counsel discuss the question whether the assessments Nos. 34, 35, 38, and 40 were legally levied,

and whether the notices thereof are such as that Mr.
Christie forfeited his certificate by failure to pay said
assessments within the time required. It is not disputed that these assessments were on account of the
death of members in good standing, and that Mr.
Christie was liable therefor in the amounts
3 assessed. In view of this fact and our conclusion
with respect to the notice, we do not inquire as
to the regularity of the manner in which assessments
were made, but accepting them as regular, we inquire
as to the notices. The certificate recites, as one of the
considerations therefor, the prompt payment of such
benefit assessments as may be legally levied by its
board of directors, and that the certificate shall be void
if the amount of any assessment made under said certificate is not received at the Waterloo office within
thirty days from the date of notice thereof. Section 19
of the by-laws in force at the time Christie became a
member provided that "such assessments shall be paid
to the secretary within thirty days from the notice
thereof. Five days shall be allowed after mailing such
notice by the secretary before members shall be considered to have received such notice." Said section
was amended August 5, 1884, to read as follows: "Such
assessments shall be paid to the secretary within thirty
days from the day on which the notice bears date. Five
(5) days shall be allowed the secretary for mailing
such notices after the date thereof, and five (5) days of
grace shall be allowed the member in addition to the
time mentioned in the notice." The dates of the notices
of these assessments and of the mailing and payment
thereof are as follows: No. 34 dated October 1, mailed
October 8, 1885, and paid January 6, 1886; No. 35, dated
November 1, mailed November 9, 1885, and paid
January 6, 1886; No. 38, dated February 1, mailed February 8, and paid March 12, 1886; No. 40, dated April
1, mailed April 7, and paid May 18, 1886. Each of these

notices required that the assessment must be received
"within thirty days from the day on which this notice
bears date." If we allow to the member in addition to
the thirty days, the five days allowed for mailing and the
five days of grace, still it will be seen from the above
dates that none of these assessments were paid within
forty days from the date of the notice thereof. It will be
observed that said notices required payment within
thirty days from their date, thereby not allowing the
time given for mailing, nor the five days of grace, and
that none of said notices were mailed within five days of
their date. If the secretary might withhold mailing
the notices for seven, eight or nine days after their date,
as he did, he might for a longer time, and thus deprive
the member of the time for payment to which he was
entitled, as that time must be counted from the date of
the notice. The defendant received these payments at
the dates named, and did not return the same, but
retained them. Therefore, if nothing further appeared,
it would be held to have waived the time for payment,
and consequently a forfeiture of the certificate if the
notices had been as required. It appears, however,
that, upon receipt of each of these payments, the defendant sent to Mr. Christie its receipt therefor, as follows:
"The time having expired for the payment of the above
assessment, and payment being tendered after the same
was due, this receipt is given by the association, and
accepted by the member, upon the following conditions,
and not otherwise: *First.* That said member is now
living and of temperate habits, and in as good health
as when originally received a member of this association; otherwise, said payment and this receipt and said
certificate shall be null and void. *Second.* The receipt
of the above sum after the same is due shall not establish or be considered a precedent for the payment of
future assessments or dues under said certificate.
Third. No payment of subsequent dues or assessments

under said certificate shall in any way impair, alter, or
change the terms or affect the conditions of this receipt,
or the payment thereunder, or re-establish membership
in this association, except upon the fulfillment of the
first condition of this receipt." It is alleged and
abundantly proven that, at the time of these payments,
Mr. Christie was not in as good health as when originally received as a member, but was declining with con-
sumption, and that defendant had no knowledge of that
fact until after his death. It also appears that Mr.
Christie retained these receipts without making any
protest or objection thereto. A contention in this case
is as to the effect that should be given to this condition
in those receipts. While provision is often made by
insurance companies that reinstatements shall be on
condition that the assured is in good or usual health,
there is no such provision in the articles of incorporation. or by-laws of the defendant, nor in this certificate
or the application of Mr. Christie therefor. The contract, as originally made, was made in contemplation of
sickness and death. It is a contract to pay to the plaintiff the net proceeds of one full assessment, not exceeding two thousand, five hundred dollars, within ninety
days after the death of Ira Christie, conditioned only
that semi-annual dues and benefit assessments should
be paid within the time required, and that the assured
would not impair his health by the use of alcoholic
liquors and that he had not concealed any material
fact as to his health. We do not understand appellant
to contend that the decline in Mr. Christie's health was
cause for forfeiting the contract, as evidenced by the
certificate. The claim is that by receiving and retaining these receipts with that condition expressed
therein, without objecting thereto, a new contract was
entered into, conditioned that the health of Mr. Christie
was then as good as at the time he became a member.
Appellee contends that the secretary who sent out these

receipts had no authority to make such a contract, nor
to receive payment upon such condition. The only
authority the secretary had was that this form of
receipt was examined and approved by the board of
directors, but without any record of their action, and
without any change in the articles or by-laws of the
company. As we have said, the contract, as evidenced
by the certificate, is that the defendant would pay the
proceeds of an assessment to the plaintiff on the death
of Ira Christie, on the conditions therein named. The
future state of Ira Christie's health was not made a
condition upon which the contract was to continue, but
it was to continue subject only to the conditions we
have named.

We do not think it should be held that, by merely
retaining the receipts without protest, Ira Christie consented to a new contract on the conditions named in the
receipt. Of the many cases cited by appellant, we notice
the following: *Garbutt v. Association*, 84 Iowa, 293, is
a case somewhat similar to this, but the question of the
authority to make a new contract, or whether a new
contract was made, was not considered in the case.
The principal questions there considered were whether
there was a forfeiture or waiver of a forfeiture, as
affected by the time of the death for which the assessment was made, and whether the plaintiff was entitled
to notice of the dues and assessments payable, her name
being omitted from the defendant's books. There are
a number of cases cited wherein receipts, conditioned
as these, are sustained; but in those cases it will be
found that some provision had been made for such
conditional reinstatements, or where the original contract had been treated as waived and at an end. In
view of the facts that the notices were not mailed within
the time required after their date, did not allow to the
assured the full time in which he was entitled to make
payment, and that the payments were retained, we do

not think that the defendant should be heard to assert said conditions in the receipts to defeat recovery upon this certificate.

IV. Appellant complains that the decree requires it to collect and pay over interest from November 10, 1888. The amount to which appellee is entitled is "the

4   net proceeds of one full assessment at schedule rates, upon all the members in good standing, at the date of said death to an amount not exceed-

ing $2,500." There is no provision in the schedule for assessing for the payment of interest, but simply of a specific sum for each death, according to the age of the person assessed. We think that interest should not be allowed in such case.

Appellant complains that the court entirely dis-regarded the counter-claim pleaded in the answer. It

5   was not denied that the amount of the two judg-ments was due from the plaintiff to the defend-ant, and we think that amount should be allowed

as an offset against the amount that is realized from the assessment ordered.

Appellant also complains that it is not protected against the assignment of the two hundred and fifty dollars of this claim, made by plaintiff to Mr. McGee.

6   Mr. McGee, though testifying as a witness in the case, and knowing of its pendancy, makes no claim therein, and, so far as appears, the defend-

ant has never become liable to Mr. McGee, and therefore there is nothing against which it needs to be protected in this matter.

It is also contended by appellant that as defendant Mabie, its former secretary, is deceased, the present secretary should have been made a party to this action.

7   We see no reason for having made Mr. Mabie a party. This action is against the corporation, and, in so far as it may go to control the official

action of its officers, it is unnecessary that they, as indi-viduals, be parties to the action.

The decree of the district court will be modified as
to the allowance of interest, and so as to provide that
the amounts of said judgments shall be deducted from
whatever amount is realized on the assessment ordered;
and thus *modified*, the decree is AFFIRMED.

MARY WOOD, *et al.*, Appellants, v. SAMUEL E. BROWN.

Quieting Title: EVIDENCE. In an action to quiet title the plaintiff's
chain of title showed a transfer of the title from a widow of one
1 former grantee, and from the heirs of another former grantee,
but there was nothing to show by what authority the transfers
were made. *Held*, plaintiff has failed to establish his allegation
of ownership.

ADMISSIONS: *Plea and proof.* An admission by defendants in an
action to quiet title to land, that plaintiffs are seized of the
2 "interest if any" owned by a specified person at his death, does
not relieve plaintiff of the burden of proving title to the land,
where an allegation that such person died seized of the land, was
put in issue by a general denial.

RIGHTS OF CLAIMANT: *Mortgages.* Plaintiff in an action to quiet
title to land cannot, where he shows no title to the land, question
4 the right of defendants to a foreclosure of the mortgage on the
land, on the ground that the latter had released part of the land
from the mortgage.

Mortgage: RELEASE: *Construction.* An instrument acknowledging
"full and entire satisfaction for a mortgage" on specified land,
8 does not operate as an entire satisfaction of the mortgage debt,
but only as the release of the land described in such instrument,
where the mortgage covered other land, and had not in fact been
paid.

Pleading: STRIKING OFF. It is not error to sustain a motion to
8 strike an amendment to the petition which alleged matter, not in
support of the cause of action, but in reply to matter alleged in
defendant's cross-petition.

Appeal from Jasper District Court.—HON. D. RYAN,
Judge.

FRIDAY, DECEMBER 17, 1897.

ON November 5, 1892, plaintiffs filed their petition to quiet the title in them to the southwest quarter of the southeast quarter of section 11, township 79, north of range 21, west of the fifth P. M., Iowa, making Samuel E. Brown, Alfred Sully, W. B. Smith, Rebecca Smith, Elizabeth Martz, and the unknown husband and children of Elizabeth Martz, and the legatees or devisees of the children of Elizabeth Martz, defendants. They alleged that they are the absolute owners in fee simple of said land, and are informed and believe that the defendants make some claim adverse to the plaintiffs thereto; that John Martz died April 1, 1869, leaving Elizabeth Martz, his widow, and some children, surviving him; that on the twenty-third day of June, 1869, said Elizabeth Martz sold and conveyed said land to Peter Cragan, without reference to any children; that on February 1, 1872, Cragan sold and conveyed the same to George B. Wood, who has since died, and from whom plaintiffs obtained title, being the only heirs at law of said Wood; that on October 14, 1867, Alexander Kannady executed a mortgage on said land to defendants Brown and Sully, and on the same day another mortgage to defendants W. B. and Rebecca Smith, which mortgages were duly recorded. Defendants W. B. Smith and Rebecca Smith answered, denying each and every allegation made in plaintiffs' petition, except those expressly admitted. "The defendants admit that plaintiffs have some claim or title in the lands described, but aver the same is junior and inferior in equity and to title of defendants." By way of cross-petition they allege the execution to them by Alexander Kannady and wife of the mortgage mentioned in the petition, and allege that the same is still due, and wholly unpaid, and pray that the same be established as superior to the claims of all the parties hereto, and that the same be foreclosed. Thereafter plaintiffs filed an amendment to their petition, alleging that said mortgage was without consideration, and for the purpose of disposing of the property in a testamentary capacity; and that afterwards said Kannady and wife rescinded the same by the execution of a warranty deed to said land to John Martz. Plaintiffs filed a second amendment to their petition in four paragraphs. In the first they set out by reference the mortgage set out in the answer of these defendants. In the second they allege that Kannady died in October, 1883, and that the cause of action under said mortgage is barred. In the third they allege that said mortgage was released, satisfied, and discharged of record by W. B. Smith on the twenty-eighth of November, 1870, and in the fourth that these defendants are not entitled to relief, for the reason that the mortgage shows on its face that it is null and void, because, by its terms, it creates an estate to commence in the future, upon the death of the grantor, reserving to him its use, enjoyment, and possession. These defendants moved to strike this amendment, on the ground that the matters set up were no part of plaintiffs' cause of action, are in avoidance of the matters alleged in the cross-petition, and could only be properly pleaded in reply thereto. This motion was sustained, and thereupon plaintiffs replied, in substance as follows: That defendants' mortgage covered two other tracts of land than that in controversy, and that, after recording of the deed to Martz, and the subsequent conveyances thereof, these defendants, on the twenty-eighth of November, 1870, without the knowledge or consent of said grantors, released and canceled said mortgage so far as it covered the land in controversy, which land was worth six hundred dollars, whereby defendants' rights under said mortgage have been postponed to and made junior and inferior to the conveyances under which plaintiffs and their grantors held the land. They renew their allegation that defendants' cause of action is barred, and allege that said

claim was never filed, proven, or allowed against the
estate of Alexander Kannady, and that the administrator of Kannady is a necessary party. Decree was
entered in favor of the defendants W. B. Smith and
Rebecca Smith, from which plaintiffs appeal.—
Affirmed.

Cragan Bros., E. J. Salmon, and *H. S. Winslow*
for appellants.

W. O. McElroy for appellees.

GIVEN, J.—I. Both parties claim through Alexander Kannady; appellees under said mortgage executed to them by Kannady, October 14, 1867, and the
appellants under the following chain of title: Deed
dated June 15, 1868, from Kannady and wife to John
Martz; deed, June 23, 1869, from Elizabeth Martz to
Peter Cragan; deed from Peter Cragan and wife to
George B. Wood, no date appearing; deed, dated November 12, 1873, from George B. Wood to Peter Olson; deed
of the only heirs at law of Peter Olson to George B.
Wood, no date appearing. Each of these deeds
1   appears to have been a warranty deed, and to
have been recorded within a short time after its
date. It will be observed that it does not appear by
what authority Elizabeth Martz conveyed to Peter Cragan, or the heirs at law of Peter Olson conveyed to
George B. Wood, from whom plaintiffs claim title. It
is certainly clear that they have failed to establish their
allegation of ownership. They contend, however, that
under the admission made in defendants' answer, and a
further admission made on the trial, it was conceded
that they held title subject to appellees' mortgage. On
the trial "the defendants admitted that the plaintiffs

are seized of the interest, if any, owned by Geo. B.
Wood at his death, in said real estate." By the
2   general denial appellees put in issue the allegation that George B. Wood died seized of this land,
and by these admissions they only conceded that appellants are seized of whatever interest Wood had at his
death; or, in other words, that they are his heirs. We
do not think that these admissions relieve appellants of
the burden of proving title, and they seem to have so
regarded it on the trial, as they then introduced the
record of the deeds we have mentioned.

II. Appellees' mortgage was executed and recorded
prior to the conveyance from Kannady to Martz; therefore Martz and his grantees took with notice thereof.
Said mortgage was executed to secure the payment of
four hundred dollars, consideration for lands in Missouri sold to Kannady; said sum to be paid on the death
of Kannady, to appellees in trust, the same to be divided
by them, when collected, as follows: One hundred dollars thereof to Rebecca Smith, one hundred dollars to
Mary J. Steel, one hundred dollars to Ellen M. Scott,
and one hundred dollars to Sophia Lawson,—daughters
of Kannady. Appellants do not question, in argument,
the validity of this mortgage, but insist that by reason
of the alleged satisfaction and cancellation thereof of
record appellees are not entitled to enforce the same as
    against the land in controversy. On November
3   28, 1870, which was after the conveyance from
    Martz to Cragan, and before the last conveyance
to George B. Wood, appellee W. B. Smith, not as trustee, but in his individual capacity, executed and
acknowledge an instrument in writing as follows,
which was recorded December 2, 1870: "For value
received, I hereby acknowledge full and entire satisfaction for a mortgage given by Alexander Kannady to
W. B. Smith on the undivided half of the south half of

the northeast quarter of section 12, township 79 north, range 21 west 5 P. M., Iowa." Question is made in argument whether this relates to the mortgage under consideration, but that it does cannot be doubted under the pleadings and proofs. This mortgage covers the land described in said writing as well as that in controversy, and one other separate tract of land. Construed in the light of attending circumstances, it seems to us quite clear that said writing was not intended as a full and entire satisfaction of this mortgage, but simply as a release of the lands described therein from the mortgage. The evidence is undisputed that no part of the debt has ever been paid, and the "full and entire satisfaction" acknowledged is not of the mortgage debt, but is as to the tract of land described. We are in no doubt that, as between appellees and the heirs of Kannady, appellees are entitled to enforce this mortgage as against the land in controversy and the other tract described, not embraced in the release. We may here add that there was no error in sustaining appellees' motion to strike appellants' first so-called amendment to their petition, as the matters alleged are not in support of their cause of action, but in reply to the matters alleged in appellees' cross-petition.

III.   The only remaining contention of appellants requiring notice is that by releasing part of the security the land in controversy stands released in the hands of these grantees from the lien of the mortgage.
4   How this might be if appellants had sustained their allegation of ownership, we need not determine, for, as we have seen, they have failed to do this; therefore they may not question appellees' right to foreclosure as to the lands in controversy. Thus viewing the case, we reach the conclusion that the judgment of the district court should be AFFIRMED.

In the Matter of the Estate of John Allison, Jr.,
John Allison, Sr., Contestant, Appellant, v.
Elizabeth Allison, Proponent.

Evidence: WILL CONTEST: *Due execution.* The testimony of a pro-
1 ponent, to the effect that she was present when the will was
2 executed and that the subscribing witnesses reside without the
3 state, is admissible to show, *prima facie,* the execution of the
will and to cast the burden of proof upon the contestant,
although the depositions of the subscribing witnesses are on file
in the case upon other issues and though proponent took one of
such depositions and all were taken by agreement.

COMPETENCY. A will in favor of deceased's wife, and offered by her
for probate, was contested by his father on the ground of incompetency and undue influence It appeared that the will was
executed in a town in Arkansas two days before deceased's death;
that the wife was there at the time; that contestant resided in
Iowa; and that deceased's only brother resided near contestant. A witness for the latter testified that she was at said town
during deceased's sickness, and that she then asked the wife why
4 she did not send for her husband's brothers, and the wife said
she did not want them. The wife's cousin, who lived near contestant, was permitted to state the contents of a lost letter she
received from the wife during deceased's sickness, and which she
read to contestant and his daughter when received. to the effect
that he was very poorly, and requesting her to take the letter to
contestant and daughter, for the reason that she had no time to
write to them, and to repeat a conversation with them to the
effect that they desired the witness to go to Arkansas, as contestant was too old, and the daughter could not go *Held,* that
the cousin's evidence was competent and material

JURY QUESTION. The finding of the jury as to competency to make a
will should stand, where it cannot be properly said that the evi-
8 dence is conclusive either way, especially after the trial court has
declined to interfere.

INSTRUCTION CONSTRUED In a proceeding for the probate of a will
an instruction to the jury that if the testator did not adopt the
signature to the instrument as his own after his name was signed
for him, it will be "proper" to find that it is not his will, is not
8 objectionable as leaving the nature of the finding upon such facts
discretionary with the jury, where, in view of preceding instructions, the word could only have been understood in the sense that

it was the right or duty of the jury, under such facts, to find there was no will.

Appeal: HARMLESS ERROR: *Evidence.* An appellant cannot com
plain that a question asked a witness whose deposition was taken
5 at the instance of appellee was erroneously overruled, as not a
proper cross-examination, when the subject was fully inquired
into by a deposition of the same witness, taken by appellant.

REQUESTED INSTRUCTIONS. An appellant cannot complain of the
failure of the court to give a requested instruction when the facts
6 assumed in it sufficiently depart from the record to make it partial and unfair, and the court, in a minute and correct charge,
dealt with the same subject in a way that was fair to both
parties.

Appeal from Des Moines District Court.—HON. JAMES
D. SMYTH, Judge.

FRIDAY, DECEMBER 17, 1897.

PROCEEDING for the probate of a will. Objections on
the grounds of incompetency and undue influence. Verdict for proponent, and the contestant appealed.—
Affirmed.

J. H. Scott and *Seerley & Clark* for contestant,
appellant.

Power, Huston & Power for proponent, appellee.

GRANGER, J.—I.   John Allison, Jr., residing in Des
Moines county, Iowa, died at Hot Springs, Ark., November 10, 1894, without issue, leaving as his widow the
proponent, Elizabeth Allison. November 8, 1894, at
Hot Springs, he executed the will in question, with Drs.
Walker and McClenden as subscribing witnesses. The
contestant was his father. By the terms of the will, he
gave his entire estate to his widow, and constituted
her the executrix of his will. The will was presented to
the district court for probate on the thirteenth day of
November, 1894, and objections were filed thereto on the
grounds of incompetency and undue influence. The

issues were tried to a jury, that returned a finding for proponent.

II. To prove the due execution of the will, the proponent offered herself as a witness, and against objections was permitted to testify that she was present

1

when the will was executed, and that she knew Drs. Walker and McClenden, and that they resided at Hot Springs, Ark. She was then shown the will, and asked if she saw them sign their names thereto, and she answered that she did. Proponent then offered in evidence the will, signed by John Allison, Jr., with the attestation signed by J. J. Walker and J. W. McClenden, which, against objections, was admitted. Proponent then put in evidence the notice and service thereof, and rested. Contestant then moved the court to instruct the jury to find against the admission of the will to probate, on the ground that there was no proof of the due execution of the will, or that John Allison, Jr., was, at the time of the purported execution, in a condition to make a valid will, which motion the court overruled. Thereupon the contestant presented evidence upon the issues of incompetency and undue influence, followed by rebutting evidence on the part of the proponent. Among the evidence introduced were depositions of Drs. McClenden and Walker, the contestant having taken the depositions of both, and proponent that of Dr. McClenden, and in both cases by a stipulation of the parties. The court gave to the jury the following instruction: "(3) It appears from the undisputed evidence in the case that there is attached to the document in controversy, offered for probate as the will of the said John Allison, Jr., a certificate in proper form, and signed by two competent witnesses, which recites that the paper in question was duly executed as the will of the said deceased, and this attestation, under the circumstances of this case, creates a presumption that the said document was duly executed as certified, and the burden of proof is consequently upon the contestant, and it is incumbent upon him to establish the invalidity of the said alleged will by a pre-ponderance of evidence." In another instruction

2   it told the jury that the presumption arising from the will, as put in evidence, might be overcome or satisfactorily explained by other evidence showing that the will was not executed as it purported to be, and that if the jury so found from the greater weight of evi-dence, or if it found from the greater weight of evidence that John Allison, Jr., at the time of the making of the will, was not of sound mind, or executed the will under undue influence, it would be proper to find that it was not his will. Contestant presents the following proposi-tions for consideration: "(1) Can secondary or inferior evidence be introduced to prove the due execution of a will, when, by consent of both parties, the depositions of the subscribing witnesses are on file in the case? (2) Can inferior testimony be introduced to prove the due execu-tion of a will, when the proponent has set in motion the process of the court, and taken the deposition of one of the subscribing witnesses to the will on other questions, and also when depositions of both are on file? And, (3) by this inferior testimony can the burden be cast upon the contestant when by agreement the process of the court had issued, and the deposition of the subscrib-ing witnesses has been taken and filed, in the case?" It should be remembered that both subscribing witnesses resided in Arkansas, and were beyond the jurisdiction of the courts of this state. The great weight, if not the entire current, of authority is with the proposition that, where subscribing witnesses are dead, or beyond the jurisdiction of the court, proof of their handwriting is a compliance with the law as to due execution. Beach, Wills, 66; *Ela v. Edwards*, 16 Gray, 91. In Lawson, Rights, Remedies & Prac., section 3198, it is said: "Where the witnesses are all dead, or cannot be had

because beyond the jurisdiction of the court, or being
present they deny their signatures, or do not remember,
proof of the handwriting of the witnesses and of the
attestation may be given." This text takes for its support *Tynan v. Paschal*, 27 Tex. 286; *Dean v. Dean*, 27
Vt. 746; *Jackson v. Vickory*, 1 Wend. 406; *Transue v.
Brown*, 31 Pa. St. 92; and other cases. In 29 Am. & Eng.
Enc. Law, 203, it is said: "While subscribing witnesses
are most proper to establish the execution of a will, and
the failure to call one within reach is a subject worthy
of consideration, yet in the case of their death, non-residence, failure to remember the circumstances of the
execution, or unfavorable testimony, the will may be
established by other evidence." This text, also, cites
numerous cases for its support. These authorities, as
well as reason, to our minds, make clear the proposition
stated.

It remains to be seen how the fact of the depositions
being taken by consent of parties affects the situation.
We do not see why that fact should change the rule. At
the inception of the proceeding for the probate of the
will the law fixed the right of the proponent as to the
character of the evidence required to show *prima facie*
the execution of the will. Other evidence was made
necessary by the objections to the probate, and the depositions were taken because of the objections. It was the
fact that the subscribing witnesses lived out of the state
that made the testimony of Mrs. Allison proper. The
right to so use her testimony did not depend on her
inability to obtain the testimony of the subscribing witnesses, but of the simple fact of their non-residence. It
thus appears that she was not bound, as a condition
precedent, to use diligence or exhaust legal means to
obtain such testimony. With the fact of non-residence
fixed, it was her right to use other evidence. So it may
be said that, even though the testimony of such non-
resident witnesses is obtainable, other evidence may be

used. The fact that proponent desired and took the deposition of one of such witnesses upon other questions, or consented to the taking of depositions by the contestant, in no way affects the right otherwise given by law. To our minds, the evidence of Mrs. Allison was proper to show *prima facie* the execution of the will, and the effect was to cast upon the contestant the burden of overcoming such *prima facie* effect, or of showing incompetency or undue influence to defeat the will. It follows that in the admission of the evidence and the giving of instructions there was no error.

3

III. A Mrs. Smith, cousin of the proponent, who resides near contestant in Des Moines county, was a witness for proponent, and was permitted, against objections, to state the contents of a letter received by her from proponent, written at Hot Springs, during her husband's sickness, and a little while before he died. When the letter was received by Mrs. Smith she took it to the home of contestant, and read it to him and his daughter, and, as the letter was lost, she was permitted to state the contents, which was, in substance, that her husband was very poorly, confined to his bed most of the time, and asked her (Mrs. Smith) to take the letter to her father and sister, and read it to them, for the reason that she had no time to write to them. She was also permited to state in evidence a conversation with contestant and his daughter to the effect that they desired her (Mrs. Smith) to go to Hot Springs, as contestant was too old, and the daughter could not go. It is urged that such evidence was immaterial and incompetent, because it did not contradict any evidence offered by contestant, and that what John Allison, Sr., might have said in no manner tended to show the circumstances under which the will was executed. A Mrs. Gobile was a witness for contestant, and testified that

4

she was at Hot Springs during the sickness of Mr. Allison, and that she had a conversation with proponent,
in which she asked her why she did not send for Mr.
Allison's brothers, as her husband was dying, and proponent answered that she did not want them there, but
that she would send for her cousin. The object of this
testimony must have been to show that for some reason
proponent was evading her husband's relatives, and
especially his brother, and he had but one. There is
evidence that John Allison, Jr., was not on speaking
terms with his brother James. As to the proof of the
contents of the letter by parol, its loss was sufficiently
accounted for to permit it, if the letter itself would have
been admissible as bearing on the question of undue
influence by her after an attempt to show that she was
avoiding the presence of her husband's brother. The
brother James lived at Mediapolis, near the father, and,
if proponent was thus sending information to the father,
the fact tends to rebut any claim that she was withholding information from relatives to further a scheme
to secure the property. It is to be borne in mind that
the letter was read to, and the conversation was with,
contestant, a party to this proceeding. Mrs. Smith was
also permitted to testify that contestant told her of the
unfriendly relation between the brothers. It is thought
that the testimony was immaterial and incompetent,
but we think not. With the evidence on the part of the
contestant as to what proponent said about wanting the
brother there, it was proper to put all the facts before
the jury, and let it determine the motive that prompted
the remark, if it was made.

IV. In a deposition of Dr. McClenden, taken by
proponent, he testified that he performed a surgical
operation one day after he arrived at Hot Springs, and
that only one operation was performed. No other
questions were asked in his direct examination. The
cross-examination disclosed that the operation was for

stricture of the urethra; that the patient was out about seven or ten days before his death; and that a rubber catheter was used during the last days of his sickness to draw urine. It was then sought, on cross-examination to show that Mr. Allison was affected with uremic poisoning, and, if so, the effect of it on him.

5   The right to do so was refused, on the ground, as we understand, that it was not a proper cross-examination. We do not find it necessary to determine the question, for the reason that the subject was fully inquired into in deposition of the same witness taken by contestant.

V. It is claimed that instruction No. 2, asked by contestant, should have been given. The instruction deals with the physical and mental condition of Mr. Allison at the time of making the will, and con-

6   ceding the correctness of the legal propositions, upon the facts assumed, it may be said that there is just enough of a departure from the record condition as to facts, to make it partial and unfair. The court quite minutely and correctly dealth with the same subject, and in a way that was fair to both parties.

VI. John Allison, Jr., did not attach his own signature to the will, but it was placed there by another, and the court, after specifying the statutory rule in such cases, said: "And if in this case you find,

7   by a preponderance of evidence, that the said John Allison, Jr., did not direct the signing of his name to the paper in controversy, as and for his will, and you further find that he did not expressly approve or adopt the signature of the said paper as his own after his name had been signed to the same for him, it will then be *proper* for you to find that he did not execute the document in question, and that it is not his will." The criticism is upon the use of the word "proper," and it is thought the court should have directed the jury that it *should* find that the instrument

was not his will under such a state of facts. It is said that the use of the word "proper" left it to the jury to find that he either did or did not execute the instrument, and that it was or was not his will, as the jury might elect. The abstract use of the word might justify some such conclusion, but words, in instructions, are not always to be considered with reference to their technical accuracy, but relatively, and that meaning accorded to them that such a consideration shows to have been intended. The instruction under consideration in terms referred to the preceding one, in which the subject of a due execution of the will, as to signing the same by the testator, was considered, and the court expressly said to the jury that if it found in the negative upon the following proposition: "Was the name of the said John Allison, Jr., signed to the document in controversy, as and for his will, in his presence, by a person acting for him and under his express direction, or was the signature of the said paper adopted by him as his signature after it was signed?" it would be its duty to find in favor of the contention of the contestant, and that the paper in controversy was not the will of the said John Allison, Jr. The thought is prominent throughout the instructions that if the instrument was not executed in a legal manner it was not the will of Allison. In view of the situation, the use of the word *"proper"* could only have been understood by the jury in the sense *of right or its duty*, and with that understanding there was no error.

VII. It is also claimed that there was really no execution of any will by John Allison, Jr., and that the finding of the jury is not supported by the evidence. Both claims depend on the state of the evidence for support. No partial review of the evidence would illustrate the situation. One view of it, as is nearly always the case, leaves no doubt of the incompetency; but, when all is considered, it is not to

be said that it is not an open question about which there
is room for a difference of opinion.   The conclusion
depends much on the credit to be given to particular
witnesses, not so much with reference to their veracity,
as with reference to their conclusions from observations
and particular facts coming to their knowledge. The line
between competency and incompetency, or that shows a
testamentary capacity, is always traced with uncertainty, and the findings in most cases are justified only
as the best solution of a doubtful problem.   It is true of
this case. However the fact might be found, there would
be the conviction that it was doubtful.   It is not to be
properly said that the evidence is conclusive either
way.   With such conditions the finding of the jury
should stand, and especially after the district court has
declined to interfere.   The judgment is AFFIRMED.

BERT McLEOD, Appellant, v. THE CHICAGO & NORTH-
WESTERN RAILWAY COMPANY.

Master and Servant: CONTRIBUTORY NEGLIGENCE: *Jury question.*
A railway employe who is directed by his superior to walk from
the rear end of the train on a particular side of the same is not as
1 matter of law guilty of contributory negligence in walking so
3 near the adjoining track, only six feet distant, that he is struck
by a switch engine thereon, where it was the duty of the employe
in charge of such engine to be on the lookout for employes on or
near the tracks and warn them of the approach of the engine, and
no such warning was given. Such employe need not look and
listen as a stranger or trespasser must.

NEGLIGENCE: *Jury question.* Employes operating a switch engine,
whose duty it is to be on the lookout for employes on or near the
1 tracks and to warn them of the approach of the engine by ringing the bell or blowing the whistle, or in some other manner. are
3 not as matter of law free from negligence toward an employe
4 walking along the track in the course of his duty, where no signal
of any kind is given of the approach of such engine.

DIRECTED VERDICT.   A verdict should not be directed for defendant in
2 an action for personal injuries, on the ground that plaintiff was

8 guilty of contributory negligence or that defendant was free
from negligence, unless the facts are such that all reasonable
men must so conclude.

Appeal from Clinton District Court.—Hon. A. J. House,
Judge.

Saturday, December 18, 1897.

This is an action to recover damages for a personal
injury to the plaintiff. At the close of the evidence for
plaintiff, the court directed a verdict for the defendant,
which was returned accordingly, and a judgment
entered thereon. Plaintiff appeals.—*Reversed.*

Charles A. Clark & Son for appellant.

Hubbard, Dawley & Wheeler for appellee.

Kinne, C. J.—I. The facts as disclosed by this
record are as follows: The defendant, on August 1,
1893, was operating its line of railway between Clinton
and Council Bluffs, Iowa, through the city of Belle
Plaine. Plaintiff was in the employ of
1   the defendant as a brakeman on a passenger train. On the morning of said day,
plaintiff was so employed on a passenger train
which was going west, and which reached Belle
Plaine shortly after daylight. On the arrival of said
train at Belle Plaine, it was his duty to remove from the
rear car of said train, and from the rear end of said
train, some lanterns, two tail lights, or "bull's eyes,"
so called, together with a can of fuzees, and to carry
them to and deposit them in the baggage car of said
train. The conductor of plaintiff's train instructed
plaintiff to carry said articles along the south side of
the train. On the south side of this train were situated

several tracks used for switching purposes. The distance between the track on which the train stood
and the nearest track south of it was six feet. Plaintiff
got off the rear end of the train with his lanterns, tail
lights, and can of fuzees, and started along the south
side of the train for the baggage car, in the space
between the train and the nearest track south of it. As
he started, he looked to the rear, and did not see any
engine or cars coming. After he had gone about three
car lengths, without again looking back, and without
seeing any engine or train, he heard an engine. He
turned around to the left, and was struck by the foot-
board of a switch engine, which was approaching from
the east, and was thrown into the air and severely and
permanently injured. It appears that, by custom,
usage, and the rules of the defendant company, it was
the duty of the engineer and the fireman operating the
switch engine to keep a lookout ahead, and to warn any
of the defendant's employes, including plaintiff, who
might be exposed to danger from said approaching
engine. The negligence charged is in negligently running said switch engine at a high and dangerous rate of
speed, without ringing the bell or sounding the whistle,
or giving plaintiff any notice of its approach upon and
against the plaintiff, and in failing to keep a lookout to
see and observe plaintiff and his position of danger, or
to warn him of the approach of the engine, and in
running said engine at a speed of more than four miles
an hour, without ringing a bell or sounding a whistle,
in violation of the rules of the defendant company. The
defendant filed a general denial.

II.   The main question in this case is as to whether
or not the trial court erred in refusing to submit the
case to the jury, and in directing a verdict. In *Meyer v.
Houck*, 85 Iowa, 327, this court, in considering the
question as to when a motion to direct a verdict should

be sustained, laid down the following rule, which has
ever since been adhered to: "Our conclusion is
2   that, when a motion is made to direct a verdict,
the trial judge should sustain the motion when,
considering all of the evidence, it clearly appears to
him that it would be his duty to set aside a verdict if
found in favor of the party upon whom the burden of
proof rests." This rule is followed in these and other
cases. *Moore v. Railway Co.*, 93 Iowa, 484; *McFall v.
Railway Co.*, 96 Iowa, 723; *Mellerup v. Insurance Co.*,
95 Iowa, 317; *Phillips v. Phillips*, 93 Iowa, 618; *Beckman v. Coal Co.*, 90 Iowa, 255; *Anderson v. Wedeking*,
102 Iowa, 446; *Hurd v. Neilson*, 100 Iowa, 555. We have
held that, under this rule, the trial court cannot pass
upon the question as to whether or not the preponder-
ating weight of the evidence is in favor of or against a
party, nor upon the weight of the evidence or the credibility of the witnesses. All these matters are for the
consideration of the jury. *Phillips v. Phillips*, 93 Iowa,
618. And see, further, *Ramm v. Railway Co.*, 94 Iowa,
300; *Kerns v. Railway Co.*, 94 Iowa, 126. It is also well
settled that when, in view of all of the facts and circumstances, the question of negligence is one as to which
men may honestly differ, the case is one for the jury;
and this is true also when the facts are not in dispute.
It is only when the facts are such that all reasonable
men must draw the same conclusion from them that the
question of negligence becomes a question of law for
the determination of the court. *Moore v. Railway Co.*,
93 Iowa, 484; *McFall v. Railway Co.*, 96 Iowa, 723;
Kerns v. Railway Co., 94 Iowa, 126; *Waud v. Polk
County*, 88 Iowa, 617; *Mathews v. City of Cedar Rapids*,
80 Iowa, 463; *Lichtenberger v. Town of Meriden*, 91
Iowa, 48; *Railroad Co. v. Powers*, 149 U. S. 45 (13 Sup.
Ct. Rep. 748); *Railway Co. v. Ives*, 144 U. S. 417 (12 Sup
Ct. Rep. 679).

In view of these rules, did the court err in directing
a verdict? Can it be said that honest men, considering
all of the evidence, fairly, would reach but one conclusion, and that, that defendant was not negli-
3   gent, or, if it was, that plaintiff was guilty of
contributory negligence? It occurs to us that
there was much evidence tending to establish the
defendant's negligence. It was, as the evidence shows,
the duty of the employes operating the switch engine
to be on the lookout for employes on or near the tracks,
and to warn them of the approach of the engine, by
ringing the bell, blowing the whistle, or in some other
manner to notify them of its approach. The bell was
not rung, nor the whistle sounded, nor was the plaintiff
in any way warned of the approach of the engine. In
view of this and other-evidence, it cannot be said that
honest men must reach the conclusion that the defendant was not negligent. Therefore the question of the
defendant's negligence was not one of law for the determination of the court. The verdict was properly
directed, however, if, as a matter of law, the plaintiff
was guilty of negligence contributing to his injury. He
was acting in the line of his duty and under orders from
his superior. True, his superior did not tell him to walk
so near the track as to expose him to injury from
passing engines and trains, but did tell him to proceed
along the side of the train, which he did. He looked for
approaching trains when he got off of the car and began
his walk to the baggage car. He saw no engine or train.
He heard none until it was so near him that, upon turning partly around, he was struck. He did not look while
he was walking the three car lengths, and it cannot be
doubted, if he had so looked in time, he must have seen
the engine, and would have avoided the accident. The
question really is: Was his failing to look, under all of
the surrounding circumstances, legal negligence, which

should bar his recovery? If so, the verdict was properly directed. Had he been a mere trespasser or a
stranger to the defendant passing along the track in a
place of danger for his own convenience, there can be
no doubt that his failure to look would, under such circumstances, preclude his recovery. But the same rule
does not obtain as to an employe who is engaged in the
discharge of his duty; that is, it cannot be said that an
employe passing along the side of the track in the performance of a duty enjoined upon him, is in duty bound
to look and listen for an approaching engine or train, to
the same extent or with the diligence of a traveler at a
crossing. As was said in *Baldwin v. Railway Co.*, 63
Iowa, 212: "In an action for a personal injury, the plaintiff (an employe) cannot be deemed to have been necessarily guilty of contributory negligence, if the danger
might have been seen, and avoided if seen. *Greenleaf
v. Railroad Co.*, 33 Iowa, 52. Somewhat depends upon
the duty which the injured person was discharging, and
somewhat upon the obviousness of the danger." In
Perigo v. Railway Co., 55 Iowa, 329, it was said that a
person is not necessarily guilty of negligence because he
does not avoid a known danger, but the "fact of knowledge of the danger on the part of the plaintiff may be
given in evidence as a circumstance tending to show
negligence." *Pringle v. Railway Co.*, 64 Iowa, 616.
In *Bucklew v. Railway Co.*, 64 Iowa, 608, we said of a
railway employe engaged in the performance of his
duty that, if "absolutely required to look and listen for
approaching trains or unexpected movements of the
train in his charge, his usefulness would be greatly
impaired. We think the question as to the duty of such
an employe to look and listen for the movement of trains
before he steps or walks on the track must be left for
the jury to determine." And in *Crowley v. Railway Co.*,
65 Iowa, 662, in speaking of the duty of an employe to
watch for approaching cars, we held that his duty was

not like that of a traveler at a crossing, "because such an obligation would be inconsistent with his proper attention to his work."

Whether the plaintiff was negligent in walking where he did, and in failing to look, for three car lengths, for approaching engines or trains, is a question to be determined from a consideration of all of the evidence. Among other matters to be considered is the fact that he was in the performance of a duty; that he was carrying lamps and lights and fuzees, and the size of these lights; that the distance between the two tracks was only six feet. How much of this six feet was taken by the cars extending over the track on one side towards the plaintiff, and how much by the extension of the engine over its track towards him, is not shown by the evidence; but jurors in considering evidence, have a right to apply to it their judgment and reason as to matters which are known to all men, and it is a matter known to everybody that all cars and engines do extend somewhat outside of the track or rails. So, it would have been proper to consider the width of the space, so far as it could be determined from the evidence, in which plaintiff had to safely walk; whether, under all of the circumstances, he was guilty of negligence in walking too near the track on which the engine approached; and, in brief, whether, in view of the duty he was discharging and the circumstances and place in which he was required to go, he was guilty of negligence. We do not think it can be truthfully said that honest men, viewing and fairly considering them all, must arrive at the same conclusion, viz.: that plaintiff was negligent; and, if that be so, then the question of his negligence should have been submitted to the jury. Again, being an employe, and engaged in the performance of his duties, he had a right to expect that the employes of the defendant would keep a lookout, and

warn him of the approach of the engine, as the evidence
shows it was the usage, custom, and their duty to do,
and was only bound to exercise such care as would be
sufficient to protect him if the defendant on its part had
given the warning to which he was entitled. *McGovern
v. Railway Co.*, 123 N. Y. 281 (25 N. E. Rep. 373); *Ford
v. Railway Co.*, 124 N. Y. 493 (26 N. E. Rep. 1101). It
may be that, when plaintiff did discover that the engine
was approaching, had he stepped towards the train, he
would have escaped injury. But he was suddenly placed
in peril, and overcome with fright, and it cannot be
said that one who under such circumstances acts negligently is, as a matter of law, guilty of contributory
negligence. The fact that plaintiff's evidence touching
the facts surrounding the accident is not in all respects
in harmony with certain written statements made by
him to the defendant's officers cannot, in view of his
explanations of such statements, be said to show contributory negligence on his part as a matter of law.
Whether, under the evidence, plaintiff was guilty of
negligence contributing to the injury of which he complains, was, we think, a question for the jury. While
it may be that the trial court, sitting as a jury, would
have found, upon all of the evidence, for the defendant,
still it by no means follows that had the case been submitted to the jury, and a verdict been returned for the
plaintiff, the court would have been justified in setting
it aside. It seems to us, under the evidence, it is one of
those cases in which, if a jury should find for either of
the parties, its verdict would not be disturbed upon
the facts. We think the court erred in directing a
verdict.—REVERSED.

G. A. SMITH v. THE CHICAGO & NORTHWESTERN RAILWAY COMPANY, Appellant.

Principal and Agent. A telegram from the chief surgeon of a railway company directing the sendee, a district surgeon in another district. to go to a specified employe who had been injured, as
1 soon as possible, and notify the agent and local surgeon of the company at the place when he will be there, does not give such sendee any apparent authority to employ another physician to assist him.

Estoppel by Testifying. The court instructed that if, on the trial of another cause, plaintiff in this cause, *for the purpose of enabling another to recover against the defendant for personal injuries,* gave testimony that he was the physician in attendance, and per-
8 formed the services, and of their value, thus enabling that other to recover of the defendant for such services, he was estopped to recover in this suit. It was also charged that if, when plaintiff testified in the prior case as to the value of his services, he added that he had a suit pending against the defendant for the services, and that he expected to collect for the services from the defendant, then there would be no estoppel. *Held,* that both instructions were proper.

SAME. Failure of a physician who attended an employe of a railway company to state while testifying as a witness for such employe in an action against the company, that he has a suit pending
4 against the company for his services, does not estop him from subsequently recovering from the company for such services, on the ground that the employe was enabled by his testimony to recover therefor from the company. It was not the duty of the witness to decline to answer nor to inform the court that he had a suit pending for such services.

Instructions: CONFLICT. An instruction authorizing the jury to consider. for the purpose of determining whether a physician employed by defendants to attend an injured employe had appar-
1 ent authority to employ plaintiff to assist him, the facts that the
2 physician said to plaintiff that the company would pay him for his services and that he was only to assist the company's physician who was to remain in charge of the case, and that plaintiff was to report the condition of the patient to the company's physician and to make such reports and have the free use of the telegraph service of the company, is improper and irreconcilable with another instruction correctly stating as the law that, "none

of the declarations or statements" of, the company's physic'an to plaintiff can be considered by the jury as any evidence that he had any authority to employ plaintiff.

Appeal from Clinton District Court.—HON. P. B. WOLFE, Judge.

SATURDAY, DECEMBER 18, 1898.

THE plaintiff is a physician residing at Clinton, Iowa. In December, 1891, one Denton Olney was a fireman in the employ of the defendant company, and was injured by his knee striking a switch target. Dr. Hobart, who was the company's district surgeon at Clinton, was called to see Olney, and treated him for a short time, when, because the family was dissatisfied, he was discharged, and one Dr. Finley was employed. The condition of the patient became serious, and a brother of his went to Chicago and saw the chief surgeon of the company, Dr. Owens. Upon consultation, Dr. Owens telegraphed Dr. Fairchild, who was the company's district surgeon at Ames, Iowa, to go to Clinton and see the patient, Olney, which he did. After an examination of the patient, and dressing his wound, Dr. Fairchild had a consultation with the plaintiff as to the treatment to be given, and the plaintiff rendered professional services until the case was discharged; and this action is for the value of such service. The theory on which it is sought to hold the defendant liable is that Dr. Fairchild employed plaintiff, on behalf of the company, and that the service was rendered in pursuance of such employment. The defendant presented a general denial, and also, by way of estoppel, pleaded that the said Olney brought a suit against the defendant company for his damages because of such injury, which was tried in the United States circuit court, and claimed as a part of his damages the amount alleged to be due plaintiff in this suit, and recovered the same, and that

plaintiff was a witness in that suit, and gave testimony
showing the service rendered, and the value thereof, for
the purpose and object of enabling Olney to recover
therefor. The issues were tried to a jury, that returned
a verdict for plaintiff, and from a judgment thereon
the defendant appealed.—*Reversed.*

N. M. Hubbard for appellant.

Hayes & Schuyler and *G. B. Phelps* for appellee.

GRANGER, J.—I. We first notice the question arising, and argued, presented by the denial in the answer,
which is a claim that the services were not rendered
under an employment by the defendant company. The
testimony as to the fact of an employment by Dr. Fairchild is in conflict, but there is a frank concession by
counsel for appellant that its condition is such that this
court cannot interfere with the finding, if Dr. Fairchild
had authority to bind the company by his acts in
that respect. It may be stated, as without dispute,
that, prior to being summoned to Clinton to see
Olney, Dr. Fairchild had no business connection with
the defendant in what is known as the "Clinton District," his duties for the company being confined to
other territory in the state. The following is the telegram in pursuance of which he went to Clinton: "D. S.
Fairchild: Please go to Clinton, as soon as you can, to
see C. H. Olney. Notify the agent and Dr. Hobart when
you will be there. John E. Owens." A published rule
of the company is that "the company will not pay for
the services of any other surgeon, after the arrival of
their own local surgeon, except by special arrangement in writing with the chief surgeon or general claim
agent." It does not appear that the plaintiff knew of
this rule, but it is important, as showing the actual
authority of local surgeons to employ others. An

instruction, in effect, took from the jury any question
of ratification by the company of what Dr. Fairchild
did, and also instructed that there was no evidence
tending to show that, at the time in question, "district
surgeons either had or exercised any authority in
employing surgeons outside the limits of their respective districts." With this condition of the record, the
question comes to this: Had Dr. Fairchild such apparent authority as that the company is bound by his acts,
assuming that he did employ Dr. Smith? The
2   court, in express terms, told the jury that "none
of the declarations or statements of Dr. Fairchild to the plaintiff or to Olney can be taken or considered by you as any evidence that he had any authority
to employ the plaintiff." It then, in the same instruction, said to the jury that such declarations and statements were only for the purpose of showing that Dr.
Fairchild did or did not employ Dr. Smith, and as to
such a rule there is no complaint. On the question of
Dr. Fairchild's apparent authority, the court gave the
following instruction: "(10) When a principal has, by
his voluntary act, placed an agent in such a situation
that a person of ordinary prudence, conversant with
business usages and the nature of the particular business is justified in presuming that such agent has
authority to perform, on behalf of his principal, a particular act, and such act having been performed, the
principal cannot deny, as against the innocent third
party, the agent's authority to perform; and in this
case, if you find from the evidence that Dr. Owens told
Mr. Olney's brother, when he called to see him, in Chicago, that he would send a physician to Clinton to see
his brother, knowing at the time that the district surgeon of the company had been for some weeks discharged, and was not in care of the patient, and that,
in pursuance of said promise, Dr. Fairchild came to
Clinton, and operated on said Olney, and that he agreed

to take charge of the case, and that the plaintiff knew that fact, and knew that the defendant paid for assist- ance rendered to the district surgeons in cases in their district, and also that when he was employed, if you find that Dr. Fairchild did employ him, he was told by Dr. Fairchild that the defendant would pay him for his services; that he was only to assist Dr. Fairchild, who was to remain in charge of the case; that he was to report the condition of his patient to Dr. Fairchild, and, to make those reports, he was to have free of charge the telegraph service of the defendant,—and that he so reported to Dr. Fairchild, using the defendant's tele- graph, and sending the reports through their assistant superintendent at this place, it is for you to say, from those facts, if you find them established by the evidence, and from all the facts and circumstances in evidence in the case, whether or not the plaintiff, as a reasonably prudent man, had a right to believe that Dr. Fairchild had authority to employ him as an assistant in the case, or not." It is said by appellant that this instruction, and the one excluding the declarations and statements of Dr. Fairchild from the consideration of the jury in determining his authority, are inconsistent. It seems to us that there is no avoiding the conclusion. It was likely the view of the court that the statements in the instruction quoted, or what Dr. Fairchild said to the plaintiff, as expressed therein, are not of the character which the law would exclude. We assume this, because otherwise there would be a want of consistency in the court's expression of its own views. It is important to have in mind that there is but a single purpose in the instruction, which is to direct the jury as to facts that might be considered, and that would warrant a finding that Dr. Fairchild had apparent authority to employ plaintiff. The instruction, in express terms, authorized the jury to consider for that purpose the facts that Dr. Fairchild said to plaintiff that the defendant would pay him for his services; that he was only to assist Dr. Fairchild, who was to remain in charge of the case; that he was to report the condition of the patient to Dr. Fairchild, and, to make those reports, he was to have free use of the telegraph service of the defendant. It seems to us that these facts are of the class that cannot be considered to show authority, under the rule given by the court. That the instruction only permits the conclusion that there was apparent authority by these facts being considered with other facts, does not change the rule. The effect is to aid facts proper for consideration, by those that are not. It is to be understood that, as to these facts, their effect is not made to depend on the company's knowledge of them, as is true of one or more of the other facts stated, but that they are for consideration absolutely, without regard to that fact. In Mecham, Agency, section 276, it is said of an agent that he "cannot establish his own authority, either by his representations, or by assuming to exercise it." If Dr. Fairchild said these things, and he had no authority, he was assuming to exercise authority, and that fact cannot be shown to establish his right to do so. A rule very applicable to this case, whether invariable or not, is stated in *Kane v. Barstow*, 42 Kan. Sup. 465 (22 Pac. Rep. 588), as follows: "The rule that a principal is bound by the acts of his agent which are within apparent scope of his authority is applicable only where there have been previous transactions of a similar character, in which the agent exceeded his powers, but which the principal ratified without question, the other party being ignorant of the limitation of the agent's authority, thereby leading him to believe that the agent had all the powers claimed."

Having in view the language of the telegram by which Dr. Fairchild was authorized to go to Clinton, and other undisputed facts, it may be stated as established conclusively that his authority was to render his personal service, and no more.   His duty was of a professional nature, not involving such business transactions as are common to agents, where implied powers attach because within their apparent scope.   The ser vice he was authorized to render justified no inference of an authority to employ another, and it is quite impossible to understand what he could have done at that time to properly indicate an apparent authority, if his own statements would be incompetent for that purpose. It would seem, as held in the Kansas case, that, to give his acts the force of apparent authority, there must have been previous transactions of a character to have justified the plaintiff in believing that such authority did exist.   Appellee cites us to no authority to sustain the rule of the instruction, and it seems to us that the general rule is against it.   There is really no controversy as to the general rules of law.   The contention is as to their application to the facts of this case.   With the objectionable evidence out, the remaining evidence is not sufficient to justify a finding of authority on the part of Dr. Fairchild.

II.   As to the estoppel pleaded, the court instructed that if, on the trial in the federal court, the plaintiff in this case was a witness, and for the purpose of enabling Olney to recover against the defendant, he gave testimony that he was the physician in attendance and performed the services, and of their value, thus enabling Olney to recover of the defendant for such services, he was estopped to recover in this suit. This was followed by an instruction in these words: "(14) If you believe from the evidence that at the trial at Dubuque, and when the plaintiff was examined as a witness, in answer to the question with reference to his bill for services in attendance upon said Olney he said: 'I have a suit pending against the company for my services, and I expect to collect for my services from

the defendant,' or words of a similar effect or import,
then, and on your so finding, there would be no estoppel,
and the defendant would fail as to this branch of its
defense." The complaint is as to the instruction quoted.
We think the instruction correct. If the witness so
stated, there could have been no finding that he gave
his testimony for the purpose of enabling Olney to get
a judgment for such services in the federal court, in any
illegal or wrongful sense. The plea of estoppel is made
to depend on the *purpose* and *object* with which Dr.
Smith gave his testimony, and the court submitted
Smith gave his testimony, and the court submitted
this branch of the case on that theory. It is
4   thought that it was the duty of Dr. Smith, when
asked in the federal court about his services to
decline to answer, and inform the court that he had a
suit pending for such services. We think that Dr. Smith
owed no such duty to the defendant. He was a witness
in court, and, in a sense, under the direction of the law.
The defendant was present, with full opportunity to
insist upon a disclosure of the facts; and if the witness
gave them, and in so doing, it was made to appear that
he was a claimant for such services himself, the basis
for an estoppel failed. For the reasons stated in the
first division of the opinion, the judgment will be
REVERSED.

FRANKLIN FLOETE, Appellant, v. MARY A. BROWN, *et al.*

Mechanic's Lien: ESTOPPEL BY FRAUD OF PURCHASER. Where mate-
1 rials for improvements were furnished to one in possession of
   land on his false representation that he owned the land, or had
2 an interest therein to which a lien could attach, and he afterwards acquired a life estate therein, and more materials were
   thereafter furnished under the same contract, a lien for all the
   materials attached to the life estate.

PRIORITIES: *Lease.* Where a lease of a life estate was made before
  5 the statement of a mechanic's lien for materials furnished prior
to the lease, was filed, and after the expiration of the time during
which the statute protects such liens without statements, and the
lessee had no actual notice of the mechanic's lien, the lien of the
lessee is superior to the mechanic's lien.

ASSIGNMENT: *Notice.* The assignee for value of a lease which is
  5 prior to a mechanic's lien by reason of the fact that the assignor
took the same without notice of the lien is protected to the same
extent the assignor would be, notwithstanding any actual knowledge such assignee may have had.

Judgment: CONSTRUCTION FOR APPEAL A judgment for some of the
  3 relief prayed which does not grant other relief prayed but does
not expressly deny it, is a judgment against plaintiff as to such
relief, so that on appeal from the judgment rendered, his right to
such relief may be considered.

Appeal: ESTOPPEL AS TO REVIEW. A party cannot question on
  4 appeal an express statement or admission in his pleadings.

Appeal from Clay District Court.—HON. W. B. QUAR-
TON, Judge.

SATURDAY, DECEMBER 18, 1897.

ACTION on a note and account, and to establish a
mechanic's lien. The district court gave judgment for
plaintiff on the note and account, but only partial relief
as to the lien sought, and the plaintiff appealed.—
Modified and affirmed.

Cory & Bemis for appellant.

Carr & Parker and *Richardson, Buck & Kirkpatrick*
for appellees.

GRANGER, J.—I.   John Brown died, testate, July 4,
1891, in Illinois, leaving as a part of his estate, a quarter
section of land in Clay county, Iowa. He left several
children surviving, and among them Vincent D. Brown.
In the spring of 1891, and before the death of his father,
Vincent D. Brown became a tenant of the land in Clay

county, and was in such occupancy when his father
died.   The right of Vincent D. under the lease
1   was only from year to year.   The will of John
Brown gave to Vincent D. a life estate in the
land, so that, after July 4, 1891, his estate was one for
life.   In April, 1891, without the knowledge of John
Brown, Vincent D. contracted with the plaintiff for
lumber to be used in erecting buildings on the land,
and the lumber was delivered and so used.   Most, if
not all, of the lumber, had been furnished before the
death of John Brown.   There is some dispute as to
where the lumber was used, it being appellant's claim
that a part of it was used in the house; but the court
found, and we think correctly, that it was used only in
the barn and hog pen.   Appellant, in his petition, sought
to establish his lien on the real estate on which the
buildings are situated.   The defendants are quite
numerous, including the widow and heirs at law of
John Brown, and also the John Paul Lumber Company,
F. H. Helsell, and the Bank of Sioux Rapids.   The interest of Helsell and the bank is because of a lease executed by Vincent D. Brown in November, 1892, to Helsell to secure a loan of one thousand dollars from the
bank.   On the fifth day of April, 1894, a balance of the
one thousand dollar claim was paid by A. H. Brown,
and the lease was assigned to him by Helsell, and he
(Helsell) also quitclaimed to A. H. Brown his interest
in the land.   On the same day, Vincent D. Brown and
wife, by deed, conveyed their interest in the land to A.
H. Brown.   It thus appears that from and after April
5, 1894, A. H. Brown was the owner of the life estate,
by a conveyance from Vincent D. Brown and wife, and
also the owner of the leasehold interest of Helsell,
which included the interest of the bank.   This suit was
commmenced August 5, 1893, and before A. H. Brown
obtained the title from Vincent D. or the interest of
Helsell; and hence he took from them with knowledge

of plaintiff's claim, but would be protected in so far as
his grantor would be protected. The statement for the
mechanic's lien was filed August 3, 1893. The cause is
continued as to the John Paul Lumber Company, so
that the company does not appear in this court. The
district court, so far as the lien concerned, sustained it
as to the barn and hog pen, and denied it in other
respects, and it is mainly because of a refusal to sustain
it as to the life estate of Vincent D. Brown that the
appeal is prosecuted.

II. The answer of the defendants admits the right
of plaintiff to a lien upon the buildings in which the
lumber was used, and they do not resist the establishment of such a lien; but the right to a lien on the land
is denied by them, and the contention comes to this:
Are the facts such that had Vincent D. Brown retained
his life interest in the land, the lien of plaintiff would
have attached thereto? For the present we leave out
of consideration how the lien, if it would attach, would
be affected by the leasehold interest of Helsell, that
was assigned to A. H. Brown. The sale by Vincent D.
to A. H. Brown was in 1894, long after the material
was furnished and the life estate was acquired, so that
the lien had attached so far as it would, of which A. H.
Brown was required to take notice in his purchase from
Vincent D. The equities of this case speak loudly for
the plaintiff, but this should not lead to an erroneous
announcement of the law. The facts are, we
2   think, beyond serious dispute, that, when the
contract was made between plaintiff and Vincent
D. Brown, both supposed that he (Vincent) had the
right to make the improvement on the land; that part
of the material was furnished before and part after the
life estate was acquired; that plaintiff did suppose
and Vincent D. had reason to suppose, at least after he
had his life estate, that the lumber was furnished so
that the lien would be upon his (Vincent's) interest, be

it greater or less. It does not appear that the contract
was for a specific amount of lumber to be delivered at a
specified time, but it seems that the period of its
delivery was from April 15 to December 10, 1891, quite
a proportion being delivered after the life estate was
acquired. Plaintiff states, and we think truthfully,
that, when the contract was made for the lumber, Vincent told him that he owned the farm. It may be
doubted if he meant more than that he was in possession, expecting the title, at least, to the extent of a
life estate. In view of these facts, we do not regard the
legal proposition as doubtful that, as between plaintiff
and Vincent D., the lien should attach to the life estate,
which he had when he took, in part at least, the fruits
of his contract. It was but one contract and one performance. We do not find that the precise question has
ever been determined. The statute does not seem to be
explicit in this particular. Apellees concede, in argument, that the lien attaches to "such interest as the
owner had at the time of entering into the contract and
the furnishing of the material." We need not express
an opinion as to the correctness of such a rule, for, if
correct, it is against the thought that it attaches only
to the interest at the time the contract is made, and
favors our conclusion; but we may say that where a
party is led to believe that one has a title or interest, to
which the lien will attach, and he has not, but obtains
it while the contract is being performed, the lien does
attach. Of such a rule we have no doubt.

III. It is thought by appellees that the appeal is
not from that part of the judgment, so that the question
we have considered is not involved in the appeal. The
prayer of the petition is in part that a lien may be
3   established against said land and the buildings
according to law, and concludes with a prayer
for such other and further relief as may be adjudged
equitable. The effect of the judgment was to deny all

relief against the land. There are no express words of denial, but there are express words of the relief granted, which would operate to deny what is not expressed, and that is, in legal significance, a judgment of denial. The notice of appeal is that plaintiff appeals from the judgment and decree rendered against him. We think that, wherein the court either expressed or by legal inference denied relief asked by plaintiff, it was a judgment against him; so that, on appeal, generally, from a judgment against him, he may have such questions considered.

IV. It is said that the devise in the will is too indefinite to vest a life estate in the particular land in question. We think that question is definitely settled, for the purpose of the case, by the answer of the defendants. It is therein expressly stated that the will left a life estate in said real estate to Vincent D. Brown.

4

V. With the life estate affected by the mechanic's lien, we should settle the question of priority between plaintiff and A. H. Brown, in so far as his leasehold interest is concerned, that he obtained by assignment from Helsell. The lien of this lease attached in November, 1892, which was after the life estate attached, and before the statement for the mechanic's lien was filed, and after the period in which the statute protects such liens without the statement. Helsell took his lease without actual notice of the mechanic's lien, and hence he is protected, and the lien of the leasehold interest, as to Helsell, is prior to the mechanic's lien. A. H. Brown is the assignee of the lease, for value, and, as we understand, is protected as Helsell would be, notwithstanding any actual knowledge he may have had. This rule is familiar. We think the judgment should be so modified as that the plaintiff's lien will attach to the life estate,

5

subject, however, to the lien of A. H. Brown by virtue of the lease obtained from Helsell.

The main contention in the case has been as to the right of the plaintiff to a lien other than on the buildings. The costs, in other respects, are but a small proportion. The defendants Helsell and the Sioux Rapids Bank are entitled to their costs, and as to the plaintiff and other defendants who have answered, and are in this court, the costs will be taxed in both courts, one-fourth to the plaintiff, and the remainder to the defendants. With the modification of the judgment as suggested, it will stand AFFIRMED.

CHARLES OSBURN, *et al.,* v. THE CITY OF LYONS, *et al.,* Appellants.

Public Improvements: CONSTRUCTION OF CONTRACT: *Guaranty.* A provision in a contract for grading, curbing, guttering and paving a street, that the contractor shall, without further compensation, keep in continuous good repair all pavements laid under the contract for a period of five years, except as to defects or repairs required by excavations or disturbances of the street not caused by the contractor, and requiring the pavement to

3   remain during such time a good, substantial, reliable and durable pavement in all its parts ' except ordinary wear," does not invalidate the contract, although Code 1873, section 465, requires the city to pay the expense of repairs—as such provision is a mere guaranty of the proper construction of the pavement.

NOTICE: . *Validity of contract.* Acts Twenty-third General Assembly, chapter 14, section 8, as amended by Acts Twenty-fourth General Assembly, chapter 12, provides that all contracts for public

1   improvements shall be made after public notice of the extent of the work, the kind of materials used, and the time when the work shall be completed. A notice provided for sealed proposals for paving, and referred to an ordinance of the city fixing November 1, 1893, as the time for completion of the work. Four

2   months after notice was published, two bids were received, and six months before either of them was accepted, the council changed the time for completing the work to August 1, 1894. The bid of the contractor was not accepted until May 1, 1894. *Held,* that as the bid of the company was originally made under

the proposition that the work should be completed November 1, 1893, and as no bid had been secured to do the work to be completed at the second date fixed, the contract, as finally made, was entered into without notice and without the competition required by the statute.

Appeal from Clinton District Court.—Hon. P. B. Wolfe, Judge.

Saturday, December 18, 1897.

Action in equity to restrain the collection of a tax levied to pay for the improvement of a street. There was a hearing on the merits, and a decree in favor of the plaintiffs. The defendants appeal.—*Affirmed.*

S. C. Scott and *Hayes & Schuyler* for appellants.

F. W. Ellis and *L. A. Ellis* for appellees.

Robinson, J.—On the thirtieth day of May, 1893, the council of the city of Lyons ordered that Sixth street, from the south line of improvement district No. 1 to the city limits of the cities of Lyons and Clinton, be graded, curbed, guttered and paved by the first day of the next November. The portion of the street ordered paved was designated "Improvement District No. 3" in the city of Lyons. A notice to contractors, inviting sealed bids for furnishing the materials for and making the improvements ordered, was published, and on or before the fifth day of July, 1893, the time fixed for filing bids, two were received by the city, that of the Lyons Construction Company being the lowest and best bid. On the thirty-first day of October, 1893, the resolution adopted May 30, 1893, was amended by changing the date on or before which the improvement should be completed from November 1, 1893, to the first day of August, 1894. On the fifteenth day of May, 1894, the city council

ordered the issuing of bonds in two series, on account of
the improvement, and not to exceed the contract price
thereof. One series, to the amount of seven thousand
dollars, was for the payment of that portion of the work
covered by the intersections of streets and alleys, and
the other series, to the amount of thirty-three thousand
dollars, was to cover the remainder of the cost of the
improvement. All of those bonds were issued and sold.
In July, 1894, the improvement was completed and
accepted by the city, the amount of the assessment was
fixed, and apportioned to the city, to the street railway company, and to the abutting property owners,
and a time fixed for making objections to the assessments, notice of which was published in two newspapers
of the city. The plaintiffs are the owners of property
against which assessments were made, and they allege
that the tax levied by the city for the improvements is
invalid for various reasons, and ask that the collection
thereof be restrained, and that it be declared not to be
a lien upon their property. The district court found
that the taxes so levied were illegal, and enjoined their
collection.

I. The first objection to the validity of the tax
urged is that the requirements of the law with respect
to letting contracts for such improvements were not
fulfilled. Chapter 14, Acts Twenty-third General
Assembly, as amended by chapter 12, Acts Twenty-
fourth General Assembly, gave to all cities of the state
having a population of more than four thousand, and
all cities acting under special charters, power to make
certain contracts in regard to paving and curb-
2   ing streets. Section 3, of the chapter 14 specified,
provides that "all such contracts shall be made
by the council, * * * and shall be made with the
lowest bidder or bidders upon sealed proposals after
public notice for not less than ten days, in at least two
newspapers of the said city, which notice shall state as

nearly as practicable the extent of the work, the kind
of material to be furnished, when the work shall be
done, and at what time the proposal shall be acted
upon." It is claimed that the notice to contractors published in this case failed to state at what time the bids
would be acted on and when the work should be done.
The portion of the notice thus called in question is as
follows: "State of Iowa, Clinton County:—ss: Sealed
bids or proposals are hereby invited by the undersigned,
city clerk of Lyons city, in said county, to be filed with
him at his office in said city on or before the fifth day
of July, A. D. 1893, at 7:30 o'clock P. M., for grading,
curbing, guttering, and paving improvement districts
numbers 2 and 3, in said city, according to the resolution and ordinance of said city heretofore adopted,
ordering the same, and the specifications of the city
engineer of said city on file in the office of the said city
clerk, which, together with his estimate of approximate
quantities are hereby included in this notice and made
a part hereof." The statute also required the notice to
state when the work should be done, but the notice in
question did not refer to that subject. It is true that
the paving resolution referred to in the notice fixed
November 1, 1893, as the time for completing the work;
but about four months after the notice was published
and the bids were received, and six months before either
of them was accepted, the council changed the time for
completing the work to the first day of August, 1894,
as already stated. The bid of the Lyons Construction
Company was not accepted until the first day of May,
1894. At that time the company was not under any
obligation, on account of the original bid, to do the
work, for the reason its bid was based on the proposition that the work should be completed on the date
first fixed, and the bid of its competitor was founded
upon the same proposition. No bid had been asked
nor made to do the work during a period of time which

would expire on the second date fixed, and the contract
as finally made was entered into without notice, and
without the competition for which the statute provides.
It is not a case where a contract has been entered into
in good faith, and for some good and sufficient reason
the time of performance has been extended, but where
a new contract has been made. By the terms of the
first notice, a certified check for five hundred dollars
was required to be deposited by each bidder, and that of
the construction company was not surrendered to it,
but that fact did not affect the character of the transaction. We are of the opinion that the notice given was
wholly insufficient to meet the requirements of the
statute. It was said in *Coggeshall v. City of Des Moines*,
78 Iowa, 235, of statutory provisions in character somewhat like those in question, that they were mandatory,
to be strictly followed. See, also, *Windsor v. City of
Des Moines*, 101 Iowa, 343. We conclude that the failure to give notice in this case required by statute was
a defect which made the contract for the improvements
in question invalid.

II. The contract which the city attempted to
make with the construction company contains the following: "The said Lyons Construction Company
        hereby guarantees that said curbing, grading,
3   guttering, and paving in said district shall be
        done and completed according to the contract
and specifications hereto attached (no acceptance of or
payment for the same being a waiver for any failure to
comply substantially with such specifications), and in
addition thereto that the same shall be and remain
(except as to the defects which may appear, or repairs
which may be needed by reason of excavations or disturbances of the streets not caused by said contractors,
their agents, servants, or employes), at the end of five
years from the completion thereof, in as good condition in all respects as when completed and as required

by such specifications; and shall be and remain good, substantial, reliable, and durable pavement in material and workmanship as a whole and in all its parts, except ordinary wear; and in case any repairs are necessary or proper, except as aforesaid, during said five years, said contractors shall make the same annually, when not of a serious or expensive character, otherwise promptly on the notification by the said Lyons city, use the same material required by these specifications, and all without expense to said city. And, in case said contractors shall fail to make such annual repairs within ten (10) days after such notification, said city may cause the same to be made, and charge the cost thereof to the con- tractors, for which they and their bondsmen shall be liable, and which they shall pay promptly to said city upon completion of such repairs." It is claimed that this portion of the contract was invalid because it pro- vided for maintaining the improvement in good condi- tion for the term of five years, the effect of which was to include in the contract price the cost of keeping the improvement in repair for the term stated, whereas section 465 of the Code of 1873, in force when the con- tract was entered into, required the city to pay the expense of such repairs. The contract refers to annual repairs, but a careful examination of its provisions shows that the contractor was not to be liable for defects caused and repairs made necessary by reason of excavations or disturbances of the streets not caused by the contractor, nor for ordinary wear. The contract was, in effect, a guaranty that the improvemeht should be of such character that they would remain in the con- dition they were in when first completed, for the term of five years, excepting as to the defects and repairs specified, and ordinary wear. It was not a contract for keeping the improvement in repair for a fixed term of years, but a guaranty of its quality and durability, coupled with an obligation to make the guaranty good.

Had the undertaking been to keep the improvement in
repair for the time specified, in terms sufficiently comprehensive to include repairs by whatever cause made
necessary, a different question would be presented.
Thus, in *Boyd v. City of Milwaukee*, 92 Wis. 456 (66
N. W. Rep. 603), a contract which required the contractor to keep in good order and repair all the work
done for a period of five years, only excepting repairs
made necessary by cutting through the pavement for
the laying or repairing of sewers, drains, gas, water, or
electric service pipes, or other work authorized by the
board of public works, was held to include a charge for
repairs, and to that extent to have been unauthorized;
but it is said that, had the agreement to repair been
confined to repairs made necessary by defective
workmanship or material, the claim that the contract
as to repairs was, in effect, but a guaranty of workmanship and material, would be entitled to serious
consideration. The cases of *Brown v. Jenks*, 98 Cal. 10
32 Pac. Rep. 701); *Verdin v. City of St. Louis*, 131 Mo.
Sup. 26 (27 S. W. Rep. 447, and 33 S. W. Rep. 480), and
Fehler v. Gosnell (Ky.) 35 S. W. Rep. 1125, involved
contracts somewhat like the one construed in *Boyd v.
City of Milwaukee*, and are not authorities against the
conclusion we reach. The case of *Cole v. People*, 161
Ill. Sup. 16 (43 N. E. Rep. 607), holds that a condition
in the contract that the contractor should "without
further compensation, keep in continuous good repair
all pavement laid under this contract for a period of
five years from September 1, 1894," was merely a warranty or guaranty of the fitness of the material for the
use intended, and that the pavement was properly constructed. The Illinois court goes further than we are
required to go to sustain the provision in question. The
case of *Barber Paving Co. v. Ullman*, 137 Mo. Sup. 543
(38 S. W. Rep. 458) tends strongly to sustain our
conclusion.

III. The appellants contend that the plaintiffs knew that the improvement in question was being made, but did not object thereto, and are therefore estopped to claim that the proceedings connected therewith are void. We do not find that any of the plaintiffs have so conducted themselves as to be estopped to assail the validity of the assessments. Some of them may have known that the improvement was being made, but it is not shown that they knew of the illegalities in the letting of the contract, nor that the improvement was the result of anything they did or refrained from doing. Some of them may have asked for it, but, if so, it must be assumed, in the absence of a showing to the contrary, that they asked that it be made according to law. Some of them protested against the improvement before the contract therefor was made. We find no ground upon which the decree of the district court should be disturbed, and it is AFFIRMED.

GEORGE DEE & SONS COMPANY v. THE KEY CITY FIRE INSURANCE COMPANY, Appellant.

Insurance: APPRAISEMENT: *Condition precedent.* An appraisement and award is a prerequisite to the maintenance of an action on an insurance policy unless such appraisement is waived or sub-
1 mission and award prevented by the company, where the policy provides that the ascertainments and estimates shall be made by the parties, or if they differ, by the appraisers, and that the loss shall not be payable until sixty days after the award of the appraisers has been rendered.

SAME: *Right of assured to appraisement.* An insured has the right to insist that if an appraisement of the amount of damages pro-
2 vided for by the policy is made it shall embrace all property claimed by him to be covered by the policy, although the company denies that it is so covered.

WAIVER. A condition in an insurance policy making an appraisement a prerequisite to the bringing of a suit on the policy is
3 waived where the company refuses to permit an agreement of

submission to appraisements to be so changed as to embrace certain property claimed by the insured to be covered by the policy,
although the company denies that such property is within the
policy.

Of proof of loss. Proofs of loss are waived by an insurance company where the secretary of the company, empowered to waive
3   such proofs, leads the insured to believe that he has done all in
that respect that is required and promises an early payment of
the loss.

Appeal from Dubuque District Court.—HON. J. L. HUS-
TED, Judge.

SATURDAY, DECEMBER 18, 1897.

ACTION on a policy of fire insurance. Verdict and
judgment for the plaintiff. The defendant appeals.—
Affirmed.

Longueville & McCarthy for appellant.

D. E. Lyon and *Henderson, Hurd, Lenehan & Kiesel*
for appellee.

KINNE, C. J.—I Plaintiff corporation was, on and
prior to June 28, 1894, the owner of a plant in the city
of Dubuque, consisting of a brick building containing
certain fixed and immovable machinery, engines, and
boilers, a stock of baskets and lye, manufactured and
in process of manufacture, all of which machinery,
engines, and boilers were used in the manufacture of
baskets and lye. On that date, and prior thereto, plaintiff held a policy of insurance covering said property in
the defendant company for two thousand dollars.
There was other concurrent insurance upon the property, so that it is conceded that the defendant's liability, if any, is for only one-fourth of the loss or damage sustained under said policy. The pleadings and
amendments thereto present several issues, but the
following are the important questions presented for

consideration: (1) Did the policy require arbitration
as a prerequisite to the payment of the loss, and to the
maintenance of the action? (2) Was such requirement,
if it existed, waived by the acts of the defendant company? (3) Was there such fraud on plaintiff's part as
would forfeit all claim under the policy? (4) Were
proofs of loss furnished in time, or were they waived?
(5) Did the court err in the ruling upon the evidence?
(6)Was it error to refuse the defendant a continuance?
(7) Was there error in giving or refusing instructions?

Touching the ascertainment of the loss, the policy
provides: "Said ascertainment or estimate shall be
made by the insured and this company, or, if they differ,
then by appraisers as hereafter provided; and,
1   the amount of loss or damage having been thus
determined, the sum for which the company is
liable pursuant to this policy shall be payable sixty days
after due notice, ascertainment, estimate, and satisfactory proof of the loss have been received by this company, in accordance with the terms of this policy
* * * The amount of sound value and of damage
shall be determined by the mutual agreement of the
company and assured, or, failing to thus agree, the
same shall then be determined by appraisal of each
article by two competent and disinterested appraisers,
one to be appointed by assured, and the other by this
company, and the two so chosen shall first select a competent and disinterested umpire. * * *" After providing that they shall make the appraisement, and, if
they do not agree, that they shall submit their differences to the umpire, and that the award of any two of
them shall be final, and that the company may repair,
replace, or rebuild the property, it is further provided
that "until sixty days after the proofs, certificates,
plans, and specifications and award of appraisers

herein required shall have been rendered, and examination perfected by assured, the loss shall not be payable." Now, the rule which governs such stipulations
is stated in *Hamilton v. Insurance Co.,* 137 U. S. 370
(11 Sup Ct. Rep. 133), in the following language: "A provision in a contract for the payment of money upon a
contingency that the amount to be paid shall be submitted to arbitrators, whose award shall be final as to
that amount, but shall not determine the general question of liability, is undoubtedly valid. If the contract
further provides that no action on it shall be maintained until after such award, then * * * the
award is a condition precedent to the right of action.
But when no such condition is expressed in the contract, or necessarily to be implied from its terms, it is
equally well settled that the agreement for submitting
the amount to arbitration is collateral and independent,
and that a breach of this agreement, while it will support a separate action, cannot be pleaded in bar to an
action on the principal contract." This rule has been
cited with approval by this court. *Lesure Lumber Co.
v. Mutual Fire Ins. Co.,* 101 Iowa, 514; *Zalesky v. Insurance Co.,* 102 Iowa, 613; *Read v. Insurance Co.,* 103
Iowa, 307. Now, this policy does not in express terms
prohibit the bringing of an action until an arbitration
is had; but it does provide that, when the parties cannot agree, the loss shall be determined by arbitration,
and that the sum for which the company is liable "shall
be payable sixty days" thereafter; and in another place
it provides that, "until sixty days after the * * *
award of appraisers herein required shall have been
rendered, * * * the loss shall not be payable."
These provisions of the policy clearly imply that the
loss is not due or payable until sixty days after the
appraisement or award is returned. If the loss is not
payable until such time, it is equally clear that suit
cannot be maintained until sixty days after the award

is returned. Under the wording of this policy, we think
the appraisement and award was a prerequisite to the
maintenance of the action, unless it was waived, or
submission and award was prevented, by the acts of the
defendant.

II.   That such a provision in a policy of insurance
may be waived is well settled. It appears that the
provision touching arbitration was not the same in all
of the policies.   It also appears that the interested
companies served a joint notice demanding an appraise·
ment. Plaintiff was not bound to agree to or to
2   enter into a joint arrangement with all of the
companies for a single appraisement. He had a
right to insist upon a separate appraisement in this
action, in accordance with the terms of the policy. If
he did assent to a joint appraisement, he had the
undoubted right, in view of the difference in the provis·
ions of the several policies, to protect himself against
subsequent misunderstanding which might arise in
consequence of these differences in the several policies.
If, as he claims, defendant would submit to no changes
in their printed agreement of submission in that
respect, we think it should be held to be a waiver on its
part of any right to insist upon the appraisement and
award.   The agreement of submission presented to
plaintiff for his signature provided that the appraisement should not "determine, waive, or invalidate any
other right or rights of either party to this agreement,"
except the loss or damage. After the quoted words,
the plaintiff's attorney added "except as per provision
of policy or proper construction of terms thereof." We
suppose the thought was to make it certain that plain·
tiff would not, by signing the agreement to submit,
waive any right he might have by virtue of the provis·
ions of the policy. It does not seem to us that this
added claim in any way changed the agreement for sub·
mission or its legal effect, and whether it was inserted

or not was immaterial. The agreement for submission provided: "The property on which the sound value and the loss or damage is to be determined is as follows:" [Then followed a description of the property as it is found in the policy.] This, plaintiff's counsel struck out, and, in lieu thereof, inserted "as shown in policies and claim of assured attached hereto." We think this was a change which the plaintiff had a right to insist upon.

The chief controversy between plaintiff and defendant was this: Plaintiff was insisting upon pay for certain articles as being covered by the policy, though not expressly specified in the policy. The defendant was denying any liability therefor, because they were not expressly enumerated in the policy. Now, it was no part of the duty of the appraisers to determine this controversy, or to determine what property, in fact, the policies covered. Clearly, we think plaintiff had a right to insist that, if an appraisement was made, it should embrace all property claimed by him to be covered by the policy. It would then leave to be determined by the parties, or by litigation, the question as to whether or not these articles of property were really embraced within the provisions of the policy, though not specifically enumerated. In any event, it could have worked no injury to the defendant, and it can readily be seen that it was necessary or might be necessary for the protection of plaintiff's rights, in the event that it should thereafter be established that said items of property were embraced within the provisions of the policy. Again, if at any time thereafter plaintiff's right to recover for said articles should be established, it might be claimed that, by entering into the agreement for a submission which did not specifically enumerate said articles, he had waived any right to claim compensation for them. He was not obliged to permit himself to be placed in such a situation. His insistence in this respect was reasonable, and as there was no conflict in the evidence touching this particular matter, and it showed conclusively that the plaintiff was demanding an appraisement of all articles of property which he claimed were covered by the policy, and that the defendant refused to permit the agreement to be so changed as to embrace them, the court did not err in instructing the jury not to consider the defense of want of arbitration. The defendant must be held by its acts to have waived the right to insist upon the arbitration.

III. The court did not err in refusing to submit the issue of fraud to the jury. Without entering into a discussion of the evidence, it is sufficient to say that there was no evidence of fraud which would warrant the court in submitting such an issue to them.

IV. The secretary of the defendant company had the right to waive proofs of loss, and did so. He led the plaintiff to believe that he had done all in that respect that was necessary, and promised an early payment of the loss. He made no objections to the proofs in fact furnished. The demand for arbitration, which is not controverted, was of itself a waiver of proofs of loss. *Walker v. Insurance Co.*, 51 Kan. Sup. 725 (33 Pac. Rep. 597); *Insurance Co. v. Bean*, 42 Neb. 537 (60 N. W. Rep. 907). No plea in abatement was entered, and, if it had been, it would have been unavailing, as more than ninety days had elapsed after the proofs of loss were waived, and before this action was commenced. The waiver took place within the thirty days provided in the policy within which proofs of loss must be furnished. As the action was not prematurely brought, and the furnishing of proofs of loss was waived, the court correctly took the question of waiver from the jury.

V. We have examined the record as to the other errors assigned, and discover no reason for disturbing the judgment below. The judgment below must be AFFIRMED.

L. H. NOYES, *et al.*, Appellants, v. THE BOARD OF SUPERVISORS OF HARRISON COUNTY, *et al.*

Accretions: NON-NAVIGABLE WATERS: *Riparian rights.* Riparian owners of lands bordering on non-navigable lakes, which were
1 meandered by the government surveyors in 1851 and 1852, and did not become wholly dry and fit for cultivation until 1890 and 1891, are not entitled to the bed of the lake, under the law of accretions

SAME. The rule that a riparian owner of land bordering on rivers
2 or streams, in the absence of limitations in his title, takes to the center thread of the stream, does not apply to the case of a lake or pond.

Appeal from Harrison District Court.—HON. GEORGE W. WAKEFIELD, Judge.

SATURDAY, DECEMBER 18, 1897.

ACTION to enjoin the defendant county from selling certain lands in the beds of Round and Dry Lakes. Decree for defendants. Plaintiffs appeal.—*Affirmed.*

S. H. Cochran and *J. T. Davis* for appellants.

L. R. Bolter & Sons and *C. W. Kellogg* for appellees.

KINNE, C. J.—I. The plaintiffs claim by accretion, and also under conveyances, title to certain portions of the bed of Dry and Round Lakes (so called), in Harrison county, Iowa, by reason of being the owners of lands bordering on said lakes under conveyances without reservation. All parties claim through the swamp land grant of 1850. It is admitted that these lakes were never navigable; and it appears without conflict that the defendant county has from time to time, for many years, surveyed portions of these lake beds, has platted

1   the same in lots, and sold said lots to various parties.   It is conceded that these lakes were meandered by the general government surveyors in 1851 and 1852, and that they never became wholly dry, and their entire beds fit for cultivation, until along about 1890 or 1891.   The county having ordered the remaining unsurveyed portions of these lakes to be surveyed into lots, and caused the same to be appraised and offered for sale, plaintiffs applied for and obtained a temporary injunction restraining the sale of the lots. On final hearing, the injunction was dissolved, and from that decree the plaintiffs appeal.

II.   It is contended by appellees that the facts of this case bring it within the application of the rule announced in *Noyes v. Collins*, 92 Iowa, 566.   The claim in that case was the same as in this,— that by reason of being riparian owners of lands bordering on these lakes and in the absence of limitations in the conveyance to them, they took title to the center thread of the lakes; and they also claimed title to the land lying in these lake beds under the law of accretion.   In the *Noyes-Collins Case* the title to a portion of the bed of

2   this same Dry Lake was in controversy; and it was held, under the facts, that the land lying in the lake bed was not an accretion to the lands of plaintiff in that case, and that the rule that a riparian owner of land bordering on rivers or streams, in the absence of limitations in his title, takes to the center thread of the streams, does not apply in this state to the case of a lake or pond.   If, then, the facts of the two cases are substantially alike, the rule is controlling in the case at bar.   While there is a conflict in the evidence in this case as to the effect of the artificial drainage upon the waters of Dry and Round Lakes, still we

think that the facts established by a preponderance of
the evidence bring the case within the rue of the *Noyes-
Collins Case*. The decree below is AFFIRMED.

THE EXCHANGE BANK OF LEON, *et al.*, Appellants, v. C.
E. GARDNER, *et al.*

Banking Partnership: DUTY OF CASHIER. It is the duty of a partner
in a banking business, to whom is left the active management of
the business, to act in good faith, and with entire honesty, in
transacting all the business of the bank, and to exercise as high
a degree of care and skill as is generally exercised by business
men, in the management of such business; but he is not liable for
honest errors in judgment, nor for the failure to take the utmost
precaution possible, in making investments for the bank.

RULE APPLIED to a case where an attempt was made to incorporate
a bank under Iowa law which was never so incorporated, though
it was, for a time, managed according to the articles of incorporation. The bank had a large amount of idle money on which
it was paying interest and one partner acting as cashier, bought
Kansas City paper which proved almost wholly worthless.
While some inquiries were made, more thorough ones would have
disclosed the truth. The president knew or should have known
that outside investments were being made, and no objection was
made to the practice.

KINNE, C. J., taking no part.

Appeal from Decatur District Court.—HON. H. M.
TOWNER, Judge.

SATURDAY, DECEMBER 18, 1897.

ACTION in equity for an accounting, and to recover
of the defendant C. E. Gardner, fifteen thousand dollars
on account of poor investments made by him as cashier
of the plaintiff bank. There was a hearing on the
merits, and a judgment in favor of the defendants for
costs. The plaintiffs appeal.—*Affirmed.*

Harvey & Parrish for appellants.

Hoffman & Baker and *T. M. Stuart* for appellees.

ROBINSON, J.—The plaintiff the Exchange Bank of
Leon is a co-partnership, which was organized in the
year 1888, with a capital of thirty thousand dollars, and
is engaged in business at Leon. The partners who composed the firm were the plaintiffs S. W. Hurst, I. N.
Clark, H. J. Vogt, Orr Sang, C. S. Stearns, and the
defendants C. E. Gardner and R. D. Gardner. The
person last named is the father of his co-defendant, and
is made a defendant because he would not join as
plaintiff. No relief is asked as against him. Therefore,
when we refer to "Gardner," C. E. Gardner is the person intended. Gardner was cashier of the bank from
the time it was organized until the summer of 1894,
when he was discharged. In October, 1890, he purchased of a Kansas City corporation, known as the
Winner Investment Company, two promissory notes,
one of which was for two thousand dollars, and the
other for four thousand dollars. They purported to
be signed by one J. R. Anderson, and were indorsed by
the Winner Investment Company, and by W. E. Winner, and were secured by bonds of the Winner Building
Company, a Kansas City corporation, to the amount of
six thousand dollars. The larger of the two notes was
renewed in the form of two notes, each of which was for
the sum of two thousand dollars. In the latter part of
November of the same year, Gardner purchased two
promissory notes, made by Martin O. Ellis, of Kansas
City, one of which was for the sum of two thousand,
five hundred and seventy-six dollars and seventy-seven
cents, and the other for ninety-one dollars. Both were
indorsed by the persons of whom they were purchased.
In February, 1891, the larger of the two notes was

exchanged for a note of the Western Lumber Company
of Kansas City; new security was taken; and the maker
and indorsers of the note exchanged were released. In
November, 1890, Gardner purchased of D. R. Emmons
a promissory note for two thousand, five hundred dollars, made by one E. L. Brown of Kansas City, and
indorsed by Emmons. At about the same time, Gardner
also purchased a note made by one W. B. Grimes, of
Kansas City, for about one thousand, three hundred
dollars, which was secured by shares of stock in two
Kansas City corporations. A considerable portion of
the Grimes note has been paid, and the security which
is held for the unpaid portion is nearly or quite sufficient to satisfy it. But a small amount has been
realized on any of the other notes, and they are of little,
if any, value. Considerable expense has been incurred
in efforts to collect them, and judgments have been
obtained on some of them. In all that Gardner did in
purchasing the notes, in renewing some of them, and in
attempting to collect them, he acted for and as cashier
of the bank. The plaintiffs claim that he exceeded his
authority in purchasing Kansas City paper, and was
negligent in not ascertaining the financial condition of
the parties liable on account of it, and its real value and
the value of the securities which were obtained with it,
in releasing some of the securities, and in making the
investments without consulting any of his co-partners.
The plaintiffs seek to recover of him the amount of the
unpaid portions of the notes, and of the expenses
incurred in the attempts which have been made to collect them.

When the bank was organized, the persons interested intended to incorporate it under the laws of this
state, and articles of incorporation and by-laws were
prepared for that purpose; but the plan of incorporating
was abandoned, and the business was carried on by the

persons who had intended to incorporate, each one contributing to the fund of thirty thousand dollars, which
was raised as the capital of the bank. Each person who
thus contributed was regarded as a stockholder to the
amount of his contribution, and dividends were declared
accordingly; but the persons interested in the business
were in fact co-partners, with interests in proportion
to the amount of the aggregate contributions to the
capital. It is claimed, however, that it was agreed
between the partners that the business should be conducted in all respects according to the articles of
incorporation and by-laws which had been prepared,
and that Gardner made the investments in question in
violation of the provisions of those instruments which
were designed to control the making of investments.
There was some attempt made for a short time after the
business was commenced to conduct it according to
the articles and by-laws, but the attempt was soon
abandoned, and no attention was thereafter paid to
them in carrying on the business of the bank. The
larger part of that business was intrusted to Gardner as
cashier, and he made investments and transacted the
business intrusted to him according to his own judgment, rarely consulting his associates to ascertain
their views in regard to what should be done. This
practice was so continuous, and of such long standing,
that it must be regarded as well known to and approved
by all parties in interest. Hurst, who had contributed
more than one-half of the capital of the bank, habitually occupied a place in the banking room. He acted
as president, and assisted somewhat in the business,
and occasionally gave directions as to what should be
done. The books of the bank were at all times open to
his inspection, and he frequently examined them or
some of them. The affairs of the bank were examined
twice each year by a committee composed of two of
the partners, and their report was presented to and

acted upon by the partners who constituted the board
of directors, at their semi-annual meetings, but no
report was required of Gardner, excepting as it was
made in the books of the bank. At about the time the
investments in question were made, the bank was
holding idle capital to the amount of more than fifty
thousand dollars, and Hurst was urging that a large
part of it should be invested. Nearly one-third of it
was money deposited by the treasurer of Decatur
county, under an agreement with the county that the
bank should pay seven and three-fourths per cent. per
annum as interest on all time deposits which should
remain in the bank six months or more, and three per
cent. per annum on daily balances in excess of two thousand dollars. Opportunities for local investments were
not sufficient to absorb the portion of the idle money of
the bank which it desired to invest. It was under those
circumstances that the promissory notes in question
were offered to the bank on terms which were favorable
if the notes were good. Gardner made some inquiries
in regard to the value of the notes, and purchased them
in the belief that they were good. From facts now
known and shown in the record, it is evident that a careful investigation made in Kansas City, as to the business transactions and solvency of the various makers
and indorsers of the notes and the value of the collateral securities which accompanied them, would have
disclosed facts which might have caused a prudent person to decline to purchase the notes. But the evidence
in regard to the financial standing of the several persons and corporations who were liable for their payment is conflicting. Some of the business men of
Kansas City who were engaged in banking and other
financial pursuits in the year 1890 state that such persons and corporations were considered insolvent in
October and November of that year, while others,
constituting the larger number, testify that they

were regarded as solvent. It appears that Winner and the investment and building companies which bear his name continued to be actively engaged in carrying on business enterprises some time in February, 1891, and that they did not fail until some months later. Anderson was a mere accommodation maker of the notes which Winner indorsed, and was his teamster. That fact was not known to Gardner when he purchased the notes, and he relied, in purchasing them, upon a telegram from a reputable banker of Kansas City, in answer to an inquiry by Gardner as to whether Anderson had deposited first mortgage bonds to the amount of six thousand dollars to secure his notes for that sum, indorsed by Winner and the Winner Investment Company. The telegram read as follows: "James R. Anderson has deposited with us bonds certified to be first mortgage to secure his notes for equal amount. Our receipt issued therefor. Consider same, with indorsement, would be good." The bonds were not secured by a first mortgage, and it is claimed that Gardner was negligent in accepting the telegram as sufficient evidence that the notes were good. In purchasing the note of E. L. Brown, Gardner relied in part upon a property statement made by Brown in April, 1890, which showed that at that time his assets exceeded his liabilities by more than fifty thousand dollars, and it is said that Gardner was negligent in relying upon a property statement made so long before the purchase.

It must be admitted that Gardner did not exercise the highest decree of care and diligence which was possible in purchasing the notes in controversy; and the question we are required to determine is whether, in view of the facts disclosed by the record, his failure to exercise greater care and diligence than he did makes him liable for the loss which followed the investments. There is no evidence whatever that he acted in bad faith, nor do we think he exceeded his authority in purchasing the Kansas City paper. Money of the bank was invested in Chicago, and, a little later, investments were made in Sioux City and Minneapolis paper. It is not at all propable that all of those investments were made without the knowledge of the president of the bank; and, even if not known at the time they were made, they were certainly known within a short time thereafter, and we are satisfied that Gardner's authority to make them was not then questioned. That he was making an honest effort to invest properly a portion of the idle money of the bank is clearly shown, and that no question in regard to the Kansas City investments was made until after the Winner failure is, we think, also established. It was the duty of Gardner to act in good faith and with entire honesty in transacting all the business of the bank, and to exercise as high a degree of care and skill as is generally exercised by business men in the management of such business. *Bank v. Johnson,* 94 Iowa, 220. But he was not liable for honest errors in judgment, nor for the failure to take the utmost precaution possible in making the investments for the bank. See *Charlton v. Sloan,* 76 Iowa, 288; *Knapp v. Edwards,* 57 Wis. 196 (15 N. W. Rep. 140). Applying these rules, we conclude that he was not so negligent in the transactions in question as to be liable for the resulting losses. This conclusion makes it unnecessary to determine questions in regard to ratification and waiver discussed in the arguments of counsel. The judgment of the district court appears to be sustained by the evidence, and is AFFIRMED.

KINNE, C. J., taking no part.

J. S. REED v. THE CITY OF MUSCATINE, Appellant.

OBJECTION BELOW. An objection that plaintiff in an action for personal injuries caused by a defective street did not give notice of the accident to the city within six months as required by Acts
1 Twenty-second General Assembly, chapter 25, section 1, cannot be first taken on appeal, on the ground that such notice is jurisdictional and may be raised at any time; as the court has jurisdiction of the general subject, and lack of the jurisdiction of the particular case cannot be first raised on appeal.

Appeal: ASSIGNMENT OF ERROR. An assignment on a motion for a new trial, that the verdict is not sustained by sufficient evidence,
2 does not sufficiently present the objection that notice of the injury to the plaintiff by a defect in the street of the defendant city was not given within six months as required by Acts Twenty-second General Assembly, chapter 25, section 1.

Appeal from Muscatine District Court.—HON. A. J. HOUSE, Judge.

SATURDAY, DECEMBER 18, 1897.

ACTION at law to recover damages for personal injuries sustained by plaintiff while driving along one of the streets of the defendant city,—due, as is alleged, to a defect therein for which defendant is responsible. Trial to a jury. Verdict and judgment for plaintiff, and defendant appeals.—*Affirmed.*

E. F. Richman and *J. F. Devitt* for appellant.

Titus & Jackson and *J. R. Hanley* for appellee.

DEEMER, J.—There is but one question in the case which is of sufficient importance to be noticed in an

opinion. The petition was filed on the twenty-second
day of March, 1895; and it is alleged that the
1   injury occurred on the twenty-fourth day of
August, 1894,—more than six months prior to
the filing of the petition. There is no allegation that
plaintiff gave the defendant notice of the happening of
the accident, as required by section 1, chapter 25, Acts
Twenty-second General Assembly. Defendant did not
demur to the petition, nor did it raise the question of
want of notice, in any manner, in the trial court. It
has filed in this court, however, what its counsel have
seen fit to denominate a "motion to reverse the judgment and dismiss the case." This motion is bottomed
upon the proposition that the notice is jurisdictional,
and that in the absence of allegations that notice
was given, the trial court had no right or authority to
hear the case, and that, as the question is jurisdictional,
it may be raised for the first time in this court. "Jurisdiction" has been defined to be the "power to hear and
determine the subject-matter in controversy between
parties to a suit; to adjudicate or exercise any judicial
power over them." *Rhode Island v. Massachusetts*, 12
Pet. 718. It is conceded that the court had jurisdiction
over the parties, but it is argued that it had no jurisdiction over the subject-matter. The subject-matter is
that right which one party claims against the other, and
demands judgment of the court upon. *Jacobson v.
Miller*, 41 Mich. 93 (1 N. W. Rep. 1013). In this case it
was the right which plaintiff had to compensation for
injuries received through the negligence of the defendant. The district court had the right to consider the
question, and therefore had jurisdiction of the subject-
matter. In determining such questions, it is important
to distinguish between jurisdiction of the general subject and jurisdiction of the particular subject; for, if it
be found that the case under consideration belongs to
the former class, then it is within the jurisdiction of

the court, and neither insufficiency of allegation nor
informality in proceedings will affect that jurisdiction.
See Brown, Jurisdiction, section 1; *Yates v. Lansing*,
5 Johns. 282; *Hunt v. Hunt*, 72 N. Y. 217. As said by
Judge Elliott in his work on General Practice (volume
1, section 240), "Where there is authority to make a
judicial inquiry, there is jurisdiction, and it is evident
that this authority exists wherever there is power over
a general class of cases." The distinction is also pointed
out in Brown, Jurisdiction, section 10. Objections to
the jurisdiction of the general subject may be made at
any stage of the proceedings, for they cannot be waived.
But, as a general rule, if there is jurisdiction of the
general subject there may be waiver of objections to
the jurisdiction of the particular subject. That is to
say, if the court has the right to decide the general
class of cases to which the one in question belongs, its
decision, although erroneous, cannot be collaterally
attacked, and, if no objection or exception be taken it
will be considered as waived. The difference between
a right to decide and a right decision clearly and briefly
illustrates the distinction we are trying to elucidate.
We have a case where there is unquestioned authority
over the general subject, but it is claimed that there
is no jurisdiction of the particular case, because of the
absence of allegations as to notice. Such objection
does not go to the jurisdiction of the subject-matter,
but rather to the correctness of the decision in the particular case, and cannot be raised for the first time in
this court. Plaintiff's failure to give notice simply
affects his right to recover, and does not go to the jurisdiction of the court. The case is quite like that of
Sheel v. City of Appleton, 49 Wis. 125 (5 N. W. Rep. 27),
wherein it is held that failure to give notice simply
affects the plaintiff's right to sue, and does not deprive
the court of jurisdiction of the subject-matter. See,
also, *Gould v. Hurto*, 61 Iowa, 47; *Bridgman v. Wilcut*, 4

G. Greene, 563; *Oskaloosa College v. W. U. Fuel Co.*, 90 Iowa, 387. None of the authorities relied upon by appellant announce a contrary doctrine. In each and every of them the question was raised in the trial court by demurrer, motion in arrest, or otherwise. The motion to reverse and dismiss is overruled.

Counsel present the same question in their brief as a reason for reversing the judgment. It is insisted that want of notice was raised by the motion for a new trial, under the assignment that "the verdict 2 is not sustained by sufficient evidence." We do not think that this was sufficiently specific, but, if it was, the assignments of error do not properly raise the question. *Duncombe v. Power*, 75 Iowa, 185; *Insurance Co. v. Henderson*, 38 Iowa, 450. Counsel also argue that it was not necessary to raise the question in the trial court, and cite us chapter 96, Acts Twenty-fifth General Assembly, which says that "no pleading shall be held sufficient on account of a failure to demur thereto," and also strikes out a provision of the Code of 1873, to the effect that, if an objection to a pleading is not raised by demurrer or waiver, it shall be deemed waived. We have heretofore held, in at least two cases, that, notwithstanding the provisions of this act, questions not made in the court below will not be considered on appeal. *Boyd v. Watson*, 101 Iowa, 214; *Weis v. Morris*, 102 Iowa, 327. No prejudicial error appears, and the judgment is AFFIRMED.

ALTA Z. MILLER v. SAMUEL MILLER, Appellant.

Husband and Wife: CONTRACTS BETWEEN. A written obligation for the payment of money given by a husband to a wife in consideration of her joining in a deed and conveying her contingent interest in the husband's land, is an unenforceable contract, under Code 1873, section 2203.

Appeal from Plymouth District Court.—HON. F. R. GAYNOR, Judge.

SATURDAY, DECEMBER 18, 1897.

THE parties are husband and wife. The defendant owned certain lands, and, desiring to convey the same to third parties, agreed with his wife (plaintiff) to pay to her the sum of two thousand dollars if she would join in the deed, so as to convey her contingent right. The conveyance was made, signed by the wife in pursuance of the agreement, and she was paid, of the amount agreed upon, one thousand, five hundred and ninety-seven dollars; and, for the remainder of the two thousand, defendant gave to her the following instrument in writing: "Know all men by these presents, that I hereby agree to pay Alta Z. Miller, within ninety days from this date, the sum of four hundred and three dollars; and, in the event I should fail for any reason to make said payment of said sum promptly when due, then I agree to secure the payment of said sum by proper security on the stock of livery this day purchased by me of Hoyt & Goudie. Dated this first day of February, 1894. Samuel Miller." The defendant refused payment, and this action is to recover on the written obligation. The cause was submitted to the court on a stipulation of facts that gave judgment for plaintiff, and the defendant appealed.—*Reversed.*

Zink & Roseberry for appellant.

I. T. Martin for appellee.

GRANGER, J—There are few, if any, important facts, other than those above stated. It appears that the parties, though husband and wife, at the time of the commencement of the action, and now, are living apart

from each other. It also appears that plaintiff refused
to join in the conveyance unless the defendant would
pay her two thousand dollars, and that thereupon the
agreement was made to do so, resulting in her signing
the deed, receiving the amount stated, and the execution of the written agreement sued on, for which there
was no other consideration than her agreement to sign
the deed. The defendant was the owner of the land
conveyed. The following is section 2203 of the Code of
1873: "When property is owned by either the husband
or wife, the other has no interest therein which can be
the subject of contract between them, or such interest
as will make the same liable for the contracts or liabilities of either the husband or wife, who is not the owner
of the property, except as provided in this chapter."
The section is in the title of the Code designated, "Of
the Domestic Relations," and in a chapter thereof
devoted to husband and wife. It permits a married
woman to own in her own right both real and personal
property, and to manage, sell, convey, and devise the
same by will, to the same extent and in the same manner
that a husband can property belonging to him. Section
2202. It provides that either husband or wife may
maintain an action against the other for the possession
or control of property belonging to him or her. Section
2204. It provides that the wife alone shall be liable for
civil injuries committed by her. Section 2205. It
makes conveyances, transfers, or liens executed by one
to the other valid, to the same extent as between other
persons. Section 2206. The chapter contains other
provisions not important to be noticed. It will be seen
that the chapter undertakes to define quite particularly
the rights of married women as to property owned by
them, and what rights the husband or wife has in the
property of the other. That the plaintiff in this case
had in the property in question but a contingent interest, being her distributive share, available to her only

after her husband's death, there is no question. Section 2203, above quoted, says that in such a case she has no interest that can be the subject of contract between herself and her husband. Was this contingent interest the subject of the contract out of which the obligation sued on arose? The question is not debatable. One definition of "subject" is, "That concerning which something is done." The contract was concerning this contingent right. The statute is, that such property cannot be the subject of contract between husband and wife. If the statute means anything, it means that such a contract is void; that it is forbidden. Appellee refers to the extended rights of married women under the statute, in support of the judgment. The statute, as a whole, is both a grant and denial of right. We should, and are disposed to, respect it in all particulars, but no right granted is impaired by the denial of the one we are considering. The statute is preservative in its nature, as to an unmatured right, so that its relinquishment shall be voluntary, in the sense of being uninfluenced by fear, fraud, or promise of reward. As the written obligation has no other consideration for its support than the contract in question, which is forbidden, it cannot be the basis of an action, and the judgment must be REVERSED.

THE CITY OF CEDAR FALLS, Appellant, v. MADS HANSEN.

Waters: DIVERSION BY GRADING. An owner of a city lot has the right to bring his lot to grade although the flow of surface water may thereby be diverted to the lots owned by other persons

ESTOPPEL. The owner of a city lot below grade does not by acquiescing in the construction by a city of ditch conveying surface water over his premises estop himself to obstruct the flow of the water in such ditch by raising his lot to grade.

Appeal from Black Hawk District Court.—HON. A. S.
BLAIR, Judge.

SATURDAY, DECEMBER 18, 1897.

THE defendant is the owner of lots 6, 7, and 8, in
block No. 5, Jackson Taylor's addition to the city of
Cedar Falls. These lots front on State street, which runs
north and south. Number 8 is the lot lying north and
it borders on Thirteenth street, which runs east and
west. Lots 7 and 6 are south of No. 8, and in the order
named. It is made to appear from the petition that
defendant has long used and occupied a house on lot
No. 8, and that, of late, he has moved the same house
onto lot No. 6, and has placed a foundation thereunder,
and is about to bring said lot to a level of the street
in front thereof, which is State street. It is further
made to appear that across said lot 6 there is a natural
depression, through which water has always flowed
from higher land, lying to the north and west of said
lots, to lower lands south of them; that the land to the
north and west, drained by the depression, is about
forty acres; that defendant has placed his house
directly in the path of the water course; and that the
completion of his work will obstruct the flow of the
water along said course, and turn it back into the
street, and onto the premises of the owners of many
lots, and thereby create a public and private nuisance,
to the damage of the plaintiff and others; and it is
asked that the defendant be enjoined from making said
obstruction. The answer admits most of the averments
of the petition, but denies the conclusions pleaded, and
it pleads other facts, some of which may be noted in the
opinion. On the trial the court dismissed plaintiff's
petition, and it appealed.—*Affirmed.*

H. C. Hemenway for appellant.

Alfred Grundy for appellee.

GRANGER, J.—It will be well to somewhat particularize the facts at the outset. It seems that north and west of the lots of defendant, many years ago, was a tract of some forty acres of land on which was a low place or basin that, because of surface water coming thereon from adjacent lands, made a pond, the overflow from which ran down across the lots of defendant, because of the natural lay of the ground. This natural passageway was not like the bed of a stream with defined banks, but such a hollow as to be followed by water, when flowing from the tract described. It may be said that, beyond question, it was surface water flowing only at times. This hollow or passageway for the water grew narrower in going south, till, on lot 6, it was comparatively narrow. The pond referred to we understand to have been filled by the city, but surface water still flows from the tract of land. The city, in 1871 and 1872, made improvements in this section, and in so doing made a ditch along the west side of lots 7 and 8, and turned the same in onto lot 6 for a short distance, so that the water passed from the ditch on lot 6 into the hollow or passageway we have described. Since the ditch was constructed the water has passed through it, and not across lots 7 and 8, except at times of the heaviest storms. The defendant has owned and occupied lots 7 and 8 since about 1871, and has owned lot 6 since 1884. The ditch constructed along the west side of the lots has been enlarged and kept in repair by the city since its construction. Since the ditch was made defendant has filled lots 7 and 8, and they have been used for gardening and a place for residence, and it is the house thereon, in which defendant lived, that is now being placed on lot 6.

It is appellant's claim first "that the drainage channel of the basin constituted a water course, which neither the city nor any person may interrupt or obstruct to the damage of any other person who objects thereto." In support of this claim we are especially referred to Angel, Water Courses (6th ed.), sections 108a-108s, where the subject of ancient water courses is considered. This court in *Livingston v. McDonald*, 21 Iowa, 160, considered the question of surface water, and as we understand, followed the rule cited in Angel on Water Courses. The subject there, as here, was that of surface water. The rule of the Livingston Case is that the owner of the higher land has no right to collect the surface water into a ditch or drain in increased quantity, or in a manner different from the natural flow, and discharge it upon the land of another, even though it be done in the course of the improvement and use of his farm; but the owner of such higher land may, for the proper use of his farm, so drain his land of surface water as to divert it from going onto the lower land owned by another. These rules are well established. It is, however, said in that case that the rule is not laid down as applicable to town or city property. The later case, in this state, of *Freburg v. City of Davenport*, 63 Iowa, 119, deals with the rights of the city in the improvement of streets and abutting property owners as to surface water. It is true that the case does not present the precise question involved in this case, but it does present one as to the liability of the city for damage for negligence of the city in failing to provide sufficient outlets for surface water. Incidentally, the question of the rights of the city to bring its streets to grade, and the abutting property owner to bring his lot to grade, are involved and considered, with the conclusion that both have the right, and damage was denied

to the lot owner because of water being diverted from
its natural course by the street improvement, because
the city had the right to presume that the owner would
bring his lot to grade, and thus protect himself from
damages. The case plainly recognizes the rule that
the city may, in bringing its street to grade, divert surface water from its natural course without liability for
damage to abutting property not at grade. The recent
case of *Knostman & P. Furniture Co. v. City of Davenport*, 98 Iowa, 589, is in some respects applicable, and is
in line with the former cases. As facts in this case, we
should have stated that the grade of State street had
been established, and the lot in question was below it.
The grading complained of was to improve the lot and
bring it to grade. It is the law, then, that the city had
the right to bring its street to grade, and in so doing
it might discharge surface water on the lot, without
liability, because defendant had not brought his lot to
grade, as the city had a right to presume he would. It
is to be remembered that the city in the improvement
of its street, changed or diverted the water from its
natural course across lots 7 and 8 and a part of lot 6,
and it is now in the position of asserting a right for
itself to change the course of the water on defendant's
land, but denying to him the right to obstruct it. Conceding that the rights of the city and the individual
may not always be the same it still remains that the city
may not divert water to its liking, and say to the defendant, "You cannot improve your lot so as to interfere
with the flow of water as it now is." It is the established
right of the city, in the improvement of its streets, to
turn surface water, even from its natural course, and
owners of lots below grade cannot complain, because
of their right to bring their lots to grade for protection.
The same right must certainly belong to the lot owner,—
that is he may exercise the right to brings his lot to
grade; and, however these changed conditions may

affect the flow of surface water, he is not responsible for
consequences, nor can he, to avoid consequences, be
denied the right to improve and enjoy his property.
The situation is within the rule, so often stated, that
surface water is a common enemy against which all
may contend.   It would not do to apply to cities the
general rule applicable to rural districts as to surface
water.   Such a rule is founded largely on the proper
enjoyment of lands, with their natural formation, while
in cities the use and enjoyment of real property is made
to depend very much on changes prescribed by the constituted authorities. Municipal regulations necessi-
tate the bringing down of higher land, and the
bringing up of lower land, to grade. Appellant
places some stress upon the rule as to easements,
but we cannot see how it can base a right on such a
claim. It is thought that the acquiesence of defendant
in the construction of the ditch, and taking the
advantage of it, should now prevent him from obstruct-
ing the flow of the water as fixed by the ditch and the
regular channel. He could do nothing else than accept
it. It was, as we have said, the city's right, so far as the
street was concerned, to change the flow of surface
water. The acquiesence was a legal necessity. The
judgment must stand.—AFFIRMED.

F. M. DAVENPORT, Contestant and Appellant, v. A. T.
    OLERICH, Incumbent.

Election Contest: BURDEN OF PROOF. Where an official count has
been made, it is better evidence of who was elected than the bal-
1 lots, unless he who discredits the count shows affirmatively that
the ballots have been preserved with a care which precludes the
opportunity of tampering and all suspicion of change, abstraction
or substitution.

RULE APPLIED. Ballots cast were placed in the custody of the
auditor until removed to that of the clerk under the order of

court They were properly protected, except those from two pre-
2 cincts, which were wrapped in paper, and placed on the floor
under the table in the vault in the auditor's office, where the
inmates of the office did not at all times have them in sight
Some of these packages were unsealed and the seals of others
were broken At one time three of the packages were mislaid;
the vault in which they were placed was left open, and many
people had access thereto. *Held*, that the ballots had not been so
preserved as to be competent as evidence for the purpose of overthrowing the official count.

Appeal from Carroll District Court.—HON. Z. A. CHURCH,
Judge.

SATURDAY, DECEMBER 18, 1897.

ELECTION contest for the office of county attorney.
From judgment declaring the incumbent entitled to the
office, the contestant appeals.—*Affirmed.*

F. M. Davenport pro se, and *M. W. Beach* for appel
lant.

B. I. Salinger for appellee.

LADD, J.—The board of supervisors, as county canvassers, found Olerich duly elected to the office of
county attorney of Carroll county at the general election of 1896. This finding was contested by Davenport, and the court of contest, organized under the
statute, decided that Davenport had received more
votes than Olerich, and was entitled to the office. Olerich appealed to the district court, where it was held
"that the ballots offered in evidence in this cause were
preserved so carelessly as to expose them readily to
fraudulent alterations, abstraction, substitution and
destruction; and that the finding made by the board of
supervisors of Carroll county, Iowa, acting as a board
of canvassers, that A. T. Olerich was duly elected county
attorney * * * is better evidence than the said

ballots." Subject to this conclusion, the court found Olerich to have received a majority of the votes cast, and to have been duly elected.

I. The ballots, when properly authenticated, afford the very best evidence of who has been chosen by the electors to perform the duties of an office. But

1   before these may be received or considered, it must affirmatively appear that they have been preserved with that jealous care which precludes the opportunity of being tampered with, and the suspicion of change, abstraction, or substitution. McCrary, in his work on Elections (page 209), says: "Before the ballots should be allowed in evidence to overturn the official count and return, it should appear affirmatively that they have been safely kept by the proper custodian of the law; that they have not been exposed to the public, or handled by unauthorized persons; and that no opportunity has been given for tampering with them." The same rule is laid down in Cooley, Constitutional Limitations, 625, and approved by the following authorities: *Coglan v. Beard*, 65 Cal. 58 (2 Pac. Rep.) 737); *Albert v. Twohig*, 35 Neb. 563 (53 N. W. Rep. 582); *Newton v. Newell*, 26 Minn. 529 (6 N. W. Rep. 346); *Hartman v. Young*, 17 Or. 150 (20 Pac. Rep. 17); *Powell v. Holman*, 50 Ark. 85 (6 S. W. Rep. 505); *People v. Livingston*, 79 N. Y. 290. After the election it is known how many ballots must be interfered with in order to affect the result, and, before any are received against the finding of the duly authorized board of canvassers, their genuineness should be fully established. As said by Church, C. J., in *People v. Livingston, supra:* "The returns may be impeached for fraud or mistake, but in attempting to remedy one evil we should be cautious not to open the door to another, and far greater, evil. After the election it is known just how many votes are necessary to change the result. The ballots themselves cannot be identified; they have no earmarks. * * *

Every consideration of public policy, as well as the ordinary rules of evidence, require that the party offering this evidence should establish the fact that the ballots are genuine. .* * * If the boxes have been rigorously preserved, the ballots are the best and highest evidence, but, if not, they are not only the weakest, but the most dangerous evidence." The rule is recognized, rather than abrogated, in *Furguson v. Henry*, 95 Iowa, 439. Our statute provides that: "The judges shall fold in two folds, and string closely upon a single piece of flexible wire, all ballots which have been counted by them, except those marked 'Objected to,' unite the ends of such wire in a firm knot, seal the knot in such manner that it cannot be untied without breaking the seal, enclose the ballots so strung in an envelope and securely seal such envelope in such a manner that it cannot be opened without breaking the seal, and return said ballot, together with the package, with the ballots marked 'Defective' or 'Objected to,' in such sealed package or envelope, to the proper auditor, clerk or recorder, as the case may be, from whom same were received, and such officer shall carefully preserve such ballots for six months, and at the expiration of that time shall destroy them, by burning without previously opening the package or envelope." Section 25, chapter 33, Acts Twenty-fourth General Assembly. It is also provided that, in event of contest, such ballots "shall be opened only in open court, or in open session of such body, and in the presence of the officer having the custody thereof." It will thus be observed that the strictest vigilance in the care and preservation of the ballots is enjoined by the legislature, and the possibility of any interference with them carefully guarded against. Security of the ballot after being cast is quite as important as freedom in casting it, if the result as finally announced shall represent the actual choice of the electors. To this end we hold, in harmony with the

authorities cited, and the evident purpose of the legislature, that the onus is on him who would discredit the
official count, before resorting to the ballots as the best
evidence of who has been elected, to show that these
have been preserved with that care which precludes the
suspicion of having been tampered with, and the opportunity of alteration or change.

II.   The parties agreed that of the ballots cast contestant received two thousand, and sixty-three, and
the incumbent two thousand and thirty-three, and these
were separated from the rest, and only those remaining
submitted to the court; that the ballots cast
2   were placed in the custody of the auditor, and
removed to that of the clerk under the order of
court; but the incumbent did not waive objections to
the identity of the ballots, and that they were not the
best evidence. He expressly reserved the right to urge
these, and still insists upon them. It appears that the
ballots were returned to the auditor by the proper election officers, in sacks prepared for the purpose, except
those from two precincts, where they were wrapped in
papers, and tied up in wires, with ends sealed. All were
placed on the floor under the table in the vault of his
office. Four or five packages were unsealed, but were
tied with wire or cotton strings. The seal of another
package had been broken, and partly torn open. At
one time only seventeen of the twenty packages were
to be found, but subsequently the remainder were discovered locked in ballot boxes, under the table, as
returned by the judges of election. In taking one sack
out, it was pulled nearly open, and so left. These ballots remained in this condition until taken before the
court of contest. The vault was so situated that the
auditor or his deputy could observe the ballots from
only a portion of the office. After the trial before the
court of contest, the sacks, without being again sealed
or protected in any way, were again placed under the

table and there remained until transferred to the clerk of the district court. During all this time people generally had access to the vault, and were allowed to examine the records, and do their work therein, unaccompanied by any one. From this state of facts, established on the trial, it appears that ample opportunity was offered to tamper with the ballots. It is idle to say they were continually under the notice of the custodian whose duty it was to guard them. His attention was diverted by his work, much of which was performed where necessarily ignorant of what was going on in the vault. Individuals remained therein alone considerable time nearly every day. If evily disposed, the ballots at such times were not safe. The auditor was not responsible for the condition of the ballots when delivered to him, but, owing to their condition, was required to exercise greater precaution for their care and protection. This could have been done by re-sealing, or by placing securely under cover. The duty of preserving the ballots is not a negative one of non-interference, but a positive requirement to do whatever may be necessary in order to accomplish the purposes of the law in keeping them inviolate. The court rightly ruled that the ballots, not having been properly preserved, were not competent as evidence for the purpose of overthrowing the official count.—AFFIRMED.

IN THE MATTER OF THE APPLICATION FOR REBATE OF LIQUOR TAX OF MRS. ATHELIA SMITH AND C. L. SMITH, Appellants.

Intoxicating Liquors: MULCT TAX   That one who sells intoxicating liquors does not obtain a consent or comply with other provisions of Acts Twenty-fifth General Assembly. chapter 62, imposing a
1   tax against all persons selling intoxicating liquors does not relieve him from liability for such tax, although section 17 provides that after obtaining a written statement of consent the payment of

such tax shall on certain conditions bar proceedings under the statute prohibiting the business.

Notice of. No notice of the assessment and levying of a tax on premises in which intoxicating liquors are sold by a lessee thereof
8 need be given to the owner under Acts Twenty-fifth General Assembly, section 11, which contemplates that the person liable to the tax shall appear and pay the same without notice.

Rights of lessor. A lessor of premises under a lease expressly providing that they shall be used for hotel purposes, only, cannot
2 escape liability for a tax for the sale of intoxicating liquors on such premises under an act passed after the execution of the lease, on the ground that the lease was in existence at the passage of such act, where he knew of the sale of liquors on such premises before the tax was levied and took no steps to terminate the lease for violation of its terms.

Appeal from Hamilton District Court.—Hon. D. R. Hindman, Judge.

Saturday, December 18, 1897.

George Wambach for appellant.

George C. Olmstead, county attorney, for appellee Hamilton County.

Kinne, C. J.—I. C. L. Smith and Jacob M. Funk are the owners of a brick building and the ground upon which the same is situated, in Webster City, Iowa. They acquired the ownership of the property in 1893. On July 10, 1893, they leased it to one Wright, for a term of five years from August 1, 1893; said lease being in writing, and expressly providing that the property should be used for hotel purposes only. In 1894, and while Wright was in possession under his lease, a mulct tax of one hundred and fifty dollars was assessed against the property. August 31, 1894, appellants filed a petition with the county auditor asking the board of supervisors to rebate and cancel said tax. The board, on a hearing of the application, confirmed the levy of said tax. From the action of the board an appeal was taken to the district court, which resulted in a judgment confirming the assessment and levy of said tax. From the judgment of the district court this appeal is taken.

II. Appellant's contention is (1) that the tax is invalid because no petition of consent has been secured, or filed with the proper officer; (2) that none of the other provisions of the statute preliminary to the right

1   to sell have been had; (3) that, as the lease was made prior to the passage of the mulct law, the lessors were not bound to anticipate such legislation, and their rights must be determined by the law in force when the lease was executed; (4) that the assessment was void because no notice was given the property owners. We proceed to consider the points made in the order of their presentation:

In section 1 of chapter 62 of the Acts of Twenty-fifth General Assembly it is provided: "There shall be assessed against every person, partnership, or corporation, other than registered pharmacists holding permits, engaged in selling or keeping with intent to sell, any intoxicating liquors, and upon any real property and the owner thereof, within or whereon intoxicating liquors are sold, or kept with intent to sell in this state, a tax of six hundred dollars per annum. * * *" Section 2 of the same act provides: "It shall be the duty of the assessor of each township, incorporated town or city, in the months of December, March, June and September of each year, to return to the auditor of each county a list of places with name of occupant or tenant, and owner or agent, where intoxicating liquors are sold, or kept for sale as herein contemplated, with a description of the real property wherein or whereon such traffic is conducted." Section 9 provides for levy by the board of supervisors at their September meeting of an annual tax of six hundred dollars against each person carrying on or conducting a place for the sale of intoxicating loquors, and also against the real property, and the owner thereof, in which, or upon which, said place is located. Sections 10 to 15 provide for the collection of the tax. In section 17 it is provided that, in any city of five thousand or more inhabitants, the tax may be paid quarterly in advance, and that after a written statement of consent, signed by the requisite number of voters, is filed with the county auditor, such payment, upon certain conditions named, shall bar proceedings under the statute prohibiting such business. Section 16 expressly provides that the act shall not be construed to mean that the business of selling intoxicating liquors is legalized. Under the provisions of this statute, the tax provided for is to be assessed against every person, other than registered pharmacists holding permits, who is engaged in selling, or in keeping with intent to sell, intoxicating liquors, and upon the real property, and the owner thereof, in or upon which such liquors are sold, or kept with intent to sell. The tax is to be assessed regardless of the fact that no petition of consent has been secured and filed. The tax is on the traffic, and is to be assessed whether the one who sells or keeps for sale the liquors has complied with the other provisions of the act which would exempt him from prosecution or not. This taxing feature of the law is general, and the only case in which it does not apply is to registered pharmacists holding permits. It is therefore of no consequence, so far as assessing and collecting the tax is concerned, that the seller has not complied with the other provisions of the act. What we have said disposes of the first two points made by the appellant. It is to be remembered that the provisions of the act, a compliance with which bars prosecution under the prohibitory liquor laws, are independent of the taxing provisions, and the only effect of a compliance with them is to release the seller from the penalties to which he would otherwise be liable.

III.   There is no force in the claim that, as the parties entered into the lease prior to the enactment of the law, they cannot be affected by its provisions.   The lease expressly provides that the premises should
2   be used for hotel purposes only.   The evidence shows that the owners of the property knew in 1894 of the seizure of liquors on this property, and it affirmatively appears that, although such keeping of liquor for sale by their tenants was in violation of the terms of the lease, they took no steps to terminate the lease.   The seizure was made only two or three months after the law took effect.   We do not determine whether the tax could be levied against the property of the appellants, for the sale of liquors by their tenant, if they had no knowledge of such illegal sales.   Having knowledge of such sales only a short time after the law went into effect, and having power, under the terms of their lease, to terminate the tenancy for a violation of its provisions, and failing to take any steps in that direction, they are in no situation to complain of the assessment of the tax against their property.

IV.   As we have said, this taxing feature of the statute applies to all cases of the sale or keeping for sale of intoxicating liquors, except as to registered pharmacists having permits.   No notice to the
3   lot owner of the assessment and levy was necessary.   It was a tax to be assessed and levied, by virtue of a general law, upon certain persons and property which came within the provisions of the act. The statute contemplates that the person liable to the tax shall appear and pay the same without notice. Acts Twenty-fifth General Assembly, chapter 62, section 11.   There was no more necessity for notice to the property owner than in case of taxes generally.   We

have not discussed the cases cited by counsel, as they are not applicable to the questions presented.—AFFIRMED.

IN THE MATTER OF THE LIQUOR TAX AGAINST DAVID & GERMAN, and LOT 1, BLOCK 1, RIVER ADDITION TO ALDEN, IOWA. MRS. H. J. DAVID, Applicant for Cancellation of Tax, and JOHN HOSKINS, Mortgagee, Intervener, Appellant, Hardin County.

Intoxicating Liquors: ASSESSMENT OF MULCT TAX. Section 1, of Acts Twenty-fifth General Assembly, chapter 62, provides for a tax of
4 six hundred dollars per annum for selling liquor. Section 7, that if on a trial to rebate the tax it appears that sales were not continued for more than six months in the "year" for which the tax was assessed, the total tax for the year may be reduced *pro rata*, and section 9 provides that the board shall at the September meeting levy an annual tax of six hundred dollars, payable semi-annually and that it shall at each regular meeting examine the assessment books and levy a tax against such persons as have not
5 previously been taxed, but that there shall be "only a *pro rata* tax for the *remainder of the year*," depending on the time of the assessment. The board made an assessment December 27, in a case where sales had not continued for six months. *Held*, in view of section 45, Code 1873, providing that, where not repugnant to the context, the word "year" means the year of our Lord, the said annual tax assessed should have been rebated to six dollars and sixty cents. or enough to pay for the time between December 27, 1895, and the end of the year 1895.

JURISDICTION: *Rebating tax*. The district court has no jurisdiction
1 to determine priorities of liens on appeal from a decision of the board of supervisors in proceedings under Acts Twenty-fifth
2 General Assembly, chapter 62, section 3, to assess property on the ground that intoxicating liquors were sold on the premises, as the board of supervisors had no such authority.

SAME. The board of supervisors has no jurisdiction to determine priority of liens on property listed for assessment, on the ground
3 that intoxicating liquors are sold on the premises under the provisions of Acts Twenty-fifth General Assembly, chapter 62, section 3.

EVIDENCE. Intoxicating liquors were sold upon leased premises during the summer and fall of 1895, and during all the years of 1895 and 1896 the place had the reputation of being a place where

8 intoxicating liquors were sold in violation of law. The lessor, who had leased the premises to be lawfully used as a pharmacy, had no actual notice of the sale of liquor until December, 1895, when she canceled the lease, and released the property to another for lawful purposes. She was in the store where the liquors were sold from three to six times per week, but testified that she did not see or hear of liquors being sold therein. *Held*, she "might have known of the sale of intoxicating liquors," within Acts Twenty-fifth General Assembly, chapter 62, section 6, so as to render the property liable for the tax.

*Appeal from Hardin District Court.—*HON. B. P. BIRD-SALL, Judge.

SATURDAY, DECEMBER 18, 1897

APPEAL from an order made on application of Mrs. H. J. David, owner of certain property in the town of Alden, for rebate of liquor tax, in which proceeding John Hoskins, a mortgagee, intervened. The district court denied the application, and Mrs. David and Hoskins appeal.—*Modified and affirmed.*

H. F. Schultz and *Milchrist & Robinson* for appellants.

No appearance for appellee.

DEEMER, J.—The property was listed for assessment under the provisions of section 3, chapter 62, Acts Twenty-fifth General Assembly—the statements of the three citizens having been filed on the twenty-seventh day of December, 1895. On the first day of January, 1896, Mrs. David, the owner of the property filed her petition to rebate and cancel the tax, which was fixed by the board at four hundred and fifty dollars, on the ground that she leased the same to Laura B. David and Theodore German, for the period of one

year from the first day of January, 1895, for the purpose of conducting a lawful business; that, if intoxicating liquors were sold or kept by them upon the premises, it was without her knowledge or consent; and that,
if she is liable for any tax it cannot exceed the sum of
one hundred and fifty dollars. On the twenty-first of
the same month, Hoskins, a mortgagee, filed a petition
of intervention before the board of supervisors, asking
that the liquor tax, if it be confirmed, be held inferior
and junior to his mortgage. At the hearing before the
board, the tax, to the extent of four hundred and fifty
dollars, was confirmed, and the petition of Hoskins was
denied. Upon appeal to the district court the tax was
confirmed, but no order seems to have been made on
the petition of intervention. Intervener's mortgage
was executed in the year 1891, and was superior to the
tax lien. *Smith v. Skow*, 97 Iowa, 640. But, as the
district court made no order with reference to the
        matter, there seems to be nothing from which to
1   appeal. The probabilities are that the court dis-
        regarded this petition, because unauthorized;
and, if such be the case, we think it did so advisedly.
The proceedings were before the district court on
appeal, and it had no authority to consider anything
not properly in issue before the board of supervisors.
The proceedings before the board were special, and it
        had no other authorirty than the statute confers.
2   Petitions of intervention are not recognized by
        statute in such matters, and we do not think the
board had jurisdiction to determine piorities of liens.
Intervener must resort to some court having jurisdiction for an adjudication of his claims. The board had
no such power, and, as it did not have, the district court
had none on appeal.

Mrs. David contends that the tax should be canceled, for the reason that she did not have knowledge,
nor could she have known, by the use of reasonable care

and diligence, that intoxicating liquors were kept or
sold upon the premises. By an agreed statement
3   of facts, it is shown that liquors were sold upon
the premises by one J. W. David during the summer and fall of the year 1895, and that during all of the
years 1895 and 1896 the place had the reputation of
being a place where intoxicating liquors were sold in
violation of law. J. W. David is a practicing physician
and surgeon, but he had no connection, so far as shown,
with the firm of David & German, which leased the building. Mrs. David had no actual notice that liquors were
sold at the place in question until the month of
December, 1895. She thereupon canceled the lease, and
re-leased the property to another firm for lawful purposes. She was in the store where the liquors were sold
from three to six times per week, but testified that she
did not see or hear of any liquors being sold therein.
She leased the premises for a pharmacy, to be used by
the lessees for lawful purposes. The material part of
the statute with reference to the matter is as follows:
"Should it appear, either on the trial before the board
of supervisors or in the district court, that there have
been sales of intoxicating liquor made in or upon the
premises listed for taxation, the tax shall be confirmed
against the person, corporation or partnership conducting the business; * * * and if it shall appear
* * * that the owner or his agent had, or, by
use of reasonable, care and diligence, might have
known of the sales of intoxicating liquors, * * *
the tax shall be confirmed against the property.
* * *" Acts Twenty-fifth General Assembly, chapter 62, section 6. "And evidence of the general reputation of the place may be introduced." Section 5 of the
same chapter. The tax was properly levied against
David & German, and we think the trial court was

justified in finding that Mrs. David, by the use of ordinary care and diligence, might have known of the
unlawful sales.

A further question is made as to the amount of tax
that should be assessed. The board levied a tax of
four hundred and fifty dollars, and the district court
confirmed the levy. Appellant contends that
4   the tax should have been *pro rata* for that part
of the year 1895 remaining after the listing of the
property, amounting to six dollars and sixty cents.
This contention calls for the construction of some very
ambiguous legislation. The act of the general assembly to which we have referred was approved March 29,
1894, and took effect upon its publication, which
occurred on April 3 and 4, of the same year. Section 1
of the above chapter provides for the assessment of a
tax of six hundred dollars per annum against every person engaged in selling, or keeping with intent to sell,
any intoxicating liquors, and upon the real property
and the owner thereof within or whereon the intoxicating liquors are kept or sold. Section 2 of the same
chapter makes it the duty of the assessor, in the months
of December, March, June, and September of each year,
to return a list of the places wherein the intoxicating
liquors are sold. Section 9 makes it the duty of the
board, at its regular meeting, in September, to levy an
annual tax of six hundred dollars, payable semi-annually, on or before the first days of April and October of
each year, against the person conducting the business,
and against the real property and the owner thereof,
and further provides that, at each regular meeting of
the board, it shall examine the assessment books,
and levy a tax against such persons as have become
liable thereto, and who have not been taxed as hereinbefore provided, for the same year, "but only a *pro rata*
tax for the remainder of the year depending upon the

time of the assessment." Section 17 of the chapter provides that in cities of five thousand or more inhabitants the tax may be paid quarterly in advance on January, April, July, and October of each year; and, upon certain conditions, such payments may be a bar. Sections 4, 5, and 6 of the same chapter relate to applications to rebate the tax, the trial thereof before the board of supervisors, and to appeals to the district court; and section 7 is as follows: "Should it be found in the trial before the board of supervisors, or on appeal, that sales of intoxicating liquors in or upon the premises described, had not continued for more than six months in the year for which the taxes were assessed, then the total tax for the year, exclusive of costs may be reduced *pro rata.*" The assessment in this case was not made in time so that the board could make the levy at its September meeting. Not having been made until December 26, the board could not make the levy until the January meeting; and the statute says that, when so levied, it shall be but a *pro rata* amount of the tax for the remainder of the year, dependent upon the time of the assessment. Section 7 also says that, if the sales had not continued for more than six months of the year for which the taxes were assessed, the total tax for the year may be reduced *pro rata.*

Now, it appears in this case that the sales had not continued more than six months in the year 1895, and it follows that the total tax *for the year* may be reduced *pro rata.* The ultimate question to be determined 5   is, what is meant by the word "year" as used in this statute? Does it mean from January to January, from April to April, from October to October, or from the time when the tax is assessed to a corresponding period in the next year? Paragraph 11 of section 45 of the Code of 1873 says that, in construing statutes, the following rules shall be observed, unless such construction would be inconsistent with or repugnant

to the context: "The word 'month' means a calendar
month, and the word 'year,' and the abbreviation 'A. D.,'
are equivalent to the expression' year of our Lord.'"
Unless, from the context or otherwise, a different intent
is gathered, the word "year," when used in a statute, is
construed to mean a calendar year. *U. S. v. Dickson*,
16 Pet. 162; *Engleman v. State*, 2 Ind. 91 (51 Am. Dec. 494).
With this rule in mind, we turn to the statute, and find,
from a reading of sections 7, 9, and 17 of the chapter, that
no other than the calendar year was intended. Indeed, it
appears from these sections that such was the period of
time the legislature had in mind, for it said in section
17 that the tax may be paid quarterly in advance on
the first days of January, April, July, and October of
each year; and in section 9 it is said that if the tax be
not levied at the regular September meeting of the
board, it should be only for a *pro rata* amount of the
tax for the remainder of the year; and in section 7 it is
said that, if the sales had not continued for more than
six months in the year for which the taxes were
assessed, they may be reduced *pro rata* upon the trial
before the board or upon appeal to the district court.
We think it clear that the calendar year is the one
intended. There is an apparent conflict between sections 7 and 9 of the chapter, but it is not necessary in
this case to attempt a reconciliation. The tax was
levied at the January, 1896, meeting for the year 1895;
and by section 9 it is provided that, when so levied, it
shall be only a *pro rata* tax for the remainder of the
year, dependent upon the time of the assessment. The
assessment was made on December 27, 1895. The
remainder of the year was but four days, for which a
levy might be made. The tax was not payable in
advance, as provided in section 17 of the chapter, for
the town in which the business was conducted did not
have the necessary population for this section to apply.
It is unnecessary for us to determine whether section 7

or section 9 applies to this case, for under either the tax
should be levied for but the four remaining days of the
year.   The amount which should have been levied was
six dollars and sixty cents, and to this extent the levy
will be sustained.   Appellant will pay one-fifth of the
costs of this appeal, and appellee the remainder.—
MODIFIED AND AFFIRMED.

J. L. CAMERON, Appellant, v. JAMES TUCKER, *et al.*, and a Certain Place in Winneshiek County.

Injunction: INTOXICATING LIQUORS: *Parties.* The granting of an
injunction against the sale of intoxicating liquors will not prevent the granting of a subsequent injunction against the sale of
2   intoxicating liquors by the sureties on the bond of the person
enjoined in the prior action, where the first injunction was not
directed against said bondsmen.

COLLUSION.   An injunction to restrain the sale of intoxicating liquors
1   will not be refused on the ground that an injunction against such
sale has previously been obtained by another person, where the
prior injunction was fraudulently obtained for the purpose of
shielding the liquor seller.

Appeal from Winneshiek District Court.—HON. L. E. FELLOWS, Judge.

SATURDAY, DECEMBER 18, 1897.

PLAINTIFF, a citizen and resident of Winneshiek
county, Iowa, brings this action to enjoin the defendants from maintaining a certain place in said county
described, for the sale and keeping for sale of intoxicating liquors.   He alleges that defendant James Tucker is,
and has been for some time, the owner of said premises,
and that he is, and has been for some time, keeping
for sale and selling therein intoxicating liquors in violation of law; that said defendant, with the defendants
Lewis F. Nelson and Peter Holland as his sureties,
has filed with the county auditor a bond as provided by

paragraph 2, section 17, chapter 62, Laws Twenty-fifth
General Assembly; that defendant Tucker has failed
and neglected to comply with the conditions of said
chapter 62 in this respect; that he has not now on file
with the county auditor a written statement of consent of the resident freeholders, as required; that said
business of selling intoxicating liquors is not carried on
in a single room, as required; that said place is open,
and sales are made therein, later than 10 o'clock P. M.
on Sundays; and that he has not filed with the county
auditor a written statement of consent, signed by sixty-
five per cent. of the legal voters of said county. Plaintiff prays that the defendants and all other persons
may be enjoined from maintaining said nuisance.
Defendants answered, denying all the allegations of
the petition except that defendant Tucker is the owner
of said premises. They allege that he has been com-
plying strictly with all the requirements of said chapter
62. Further answering, they say "that the plaintiff
cannot have and maintain this action, for the reason
that heretofore, to-wit: on or about October 1, 1895,
a perpetual injunction was granted by the district court
of Winneshiek county, Iowa, against the defendant
Tucker and the property described in the petition, and
that said injunction is still in full force and effect.
Plaintiff, in reply, admits that said injunction was
granted, and alleges as follows: "Par. 3. That the
plaintiff in said injunction cause is a pronounced enemy
to the enforcement of the prohibitory law, and a friend
to the saloon and liquor interests of the community
where defendant resides. Par. 4. That the plaintiff's
attorney in said injunction case was, and still is, a bitter
and outspoken enemy of the Iowa prohibitory laws, and
averse to its enforcement, and that said injunction was
not brought by plaintiff or any of the parties therein in
good faith. Par. 5. That said above-named injunction
cause was brought with a fraudulent intent and purpose

of shielding defendants and the property in question
from *bona fide* suits commenced by law-abiding citizens
of this community to abate the liquor nuisance now
maintained on said premises, and to protect them and
the said premises from the costs and damages which
would result from any and all *bona fide* prosecution.
Par. 6. That said preceding injunction is the result of an
understanding and conspiracy of said parties, and all
of them, both plaintiff, defendants, and their attorneys,
for the fraudulent purpose of defeating the enforcement of the prohibitory law of the state of Iowa against
said defendants and the premises aforesaid, and for
the purpose of holding a shield above said defendants;
and that the same was procured by collusion and fraud;
and that the same is held fraudulently as a shield to
protect said defendants and said property from the
penalties that they would otherwise be subject to under
the prohibitory law of Iowa." Defendants moved to
dismiss the action, for the reason that the pleadings
show that said injunction is still in full force and effect.
This motion was sustained, and judgment rendered
accordingly, from which judgment the plaintiff appeals.
—*Reversed.*

A. L. Himle and *J. J. Cameron* for appellant.

Dan Shea and *H. F. Barthell* for appellees.

GIVEN, J.—The motion is in the nature of a
demurrer to the allegations of plaintiff's petition and
reply, and, for the purpose of the motion, we must take
said allegations, in so far as they are well pleaded, to
be true; in other words, if the plaintiff's pleadings show
him entitled to the relief asked, the motion should not
be sustained, even though those allegation are
1   denied. On the face of the pleadings, we have
this state of facts: The defendant Tucker is
maintaining the place described for the sale and keep-

ing for sale of intoxicating liquors, but whether or not lawfully depends upon whether he has failed to comply with said chapter 62, Acts Twenty-fifth General Assembly, in the respects alleged in the petition. If this issue should be found with the defendants, then they are not open to injunction; but, if otherwise, they may or may not be, according as effect is given to the injunction of October 1, 1895. The contention presented in argument is whether, because of said matters alleged in the reply, we should hold that said injunction is not a bar to granting another injunction, as prayed by the plaintiff. In *Dickinson v. Eichorn*, 78 Iowa, 710, a case like this, it was held that a second injunction would not be granted when there was one in full force. It is said in that case: "The question for determination is, can this second action be maintained, and another decree entered for precisely the same thing,—that is, for enjoining and abating the same nuisance which is already enjoined and ordered to be abated? It is to be observed that it is conceded that the former decree is in full force, and no reason is stated anywhere in the record, nor even suggested in argument, why it has not been enforced. If a showing were made that the decree was obtained by collusion with the defendant, for the purpose of allowing it to remain without enforcement, and the same is therefore a fraud upon the court, and intended as an evasion of the law, there might be some ground for maintaining this action; but we need not determine that question, because it is not presented in this record." It is further stated: "But it is apparent that in this class of actions one valid injunction is as effective as a thousand would be. * * * The plaintiff, as a citizen of the county, stands for and represents the public."

Defendant Tucker is maintaining a place for the sale and keeping for sale of intoxicating liquors, and, if the allegations of the petition be true, he is doing so in violation of the law. If the allegations of the reply are true, it is manifest that the obtaining of the injunction upon which defendant's rely for protection was by fraud upon the court that granted it, and upon the public, and that it is not in fact effective in protecting the public against the alleged nuisance. Where such are the facts, surely, the public should not be deprived of the protection the law contemplates, nor violators of the law be permitted to shield themselves by such

2   frauds. Lewis F. Nelson and Peter Holland are defendants in this action, because of their being sureties for defendant Tucker on said bond, and, as we understand the record, join in the answer and motion. They are not parties to the injunction granted October 1, 1895, but are sought to be enjoined in this action, together with the defendant Tucker. In *Carter v. Steyer*, 93 Iowa, 533, it was held that an injunction restraining the defendant from keeping intoxicating liquors for sale on certain premises, and within the judicial district, did not bar a suit to enjoin the maintenance by him of a similar nuisance in the same disrict,—but on other premises owned by his co-defendant, against whom no injunction is in force. Applying this rule, plaintiff is entitled to an injunction against the defendants Nelson and Holland. Therefore the motion should have been overruled. We are of the opinion, however, that, because of said matters set up in the reply, the injunction of 1895 is not a bar to plaintiff's right, upon establishing said facts, to have a perpetual injunction in this action against all the defendants. It follows from this conclusion that the judgment of the district court must be REVERSED.

WILLIAM MORAN, Executor, v. WILLIAM D. MORAN, *et al.*, Appellants.

Wills: TRUSTS: *Evidence.* Parol evidence is inadmissible to show
that, in making an absolute devise, the testator intended that the
1 devisee should hold the property in trust for others, under Code,
1873, section 2326, requiring wills to be in writing; and this is so
2 though the devisee acknowledges the trust in writing and defines
its extent.

CHARITIES: *Certainty.* A bequest of money "to be divided among
the Sisters of Charity," without any limitation as to locality,
3 state or nation, and without any provision for the exercise of discretion by the trustees, is void for uncertainty.

CERTAINTY: A bequest for a known and lawful purpose, where the
4 power of execution is prescribed and available, should never fail
5 for want of name or a legal classification, unless it is in obedience
to a positive rule of law.

RULE APPLIED. A bequest to the pastor of a specific church, "that
4 masses be said for me," although not a charity, creates a valid
5 private trust.

Apeal from Dallas District Court.—HON. J. H. APPLE-
GATE, Judge.

SATURDAY, DECEMBER 18, 1897.

THIS is a proceeding asking for the construction of
the will of John Moran, deceased. The will is in the
following language, so far as it is important for the
purpose of this proceeding: "Will of John Moran.
Before these present, I will and bequeath to Patrick
Moran five hundred dollars of money. I will and
bequeath to William Toomey nine hundred dollars of
money. I will and bequeath to Patrick Doyle three
hundred dollars of money. I will and bequeath to the
Catholic priest who may be pastor of the Beaver Catholic church, when this will shall be executed, three hundred dollars, that masses may be said for me. I will

and bequeath to my brother William five hundred dollars, and to my brother Michael fifteen hundred dollars, and to my sister, Mary Moran, five hundred dollars, and to be divided among the Sisters of Charity, by William Toomey, William Moran, and Rev. H. V. Malone, five hundred dollars. And I will to William Moran, my nephew, a son of my sister, Mary, my farm." The witnesses to the will are William Moran and William Toomey, both of whom are legatees in the will. The probate of the will was contested on the ground, among others, that the subscribing witnesses were legatees thereunder. The testator died without issue and unmarried. He left surviving him William D. and Michael and Mary Moran, as brothers and sister, who, in the absence of the will would inherit the estate. They are defendants in this proceeding, with others, and each is a legatee under the terms of the will. After the filing of the objections to the probate of the will, William Moran, who was a legatee under, and subscribing witness to, the will, filed his answer to the objections, in which he expressly denied that he had any interest in any devise or legacy provided by the will, and alleged that the devise of the farm to him was in trust, only, for the children of his sister, Bridget Tiernan, which trust was declared by parol by the testator, and by the parol agreement on his part to accept said trust. William Toomey, the other subscribing witness, also filed his written relinquishment of any provisions of the will in his favor, and upon a hearing the will was admitted to probate. The plaintiff, as executor, institutes this proceeding, with all parties in interest as defendants, and asks the court to determine what provisions of the will are valid and should be executed. Defendant William D. Moran answers the petition, representing that the bequest of three hundred dollars, that masses might be said, and also of five hundred dollars, to be divided among the sisters of charity, are void, and also that the

devise of the farm to William Moran cannot be established and treated as a trust in favor of the children of
Bridget Tiernan, but that, because of the relinquishment by William Moran, the same becomes a part of
the estate, for distribution among the heirs at law as
if the said john Moran had died intestate. Other pleadings were filed, by other parties, presenting their
respective claims for construction in accord with their
interests. The district court adjudged the bequests
for masses and to the Sisters of Charity valid, and that
the devise to William Moran, of the farm, was in trust
for the children of Bridget Tiernan. The defendant
William D. Moran appealed.—*Modified and affirmed.*

Bobt. S. Barr and *Shortley & Harpel* for appellant.

White & Clarke for appellees.

GRANGER, J.—I. We first notice the question
whether or not what appears by the terms of the will
to be an absolute devise to William Moran of the farm
can be shown by parol evidence to be in trust for the
children of Bridget Tiernan. It appears that the
will was drawn by Father Malone, a Catholic
priest. There were present, other than the
priest and the testator, William Moran and William
Toomey, who were subscribing witnesses. The situation will be best seen by quoting from the record a little
of the evidence. Father Malone testified: "When I sat
down, I told him now we were ready to write anything he wanted us to write; and he says to me, the
very first thing, 'I want Billy, here, to take that farm,
and give the benefit to those children.' I says, 'What
children do you mean?' and he says, 'The Tiernan
children.' We didn't understand how he wanted the
title fixed,—whether he wanted it left to the Tiernan
children by will, or leave it to William in trust. Q.

What was said by him? What did he say in reference
to that? A. I stopped and hesitated quite a bit,
because I didn't want to disturb the man any more
than was necessary. I remember I said: 'John, you
don't fix the title to that property, and, if we write it
down the way you say it would be very vague. Can't
you make it clearer?' He says: 'Billy can explain it
to·you, if you want it.' And it seemed to worry him
when I said that. I says : 'Let us drop that out until
we write the rest, and leave that to the last.' When we
had writen the other items, I says: 'I believe we have
written all but that.' He says: 'I want it left to Billy,
simply.' I wrote it down, and says: 'Is that what you
want?' He says: 'Yes, sir; that is it exactly. Billy
will know what to do with the children.' In order to get
more information without questioning, I says: 'That
is a very good idea. Some of the children are very
young, and they might squander it.' He says: 'That is
it, exactly. Some of them might not be as good as they
might be, and, if they got any part of this property,
they might squander it; and, in order to prevent it, I
want him to have that title, so that he can discriminate
among them as he sees fit.' And then he made the
remark that it would prevent litigation and keep it out
of court." William Moran, the devisee, testified as follows: "He said he wanted to leave it to these children,
for their use and benefit, and he wanted to put it in
my name, so there would be no costs or court expense.
For that reason it was put as it was." "I asked him if
he had any particular choice, that he should leave more
to one than to others. He said, 'No;' if they were all
good, he wanted them to get equal amounts, and, if
there was any poor ones (that is, ones of bad character),
he didn't want them to have anything. I consented I
would carry out his instructions if I was permitted to
do so."

While there is a claim otherwise, we think it clearly appears, by parol evidence, that the testator's intention was to devise the farm to Moran, only for the use and benefit of the Tiernan children. With this expression of opinion as to the sufficiency of the evidence if admissible, we may better consider the legal proposition whether, under the provisions of our statute, such evidence is competent to show the fact. It will be remembered that the devise is absolute to Moran of the farm, in the following language: "I will to William Moran, my nephew, son of my sister, Mary, my farm." Can the devise so made, by evidence like the above, be so affected, changed, or modified as to give it the effect of a devise in trust to Moran for the use and benefit of said children? Upon this question the parties are in very earnest contention; appellant saying it cannot, because of the following provision of the Code of 1873, in force at the time of the execution of the will, and of the trial of the case in the district court.

"Sec. 1934. Declarations, or creations of trusts or powers, in relation to real estate, must be executed in the same manner as deeds of conveyance; but this provision does not apply to trusts resulting from the operation or construction of law."

"Sec. 2326. All * * * will, to be valid, must be in writing, witnessed by two competent witnesses and signed by the testator, or by some person in his presence, and by his express direction."

Reliance is also placed on the statute of frauds.

Appellees maintain that the devise can be so affected, and state two propositions, either of which is said to be sufficient to support the conclusion,—first, that "the case is not within the statute of frauds or of wills," and "that it has been held universally, in such cases as the one at bar, that the statutes are inapplicable and are not to be invoked to accomplish a

fraud." A little sifting out of claims that we are dis·
posed to disregard, will tend to simplify the disposition
of the question. The statute of frauds seems, by its
express language, to prescribe a rule of evidence
applicable to contracts; and, without any holding on
the question, we may say that it is a matter of serious
doubt if it was ever intended to apply to testamentary
dispositions of real estate. Section 1934 of the Code of
1873, providing that "declarations or creations of
trusts or powers in relation to real estate must be executed in the same manner as deeds of conveyance," is a
section of a chapter on real estate, the purport of which
seems to be as to transactions other than those of a
testementary nature; and, without placing any construction on the scope of either of those statutory provisions, they may be understood as in no way influenc-
ing our conclusion on this question. The statu-
2   tory law that we do regard as applicable and
controlling is that "Of Wills and Letters of
Administration," wherein it is provided who may dispose of his property by will, and how it shall be done.
After specifying the circumstances under which personal property may be disposed of by verbal will is
the provision we have quoted above, that "all other
wills, to be valid, must be in writing, witnessed by two
competent witnesses and signed by the testator, or by
some person in his presence, and by his express direction." This provision as to wills being in writing is a
general, if not a universal, statutory requirement in this
country; and hence judicial determinations and general
rules of construction may prove valuable aids to a
conclusion. Looking at the question solely in the light
of our statutory language, if we permit the evidence in
this case to ingraft on the will the modification sought,
the effect will be to change the absolute devise to Wil·
liam Moran of the farm into a devise as follows: "*I
will to William Morgan* * * * *my farm, in trust*

for the children of Bridget Tiernan." The provision
established by oral evidence, and without which it
could not be even thought of, entirely destroys the
devise manifest from the language of the will, and
makes another. Can such a devise properly be said to
be in writing? From an extended examination of
authorities, we are led to regard the rule as universal
that the plain effect of the language as used in the
will is not to be varied by external proof of what effect
was really intended. Parol evidence may, indeed, be
resorted to for the purpose of making intelligible in the
will that which cannot without its aid be understood, or
resolving a doubtful interpretation; but if the language
of the will, in point of legal construction, requires one
interpretation, and can be understood in that sense, evidence of intention cannot be adduced to give it another
and different interpretation. Such is the rule as stated
in Schouler, Wills, section 587. Mr. Redfield, in his
work on Law of Wills (volume 3, page 59), in a connection to make the language entirely applicable, uses this
language: "The very purpose of requiring wills to be
in writing would be wholly defeated if courts of equity
were allowed to ingraft upon their provisions such parol
trusts as seemed probably to have existed in the mind
of the testator." It is to be said that such a rule has
general support in authority, but we are cited to a
larger number of cases said to sustain the rule of appellee's contention. We cannot agree with appellees in the
claim that they apply to the facts of this case. That there
are authorities to the effect that where a testator,
because of the fraud of a devisee, is induced to make the
devise on the representation by the devisee that he will
take the devise in trust for another, who was the real
object of his bounty, equity will enforce the trust, is not
to be questioned. See *Hooker v. Axford*, 33 Mich. 454;
Hoge v. Hoge, 1 Watts, 216; *Dowd v. Tucker*, 41 Conn.

197; *Williams v. Vreeland*, 29 N. J. Eq. 417; *Tee v. Ferris;* 2 Kay & J. 357. Numerous other cases could be cited, but it is not important to do so. In these cases,—and, if there are exceptions, we have not noticed them,— equity has interfered to enforce a trust on the ground of fraud, in the practice of which the devisee has, by his acts or silence, prevented the testator from, or led him to avoid, making provisions in his will which he intended; and the cases cited were not for the construction of the wills, but to declare a trust based on the fraudulent acts by which the making of the will, as intended, was prevented. The cases do not attempt to change the wills, or to construe them, but to fix obligations because of the acts of the devisee. In this case there is no claim of fraud, nor that the devisee in any way induced the devise. The will was written just as the testator desired it. He wanted Moran to have the title, and he gave it to him. He also wanted Moran to hold and use the property for specified purposes, and neglected to make any provision for it in his will, and that is what the authorities say cannot be ingrafted onto the will by oral proof. If, in this case, we sustain the trust, we must say that the testator intended by his will to create the trust, while we know at its making, and all present knew, that he did not so intend, but he did intend verbally to create the trust. In fact, all was done as he intended to do it, but not in a way to give his intentions effect. Assuming that he knew the law, as we must, he purposely departed from its requirement to make the devise in writing. It is also to be said that the objector, who is a brother of the deceased, and urges the invalidity of the devise, had no part in, and, so far as the record discloses, had no knowledge of, the making of the will. He is in no way in fault that the will does not express the intention shown by the verbal proof. In this respect the case is unlike those in which a trust is sustained. We think the cases all

expressly or impliedly guard the exercise of authority
to maintain or enforce such a trust by the fact that the
testator would have done what the trust is maintained
for, had not fraud prevented it. That is not true of this
case. It is also said by appellees that, if further writing
is necessary to prove the trust, it is found in the answer
of William Moran in the probate proceedings, in which
he acknowledged the trust and defined its extent. Mr.
Moran is to be commended for his unselfish and faith-
ful course in the matter, by declining so generous a
bounty at the expense of a breach of confidence, but he
cannot by his writing do what the testator should have
done. The conditions of the will were fixed by the
expressed intentions of the testator in the way provided
by law. Inasmuch as William Moran has relinquished
all claims under the will, except such as should come
from the trust sought to be shown, and as no trust can
be sustained, the devise of the farm must fail; and it
becomes a part of the residuary estate, to be disposed
of as if no devise of it had been attempted.

II.   Objection is made to the provision of the will
in favor of the Sisters of Charity, which is in these
words: " I will and bequeath,   *   *   *   to be divided
among the Sisters of Charity by William Toomey, William Moran, and Rev. H. V. Malone, five hundred dollars." It is said that the bequest is void because
3   of uncertainty, and we think the objection must
be sustained. We do not question the rule that
it is competent for a testator to bestow a charity on a
person or institution to be chosen by a trustee or
executor, and that such bequests will be upheld. It is a
historical fact, of which we may take notice, that Sisters
of Charity are general throughout the state and country.
It appears in evidence that they constitute a charitable
sisterhood of the Catholic church. The provision of
the will is that the bequest is to be "divided among the
Sisters of Charity." If the bequest should be sustained,

how would the trustees execute it? No one would say that it should be divided among all of them, for such, in reason, could not have been the intention. There is no limitation as to locality, state or nation. We infer that appellees think the trustees may select to whom the bequest shall be given. The will does not so provide. In *Lepage v. McNamara*, 5 Iowa, 124, with a very similar question under consideration, as to the legal proposition it is said: "If there is such uncertainty as that it cannot be known who is to take as beneficiary, the trust is void; and the heirs, by operation of law, will take the estate, stripped of the trust." That rule is decisive of the question. There is no attempt in argument to say who the beneficiary of this bequest is, in language less uncertain than the will itself. There is no contention that the will is sufficiently specific, if the trustees may not use a discretion, and no such right is granted. The bequest is void for uncertainty.

III. It is also urged that the provision of the will, in order that masses might be said for him, is void. The bequest is as follows: "I will and bequeath to the Catholic priest who may be pastor of Beaver Catholic Church, when this will shall be executed three hundred dollars, that masses may be said for me." The testator was a member of Beaver Catholic Church. It had a definite and known location. It is not to be doubted that the words of the bequest "when this will shall be executed" mean when the will should be carried into effect. An objection to the bequest is that it contained no element of a charitable use. That is true, but bequests are not limited to such purposes. We must assume that the bequest was inspired by his religious convictions as to duty in the way of furthering his hopes and purposes for security and happiness hereafter. Promises and pledges made in life for the support of religious observances to the same end are usual, and supported by undoubted

authority. Why is not a bequest to secure such observance after one's death, for the same purposes, valid?
It is said that "the soul of the deceased being a use not
recognized in law, and the donor and use being the
same, and not in life, the bequest should be held void." It
is thought that *Russell v. Allen*, 107 U. S. 163 (2 Sup. Ct.
Rep. 327), sustains appellant's view, but a careful examination of the case shows otherwise. The case has to do
with charitable bequests, and where they are void,
because the object of the charity is not so defined as
that it may be known. We have in this case recognized
the rule of that case in the respect stated; but, as we
have said, this bequest is not a charity. It is an expenditure directed by the testator for a service promised to
him, and the fact that, when the service is to be
rendered, he will not be living, so as to be a beneficiary
in this life, is a matter of no concern to the courts. His
soul's welfare in the hereafter is a matter of his personal concern, for which, when not contravening public
policy, he may act as his judgment and beliefs shall
direct. It is not the province of the courts to inquire
as to the soundness or reasonableness of religious
beliefs, but to respect all such, and the ceremonies of
their observance, wherein they do not militate against
the public peace and security. The provision is little
different from one for the erection of a monument after
his death, or the doing of any other act that he might
desire, not intended for the benefit of any one living,
but which, if living, he might lawfully do. Such
bequests, if made so definitely as that the intent may
be known and carried into effect, are valid. In a somewhat recent case in Alabama [*Festorazzi v. St. Joseph's
Catholic Church*, 104 Ala. 327 (18 South. Rep. 394)], the
legal effect of such a bequest is considered. The bequest
there considered was in these words: "I give and
bequeath to the Roman Catholic Church of St. Joseph,
in the city of Mobile, the sum of two thousand dollars,

to be used in solemn mass for the repose of my soul."
The case treats the bequest as a private trust, which,
we think, is the proper class in which to place such a
bequest. In holding the bequest invalid as such a trust,
it is said: "It is not valid as a private trust, for the
want of a living beneficiary. A trust in form, with no
one to enjoy or enforce the use, is no trust." The latter
proposition is not to be doubted. The former we need
not consider, for that branch of the case is made to turn
on the fact that "there is no imaginable being possess-
ing power to enforce the use declared in the bequest."
The statement as to such a bequest being void for want
of a living beneficiary is not argued. It will be noticed
that in that bequest the trustee is the church, because of
which it is said there is no imaginable person to enforce
the trust. That is not true of this case. The priest of
the church designated, at a specified time, is made the
person to execute the trust; and, when he accepts the
money he becomes repsonsible to the court for the
proper discharge of his duties as trustee.

The cases on this subject are not in accord. Some
of the courts have been slow to get away from the rule
of the English cases in which, under their amalgamated
condition of church and state, such bequests and
devises were held void, as superstitious uses or creating
perpetuities. In *Festorazzi v. St. Joseph's Catholic
Church, supra,* it is said: "Under our political institutions, which maintained and enforced absolute separa-
tion of church and state, and the utmost freedom of
religious thought and action, there is no place for the
English doctrine of superstitious uses." Similar
language has been repeatedly used by the courts if this
country. In *Gilman v. McArdle,* 99 N. Y. 451 (2 N. E.
Rep. 464), the question was to the effect of an agreement by which money was accepted during the lifetime
of the decedent, to be applied to certain purposes, and
the residue to be expended for Roman Catholic masses,

to be said for the repose of her soul, and that of her husband. The court declined to definitely settle the question as to the application of the residue, for masses, but the opinion contains a discussion of bequests for such purposes, incidental to other questions, that is worthy of notice. The lower court in that case had held that, as to the surplus to be used for masses, it was held by one as mere agent, whose authority was revocable, and that no valid trust had been created; that there was nothing illegal or contrary to public policy in the purpose to which the money was intended to be applied, but that, as a trust, it was void for want of a beneficiary who could enforce it, both of the persons for whose benefit the masses were to be solemnized being dead. The same court expressed the opinion that the disposition of such surplus would have created a valid trust if contained in a will. This holding and language of the court is made the basis on which the court of appeals based its discussion and conclusion. The argument is clear to the effect that there is no such distinction in law as that an agreement during life, for the expenditure of money for masses after death, is invalid, but that a testamentary provision to that effect would be valid. The two methods are unmistakably made of equal validity, for the court, after specifying the facts, says: "Such a contract could be enforced by the legal representatives of the promisee, and, in case of a refusal to perform, they could recover the consideration paid. It certainly must be in the power of a person to provide, either by will or contract, for matters of this description, and I can see no legal reason why he should be confined to a testamentary direction." This conclusion follows some argumentative language that gives to it an added value, and we quote it as follows: "But in the case before us, even if it should be conceded that the agreement under which the defendant received the money could not be sustained strictly as a trust, on the

ground of the want of a beneficiary to enforce it, it
would not follow that it was of no effect whatever. As
a trust, the same objection, if valid, existed to the undertaking to apply the fund to defraying the funeral
expenses of the deceased and her husband, and to the
erection of a monument to their memories, but it would
be a great abridgement of the rights of property to
deny to any person the power, in his lifetime, to enter
into a contract to be performed after his death by
another person, to do or procure to be done any act not
objectionable as against any rule of law, morals, or public policy, and to pay the consideration for the performance of such a contract. It appears in this case that the
defendant was an undertaker; that the deceased selected
the kind of a coffin she desired, and described the
monument she wished erected, and specified the times
at which the masses were to be solemnized; and the finding of the court is that the defendant received the
money on the terms stated by the deceased, and promised to apply it to the uses and purposes therein mentioned. There was no indefiniteness about this contract, and it was easy of performance. There certainly
can be no legal objection to a person contracting in his
lifetime for his funeral, his coffin and his monument,
and even for the solemnization of masses, and paying
for them in advance. And, if so, what reason can there
be for denying him the power of paying a sum of money
to a third person on his agreement to procure those
things? Suppose a person should desire in his lifetime
to provide for the writing of his biography, the publication of his literary works, the painting of his por-
trait, or the erection of a statute to his memory after
his death? He certainly can make a valid contract with
any person to do either of those things, and pay for
them; and although they may be personal to himself,
and for the gratification of his own feelings and perhaps his vanity, and he cannot, in strictness, create a

trust for the purpose, because there will be no beneficiary, as he will not live to enforce it, why should he
not be at liberty in his lifetime to contract with some
person of his confidence to procure them to be done,
and, as a consideration for such agreement, to pay him
the sum necessary to defray the expense?" We may
assume that if such an agreement has the sanction of
the law, because it has the elements of a valid contract, so would a testamentary provision with precisely
the same elements for its support. It is not wise, in
such cases, for courts to quibble about technical
trusts or beneficiaries. Results are of greater
importance than technical names, and a bequest for
a know lawful purpose, where the power of execution
is prescribed and available, should never fail for want
of a name or a legal classification, unless it is in obedience to a positive rule of law.

We have said that this bequest, if the priest should
accept the money, is a private trust; and we think it
possesses the essential elements of such a trust, as much
as it would if the object were the erection of a
5   monument or the doing of any other act intended
alone to perpetuate the memory or name of the
testator. But even if there is a technical departure,
because of no living beneficiary, still the bequest is
valid. We have also said that it is not a charity, and
we can discover no element of a charity in it. It seems to
be a matter entirely personal to the testator. In one
or more cases the courts have felt the necessity, in order
to sustain such a bequest, to denominate it a "charity,"
because charitable bequests have had the sanction of
the law. We know of no such limitation on testa
mentary acts as that bequests or devises must be in the
line of other such acts, if otherwise lawful. Such a
bequest has direct support in *Seibert's Appeal* (Penn.),
18 Wkly. Notes Cas. 276. *In re Schouler*, 134 Mass.
426, such a bequest is sustained, and it is said: "Masse:

are religious ceremonies or observances of the church,
* * * and come within the religious or pious uses
which are upheld as public charities." Our conclusion
is that, as to the devise of the farm and the bequest to.
the Sisters of Charity, the will must be held inoperative,
and the property passes to the residuary estate. As to
the bequest for the saying of masses for the testator,
the will is sustained. The judgment will stand MODI-
FIED AND AFFIRMED.

J. W. TWINAM, Appellant, v. LUCAS COUNTY.

Peace Officers: WHO ARE NOT. A deputy marshal of a city of a
second class is not a peace officer within the meaning of Acts
Twenty-third General Assembly, chapter 43, section 6, designating
those entitled to compensation from the county for services rendered in the arrest and commitment of vagrants; neither is he one
within section 4109, Code 1873, which makes the marshal such an
officer.

*Appeal from Lucas District Court.—HON. M. A. ROB-
ERTS, Judge.*

SATURDAY, DECEMBER 18, 1897.

ACTION at law, in which plaintiff, as a deputy
marshal of the city of Chariton, seeks to recover compensation for services as a peace officer in arresting
certain vagrants in Lucas county. The trial court sustained a demurrer to his petition, and he appeals.—
firmed

Will B. Barger for appellant.

No appearance for appellee.

DEEMER, J.—The case comes to us upon a certificate
from the trial judge, the material parts of which are as
follows: "On the sixth day of July, 1896, the plaintiff,

J. W. Twinam, a deputy marshal of the city of Chariton,
Iowa, filed a petition in the office of the clerk of the district court of Lucas county, Iowa, claiming that the
defendant, Lucas county was indebted to him in the
sum of fifty-six dollars and ten cents for services performed by him as a peace officer, from the first day of
October, 1895, to the first day of April, 1896, during his
term of office as a deputy marshal, in the arrest, trial,
and commitment of certain persons commonly called
tramps or vagrants, there being fifty-one different
arrests, trials, and commitments, all of the said persons
having been convicted in the justice courts in the said
city of Chariton, Iowa, and that afterwards the fee bills
for said services were transcripted by the justices of
the peace to defendant's county board of supervisors for
allowance, and that said board of supervisors rejected
the said claim for fees, and refused to allow the same;
and that said board of supervisors, at their June session
in the year 1895, and before the said services were
rendered, fixed the amount of fees to be received by the
peace officers for the fiscal year ending June, 1896, which
said fees were so fixed at the sum of twenty-five cents
for all services performed in the trial and the commitment of vagrants or tramps to the county jail, and the
sum of seventy-five cents for serving warrants of arrest,
and ten cents per mile for mileage in each case,—making
in all the sum of one dollar and ten cents as fees in each
case tried, as fixed by the board of supervisors of defendant county as full compensation for said services.
* * * The trial judge desires the opinion and determination of the supreme court upon the following question of law: First. Is the deputy city marshal of a city
of the second class a peace officer, within the meaning
of section six (6) of chapter forty-three (43), Acts of
the Twenty-third General Assembly of the state of
Iowa? Second. Is a deputy marshal of cities of the second class entitled to compensation from the counties

in which such cities are located for services performed as a peace officer in the arrest, trial, conviction, and commitment of vagrants or tramps brought before justices of the peace for trial under chapter 43, Acts of the Twenty-third General Assembly of the state of Iowa?"

Section 6, chapter 43, Acts Twenty-third General Assembly, makes it the duty of the board of supervisors to fix the compensation to be allowed to all officers in the enforcement of the statutes relating to vagrancy, and further provides that the amount allowed the "peace officer" for all services except making the arrest shall not exceed a certain amount. The whole chapter relates to the arrest and punishment of tramps and vagrants. Code 1873, section 4109, is in the following language: "The following persons respectively are designated in this Code under the general term 'peace officer': 1st: Sheriffs and their deputies; 2nd: constables; 3rd: marshals and policemen of incorporated cities and towns." Chariton is a city of the second class, and section 3 of chapter 13 of the Acts of the Twenty-fifth General Assmbly provides that "in all such cities the marshal, deputy marshal and police shall be appointed by the mayor, with the approval of the council, and hold their offices during his pleasure;" thus recognizing a deputy marshal as one of the proper officers of such a municipality. Chapter 43 of the Acts of the Twenty-third General Assembly makes it the duty of all *peace officers* to arrest any vagrant whom they may find at large, and take him before some magistrate of the county, city or town in which the arrest is made. To be entitled to any compensation for his services, the plaintiff must show that he is a "peace officer," within the meaning of that term as used in the Acts of the Twenty-third General Assembly, to which reference has been made, for

it is the universal rule that in the absence of some statute clearly authorizing it, a public officer is not entitled
to compensation.   *White v. Levant*, 78 Me. 568 (7 Atl.
Rep. 539); Mecham, Public Officers, section 856; *Troup
v. Morgan County*, 109 Ala. 162 (19 South. Rep. 503).
The statutes do not define the duties of deputy marshals, nor do they fix their compensation.   The ordinances of the city are not before us, and we are unable
to say whether or not they define plaintiff's duties, and
fix his compensation.   It may be assumed, however,
that his duties are the same as those of the marshal.
Abrams v. Ervin, 9 Iowa, 87.   The marshal is a peace
officer, and it is his right, as well as his duty, to arrest
vagrants.   This his deputy might also do, in the absence
of any showing to the contrary.   But this does not solve
the problem here presented.   Plaintiff's right to make
arrests is unquestioned.   The point in dispute is his
right to compensation from the county.   In the case of
Upton v. Clinton County, 52 Iowa, 311, we held that,
while the mayor of a city was a magistrate, and a con-
servator of the peace, and might perform the duties of
justice of the peace, yet, as there was no statute allowing him compensation for work so done, he could not
recover from the county.   We then said: "Because a
mayor is vested with the jurisdiction of a justice of the
peace, it does not follow that he must have the same
compensation, and be paid in the same manner.   Fees
and compensation of officers are fixed by statute, and
are arbitrary, and subject to the legislative will."   See,
also, *Christ v. Polk County*, 48 Iowa, 302; *Ripley v.
Gifford*, 11 Iowa, 367.   We look, then, to see whether
there is any statute fixing plaintiff's compensation, and
find that there is none, unless he is comprehended
within the term "peace officer," as used in the Acts of
the Twenty-third General Assembly.   In section 4109
of the Code of 1873 the legislature has said that the
term "peace officer," as used in the Code, comprehends

sheriffs and their deputies, constables, marshals, and policemen of incorporated towns and cities. Deputy marshals are not included, unless by implication. We do not think it was the intent that they should be included, for in naming sheriffs the legislature also says "their deputies." If any deputy was to be included by implication, it certainly would be a deputy sheriff; but that it did not so intend is manifest from the fact that deputies áre named. When in the same section the legislature names marshals, and neglects to include their deputies, it is manifest that deputy marshals are not to be included. In the case of *Foster v. Clinton County*, 51 Iowa, 541, we held that a special constable, appointed by a justice of the peace under section 3630 of the Code of 1873, was not a peace officer, although he performed some of the duties of constable. As a deputy marshal is not a peace officer within the meaning of section 6, chapter 43, Acts Twenty-third General Assembly, he is not entitled to the compensation fixed by the board of supervisors. Both questions certified should be answered in the negative, and the judgment is AFFIRMED.

JAMES RILEY v. THE CHICAGO, MILWAUKEE & ST. PAUL RAILWAY COMPANY, Appellant.

Stock Killing: RAILROADS: *Instructions.* An instruction to the jury, in an action against a railway company for the killing of a horse to find for the defendant if the animal was struck upon the highway crossing, and not within the right of way, and his death was
1 not due to the defendant's failure to maintain a safe and sufficient cattle guard at the place where the accident occurred, is properly given when the testimony shows that the cattle guard was not out of repair, and the evidence is conflicting as to the exact point where the horse was struck.

DAMAGES: *Proximate cause.* Where a horse had crossed a defective cattle guard on the right of way of a railroad, and, after crossing
2 onto the highway, was killed, the defective cattle guard will be held to be the proximate cause of the injury, where the immediate

cause of the horse being on the highway was the defective cattle
guard.

Appeal: REVIEW OF VERDICT: *Damages.* The damages awarded
against a railroad company for the killing of a horse will not be
8 adjudged excessive when the evidence as to the animal's value is
conflicting, some witnesses placing it above and some below the
amount for which judgment was rendered.

Appeal from Allamakee District Court.—HON. A. N.
HOBSON, Judge.

SATURDAY, DECEMBER 18, 1897.

ACTION at law to recover the value of a horse, killed
by a locomotive engine of the defendant. There was a
trial by jury, and a verdict and judgment for the plaintiff. The defendant appeals.—*Affirmed.*

H. H. Field and *J. C. Cook* for appellant.

F. S. Burling for appellee.

ROBINSON, J.—I.   The horse in question passed
from a highway, over a cattle guard, into the right of
way of the defendant. An east-bound train approached
a short time thereafter. The horse attempted to leave
the right of way for the highway, and was struck by the
engine and killed. The evidence for the plaintiff tended
to show that the cattle guard was out of repair and in
bad condition; that the horse was enabled to cross it
for that reason; and that he was on the cattle guard,
or west of it on the right of way, when he was struck by
the engine. The evidence for the defendant tends to show
that he had re-crossed the cattle guard, and was struck
        east of it, in the highway. The defendant asked
1   the court to instruct the jury as follows: "The
        jury are instructed that, if you find the horse was
struck on the highway crossing, then your verdict must
be for the defendant, as there is no negligence claimed in

regard to the operation of the train, or of the employes
in charge thereof." The court refused to give that
instruction, but charged the jury as follows: "(5) If you
find by a preponderance of the evidence that the defendant had the right, and that it was its duty, to construct
a good and sufficient and safe cattle guard at the place
where the injury is said to have occurred, and you find
that the injury occurred without the plaintiff's fault,
and on account of the failure of the defendant to make
or maintain such good, sufficient, and safe cattle guard,
and that the plaintiff has sustained damage on account
of such neglect and failure, then your verdict will be for
the plaintiff; and, if you do not so find, then your verdict
will be for the defendant. (6) If you find from the evidence that the horse in question was struck upon the
highway crossing, and not within the right of way, and
that he was killed without any neglect or failure of the
defendant in making or maintaining a good, sufficient,
and safe cattle guard at or near the place where the
injury occurred, then your verdict should be for the
defendant, as there is no neglect charged in regard to
the operation of the train or the employes thereof." The
appellant complains of the refusal of the court to give
the instruction asked, and of the giving of the sixth paragraph of the charge. It will be observed that the paragraph objected to includes the instruction refused,
with some modifications. We think the two paragraphs
of the charge we have set out were correct and not misleading, as applied to the facts in the case. The
2   appellant claims that if the horse had re-crossed
the cattle guard, and was killed in the highway,
the defective condition of the cattle guard could not
have been the proximate cause of the injury. We do not
think that is necessarily true. If the horse was in the
highway when killed, but the immediate cause of his
being there was the defective condition of the cattle
guard, the defendant would be liable. Its liability did

not depend upon its ability to anticipate with certainty the movements of the horse, which led to the accident. See *Ward v. Railroad Co.*, 97 Iowa, 50.

It is claimed that the amount of the plaintiff's recovery is excessive. There was a conflict in the evidence, some of the witnesses placing the value of the horse above, and others below that which the jury found it to be. We cannot say that the amount of the recovery fixed by the verdict, and for which judgment was rendered, was excessive. No ground for disturbing the verdict is shown, and it is AFFIRMED.

3

ALBERT T. CHAMBERS v. THE ILLINOIS CENTRAL RAILROAD COMPANY, Appellant.

Removal of Causes: STATE COURT'S POWER OVER. A state court has no jurisdiction to sustain a motion by plaintiff to dismiss the case after defendant has filed a proper petition and bond for removal of the cause to a federal court, under Twenty-fifth United States Statute, chapter 866, sections 2, 3, providing that when such petition and bond are filed "within the time it shall be the duty of the state court to accept the same and proceed no further" in the suit.

Appeal from Woodbury District Court.—HON. SCOTT M· LADD, Judge.

SATURDAY, DECEMBER 18, 1897.

THIS case is submitted on appellant's abstract and argument alone, there being no appearance by the appellee. The abstract shows that on December 27, 1895, plaintiff filed his petition, asking to recover six thousand dollars from defendant on account of personal injuries; that on January 4, 1896 (being within the time required), defendant answered, joining issue upon the allegations of said petition; that at the same time the defendant filed its petition and bond for the removal of this case to the circuit court of the United States for the Northern district of Iowa, Western division; that there-after, to-wit: on January 11, 1896, plaintiff applied to said district court, by motion, to dismiss this case without prejudice to further action, which motion was sustained, to which defendant excepted, and from which ruling it appeals.—*Reversed.*

John F. Duncombe and *S. M. Marsh* for appellant.

No appearance for appellee.

GIVEN, J.—The petition for the removal of this cause was made under sections 2 and 3 of chapter 866, 25 U. S. Statutes at Large. The abstract shows that the application was as required by these sections, and presented a proper case for removal; also, that the bond was in proper form and amount, and conditioned as required. The application and bond were filed with the answer within the time allowed for answering, and the bond was approved by the clerk, by order of the court. Appellant insists that, as the case is a proper one for removal, by the filing of the application and bond, and approval of the bond, within the time required, the jurisdiction of the state court ceased, and that of the United States court immediately attached. Said section provides that when such a petition and bond are filed within the time required, "it shall then be the duty of the state court to accept said petition and bond, and proceed no further in such suit; and the said copy being entered as aforesaid in the circuit court of the United States, the cause shall then proceed in the same manner as if it had been originally commenced in the said circuit court." In *Stone v. South Carolina*, 117 U. S. 431 (6 Sup. Ct. Rep. 799), it is said: "It is undoubtedly true, as was stated in *Steamship Co. v. Tugman*, 106 U. S. 118-122 (1 Sup. Ct. Rep.

58), that upon the filing of the petition and bond, the
suit being removable under the statute, the jurisdiction
of the state court absolutely ceases, and that of the
United States Court immediately attaches; but, still, as
the right of removal is statutory, before the party can
avail himself of it, he must show upon the record that
his is a case which comes within the provision of the
statute. * * * If he fails in this, he has not, in
law, shown to the court that it cannot proceed further
with the suit. * * * To accomplish the removal,
the suit must be one that may be removed, and the petition must show a right in the petitioner to demand a
removal. This being made to appear on the record, all
the necessary security having been given, the power
of the state court in the case ends, and that of the United
States circuit court begins." In *Van Horn v. Litchfield*,
70 Iowa, 12, this court said: "It is a rule settled by the
decisions of the United States supreme court that, upon
the filing of a petition in a state court presenting a sufficient cause for removal to the United States court, the
rightful jurisdiction of the state court comes to an
end. The state court must stop when the petition and
security are presented;" citing cases. Further citations
are unnecessary to show that, when this petition and
bond were filed, on January 4, 1896, the district court
immediately ceased to have jurisdiction of this case for
any purpose, and that jurisdiction thereof immediately
passed to the United States court. This being true the
state court had no jurisdiction to thereafter, on January 11, 1896, entertain or sustain plaintiff's motion to
dismiss the case. The case was then pending in the
United States court, and could only be dismissed in
that court. Appellant suggests the inquiry whether it
is prejudiced by this error of the district court, and
answers it by insisting that, as plaintiff could not defeat
the removal by reducing the amount of his demand after

the removal was asked, he could not defeat it by dismissing after removal was made, and suing for lesser sum. While there is force in this answer, another is that defendant is prejudiced by the error in that it cannot know until this appeal is determined whether the case is still pending against it or not. This being the proper court to review the action of the district court, and its action in sustaining the motion to dismiss being erroneous and prejudicial to appellant, it is REVERSED.

LADD, J., takes no part.

104
104

J. R. FAUST v. THE CHICAGO & NORTHWESTERN RAILWAY COMPANY, Appellant.

Shipment: DUTY OF SHIPPER IN ATTENDANCE. Mere failure of a shipper of live stock to remain on the train as required by the shipping contract does not preclude him from recovering for the loss of such live stock by the 'burning of the car in which it was carried, where his contract did not require him to ride in such car but in the caboose.

SAME: *Burden of proof*. Under such circumstances it was not the duty of the shipper to prove that the loss was not caused by his failure to remain on the train, nor by his failure to care for the property while in transit. He could recover on proof that the fire was not due to any act or negligence of his.

Plea and Proof. Evidence that plaintiff in an action to recover the value of horses and other property lost in transportation over defendant's road did not have time to read the shipping contract before signing it, is inadmissible under an allegation that, after the property was loaded, defendant's agent presented the contract to plaintiff, representing it to be a pass to carry him to the place of delivery and requested him to sign it.

Appeal: HARMLESS ERROR: *Evidence*. Admission of incompetent evidence that plaintiff in an action for loss of property during shipment did not have time to read the shipping contract before signing it, is harmless error to defendant, where the charge to the jury requires them to consider the contract as in force

REVIEW OF VERDICT. In an action to recover the value of horses and other property burned on defendant's train, the evidence showed that, at a certain station where the train stopped, plaintiff, shipper, who by the contract was to accompany the stock, left the car and went to the caboose, but left it before the train started, to return to the stock car. He was not thereafter seen on the train. After the train started the car was found to be on fire, and the stock therein was destroyed. Plaintiff claimed to have been left at the station at which the train stopped, but his testimony was uncertain and contradictory There were not as many carcasses of horses found in the car as plaintiff claimed to have shipped, and his reputation for truth was bad. The evidence tended to show that he set the fire. *Held*, that he was not entitled to recover or hold his verdict.

Appeal from Story District Court.—HON. S. M. WEAVER, Judge.

SATURDAY, DECEMBER 18, 1897.

ACTION at law to recover the value of horses and other property placed in a car of the defendant for transportation over its railway, and never delivered. There was a trial by jury, and a verdict and judgment for the plaintiff. The defendant appeals.—*Reversed.*

Hubbard, Dawley & Wheeler for appellant.

J. F. Martin for appellee.

ROBINSON, J.—On the twenty-fourth day of January, 1894, the plaintiff placed in a box car of the defendant at Lisbon, Iowa, several horses, harness, a wagon, a buggy, and other articles, all of which were consigned to the plaintiff for delivery at Carroll. The car thus loaded was taken by the defendant, and hauled to a point a short distance west of Ames, where its contents were discovered to be on fire. Efforts were made to extinguish the fire, and to prevent damage to other cars of the train, and the burning car was hauled to Ontario, the first station west of Ames, and the fire was there extinguished, but not until the sides and roof of the car were burned, and its contents were destroyed. The plaintiff seeks to recover the value of the property which he placed in the car.

The defendant denies that the property destroyed was in its possession, denies that it was negligent in what it did concerning it, denies that it is in any manner responsible for the loss of the property, and avers that the fire which destroyed it was caused by the act of the plaintiff. In a counter-claim the defendant asks judgment for the amount alleged to have been agreed upon for hauling the property from Lisbon to Carroll. In connection with the shipment of the property, the plaintiff signed a contract which contained the following provisions: "Shipment of live stock in car loads, or less than car loads, will only be taken at the rates named herein, after this contract or agreement shall have been signed by the company's station agent and the owner or shipper, by which it is agreed and understood that such owner or shipper shall load, feed, water, and take care of such stock at his own expense and risk. * * * All persons in charge of live stock will be passed on the train with and to take care of the stock, and will be expected to ride in the caboose attached to the train." The plaintiff claims that the train containing his car left Lisbon at 3 o'clock in the afternoon of January 24, and that he rode in his car to Cedar Rapids, where he purchased a lantern; that he rode in the caboose from Cedar Rapids to Belle Plaine, where there was a change of conductors and cabooses; that there was considerable delay at Belle Plaine; that he went into a restaurant for a few minutes, and when he came out could not find his car; that he then purchased a ticket for Nevada, and took the first west-bound passenger train for that place in order to catch his car; that he reached Nevada a little before daylight, and failing to learn anything in regard to the train which contained his car, went to a hotel and waited until the next train for the west arrived; that he took that train and went on to Carroll, and there learned that his property had been destroyed as stated.

I. The plaintiff testified that he did not read the shipping contract before he signed it, and was asked, "Why didn't you?" An objection by the defendant was overruled, and the plaintiff was permitted to answer: "Why, the freight was right there, and the agent says, 'Now, you want to get right on, or you will have to wait until night.' I was not quite ready for it yet. I left a coat down to the hotel, and a lantern I bought at Lisbon I did not get. I wanted to go after it, but could not do it, and a man said, 'You are a fool to have that agent run you out of town before you are ready.' I did not have time to read it before the freight started." A motion of the defendant to strike out the answer as immaterial and irrelevant was overruled, and the defendant complains of the ruling which permitted the jury to consider that evidence. We do not think it was material to any issue presented by the pleadings. In an amendment to his petition the plaintiff alleged that, after the property was loaded, the agent of the defendant presented to him the contract, and represented it to be a pass to carry him to Carroll, and requested him to sign it, and that he understood that it was a pass; that it seeks to change the liability of the defendant in regard to receiving, transporting, and delivering the property, and to excuse the defendant for negligence, and is void and of no effect; and that the only purpose for which it was given was to pass the plaintiff as a passenger in the caboose of the train. There is no controversy over the fact that the contract included a pass, and the testimony in question did not tend to support any statement contained in the petition in regard to the contract, excepting that it was intended to pass the plaintiff as a passenger, and should not have

been admitted. See *Mulligan v. Railway Co.*, 36 Iowa,
188; *Wilde v. Transportation Co.*, 47 Iowa, 274.

3   But we think that the evidence could not have
been prejudicial, for the reason that the charge
to the jury treated the contract as in force, and required
the jury to so consider it.

II.   The defendant asked the court to instruct the
jury that "the burden is upon the plaintiff to show, by a
preponderance of the testimony, that his loss did not
occur by reason of his acknowledged failure to
4   remain upon the train with his stock and care for
it.   If he has failed to show you by such preponderance that the loss was not occasioned by such
failure upon his part, then he cannot recover in this
action."   The defendant also asked the court to instruct
the jury that the burden was on the plaintiff to show
that his loss did not occur by reason of any failure on
his part to carry out his agreement to take care of the
horses while in transit, and that the mere fact that he
remained at Belle Plaine when his car went west,
whether left accidentally or by reason of his own negligence, would not excuse him from his contract to accompany the stock, or notify the proper officers of the
defendant that he had been left, and could not care for
the stock.   The court refused to so instruct, and charged
the jury that, to entitle the plaintiff to recover, he must
establish by a preponderance of the evidence that the
fire which destroyed his property was not occasioned by
any act of negligence on his part, and that, if he established that fact, he was entitled to recover for the property which he delivered to the defendant.   It is said in
4 Elliott, Railroads, section 1549, that, "where the owner
accompanies the stock under a special contract to care
for them himself, he may well be presumed to be as
well acquainted with the facts in regard to their loss
or injury as the carrier, and as they may have been
injured because of his own negligence, or because of

their inherent nature and propensities, and not by the negligence of the carrier, it is but just to require him to show the facts. The rule in such cases, therefore, is that the burden of proof is upon the plaintiff to show that a breach of duty upon the part of the carrier caused the injury or loss, and, if the carrier is liable only for negligence, the burden is upon the plaintiff to show such negligence." See, also, *Railroad Co. v. Sherwood*, 132 Ind. 129 (31 N. E. Rep. 781). But we do not think this case is within the rule of the authorities cited. Of course, the plaintiff should be held to the performance of his part of the agreement, but there was nothing in the circumstances or character of the loss shown to justify the conclusion that it resulted from the absence of the plaintiff. His contract did not require him to ride in his car, but in the caboose, and, had he been in the latter, he could not have prevented the fire if it was not caused by his agency. Therefore, if he showed, as the charge required him to do, that the fire was not occasioned by any act or negligence on his part, he was entitled to recover. We do not find that the court erred with respect to instructions refused or the charge given.

III. The appellant contends that the verdict and judgment are not sustained by the evidence. There is much in the record to sustain the claim thus made. The testimony of the plaintiff is in some respects 5   unreasonable, and in conflict with facts which must be regarded as established. He states that the train which contained his car reached Belle Plaine about midnight; that he then went to his car and remained in it probably half an hour or longer; that there were three bales of hay in the middle of the car, only one of which had been opened; that he found everything in it in good order, and when he left extinguished the light in his lantern, placed it on the seat of the buggy, closed the car door, and probably fastened it, although he says he is not sure as to that, and then went into a restaurant for warmth and something to eat; that he remained in the restaurant probably "twenty minutes, or so;" that there were several trains in the yard, and switching being done; that he went to the place where he had left his car, but could not find it; that he made inquiries, but could not learn anything of it; that he finally went to the ticket office, purchased a ticket for Nevada, and remained at the station, most of the time in the waiting room, for three-quarters of an hour, or an hour, when a passenger train from the east arrived; that he entered one of the cars before daylight, and went to Nevada to catch his car; that when he arrived at that place he did not enter the depot, although he inquired for the train his car was in, but did not learn anything of it; that he went to a hotel, remained there an hour or two, without registering, procured something to eat in a candy store, and went to the depot about 9 o'clock; that he asked for a ticket for Carroll, but was given one for Glidden; that he took the train for Carroll, but was obliged to pay twenty-two cents fare from Glidden. He introduced in evidence a railway ticket from Belle Plaine to Nevada, which he states he purchased in the former place, before leaving it on the morning of January 25, but which he says the conductor failed to take up. The evidence on the part of the defendant shows the following: The freight train which contained the car of the plaintiff was known as "No. 31," and left Belle Plaine for the west at twenty-seven minutes after 12 o'clock midnight. It contained seventeen loaded and empty cars, and the car of the plaintiff was the second one from the caboose. During the night three cars were set out, one at Tama, one at Nevada, and one at Ames. A brakeman of the train states that a few minutes before the train left Belle Plaine the plaintiff came into the caboose, warmed himself, stated that he was with the car in question, and asked how soon the train would leave; that he was told that it

would leave soon, and he then prepared to go out; that
in response to a question, he said he was going to his
car; that he was told he had better remain in the caboose
on account of the cold, but that he took his lantern and
went out through the forward door, as though he were
going to his car; and that he was not in the caboose
again. The train stopped for coal and water at Lamoille,
about twenty-two miles east of Nevada, and while there
the conductor saw a light in the plaintiff's car. At
Nevada a light was seen in the car by the conductor, a
brakeman, and the fireman. The train arrived at Ames
a few minutes after 5 o'clock, and remained there a little
more than half an hour. It does not appear that any
light was seen in the car at that place. Although the
conductor passed the car while there, he did not notice
anything unsual about it. Just after the train commenced to move from Ames, smoke was noticed by men
in the caboose, and within a minute or two a fire was
discovered in the car in question. The train was stopped,
and the trainmen went to the car and looked for the
plaintiff, thinking he might be in it. The south door
of the car was found open far enough to permit a man to
pass through the opening. Not finding the plaintiff in
the car, one of the trainmen looked along the track for
him, thinking he might have jumped from the car. An
investigation of the car, after the fire was extinguished,
showed that the fire had not originated below the car,
as from a hot box, but inside. No bales of hay were
found, although it is shown to be difficult to burn baled
hay, and that it burns slowly. Wire used for baling
was found scattered about, but not together, as though
around bales which had been burned. The bodies of but
three horses were found, although four were billed, and
recovery for four is sought. The first passenger train
which went west from Belle Plaine after midnight,
January 25, was No. 5, which left at 3:23 o'clock A. M.,
and did not stop at Nevada, and reached Ames at 5:40

o'clock A. M., leaving three minutes later, and seven minutes before No. 31 left. No ticket for Nevada was sold at Belle Plaine before No. 5 left. A man who rode in the waycar with the plaintiff, just before reaching Belle Plaine, waited at the depot until the next passenger train for the west left and went out on it, going in the car, which the plaintiff says he was in, but did not see him at the depot nor in the car. The ticket offered in evidence was so mutilated that all means of ascertaining from it the date on which it was issued were destroyed. There are other circumstances which tend to contradict the claim of the plaintiff that he did not leave Belle Blaine on No. 31. Four witnesses testified that they knew the reputation of the plaintiff for truth and veracity in the neighborhood where he had lived, and that it was bad, and they testified to the same effect in regard to his moral character. No attempt was made to rebut that evidence. After a very careful examination of the entire record in this case, we reach the conclusion that it is so clearly established by the evidence that the statements of the plaintiff with respect to his leaving Belle Plaine, and his arrival at Nevada, are untrue, and that he was responsible for the fire which destroyed his property, that the district court court should have set aside the verdict. For it its failure to do so the judgment rendered is REVERSED.

CARRY E. CHENEY, et al., Appellants, v. AMELIA McCOLLOCH, et al.

Continuances: DISCRETION: *Partition Suit.* In an action for a partition of defendant's land, plaintiffs moved for a continuance on the ground that it could not at that time be determined whether the personalty would be sufficient to pay the debts It appeared
8 that, at the time of the motion, a previous order authorizing the sale of the lands, to pay the debts, was in force; but plaintiffs asserted that this order had been abandoned, and was void because no statement of claims was made or disposition of personalty

shown at the time the order was made There was no showing
that the administrators had not filed their reports, nor that the
sufficiency of personalty to pay the debts could not then be determined. *Held*, that there was no error in overruling this motion.

-COLLATERAL ATTACK. An order for the sale of defendant's land,
4   made in the absence of a statement of the claims filed or a showing as to the disposition of the personalty, if irregular, is not void.

Appeal: TRIAL DE NOVO. A certificate by the trial judge in a case
tried as in equity, that the foregoing record contains all the evi-
1   dence "offered and introduced" on the trial, is insufficient to
present the case for trial *de novo*. It must appear that all the
evidence offered, introduced and rejected, is up.

REVIEW: *Evidence.* Alleged error in dismissing a petition for parti-
2   tion of land cannot be determined on appeal, where all the evidence
offered on the trial is not in the record.

Appeal from Keokuk District Court.—HON. D. RYAN,
Judge.

SATURDAY, DECEMBER 18, 1897.

SUIT to partition certain real estate belonging to
the estate of Martin Pfaff, deceased. The trial court
dismissed plaintiffs' petition, and they appeal.—
Affirmed.

C. M. Brown for appellants.

Woodin & Son and *Hamilton & Donohue* for appellees.

DEEMER, J.—The case was tried as in equity, and
the trial judge made a certificate in which he said "that
the foregoing record contains all the evidence offered
and introduced on the trial." The abstract
1   recites that it contains all the evidence offered
and introduced upon the trial. Neither of these
statements is sufficient to present the case for trial
de novo. *Wallick v. Pierce,* 102 Iowa, 746; *Reed v.*

Larrison, 77 Iowa, 399; *Bank v. Ash,* 85 Iowa, 74, and cases cited therein.

Appellants' counsel have assigned errors, but with one exception, a solution of the errors complained of depends upon a consideration of the evidence. This

2   exception is a complaint that the court erred in overruling plaintiffs' motion for a continuance.

The motion was based upon the ground that it could not at that time be determined whether the personal assets would be sufficient to pay the debts of the deceased; or all the debts, except such as were secured

3   by the mortgages upon the real estate sought to be partitioned. A request that the administrator be required to file a report at the next term of court, showing the amount of assets, and to the extinguishment of what debts the assets had been applied, was also embodied in the motion. At the time this motion was filed, the issues had been made up, and from the pleadings we gather the following: Plaintiff and defendants are the representatives, and mortgagees of Martin Pfaff, who departed this life on the second day of January, 1894, seized of the real estate sought to be partitioned. The mortgagees answered setting forth their claims, and further pleading that the claims against the estate amounted to more than six thousand, eight hundred dollars, and the personal property belonging thereto amounted to but one thousand and twenty-two dollars; that, at a former term of court, an order was made authorizing the administrator to sell the real estate in controversy, except the homestead for the purpose of paying the debts; and that this order was in full force. The widow answered that she was unable to elect as to which she would take—homestead or dower,—until the debts of the estate were fully settled. And the administrators pleaded an order of court, dated April 11, 1894, authorizing them to sell the real estate described in the petition for the payment

of the debts of the deceased; that the debts amounted to four thousand, eight hundred dollars, and that they had but nine hundred dollars with which to pay them; that they had made every effort to sell, but, on account of the financial depression, were unable to do so. In reply, the plaintiffs denied the validity of the order to sell, for the reason that no statement of the claims filed was made, or disposition of personal property shown, at the time the order was made, and further pleaded that the administrators had abandoned their efforts to sell under the order made. They further pleaded that the widow had elected to take homestead in lieu of dower, and that she was able to determine the situation of the estate, for that the time had long since expired for the filing of claims. They also pleaded that there was sufficient personal property on hand with which to pay all claims. They further pleaded that there were sufficient assets from the personal property to pay all unsecured debts, and that the proceedings to sell had been abandoned.

An application for a continuance is addressed peculiarly to the sound discretion of the judge, and his ruling thereon will not, as a general rule, be interfered with, unless it clearly appears that this discretion has been abused, and injustice done thereby. *Widner v. Hunt,* 4 Iowa, 355; *Boone v. Mitchell,* 33 Iowa, 45; *State v. Wells,* 61 Iowa, 629. That there was no abuse of discretion is clearly shown when we consider the status of the case at the time the motion was filed. Here an order had been made to sell this very real estate for the payment of debts; and, while the plaintiffs were insisting that the order was void and had been abandoned, yet they did not need any time in which to prepare to meet this issue. Moreover, the order for the sale was not subject to the attack made upon it. It may have been irregular, but was not void. *Morrow v. Weed,* 4 Iowa, 77; *Myers v. Davis,* 47 Iowa, 325.

There is no showing that the administrators had not filed their reports as required by law, and it does not appear that the court could not at that time determine whether the personal assets were sufficient to pay debts. There was no error in overruling the motion.

Appellants contend that the court erred in dismissing their petition. We cannot determine this question nor any other question argued, for the reason that we do not have all the evidence offered upon the trial. No error appears, and the judgment is AFFIRMED.

PATSY SHEROD v. JENNIE K. EWELL, Appellant.

Real Property: ACKNOWLEDGMENT OF DEED: *Forged deed.* The
2   fact that a deed to which the signature of a wife was forged was
    recorded, does not give one the right to rely upon her execution of
3   the instrument when there is no protense that she acknowledged
    it, for an unacknowledged deed is not entitled to record. Code
    (McClain's) section 8113.

Partition: PRIORITY OF TITLE. The fact that real property was sold
    upon execution sale and the plaintiff's dower right thereby cut
4   off, under McClain's Code, section 3044, cannot be urged by the
    defendant in an action for partition when such defendant does
    not stand in privity with the purchaser at such sale, but claims
    under a hostile title.

Evidence: PRESUMPTION OF DEATH   Undisputed evidence that a
1   man has been absent from home and unheard from for seventeen
    years, although his family have continued to reside in the same
3   place, will warrant the conclusion that he is dead; and his wife is
    entitled to dower in his lands.

Adjudication: ESTOPPEL: *Parties.* One not made a party defendant
3   to an action is not concluded by the decree rendered therein.

Pleading: ESTOPPEL. An estoppel which is not pleaded cannot be
2   taken advantage of.

Appeal from Wayne District Court.—HON. W. H. TED-
FORD, Judge.

SATURDAY, DECEMBER 18, 1897.

Action for partition of certain land. Decree that plaintiff is the owner of the undivided one-third part of said land, and that the defendant is the owner of an undivided two-thirds part of said land, and confirming said respective shares, and ordering partition. The defendant appeals.—*Affirmed.*

Freeland & Evans for appellant.

Miles & Steele for appellee.

Kinne, C. J.—I. From the pleadings and evidence the following facts are established: On and prior to September 25, 1877, plaintiff was the wife of Charles M. Sherod, and said parties lived together as husband and wife, in Wayne county, Iowa, on the land in controversy. As the fruit of said marriage, there were born to plaintiff and her said husband three children, who have always lived with the mother. On August 16, 1876, said Charles M. Sherod conveyed by warranty deed, to Amos C. Sherod, the land in controversy. Said deed purported to be signed by the plaintiff, but did not purport to be acknowledged by her. In fact, she never signed said deed, nor did she authorize any one to sign it for her. February 8, 1877, Amos C. Sherod (unmarried) executed and delivered to C. M. Sherod a warranty deed to said land. Prior to executing said last-mentioned deed, and on January 1, 1877, Amos C. Sherod (unmarried) executed a note to John M. Ewell for one thousand dollars, due January 1, 1882, and secured by a mortgage on the same land. September 25, 1877, Charles M. Sherod left his home, wife, and family, without cause, and has not been heard from by the wife or children since August, 1878. In 1879 said John M. Ewell procured a judgment and a decree of foreclosure of his mortgage on the land in controversy, and on March 13, 1880, received a sheriff's deed to the same on a sale had on an execution,

issued on said decree. Ewell and the defendants have
had possession of said land under said sheriff's deed
since its execution. October 23, 1877, one Lloyd Selby
recovered a judgment in the district court of Wayne
county, Iowa, against C. M. Sherod, and under an execution issued on said judgment said land was sold, and on
December 18, 1878, he received a sheriff's deed therefor.
Selby never went into possession of the land, or exercised any acts of ownership over it. June 15, 1895, Selby
made a quit-claim deed of said land to the plaintiff.
John M. Ewell died prior to the commencement of this
action, and by his will he devised to the defendant all the
right, title, and interest he had in said land. Appellant
contends (1) that plaintiff relinquished her dower in
the deed of date August 16, 1876; (2) that, if she did not
sign the above-mentioned deed, she afterwards ratified
the signing of her name thereto; (3) that the dower right
of plaintiff (if any remained) was extinguished by the
sale under the Ewell execution; (4) that the sale under
the Selby execution extinguished plaintiff's right of
dower.

II.   Claim is made that the evidence does not warrant the conclusion that C. M. Sherod is dead. The rule,
as laid down in 1 Greenleaf, Evidence (15th ed.), section
41, is: "But, after the lapse of seven years, without
intelligence concerning the person, the presump-
1   tion of life ceases, and the burden of proof is
devolved on the other party." So, in 1 Jones,
Evidence, section 57, it is said: "If a man leaves his
home, and goes to parts unknown, and remains unheard
from for the space of seven years, the law authorizes
to those that remain the presumption of fact that
he is dead." "A presumption of the death of a party
does not arise until he has been absent, without intelligence concerning him, for the period of seven years."
State v. Henke, 58 Iowa, 458; *Tisdale v. Insurance Co.,*
26 Iowa, 176; *Seeds v. Grand Lodge,* 93 Iowa, 175. A

multitude of authorities might be cited in support of the above rule. In this case C. M. Sherod had, at the time of the trial, been absent from his home for a period of almost seventeen years. The evidence is abundant and undisputed as to his absence, and that he has not been heard from by his wife or children for nearly seventeen years, though they have all of this time continued to reside in Wayne county.

III. It appears without conflict that plaintiff never signed, nor authorized her name to be signed to, the deed. The pretended signature of her name was a forgery. The pretended signature was not acknowledged. Whether or not plaintiff would be estopped by her silence, after knowing of the pretended signature of her name to the deed, we need not consider. It is sufficient to say that no estoppel is pleaded.

2

IV. The dower right of the plaintiff was not affected by the sale under the Ewell mortgage. She was not made a party to that action, and hence could not be concluded by the decree. Not having, in fact, signed the deed, and there being no pretense that she had acknowledged it, it was not properly or lawfully recorded, and it therefore imparted no notice, and no one had a right to rely upon the fact that the plaintiff had apparently signed the deed. McClain's Code, section 3113; *Willard v. Cramer*, 36 Iowa, 22; *Greenwood v. Jenswold*, 69 Iowa, 53.

3

V. Finally, it is said that the execution sale to Selby bars the plaintiff's right to any interest in the land. This claim is based upon the provisions of McClain's Code, section 3644, which reads: "One-third in value of all the legal or equitable estates in real property, possessed by the husband at any time during the marriage, which have not been sold on execution or any other judicial sale, and to which the wife has made no relinquishment of her right, shall be

4

set apart as her property in fee simple, if she survive him." It will be remembered that Selby sold this land on a judgment against the husband alone. Manifestly, this statute applies to the case of one holding an interest in land under or by virtue of the execution sale referred to, or who at least stands in privity to the purchaser under such execution and sale. Now, appellant derived her right, title, and interest to this land, if she had any, through the will of her father. That interest is not only not one of privity with Selby, but it is hostile and adverse to any interest he might have had by virtue of this sale and deed under his judgment. Appellant is not claiming title under Selby. She received no right from him, or by virtue of the sale to him, and therefore is in no sense in privity with him. She cannot, therefore, predicate a claim to this land upon a title to which she is not only a stranger, but which was held in hostility to the title under which she claims. The Selby sale is not, then, such a sale on execution as, in favor of the appellant, will bar plaintiff's dower claim. Our construction of the statute finds support in principle in the following cases: *Kitzmiller v. Van Rensselaer*, 10 Ohio St. 63; *Pixley v. Bennett*, 11 Mass. 298; *Robinson v. Bates*, 3 Metc. (Mass.) 40; *Malloney v. Horan*, 49 N. Y. 111. The decree below is AFFIRMED.

S. A. Hoyt v. M. W. Beach, Appellant.

Pleading: REPETITION: *Judicial notice.* The court will grant a motion to strike out an answer when the matter contained therein
1　is the same in substance as the allegations in former answers to which demurrers have been sustained, although it contains a preliminary statement withdrawing all former answers and amendments. The court still takes judicial notice that the withdrawn pleadings stated matter vulnerable to demurrer.

Interest: JUDGMENTS. Interest may be allowed on a judgment for costs and attorney's fees, from the date of the entry of the judg-
2   ment (Code 1873, section 2078), citing *Parker v. State,* 85 N. E. Rep. (Ind.) 1105; *Galbraith v. Walker,* 95 Pa. 481; *Hayden v. Heffaran,* 58 N. W. Rep. (Mich.) 59; *Linck v. Litchfield,* 31 Ill. App. 104; *Palmer v. Glover,* 73 Ind. 532; *Bates v. Wilson,* 18 Colo. 287; *Emmitt v. Brophy,* 42 Ohio St. 82.

Appeal from Carroll District Court.—HON. Z. A. CHURCH,
Judge.

SATURDAY, DECEMBER 18, 1897.

ACTION at law upon promissory notes. Verdict and judgment for the plaintiff. Defendant appeals.— *Affirmed.*

F. M. Davenport for appellant.

J. P. Conner for appellee.

KINNE, C. J.—I. Without reciting all the facts of the case, it may be said that this appeal is from an order of the trial court sustaining a motion striking counts 2 and 3 of the defendant's answer. Some
1   four grounds were stated in the motion as to each count. It does not appear from the record upon what ground the motion was sustained. The principal ground of the motion was that the answer was a repetition, in substance, of the former answer and amended and substituted answers filed by the defendant, to which demurrers had been sustained. The appellant claims that the last answer is not, in fact, a repetition of the former answer, and that if it was, as by a preliminary statement in the last answer to which the motion was directed, all former answers and amendments were withdrawn, the last answer could not be stricken as being a repetition of matters contained in former answers, as such answers

could no longer be considered. An examination of the record shows that the last answer differs in no material respect from those to which demurrers were sustained. Some new matter is found in this last answer, but it is simply a conclusion drawn from the same facts pleaded in both answers. Under the established rule of pleading, it is proper to strike an answer which is, in substance, a mere repetition of allegations which have been held insufficient on a demurrer to a former answer in the same case. *Epley v. Ely*, 68 Iowa, 70; *Mayer v. Woodbury*, 14 Iowa, 57; *Robinson v. Erickson*, 25 Iowa, 85; *Phoenix Ins. Co. v. Findley*, 59 Iowa, 591. Whether the operation of the rule would be affected by the statement in the last answer that all former answers and amended answers are withdrawn has not been determined by this court. Now, an answer may be withdrawn; but the fact that it has been once filed, and that the facts set forth therein have been held insufficient on a demurrer, remains a matter of record, and is within the judicial notice of the court, acting upon the motion to strike the pleading; and the operation of the rule mentioned cannot be affected by the withdrawal of the former pleading, which is made in the latter pleading. Any other rule would permit parties to continue indefinitely to file pleadings which were mere repetitions of former pleadings, which had been held bad on demurrer. Such a construction would tend to disorder and a disrespect for the rulings of the court, would delay judicial procedure, and interfere with the orderly administration of justice. The matter contained in the answer last filed being the same, in substance, as the allegations contained in former answers, to which demurrers had been sustained, the court properly sus tained the motion to strike.

II. In entering the judgment, the court provided that the judgment for costs and attorney's fees should draw interest at six per cent. per annum from the date

of entry of the judgment. Appellant contends that this
was erroneous. No authorities are cited to show
that interest should not be allowed on attorney's
fees and costs. The allowance of interest on
judgments is controlled entirely by statute. At common
law, judgments carried no interest. 2 Black, Judgments, sections 880, 981. Our statute provides that
interest shall be allowed on all money due on judgments
and decrees of courts at the rate of six cents on the one
hundred by the year, unless a different rate is fixed
by the contract. Code 1873, section 2078. But few
adjudicated cases are to be found which determine the
right to interest on costs, and these are by no means
in harmony. In Indiana it is held that a judgment for
costs bears interest, but that there is no statute authorizing the allowance of interest on "fees," and that a witness or officer takes his fees as taxed without interest.
Parker v. State, 135 Ind. 534 (35 N. E. Rep. 1105). See
Galbraith v. Walker, 95 Pa. St. 481. In some of the
states interest on costs, which seem also to embrace
fees, is allowed. *Hayden v. Hefferan*, 99 Mich. 262 (58
N. W. Rep. 59); *Linck v. City of Litchfield*, 31 Ill. App.
104; *Palmer v. Glover*, 73 Ind. 532; *Bates v. Wilson*, 18
Colo. 287 (32 Pac. Rep. 615); *Emmitt v. Brophy*, 42
Ohio St. 82. Money due on a judgment for costs is as
much money due on a judgment as is money due on a
judgment for damages, and this is true whether such
costs embrace the fees of witnesses or officers or
attorney's fees. While we think it has been the under-
sanding that costs did not draw interest, still we discover nothing in our statute allowing interest on judgments which limits its allowance to the judgment for
damages only. There was therefore no error in providing that the costs and attorney's fees should draw interest.—AFFIRMED.

LANDON DAVIS, Executor, v. W. T. CLOSE, *et al.,* Appellants.

Wills: ADEMPTION OF LEGACY. A bequest of a specific amount to testator's son to be paid by deducting the same from the amount due from the son to the testator, as evidenced by notes, is specific, and is adeemed by the father's returning the notes to the son, during his lifetime.

Appeal from Wayne District Court.—HON. W. H. TEDFORD, Judge.

SATURDAY, DECEMBER 18, 1897.

THIS is a proceeding to obtain a construction of the will of Joseph Close, deceased. The trial court held that a certain legacy to W. T. Close was specific, and had been adeemed before the testator's death. The legatees appeal.—*Affirmed.*

Freeland & Evans for appellants.

Miles & Steele for appellee.

DEEMER, J.—The fourth clause of the will is as follows: "I give, will, and bequeath unto my son William Thomas Close the sum of one thousand dollars, to be paid by deducting the same from the amount he owes me, as evidenced by notes I hold on him." In the third clause he gave a granddaughter one thousand dollars in bank stock, as well as some real estate; in the fifth, to a son, a certain forty acres of real estate ;in the sixth, a certain forty acres of real estate to a daughter; in the seventh, eighth, and ninth, one thousand dollars to each of three daughters; and in the tenth he gave the residue of his estate to his sons and daughters and granddaughter, share and share alike. At the time of the

execution of the will the testator held a note for seven
hundred dollars executed by W. T. and J. F. Close
jointly, and a note for three hundred dollars executed
by W. T. Close individually. Shortly before his death
the deceased surrendered these notes to his son W. T.
Close. Appellant contends that the will did not take
effect until the death of the testator, and that the legacy
to W. T. Close is not specific, but demonstrative, and
that he is entitled to one thousand dollars from the general estate of his father; while, on the other hand, appellee insists that the legacy is specific, and that it was
adeemed by the testator before his death.

"A legacy is said to be general when it is not
answered by any particular portion of, or article belonging to, the estate, the delivery of which will alone fulfill
the intent of the testator; and when it is so answered it
is said to be a specific legacy, because it consists of some
specific thing belonging to the estate, which is by the
legacy intended to be transferred in specie to the legatee." *Smith v. McKitterick*, 51 Iowa, 548. See, also,
Evans v. Hunter, 86 Iowa, 416. Whether a legacy is
specific or general depends upon the intention of the
testator, to be derived from the language used in the
bequest, construed in the light of all the provisions of
the will. *Davis v. Crandall*, 101 N. Y. 311 (4 N. E. Rep.
721). If the intent is to have it paid without reference to
the fund upon which it is primarily a charge, it is general; but when it is to be paid out of a particular fund,
and not otherwise, it is specific. *Stevens v. Fisher*, 144
Mass. 114 (10 N. E. Rep. 803). Applying these rules to
the case at bar, it is clear, we think, that the legacy
was specific; for the one thousand dollars bequeathed to
W. T. Close was to be satisfied by deducting the same
from the amount of the notes the testator then held
against him. It was not intended that he should be
paid one thousand dollars out of the general estate, and
without reference to the notes upon which it was made

a charge. The other provisions of the will tend to strengthen this conclusion; for it is evident that the testator intended to bequeath to each of his children one thousand dollars, or its equivalent, and thus place them practically upon an equality. To hold that W. T. Close should not only have the notes, but an additional one thousand dollars as well, would be taking from the other children to benefit him. Evidently, this was not the testator's intention. But, whether this be true or not, the rule seems to be well settled that if a legacy be given by a parent, or one standing in *loco parentis*, and the testator afterwards make an advancement or gift of money or property *ejusdem generis* to the same beneficiary, the presumption will arise that the gift was intended in satisfaction of, or substitution for, the prior legacy, and, unless this presumption be rebutted, an ademption, in full or *pro tanta*, as the gift is equal to or less than the prior benefit, will occur. *Richardson v. Eveland*, 126 Ill. Sup. 37 (18 N. E. Rep. 308; 1 L. R. A. 203); 1 Pomeroy, Equity Jurisdiction, sections 554-557; Story, Equity Jurisdiction, sections 1111, 1112; *Richards v. Humphreys*, 15 Pick, 133; Beach, Modern Equity, sections 1047, 1050. When the testator surrendered the notes to his son, he made him a gift of the same general nature as he intended to confer upon him by will, and the presumption that it was intended as a satisfaction of the legacy is not met by any showing on the part of the legatee to the contrary. It was practically the same amount as bequeated by the will; for it is evident that the testator, in the fourth paragraph of his will, considered the note for seven hundred dollars as an individual liability of W. T. Close, as it in fact was in law. There was therefore an ademption in full. The case of *Wheeler v. Wood*, 104 Mich. 414 (62 N. W. Rep. 577), is quite like the one at bar; and it was there held that a legacy similar to this one was specific, and had been satisfied or adeemed. *Frank v. Frank*, 71 Iowa,

646, is not in conflict with these views. In that case the
devise was of real and personal property to a certain
amount, and was thus qualified: "This amount is in
notes such as Mary P. Frank, the executor of my will,
may turn over to them." We said in that case: "The
will clearly expresses the intention of the testator to
give to each legatee six hundred dollars, and a different
intention is not expressed in the clause speaking of the
notes. * * * In our opinion, the testator intended
that each legatee should have $600, which the executor
could pay in notes of that value, or which would yield
that sum. If the notes do not yield that amount, or
there should not be good notes of that value in the hands
of the executor, the sum is to be made up from other
property of the estate." Such is not the case at bar.
Here the one thousand dollars is to be paid by deducting
that amount from the sum due from the legatee, which,
as we have seen, was of the same amount as the legacy,
and not from any other fund. In the cited case there
was no intent to relieve the general estate from liability,
while in the case at bar the bequest is, in effect, a gift
of the debt itself, as distinguished from a definite sum of
money. A careful examination of the case *In re Newcomb's Will*, 98 Iowa, 176, relied upon by appellant,
will disclose that it is in entire harmony with the conclusions reached in this opinion. The trial court properly construed the will, and its judgment is AFFIRMED.

THE SECURITY FIRE INSURANCE COMPANY v. CHRIST
HANSEN, *et al.*, Appellants.

Bonds: DEATH OF OBLIGOR: *Estates.* The liability of a surety on a
bond of an insurance agent, conditioned that such agent will perform all duties as such, and at the termination of the agency, by
3 resignation, removal or otherwise, faithfully account with the
company and pay over all money due, is not terminated by the

death of the surety, but continues against his estate and its distributees, where the bond provides that such surety binds himself, his "heirs, executors and administrators."

Claims Against Estates. Code 1873, section 2421, fixing a period in which claims against the estate of a deceased person shall be
1 filed, does not apply to contingent and undetermined claims grow-
2 ing out of a bond given by decedent to stand good for the business conduct of an insurance agent, such claims arising after that period has expired.

Appeal from Clinton District Court.—HON. W. F. BRENNAN, Judge.

SATURDAY, DECEMBER 18, 1897.

DEFENDANTS' demurrer to plaintiff's petition being overruled, and defendants electing to stand upon their demurrer, judgment was entered against John, Anna, Henry, and William Teege and their guardian, O. T. Nelson, for two hundred and twenty-one dollars and thirty-one cents, and costs. Defendants appeal.— *Affirmed.*

R. B. Wolfe for appellants.

Holleran & Scott for appellee.

GIVEN, J.—I. The allegations of the petition are, in substance, as follows: That about July 23, 1885, Christ Hansen was appointed agent for the plaintiff corporation, and continued to act as such up to November, 1895. That on July 23, 1885, he, with John R. Merrill and Theodore Teege, now deceased, as his sureties, executed and delivered to the plaintiff a bond in the sum of five hundred dollars, for the payment of which they obligated "ourselves, our heirs, executors, and administrators, jointly and severally, by these presents," upon this condition. "The condition of this obligation is such that whereas, Christ Hansen has been duly appointed agent of the Security Fire Insurance Company at Lost

Nation, county of Clinton, and state of Iowa, and as such agent authorized to receive money for said Security Fire Insurance Company, for premiums on policies, payment of losses, salvages, collections or otherwise, and has agreed to keep a true and correct account of the same, and make regular reports to said Security Fire Insurance Company of the business of said Security Fire Isurance Company transacted by him, and to pay over all money due to said company, and to in every way truly and faithfully perform all duties as such agent in compliance with the instructions received from time to time through the proper officers of said company, and, at the termination of said agency, by resignation, removal, or otherwise, to truly and faithfully account with said company, and pay over all moneys then due to said company, and also to return all books, supplies, and property in his possession belonging to said company." The petition shows that there is due and owing to the plaintiff from defendant Hansen, on account of moneys received by him up to November, 1895, the sum of two hundred and sixteen dollars, which he fails and refuses to pay, and which he has converted to his own use. That on the ninth of June, 1892, said Theodore Teege died intestate, possessed of an estate of personal property valued at about two housand, five hundred dollars. That administration was granted on the said estate, June 20, 1892, and that administration thereon was closed on the twenty-sixth day of July, 1893, and the administrator discharged. That said deceased left, as his children and only heirs, the defendants John, Anna, William, and Henry Teege, all of whom are minors, and each of whom received from said estate one-fourth part of one thousand, two hundred and seventy-nine dollars and sixty cents. That defendant O. T. Nelson is the duly appointed and qualified guardian of said minor heirs, and as such received said sum from the administrator on the twentieth day of July, 1893. That the defendant Mary Voss, as the widow of said deceased, received from the administrator six hundred and thirty-nine dollars and eighty cents from said estates on the twentieth day of July, 1893. That the indebtedness which is the basis of this action arose from the aforesaid breaches of said bond after the administration of said estate had closed. The payment of said balance due to plaintiff was demanded from said defendants, an that each and all of them failed, neglected, and refused to pay the same or any part thereof. Plaintiff asked judgment against the defendants for two hundred and sixteen dollars and ninety-nine cents and interest.

Defendants demurred to the petition on four grounds, namely: That the petition shows that the breaches of said bond took place after the death of Theodore Teege, and after his estate had been fully administered upon; that the petition shows that during the lifetime of Theodore Teege, and during the time there was an estate of his in existence, there was no default on said bond; that the death of Theodore Teege, the administration upon his estate, the closing of said estate, and the discharge of the administrator terminated all liability upon the bond against the heirs of said Theodore Teege; that said contract of suretyship is null and void in law, for that it undertakes to bind the heirs upon a bond after the estate of the surety has been fully administered upon and closed before the default occurred upon said bond.

Appellants' counsel say, and correctly so, we think, that the only question to be determined is whether these heirs are liable on this bond for a breach thereof that did not take place until more than three years after the surety's death, and more than two years after his estate had been fully administered upon and closed, said claim never having been filed against his estate. Appellants' counsel state their contentions as follows: "First, that there can be no liability against

the estate of Theodore Teege, for the reason that it
nowhere appears from the pleadings that the bond was
ever filed, or filed and allowed, as an additional liability
against the estate of Theodore Teege, and not having
been so filed, under section 2421 of the Code of Iowa, it
cannot now be asserted against his heirs and collected
of them; second, that the death of Theodore Teege, the
administration and closing of his estate, terminate all
of his liability and that of his heirs upon the bond."

The first contention is directly answered in the negative in the opinion of this court announced in the recent
case of *Wickham v. Hull*, 102 Iowa, 469, wherein we
held that said section 2421 of the Code of 1873 did not
apply to claims arising after the period fixed in that
section for filing claims had expired. This, like
2   that, was a contingent and undetermined claim
until after the time allowed for filing claims, and
therefore not subject to the limitations provided in said
section. By the language of this bond, Theodore Teege
not only obligated himself, but his estate in the hands of
his heirs, executors and administrators. The obligation
is not limited to the life of the surety, but by the termination of the agency. The bond set out in the petition,
though varying in language, is identical in substance
with the bond sued upon in the case of *Royal Ins. Co. v.
Davies*, 40 Iowa, 469. In that case the defendant
answered, alleging as defenses that John L. Davies, the
surety, died on the twenty-third day of April, 1872; that
thereby his estate was discharged from any further
liability on said bond; and that up to the time of his
decease the conditions of the bond had not been broken,
but that the breaches alleged in the petition happened
after the death of Davies. To this plaintiff demurred,
which being overruled, and plaintiff standing thereon,
judgment was rendered for the defendant, and plaintiff
appealed. This court said: "By the terms of the bond
the surety, Davies, bound himself, his heirs, executors,

and administrators, as surety for his principal, Kidder.
This language shows no intention to limit the liability to
the lifetime of the surety.   On the contrary, it imports
that the liability shall continue after his death, and
bind his heirs and personal representatives." It is said
that this intention is further manifested by further
language of the bond, to the effect that Kidder will perform all his duties "for and during the time he offici-
ated as said agent." It is argued that, as this language
does not occur in the bond under consideration, the
cases are distinguishable.   It will be seen, by the
language quoted above, that the time to which this bond
was to run was the termination of the agency of Hansen "by resignation, removal, or otherwise."   We see
no distinction between the cases, and think the contentions of appellant are answered in the negative by said
case against Davies.   There was no error in overruling
said demurrer ,and the judgment of the district court
is therefore AFFIRMED.

THE HARTMAN STEEL COMPANY, Limited, v. E. HOAG &
    SON, E. HOAG, and A. HOAG, Appellants.

Directed Verdict. A verdict is properly directed for plaintiff in an
    action for a balance due on account, where plaintiff's claim is
  8 admitted by the answer and defendant's claim for damages,
    because of plaintiff's negligence in delaying to foreclose a chattel
  8 mortgage, assigned by plaintiff to defendants, by reason of which
    the collateral security is lost under a sale on a junior lien, is not
    sustained by evidence, but it is shown that the property covered
    by such mortgage was sold on a valid judgment against defend-
    ants and applied in liquidation thereof.

Attorneys: AUTHORITY. An attorney who has no other authority
  8 than to collect a debt, cannot ratify the acceptance by an agent of
  6 the creditor of a bill of sale from the debtor as a payment.

Representations: ESTOPPEL. Reliance by a debtor on the advice of
    an attorney for the creditor, that a bill of sale of personal prop-
  2 erty by the debtor to the creditor was sufficient to fully and legally
  8 transfer the property to the creditor, does not estop the creditor to

6 subsequently set up that the title to the property did not pass by
   such bill of sale, and that the debt was therefore unpaid, as the
   debtor has no right to rely on the advice of the creditor's attorney
   in such matter.

President of Corporation: RATIFICATION. A creditor of a corporation cannot ratify the unauthorized act of the president of such
7 corporation in executing a bill of sale of corporate property for
   payment of a debt.

Pledges: RIGHT OF PLEDGEE OF MORTGAGE. One to whom a chattel
8 mortgage is assigned as collateral security is not required to
5 accept an offer by the purchaser of the mortgaged property. at a
   sale under a junior lien, to give security on such property.

Evidence: ADMISSION BY PLEADING. Evidence that the claim of plaintiff was, from its inception, a debt of a corporation. in which
5 defendants had an interest, instead of a debt of the defendants
   themselves, is properly excluded where defendants admit in their
   answer that it was their debt from its inception.

CROSS-EXAMINATION. A witness, having testified to a conversation
   had with plaintiff's attorney relative to the mortgage in question,
4 stated that he had told them what he thought about it. On
   cross-examination it is proper to ask him "what" he told them

Pleading: STRIKING OFF. It is not error to strike out an amendment
1 to an answer alleging want of diligence in collecting collateral
   security on the part of the plaintiff, where such fact had already
   been sufficiently alleged.

Appeal from Delaware District Court.—HON. J. J.
TOLERTON, Judge.

SATURDAY, DECEMBER 18, 1897.

PLAINTIFF brings this action to recover one thousand
three hundred and fifty dollars and fifty-five cents, with
interest, a balance alleged to be due on account for wire
sold by the plaintiff to the defendants. Defendants
answered as follows: "The defendants, for answer to
plaintiff's petition on file herein, say that on or about
the twenty-second day of September, 1888, they settled
with the plaintiff, and paid the said plaintiff the balance due on the said account, upon which this action
is founded." Defendants, by way of amendment, filed

two additional counts, entitled second and third counts, in which they alleged, in substance, as follows: In the second, that prior to said twenty-second day of September, 1888, they assigned to plaintiff, as collateral security for said indebtedness, a certain chattel mortgage owned by them, which assignment was duly recorded; that plaintiff orally agreed to proceed at once to foreclose said mortgage, and to apply the avails on said indebtedness; that said security was of an actual value largely in excess of said indebtedness; that plaintiff continuously retained said security, and has negligently, carelessly, and recklessly suffered and permitted the property upon which such lien was held, to be sold under a junior and inferior lien, whereby said collateral security became and was wholly lost, and is now valueless, to the damage of the defendants in the sum of four thousand dollars. Defendants ask judgment to an extent equal to plaintiff's claim, with interest and costs, but do not ask any affirmative relief other than as in extinguishment of plaintiff's right of action. In the third count they allege that subsequent to said assignment, to-wit, on or about September 21, 1888, plaintiff, by its agent, N. B. Williams, orally agreed with the defendants to take a bill of sale from defendants of certain personal property in full satisfaction of said debt; that plaintiff's counsel prepared a bill of sale, which defendants executed, and which was duly placed on record; that thereafter plaintiff took proceedings under and by virtue of said bill of sale, assuming to be the owner and entitled to the possession of the chattels therein described, and that, but for said acts of plaintiff, defendants would have taken measures to protect such rights of property; that defendants were damaged thereby to the value of said property, which was agreed upon as equal to plaintiff's claim. Defendants aver that the plaintiff is, by said acts, estopped to deny that such bill

of sale so received was not in full satisfaction and discharge of defendants' obligation. Defendants pray that
they may have their damages herein allowed in cancellation of plaintiff's claim, and that plaintiff be estopped
from recovering any judgment herein.   Thereafter,
defendants filed a second amendment to their answer,
amending said second count, in substance as follows:
That at the time of the sale under said junior lien plaintiff was offered by the purchaser security on the property included in the sale, which was ample security for
said claim, and the plaintiff refused such security, and
failed to take adequate measures to protect the superior
lien held by plaintiff under the assignment of said mortgage. The third count was amended by alleging that
in making said bill of sale defendants acted under the
advice and direction of plaintiff's counsel, and with the
full understanding and belief that said property covered
by said bill of sale was fully and legally transferred to
plaintiff, and that they and plaintiff thereafter acted
upon such understanding, wherefore they aver that
plaintiff is estopped to maintain that said writing so
executed was not legally sufficient. Plaintiff moved to
strike said second amendment upon the following
grounds: That the averment of want of diligence of the
plaintiff to enforce the securities and damage resulting
to defendants therefrom is surplusage, and redundant,
and fully covered by the allegations of the first amendment; that the offer by the holder of the junior lien to
secure plaintiff's claim is immaterial, as plaintiff was
not bound to accept such security; that defendants
could not rely upon the advice of counsel adversely
interested; that the allegations of said second amendment do not show that defendants were misled to their
prejudice by any act of plaintiff or its counsel upon
which they were justified in relying, and that such allegations show no estoppel; that all the allegations of said
second amendment are immaterial. This motion being

sustained, plaintiff replied to said second count, denying that defendants suffered any damage by reason of
the failure to foreclose said chattel mortgage, for that
the property referred to as covered by said mortgage
was sold upon execution against the defendants, and
the proceeds applied to the satisfaction of their lawful
and valid indebtedness; that said chattel mortgage was
without consideration and void and for that reason
plaintiff could not enforce it; that said chattel mortgage
was never delivered to plaintiff, and that long before
the execution of said pretended assignment said mortgage had been destroyed, canceled, and surrendered,
and that only a certified copy of the record thereof was
delivered to plaintiff. Plaintiff denies that the securities in said second count referred to were of the value
of plaintiff's claim, or of any value whatever, and denies
that it made the agreement in said count set out. In
reply to the third count plaintiff denies that the bill of
sale therein referred to was accepted in satisfaction or
discharge of defendant's obligation, and avers that said
bill of sale was accepted, if at all, only as security.
Further replying, plaintiff says that said bill of sale was
unauthorized by any act or resolution of the board of
directors of the corporation owning the property in said
bill of sale described. Plaintiff denies that it is estopped
by any act upon the part of plaintiff alleged in said
count, and alleges that the personal property described
in said bill of sale was sold upon execution against the
defendants, and the proceeds applied to the satisfaction
of the judgment against them, whereby defendants
received full benefit of said property. Plaintiff denies
every allegation contained in said counts not expressly
admitted. Upon these issues the cause came on for trial
before the court and jury, the court holding that
the defendants had the burden of proof. At the

conclusion of the evidence, plaintiff's motion for a verdict was sustained, and verdict returned in favor of the plaintiff, from which the defendants appeal.— *Affirmed.*

Bronson & Carr, Yoran & Arnold, and *W. E. Bauer* for appellants.

Boies, Couch & Boies and *Dunham & Norris* for appellee.

GIVEN, J.—I. Appellants' first complaint is of the ruling of the court sustaining appellee's motion to strike said second amendment to the answer. We think there was no error in the ruling. The averment of want ·1   of diligence on the part of plaintiff had already been sufficiently alleged, and, in so far as it alleges an offer by a third party of security to the plaintiff, it is immaterial, for that the plaintiff was not bound to accept such offer. Defendants had no right to rely upon the advice of plaintiff's counsel as to the 2   legal sufficiency of the bill of sale, and such reliance upon his advice upon a question of law constitutes no estoppel against the plaintiff. *Cedar Rapids & M. R. Co. v. County of Sac,* 46 Iowa, 243; *District Tp. of Clap v. Independent Dist. of Buchanan,* 63 Iowa, 188. Appellants' counsel cite in this connection a number of authorities as to the extent to which a principal is bound by the acts of an agent, but this does not seem to us to have any bearing upon the questions presented by this motion to strike.

II. A further consideration of the case requires that we notice in a general way the facts developed on the trial. E. Hoag & Son assumed and paid an indebtedness of Thompson and Farrell to one Percival, 8   who was then engaged with Thompson and Farrell in the manufacture of barbed wire. Thompson and Farrell gave Hoag & Son their note for two thousand five hundred dollars, secured by a chattel mortgage on their interest in the machines, tools, furniture, stock, etc., of the barbed-wire company, and Hoag & Son subsequently paid said debt of Thompson and Farrell. Afterwards, the barbed-wire company became incorporated under the name of the "Beat 'Em All Barbed-Wire Company," and E. Hoag was elected president, and was acting in that capacity, when the company failed, and when said bill of sale was executed by him to the plaintiff. Hoag & Son ordered from plaintiff the wire charged for in the account sued upon, and the same was turned over to the barbed-wire company for its use. The barbed-wire company failed in the fall of 1888, and one N. B. Williams appeared as representing the plaintiff to effect a settlement of their claim against defendants, E. Hoag & Son, whereupon E. Hoag assigned to plaintiff, by separate writing, said chattel mortgage from Thompson and Farrell as collateral security for the claim sued upon, plaintiff, by said Williams, giving to E. Hoag & Son a written agreement to apply the proceeds of said mortgage to defendants' indebtedness, less charges and expenses necessary to protect the mortgage, and to pay any residue to Hoag & Son. On the next day,—September 22, 1888,—E. Hoag, as president of said corporation, in pursuance of an agreement with said Williams, executed to the plaintiff an unconditional bill of sale of the machines, tools, belting, shafting, and all other personal property of the corporation in its building in Cedar Falls, Iowa. On the eighteenth day of September, 1888, an execution in favor of A. S. Blair and against the said barbed-wire company, E. Hoag, and A. A. Hoag, S. Thompson and W. E. Farrell, was placed in the hands of the sheriff, and on the twenty-second day of September, 1888, he levied the same upon the property of said corporation in its factory at Cedar Falls. Thereafter plaintiff, by its attorneys, notified said sheriff that it claimed to be the qualified owner of said property by virtue of said assignment of said chattel mortgage thereon, and said bill of sale. A. S. Blair gave an indemnifying bond, whereupon the sheriff proceeded to sell said property under the execution, and sold the same to A. S. Blair for over two-thirds of the appraised value thereof.

III. Appellants complain of certain rulings in taking the testimony of A. S. Blair and of E. Hoag. Mr. Blair, having testified to a conversation with plaintiff's counsel about said mortgage, stated that he had
4   told them what he thought about it. On cross-examination he was asked to state what he told them, to which defendants objected, and the objection was overruled. What he said was a part of the conversation, and the proper subject of inquiry, as it went to make intelligible the other parts thereof. Appellants complain that Mr. Hoag was not permitted to state what offer Mr. Blair had made to the plaintiff's attorney in the way of security. We have seen that that
5   part of the answer was properly stricken out; therefore the inquiry was immaterial. It is further complained that Mr. Blair was permitted to testify, over defendants' objection, that he never offered plaintiff any security. If this was error, it was without prejudice, for, as we have seen, it is entirely immaterial whether or not Mr. Blair had offered security as claimed. It is assigned as error that the court excluded evidence offered to establish the fact that plaintiff's claim was, from its inception, the debt of the barbed-wire company. There was no error in excluding this evidence under the pleadings, for, by the answer, the defendants admitted that it was their debt from its inception. Other errors assigned on the taking of testimony are not of sufficient importance to require further notice.

IV. At the close of the evidence, plaintiff moved to strike all evidence of negotiations between the

defendants and Williams, or any other person, claiming to represent the plaintiff, relative to said bill of sale, upon the following grounds: That there is no evidence of any authority upon the part of Williams or others to accept said bill of sale in liquidation of this debt, and that there is no evidence of authority from the barbed-wire company to Hoag to execute said bill of sale. Defendants contend that the plaintiff is
6 estopped from denying the authority of Williams and of its attorneys, because of the giving of said notice of qualified ownership to the sheriff. There is no evidence of other authority to either Williams or to plaintiff's attorneys than simply to collect this claim, and it is not contended that such authority would authorize the taking of anything else than money in payment. See *Harbach v. Colvin*, 73 Iowa, 638. The claim of defendants is that the bill of sale was taken in payment of the debt, while the notice given by plaintiff's attorneys only claimed it as security. The evidence fails to show that these attorneys had any other authority from the plaintiff than to collect; therefore they could not ratify the acceptance of the bill of sale as a payment. Mechem, Agency, section 121. Again,
7 there is an entire absence of evidence showing authority to E. Hoag, as president, to execute that bill of sale on the property of the corporation for the payment of a debt owing by E. Hoag & Son, and, therefore, we think, plaintiff could not ratify that unauthorized act. Mechem, Agency, section 168. If the bill of sale is to be held effective only by reason of the ratification, it will be observed that that ratification was not until after the property had been levied upon under Mr. Blair's execution. As already stated, there is no evidence of authority from the barbed-wire company to E. Hoag, to execute said bill of sale; therefore,

the second ground of the motion was properly sustained.

This evidence being stricken out, the court prop-
8   erly sustained plaintiff's motion for a verdict.

The plaintiff's claim was admitted by the answer, and defendants' claim for damage was not sustained by evidence, but, on the other hand, it is shown that the property described in the chattel mortgage was sold upon a valid judgment against the defendants, and applied in liquidation thereof. We do not discover any error prejudicial to the defendants in either of the respects complained of, and the judgment of the district court is AFFIRMED.

GEORGE CHAMBERS, Appellant, v. HENRY OEHLER, *et al.*

Pleading: JOINDER OF CAUSES. A complaint in an action to recover damages for an alleged unlawful arrest for failure to obey a subpena brought against the justice who issued the subpena and the warrant, the parties who served them, the sureties on the official bond of the justice and one who filed an affidavit in reference to which the subpena was issued, which complaint charges in one count oppression, annoyance and extortion, and in another a conspiracy to cheat and defraud, is not, after a dismissal of the suit as to the sureties, demurrable for misjoinder of causes of action and misjoinder of parties, under Code 1873, section 2630.

Appeal from Delaware District Court.—HON. J. J. TOLERTON, Judge.

SATURDAY, DECEMBER 18, 1897.

ACTION at law to recover for the alleged wrongful arrest of the plaintiff in proceedings intended to punish him for an alleged contempt of court. The defendant Wessel demurred to the petition on two grounds. The demurrer was sustained as to the first ground, and overruled as to the second. The plaintiff elected to stand on his petition as to Wessel, and as to him the cause

was dismissed by the court. The plaintiff appeals.—
Reversed.

S. T. Richards, E. C. Perkins, and *Arthur A. House*
for appellant.

Bronson & Carr for appellee Wessel.

ROBINSON, J.—The petition contains two counts. In
the first, plaintiff alleges that on the fourth day of July,
1893, the defendant and Oehler, a justice of the peace
within and for Dubuque county, issued a subpoena com-
manding the plaintiff to appear forthwith before him, at
his office in Dyersville to testify in a certain suit wherein
one Sarah Jane Galloway was plaintiff, and the Chicago, Milwaukee & St. Paul Railway Company was
defendant; that on the same day the subpoena was
served on the plaintiff by the defendant Wessel; that
afterwards, and on the same day, Oehler issued a warrant for the arrest of the plaintiff, and that he was then
and there taken into custody by the defendant Meyers,
under and by virtue of the warrant, and compelled by
Meyers to go with him as a prisoner to the town of New
Wine or New Vienna, and through the public streets
thereof, before the justice, by whom the plaintiff was
then accused of contempt of court, for disobeying the
subpoena; that the justice, after denying the plaintiff
the rights of counsel and of making defense in his own
behalf, adjudged him guilty of the offense charged, and
assessed a fine of five dollars and costs against him,
which he then paid. The count further alleges that the
plaintiff could not legally be required to appear before
the justice on the day stated; that no proceeding or trial
in which process could lawfully issue was then pending
before the justice; that the subpoena and warrant and
all proceedings thereunder were wholly without jurisdiction, and the acts of the defendants were willful,

malicious, wholly without cause or jurisdiction, and for the purpose of oppressing and annoying the plaintiff, and to extort money from him, in violation of law; that the plaintiff sustained damage by reason of the treatment, indignity, insult, and outrage, in the sum of two thousand dollars; that the justice executed an official bond in the sum of five hundred dollars, with the defendants Gehrig and Freyman as sureties, the conditions of which were broken by reason of the alleged fraud and oppression practiced upon the plaintiff. A copy of the bond is made a part of the petition. The second count is based upon the same transaction, and alleges that the defendants Oehler, Wessel, Meyers, and one M. C. Lane, fraudulently and maliciously conspired and confederated together for the purpose of cheating and defrauding the plaintiff, and obtaining money from him, as fees, unlawfully, by means of the willful and malicious oppression of the plaintiff by Ochler in pretending to act in his official capacity; that, in furtherance of the conspiracy, and as part of the common design, Lane appeared before the justice on the fourth day of July, 1893, and filed with him an affidavit in which Lane falsely and fraudulently pretended and assumed to represent the Chicago, Milwaukee & St. Paul Railway Company, in the capacity of a claim agent, and falsely and fraudulently claimed that it was necessary that papers be served upon the railway company on that day. The averments of the first count are then repeated in substance, and a copy of the affidavit of Lane is attached to the count.

The ground of Wessel's demurrer, which was sustained by the court, is as follows: "The facts stated in the first and second counts of said petition, and each of them, show that plaintiff is not entitled to the relief demanded against this defendant, in this, that said counts, and each of them, show upon their face that several causes of action are joined therein against different parties; that each of said counts shows, not only that there is a misjoinder of causes of action, but of parties also." After the demurrer was filed, but before the ruling thereon was made, the plaintiff dismissed the action as to the sureties Gehrig and Ferguson. Before the action was dismissed as to the sureties, each count stated a cause of action against Oehler, Wessel, and Meyers, independent of the official bond of the justice, and another cause of action on the bond against the sureties. But one cause of action was stated against Oehler in each count, although the plaintiff had the right to seek a recovery on the bond, or without regard to it, as he should elect. All of the facts upon which the plaintiff relied to show fraud and oppression contrary to the conditions of the bond were shown by the averments which were designed to state a cause of action against Oehler independent of the bond, and the statements with reference to that added nothing to the averments which showed liability on his part. The prayer for relief applied to both counts, and was in words as follows: "Wherefore plaintiff demands judgment against all of said defendants in the sum of five hundred dollars, and also judgment against Henry Oehler, Barney Wessel, and Frank Meyers for fifteen hundred dollars in addition to the above sum, with costs." It will be observed that the prayer as against all of the defendants but the sureties is in precisely the same language, and no reference is made therein to the bond. The statements respecting it made in the petition were designed to show that the sureties were liable. The dismissing of the action as against the sureties did not, it is true, withdraw all references to the bond contained in the petition, but they then became mere surplusage, without legal effect. Section 2630 of the Code of 1873 contained the following: "Causes of action of whatever kind, where each may be prosecuted by the same kind of proceedings, provided that they be by the same party, and against the same party in the same rights, and if suit on all may be brought and tried in that county, may be joined in the same petition." This is sufficiently broad to permit the joinder of the two causes of action against Oehler, Wessel, and Meyers, which are set out in the two counts of the petition.

It follows from what we have said that, after the case was dismissed as to the sureties, there was no mis-joinder of causes of action nor of parties, and that for that reason, if for none other, the demurrer was improp-erly sustained upon the ground in question. Attention is called to the fact that Oehler was a justice of the peace of Dubuque county, and that, under section 2579 of the Code of 1873, an action on the official bond of a public officer must be brought in the county where the cause of action arose, and that the causes of action alleged in this case arose in Dubuque county. It is said that for that reason Oehler was wrongfully made a party in Delaware county. But the objection thus made was not presented by the demurrer, and, as we have seen, when it was sustained, the action was not on an official bond. In view of the conclusions we have stated, it is unnecesssary to determine whether the proper method of presenting the objections upon which Wessel relied was by motion or by demurrer. For the reason shown, the judgment of the district court is REVERSED.

C. L. Hipsley v. T. J. Price, Sheriff, *et al.*, Appellants.

Landlord's Lien: EXEMPTION FROM. In Code 1873, section 2017, read-ing, "a landlord shall have a lien for his rent upon all crops
2 grown upon the demised premises, and upon any other personal property of the tenant which has been used upon the premises during the term, and not exempt from execution," the words "not exempt from execution," refer only to "other personal property," and not to "crops grown upon the demised prem-ises," and no part of said crops is exempt from the lien.

INTERVENTION BY LANDLORD. In an action by a mortgagee of chattels against a sheriff who has sold the chattels on attachment by
8 a landlord for rent, the landlord can intervene, and assert his interest in the property, whether the attachment was valid or not.

Appeal: OBJECTION BELOW. An objection that the levy of a landlord's attachment was invalid, because written notice thereof was
1 not served on the attachment defendant, cannot be first presented on appeal from a judgment for plaintiff in an action to recover as mortgagee the attached property, or plaintiff's interest therein.

Appeal from Mahaska District Court.—HON. BEN McCOY, Judge.

SATURDAY, DECEMBER 18, 1897.

ACTION at law to recover the possession of specific personal property. There was a trial by jury, which resulted in a verdict and judgment for the plaintiff. The defendants appeal.—*Reversed.*

Searle & Keating and *Liston McMillen* for appellants.

Dan Davis and *Bolton & Bolton* for appellee.

ROBINSON, J.—In October of the year 1893, Moses Nowels and W. Martin entered into an agreement, in writing, by which the former leased to the latter, for the term of five years from the first day of March, 1894, certain land in Mahaska county. The rent to be paid therefor was three hundred and fifty dollars, on the twentieth day of October, 1894, the same amount on the first day of February, 1895, and like sums on corresponding dates during each year of the term of the lease, and for each sum to be so paid Martin gave his promissory note to Nowels. On the twenty-fourth day of October, 1894, Nowels commenced against Martin an action, aided by a landlord's attachment, to recover rent then due and unpaid. The writ of attachment was

delivered to the sheriff or his deputy, levies thereunder
were made on the twenty-fifth and twenty-ninth days
of October, on one hundred and twenty acres of corn
and other property, an order for the sale of the attached
property as perishable was obtained, and the property,
or a part thereof, was sold by the sheriff in December.
Judgment was subsequently rendered in the action by
Nowels against Martin for the sum of four hundred and
twenty-five dollars and costs. On the seventeenth day
of November, 1894, Martin gave to the plaintiff a chattel
mortgage on one hundred and ten acres of the corn upon
which the landlord's attachment had been levied, to
secure the payment of a note for two hundred and fifty
dollars. This action was commenced against the sheriff
at about the time the property was sold, to recover possession of the corn mortgaged to the plaintiff, or for the
value of the plaintiff's alleged interest therein, and
costs. Nowels intervened, and claimed the corn, and
the proceeds thereof, by virtue of his lease and his landlord's attachment. The jury returned a verdict for the
plaintiff, and found the value of his interest in the corn
to be the sum of two hundred and seventy dollars. He
elected to take a judgment for that amount in lieu of the
property, and judgment was so rendered. The sheriff
and the intervener appeal.

I. The plaintiff claims in argument that the levy
of the landlord's attachment was invalid, because
written notice thereof was not served on Martin, the
defendant in the attachment proceedings. See *Hicks
v. Swan*, 97 Iowa, 556. The only answer which
1   need be made to that claim is that it is presented
for the first time in this court. The record submitted to us shows that the intervener based his claim
to the property upon the levy of his landlord's attachment, upon an alleged change of possession by virtue of
the levy and proceedings thereunder of the officers who
served it, and upon a provision in the lease, in words as

follows "* * * All accrued rent on said premises,
and unpaid, the same shall be a lien on any and all crops
raised and belonging to the said party of the second part,
on the above described premises, whether the same be
exempt from execution or distress by law or not; and in
such event the second party [Martin] waives all legal
rights which he may have to hold or retain 'any such
property under an exemption law in force in this state."
The record also shows that the claims made by the plaintiff in the district court were that the corn in question
was exempt from execution; that it was exempt for that
reason from seizure under a landlord's attachment; and
that he obtained the mortgage on which he relies without notice of the claim or rights of the intervener, under
the mortgage clause of his lease. See *Bank v. Honnold*,
85 Iowa, 352. The pleadings, the evidence, and the
charge of the court show that the plaintiff was permitted
to obtain judgment on the theory that his claim with
respect to exempt property was well founded. Martin
at the time of the levy of the attachment, was a resident
of this state, a farmer, the head of a family, and entitled
to all the exemptions which the law allows to such persons. He had a considerable amount of live stock
exempt from execution, and claimed as so exempt the
corn in question, on the ground that it was necessary
food required for his exempt stock for the period of
six months. Section 2017 of the Code of 1873, which
was in force when the rights of the parties to
2   this action became fixed, contained the following:
"A landlord shall have a lien for his rent upon all
crops grown upon the demised premises, and upon any
other personal property of the tenant which has been
used on the premises during the term, and not exempt
from execution. * * *" Does the clause, "and not
exempt from execution," apply only to "other personal
property of the tenant which has been used on the
premises during the term," or to such property and also

to "all crops grown upon the demised premises?" It
was said in *Thompson v. Anderson*, 86 Iowa, 706, that
the reason upon which the lien provided for by the
statute is grounded is that "the use of the landlord's
premises has contributed to the production, improvement, or maintenance of the property upon which the
lien attaches." That reason applies with especial force
to crops raised upon the premises. Other personal
property may derive little, if any, benefit from the premises, but crops raised thereon draw in large part their
sustenance, and the elements which are necessary to
their growth, from the soil, which is to some extent
impoverished, and made less productive, by each suc-
cessive crop which it yields. There is ample reason for
not permitting the lien to attach to property which the
tenant needs for the maintenance of himself and family,
and to the production and preservation of which the
leased premises have contributed little or nothing; but
on what theory of reason or justice can it be said that
the lien should not attach to crops which could not have
been produced but for the leased premises? It is quite
clear that the general assembly intended to make a distinction between crops grown on leased premises and
other personal property, and that the clause, "not
exempt from execution" applies only to the property
referred to in the sentence immediately preceding it,
and not to the crops specified in the first sentence of
the section. This interpretation is fully authorized
by the language used, will give force to what we
are satisfied was the legislative intent, and will
do justice. It follows that, whether the plaintiff
had knowledge of the mortgage clause in the lease of
Nowels to Martin, or whether written notice of the landlord's attachment was given to Martin, is not material
to a determination of this case. The crops in question
were grown upon the leased premises. Nowels was
entitled to a lien upon them for that reason, and the

lien had not been terminated when the mortgage to the plaintiff was executed, and the interest he thereby acquired was subject to the lien of Nowels. If

3   the attachment was, for any reason, invalid, Nowels had the right to assert and have protected his interest in the property, and the proceeds thereof, by intervening in this case. The judgment rendered by the district court rests upon an erroneous theory of the statute to which we have referred. The facts which determine the application of the statute are not in dispute, and the judgment must therefore be, and is, REVERSED.

J. E. REIZENSTEIN v. EZEKIEL CLARK AND EARL CLARK, Appellants.

Joint Assault: EXEMPLARY DAMAGES. In a joint malicious assault,
8   if one of the participants was actuated by malice, each will be liable for damages, both actual and exemplary, resulting from the assault.

EVIDENCE. Plaintiff in an action for wanton, malicious assault com-
9   mitted by two persons, need not show that either defendant expressly directed the other to make the assault or that they struck him at the same moment of time, or that one struck him after the other.

SAME. Evidence tha' plaintiff, in an action for malicious assault, had been assaulted at another time, before the assault in question is
4   inadmissible in the absence of any contention that any of the disorders from which the plaintiff claims to be suffering were due to the prior assaults.

EXEMPLARY DAMAGES: *Instructions.* An instruction in an action for
6   assault that the jury may award exemplary damages if they find
8   the assault was malicious, and that the amount thereof rested solely in the discretion of the jury, is proper, although the verdict might be reversed as excessive.

PLEADING AND PROOF. Under Code 1873, section 2729, which provides that a party shall not be compelled to prove more than is neces-
5   sary to entitle him to the relief asked, it is only necessary, in an action for assault, to prove that it was unlawful, although the petition alleged that it was wanton and malicious.

REQUESTING INSTRUCTIONS. In an action for malicious assault, failure, in an instruction, to define "malice," or to state that the
7 burden of, proving it is on plaintiff, is not error, where no such
instruction was asked by defendant.

Evidence: HARMLESS ERROR: In an action for damages resulting
from an assault, the exclusion, on cross-examination of plaintiff,
8 of evidence that plaintiff was suffering from the injury complained of before the alleged assault, is harmless error, where
such facts are subsequently testified to by other witnesses.

Witness: IMPEACHMENT. Plaintiff, in an action for malicious assault,
who testified on his cross-examin·tion that on the trial of a criminal case against defendant, growing out of the assault, he had
9 not refused to answer a question of defendant's attorney as to
whether he was ruptured at the time of the alleged assault, but
that an objection to the question was sustained, and that he does
not remember all the questions that were asked on the criminal
trial, cannot be impeached by reading the answers made by him
on such trial.

Appeal: OBJECTION BELOW. An objection by defendants in an action
for malicious assault, that they were not, from the allegation of
1 the petition, bound to anticipate a claim by plaintiff that he had
been injured in a certain manner, cannot be first taken on appeal.

Appeal from Johnson District Court.—HON. M. J. WADE,
Judge.

SATURDAY, DECEMBER 18, 1897.

ACTION at law for an alleged wanton and malicious
assault. Defendants denied the alleged assault, and
pleaded that whatever they did was in self-defense; and
other matters which might be considered in mitigation
of damages. Trial to a jury. Verdict and judgment for
plaintiff, and defendants appeal.—*Affirmed.*

Ranck & Bradley, G. A. Ewing, and *John W.
Slater* for appellants.

Remley & Ney and *Bailey & Murphy* for appellee.

DEEMER, J.—I. In his petition, plaintiff alleged
that he received serious and dangerous injuries, some

of which were permanent in their nature and character. He proved upon the trial, without objection, that he was ruptured in the assault made upon him by defendants.

Appellants contend that they were not bound to
1　　anticipate the claim of such injury from the averments of the petition, and that all evidence relating thereto was incompetent. They made no such objections in the lower court, and cannot present them here for the first time.

II. On cross-examination, plaintiff was asked as to certain statements (or, rather, as to the want of certain statements), made by him, as to the extent of his injuries, upon the trial of a criminal case, growing out of the assault. These questions followed, which were
2　　disposed of in the manner indicated: "Q. Did you, on that trial, when asked if you were injured, say that you were ruptured at the time of that occurrence? (Same objection. Sustained. Defendants except.) Q. What did you say? A. I started to answer your questions, and the attorney objected, and the court sustained the objection; so the question was not repeated to me. Q. Did you not refuse to answer? A. No, sir; it came about just as it did this time. You asked the question, and I was getting ready to answer you, and the attorneys objected. You asked me then if I refused to answer, and I said, 'No;' but the objection had been made, and the court sustained it." The witness further testified: "I cannot recollect all the questions, that way, that was asked me at the trial before 'Squire Dodder. I do not remember what was asked, and I do not remember what answer I made. I would tell you if I could think of it." The shorthand reporter who took down the evidence at that hearing was called as a witness for the defendants, and asked to read certain questions propounded to, and answers made by, Reizenstein. To this an objection was interposed, upon the ground that it was in no manner contradictory of

what he had said upon the witness stand in this trial, and the objection was sustained. Surely, there was no error in this. Appellants were granted all they were entitled to.

III.   Appellee was asked upon cross-examination if he had not stated to one Bradley, prior to the alleged assault, that he was ruptured, and also if he had not filed a petition before the city council, asking to be relieved from working poll tax, on account of physical

3
infirmity. Objections to these questions were sustained, and, as we think, erroneously. But we find, on turning to the record, that the witness answered in response to further interrogatories as follows: "I do not remember of ever having a conversation with Bradley, while he was a member of the city council, in 1893, with reference to getting poll tax remitted. I never made application to the city council to have my poll tax remitted. I do not know whether I was at the city council on the third day of July, 1893, or not." Whatever error there may have been was cured by the subsequent proceedings. Moreover, defendants proved by Bradley the statements made to him, and introduced evidence to the effect that appellee had presented to the city council the petition referred to; and the whole matter was again inquired about when plaintiff was placed upon the stand in rebuttal.

IV.   Apellants sought to show, upon cross-examination, that appellee had been assaulted at other times prior to the assault in question. They did not contend, however, that these assaults resulted in permanent injury, or that any of the disorders from which plaintiff

4
then claimed to be suffering were due to these prior assaults. The objections to the questions were properly sustained. *Lorig v. City of Davenport*, 99 Iowa, 479. Moreover, appellants were permitted to prove, as a part of their case, that appellee had

been assaulted on the two occasions referred to. And there was no prejudice in any event.

V. At the close of the introduction of appellee's evidence, appellants moved for a verdict on the ground that the assault was not a joint one. Their motion was overruled, and exception taken. We will not review the evidence bearing upon this question, and content ourselves by saying that there was no error in the ruling.

VI. The petition alleges that the assault was wantonly and maliciously committed, but the court did not charge that plaintiff must prove that it was so done, in order to recover. This is said to be error, and *Cottrell v. Piatt*, 101 Iowa, 231, is relied upon. That case does not go to the extent claimed. All that it holds is that plaintiff must prove that the assault was intentionally committed. It has never been held that the plaintiff 5 must prove that an assault made upon him was malicious, in order to recover. And the fact that the assault is charged to have been done maliciously does not change the rule, for the Code of 1873 (section 2729), provides that a party shall not be compelled to prove more than is necessary to entitle him to the relief asked. The trial court instructed that plaintiff must prove that the assault and battery was unlawfully made. This was sufficient.

VII. The court instructed that, if the jury found the assault was malicious, they might award exemplary damages (that is, a sum sufficient to show disapproval of the act, or as an example to deter others from doing likewise), and that the amount thereof, in case they should be awarded, rested solely in the discretion of the jury. Claim is made that the instruction is erroneous, because there was no evidence of malice, 6 and for the further reason that it is not true that the whole matter is left to the discretion of the jury. We think that there was sufficient evidence to justify the giving of the instruction, and that the instruction, as

given, is correct. It is true that we have said, in considering allowances made by juries in some cases, that this discretion is not unlimited,—which is, no doubt, true; but these statements were made when considering the question as to excessiveness of verdict, and had no reference to what should be embodied in an instruction given by a trial judge. The paragraph of the charge which is challenged is in accord with instructions approved by the almost universal voice of authority. *Goodenough v. McGrew,* 44 Iowa, 670; *Root v. Sturdivant,* 70 Iowa, 55. Further, it is contended that
7   the instruction does not define "malice," and that the burden of proving it was not placed upon the plaintiff. The instruction was correct so far as it went. If appellants desired more specific reference to the matter, they should have made request therefor. Again, it is said that it directs the jury to assess exemplary damages against both defendants if they found but one was actuated by malice. We do not think that this is a proper construction of the instruction. It certainly does not say so in express terms, and, when we look to the charge as a whole, we find that such a thought is clearly excluded. But, in any event, the charge, as applied to the facts of this case, was correct. The jury must have found, under the instructions, that
'   the assault was a joint one. If so, and if one of
8   the participants was actuated by malice, this condition of mind will be attributed to the other, and each held liable for all damages, both actual and exemplary, resulting from the assault. So the court instructed, and such is undoubtedly the law. *Turner v. Hitchcock,* 20 Iowa, 310; Sutherland, Damages (2d ed.), section 140.

VIII. In answer to special interrogatories, the jury found that Ezekiel Clark did not strike plaintiff at any time after his son, Earl, took hold of him; that

Ezekiel Clark directed his son, Earl Clark, to take plaintiff away; and that Ezekiel Clark and Earl Clark did not strike plaintiff at the same time. Counsel contend that the special findings are inconsistent with the general verdict, and that a new trial should have been granted. Assuming, as we must, that all these facts specially found by the jury are true, yet it does not follow that the general verdict is inconsistent with them.

9 The jury may very well have found that the defendants were jointly engaged or concerned in the assault, or that one aided or abetted the other therein, and such finding would not be inconsistent with the general verdict. It was not incumbent on plaintiff to show that either defendant expressly directed the other to make the assault, or that they struck him at the same moment of time, or that one struck him after the other. These were largely evidentiary, and not ultimate, facts, and are not controlling.

IX. Some other matters are discussed, but they are not of sufficient importance to demand separate consideration. We find no prejudicial error, and the judgment is AFFIRMED.

ENGELTHALER & HASEK V. LINN COUNTY, Appellant.

Mulct Law: REBATE. Under Acts Twenty-fifth General Assembly, chapter 62, section 7, providing that in case sales of intoxicating liquors have not continued for more than six months of the year for which the taxes are assessed, the total tax for the year may be reduced *pro rata*, the year referred to is the calendar year, and therefore it is immaterial that sales have not continued for more than six months before levy of the tax. If, therefore, a party sells liquors for more than six months of the calendar year 1895, and a mulct tax is levied on him at the September meeting of that year, he can have no rebate from the payment of six hundred dollars for the year 1895.

SAME Acts Twenty-fifth General Assembly, chapter 62, section 9, providing that if a tax for selling intoxicating liquors on premises be not levied at the September meeting of the board of supervisors,

It shall be levied for a *pro rata* amount of tax for the remainder of the year, does not authorize the board to levy a *pro rata* tax at a September meeting.

Appeal from Linn District Court.—HON. WILLIAM G. THOMPSON, Judge.

SATURDAY, DECEMBER 18, 1897.

APPLICATION for rebate of tax levied under the provisions of what is known as the "Mulct Law." A tax of six hundred dollars was levied by the board of supervisors of Linn county at its regular September meeting against the plaintiff and the property in which they were doing business. At the time of the levy, plaintiffs had on file a petition for the rebate of the tax for the months of January, February, and March. The board denied the petition, but, upon appeal to the district court, it was sustained, and the county appeals.— *Reversed.*

J. M. Grimm, county attorney, and *J. H. Rothrock, Jr.,* for appellant.

Heins & Heins for appellees.

DEEMER, J.—From the agreed statement of facts upon which the case was tried in the district court, we find that appellees sold no liquors in the county of Linn in the year 1895, prior to the month of April. They commenced to sell on the first day of that month, and continued in business down to the time of the trial in the district court. On this record the trial court held that the year referred to in the Acts of the Twenty-fifth General Assembly, chapter 62, relating to sales of intoxicating liquor, commenced, in so far as these appellees are concerned, on the first day of April, and that they were entitled to a rebate of one hundred and fifty dollars. It is from this order that the appeal is taken.

In the case of *David v. Hardin County*, 104 Iowa, 204, we held that the word "year," as used in the acts of the general assembly under consideration, meant "calendar year," and that, when the assessment was made at other than the regular September meeting of the board, it should be *pro rata* of the annual levy "dependent upon the time of the assessment." This case not only involves a determination of what is meant by the word "year," but also a construction of sections 7 and 17 of chapter 62, Acts Twenty-fifth General Assembly. We have set out the substance of these sections in the opinion just referred to, and need not repeat them here. With reference to section 17, it need only be said that it relates to the time of payment of the tax, and to what it is necessary to do in order that such payment may constitute a bar to proceedings for violation of the general statutes prohibiting the traffic in intoxicating liquors. We may also observe that the case of *Clark v. Riddle*, 101 Iowa, 270, wherein we held that section 17 did not apply to cities acting under special charters; and the act passed at the recent special session of the legislature, and known as chapter 7, Acts Twenty-sixth General Assembly (Ex. Sess.), which undertook to legalize all sales made in cities acting under special charters, and all proceedings with reference thereto, have no bearing upon the question now before us. The whole matter is solved by a construction of section 7, which says, in effect, that, if it should be found on appeal that sales of intoxicating liquor had not continued for more than six months in the year for which the taxes were assessed, then the total tax for the year may be reduced *pro rata*. It is conceded that appellees sold liquor for more than six months of the year 1895. There can, therefore, be no remission under section 7. Claim is made, however, that section 9 applies, and that appellees should pay no more than four hundred and fifty dollars. It is manifest, however,

that the latter part of this section, being the part upon
which appellees rely, has no application to this case, for
the reason that it has reference to levies made at other
than the September meeting. We are of opinion
2   that the year referred to in this so-called "Mulct
Law" is the calendar year; that appellees are not
entitled to the rebate claimed, for the reason that they
had continued their sales for more than six months of
the year for which the taxes were assessed; and that the
latter part of section 9 has no application, for the reason
that the taxes were levied at the regular September
meeting of the board.—REVERSED.

JAMES W. ROBINSON AND MARGARET J. ROBINSON, Appellants, v. C. A. CHARLETON.

Homestead: ABANDONMENT. The formation of a purpose by the
    owner of a homestead to sell the land and invest the proceeds in
5   another home, does not operate as an abandonment of the home-
    stead, under code, section 2000, permitting the owner to do so,
    and also entitling him to a reasonable time within which to
    accomplish such object.

RULE APPLIED. In an action to set aside a sheriff's sale on the
    ground that the land sold was a homestead and exempt, the evi-
    dence showed that plaintiff purchased the land in 1887, and
    occupied it as a home until December 10, 1890, when he moved to
    another place to educate his children, intending to return to the
2   homestead, which intention he retained until the death of his son,
    in September, 1893. Thereafter, he thought it desirable to sell the
    homestead and invest the proceeds in another home, though it
    is doubtful whether this conclusion was reached before or after
    the sheriff's sale, December 29, 1893. Held, that under Code, sec-
    tion 2000, plaintiff was entitled to a reasonable time, after con-
    cluding to sell the homestead, to accomplish it, and that in this
    case such reasonable time had not elapsed, and the sheriff's sale
    was void.

SAME   That the owner of a farm, which has been occupied as a
3   homestead, talked about exchanging the farm, or said he was not
    built for farming, or told what he considered the land worth, does -
    not of itself show a purpose to abandon the homestead.

SAME. The mere fact that the owner of a homestead, who is tem-
4 porarily absent therefrom, with the intention of returning, votes
at the place where he temporarily resides, is not of itself conclusive of an intention to abandon the homestead, though it is strong
evidence of abandonment.

BURDEN OF PROOF. The burden of showing the abandonment of a
homestead after the homestead character has once been estab-
1 lished, rests upon one who seeks to subject the land to a judgment in his favor, and where the debt for which the judgment is
rendered is contracted while the land was occupied as a homestead, so that no credit was extended on the faith of its being subject to the payment of debts, the evidence of abandonment should
be more satisfactory.

Appeal from Pocahontas District Court.—HON. W. B.
QUARTON, Judge.

SATURDAY, DECEMBER 18, 1897.

ACTION to set aside sheriff's sale and deed on the
ground that the land sold contained a homestead exempt
to the judgment debtor. Relief denied, and plaintiffs
appeal.—*Reversed.*

J. A. O. Yeoman, R. M. Wright, and *S. H. Kerr*
for appellants.

No appearance for appellee.

LADD, J.—Execution was issued November 25, 1893,
on a judgment for twenty-two dollars and sixty cents,
with costs and interest, against James W. Robinson,
and levied on eighty acres of land in Pocahontas county.
This land was sold as an entirety for fifty dollars and
five cents, December 29, 1893, and a sheriff's deed executed therefor a year later to Charleton, the judgment
plaintiff. There was a mortgage which, with interest
and taxes, amounted to nearly eight hundred dollars,
constituting a prior lien. At the time of the sale the
land was worth twenty-seven dollars and fifty cents per

acre. Robinson did not learn of the levy and sale till several days after the execution of the sheriff's deed. This action is brought to set aside the sale and deed because the land sold contained the homestead of the plaintiffs, which was not in any way platted or set apart to them. The defendant answered that the plaintiffs had abandoned their homestead interest in the land. Other issues are raised by the pleadings, but, owing to the view we take of the case, need not be con-

1   sidered. Robinson purchased the land in 1887, and occupied it, with his family, as a home, from April, 1888, till December 10, 1890. The homestead character of the land having been thus established, the burden of proof was on the defendant to show its abandonment. *Bank v. Baker*, 57 Iowa, 197; *Bradshaw v. Hurst*, 57 Iowa, 745; *Boot v. Brewster*, 75 Iowa, 631. And, as the debt was contracted while the land was occupied as a homestead, more satisfactory evidence of its abandonment is required than if credit had been extended on the faith that it was subject to the payment of debts. *Davis v. Kelley*, 14 Iowa, 523. The period of absence is important, but not con-

2   clusive. *Dunton v. Woodbury*, 24 Iowa, 74. The evidence shows that the plaintiffs moved to Humboldt for the purpose of educating their children, and intended, as soon as this was accomplished, to return to the farm. The stock was sold, but the implements were retained for some time, and finally disposed of because nothing could be obtained for their use. A harrow, corn cultivator, and plow were kept and the last repaired in the summer of 1893, with a view of using it the following spring. Robinson repeatedly refused to sell or exchange the land, giving as a reason that he expected to move on it again. He declined to rent it for more than one year, because he expected to return. The family arranged to do so in the spring of 1894, when the

son was to perform the farm work, and Robinson continue in his employment as traveling salesman.   No
other home was purchased.   Both Robinson and his
wife testify to their intention of moving back to the
farm, and that this was their abiding purpose from the
time they went to Humboldt, in 1890, to the date of their
son's death, in September, 1893, is fully established by
the evidence.   The testimony of alleged statements and
admissions either relate to a time subsequent to the sale,
or else is discredited or overcome by the weight of
3   evidence.   That Robinson talked about exchange
of property with those proposing a trade, or
said he was not built for farming, or stated what he
considered the land worth, if true, does not establish his
purpose of abandoning it, when considered in the light
of the surrounding circumstances.   He voted in
4   Humboldt in 1891 and this is a very strong
circumstance tending to show a permanent
change of residence.   He explains it, however, by saying
he supposed one might vote "where he resided temporarily and got his washing done."   This erroneous impression is quite common, and we cannot regard the mere
fact of voting in a precinct other than that of the homestead conclusive of an intention to abandon it.   The
point was not decided in *Painter v. Steffen*, 87 Iowa, 171,
and was not regarded controlling in *Conway v. Nichols**
(Iowa) (71 N. W. Rep. 183).   While, as a general rule, a
man will be·presumed to reside where he exercises the
right of suffrage, this is subject to such explanations as
will show the real intention of the party in removing
from the former residence, whether *animo revertendi*.
See *Dennis v. Bank*, 19 Neb. 675 (28 N. W. Rep. 512).
After the son's death Mrs. Robinson went to the eastern
part of the state, where she remained over two months,
and not until her return was the purpose of moving

*Decided May 14, 1897, and held out on rehearing. —Reporter.

back to this land ever questioned in the family. It was
then thought desirable to have a home near Humboldt,
though the evidence leaves it in doubt whether
5   this conclusinon was reached before or after the
sale under the execution. The purpose was to
sell, and invest the proceeds in another home; and they
not only had the right to do this, but were entitled to a
reasonable time within which to accomplish their object.
Code, section 2000; *Benham v. Chamberlain*, 39 Iowa,
358; *Cowgell v. Warrington*, 66 Iowa, 666; *Mann v. Corrington*, 93 Iowa, 109; *Schuttloffel v. Collins*, 98 Iowa,
576. What will be a reasonable time must depend on
the facts of each particular case. If it be conceded that
Robinson had concluded to sell and buy another home,
the time to which he was entitled, in order to do so, had
not elapsed. When the sale occurred, the land included
the homestead of the plaintiffs, and must be adjudged
void; *Linscott v. Lamart*, 46 Iowa, 312; *Goodrich v.
Brown*, 63 Iowa, 247; *Visek v. Doolittle*, 69 Iowa, 602;
and, being void, the intention of the plaintiffs thereafter is not material.—REVERSED.

REPORTS

OF

CASES AT LAW AND IN EQUITY

DETERMINED BY THE

SUPREME COURT

OF

THE STATE OF IOWA

AT

DES MOINES, JANUARY TERM, A. D. 1898,

AND IN THE FIFTY-SECOND YEAR OF THE STATE.

DANIEL COOPER, Appellant, v. C. M. MOHLER, Intervener.

Foreclosure: OWNER OF ONE NOTE: *Protection of.* A land owner
agreed that if an agent for wire fencing should furnish him a
purchaser for his land at a certain price, he would purchase a
2 fence from the agent. The purchaser was obtained, and an
agreement was made for building the fence, and one of the notes
for the price of the land was for the exact contract price of the
fence. The notes were all secured by a mortgage on the land.
Held, that a decree was justified, finding the agent to be the owner
of the note given for the price of the fence, and entitled to the
protection of said mortgage.

Intervention: MORTGAGE NOTES. The holder of one of several notes
secured by the same mortgage, which is entitled to a priority over
1 the other notes, is entitled to intervene in an action for the foreclosure of a mortgage, under Code 1873, section 2683.

(301)

*Appeal from Carroll District Court.—*HON. S. M. ELWOOD, Judge.

TUESDAY, JANUARY 18, 1898.

ACTION in equity against John Wasmund to recover the amount of certain promissory notes, for the foreclosure of a mortgage given to secure their payment, and for other relief. C. M. Mohler intervened, claiming to be the owner of one of the notes which the mortgage was given to secure, and demanded judgment for the amount due thereon, and asked that it be decreed a first lien upon the mortgaged premises. There was a hearing on the merits, and a decree in favor of the intervener, as prayed. The plaintiff appeals.—*Affirmed.*

M. W. Beach and *F. M. Powers* for appellant.

George W. Bowen for appellee.

ROBINSON, J.—In December, 1893, the plaintiff was the owner of two hundred and twenty acres of land, upon which the mortgage in controversy was afterwards given; and the intervener was engaged in the business of selling woven wire fence. He attempted to sell to the plaintiff fences for the land, but was told by the latter that he preferred to sell his farm for thirty-five dollars per acre. The intervener told him that he could sell the farm for forty dollars per acre if it were fenced. The plaintiff then said that he would have the fence built if the intervener would secure a purchaser for it at the price last named. The intervener undertook to furnish such a purchaser, and in the latter part of January, 1894, went to Cooper with the defendant, Wasmund, and a sale of the farm to him at forty dollars per acre was effected, and an agreement was made for building the fence. The contract price of the fence to be built was six hundred and fifty-one dollars. A note for that amount was made by Wasmund to the plaintiff, with other notes, and a mortgage to secure all of the notes thus given was executed by Wasmund. The fence was afterwards constructed, and the note given for the contract price therefor was surrendered to Wasmund, although he did not pay anything for it. The right of the plaintiff to the relief he demands against Wasmund does not appear to be questioned, and is not involved in this appeal.

I. The plaintiff demurred to the petition of intervention, but his demurrer was overruled. He now insists that it should have been sustained, for the alleged reason that the petition did not show

1   sufficient grounds upon which to intervene. We do not think the claim thus made is well founded. The petition alleged that the intervener was the owner of one of the notes secured by the mortgage which the plaintiff was attempting to foreclose, and that it was the first note thus secured to become due. It thus appeared that the intervener had a direct interest in the mortgage, and in having determined the priority of the various claims which it secured, and it is the policy of the law to permit conflicting claims of priority growing out of a single mortgage to be settled in one action. The authority to have that done by means of proceedings by intervention is ample. Code 1873, section 2683; *Taylor v. Adair*, 22 Iowa, 279; *Dyer v. Harris*, 22 Iowa, 268. We are of the opinion that the demurrer was properly overruled.

II. The intervener and Wasmund are brothers-in-law, and it is the theory of the plaintiff that Wasmund was to pay the intervener for the fence, and that the note in controversy was given to secure the building of the fence. There is some testimony which tends

2   to support that theory, but there are some facts, which are not seriously disputed, which, with other evidence for the intervener, satisfy us that the

theory is not correct, and that the note was to become the property of the intervener when he should have built the fence. The plaintiff was willing to sell his farm for thirty-five dollars per acre, and agreed to have the fence constructed if he could sell the farm for forty dollars per acre. The intervener found a purchaser at that price, and agreed to construct the fence. The sale was effected, and notes given for the purchase price, on the basis of forty dollars per acre for the farm. The fence was not to be constructed until later in the year, and, if the theory of the plaintiff be correct, there could not have been any object accomplished by giving him the fence note. If the purchaser was to pay the intervener for the fence in any other manner than by paying the note, the reasonable and direct method of accomplishing what was designed, so far as the plaintiff was concerned, would have been to deduct the price of the fence from the price of the farm, and accept the notes only for the remainder due. The only reasonable purpose to be accomplished by giving the fence note to the plaintiff was to have the price of the fence secured by the mortgage. There was no occasion to secure the plaintiff for the cost of the fence, if he was not under any obligation to pay the intervener for it. It is probable that the note was surrendered to Wasmund in consequence of some mistake. He was to pay for the fence it is true, as some of the witnesses for the plaintiff state; but he was to do so by paying the fence note, and that he has not done. We are well satisfied that the fence note belonged to the intervener when he completed the fence, and that it should have been delivered to him by the plaintiff. The decree of the district court effects justice, and is sustained by the evidence. It is therefore AFFIRMED.

State of Iowa v. Victor Repp, Appellant.

Bees: larceny. A trespasser, who finds bees on the land of another, and hives them, but is not the owner of the hive in which he puts them, has no interest in them which is the subject of larceny.

Same. The mere finding of bees in a tree on the land of another person gives the finder no right to the bees or to the tree.

Appeal from Monroe District Court.—Hon. Frank W. Eichelberger, Judge.

Tuesday, January 18, 1898.

The defendant was convicted of the larceny of a swarm of bees, and from the judgment, imposing a fine of five dollars, he appeals.—*Reversed.*

T. B. Perry for appellant.

Milton Remley, attorney general, and *Jesse A. Miller* for the state.

Ladd, J.—In July, 1895, Stevens found a bee tree on the land of Cody, and, without the latter's permission, chopped it down, and put the bees in a gum obtained from Mosely. These were left near the fallen tree, on Cody's land. The gum was cut from a tree on defendant's land, without his knowledge or consent; and finding it, with the bees, where left by Stevens, he removed them, at dusk of day, to the orchard of his mother, and inclosed them in a telescope gum, about thirty-three inches square, nailed to that procured from Mosely. This was unknown to the mother, whose residence was about one mile from the bee tree, while that of the defendant was three miles further away. It does not appear that the defendant knew who hived the bees, or

that Stevens was aware that Mosely was not owner of
the gum. When Stevens discovered the bees, after several days' search, the defendant refused to do more than
return them, and after some parley this prosecution
was begun.

Wild game is under the control of the state, and only
becomes the subject of private ownership when
reclaimed by the art and industry of man. A somewhat
different rule applies to bees, though *ferae naturae*.
These have a local habitation. Blackstone states: "It
hath also been said that with us the only ownership in
bees is *ratione soli;* and the charter of the forest, which
allows every freeman to be entitled to the honey found
within his own woods, affords great countenance to this
doctrine that a qualified property may be had in bees,
in consideration of the property of the soil whereon they
are found." The same rule is laid down in Cooley on
Torts, 435, where it is said that bees "have a local habitation, more often in a tree than elsewhere, and while there
may be said to be within control, because the tree may
at any time be felled. But the right to cut it is in the
owner of the soil, and, therefore, such property as the
wild bees are susceptible of is in him, also." And it has
been so adjudged in *Ferguson v. Miller*, 13 Am. Dec. 519,
and *Rexroth v. Coon*, 15 R. I. 35 (23 Atl. Rep. 37), (2 Am.
State Rep. 863). By the law of nature, the person who
hived the swarm would be entitled to it; but, under the
regulation of property rights, since the institution of
civil society, the forest, as well as the cultivated field,
belongs to the owner thereof, and he who invades it is a
trespasser. *Goff v. Kilts*, 15 Wend. 550. See *Adams v.
Burton*, 43 Vt. 36. The mere finding of bees on the land
of Cody gave Stevens no right to them, or to the tree.
Merrils v. Goodwin, 1 Root, 209; *Gillet v. Mason*, 7
Johns. 16. In cutting down the tree and taking the
bees, he was a wrongdoer. Had he acted with the
license of Cody, he might have acquired ownership, but

he could obtain no title by his wrongful acts as a mere trespasser. *Rexroth v. Coon, supra.* In that case the plaintiff had placed a box in the crotch of the tree belonging to Green, without permission, and later the defendant, without the consent of either, took the box from the tree, emptied it of bees and honey, and then replaced it. In holding that the plaintiff was not entitled to recover, the court said: "The plaintiff was a tres· passer upon the land of Green. He had no right to place the box or hive in the tree, and by placing it there he acquired no title to the bees which subsequently occupied it, or to the honey which they produced." No better title would be acquired by removing the bees from the tree top to a box on the land, than by luring them to a box placed in a tree top. Title to a thing *ferae naturae* cannot be created by the act of one who at the moment is a trespasser, and Stevens obtained no inter· est in the bees by the mere wrongful transfer from the tree to the gum. He neither owned the land on which he left them, nor the gum in which they were hived. Having neither title nor possession, he had no interest therein, the subject of larceny. As the information alleged ownership in Stevens, and the case was tried on that theory, we need make no inquiry as to any taking from Cody. But see *Wallis v. Mease,* 3 Bin. 546.— REVERSED.

THE FRED MILLER BREWING COMPANY, Appellant, v. HARRY O. HANSEN, JOHN WESTFIELD, and J. O'DONOVAN ROSSA.

Judgment: ASSIGNMENT. An assignee of a judgment acquires no greater rights as against the judgment debtor than his assignor has.

Appeal: TRIAL DE NOVO. The record as set out in the abstract con· tained a stipulation that affidavits filed on a motion to dissolve a temporary injunction should be taken as the testimony of affiants. Following it was a statement that the cause came on for trial on

the evidence, "as shown by this abstract, "which contained all the
evidence offered, all of which evidence was certified by the judge
and filed, and made a part of the record. Then followed what
purported to be evidence, and after it a statement that the trial
judge duly certified the same to be all the evidence offered at the
trial. The abstract then recited that it contained all the evidence
offered, but no affidavits, as such, or purporting to be testimony
or depositions of affiants, appear in the abstract. *Held*, sufficient
to present the case for trial *de novo*.

OBJECTION BELOW. The objection that no answer was filed to an
2   amendment to a petition cannot be raised on appeal where the
case was tried in the lower court as if such answer had been filed.

Appeal from Woodbury District Court.—HON. JOHN F.
OLIVER, Judge.

TUESDAY, JANUARY 18, 1898.

SUIT in equity to enjoin the collection of, and to set
aside, a judgment. From a decree dismissing plaintiff's
petition, it appeals.—*Reversed.*

· *T. F. Griffin* for appellant.

J. O'Donovan Rossa for appellees.

DEEMER, C. J.—I. This suit was brought to enjoin
the defendant from collecting a certain judgment which
had previously been rendered against appellant, in justice court, upon a counter-claim interposed by appellee
Hansen to a suit brought by appellant, for the collection
of a bill alleged to be due it on account for liquor sold
and delivered. In the main suit, appellant sued out a
writ of attachment, and garnished one Nead, who was
then owing Hansen the sum of forty-seven dollars.
Appellee filed a counter-claim, upon which he recovered
judgment; and, by reason of some mistake or misunderstanding, appellant's counsel did not appear at the trial
before the justice. Appellant immediately took the
necessary steps for taking an appeal from the judgment

of the justice of the peace; and it claims that, before perfecting it, it entered into an agreement with Hansen to the effect that it should release the garnishee, and permit him to pay the money to Hansen, and Hansen should, in turn, satisfy and release the judgment he had obtained upon his counter-claim, and thereupon appellant should dismiss his appeal. Appellant further contends that it complied with its part of the agreement, but that Hansen neglected to satisfy the judgment, and, disregarding his agreement, assigned the same to appellee Rossa, who was proceeding to enforce it when this action was commenced.

Appellees contend that we cannot consider the case upon its merits, for the reason that we do not have all the evidence offered in the court below. The abstract contains a certificate that we have all the evidence given, offered, or submitted upon the trial, and there is no denial, except in argument. Ordinarily, this would not be held sufficient. But counsel contends that the abstract shows affirmatively that the evidence is not all before us. The record contains the following: "Stipulation. It is agreed that the affidavits which have been filed in support of the motion to dissolve the temporary injunction, and those filed in resistance of the motion, may be taken and considered as the testimony of the witnesses and the depositions of the affiants, and the case now be heard, and finally, on the evidence now introduced and that contained in those affidavits." Following this is a statement that "this cause came on for hearing and trial upon the pleadings and evidence therein adduced and submitted, as shown by this abstract, which contains all the evidence offered, produced, or submitted, or offered to be given or submitted, by either plaintiff or defendants, upon the trial of said cause, all of which evidence was duly certified by the trial judge, John F. Oliver, on April 28, 1896, and on March 1, 1896, was duly filed in the Woodbury district court, and made a part of the records thereof." Then follows what purports to be evidence, and after this is a statement that the trial judge duly certified the same to be all the evidence offered, given, or introduced upon the trial. And the abstract then recites that it contains all the evidence given, offered, or submitted upon the trial. Surely, this is sufficient to present the case for trial *de novo*. It may be · the affidavits were not offered upon trial; or, if they were offered, the stipulation says that they should be treated as the testimony and depositions of the affiants. The abstract contains the testimony of various witnesses, and we must presume, in the absence of a showing to the contrary, that it includes the contents of the affidavits referred to in the stipulation.

II. Appellant filed an amendment to its petition, pleading an estoppel by reason of some statements of appellees' attorneys, and setting forth at more length the terms of the alleged agreement of settlement.

2 No answer seems to have been filed to this amendment. The case was tried in the lower court as if an answer had been filed, and will be so regarded here. Appellant cannot raise the question of failure to answer for the first time, in this court.

III. The trial court denied the relief asked, on the theory that appellant had failed to establish the agreement relied upon. In this we think there was error. The decided preponderance of the evidence is in favor of apellant's claim. Hansen received the money by virtue of the agreement, and should have satisfied the judgment, instead of assigning it to Rossa. The conceded facts tend strongly to confirm appellant's contention, and it produced at least three witnesses to testify to the making of the agreement. As against this we

3 have nothing but the denial of Hansen. Rossa gained no greater rights by reason of the assignment than his assignor, Hansen, had at the time of the

assignment. *Burtis v. Cook*, 16 Iowa, 194; *Balinger v. Tarbell*, 16 Iowa, 491. The judgment of the district court is reversed, and the cause is remanded for a decree in harmony with this opinion.— REVERSED.

THE BOSTON INVESTMENT COMPANY, Appellee, v. THE PACIFIC SHORT LINE BRIDGE COMPANY, THE MIS-SOURI RIVER BRIDGE COMPANY, THE MANHATTAN TRUST COMPANY, Defendants and Appellees, SOOY-SMITH & COMPANY, J. A. L. WADELL, Defendants and Cross-petitioners, Appellees, E. H. HUBBARD AND H. J. TAYLOR, Receivers in this Cause, Appel-lee, THE CREDITS COMMUTATION COMPANY AND C. L. WRIGHT, Defendants in Intervention, and Appel-lees, E. H. HUBBARD, Assignee of THE UNION LOAN AND TRUST COMPANY, Intervener, Appellee, W. H GOODWIN, Intervener and Appellant.

Receivers: WHEN APPOINTED. Under McClain's Code, section 4118, which provides that a receiver may be appointed on petition of a 1 person holding an interest in property which is in danger of being lost or impaired, a court can appoint a receiver of an insolvent corporation (all creditors, most of whom have liens, consenting, 8 except one), which corporation was organized to build a bridge, in which the public was largely interested, under a charter granted by congress, where the property consisted of two com-pleted and one incompleted piers and some real estate connected with the bridge all of which would be of little value without the franchise, which would be forfeited in less than a year unless the bridge was completed.

SAME. The court will not decline to appoint receivers and direct the 1 sale of the property and franchises of a corporation organized to construct a public bridge, pending suit by a creditor to set aside a 2 conveyance thereby, upon the intervention of an officer of the corporation, who prefers a claim for salary and advances, more 8 than two years after the commencement of the suit, where an early sale is imperative to save the franchises from forfeiture for noncompletion of the bridge.

SAME. An order of sale of property in the hands of the receivers 7 cannot be said to be in effect a foreclosure of a trust deed on the property, where it has no other effect than to bring the proceeds of the sale into court, instead of the property.

SAME. That the sheriff is in possession, under plaintiff's execution,
of the property involved in a suit to set aside a conveyance of
1   property and franchises, does not prevent the appointment of a
4   receiver to sell the property, pending the action, where it is in
danger of being lost or destroyed. He could not avoid a forfeiture, and need not be made a party.

EVIDENCE. Findings by the court, in an order appointing receivers of
an insolvent bridge corporation's property, that the property is
3   without care and abandoned and going to waste, are supported by
evidence that the property has been in the hands of the sheriff for
about two years and the work on the property has ceased during
all that time.

SAME. An objection that no evidence was introduced to support the
finding upon which an order appointing receivers was made,
5   cannot be sustained when the pleadings show facts to sustain
the findings, and the order was based upon facts admitted in
open court by all the parties to the action, and made with their
consent.

SAME It was not error for the court to order a sale of the property
immediately on the appointment and qualification of the receivers
7   and upon their application, where the property was an uncompleted bridge, which would be, when completed, a public benefit,
and the franchise to build same was about to expire.

*Appeal from Woodbury District Court.—*HON. F. R.
GAYNOR, Judge.

TUESDAY, JANUARY 18, 1898.

ACTION in equity to set aside a certain deed of conveyance, and to determine the amount and order of
priority of the claims of creditors of the Pacific Short-
Line Bridge Company who are parties to this action.
Pending the action, an order was made appointing E. H.
Hubbard and H. J. Taylor joint receivers of the property and franchises of the Pacific Short-Line Company,
and thereafter a further order was made, upon their
application, for the sale of said franchises and property.
Thereupon W. H. Goodwin intervened in the action,
setting up his claim to a lien upon certain parts of said
property, and moved the court to restrain the receivers
from executing said order of sale, which motion was

overruled. Said Goodwin then filed his exceptions to the appointment of said receiver, and to the order of sale and report of sale, which exceptions were overruled, and the report of the receivers of the sale made by them was confirmed. Intervener, Goodwin, appeals from the overruling of his said motion and exceptions.— *Affirmed.*

Kean & Sherman for appellant.

Spaulding, Taylor & Burgess and *Wright, Hubbard & Bevington* for appellees.

GIVEN, J.—I. Owing to the number of the parties, and the nature of their respective claims, the pleadings are necessarily lengthy and complicated, but as the questions presented on this appeal are simply whether the court erred in appointing the receivers, and in ordering a sale of the property, and in the confimation of said sale, the following will be a sufficient statement of the cases for the purpose of these questions: The Pacific Short-Line Bridge Company was incorporated under the laws of Iowa, to build a combination railroad, wagon, and foot bridge across the Missouri river, at Sioux City, Iowa, under an act of congress granting it a charter so to do, which required the bridge to be completed on or before March 1, 1896. This company

1   acquired certain franchises from the city of Sioux City, in certain of the city's streets, for the purpose of approach to said bridge. It also acquired, for the same purpose, certain real estate. Said company executed a deed of trust to the Manhattan Trust Company, as trustee, on all its franchises and property, to secure its issue of bonds in the sum of one million five hundred thousand dollars, five hundred thousand dollars of which were certified by trustees and issued by said company. Said company entered into

contracts for plans, specifications, materials, and labor
for the construction of said bridge, and the construction
thereof was proceeded with thereunder, and said company became largely indebted therefor. This company,
being unable financially to continue the work of constructing said bridge, did, on the sixth day of April,
1893, for the consideration of one dollar, execute a deed
of conveyance of all its property and franchises to the
Missouri River Bridge Company, a corporation organized under the laws of Iowa. The plaintiff, the Boston
Investment Company, having theretofore obtained
judgment against the Pacific Short-Line Bridge Company, caused an execution to issue thereon on April 27,
1893, and to be levied on all property and franchises of
said company, whereupon all further work on the bridge
was suspended. On the same day, plaintiff brought this
action to set aside said deed of conveyance, and to subject said property to its execution. On May 13, 1893,
the court, on an application of the parties, granted an
order restraining the sheriff from selling under said
execution until the further order of the court, to the end,
evidently, that the priority of the several liens against
said property might first be ascertained. In the course
of the further proceedings, the other persons named
above as parties, except intervener, Goodwin, became
such to this action by the consolidation of their actions
herewith, or by intervention, and issues were joined
upon their respective pleadings.

On October 19, 1893, the plaintiff applied for the
appointment of a receiver, which application was set
down for hearing on October 24, following, but does not
appear to have been heard at that time. Thereafter
the defendants Sooysmith & Co., and E. H. Hubbard,
assignee, joined in asking the appointment of a receiver;
and on the twenty-seventh day of May, 1895, after all
the parties above named, except appellant, Goodwin,
had become parties to this action, the court, with their

consent, and upon the pleadings and agreements, orally
made in open court as to the facts, appointed H. J.
Taylor and E. H. Hubbard joint receivers of all said
property and franchises.   The court found that both of
said bridge companies were insolvent; that the property
was incapable of division, and should be treated as an
entirety; that it was without care; that attachments
and executions had been levied upon it; that the value
of the franchises was being lost by delay; that the
property had been abandoned by the corporations, and
was going to waste; that the charters would expire
March 1, 1896, if the bridge was not built; that the
claims of these parties required immediate protection;
and that a receiver was necessary to prevent loss and
injury.   On the twenty-seventh day of May, 1895, said
receivers, having qualified, applied for an order to sell
said property, on the ground that the two completed
piers, the one incomplete pier, and the materials on
hand were exposed to loss; that the franchises would
be forfeited unless the work was completed by the time
provided; and that, if a sale could be made, the bridge
could be completed within said time.   On the same day,
and with the consent of the then parties to this action,
the order for the sale of said property in Woodbury
county, state of Iowa, was made, the sale to be made on
the tenth day of June, 1895.

   On the eighth day of June, 1895, appellant, W. H.
Goodwin, filed his petition of intervention, claiming of
the Pacific Short-Line Bridge Company five thousand,
two hundred and thirty-five dollars, three
hundred dollars of which was for money
advanced by him for said company upon
a contract for right of way, the balance being
for unpaid salary as vice president of said company.   His petition shows that a corporation known as
the Nebraska Terminal Railway & Elevator Company
was organized under the laws of Nebraska, to purchase

certain property in Dakota county, Nebraska, necessary
to the construction of the bridge; that mortgages were
given for part of the purchase money, which were foreclosed, and the property sold; and that intervener, with
money furnished by the Pacific Short-Line Bridge Company, took assignments of the certificates of sale to himself, and thereafter received sheriff's deeds in his own
name to said property. He claims that he is entitled
to hold said Nebraska property as a mortgage to secure
the indebtedness to him for said three hundred dollars
advanced and for said balance of salary. Intervener
alleges that he executed a conveyance in blank for said
property, and deposited it with a statement of his
account with one C. L. Wright, an officer of said bridge
company, said conveyance to be used when intervener's
claim was settled; that said conveyance is still in the
hands of said Wright, the claim unsettled; and that he
has forbidden said Wright to make any use of said conveyance. Intervener then, after reciting the matters
already sufficiently stated, alleges that the decree
appointing said receivers was without jurisdiction and
erroneous, for numerous reasons that will hereafter be
noticed. He states as his only reason for delaying his
intervention that he had been negotiating with the
principal parties hereto with reference to an adjustment
of his claim, and that the negotiations were only terminated on the afternoon of June 8, 1895, by their refusal
to recognize his claim. With his petition appellant filed
his motion to restrain the receivers from executing said
order of sale, which motion was overruled, "except as to
the property situated in Dakota county, in the state of
Nebraska," being the same upon which intervener
claims a lien. The receivers having sold the property
other than that in Dakota county, Neb., intervener filed
his exceptions to the approval of said sale, upon several
grounds that will be hereafter noticed. These exceptions were overruled, and an order was made approving

the sale and ordering a conveyance of the property. Invervener, appellant, makes eighteen assignments of error, based upon the overrulings of his said motion and exceptions.

II. Appellant's first contention is that the pleadings do not show that the property, or the lands, income, and profits thereof, are in danger of being lost or destroyed. As we view the pleadings, they do
3   show that this property was in danger of being lost. Without the franchises, the two completed and one incomplete piers, as well as the material accumulated and the real estate purchased, would be of little value. The enterprise was one in which the public was concerned. If the property were left to remain as it was, a forfeiture of the franchises would follow, the value of the whole, as a unit, be largely depreciated, and the public deprived of the advantages that were to be gained from the construction of the bridge. To place this property in the hands of a receiver, and cause it to be sold, so that the enterprise might be carried to completion, was to prevent the loss that otherwise would occur. Most, if not all, these creditors, had liens upon the property, and were therefore entitled to ask for the appointment of a receiver.

It is urged that, the property being in the possession of the sheriff, a receiver was not necessary to the care of the property, and that the sheriff was a necessary
4   party to the making of the order. The care that the sheriff could bestow would not prevent the loss that would follow the forfeiture of the franchises, and his possession was not so adverse to the claims of the plaintiff and other lien-holders who asked the appointment of the receiver as to render him a necessary party to that application.

It is further contended that the order appointing the receivers is void, because the findings therein are

insufficient to support the appointment, especially the
findings that the property is without care, and
5   that it has been abandoned by the corporations,
and is going to waste. The care that this property required was that the work should be proceeded
with, and certainly the corporation had abandoned the
enterprise, and therefore the property was without the
care needed for its preservation.

It is also contended that there was no evidence
introduced to support the findings upon which the order
was made. The pleadings alone show facts sus-
6   taining the findings, and, as we have seen, the
order was based upon facts admitted in open
court by all the then parties to the action, and made
with their consent.

Appellant also contends that, for these reasons, the
order for the sale of the property was unauthorized. It
is insisted that the order is, in effect, a foreclosure of
the deed of trust, but we think not. It has no
7   other effect than to bring the proceeds of the
sale into court, instead of the property, and to
render it possible, at least, that the construction of the
bridge might go forward to completion.

Under the pressing necessities of the case, it was
not error for the court to order the sale immediately
upon the appointment and qualification of the receivers,
and upon their application.

All the errors assigned may be summed up as presenting the questions whether, under the record, the
court erred in appointing the receivers, and in ordering
and confirming the sale of the property. Appellant's
complaints of these orders are based upon purely technical grounds, and his attitude in the case is
8   without any equitable considerations to support
it. His claim is largely for an arrear of salary as
vice president. As vice president, he certainly knew of

these various claims, and of the pendency of this litigation, for more than two years prior to his intervention; yet it was not until the receivers had been appointed, the property ordered to be sold, and on the eve of the sale, that he appeared to assert his claim. For this delay and untimely intervention he gives no reason but the hope of effecting a settlement of his claim. At the last moment he intervenes to prevent the wise and judicious disposition of the property ordered by the court, and to force delays that would render it comparatively valueless. It will be observed that his claim to a lien was upon the Nebraska property, and that the court excepted it from the order of sale, thereby leaving the appellant unprejudiced by the orders of which he complains. Many authorities are cited, but the case so manifestly called for the action taken by the court that we do not deem it necessary to refer to any authorities to support that action. We are in no doubt whatever that, upon the record before it, the district court was fully warranted in making the order that it did, appointing these receivers, and in promptly ordering a sale of the property, as was done. The equities are clearly against the appellant, and his appeal without merit, and the decrees of the district court complained of are therefore AFFIRMED.

W. L. MOORE v. M. W. KLEPPISH AND DAN R. KINLEY, Appellants.

Dedication: PLATTING. The platting of land as a public square
1 amounts to a dedication thereof to public use.

REVOCATION: A dedication of a square to the public cannot be
2 revoked without the joint act of all parties interested, including
3 owners of abutting lots.

RULE APPLIED. Where land has been platted as a public square, an
2 instrument executed by the party who made the plat, and others

8   whose interests do not clearly appear, in which some of the abutting property owners did not join, is ineffectual as a vacation of such square.

Estoppel: VACATION OF PLAT. An owner of lots abutting on a public square is not estopped to attack the validity of an attempted vacation by another owner, of the dedication of the square to public use, by subsequently occupying a portion of the square, where he supposed that the attempted vacation was valid.

Right to Enjoin: TITLE. Plaintiff in an action *to restrain the sale on*
1   *execution of real property* of which he is in possession, is at most only bound to show a presumptive title, where defendant has no
4   title at all.

Appeal from Linn District Court.—HON. W. P. WOLF, Judge.

TUESDAY, JANUARY 18, 1898.

ACTION in equity to restrain the sale on execution of certain real estate. Decree for plaintiff. Defendants appeal.—*Affirmed.*

Rickel & Crocker for appellants.

John M. Redmond for appellee.

WATERMAN, J.—Plaintiff, claiming to be the owner of certain real estate in the city of Cedar Rapids, brings this action to restrain the sale of said premises under a writ of general execution against one J. M. May, on the ground that the judgment debtor has no interest in said land, and did not have at the time of the rendition of said judgment. The defendant Kleppish is the execution creditor, and Kinley is the sheriff of Linn county. Much evidence was taken upon the question of plaintiff's title to the premises, and the greater portion of the argument on both sides is devoted to a consideration of the conflicting claims on this point. In the view

1   we take of the case, we shall be spared an attempt to solve many questions of fact that are in dispute between the parties as to the length of time plain-

tiff and his grantors have been in possession of the premises, and the character and incidents of such occu- pancy. It is sufficient for our purpose to say that it is undisputed that plaintiff went into the possession of this tract on April 29, 1892, under a conveyance from his father; that he has held possession since that time under a claim of ownership, and has made valuable improvements. So much for plaintiff's interest. We will now examine the claim of defendants. It appears that one John M. May, being the owner of a tract of land in Cedar Rapids, platted the same in 1874 as an addition to said city, the plat containing a public square known as "Union Square." Prior to 1878, Martin Moore, the father of plaintiff, acquired title to lots 1, 11, and 12 in said addition, each of which abutted upon the public square mentioned. On November 7, 1878, May, joining with others, whose interest does not clearly appear, but who claim to be joint owners, filed for record an attempted vacation of said "Union Square." Martin Moore, who was at this time the owner of the three lots mentioned above, did not join in said vacation, nor does it appear that he consented thereto. After this so-called vacation, and apparently relying upon its validity, Martin Moore took possession of a part of said public square in front of the lots owned by him, and claimed title thereto. This is the tract in dispute in this case. After this, in 1892, he conveyed the same to plaintiff, as already stated.

It is obvious from what has been said that the attempted vacation of "Union Square" was invalid and of no effect. It is not necessary to cite authorities to show that the platting of such square in the addi- tion in question amounted to a dedication to pub- lic use. This dedication could be revoked only by the joint action of all parties interested, including own- ers of abutting lots. This was not had. Nothing less than this could take title from the public, and revest it in private owners. Whether Martin Moore's seizure of part of the square, and his claim of ownership thereof, might, under some circumstances, be held to estop him, or those holding under him, from claiming there was no valid vacation of said square, we will not say. We content ourselves with holding that, if he could be bound in any way other than by joining in the written instrument of vacation, the facts here disclosed are not sufficient to do so, for it appears affirmatively that he believed the attempted vacation by May was valid, and that his subsequent action was induced by such belief. The judgment against May, under which the sale of the premises in question is threatened, was rendered October 17, 1888. From what we have already said, it is apparent that May had no interest in said real estate.

The only question remaining is whether plaintiff has any such interest in the property as will give him a standing in court to enjoin the execution sale. Plaintiff does not seek to quiet title. His only prayer is that the threatened sale may be enjoined, and this was all the relief given by the decree below. Defendants insist that plaintiff must recover on the strength of his own title, and not on the weakness of defendants' claim. This undoubtedly is the rule in actions for the recovery of real property, but this is not an action of that nature. Plaintiff is in possession of the real estate under a claim of title. Defendants are seeking to subject it to the payment of a debt that cannot be legally enforced against it. It may well be doubted whether the rule contended for by defendants obtains in cases like this, or in actions to quiet title; but, if it does, it is in a modified form, and is fulfilled by plaintiff making a showing of presumptive title,—that is, of facts from which title may fairly be inferred. *Russel v. Nelson*, 32 Iowa, 215; *Railway Co. v. Lindley*, 48 Iowa, 11; *Shaffer v. McCrackin*, 90 Iowa, 578. This last was an action to quiet title. A decree was rendered by the lower court granting the relief asked, and, in affirming such action, this court said upon the subject of plaintiffs' title: "But what right, title, or interest in said premises have plaintiffs or the other parties to the suit? It may truly be said that they must recover, if at all, on the strength of their own right, and not on the weakness of McCrackin's claim. Yet they need not have a perfect title as against J. R. McCrackin. If they have any right or equity therein, they should be protected as against him, who has no right whatever. It matters not that others may be able to assert rights in said premises as against plaintiff. That fact, if it exists, cannot prejudice McCrackin, whose interest in the land may be represented by zero." As sustaining this principle, see, also, *Craft v. Merrill*, 14 N. Y. 456; *Loomis v. Roberts*, 57 Mich 284, (23 N. W. Rep. 816.) The decree below is correct, and is AFFIRMED.

STATE OF IOWA V. RICHARD ROWE, Appellant.

Criminal Law: EMBEZZLEMENT: *Accessories.* One may, independ-
2 ently of statute, be an accessory by procuring a crime, although he is incompetent to commit the crime in person.

PRINCIPAL AND ACCESSORY: *Construction of statute.* The declaration of Code 1873, section 4314, that one aiding or abetting the commission of a public offense is a principal, enlarges the scope
1 of section 3908, providing that public officers who shall convert to their own use money intrusted to their care and keeping shall be guilty of embezzlement; and therefore, one not a public officer, and who therefore, would not violate section 3908 if he took the money himself, may commit the crime of aiding and abetting another, who is such officer.

INFORMATION CONSTRUED. An information which charges one with embezzlement by aiding and abetting another in the commission
8 of such offense, does not charge defendant as an accessory before the fact

Extradition. One extradited under an information containing a single count may be prosecuted under an indictment charging the same

4 offenses in different counts, presenting different ways in which the offense was committed.

INFORMATION AND INDICTMENT. The treaty of the United States with Mexico provides for the surrender of persons "to justice * * *
4 who being accused of the crimes enumerated," etc. *Held*, that such provision means that he is to be accused in due form of law, and hence it applies to one who is accused on information, as well as one charged by indictment, since an information is one of the forms of accusation prescribed by statute.

Appeal: REVIEW. The appellate court cannot take notice of a mere remark in argument to the effect that defendant in a criminal
5 case was forced to trial before a jury that had fixed opinions as to one of the facts essential to his conviction.

Appeal from Poweshiek District Court.—HON. D. RYAN, Judge.

TUESDAY, JANUARY 18, 1898.

INDICTMENT for embezzlement. Verdict of guilty, and a judgment of imprisonment, from which the defendant appealed.—*Affirmed.*

J. T. Allensworth for appellant.

Milton Remley, attorney general, for the state.

GRANGER, J.—I. The indictment charges that Chester W. Rowe, as county treasurer of Poweshick county, Iowa, embezzled thirty thousand dollars of money belonging to the county, and that the defendant aided and abetted him in so doing. The defendant was not a public officer, and bore no trust relation whatever as to the money charged to have been embez-
1 zled. To get directly to the point, it may be said that, had he taken the money without any reference to Chester W. Rowe, he could not have been indicted and convicted of embezzlement. If the charge of embezzlement can be sustained, it is solely on the ground that he aided or abetted Chester W. Rowe to

commit such a crime. In view of this situation, the
question is presented: Can one who, by himself, could
not be a principal in the crime of embezzlement, be an
accessory to the crime, in the sense of aiding and abetting its commission? The question leads to a consideration of our statutory provisions. Section 3908 of the
Code of 1873 provides that public officers who shall convert to their own use money intrusted to their care and
keeping shall be guilty of embezzlement. The following
is section 4314: "The distinction between an accessory
before the fact and a principal is abrogated and all persons concerned in the commission of a public offense,
whether they directly commit the act constituting the
offense or aid and abet its commission, though not present, must hereafter be indicted, tried and punished as
principals." The question is urged: If Richard Rowe
could not be principal in the crime of embezzlement if
he took the money himself, how can he be if he merely
advises the taking of it? The answer is not difficult. It
is because the law makes him so. It is just as competent for the legislature to make one who aids another
to commit embezzlement an embezzler as it is to make
the principal actor one. It is merely a question of legislative intent. The difficulty of the argument is in bringing into it the thought of accessoryship, and that
there is a charge of that character when there is no
such purpose. The section quoted abrogates the
relationship of accessory before the fact to crimes in
this state, and fixes the crimes and punishment for one
who aids and abets another in the commission of a public offense. If he aids and abets another to commit a
crime, he is guilty of the same crime as the other, and
subject to the same punishment. The effect of section
4314 is to enlarge the scope of section 3908, so that other
persons than those therein specified may be guilty of
embezzlement by doing the acts specified. Stress is

placed upon the fact that section 4314 was enacted in 1843, and section 3908 not until 1851; so that, in the enactment of section 4314, reference must have been had to the rule of accessory before the fact; and, as the crime of em.. ezzlement was not know to the common law, there could have been no intent to have it apply to embezzlement. A sufficient answer is this: Both provisions were embraced in the Code of 1851, in the Revision of 1860, and in the Code of 1873. In each instance the manner of adoption was such as to make all embraced therein part of one act, so there can be no doubt of their being provisions of the law that should be considered together. *Hunt v. Insurance Co.*, 67 Iowa, 742. In *State v. Smith*, 100 Iowa, 1, in considering section 4314, we said: "The effect of this provision is to make the offense of one who at common law would have been an accessory before the fact substantive and so far independent that he may be indicted, tried, and punished, and as a principal, without regard to the prosecution of the person who at common law would have been the principal." The whole matter is concluded in this one proposition; that the statute, in effect, provides that one who aids and abets another to commit embezzlement is himself guilty of embezzlement, and shall be punished accordingly. The authority of the legislature to so provide is not doubted. But, independent of our statute, appellant's position is not sound. One may be an accessory by procuring a crime, although such procurer is incompetent to commit the offense in person. *State v. Comstock*, 46 Iowa, 265; 1 Am. & Eng. Enc. Law. (2d ed.) 260, and cases there cited.

II. Preliminary information was filed before a justice of the peace in July, 1895, charging the offense of embezzlement in the manner we have stated, and

such information was made the basis of proceedings by
which defendant was extradited from the repub-
3   lic of Mexico. The point is made that in the information he was charged as an accessory before the
fact, and was brought to Iowa, and tried on an indictment charging him as principal. The mistake is in the
facts. He was not charged as accessory in the information, but as counseling and advising the commission of
the crime of embezzlement by Chestr W. Rowe. As to
that particular fact, there was no difference between
the information and indictment. By the information
the defendant was, in express terms, charged with the
crime of embezzlement, followed by the averment of
facts that constituted the offense. This information was
before the authorities of Mexico, and they could judge
of its sufficiency under its treaty with our government.
It is true that in *U. S. v. Rauscher.* 119 U. S. 407 (7 Sup. Ct.
Rep.234,) it is held that a treaty to which the United
States is a party is a law of the land, of which all courts,
federal and state, are to take judicial notice, and by the
provisions of which they are to be governed, so far as
they are capable of judicial enforcement; and that,
under our treaty with Great Britain, where a defendant
was extradited on a charge of murder, the extradition
proceedings clothed him with an exemption from trial
for any other offense until he has had the opportunity
to return to the country from which he was taken for
the purpose alone of trial for the offenses specified in the
demand for his surrender. In that case the charge on
which extradition was obtained was murder on the
high seas, and the defendant was placed on trial under
an indictment charging cruel and unusual punishment.
The rules we have stated were announced under such
facts. In this case the defendant was extradited on
a charge of embezzlement, and tried for the same
offense, and the case seems to be clear authority for the
procedure. The rule of the *Rauscher Case* seems

to be applicable only to international extradition. *Lacelles v. Georgia*, 148 U. S. 537, (13 Sup. Ct. Rep. 687); *State v. Kealy*, 89 Iowa, 94.

III. Our treaty with Mexico provides for the surrender of persons "to justice * * * who being accused of the crimes enumerated," etc. It is urged

4   that the treaty means charged or accused in an indictment where the crime, is so punishable, and not accused or charged with the offense in an information on which he cannot be tried. That he is to be charged or accused means no more than that he is to be charged or accused in due form of law. Spear, Extradition p. 360. The charge is to be made in the state or country in which the alleged crime is committed, and by "due form of law" is meant due form of law in that state or country. The charge upon information, as in this case, is one of the forms prescribed by our law, as is also the further proceeding on indictment. The information contained but a single count, and it is true the indictment contained five counts, but all charged but the one offense of embezzlement. The different counts in the indictment but charged the offense to have been committed in different ways, and no authority coming to our notice denies the right to such a procedure.

IV. It is said the defendant had the right to contest the guilt of Chester W. Rowe on the trial of this indictment. The cause was submitted to the jury, on

5   the theory that there could be no conviction unless the evidence showed beyond a reasonable doubt that Chester W. Rowe embezzled the money, as stated in the indictment, and the cause was tried throughout on that theory. A mere remark in argument refers to the right of defendant to an impartial jury, and it is said defendant was forced to trial before a jury that had fixed opinions as to the guilt of Chester W. Rowe. There is no reference to any ruling

or facts to guide us, and we do not discover any error in the respect suggested.

V. It is next said that the verdict has not support in the evidence. The evidence on which the verdict rests is entirely circumstantial, because of which less than a presentation of the whole would not correctly and fairly disclose the basis of our conclusion. It so happens at times that the convincing or conclusive force of evidence, as disclosed by a record, consists largely of minor details and undisputed facts, that carry conviction, and leave little room for doubt, when less than an entire presentation would fail to justify a conclusion otherwise fully warranted. Of the guilt of the defendant there is little room for doubt. The evidence in the case, fairly considered by an impartial person, would leave no reasonable doubt of guilt. That Chester W. Rowe was guilty of embezzlment no one questions. The presence of defendant at Montezuma just before the departure of his brother with the money, their somewhat strange conduct, the times of their leaving, their meeting and journeying to Mexico, their false statements as to their previous places of residence and business, their having money, and engaging in business under assumed names, and the defendant's manifest desire to conceal his identity when the question of who was guilty of the offense was being considered or talked of, with many incidental facts, satisfy us that the finding of the jury is warranted. The instructions are a fair presentation of the law, and in a way that there was no error in refusing instructions asked. The result is a clear vindication of the law, and the judgment will stand AFFIRMED.

THOMAS S. CATHCART, Appellant, v. JAMES G. GRIEVE, JANET GRIEVE, and JOHN POLLOCK.

Fraudulent Conveyance: RIGHTS OF CREDITORS. A creditor has the
6 right to secure himself, though he knows that in so doing he will
delay other creditors in the collection of their claims, unless he
participates in a fraudulent intent by the debtor.

BADGES. Mere relationship between the parties to a transfer is not a
1 badge of fraud, as against creditors, which calls for explanation.

DEEDS AS MORTGAGE: *Consideration.* Inadequacy of consideration
3 for a deed is not material on the question of fraud as against the
6 grantor's creditors, where the deed, though absolute on its face,
was intended as a mortgage.

SECRET TRUST: *Rental.* The execution of a lease, by a grantee to the
2 grantor, is not a badge of fraud as against the grantor's creditors,
4 when the lease containing such reservation is duly recorded

EVIDENCE. Shortly before judgment was obtained against him, an
insolvent debtor deeded land to his uncle, who lived at a remote
5 distance, for an adequate consideration, and at the same time he
leased the land of his uncle at a fair rental, and the deed and
lease were recorded together. The grantor occupied the land
6 under the lease the succeeding year The deed, though absolute
in form, was in fact a mortgage, and the rent reserved in the lease
was intended as additional security. At about the same time, the
grantor mortgaged all his property to other creditors, including a
chattel mortgage to his uncle. The uncle knew only of the
indebtedness to others, recited in the instruments made to him.
No concealment was made of the deed's being a mortgage, and,
when questioned, the parties declared it to be a mortgage. *Held,*
that the conveyance was not fraudulent as to the judgment creditor.

Cross Petitions: NOTICE In an action to set aside a mortgage as in
fraud of creditors, where the defendant mortgagee seeks by cross
8 petition to have the mortgage foreclosed, he must serve the cross
petition on the defendant mortgagor.

PROOF UNDER When the defendant mortgagee, in an action to set
aside a mortgage as in fraud of creditors, seeks by cross petition
9 to have the mortgage foreclosed, and the averments of such petition are denied in the reply, there can be no foreclosure, in the
absence of proof of the allegation of the cross petition.

Appeal from Clay District Court.—HON. W. B. QUAR-
TON, Judge.

WEDNESDAY, JANUARY 19, 1898.

CREDITOR'S bill to subject certain real estate, the
legal title to which is in defendant John Pollock, to the
payment of a judgment held by plaintiff against James
G. Grieve. Defendants pleaded that the conveyance of
the land from Grieve and wife to Pollock was intended
as a mortgage to secure Pollock for money loaned, and
denied all fraud in the transaction. The trial court dismissed the petition, and plaintiff appeals.—*Reversed* in
part and *affirmed* in part.

Kinkead & Kinkead and *Dale, Kinkead & Bissel*
for appellant.

F. H. Helsell for appellees.

DEEMER, C. J.—Plaintiff obtained his judgment
against James G. Grieve on March 6, 1895, upon a debt
contracted in the year 1894. On the twenty-fifth day of
February, 1895, Grieve (his wife, Janet, joining) conveyed, by warranty deed, four hundred and thirty-nine
acres of land in Clay county to defendant John Pollock,
for the expressed consideration of two thousand six
hundred dollars. The deed recites that it is subject to
two mortgages, amounting, in the aggregate, to seven
thousand four hundred dollars. This deed was recorded
March 2, 1895. At the same time, and evidently as a
part of the same transaction, Pollock executed a lease
to Grieve of all the land described in the deed, for the
term of one year, at the agreed rental of eight hundred
dollars. This lease was also recorded on March 2, 1895.
The defendants pleaded that this transaction was in
fact a mortgage to secure a debt due from Grieve to

Pollock. At or about the same time, Grieve gave Pollock a chattel mortgage upon some personal property,
to secure the sum of one thousand and thirty dollars.
Grieve also mortgaged his property, of every kind or
nature, to other of his creditors, on or about the same
date. Appellant claims that the conveyance and mortgage to Pollock are fraudulent and void, because made
with intent to hinder, delay, and defraud creditors. On
account of the loose manner in which the case was tried
in the court below, it is difficult to get at the real facts.
Plaintiff proved the indebtedness of Grieve; the recovery of judgment against him; the execution of the deed,
lease, and chattel mortgage to which we have referred;
that Pollock is a resident of Scott county, and an uncle
of Grieve; that Grieve is insolvent, and has been since
the execution of the conveyances in question; and that,
about the time of these conveyances, Grieve executed
two other chattel mortgages to residents of Clay county,
to secure debts purporting to amount to over one thousand seven hundred dollars. Plaintiff also proved that
the deed to Pollock, and probably the lease, were executed at Davenport, in Scott county, and that the land
was worth twenty-five dollars per acre. This is substantially all the evidence that was adduced, save that Grieve
was in possession and occupancy of the land during the
year 1895. At the conclusion of plaintiff's evidence,
defendants moved for judgment dismissing the petition,
because there was no evidence of fraud, and no showing
that the deed was anything other than an absolute conveyance. Thereupon plaintiff offered in evidence the
admission in defendants' pleadings that the deed was a
mortgage. This was objected to, because offered after
plaintiff had rested, and after the motion for judgment
had been made. At this stage of the proceedings, court
adjourned. We find the following record made the next
morning: "Mr. Kinkead: This now is the incoming of
court, nine o'clock this morning, and the motion having

been made last night, on its coming on now for hearing
and announcement of the decision of the court, before
that announcement is made, the plaintiff in this case
desires to place upon record the following: 'Motion No.
2, Comes now the plaintiff, pending the defendants'
motion for decree and judgment as hereinbefore stated,
and withdraws from the evidence in this case the
answer and amended and substituted answer of
the defendants, and the offer in evidence heretofore made of the same in this case by the plaintiff.
Plaintiff also further withdraws from the evidence the
deed, and his offers hereinbefore made of the same, and
all the record thereof in the evidence, and which deed is
mentioned in the plaintiff's petition in this case, as
Exhibit A. And plaintiff now moves the court, upon the
record in this case, to render judgment and decree for
the plaintiff against the said James G. Grieve, Janet
Grieve, and John Pollock, as demanded in the prayer of
plaintiff's petition filed herein March 16th, 1895.'" Following this were some more motions and objections on
behalf of defendants, and the court finally made this
ruling: "The motion to withdraw the deeds from the
record, and the answers from the record, as indicated
in motion number two, is overruled, because the said
motion is made after the cause is fully submitted to the
court and argued by the counsel to the court; and the
court has indicated to both counsel what its opinion
would be in this case, and directed a decree, declaring
that the deed was in fact a mortgage, establishing Pollock's lien to the amount claimed in the answer, declaring that plaintiff's judgment was a lien junior to the
claim of Pollock, and directing foreclosure and sale of
the premises." There are no assignments of error, and
we must try the case anew on this record, assuming, of
course, that the rulings on the motions, except in so
far as they involve the merits, are correct.

The burden is upon the plaintiff to establish the fraud pleaded by him, and evidence which merely raises a suspicion is not sufficient. Certain badges of fraud are relied upon; but appellant concedes that the rule in this state is that none of the many badges of fraud usually relied on are regarded as conclusive, citing a number of our cases. Among the badges so relied upon are: First, the relationship of the parties; second, the fact that there was a secret trust created by the lease; third, such inadequacy of consideration as indicates fraud or renders the conveyance voluntary; fourth, the making of an absolute conveyance when security only was intended; fifth, execution of a series of instruments covering all the grantor's property at a time when he was insolvent, and shortly before the recovery of plaintiff's judgment.

It has frequently been held that mere relationship alone is not a badge of fraud which calls for explanation. *Oberholtzer v. Hazen*, 92 Iowa, 602; *Allen v. Kirk*, 81 Iowa, 668. Here the relationship was somewhat distant, and the parties lived remote from each other; and, in addition, there is not the slightest evidence that Pollock knew that Grieve was indebted except as shown in the instruments given him, which referred to some prior debts and incumbrances.

1

The lease given to Grieve by Pollock was recorded at the same time as the deed, and was not kept secret. The evidence tends to show that Grieve was to pay the rent reserved, and that at the time of the trial he had part of the money deposited in a bank with which to pay it. Such transactions are not uncommon; and the rent reserved is treated as additional security for the payment of interest or interest and principal. See *Rogers v. Davis*, 91 Iowa, 730; *Jordan v. Lendrum*, 55 Iowa, 483; *Smith v. Mack*, 94 Iowa, 539. The case differs essentially from *Macomber v. Peck*, 39 Iowa, 351, relied upon by appellant. In that case there was

2

no recorded lease, and a part of the consideration for the conveyance was an agreement that the grantor should use and occupy the land for three or four years without rent. This part of the consideration was not mentioned in the deed. The conveyance was held fraudulent because of the secret reservation securing a benefit to the grantor at the expense of his creditors. Neither is the case of *Graham v. Rooney*, 42 Iowa, 567, in conflict with the views expressed in this opinion. In that case a part of the consideration was an agreement for future support of the grantees; in other words the secret reservation of a beneficial interest in the property. Such conveyances are universally held to be fraudulent. *Harris v. Brink*, 100 Iowa, 366; *Strong v. Lawrence*, 58 Iowa, 55.

No such secret trust is established as will justify us in declaring the conveyance fraudulent. The land was worth, when transferred, something over ten thousand dollars. The consideration expressed in the deed was two thousand six hundred dollars; but the land was taken subject to incumbrances amounting to seven thousand four hundred dollars. It is true, there is no direct evidence of the existence of these mortgages. The deed was offered by the plaintiff however, and defendants are not in position to deny the statement therein that the land was so incumbered. If it was so incumbered, then the consideration is adequate. Plaintiff offered no evidence as to the consideration in fact paid, except as we have stated, and made no attempt to prove that the land was unincumbered. Moreover, if it be true that the deed was intended as a mortgage,, inadequacy of consideration is of no moment in determining the issue of fraud. The conveyance was not voluntary.

The fact that the conveyance was absolute, instead of conditional, is undoubtedly a badge of fraud, and

should be regarded with suspicion. *Fuller v. Griffith,*
91 Iowa, 632. In the case at bar, however, there
4   was no disguise or concealment of the character
of the transaction. When questioned, the parties
immediately declared it to be a mortgage, and, except
in the motion made, have at all times, when required,
disclosed its purpose. The motion was made during
the progress of the trial, and was based upon an alleged
failure of proof on the part of the plaintiff. There was
no disguise in this. True, it is that the defendants did
not go upon the witness stand in their own behalf to
explain the transaction. Plaintiff relieved them of this
privilege, to some extent at least, by introducing in
evidence their admission in answer that the
5   transaction was a mortgage. But aside from all
this, the consideration was nearly, if not quite,
the full value of the property. And there is no evidence
whatever that defendant Pollock knew or had any intimation that defendant Grieve was financially embar-
rassed, except as he gained it from the statement in the
deed with reference to the mortgages upon the land. As
a creditor, Pollock had the right to secure himself, even
if he knew that, in so doing, other creditors would be
delayed in the collection of their claims. Security given
to such a creditor will not be declared fraudulent, unless
he participated in an intent to defraud other creditors.
The rent reserved is not shown to have been inadequate,
and there has been no deceit or dissembling in the transaction, except in this: that the conveyance was absolute in form, instead of a pledge or mortgage. In
6   the *Fuller-Griffith Case, supra,* we said that a
deed absolute on its face may be shown to be a
mortgage; "yet, as to creditors, the transaction must
be clean and clear as a conveyance for permanent ownership." The conveyance was of that kind, and is not
fraudulent simply because absolute in form. See, also,
Stevens v. Hinckley, 43 Me. 441.

What we have hitherto said largely answers the last claim made by plaintiff; for, if Pollock was a creditor of Grieve, he had a right to secure himself even if Grieve was insolvent, and this he could do even if the effect of the conveyance was to hinder and delay other creditors. That he took the conveyance as a mortgage was proved by the plaintiff in introducing the admission; and there is no proof whatever that Pollock participated in any fraudulent intent on the part of Grieve, even if such fraudulent intent were established.

7

II. The defendants, as we have seen, pleaded that the conveyance was a mortgage to secure certain sums advanced by Pollock. Pollock also filed a cross-petition, asking that the amounts be established, and that a decree be entered declaring the instrument to be a mortgage, and asking for a foreclosure of the same. He did not serve notice of his cross-petition upon his co-defendant, nor did he introduce any evidence upon the trial as to the amount of his advancements. The trial court undertook to establish them, however, and granted a decree of foreclosure as prayed. The only evidence tending to support defendants' claim was introduced by plaintiff and this did not go to the extent of the indebtedness. The evidence introduced by plaintiffs touching this matter had reference simply to the fact that defendants admitted that the conveyance was in fact a mortgage instead of an absolute deed. The trial court did not have sufficient evidence before it from which to determine and fix the amount of the advancements made, and could not, for that reason alone, grant the decree prayed in defendants' cross-bill. As Pollock introduced no evidence to establish the allegations of his cross-bill, he was not entitled to a decree upon the

8

statements contained therein, for the reason that they were denied in the reply. Again, he
9   was not entitled to a decree of foreclosure, for the reason that Grieve had no notice of the cross-petition. We may also observe, in passing, that we doubt whether he was entitled to such decree under the prayer of his petition. In so far as the decree fixes the amount of the advancement made by Pollock, and directs the foreclosure and sale of the premises, it is reversed, and will be remanded to the court below for further proceedings in harmony with this opinion; and so far as it declares the conveyance to Pollock to be a valid and subsisting mortgage for the amount actually found due him upon subsequent proceedings, prior and superior to the plaintiff's judgment, it is affirmed. The parties plaintiff and defendant will each pay one-half the costs of this appeal.—Reversed in part and affirmed in part.

Margaret Hyatt v. Martin Clever, *et al.*, Appellants, and Margaret Hyatt v. Mattie A. Hurlbut, *et al.*, Appellants, and Two Other Cases.

Boundaries: Deeds. Plaintiff's and defendant's common grantor, in conveying plaintiff's land, reserved land west of it, "commencing nineteen rods west of the southwest corner of out lot six" (evi-
1 dently an error, as lot five is the only one adjoining). and, in conveying the reserved land to defendant, defined its eastern boundary as commencing "nineteen rods west from the southwest corner of out lot five " which corner is one rod east of the section. *Held*, that plaintiff's western boundary was eighteen rods west of the section line.

Appeal: Supersedeas. An appellee's possession of the land in dispute, obtained by the service of a writ of possession *before* an
2 appeal bond was filed, is not affected by a subsequent perfecting of appeal and filing of a supersedeas bond, under Code 1873, section 3186, providing that an appeal shall not stay proceedings unless a bond is filed.

Injunction after appeal. Under Code 1873, section 3389, providing
    that an injunction affecting the subject-matter of an action can
3 be granted only by the court before which it is pending, an
    injunction restraining the taking of possession of land in dis-
    pute, after an appeal has been taken, can be granted only by the
    appellate court.

Appeal from Monroe District Court.—HON. M. A.
ROBERTS, Judge.

WEDNESDAY, JANUARY 19, 1898.

PLAINTIFF, the owner of lot 2 and west half of lot 3,
block 8, George's First addition to Albia, prosecutes
these actions for the possession of, and to be quieted in
the title to, a strip of land about twelve feet wide, east
and west, and eighteen rods long, north and south,
which she claims to be a part of her said lots, on the
west side thereof. The defendant Clever, owner of lot
4, block 7, of said addition, claims the south half of said
strip as part thereof; and defendant Hurlbut, owner of
lot 1, block 7, claims the north half as part of her said
lot. The defendants also claim to be entitled to said
parts of said strip, respectively, by prescription. Separate decrees were entered in favor of the plaintiff as
prayed, from which the defendants appeal. The issues
and facts being the same in the above-entitled cases,
they are submitted together. Two other cases, wherein
said defendants are plaintiffs and appellants, and said
plaintiff and L. E. Hyatt, her husband, are defendants,
are also submitted herewith.—*Reversed* in part.

W. A. Nichols for appellants.

T. B. Perry for appellee.

GIVEN, J.—I. We first inquire as to the title to the
land in dispute. This strip of land is a part of the north

one-half of the northeast one-fourth of section 21, township 72, range 17, Monroe county. The abstracts
1   of title show a number of conveyances of fractional parts of this tract by metes and bounds
that are difficult to apply to the intended parts. All
the abstracts of title show that Willis Arnold owned
said tract of land by conveyance from the owner of the
patent title. Plaintiff's abstract shows that Arnold
conveyed the same to W. T. George, excepting parts
thereof described by metes and bounds, reserved to
Arnold in the deed. On June 24, 1857, there was
recorded a survey and plat of said tract as "Plat of
George's First Addition to Albia," which was dated
June 20, 1857, and duly executed and acknowledged by
Carlos R. Kelsey, W. T. George, S. E. L. Moore, and
Nathan Draper. Plaintiff shows title from George,
through several intermediate grantors to her, for her
said lots in block 8. Defendant Clever's abstract shows
that August 1, 1856, Arnold conveyed one-half acre of
said tract to Mortimer Sellick by metes and bounds,
"commencing at a point nineteen rods west from the
southwest corner of outlot No. 5, in Albia." This one-half
acre is next west of that conveyed to George. Said
abstract also shows that on November 4, 1856, Sellick,
conveyed same one-half acre to Stephen Lofton; that
May 2, 1857, Samuel Thompson conveyed the south half
thereof to Jacob Staltz, who conveyed the same to John
I. Anderson, Anderson to Clark, and Clark to defendant
Clever It will be observed that no conveyance is shown
from Lofton nor to Thompson. Therefore, so far as this
abstract shows, the title to said one-half acre is in
Lofton, and was at the time the plat was made. The
abstract of defendant Hurlbut shows the same conveyances, down to Lofton. It also shows a conveyance of the
north one-half of said one-half acre, April 23, 1857, from
Lofton to Kelsey, and from Kelsey, through intermediate grantors, to defendant Hurlbut. It will be noticed

that Kelsey, who owned the north half, did join in executing the plat. Plaintiff's counsel insist that, as it does not otherwise appear that Draper, who joined in the plat, had any other interest in the land, we may find from the testimony of Mr. George that Lofton had conveyed this south half to Draper. Whether we may so find we do not determine, as it is entirely clear that these parties and their grantors have treated this entire one-half acre as included in said plat. While the lands of different owners were platted as "George's First Addition to Albia," each seems to have conveyed the lots formed out of the land owned by him. Mr. George owned the land out of which block 8 was formed. Block 7, in which defendant's lots are located, and which, as we have seen, includes said one-half acre, lies immediately west of block 8. The plat is bounded on the east by a section line, east of which, and opposite block 8, is outlot 5, with an alley one rod wide between it and the section line. A like width appears to have been left between the east line of the plat and section line, thus giving roadway on that line two rods wide.

Plaintiff contends that the west line of block 8 is nineteen rods west of said section line, and therefore, eleven feet six inches west of a certain fence. Defendants claim that it is nineteen rods west of the southwest corner of said outlot 5, or eighteen rods west of said section line, and that said fence is on the west line of block 8. We are unable to say from the plat and field notes from which point the measurement was made, but it seems clear, from the deeds from Arnold to George and to Sellick, that the land conveyed to George only extended nineteen rods west of the southwest corner of outlot 5. One of the reservations in that deed reads: "And commencing nineteen rods west of the southwest corner of outlot 6," etc. 6 is evidently an error, as 5 is the number of the adjoining outlot. It is clear that George's title only extended nineteen rods west of the west line of outlot 5, and not nineteen rods from the section line. The deed from Arnold to Sellick for said one-half acre commences "nineteen rods west from the southwest corner of outlot 5, in Albia." We are in no doubt but that the west line of George's land and of block 8 is but eighteen rods west of said section line.

II. The evidence shows that many years ago the then owners agreed that the west line of block 8 was where said fence was afterwards built, and that for more than ten years prior to the bringing of these actions these parties and their grantors occupied and improved with reference to that as the line. Whether this occupation was under such circumstances as to confer title by prescription we do not determine, as we are convinced that the line so occupied to is the true line. It follows that the decrees of the district court must be reversed, and the cases remanded for decrees in harmony with this opinion.—Reversed.

III. The other two cases are entitled as follows: "Martin Clever and Nancy G. Clever, Appellants, against Margaret Hyatt and L. E. Hyatt;" and "Mattie Hurlbut and E. C. Hurlbut, Appellants, against the same defendants." The plaintiffs in each case are husband and wife, and the defendants are also husband and wife. The facts concerning these cases, are, in substance, as follows: The decrees in the cases first considered were entered and excepted to on February 17, 1896, in favor of Margaret Hyatt, who caused a writ of possession to issue, which was duly served at 3 o'clock P. M. of March 5, 1896. Thereafter, and on the same day, these plaintiffs perfected their appeal in said cases by giving bonds and serving notices of appeal, said notices being served between 5 and 6 o'clock P. M. On the following day, notwithstanding the appeal, defendant L. E. Hyatt, by the direction and consent of his wife, entered upon the disputed land,

and proceeded to tear down the fence thereon. On March 9 temporary injunctions were granted on the petition of these plaintiffs (appellants) restraining Mr. and Mrs. Hyatt from interfering with appellants' pos. session. On March 14, 1896, said injunctions were, on motion of these defendants, dissolved, and from those orders these appeals are taken. Counsel for plaintiffs (appellants) contend that the perfecting of the appeal superseded the service of the writ of possession that had been made, and left the parties in *status quo* pending the appeal. By the service of that writ these defendants were put in possession of the disputed land before the decree under which the writ issued had been superseded by appeal; therefore there was nothing to .say. See Code, 1873, sections 3186, 3192, and 23 Am. & Eng.

3   Enc. Law 554. It will be observed that at the time these injunctions were granted, and also at the time they were dissolved, the cases in which the decrees for possession had been rendered has been appealed to, and were pending in this court. These injunctions should have been sought in these actions, and, under the provisions of section 3389 of the Code of 1873, the application therefor should have been to this court, as the actions were then pending therein on appeal. There was no error in rendering the judgments dissolving said injunctions, and they are therefore AFFIRMED.

STATE OF IOWA v. WILLIAM JAMISON, Appellant.

Former Jeopardy: COURT AND JURY. When, under the law, or for
2   want of evidence, a plea of former conviction is not sustained the
court may so charge the jury.

Pleading. The state may defeat a former conviction by showing that
the court in which the defendant was convicted had no jurisdiction without alleging that fact in the replication, as the rules in

1   civil cases have no application to criminal procedure and Code,
    section 4849, expressly provides that no replication or further
    pleading is necessary to a plea of former adjudication.

Appeal from Butler District Court.—HON. P. W. BURR,
Judge.

WEDNESDAY, JANUARY 19, 1898.

THE defendant was convicted of assault and
battery, and from a judgment imposing a fine of twenty-
five dollars he appeals.—*Affirmed.*

C. M. Greene for appellant.

Milton Remley, attorney general, and *J. W.
Arbuckle* for the state.

LADD, J.—After the discharge of the defendant by
the district court, as recited in *State v. Jamison,* 100
Iowa, 342, another information was filed with C. L.
Jones, a justice of the peace, accusing him of the
same offense, and to which he entered a plea of guilty.
He withdrew this on appeal, and pleaded not guilty,
and that he had been convicted of the identical offense
before the mayor of Allison. The defendant having
introduced that officer's record of conviction, the state
introduced that of the district court, adjudging the
mayor to have been without jurisdiction. It is urged
that this was in the nature of a confession and avoidance of the special plea of the defendant, and was not
admissible without a reply. See Code 1873, sec-
1   tion 2718. But the rules of pleading in civil cases
have no application to criminal procedure. The
statute expressly provides that to the plea of former
adjudication no replication or further pleading is necessary. Code 1873, section 4349. Any evidence which
tended to overcome that plea was admissible.

II. The record shows conclusively that the former
conviction was by a tribunal without jurisdiction, and
the court very properly advised the jury to disregard
        the special plea of the defendant. The only issue
2   was purely one of law, and might have been
        raised by demurrer, had the facts been fully
pleaded. *State v. Callendine*, 8 Iowa, 289; *State v. Redman*, 17 Iowa, 329. And when, under the law, or for
want of evidence, the plea is not sustained, the court
may so charge the jury. *State v. Parker*, 66 Iowa, 586,
Wharton, Criminal Pleading and Practice, 484, and
note.

The motion to retax costs was properly overruled.
—AFFIRMED.

JAMES TOWER, Appellant, v. A. A. MOORE, Appellee, C.
M. BUCKand ELIZABETH BUCK.

Mechanic's Lien: PRIORITIES: *Independent buildings.* McClain's
    Code, section 3317, sub-division 4, provides that, where a
    mechanic's lien has attached for a building erected on mortgaged
1 land, the court may order such building to be separately sold, and
    the purchaser may remove the same; but that if, in the discretion
    of the court, the buildings should not be sold, the proceeds of sale
    of the whole premises shall be ratably distributed between the
    mortgagee and the holder of the lien, and "that, in case the prem-
    ises do not sell for more than sufficient to pay off the prior mort-
    gage or other liens, the proceeds shall be applied on the prior
    mortgage or other liens " *Held,* that the holder of the mechanic's
    lien on the building has a right to priority on such building, in
    every case where the court shall find as a fact that such building
    can be removed without material injury to the security of the
    earlier lien holder, but where no such finding is made, the land
    must be sold, and the purchase price applied first in payment of
    the prior incumbrance.

CONSTRUCTION OF STATUTE. McClain's Code, section 3317, subdivision
    4, prescribing the manner in which mortgaged premises on which
2 there is a subsequent mechanic's lien shall be subject to the pay-
    ment of both liens, is merely a statement in express terms of the
    law with reference to priority of liens as it existed in judicial
    interpretation at the time the statute was passed.

Appeal from Marshall District Court.—HON. G. W.
Burnham, Judge.

WEDNESDAY, JANUARY 19, 1898.

ON April 9, 1892, the defendants C. M. and Elizabeth
Buck executed to plaintiff a mortgage on certain real
estate in Marshalltown, Iowa, to secure an indebtedness
due from them. This instrument was duly recorded
April 11, 1892. Between May 19, 1894, and July 2 of
the same year, the appellee furnished lumber and other
materials to the defendants Buck for the erection of a
new building on said premises, and on September 7,
1894, appellee filed a mechanic's lien therefor. Another
mechanics' lien for labor done on said building by one
Mead became the property of appellee by assignment.
Neither the amount or the validity of said liens is
questioned. On December 23, 1895, plaintiff began an
action for the foreclosure of his mortgage, making the
Bucks and appellee parties defendant. Appellee filed a
cross-bill, asking to have the mechancs' liens established
upon the building which was the product of labor and
material so furnished, as prior and superior to the
mortgage. The court below found in appellee's favor,
and although it is shown beyond dispute that the value
of the premises, including the improvements, does not
exceed the amount of the mortgage indebtedness, a
decree was entered establishing the mechanics' liens as
preferred claims upon the building, and ordering said
structure sold and removed. Plaintiff appeals.—
Affirmed.

Meeker & Meeker for appellant.

B. F. Cummings and Binford & Snelling for appellee.

WATERMAN, J.—A solution of the controversy here presented involves a construction of subdivision 4 of section 3317 of McClain's Code, which, so far, as material, is as follows: "The liens for the things 1 aforesaid, or the work, including those for additions, repairs and betterments, shall attach to the buildings, erections or improvements for which they were furnished or done, in preference to any prior lien or incumbrance or mortgage upon the land upon which such erection building, or improvement belongs, or is erected or put. If such material was furnished or labor performed in the erection or construction of an original and independent building, erection, or other improvement commenced since the attaching or execution of such prior lien, incumbrance, or mortgage, the court may, in its discretion, order and direct such building, erection, or improvement to be separately sold under execution, and the purchaser may remove the same within such reasonable time as the court may fix. But if, in the discretion of the court such building should not be separately sold, the court shall take an account and ascertain the separate values of the land, and the erection, building, or other improvement, and distribute the proceeds of sale so as to secure to the prior mortgage or other lien, priority upon the land, and to the mechanic's lien, priority upon the building, erection, or .other improvement. * * * In case the premises do not sell for more than sufficient to pay off the prior mortgage or other lien, the proceeds shall be applied on the prior mortgage or other liens." It is not claimed that the lower court erred in its finding that the building upon which appellee had his lien could be removed without material injury to the remaining security of appellant, and without seriously lessening the value of such structure. Such findings, we take it, were necessarily involved in the exercise of the court's discretion

in favor of the mechanic's lien holder. But it is broadly
claimed by appellant that under no circumstances can
the holder of a mechanic's lien be given a preference, as
against an independent building, over a prior mortgage
of the land, unless the value of the land, with such
improvement, exceeds the mortgage debt, and this claim
is based upon the closing paragraph of the quoted section. If appellant is correct in his construction of this
section, then, although it in terms gives to the holder of
a mechanic's lien such preference, yet it denies him the
right in all cases where priority could be of any
advantage to him. We cannot think the preference here
given the mechanic's lien holder is of this barren character. A proper construction of this statute, we think,
must give to the holder of a mechanic's lien against an
independent building a priority of right in every case
where the court shall find as a fact that such building
can be removed without material injury to the security
of the earlier lienholder; but where no such finding is
made, the land must be sold, and the purchase price
applied first in payment of the prior incumbrance.
This construction, we think, has support in former
decisions of this court. We will briefly review some of
the cases, and the statutes under which they were
decided. Section 1855 of the Revision of 1860 corresponds with the provision in question. It is as follows: "The lien for the things aforesaid, or work, shall
attach to the buildings, erections or improvements, for
which they were furnished or the work was done, in
preference to any prior lien or incumbrance, or mortgage upon the land, upon which said buildings, erections or improvements have been erected or put, and
any person enforcing such lien, may have such building,
erection or improvement sold under execution, and the
purchaser may remove the same within a reasonable
time thereafter." With some unimportant verbal
changes, this section was re-enacted in the Code of 1873.

With the law in this form, it was held that the lien of
the mechanic for repairs or additions to a building
would not be preferred to an existing mortgage on the
land, but that such priority was limited to cases where
the mchanic's lien was held against an independent or
original structure, which could be removed. *Getchell
v. Allen*, 34 Iowa, 559; *O'Brien v. Pettis*, 42 Iowa, 293.
In *Conrad v. Star*, 50 Iowa, 470, it is said: "We are of
the opinion that, under the law existing prior to the act
of 1876, the only manner of establishing the priority of
a mechanic's lien over a pre-existing incumbrance upon
the land was by the sale and removal of the building,
and that, where the nature of the improvements is such
that it cannot be removed, the lien of the mechanic must
be postponed to that of the prior incumbrance upon
the land." In *Stockwell v. Carpenter*, 27 Iowa, 119, it is
held that, in case of an independent structure that could
be removed without material detriment to the premises,
the liens of the mechanic took precedence of a prior
vendor's lien, and a sale of the building was ordered,
although the vendor's claim exceeded in amount the
value of the premises. Such was the law at the time
of the enactment of chapter 100, Laws Sixteenth General Assembly, of which section 3317, McClain's Code, is
a part. While this act effected many and radical
2   changes in the then existing law relating to
mechanics' liens, a careful reading of subdivision
4 of said section will make it manifest that the general
assembly in its adoption intended only to state in
express terms in the statute the law as it then existed,
as to priority of liens, in judicial interpretation. The
cases cited by appellant do not conflict with the construction we give to this statute. *Bartlett v. Bilger*, 92
Iowa, 732, was a case in which the mechanic's lien holder
claimed a preference as to the real estate as well as the
buildings, and this was disallowed. In *Kiene v. Hodge*,
90 *id.* 212, the lower court failed to find that the

building could be removed, but ordered a sale of the whole premises. *Miller v. Seal*, 71 *id.* 392, holds only that the lower court did not abuse its discretion in refusing to order the sale and removal of the building. In *Curtis v. Broadwell*, 66 *id.* 662, the lower court ordered a sale of the land and buildings to satisfy all liens; and in *Bank ·v. Schloth*, 59 *id.* 316, the lien claimed was for an addition to an existing building. On the other hand, we have in *Luce v. Curtis*, 77 *id.* 347, a case in which, under section 3317, this court approved an order for the sale and removal of a building as against a prior mortgage; and while it is true the value of the premises does not appear, we think it would be an exceptional case where the holder of the mechanic's lien would resort to his right to the building alone, if there was a prospect of his realizing something on a sale of the whole premises. The construction here announced is in accord with the words of the statute, and it is not inequitable, for it leaves to the prior mortgagee or lien holder all that he had when his interest attached. For the reasons stated we think the decree of the lower court must be AFFIRMED.

E. BOURRETT, Appellant, v. PALO ALTO COUNTY.

Bounty: COUNTIES: *Powers of board.* The board of supervisors has no discretion to refuse a bounty for a wolf skin, if the complainant has fully complied with the law, and the facts are undisputed, under Acts Twenty-fourth General Assembly, chapter 37, providing for the allowance of such a bounty upon a certified statement of the facts, together with such other evidence as the board may demand, showing the claimant to be entitled thereto, and if they so refuse, the bounty may be recovered in a court of law.

Appeal from Palo Alto District Court.—HON. W. B. QUARTON, Judge. ·

WEDNESDAY, JANUARY 19, 1898.

THE petition shows that Charles Baker killed, in Palo Alto county, twelve adult wolves, and one cub wolf in August, 1893; that in September, 1893, Baker filed his bill in the office of the county auditor of said county, showing him to be entitled to the bounty on said wolves, as provided by law; that he produced the whole skin of each of the thirteen wolves to the county auditor, who destroyed the same, by burning them; that the county auditor gave to Baker a receipt for said skins so received and destroyed; that plaintiff is the assignee of said account; that, at the regular meeting of the board of supervisors of said county in November, 1893, the said account was laid over till the September meeting, 1894, that, while the account was pending before said board of supervisors, it directed that other affidavits be filed showing that Baker caught and killed said wolves in Palo Alto county, which affidavits were filed, showing such facts; that all evidence demanded by the board was furnished; and that thereafter said board refused to allow the account. The petition asks judgment for one hundred and twelve dollars. To the petition there was a demurrer, which the court sustained, and gave judgment for defendant for costs, and the plaintiff appealed.—*Reversed.*

Thos. O'Connor for appellant.

John Menzies for appellee.

GRANGER, J.—The following are section of the Code of 1873:

"Sec. 1487. A bounty of one dollar shall be allowed on each scalp of a wolf, * * * to be paid out of the treasury of the county in which the animal was taken, upon a verified statement of the facts showing the claimant to be entitled thereto.

"Sec. 1488.   The person claiming the bounty shall
produce such statement, together with the scalp or
scalps, with the ears thereon, to the county auditor, or
a justice of the peace of the county wherein such wolf
*   *   *   may have been taken and killed; and the
officer before whom such scalps are produced shall
deface or destroy the scalps when so produced, so as to
prevent the use of the same to obtain for the second
time the bounty herein provided for."

In *Murray v. Jones County*, 72 Iowa, 286, in construing these sections, it is held that where it appeared that
the affidavit had been made before the justice, and he
had certified that the wolf scalps has been delivered at
his office, by the claimant, who was entitled to the
bounty, and he had destroyed the same, it was sufficient
to justify a recovery; it being the statutory intent that,
if the justice was satisfied that the bounty had been
earned, it was all that was required.   Chapter 37, Acts
Twenty-fourth General Assembly, repealed the above-
quoted sections, and enacted in lieu thereof: "A bounty
shall be allowed on the skin of a wolf *   *   *   as
follows: Five dollars on an adult wolf and two dollars
on a cub wolf,   *   *   *   to be paid out of the treasury
of the county in which the animal was taken, upon the
certified statement of the facts, together with such
other evidence as the board of supervisors may demand,
showing the claimant to be entitled thereto."   Another
section provides that the person claiming the bounty
shall produce the statement, together with the whole
skin of the animal, to the county auditor, who shall
destroy or deface the same, to prevent their further use
for the same purpose.   For the purposes of our consideration, to show whether the county is absolutely
liable where the claimant has done all that the law
requires, and the evidence is conclusive of the facts in
favor of the claimant, there seems to be no change in
the law other than the words "together with such other

evidence as the board of supervisors may demand showing the claimant entitled thereto."

The demurrer presents the objection to the petition
that the district court has no jurisdiction of the subject-
matter of the action; that the liability of the county
is purely statutory; and that the board of supervisors
alone has power to pass upon and allow or disallow
the claim. Reliance is placed on our holding in *Hodges
v. Tama County*, 91 Iowa, 578. That was an action
brought to recover for sheep killed by dogs, under the
provisions of chapter 70, Acts Twentieth General
Assembly. It was held in that case that under the
peculiar provisions of the act, because there was no
common law liability for the injury against the county,
and the payment was to be made from a special fund,
against which the claim was, instead of being against
the county, and as the board was authorized to hear evidence and determine the rights of the claimant, the
claim could not "be the subject of a civil action, nor
within the jurisdiction of the district court." The
two statutes are widely different in the particulars to be considered for the purposes of this case.
In that statute the county is not made liable for a
service rendered in behalf of the public in the interest
of the preservation of property generally. That act
does not say that there shall be compensation for such
losses upon the facts being found. It does not provide
for payment by the county, and it does provide that
"the board shall hear and determine such claims,
* * * and shall allow the same or such portions
thereof as they may deem just." The statute in this
case is that "a bounty shall be allowed on the skin of a
wolf," fixing the amount. It is a provision to encourage
and compensate the killing of animals that are a public
enemy. Without the words as to "other evidence,"
there is not room for doubt that the law intended that
the payment should be made on the "certified statement

of the facts." It cannot be that the words "together with such other evidence as the board of supervisors may demand showing the claimant entitled thereto" are intended to invest the board with a discretion to pay or not if the essential facts are established to its satisfaction. It is to be understood that the only question we have before us, is whether, with the facts conceded that the claimant has fully complied with the law, and the facts are without dispute, he may enforce his claim in a court of law, if denied to him by the board. It seems to us the statute means this: That, besides the certified statement, the board may demand other evidence, with a view of knowing if the facts justify the payment of the bounty. If so, its payment is the legal right of the claimant. So long as the facts are open to question, it is a matter within the discretion of the board, but that discretion cannot overrule undisputed facts in favor of the claimant. The judgment is REVERSED.

P. L. SCHOEP, Administrator, v. THE BANKERS ALLIANCE INSURANCE COMPANY OF CALIFORNIA, Appellant.

Insurance: ACTION BY ADMINISTRATOR. The administrator of insured cannot maintain an action on a certificate of insurance payable to
4   the legal heirs of insured, but the action must be brought by such heirs. *Distinguishing Kelly v. Mann,* 56 Iowa, 625; *Rhode v. Bank,* 52 Iowa, 375

SAME. The provisions of Code 1873, sections 2371, 2372, do not apply to
5   the avails of life insurance which do not belong to the estate of the defendant, and are not designed to authorize the administrator to collect an amount due on a policy which is not a part of the estate, in which belong to the beneficiaries named therein, who are not the legal representatives of the decedent.

PRINCIPAL AND AGENT: *Declarations of agent.* A soliciting agent of
1   an insurance company who has power to take and forward application, receive money, and to reserve fund notes in certain cases, when the certificate of insurance is delivered, has no authority to
8   bind the company by declarations as to the validity of the certificate or as to the rights and liabilities of the company, when not

made in the discharge of his duty, as agent in the transaction in question, though he had the policy in his possession when he made the statements.

RULE APPLIED   In an action on a life policy which had been sent to a bank for delivery, but was not delivered before insured died,
1   defendant claimed that it never became a valid contract. It recited payment by insured of ten dollars, but defendant's solic- iting agent testified that the money had never been paid, and that
8   the policy was not to be delivered until the money was paid. *Held,* that it was error to admit evidence of statements by such agent, after insured's death, that insured "had fully supplied the company," that the policy was all right, that the ten dollars pay- ment for which it provided belonged to him, and that whether he received it was none of the company's business.

Impeachment of Witness: Evidence of the reputation of a witness
2   for veracity in a place where he lived about a year before he testi- fied is competent, in the absence of proof of a subsequent perma- nent residence at any particular place.

Appeal from Sioux District Court.—HON. GEORGE W. WAKEFIELD, Judge.

WEDNESDAY, JANUARY 19, 1898.

ACTION at law to recover the amount of an alleged policy of life insurance. There was a trial by jury, and a verdict and judgment for the plaintiff. The defend- ant appeals.—*Reversed.*

John Wallace for appellant.

Boies & Roth and *E. W. Robey* for appellee.

ROBINSON, J.—The plaintiff is the administrator of the estate of Richard J. Buurman, deceased, and the defendant is an insurance corporation organized and existing under the laws of the state of California. In December of the year 1894, the decedent made applica- tion to the defendant, through one of its soliciting agents, named R. W. Stone, for insurance. In January of the year 1895, the application was approved, and a certificate of membership or policy was forwarded from Los Angeles, in the state of California, to a bank in Sioux Center, in this state. On the thirty-first day of January, and before there was any actual delivery of the certificate to Buurman, he died. The plaintiff claims that the decedent had performed all the conditions required on his part to give the certificate legal effect, and that it is a valid contract of insurance,

1   on which the defendant is liable. The defendant contends that it never became a valid contract, and that the plaintiff is not entitled to maintain this action.

I. The certificate recites the payment by the decedent of an admission fee of ten dollars. A portion of the deposition of Stone, which tended to show that the money had never been paid, and that the certificate was never delivered, and was not to have been delivered until the money was paid, was

2   read in evidence. Witnesses were introduced on the part of the plaintiff to show that the reputation of Stone for truth and veracity was bad in Sioux Center, where he had resided eight or nine months from about the middle of the summer of the year 1894. The defendant objected to the testimony on the ground that Stone resided at Los Angeles when his deposition was taken, and had been in Sioux Center but a short time. The evidence does not show how long he had been a resident of California, and the testimony in question was given about a year after he had ceased to reside in Sioux Center. That time was so short that, in the absence of proof of any permanent residence at any particular place, we think evidence of his reputation for truth and veracity while in Sioux Center was competent. The rule in regard to the admission of such evidence, so far as it relates to the time when the reputation existed, is somewhat flexible. *Buse v. Page*, 32 Minn. 111, (19 N. W. Rep. 736, and 20 N. W. Rep. 95.)

In the case of *State v. Potts,* 78 Iowa, 659, relied upon by the appellant, the witness whose character as a witness was sought to be impeached had been a resident of Des Moines for about five years, but testimony was introduced to show what his reputation was in the place where he had resided before moving to Des Moines. We held that such testimony was erroneously admitted, for the reason that he had been a resident of Des Moines for a sufficient length of time to have acquired a reputation as to truth and veracity there; but we recognized as an exception to the general rule that where a witness had lived at his home, at the time evidence as to his reputation was taken, so short a time as not to have acquired a reputation there, evidence as to his reputation where he was better known was admissible.

II.   Two brothers of the decedent were permitted to testify respecting conversations they had with Stone a few days after the death of their brother, to the effect that Stone had said the decedent "had fully supplied the company," that he said the policy was all right, that the ten dollar payment for which the certificate provided belonged to him, and that whether he received it was none of the company's business. The evidence was objected to by the defendant, and in admitting it we think the court erred. Stone was a soliciting agent, with power to take and forward applications, to receive money which was to be paid, applications, to receive money which was to be paid, and to receive reserve fund notes in certain cases, when the authority to bind the company by declarations as to the validity of the certificate, or as to the rights and liabilities of the company, when not made while discharging his duties as agent in the transaction in question. *Dryer v. Insurance Co.,* 94 Iowa, 471; *Bank v. Kelleog,* 81 Iowa, 126. Whether the certificate was valid was a disputed question in the case, and the testimony received was of a character to prejudice the defendant. The plaintiff does not contend that the declarations of Stone were competent, excepting to show the payment to him of the ten dollars for which the certificate provided, but the questions objected to were not limited to testimony of that character. The certificate was in the possession of Stone at the time the conversation took place, but that fact did not affect the competency of his declarations.

III. The amount of the certificate was made payable, in case of the death of Buurman, to his "legal heirs." It is shown that his mother and several brothers and sisters survived him. The appellant contends that, if it be true that the certificate became a valid and binding contract, the administrator of the estate of the decedent cannot maintain an action upon it, and that such an action can be maintained only by his legal heirs. The contract entered into between the defendant and the decedent must control. That, as we have stated, provides for the payment of the amount of the certificate, in the event of the death of the assured, to his "legal heirs," and at his death their rights became fixed. The amount due by virtue of the certificate did not belong to the estate of the decedent and the administrator of his estate not entitled to recover it. In *McClure v. Johnson*, 56 Iowa, 620, the beneficiary of the insurance was held entitled to the proceeds of it, notwithstanding the attempt of the assured, Johnson, who was her husband, to provide by will for the use of a portion of them for payment of a debt. This court said: "The contract was one of insurance, and by express terms the insurance was to be paid to the defendant if she was living at the time her husband died, and the money became payable to her. She alone could have maintained an action therefor. The estate of Johnson was not entitled to the money." In *Wendt v. Legion of Honor*, 72 Iowa, 682, a certificate

of insurance which provided for the payment of the amount of the certificate, upon the death of the assured, "to his legal heirs," was under consideration. This court said, "While the heirs during the life of the assured had no right in the policy, their interest being nothing more than in expectancy, upon his death they acquired rights which cannot be cut off except in the manner prescribed in the contract." In *Phillips v. Carpenter*, 79 Iowa, 600, a certificate of insurance was involved, which was payable at the death of the assured to "his legal heirs," and this court said, "The certificate under consideration being payable to the 'legal heirs' of Dr. J. H. Phillips, deceased, the proceeds thereof are not to be divided as personal property of the estate, but go directly to the persons designated in the certificate." See, also, *Spry v. Williams*, 82 Iowa, 61; *Bomash v. Order of Iron Hall*, 42 Minn. 241 (44 N. W. Rep. 12); Niblack Benefit Society Accident Insurance (2d ed.), sections 204, 347. The appellee contends that the administrator of the estate of the decedent is the proper person to recover on the certificate, and cites in support of his claim the case of *Kelley v. Mann*, 56 Iowa, 625. But the policy of insurance considered in that case made the amount of the policy payable after the death of the assured to his "legal representatives." As used in the policy, those words referred to the administrator of his estate or the executors of his will. The policy involved in *Rhode v. Bank*, 52 Iowa, 375, was made payable "to the assured, his executors, administrators, or
5   assigns." Sections 2371 and 2372 of the Code of 1873, also cited by the appellee, do not apply to the avails of life insurance, which do not belong to the estate of the decedent, and were not designed to authorize the administrator of his estate to collect an amount due on a policy of insurance which is not a part of the estate of the decedent, but belong to beneficiaries named in the policy, who are not the legal representatives of

the decedent. We conclude that the plaintiff is not entitled to maintain this action.

IV. Questions which we have not set out are presented in argument, but are not likely to be involved in any further proceeding upon the certificate in controversy, and need not be further considered. For the errors which we have pointed out, the judgment of the district court is REVERSED.

HANSEN'S EMPIRE FUR FACTORY, Plaintiff, v. F. TEABOUT, *et al.*, J. J. LONG, Administrator, Etc., ANGIE VALLEAU, Sole Heir, Etc., Defendants and Appellees, E. S. JAFFRAY & COMPANY, WILLIAM YOUNG & COMPANY, and HENRY WELSH, Interveners and Appellants, H. F. BROWN, *et al.*, Interveners and Appellees, and KEITH BROTHERS, Plaintiffs, v. THE SAME DEFENDANTS, Appellees, THE SAME INTERVENERS, Appellants, THE SAME INTERVENERS, Appellees.

Execution Against Decedent: JURISDICTION. Since under McClain's
6   Code, section 4321, none but the court which rendered a judgment
7   can award execution against one deceased after its rendition, the
    judgment creditor cannot enforce payment of the judgment out
    of the deceased's real estate in a county other than that in which
    the judgment was rendered.

Attack on Execution Sale: EXPIRED JUDGMENT LIEN. Since a junior
1   judgment creditor has no right to redeem from an execution sale
    after ten years from the date of his judgment, an action by him,
8   after ten years have expired, to subject real estate to the payment
    of his judgment, and to redeem from execution sales because of
    defects therein, is barred

Estates: FILING CLAIMS: *Limitation of action.* Filing and allow-
    ance of a claim of a judgment creditor against the debtor's estate
4   gives the former no additional right against the real estate of the
    decedent, when the lien of his judgment thereon has expired by
    statutory limitation.

SAME. An action to subject decedent's real estate to the payment of
    judgments rendered before his death and to redeem from execu-
8   tion sales thereof because of alleged defects cannot be maintained

after the expiration of ten years from the rendition of the judgment declared upon.

SAME: *Executors and administrators.* A judgment creditor who has
filed his claim with the debtor's administrator cannot, after the
1   expiration of the lien of his judgment upon the lands of the
5   decedent, proceed, independently of the administrator, to subject
6   the property to the payment of his judgment.

Limitation of Actions: JUDGMENTS *Filing claims.* A judgment
2   against one who has since deceased may be enforced within ten
8   years from the date of its recovery, against the real estate upon
which it is a lien, without filing it as a claim against the estate.

Executors and Administrators: ACTION FOR CREDITORS: *Laches.*
1   An action by a judgment creditor to enforce his lien against a
5   decedent's real estate cannot be maintained independently of the
6   administration proceedings, when the administrator has not
10 refused to bring it, and there has been great delay, and it does not
11 purport to be for the benefit of all the creditors.

Suit by Administrator for Creditors: ADJUDICATION. A creditor in
whose behalf an administrator brought suit to set aside a convey-
9   ance as fraudulent, and to obtain a decree that the grantee held
the property in trust for the payment of debts due from the estate,
is concluded, by an adverse determination of such suit, from
thereafter asserting that the land should be sold to pay his claim
as one of the creditors of the estate.   ·

Estoppel: LACHES. One who attacks a defective sheriff's sale more
1   than ten years after it was made is guilty of such laches as will
11 prevent him from being heard, in the absence of any excuse for
not sooner bringing his suit.

LADD, J., took no part.

Appeal from O'Brien District Court.—HON. S. M. LADD,
Judge.

THURSDAY, JANUARY 20, 1898.

THE two cases entitled as above, involving the
same issues, were tried together in the lower court, and
will be disposed of as one in this court. They are suits
in equity brought by two judgment creditors of F. Teabout and Teabout & Valleau to subject certain real

estate, the title to which is in Angie Valleau, to the payment of these judgments, on the ground that said Valleau held the title in trust for the benefit of Teabout.
Valleau denied the alleged trust, and pleaded that at
the time of the death of Teabout, which occurred in
March, 1888, she was the owner of the real estate, and
that she still held the absolute title thereto.   E. S.
Jaffray & Co., William Young & Co., and Henry Welsh
intervened, setting forth in their petitions the fact that
they were judgment creditors of Teabout, having
recovered their judgments before his death,—Jaffray
& Co. in the United States circuit court for the Northern
district of Iowa, Young & Co. in the circuit court of
O'Brien county, and Welsh in the circuit court of Winneshick county.   They each and all alleged that Valleau
held title to the land under and by virtue of an execution sale of the lands in the case of Hemphill, Hamlin
& Co. against Frank Teabout *et al.*, held on the seventeenth day of May, 1882, and that the execution sale and
deeds thereunder were and are void for the reason that
the land so sold, comprising about two thousand six
hundred acres, was purchased by one Potts, an attorney
for plaintiff in execution, for the nominal sum of seven
hundred and eighty-two dollars, whereas it was in truth
worth thirty thousand dollars; that a part of the land
so sold was the homestead of Teabout, who then occupied the same with his family; that the sheriff did not
cause the said homestead to be marked off, platted, and
recorded as by law provided; that he sold the entire
real estate *en masse*, without first offering it in
smaller tracts, and without first offering all other
real estate before selling the homestead; that Pitts
transferred the certificate of purchase to one Bullis,
who took and received from the sheriff a deed to the
land; that Bullis was the then attorney for Teabout;
that he furnished no part of the money for the purchase
of the certificate; and that Bullis thereafter quitclaimed

the said real estate to defendant Valleau without any
consideration having been paid therefor by her. Interveners further pleaded the death of Teabout, and the
appointment of one J. J. Long as his administrator, and
further alleged that the personal estate of the deceased
was insufficient to pay his debts. They asked that the
sheriff's sale and deeds be set aside, that Angie Valleau
be held to account for the rent of the real estate, that the
property be decreed to be that of Teabout and subject to
the interveners' judgments, that they be permitted to
redeem from the sale under execution, and that executions issue for the sale thereof. Defendant Angie
Valleau answered these petitions, denying the alleged
defects in the sheriff's sales and deeds, and denying that
she held the title in trust, or that she paid no consideration therefor. She further alleges that after the death
of Teabout these intervenors filed their claims with
his administrator, and that thereafter—it being discovered that the personal assets were insufficient—the
administrator brought suit to subject the real estate
to the payment of these and other claims, alleging, as
one of the grounds therefor, the same matters as are set
forth in the interveners' petitions; that this action was
tried, resulting in a decree for this defendant; and that
such determination was a final adjudication of all the
matters complained of by interveners. Defendant
further pleaded the five-year statute of limitations, the
ten-year statute, and laches on the part of the interveners. She also pleaded that, as more than ten years
had elapsed since interveners had obtained their judgments, they ceased to be liens upon the land, and that
the same could not be enforced against it; that interveners had waived their liens, and could only enforce
their claims through the administrator of Teabout.
She also pleaded that the district court had no jurisdiction to award execution on the Jaffray and Welsh judg-

ments, and that the court which awarded the judgments, alone, could do that. She also pleaded a counter-
claim, and asked that her title be quieted as against the
interveners. In reply interveners denied that they had
filed their claims with the administrator before he commenced his suit to subject the lands, denied that said
suit was based upon the same grounds as their intervention, and further denied the application of the statutes
of limitation; or that they had been guilty of laches.
On these issues the cases were tried to the court, resulting in a decree subjecting the lands to the payment of
plaintiffs' judgments, and dismissing the petitions of
intervention. Interveners, Jaffray & Co., Welsh and
Young & Co., appeal.—*Affirmed.*

H. E. Long for appellants.

No appearance for appellees.

DEEMER, C. J.—The trial court found some of the
facts which we believe to be established by the evidence,
and which we here adopt as a partial basis for this
opinion. They are as follows: "Frank Teabout,
1   defendant in this action originally, died in the
year 1888, intestate, leaving no widow, and leaving defendant Angie Valleau, his only child and heir at
law, being the owner of the following described real
estate, situated in O'Brien county, Iowa, to-wit: The
southeast one-fourth and the northeast one-fourth of the
northeast one-fourth and the southwest one-fourth of
the northeast one-fourth, all in section 35, and the west
one-half of the northwest one-fourth and the southeast
one-fourth of the northwest one-fourth and the
west one-half of the southwest one-fourth, all in
section 36,—all being in township 97 north, of
range 40 west fifth P. M. That on the first day
of May, 1883, while said Teabout was the owner of

said real estate, the plaintiff herein obtained a judgment in the district court of O'Brien county, Iowa, for the sum of one thousand five dollars and fifty cents, with interest thereon at six per cent. per annum from said date, and costs of suit, taxed at $———. That under and by virtue of an execution issued upon a certain judgment in favor of Hemphill, Hamlin & Co. against said Teabout, recovered in this court on April 28, 1881, for six hundred and forty-seven dollars and costs, the sheriff of said O'Brien county, Iowa, levied upon two thousand six hundred acres of real estate, including the real estate hereinbefore described; and, certain town lots, and thereafter, on or about June 19, 1882, sold same, all in bulk, without first offering same in smaller tracts, for the full sum of seven hundred and eighty-two dollars and thirty cents, to one G. W. Pitts, who thereafter assigned so much of the certificate of purchase to one Bullis as covered and described the real estate in question in this action (including about nine hundred and sixty acres of other land not in controversy herein) and that of Hansen's Empire Fur Factory against same defendants for the sum of five hundred and sixty dollars and eighty-five cents; the said money for the payment thereof having been furnished by the defendant Angie Valleau, herein, and he having thereafter made to her a quitclaim deed therefor without further consideration. And the court further finds said sheriff's sale and deed were invalid, and conveyed no titel to said Bullis or his grantee, Angie Valleau, defendant herein. The court further finds that on August 8 and September 20 and 21, 1883, respectively, defendant Angie Valleau paid to the clerk of this court the full sum of five thousand one hundred and twenty-five dollars to redeem the lands hereinbefore described, from sheriff's sale upon execution of a judgment in favor of Field, Lindley & Co. against Frank Teabout, under a foreclosure of mortgage upon

said real estate, with other real estate, paramount in
lien to any of said judgments upon said lands; and
under said redemptions sheriff's deeds were made to
said defendant Angie Valleau, which deeds were
invalid, and conveyed no title as against this plaintiff.
The court further finds that plaintiff's said judgment
was a lien upon said real estate junior to the judgments
in favor of Field, Lindley & Co. and Hemphill, Hamlin &
Co. against said Teabout. The court further finds that
the personal estate of said F. Teabout, deceased, is, and
has been ever since his death, insufficient to satisfy any
of the judgments herein set forth in favor of plaintiff
and interveners." On this state of facts Valleau was
ordered to pay plaintiff's judgment within ninety days,
and that if she did not do so the sheriff's sale and deeds
under which she claimed would be set aside, and general execution would issue for the sale of the land to pay
plaintiff's judgment, as well as to satisfy the amount
Valleau had advanced to procure the sheriff's certificate and to redeem from the foreclosure, and, as we
have said dismissed the petitions of intervention. We
are not favored with an argument for appellees, and
have no means of knowing upon what theory the court
acted in reaching his conclusions. It is apparent, however, that it found in favor of Valleau on one or
more of the defenses interposed by her; and we turn,
then, to a consideration of the matters so presented.

And first as to the rights of Welsh: He recovered
his judgment in the circuit court of Winneshick county
on the sixth day of September, 1881, and filed his petition of intervention on October 27, 1893.
2   He did not file his claim with the administrator of Teabout's estate, and therefore
must rely solely upon his judgment. We have
heretofore held, and it is now the settled rule in this

state, that while a judgment against one who has since deceased may be enforced against the real estate
3 upon which it is a lien without filing it is a claim against the estate, yet this must be done while the judgment lien exists. *Baldwin v. Tuttle,* 23 Iowa, 66; *Davis v. Shawhan,* 34 Iowa, 91; *Boyd v. Collins,* 70 Iowa, 296. In the case of *Davis v. Shawhan* we held that, if one seeks to enforce payment of a judgment out of real estate of one deceased, he must do so before his lien expires, and that he cannot do so afterwards. The Welsh judgment ceased to be a lien upon the land at the expiration of ten years from its date (Code 1873, section 2882), and intervener has no remedy against the real estate.

Young & Co. obtained their judgment on September 28, 1882, in the circuit court of O'Brien county, and they filed their petition of intervention on August 15, 1893, more than ten years after they recovered judgment. They are in the same position as intervener Welsh, except that they filed their claim with the administrator December 9, 1892, and the same was allowed by
4 order of the district court of O'Brien county on December 13, 1892. It is apparent that the lien of their judgment had expired when they filed their petition of intervention. The filing and allowance of their claim gave them no additional right as against the real estate, for, as said in *Davis v. Shawhan, supra:* "A judgment creditor has two remedies, or rather, has recourse to two funds. He may either seek payment out of the personal assets, or he may enforce his lien on the real estate. * * * If he adopts the former, he must file his claim, duly proved, within the time limited by the law." "He has no special claim to have his judgment satisfied out of the real estate, and can only seek payment * * * from the personal assests in the

hands of the administrator, in which case the real estate
might in the event of inadequacy of the personal
5   assets, be subjected to the payment thereof.
        * * *" We may also add, in this connection,
that such action must as a general rule, be brought by
the administrator, and, save as to exceptional cases,
within the year allowed for the filing of claims. *Creswell v. Slack*, 68 Iowa, 110; *Minear v. Hogg*, 94 Iowa,
641. Creditors must, as a rule, have a lien before filing
a bill in equity to subject real estate to the payment of
their claims. See Wait, Fraud Conveyance, section 73,
75, 87; *Buchanan v. Marsh*, 17 Iowa, 494; *Goode v. Gar-
rity*, 75 Iowa, 713; *Faivre v. Gillan*, 84 Iowa, 573. We
are aware that there are exceptions to this rule,
as where one has made a fraudulent conveyance
of his property, and thereafter dies, his creditors
may, under certain circumstances, proceed to subject the property without first obtaining judgments upon their claims. But this exception has
reference to claims not reduced to judgment during the
lifetime of the debtor, and also has reference to claims
filed at a proper time with the representative of the
estate. Moreover, as we shall see, these petitions of
intervention are not creditors' bills, but are attempts to
subject property to the payment of judgment liens.

     Jaffray & Co. obtained their judgment in the United
States circuit court for the Northern district of Iowa,
western division, on the twenty-second day of May,
1882, and they filed their petition of intervention on
May 22, 1892, which was within ten years from the time
the judgment was rendered. It also appears that they
filed their claim with the administrator, Long, and
secured the allowance thereof on the twenty-sixth day
of December, 1888. It further appears that the action
brought by Long, administrator, against Valleau, to

subject the real state to the payment of debts was for
the special benefit of this intervener. See *Long*
5   *v. Valleau*, 87 Iowa, 686. As the judgment ceased
to be a lien the next day after the filing of the
petition of intervention, it could only be enforced
in a suit independent of the administration proceedings,
by the levy of an execution upon the real estate; and,
as the judgment debtor is dead, a renewal by *scire facias*
is necessary in order that the lien may be continued and
enforced. In the case of *Albee v. Curtis*, 77 Iowa, 647,
we held that the issuance of an execution did not extend
the lien of a judgment, that the lien was statutory, and
that "the mere lapse of time annihilates the lien of a
judgment." See, also, *Lakin v. C. H. McCormick & Bro.*,
81 Iowa, 548, where it is said: "If he seeks the
advantages of his lien, he should not defer his action
until it is too late to perfect his rights thereunder. The
law fixes the period, and provides the means for rendering his lien effectual. If he neglects action until too late
to complete his work within the period, then the right
to make the levy is a barren one, —in effect, no right."
See, also, *Flagg v. Flagg*, 39 Neb. 229 (58 N. W. Rep.
109); *Denegre v. Haun*, 13 Iowa, 245; *Bertram v. Waterman*, 18 Iowa, 529; *Hendershott v. Ping*, 24 Iowa, 134;
Boyle v. Maroney, 73 Iowa, 70. *Postlewait v. Howes*, 3
Iowa, 364, is not in conflict with these subsequent cases.
If, then, Jaffray & Co.'s judgment ceased to be a lien at
the expiration of ten years from its date, and if the
issuance of an execution upon *scire facias* will not
renew it, it is clear that they have no right to proceed,
independent of the administrator, to subject the property to the payment of their judgment.

In so far, then, as these interventions are actions
brought by judgment creditors to enforce their claims
and liens against property of one deceased after the
rendition of their judgments, they are barred by reason

of the statute limiting judgment liens to the period of
ten years. It may also be said that Jaffray &
7   Co. and Welsh are not in position to enforce their
liens, as they are required to have their right to
executions renewed because of the death of the judgment debtor, and this they cannot do except in the
court where the judgments were ˙ rendered. See
McClain's Code, section 4321. Appellants' counsel contend that this section, as printed in McClain's Code, is
incorrect, that the reading as given in the original Code
of 1873 is correct, and that interveners had the right
to have execution awarded in the O'Brien county district court. We find that Mr. McClain has properly
stated the facts with reference to the passage of this
section of the Code, and that his rendering is the correct one. The original bill is as stated by Mr. McClain,
and it follows that none but the court which renders the
judgment has power to award execution against one
deceased since the rendition thereof. This, in itself,
would be a sufficient answer to the claims of interveners
Jaffray & Co. and Welsh, for it must be remembered
that this is not an action to set aside conveyances made
by deceased because of fraud, but to subject certain
real estate to the payment of judgments rendered before
his death, and to redeem from execution sales
8   thereof because of certain defects therein. In
the case of *Albee v. Curtis, supra,* we held that a
junior judgment creditor had no right to redeem after
the expiration of ten years from the rendition of his
judgment. See, also, *Long v. Mellet,* 94 Iowa, 548.
Young & Co.'s claim is clearly barred by the statute.

Long, as administrator, brought his suit to subject
this same real estate to the payment of claims filed
against the Teabout estate, claiming that the conveyance to Angie Valleau was fraudulent, and that she

held the same as a resulting or implied trust for the
Teabout estate, and that the personal estate was
9   insufficient to pay the debts. He was defeated
in his suit, and the decree rendered in that case is
binding upon the creditors whom he represented. It is
settled in this state that an administrator may bring
such a suit. *Cooley v. Brown*, 30 Iowa, 470; *Doe v. Clark*,
42 Iowa, 123; *Harlin v. Stevenson*, 30 Iowa, 371. As he
had this authority, the parties for whose benefit the
suit was brought are concluded thereby. *Perry v. Mills*,
76 Iowa, 622; Freeman, Judgments, (4th ed.) section
163; 2 Van Fleet, Former Adjudication, 925; *Mehlhop
v. Ellsworth*, 95 Iowa, 657. Interveners Jaffray & Co.
are clearly concluded by this determination,from claiming that the land should be sold to pay their claim as
one of the creditors of the estate. Young & Co. are also
concluded, if it be held that they filed their claim in
time to be entitled to any of the general assets. In
view of our holding, it is unnecessary to consider
whether or not Welsh is bound by the decree rendered
in that case.

Let it be conceded, however, that this case presents
issues, different from those presented in the case
brought by the administrator. What, then, is the situation? Clearly, those creditors who filed their claims
with the administrator are estopped from claiming that
the conveyance from Teabout to Valleau was fraudulent. They must recover, then, upon the theory that
they are judgment lien-holders (which we have seen
they cannot do), or upon the proposition that they are
creditors of Teabout's estate, that the personal assets
are insufficient to pay his debts, and that they are
entitled to have the real estate sold, or a right of
redemption given, to pay their claims. There are several insuperable objections to this last claim:
10   First, the administrator must, as a general rule,
bring such an action, and it must, ordinarily, be
brought within the year allowed for filing claims. The

administrator brought a suit for this purpose, and was
defeated. Again, the administrator did not refuse to
bring such suit, and no reason is given why the creditors
proceed, instead of the administrator. Moreover, no
excuse is given why such suit, even if it could be
brought, was delayed for nearly five years from the date
of Teabout's death. A still further objection is found
in the fact that the actions are and were independent,
and not for all the creditors,—thus evidencing the fact
that the suits are for the purpose of enforcing liens
independent of the administration proceedings.

Another cogent reason why interveners cannot
recover on any theory is found in the fact that they
have been guilty of such laches as that they
should not be heard to complain. The sheriff's sales
which they attack were made more than ten
11 years ago. They were and are defective, because
the land was sold *en masse*, and because the
homestead was not platted and set apart. They offer
no excuse for not sooner bringing their suits, and it
seems to us they ought not now to be heard to complain.
Williams v. Allison, 33 Iowa, 278; *Coriell v. Ham*, 4 G.
Greene, 455.

It is not necessary for us to determine whether the
decree rendered by the court upon Long's application
to sell was *res adjudicata* as to all matters which might
have been pleaded in that case. The decree of the district court, in so far as the interveners are concerned, is
right, and it is AFFIRMED.

LADD, J., took no part.

E. J. COLE, Appellant, v. T. M. EDWARDS, L. CRANE, and SAMUEL BOONE.

Supersedeas Bond: WHAT RECOVERABLE UNDER. Damages for defendant's continuing to practice his profession penaing his appeal from a decree enjoining his future practice are not covered by the supersedeas bond conditioned for payment of "all costs and damages that shall be adjudged against said appellant in this appeal." Nothing but damages adjudged on the appeal are recoverable on such bond.

*Appeal from Harrison District Court.—*HON. F. R. GAYNOR, Judge.

THURSDAY, JANUARY 20, 1898.

FROM an order striking the main item of damages from plaintiff's petition, he appeals.—*Affirmed.*

S. H. Cochran for appellant.

Roadifer & Arthur for appellees.

LADD, J.—After the affirmance of a decree permanently enjoining the defendant Edwards from practicing his profession in Woodbine and vicinity, (*Cole v. Edwards,* 93 Iowa, 477), the plaintiff began this action on the supersedeas bond filed in that case. conditioned for the payment of "all costs and damages that shall be adjudged against said appellant on this appeal," and alleged, among other things, that during the pendency of the appeal Edwards continued in the practice of medicine in the same locality, and that by reason thereof the plaintiff sustained damages in the sum of one thousand, five hundred dollars. All the averments of the petition with reference to this item of damages were stricken therefrom, on motion of the defendants, because "no recovery for said damages is provided for in the conditions of said appeal bond, and no legal recovery can be had for such damages." The plaintiff elected to stand on this ruling, and, having taken judgment on other items included in the bond, appeals.

This order may be upheld on either of the two grounds: (1) The damages were not covered by the bond, and (2) were not occasioned by the appeal. Liability cannot be extended beyond the terms of such an instrument. *Jayne v. Drorbaugh*, 63 Iowa, 711. See *Noyes v. Granger*, 51 Iowa, 227; 1 Enc Pl. & Prac. 1015, and notes. Damages adjudged on appeal, and not such as result from a violation of the writ of injunction, are those contemplated by the bond. An appeal or stay does not vacate or affect the judgment appealed from. Code 1873, section 3186. The decree perpetually enjoining Edwards from engaging in the practice of medicine at Woodbine and vicinity was not vacated or suspended by the appeal, or the filing of the bond. *Lindsay v. District Court*, 75 Iowa, 509. See *Allen v. Church*, 101 Iowa, 116, 2 Enc. Pl. & Prac. 326. If he did as alleged, he was guilty of contempt of court, and all the provisions of law for enforcing obedience might have been resorted to by the plaintiff as freely after as before the filing of the bond. The damages, if any, were occasioned, not by reason of, but in spite of, the procedure and orders of the court.—AFFIRMED.

JOSIAH DAY, Appellant, v. ANN GOODWIN, Appellee, H. M. STEVENS, JOSIAH DAY, Substituted as Plaintiff, v. ANN GOODWIN, RICHARD GOODWIN, *et al.*, Appellees.

Judgment Construed: EFFECT. A decree in a suit in which plaintiff
1　asks, as against all defendants, a judgment of foreclosure, is

3 good to some extent as against all the defendants, in a proceeding
4 not regularly attacking it, but expressly ignoring or denying its
existence; the entry being entitled against all the defendants, the
decree reciting due and legal service on them, adjudging them in
default, finding that plaintiff is entitled to foreclose as prayed for,
and ordering the land sold, though personal judgment is given
only against one, and his right of redemption alone is cut off.

ACTION TO ANNUL. All the parties to a judgment should be made
4 parties to a proceeding either in equity or at law, under the stat-
5 ute, to annul it.

COLLATERAL ATTACK. Service appearing on the face of the record to
2 be good, and the court having taken jurisdiction, the judgment is
4 not void; and the intrinsic facts relied on to defeat the service
6 can be shown only on direct attack of the judgment.

RULE APPLIED. A judgment rendered in a foreclosure action is not
2 void, although the notice of the pendency of the foreclosure pro-
4 ceedings was served upon one who had previously been adjudged
6 insane, without at the same time leaving a copy for her with her
husband, with whom she resided, and who was likewise a party to
the action, and served with process on the same occasion.

Appeal: REVIEW. Plaintiff having asked for a *nunc pro tunc* order
7 requiring the clerk to record a former decree, and defendant
moved for leave to answer, defendant, not having appealed, can-
8 not, on the appeal of plaintiff from the denial of the order, claim
any affirmative relief as to or by reason of the motion, relative to
which the lower court took no action.

Nunc pro tunc Orders. Where no rights of third parties have intervened or will be affected thereby, plaintiff is entitled to a *nunc pro*
9 *tunc* order requiring a clerk to record a decree which has been
prepared and signed by the judge, and given to the clerk, who
filed, but failed to record it.

Appeal from Calhoun District Court.—HON. Z. A.
CHURCH, Judge.

THURSDAY, JANUARY 20, 1898.

THESE cases were submitted and will be considered
together. The matters involved are so intimately
related that they, in effect, present but one cause. The
facts will be found in the opinion. There was a decree
and judgment below for defendants. Plaintiff appeals.
—*Reversed.*

M. W. Frick and *H. S. Winslow* for appellant.

Botsford, Healey & Healey for appellees.

WATERMAN, J.—On October 3, 1885, the defendants
Ann Goodwin and Richard, her husband, being indebted
to one H. M. Stevens, executed to him their promissory
note for the amount, and also a mortgage securing it,

1   on the real estate in controversy, situated in
Calhoun county, Iowa. An action was brought
in the name of Stevens, as plaintiff, and against
the Goodwins and one Horton and one Dautremont, as
defendants, to foreclose this mortgage, at the February
term of the Calhoun district court. The proceedings
thereafter in said foreclosure, in the order in which they
occurred, are as follows: Complete record entry: "And
now, to-wit, on this twentieth day of February, A. D.
1889, the same being the second day of the regular February, 1889, term of said court, Richard Goodwin,
defendant, files answer. Default. Personal service,
Ann Goodwin, A. A. Horton, L. A. Dautremont. Now,
to-wit, on this twenty-first day of February, A. D. 1889,
the same being the third day of the regular February,
1889, term of said court, reply to answer of Richard
Goodwin. Defendant Richard Goodwin files motion to
take evidence in form of depositions. Motion sustained,
and the evidence of defendant is ordered to be in the
form of depositions, and the plaintiff, at his election,
may take his either in form of depositions or any way on
the time of trial. Judgment for amount of one note and
attorney's fees against Ann Goodwin, defendant. To
all defendant excepts, Richard Goodwin." This entry
seems to be but a copy of the entry in the judge's docket.
On February 20, 1889, a decree was signed by the judge,
reciting due service of original notice upon Ann Goodwin, Horton and Dautremont, giving judgment against

Ann Goodwin for one thousand two hundred and ninety-
one dollars and nine cents, with interest at eight per
cent, and costs of suit taxed at sixty-nine dollars and
twenty-six cents, and decreeing a foreclosure of the
mortgage and sale of the land, and ordering special
execution therefor. This decree was filed, with the
papers in the cause, February 20, 1889, but was never
recorded. On October 10 of the same year, the matter
coming on for hearing against Richard Goodwin, a
supplemental decree was entered and recorded in
which a judgment was rendered against him for
one thousand, five hundred and sixty-one dollars and
twenty-seven cents, with interest at eight per cent, and
costs of suit, including attorney's fees, taxed a ninety-
two dollars and ninty-five cents, and foreclosing the
mortgage, and ordering special execution to issue. This
cause was known as "Equity No. 579," and will be so
referred to here. Thereafter, on November 16, 1889, the
land was sold under special execution issued on both
said decrees for the sum of one thousand six hundred
and ninety-seven dollars and thirteen cents; and plaintiff Day, as assignee of the certificate of sale, received
on November 19, 1890, a sheriff's deed. Plaintiff has
owned and occupied the premises since that time, and
has made valuable improvements thereon. It appears,
too, that plaintiff took the assignment of the certificate
of sale at the request of Richard Goodwin, and that,
upon the latter's representation that no redemption
would be made, plaintiff paid him the sum of four hundred dollars. These facts are shown by plaintiff in the
case of Day against Goodwin, and it is asked that
his title be quieted. The defendant appears by
Richard Goodwin, as her guardian, and admits
the execution of the mortgage and note. But it is
alleged that said Ann Goodwin was of unsound mind
at the time of the service of the original notice in No.
579, and has been so judicially declared. This notice, it

may be here said, was served by reading and giving a copy thereof to Ann Goodwin, as provided in section 2603 of the Code of 1873. A cross bill is also filed in which is set up the insanity of defendant, the owner-ship of the land, and a denial of the fact that any judg-ment was rendered in the foreclosure proceedings. It is also claimed that Day is liable for the rental value of said premises in the amount of one thousand eight hundred dollars; and the prayer is that she have judg-ment against him, and that her title be quieted. The lower court allowed the plaintiff the amount due on his mortgage, charged him for rents, and gave judgment for the remainder, one thousand, five hundred and forty-two dollars and forty three cents, to plaintiff, and established it as a lien on the land. It set aside the sheriff's deed to plaintiff, and decreed title to the prem-ises to be in defendant, and the real estate was then ordered sold to pay plaintiff's lien. On motion, it was ordered that all costs, including filing fee and service of original notice, except costs of witnesses who testified to improvements, be taxed to plaintiff. From this decree and order plaintiff appeals. To avoid confusion, we will consider these issues first, and state the facts in the case of Stevens against Goodwin later on.

Plaintiff, claiming title through the proceedings in the Stevens foreclosure, seeks to quiet the same as against Ann Goodwin, who was a defendant therein. It is claimed in her behalf that the sale and deed in that case were void, for that no judgment was ever ren-dered in said cause. This must be the ground
3   upon which the defendant can succeed, if at all, for the claim that the original notice was not properly served, and which will be spoken of more fully later, cannot be considered except upon application to set aside the judgment if one was rendered; and neither the answer nor cross bill suggests that any such relief is desired. The theory of the defense is that equity

cause No. 579 is still open and pending, and that Ann
Goodwin has a right to make defense therein. We may
assume that the entry apparently copied from the
judge's docket is, so far as it pretends to be a judgment,
absolutely void, and that the decree signed by Judge
Conner, but never recorded, has in such condition no
force or effect; but there is still another entry to be disposed of, and this is the supplemental decree of October
10, 1889, which was duly recorded and approved.

4   This language is found in this entry: "And the
court finds, after an inspection of the record,
that due and legal service of notice of the pendency of
this cause has been made upon said defendants, and
that said defendants having failed to appear, and
though solemnly called, came not, but made default, it
is therefore ordered by the court that said defendants
be adjudged in default." The court further finds that
"plaintiff is entitled to a foreclosure of said mortgage
as prayed in the petition." A judgment is then given
against Richard Goodwin, the land ordered sold, and
his equity of redemption decreed to be barred. This
entry is entitled against Ann Goodwin, Richard Goodwin, Dautremont, and Horton. The parties were all
adjudged to be in court. The plaintiff was asking as
against all defendants a judgment of foreclosure. Reading the decree in the light of the record, and it in terms
appears that all defendants were held to be in default,
and the land ordered sold, though personal judgment is
given only against Richard Goodwin, and his right of
redemption alone is cut off. It is, as against Ann Goodwin, certainly informal. It might not withstand a
direct attack. It may be that it was not intended to
mean all that it says, but we think it must be held good,
to some extent at least, as against all defendants in a
proceeding that expressly ignores or denies its existence.

There are two methods, either of which defendant
could have adopted to secure relief as against this judgment if it is voidable for any of the reasons she sets up.
She could have instituted proceedings at law under
sections 3154, 3157, and 3158, Code 1873, by asking to
have the judgment vacated, or she might have proceeded in equity. See *Jackson v. Gould.* 96 Iowa, 488;
Larson v. Williams, 100 Iowa, 114, and cases cited. But
in either such event the parties to the judgment
5   should be made parties to the proceeding to
annul it. In the case at bar the proper parties
were not in court to authorize relief against the judgment, even if such relief was asked. But it is claimed
by defendant, in effect, that there was no notice of the
pendency of the foreclosure proceedings served upon
her, and that, because of this fact, the judgment therein
is absolutely void as to her, and may be ignored.
6   The notice was in fact served by reading and
giving to her a true copy, as provided by section
2603 of the Code of 1873, as already said; and, although
Mrs. Goodwin had been previously adjudged insane,
she was not, when the foreclosure suit was begun, confined in an asylum, but was living with her husband;
nor had she a guardian at this time. The notice was
served both upon Ann and Richard Goodwin, who were
parties defendant. The statute (section 2615, Code 1873)
requires that in such cases the service on the insane
person "may be made upon him and upon his guardian,
and if he have no guardian then upon his wife or the
person having the care of him or with whom he lives,"
etc. A strict compliance with this provision would
have required the notice to Ann Goodwin to be served,
not only on her, but also on her husband, although, as a
matter of fact, he was present at the time, and was
served with a similar notice as a joint defendant.
Though the notice be irregular and insufficient, yet, if
the court takes jurisdiction, the judgment is not void.

De Tar v. Boone County, 34 Iowa, 488; *Woodbury v.
Maguire*, 42 Iowa, 339; *Moomey v. Mass*, 22 Iowa, 380.
There are many other cases to like effect, but we need
not cite them. The service appears upon the face of the
record to be good. The defendant relies upon extrinsic
facts to defeat it. We think it manifest on principle
that in such case the showing can be made only in a
direct attack on the judgment. It may be said in defendant's behalf that the action on her part below, in
the case of *Stevens v. Goodwin*, being "Equity No.
579," was in the nature of a direct attack. This naturally leads to a consideration of what was done in that
case.

After the action of *Day v. Goodwin* was
brought, and after the discovery that the entry signed
by Judge Conner had not been recorded, defendant, on
October 7, 1895, filed an answer of general denial in
"No. 579." Day moved to strike this answer from the
files. There was no ruling on this motion. On
October 8, 1895, Day made a motion to be substituted as plaintiff in No. 579, and for an order
nunc pro tunc requiring the clerk to record the Conner
decree. October 12, 1895, Defendant Ann Goodwin,
through her guardian, filed a motion for leave to
answer in said cause, and attached to the motion an
answer containing substantially the same facts we have
been considering in *Day v. Goodwin*. No ruling
was made on this motion. Thereafter, on October 13,
1896, the trial court entered an order allowing Day to
be substituted as plaintiff, but holding that "he had no
right to have a *nunc pro tunc* order made directing the
clerk to record in the records of the court the certain
alleged judgment and decree as of the twentieth of
February, 1889." From this order the appeal we are
considering was taken by Day. No complaint of
the lower court's action or non-action is made by
Goodwin. Conceding that Ann Goodwin's proceedings in this matter were in the nature of a direct

attack, yet her right has not been passed upon by the lower court. Not having appealed, she can claim no affirmative relief here at this time. Her motion for leave to answer still stands undisposed of in the lower court. We have, then, to consider only whether plaintiff was entitled to the *nunc pro tunc* order asked.

It is not claimed that any rights of third parties have intervened or will be affected by such order. The action of the lower court in substituting Day as plaintiff in that cause is not questioned. The right claimed to a *nunc pro tunc* order is only a right to have the records show what the court in fact did in the case. The decree was prepared and signed by the judge, and given to the clerk, who filed, but failed to record it. In passing upon the right to this order, it is immaterial whether the proceedings in the case were regular or irregular, valid or invalid. The sole matter to consider is, shall the failure of a mere ministerial officer to perform his duty have the clerk to falsify the action of the court? We think the authorities sustain the right of Day to have the order prayed for. *Fuller v. Stebbins*, 49 Iowa, 376; *Tracy v. Beeson*, 47 Iowa, 155; *Buckwalter v. Craig*, 24 Iowa, 215; *Shelley v. Smith*, 50 Iowa, 543. It is true that the order made by the court in Equity No. 579 was not entered until after the decree was rendered in Day against Goodwin, but this should not prejudice plaintiff, for his application for the relief was on file long before the disposition of the case last mentioned.

What we have said makes our conclusions apparent. Plaintiff should have had a decree on his bill to quiet title, the costs should have been taxed to defendant, and plaintiff was entitled to the order prayed for in No. 579. The action of the lower court in both cases will be REVERSED.

T. W. HARRISON V. PALO ALTO COUNTY, Appellant.

Counties: POWERS: *Deed with warranty.* A county has no authority
    to execute a deed with covenants of warranty, as no statute con-
6 fers such power, and it cannot be implied; being neither necessary
    in order to make such conveyance available, or essential to the
7 purpose of such corporation   Citing *Findla v. San Francisco,* 18
    Cal. 534; *Hamilton v. Shelbyville* (Ind. App.) 34 N. E. Rep 1007;
    Lang v. Duluth (Minn.) 59 N. W. Rep. 878.

FRAUD IN SALE BY.   Where the grantee in a deed made by a county in
    settlement of litigation pending between the parties had knowl-
8 edge respecting the title equal to that possessed by the agents of
    the county, who concealed nothing from him, and were guilty of
    no other fraud, the mere failure of the title to the land conveyed
    did not render the county liable to him as for money had and
    received

SAME.   An action for fraud will not lie against a county upon failure
7 of title to land deeded by it in compromise of a pending litiga-
    tion, when no fact was withheld from the record, or any statement
6· made to the grantee, except such as could be inferred from the
    fact that the land was offered and deeded as part consideration
    for a compromise.

Assumpsit.   In the absence of a warranty, or of fraud in inducing the
6 conveyance. the failure of the title will not support an action
7 against the grantee for money had and received.

LIMITATION OF ACTIONS   An action for deceit in the sale of land is in
9 tort, and barred in five years after the discovery of the fraud

REPAIR OF BRIDGES.   It being the duty of a county to keep its bridges
    and the approaches thereto in repair, where sand and gravel were
    taken from plaintiff's land, with his consent, by direction of the
    board of supervisors of the defendant county, for the construction
11 and repair of the approach to a county bridge, defendant was
    liable for the value thereof, as on an implied contract, and not for
    what it would cost to restore the land from which it was taken to
    its former condition.

Appeal: NOTICE.   The fact that a notice of appeal erroneously names
2 the term or fixes the time of hearing, is immaterial.

SAME.   The statute respecting notice of appeal (Code 1873, section
    3178), does not require that it name the term at which the appeal
2 will be heard; and therefore words so used, though erroneous, do

not affect the validity of the notice, but are to be regarded as surplusage.

OWNER OF CONTINGENT FEE. Attorneys who agree to present a case upon appeal for a contingent fee, do not thereby become parties
1 to the action and entitled to service of notice of appeal.

DISMISSAL. *Payment for transcript.* An appeal will not be dismissed on the ground that the clerk's fees have not been paid and can-
8 not be waived, when he had performed all the duties required of him and certified the transcript of the record.

Assignments. That no errors are assigned will not require the dis-
4 missal of an appeal, although the action is at law, when the parties treated it in the lower court, as in equity.

ABSTRACTS. Where it was certified in the abstract that it contained
5 all the evidence, and appellant filed an amendment covering the alleged defects, and reaffirming such facts, and appellee also filed an abstract setting forth some omissions and corrections, the cause was properly before this court.

REVIEW. The disallowance of a claim for damages, although pre-
10 sented in the briefs, will not be considered, when the party injured thereby has not appealed.

Appeal from Palo Alto District Court.—HON. W. B. QUARTON, Judge.

FRIDAY, JANUARY 21, 1898.

ACTION at law to recover damages for failure of title to certain land deeded by defendant to plaintiff in settlement of a claim held by him; to recover compensation for earth and gravel taken from plaintiff's land, and used by the county in building approaches to its bridges; for trespass upon his land; and for taking certain lands for use as a public highway without compensation. The case was tried as in equity, resulting in a judgment for plaintiff in the sum of one thousand, six hundred and fifty-nine dollars and eighty-five cents. The court also issued an injunction restraining defendant from committing further trespasses upon plaintiff's lands, but refused to grant an injunction restraining the county from using certain land as a highway. The county alone appeals. —*Modified and affirmed.*

John Menzies, county attorney, and *Soper, Allen & Morling* for appellant.

T. W. Harrison (pro se), McCarty & Linderman, and *George E. Clarke* for appellee.

DEEMER, C. J.— After the case was tried in the lower court, Soper, Allen & Morling, attorneys, entered into a contract with the county by which they agreed to present the case upon appeal to this court, for a contingent fee. Appellee insists that, as they had an interest in the outcome of the suit, they should have been served with notice of appeal. That this firm of attorneys have the case on a contingent fee is conceded, but it does not follow that they should be served with notice of appeal. The notice is to be served upon the adverse party. The attorneys are not parties, and, had they been assignees, it was not necessary to serve notice of appeal upon them. *Littleton Sav. Bank v. Osceola Land Co.,* 76 Iowa, 660.

The case was determined in May, 1896; and the notice of appeal (which was in the usual form), among other things, recited that the appeal would come on for hearing "at the January term of the supreme court, * * * commencing on the third Tuesday of January, 1896." This notice is said to be so defective as to amount to no notice. The law fixes the term at which a cause shall stand for hearing in this court. Code 1873 sections 3180-3182. And the fact that the notice does not name the term, or that it erroneously fixes the time of hearing, is of no consequence. *Geyer v. Douglass,* 85 Iowa, 96; *Mickley v. Tomlinson,* 79 Iowa, 385. The statute with reference to the notice does not require that it name the term at which the appeal will

be heard. See Code 1873, section 3178. If the notice
does so, the words used are to be regarded as surplusage, and do not affect the validity of the notice.

Appellee further contends that the appeal has not
been perfected, for the reason that the clerk's fees have
not been paid or secured. It appears, however, that the
clerk expressly waived this requirement. It is argued,
however, that he cannot make such waiver. We think
he may. But whether this is true or not the appeal
should not be dismissed, for the reason that the clerk
has performed all the duties required of him, and has
certified the transcript of the record to this court. This
is sufficient. See *Fairburn v. Goldsmith*, 56 Iowa, 348;
Searles v. Lux, 86 Iowa, 61; *Bruner v. Wade*, 85 Iowa,
666; *Slone v. Berlin*, 88 Iowa, 205. See, also, *Simplot v.
City of Dubuque*, 49 Iowa, 630.

It is also contended that the appeal should be dismissed because no errors are assigned. The action was
undoubtedly at law, but the parties treated it in the
lower court as if in equity, and it will be so
4   treated here. *Lemert v. McKibben*, 91 Iowa, 349;
Bryant v. Fink, 75 Iowa, 518; *Spring Co. v.
Smith*, 90 Iowa, 335.

Further claim is made that the abstract on its face,
shows that it does not contain all the evidence offered
upon the trial. There is a certificate in the abstract
that it contains all, and the appellant has filed
5   an amendment covering the alleged defects, and
re-affirms the statement made in the original
abstract. Appellee has also filed an amended abstract,
setting forth some omissions and corrections. With
these additions, the case seems to be properly before us.
Seekell v. Norman, 76 Iowa, 234; *State v. O'Day*, 68
Iowa, 213.

With these preliminaries disposed of, we now come
to the merits. It appears that plaintiff was engaged in

protracted litigation with the defendant over certain
swamp-land contracts. One of these cases
6   reached this court. See 68 Iowa, 85. While this
litigation was pending, a contract of settlement
was entered into, which lies at the basis of this controversy. By the terms of the settlement the defendant
county was to make a warranty deed to the plaintiff
for the lands in dispute, as well as other property—
amounting in all to eight hundred and forty acres of
land, and one thousand and twenty dollars in money.
The lands were all supposed to be swamp lands, but
the forty acres in controversy was high, dry land, and
the same was never patented to the county. The warranty deed agreed upon was executed, and plaintiff
seeks to recover upon the covenants, or because the title
has failed, and says that he is entitled to the value of the
land, which he claims was agreed to be worth eight hundred dollars at the time the contract of settlement was
entered into. He further says that he was defrauded
by the county, and "that in giving said deed, and representing that the said Palo Alto county had perfect
title thereto, the plaintiff was deceived and defrauded."

It is practically agreed that the county had no
title when the conveyance was made, and the first
question which arises is, is it liable upon its covenants
of warranty? Municipal corporations have and
7   can exercise only such powers as are expressly
granted to them by law, and such incidental ones
as are necessary to make those powers available, and
are essential to effectuate the purposes of the corporation; and those powers are strictly construed. *Becker
v. Waterworks*, 79 Iowa, 422; *Webster County v. Taylor*,
19 Iowa, 117; *Baker v. Washington County*, 26 Iowa,
154. Swamp lands passed to the different counties of
the state, and section 956 of the Revision provided:
"That no swamp or overflowed lands granted to the
state, and situated in the present unorganized counties,

shall be sold or disposed of till the title to said lands shall be perfected in the state, whereupon the titles to said lands shall be transferred to said counties where they are situated." After the title to such land was perfected in the state, the county had authority to sell and convey the same. But there is no statute giving it power to execute a deed with convenants of warranty. If it had such authority, it is in virtue of its implied power. Such power is not necessary to make the con· veyance available. Nor is it essential to the purposes and objects of the corporation. A conveyance or assur· ance is good and perfect without either a warranty or a personal covenant. And, as the powers granted to or implied of a municipal corporation are only such as are necessary to make those expressly granted avail· able, it seems quite clear that it has no authority to execute a deed with covenants of warranty. See, as sustaining this conclusion, to some extent, at least, *Carter v. City of Dubuque*, 35 Iowa, 416; *Findla v. City and County of San Francisco*, 13 Cal. 534; *Brockman v. City of Creston*, 79 Iowa, 589; *Stidger v. City of Red Oak*, 64 Iowa, 466; Jones Real Property, sections, 830, 831; *Hamilton v. City of Shelbyville*, 6 Ind. App. 538 (33 N. E. Rep. 1007). Again, the title to the land which the county attempted to convey had not been perfected in the state, and was not in fact swamp, but high, dry land. One of the witnesses says, "It was one of the highest hills in the country." In the case of *Findla v. City and County of San Francisco*, *supra*, it is held that the town was authorized to make a conveyance of its own land, but was not bound by a conveyance (contain· ing covenants) of a lot belonging to a stranger. See, also, *Sang v. City of Duluth*, 58 Minn. 878 (59 N. W. Rep. 878). We are well satisfied that the defendant had no power or authority to execute a deed with cove· nants. Appellee insists, however, that, if the county had no such power, yet, as it received the benefits of the contract, it is liable to him as for money had and received. It seems to be settled that in the absence of a warranty, or of fraud inducing the conveyance, there is no liability of the grantor for failure of title. If the deed be delivered to the purchaser, he has received the entire consideration for which he has bargained, and mere failure of title is not sufficient to support a plea for money had and received. *Nelson v. Hamilton County*, 102 Iowa, 229; *Allen v. Pegram*, 16 Iowa, 172; *Funk v. Creswell*, 5 Iowa, 84; Rawle, Covenants (5th ed.) sections 320, 321. In the *Nelson Case, supra*, we held that under the facts there shown the county was liable for false and fraudulent representations of its agents in the sale of land. It appeared in that case, however, that the county, through its agents, not only made false and fraudulent representations regarding the title, but also withheld from the record the fact that the title claimed by it had theretofore been adjudged invalid. In the case at bar the only allegation in the pleading which indicates that it is an action for fraud or deceit is the statement which we have before quoted, to the effect that in giving the deed the county represented that it had a perfect title to the land, and plaintiff was deceived and defrauded. There is no the record, or that any other statement was made to the record, or that any other statement was made to plaintiff, except such as could be inferred from the fact that the county offered and deeded the land to him as part consideration for the compromise. Does such a pleading sufficiently state a cause of action for fraud? We think not. In the case of *Clark v. City of Des Moines*, 19 Iowa, 199, which was an action upon certain unauthorized warrants issued by the city council of the defendant city, we held that one taking the warrants was bound, at his peril, to ascertain the nature and extent of the power of the officers and of the city, and that a representation by the municipal authorities that

the warrants were properly issued were not binding
upon the corporation, for the reason that an agent can
neither create nor enlarge his powers by his unauthorized representations. Here there is neither pleading nor
proof that the defendant, or any of its agents, knew that
they had no title to the land, nor that they had any other
or better knowledge with reference thereto than the
plaintiff. Moreover, it affirmatively appears that
plaintiff knew when he took the conveyance that the
land had not been patented or certified to the state, and
he also knew the situation and character of the land.
His knowledge was equal to that of the defendant, and
nothing was concealed from him by the agents of the
county. It must be remembered that the plaintiff took
the lands in settlement of litigation then pending
between the parties, and that he is in no other sense a
purchaser. True it is that the land was valued at eight
hundred dollars in this settlement, but that fact alone
amounts to nothing more than an estimate of the
amount received by the plaintiff in the settlement of his
disputed claim. Possibly it might fix the measure of
recovery in the event plaintiff was found entitled to
anything. But this we do not decide, as it is not necessary to a determination of the case. We are well satisfied the plaintiff is not entitled to recover
9   because of failure of title to the lands. If
recovery were allowed, it would be for deceit
in the sale of the land; and, as this would be for a tort,
the cause of action would be barred in five years after
the discovery of the fraud. The statute began to run,
according to plaintiff's evidence, sometime in the year
1888. He did not commence this action until the year
1895, and it is clearly barred, in so far as it is based
upon fraud.

II. The trial court disallowed plaintiff's claim
of damages for the use of certain of his lands for
10   highway purposes, and, as he has not appealed,
we cannot consider this question, although presented in the briefs.

III. There remains the question as to the liability
of defendant for the sand and gravel used by it in the
repair of a highway which it is claimed was used and
treated as an approach to one of the county
11   bridges, or, if not so used, that the county undertook to keep this highway in repair, and is liable
for the sand and gravel taken for that purpose. It is
the duty of the county to keep its bridges and the
approaches thereto in repair, and it may, under certain
circumstances, make improvements on the highways
out of the surplus in the bridge fund, or from taxes
levied for that purpose. Acts Eighteenth General
Assembly, chapter 88, section 1; Acts Twentieth General Assembly, chapter 200. The highway upon which
the sand and gravel was used was not repaired under
the provisions of either of these acts of the general
assembly, as we understand it; and the county is not
liable for the acts of its agents in taking and using the
property of plaintiff, unless it was used in repairing
the approach to a county bridge. What is such an
approach is purely a question of fact. We are of
opinion that the sand and gravel taken was used upon
a part of the highway which should be held to be an
approach to a county bridge, under the rule established
in *Casey v. Tama County*, 75 Iowa, 655; *Van Winter v.
Henry County*, 61 Iowa, 684, and *Jessup v. Osceola
County*, 92 Iowa, 178. The evidence shows that the
county built the grade where the material was used in
order to make the bridge available and accessible, and
has ever since kept the same in repair. The sand and
gravel were taken by direction of the board of supervisors, and the county should be held liable therefor if

it could have made a contract for the same in the first
instance. That the board could have made a contract
for material to be used in constructing an approach
to one of its county bridges, is clear. And we think
there is no question that it is liable for the sand and
gravel taken; amounting, as near as we are able to
judge, to six hundred yards. This amount was taken
after plaintiff acquired title to the land. We come next
to the amount that plaintiff should be allowed. Reference has already been made to the fact that recovery is
allowed upon the theory of an implied contract, and not
because of a trespass committed by the defendant; and
we may remark, parenthetically, that it is doubtful
whether the action of trespass would lie. But, as plaintiff is not obliged to prove more than is necessary to
entitle him to recovery, the allegations with reference
to trespass may be regarded as surplusage. See
Code 1873, section 2729. We may observe, in passing,
that the material was taken with plaintiff's consent.
Moreover, the plaintiff, in the third count of his petition, asks judgment for the value of the sand and gravel
taken. What, then, is the measure of his recovery?
The liability being upon contract, it is clear that it is
the value of the material taken, and not what it would
cost to place the land from which it was removed in the
condition it was in before the sand and gravel was
taken. The evidence shows it to have been worth from
twenty-five to forty cents a yard, but, as plaintiff claimed
but twenty-five cents in his petition, his recovery must
be limited to that amount. Under the pleadings and
proof, plaintiff is entitled to judgment for the sum
of one hundred and fifty dollars, with six per
cent. interest thereon from May 29, 1895,—amounting in all to one hundred and sixty-five dollars,—and no
more. Appellant will pay one-fourth, and apellee three-
fourths, of the costs of this appeal. At appellant's
option, exercised within twenty days from the filing of

this opinion, a judgment and decree may be entered in this court. If no such election is made, the cause will be remanded for a decree in harmony with this opinion. —MODIFIED AND AFFIRMED.

A. L. STETSON v. THE NORTHERN INVESTMENT COM-
PANY *et al.*, Appellant.

Directors: WHO DEEMED. One who, though not a stockholder in a corporation, acted as a director for two years, was treated by the officers of the company—all of whom were non-residents—as such

1   director and gave advice concerning the affairs of the company in his city, comes within the rule applicable to dealings between a director in his own interest and his corporation.

CONTRACT WITH. One occupying the relation of local director of a corporation whose stockholders were non-residents, sold property to the corporation. His valuation of the property, and his repre-

2   sentations as to its probable rental value, were in excess of the real values, but were mere expressions of opinions. The deal was not consummated until after deliber ations by the stockholders, and until after one director familiar with real estate values in that city had visited the property and made a report. The owner of the property was not present at the meeting at which it was decided to make the purchase. *Held*, that since the owner had not acquired his information as to the values by reason of his position as director of the corporation, and the corporation had not relied solely upon his representation the sale would not be set aside on the ground of fraud or bad faith.

RATIFICATION. A corporation which has purchased property of a director, had paid off incumbrances assumed by it, and had pos-

3   session, management, and control for nearly three years, will be presumed to have ratified the contract, and cannot assert for the first time, as a defense in an action for the price, that the director had acted in bad faith in his representations regarding its value.

LADD, J., took no part.

Appeal from Woodbury District Court.—HON. SCOTT M. LADD, Judge.

FRIDAY, JANUARY 21, 1898.

ACTION for judgment on three promissory notes, and for a decree foreclosing three mortgages on separate

pieces of real estate, given severally each to secure one
of said notes.   Defendants answered, admitting the
execution of the notes and mortgages, and alleged as
defense, in substance, as follows: That during the years
1891 to 1894, inclusive, plaintiff, a resident of Sioux
City, was a member of the defendant's board of seven
directors, six of whom resided in Massachusetts; that
plaintiff was actively engaged in the management of
the affairs of the company, and better informed as to the
values of real estate in Sioux City than any other of
said directors; that in 1891 he was the owner of lots 4,
5, and 6, block 26, Middle Sioux City; that he represented to the other directors that said lots were reasonably worth seventy-five thousand dollars, and that it
would be greatly to the advantage of the company to
purchase said lots, and as a director recommended their
purchase at that price; that to induce the purchase he
offered that, if the defendant company would purchase
said lots and put improvements thereon costing five
thousand dollars, he would pay as rent therefor five
thousand six hundred dollars for three years, well
knowing that said sum greatly exceeded the real rental
value; that said representations as to the value of said
lots were untrue, and known to be so by plaintiff, and
were made for the purpose of cheating and defrauding
the defendant company, said lots not being worth to
exceed thirty-five thousand dollars; that the directors,
relying thereon, entered into a written agreement on
December 17, 1891, to purchase said lots for seventy-
five thousand dollars; that, in pursuance of said agreement, the company delivered the three notes sued upon,
aggregating twenty-nine thousand six hundred and
fifty-eight dollars and twelve cents, and delivered two
hundred shares of its stock, and assumed and agreed
to pay mortgages upon said lots aggregating twenty-
three thousand eight hundred and sixty-nine dollars
and thirty-two cents, and special assessments to the

amount of eight hundred and seventy-two dollars and
fifty-six cents; that the company has paid all of said
assessments and all of said mortgage indebtedness
except about eleven thousand six hundred and eighty-
three dollars, and that said shares of stock and mortgage indebtedness greatly exceed the value of said lots
at the time said representations were made. Defendants allege that, by reason of said facts and false representations, said notes are without consideration, and
that defendants first learned of said false representations about July 20, 1895. Defendants, as counter-
claim, allege, in addition to the foregoing, that after
the sale plaintiff represented that said premises could
be used to better advantage by making more valuable
improvements; that the company, relying thereon, was
induced to make a new lease with plaintiff, whereby he
was to pay a rental of five thousand eight hundred and
fifty dollars for the use of the premises for three years;
that after making said new lease, about September 1,
1892, plaintiff falsely represented that said premises
could be rented to better advantage by the company,
and proposed, in consideration of releasing him from
all liability on said lease, to credit the sum of two thousand one hundred and eighty-six dollars and four cents
on each of said notes, and as a director recommended
the acceptance of said offer; that, believing and relying
upon said representations and recommendations, the
company, in consideration of said credits being made,
released plaintiff from said lease; that said representations were made with the intent to cheat and defraud
the company, and when made said lots could not be
leased for more than two thousand dollars per year;
and that defendants were damaged thereby in the sum
of twelve thousand dollars. As a further counter-
claim the defendants allege that, by reason of said false
and fraudulent representations as to the value of said
property, they had been damaged in the sum of forty

thousand dollars. Defendants ask that plaintiff's
action be dismissed; that said notes and mortgages
may be adjudged fraudulent and void; and that they
have judgment against the plaintiff for fifty-two thousand dollars. Defendants, by amendment, allege that
they were ready and willing to reconvey said property
to plaintiff upon receipt of the amount paid by defendants therefor, with interest, and further pray that said
contract of purchase be decreed fraudulent and void,
and that they have judgment accordingly and for damages. Plaintiff, in reply to the answer, denies that he
was ever a director of the defendant company, or acted
as such, except as follows: He avers that on the temporary organization he consented to the use of his name
as director for the purpose of filing the articles of incorporation, and that he never had any other connection
with said corporation, and that said connection ceased
as soon as the stock thereof was subscribed; that he
never held any stock in said corporation except the two
hundred shares received in February or March of 1892,
under said contract of purchase, and which he sold and
transferred the following August; and that March or
May, 1893, he attended a meeting of the directors to
elect a successor to George Leonard, deceased, as president. Plaintiff denies that he was better informed as
to the value of real estate in Sioux City than any of the
directors, and avers that Mr. Leonard gave more attention to and was better informed as to such values than
plaintiff. He denies that he ever made to defendants
any false and fraudulent statements with reference to
said property, or any statements or representations,
except such as he had a full right to make. In answer
to the counter-claim, plaintiff repeats the denials made
in his reply, and denies that the defendants have, by
reason of anything said or done by him, suffered any
damage or acquired any right of action against him.

Decree was rendered in favor of the plaintiff. Defendants appeal.—*Affirmed.*

Milchrist & Robinson for appellant.

Shull & Farnsworth for appellee.

GIVEN, J.—I. Defendants' contentions are based
upon the allegation that at the time of the transactions
under consideration plaintiff was a director in the
defendant company, and actively participating in the
management of its affairs. Plaintiff admits that
1   he was chosen a director in 1891, but contends
that, not being a stockholder, he was not qualified to act, and that he was merely nominally a director,
and did not participate in the affairs of the company.
We are in no doubt but that, whether qualified or not,
plaintiff did act as a director from his election, in 1891,
until July 19, 1893, at which date he presided at a
meeting of the directors called to elect a president to fill
the vacancy caused by the death of Mr. Leonard; also
that he was treated by the officers of the company as a
director, and gave advice concerning the affairs of the
company at Sioux City. We think that, for the purposes of this case, plaintiff should be considered as
coming within the rule applicable to dealings between
a director in his own interests and his corporation.
While many authorities are cited, there is no
2   dispute between counsel as to the rule in this
state. They cite *Buell v. Buckingham,* 16 Iowa,
284, wherein it is said: "A purchase of property by a
trustee of his *cestui que* trust is not void in equity, but is
voidable. Such sale will   set aside for fraud, or upon
a very slight showing of advantage or bad faith; but,
when it is clear that the *cestui que* trust intended that
the trustee should buy, and there is no fraud, no concealment, and no advantage taken by the trustee of

information acquired by him as such, it will be upheld and enforced." The inquiry is whether, in the sale of the lots or in the agreement as to rents, the plaintiff acted fraudulently or in bad faith. The complaint is that he falsely represented the value of the lots and the rental that could be readily realized therefrom. Now, while these were mere expressions of opinions, yet, where special confidence is reposed and the utmost fairness required, such opinions may show fraud or bad faith. That the values represented by plaintiff were excessive is clearly shown, and that they were known to him to be such. It does not appear, however, that the directors made the contracts solely upon the representations of the plaintiff. Plaintiff's offer to sell was under consideration for some time, thus affording opportunity for inquiry, and during that time one or more of the directors visited Sioux City. Mr. Leonard was well informed as to the values of real estate in Sioux City, and as to the character and value of this property, and was present at the meeting that accepted the plaintiff's offer. Plaintiff was not present, and did nothing to induce the purchase, except to state his opinion as to said values, and that it would be advantageous to the company to buy and lease as proposed. We are satisfied that the judgment of Mr. Leonard did more to influence the acceptance than the representations of the plaintiff. Plaintiff did not acquire his information as to these values by reason of his position as director, and, so far as appears, the corporation dealt with him in this matter as with a stranger.

II. Let it be said, however, that, because of his relation as director, he did not act in good faith in representing the values in excess of what he believed them to be, the inquiry remains whether defendants should now be heard to complain. The contract of purchase was made December 17, 1891, the new lease May 26, 1892, and the cancellation of the lease September 1, 1892. The defendants improved the

property, and had full possession from September 1,
1892, and yet made no complaint as to the fairness of
these transactions until shortly before the commencement of this action, April 11, 1895, when informed that
an action would be commenced if payment was not
made. For nearly three years the defendant company
continued to hold this property, and to pay incumbrances thereon, as per the contract of purchase, without a complaint. In 3 Thompson, Corporations, section
4047, it is said: "If the corporation or the stockholders
wish to disaffirm the transaction, this must be done
within a reasonable time, accompanied, ordinarily, by
an offer to put the trustee in *status quo*. The meaning is
that laches—that is to say, an unreasonable delay after
knowledge—will be tantamount to a . ratification."
Surely, a much less time was sufficient for defendants
to have found the matters now complained of, and to
have offered, as is now offered, to rescind the contract.
The offer comes too late, not only because not made in
a reasonable time, but because it is now impracticable,
if not impossible, to place the parties in *status quo*. As
we view it, the defendants are not only not entitled to a
rescission of the contract, but, under the facts, should
be held to have ratified said contracts after ample
opportunity to know the facts. Our conclusion is that
the decree is correct, and it is therefore AFFIRMED.

JOSEPH HOLMES, Appellant, v. ANNIE S. REDHEAD.

Principal and Agent: IMPLIED AUTHORITY. One authorized by the
owner to negotiate a sale or exchange of real estate is not thereby
invested with an implied or apparent authority to make a binding
contract of sale for his principal. Citing *O'Rilley v. Kein* (N. J.
Err. App.) 34 Atl. Rep. 1073; *Duffy v. Hobson*, 40 Cal. 240; *Everman
v. Herndon*, 71 Miss. 823; *Halsey v. Monteiro*, 92 Va. 581.

Appeal from Polk District Court.—HON. T. F. STEVEN-
SON, Judge.

FRIDAY, JANUARY 21, 1898.

ACTION in equity to enforce specific performance of
a contract to convey real estate. Decree for defendant.
Plaintiff appeals.—*Affirmed.*

J. L. Carney for appellant.

St. John & Stevenson for appellee.

WATERMAN, J.—The contract which is set up as a
basis for the relief sought by plaintiff is in writing, and
as follows:

"Des Moines, Iowa, December 22, 1894.
"List of Redhead's Property Offered in Exchange for
Holmes Vinegar Plant:

Double brick flat..............................$	4,000
Bixby house, barn, and land.................	4,000
Watson house and lot.......................	2,000
Lomley house and ground...................	1,500
5 lots in K, 14 lots in J, 10 lots in S, Redhead's addition	5,800
Lots 23, 22, 21, 20, 19, 18, 16, 15, Block Add.....	6,200
Lots 8, 9, 10, 11, 12, and 14, Block A, East Park Place	4,300

$27,800

"The above property to be free from incumbrance,
except $2,000 on the double brick flat. Said Redhead
agrees to take in even exchange Holmes vinegar plant,
consisting of the lot on which it stands, sixty feet by
one hundred and eighty feet, and all of the permanent
fixtures used in the manufacture of vinegar, pickles,
yeast, and cider; also, a feed lot, which contains about

two and one-half acres, four horses and harness, and
two wagons, all of which is free of incumbrance. Said
Holmes property is in Marshalltown, Iowa, and property of said Redhead is located in Des Moines, Iowa.

"Annie S. Redhead,
"By George Redhead.
"Joseph Holmes.

"Des Moines, December 22, 1894. Received on the
within contract $1, to apply on the within trade.
"George S. Redhead."

We are confronted at the outset with an issue of
fact presented by the answer, the determination of
which is decisive of this case: Was the writing in question the contract of the defendant? It is obvious that,
to answer this interrogatory, we must ascertain
whether George S. Redhead, who was the son of defendant, had authority to affix his mother's name thereto.
The testimony is not materially conflicting. Many facts
are not in dispute. We deem it unnecessary to set them
forth in detail, but will give our conclusions.

Annie S. Redhead, the defendant, is a widow, and
derived title to the real estate involved, with considerable other property, by devise from her husband. She
is not a woman of much business capacity or experience,
and has been dependent upon others for advice and
assistance in the management of her estate. Her son
George S. had charge of the making of leases to her
tenants and the collection of rents, but, when real property was sold or other transactions of magnitude undertaken, she usually went to others for advice, and princi-
pally to Mr. St. John, her attorney. It seems that negotiations were begun between plaintiff and George S.
Redhead looking to the exchange of some of defendant's
real estate for a vinegar plant belonging to plaintiff,
and which was located in Marshalltown, Iowa. After
a time these negotiations culminated in a visit of plaintiff to Des Moines, where the Redheads resided. It is

at this time that defendant first appears in connection
with the matter. Plaintiff went with George to his
mother's house for dinner. The parties do not quite
agree as to what occurred at this time, but, stating it
most favorably for plaintiff, we think defendant can be
held to nothing more than what follows: She talked
with plaintiff about the contemplated exchange, but
said nothing as to the kind or amount of property that
she was willing to put in. She spoke of her son Herbert
going into business in Marshalltown; hoped the business would be profitable, and that he would succeed,
and said that George would show the property "they
had in exchange for this." George and plaintiff left the
house soon after, and together looked at the Redhead
real estate. The next day, plaintiff went with another
person to see the property, but he had no further talk
with Mrs. Redhead. After some further negotiations
with the son, the latter agreed that the property
described in the contract should be given for the vinegar
plant, and went alone to consult his mother about it
before completing the trade. Nothing material in support of plaintiff's claim occurred at this interview.
George says in cross-examination that he informed her
in some measure as to the details of the exchange, and
that she neither gave her assent nor refused it. But it
does not appear that she knew or had reason to suspect
at this time that he intended entering into a contract
in her name. On the contrary, we are justified in finding, when we consider all the evidence, that from the
first she insisted that nothing conclusive be done without the approval of Mr. St. John, and this was never
had. Indeed, he explicitly advised against the contemplated trade when he was consulted, shortly prior to the
interview between George and his mother to which we
have just alluded. Under these circumstances the
instrument that is the basis of this action was executed,
and we may concede for present purposes that it is in

form a binding contract of sale. Taking the case as plaintiff makes it, and we think there is a complete absence of any showing of authority in George S. Redhead to bind the defendant by this agreement. Plaintiff does not claim express authority, but he does insist that there was implied or apparent authority. This, we think, cannot be successfully maintained. That the son had a right to negotiate for a sale or exchange in this case is true, but plaintiff had no reason to infer anything further from this fact. A property owner who authorizes a broker to procure a purchaser gives to the broker authority to negotiate for a sale, but it would be an unusual rule, and contrary to the current of decisions, to hold the broker's acts in this direction to be legally sufficient to warrant a belief in one dealing with him that such agent had a right to make a binding contract of sale for his principal. *Furst v. Tweed*, 93 Iowa, 300; *O'Reilly v. Keim*, N. J. Eq. & App. (34 Atl. Rep. 1073); *Duffy v. Hobson*, 40 Cal. 240; *Everman v. Herndon*, 71 Miss. 823 (15 South. Rep. 135); *Halsey v. Monteiro*, 92 Va. 581 (24 S. E. Rep. 258). The decree below was right, and will be AFFIRMED.

In the Matter of the Assignment of W. W. Doolittle, J. L. Carney, Assignee, v. Nellie T. Smith, Claimant, Appellant.

Assignment: SECURED CLAIMS: *Insolvency.* Where a claim against an assigned estate is paid in part after it is filed, out of the proceeds of collaterals held by the claimant, the claim will be reduced to the extent of the payment, for the purpose of final distribution, though no objections are made to the claim as filed, distinguishing *People v Remington*, 121 N. Y. 328; citing *Armory v. Francis*, 16 Mass 308; *Bank v. Lanahan*, 66 Md. 461.

Appeal from Marshall District Court.—Hon. G. W. Burnham, Judge.

Friday, January 21, 189○

IN June, 1895, W. W. Doolittle made an assignment for the benefit of his creditors with J. L. Carney, as assignee. Nellie T. Smith filed her claim for five thousand dollars, September 18, 1895, to which no objections were filed. In October, 1895, the assignee filed his report in the district court, giving the names of creditors and the several amounts, and among them that of Nellie T. Smith, for five thousand dollars. Prior to the assignment, Nellie T. Smith held, as collateral security for her debt, certain corporation stocks, on which she realized three thousand and forty-eight dollars and thirty-eight cents. This was in January, 1896. In August, 1896, the assignee filed his final report, showing a balance for distribution among creditors of eight hundred and sixteen dollars and thirty-three cents, and asked an order for such distribution on the claims filed with him, "without including interest, paying an equal *pro rata* on the principal of the same, still unpaid." Nellie T. Smith filed exceptions to the report, on the ground that it proposed a distribution to her on the basis of her unpaid claim after deducting the three thousand and forty-eight dollars and thirty-eight cents, instead of on the basis of the claim of five thousand dollars, as filed. The district court approved the report, and ordered distribution accordingly, and Nellie T. Smith appealed.— *Affirmed.*

Binford & Snelling for appellant.

J. M. Holt and *J. L. Carney* for appellee.

GRANGER, J.—The single question before us is: Where a claim for which collaterals are held as security is filed, in an assignment proceeding, and where the claim is afterwards partly paid from the collaterals, is the claim, because of the payment, to be reduced to that extent, for the purpose of a final distribution of the assets in the hands of the assignees, or is such distribution to be made on the basis of the claim as filed, where no objcetions to it are made? It should be conceded that, as no exceptions were filed to the claim of appellant, it stood established, by operation of law, for the amount claimed; so that without the payment in question, because of the collaterals, the distribution would be on the basis of the full claim. Such a rule is not questioned, and its statement accords with appellant's claim. It is a fact that the time for filing exceptions to claims expired before the application of the proceeds from the collaterals. In view of such fact, it is appellant's claim that, "immediately at the expiration of the time for filing exceptions to claims, if none be filed, each claim is established and proved, and each claimant has a vested interest in the property assigned in proportion to the amount of his claim, and from that date the amount of his equitable interest in the property assigned is certain and fixed." Appellant's argument in support of the proposition is that, when the five thousand dollar-claim became established for want of exceptions to it, she had a vested interest in the property assigned, and also in the property pledged as security, so that she had two securities for the debt. By combining parts of two sections from Jones, Pledges, 590, 591, appellant presents and invokes the following rule in support of her claim: "In short, in the case of a pledge, just as in the case of a mortgage, the creditor may use any remedy he has against the debtor or his property for the collection of the principal debt, without destroying or impairing his security for the debt, until it is actually paid. A creditor is entitled to hold his securities, whatever they may be, until he gets his pay. The securities belong to him, and he may enforce the debt without surrendering them. * * * It is of the very nature of collateral security that it may be resorted to for a satisfaction of

the principal debt if its payments shall not be otherwise
obtained." The language is used by the author in support of the following rules: "The holding of collateral
security for a debt does not impair or suspend the right
of action upon it, unless so agreed upon by the parties,
whether the collateral be given at the time the debt
was contracted or afterwards." "The recovery of a judgment upon a principal debt does not affect the pledgee's
right to hold and enforce a pledge taken to secure that
debt." We refer to these rules to show the connection
in which the language was used, and thus be better able
to know of its application to the question we are considering. The rules stated are, so far as we know,
nowhere doubted. There is no attempt to deprive appellant of the right to hold her collaterals and maintain
an independent action for the debt, or to deny to her
a right to use the collaterals after obtaining a judgment
on the debt. The rules seem to us to be foreign to the
question presented in this case, and it is not to be correctly said that the author used the language cited
except in the elucidation of his propositions. The following is a part of section 2122 of the Code of 1873: "If
no exception be made to the claim of any creditor, or if
the same have been adjudicated, the court shall order
the assignee to make, from time to time, fair and equal
dividends among the creditors of the assets in his hands,
in proportion to their claims." It will be seen that the
controversy is to be determined on what is meant by the
use of the word "claims."

Appellant cites and quotes extensively from *People
v. E. Remington & Sons*, 121 N. Y. 328 (24 N. E. Rep.
793). It was a case of the state against an insolvent
bank for its dissolution, and a creditor bank, holding
collaterals as security, presented and sought to prove
up its claim for the full amount; and the question was
made if the bank should not deduct from its claim what
had already been realized on the securities and the value

of the securities still held. The reasoning of the opinion commences with these words: "There are conflicting decisions upon this question in the courts of the United States; and in England, if we look back upon the current of opinions, we may find some differences in views. But the preponderance of authority is in favor of the view that the creditor has the right to prove and have his dividends upon his entire debt, irrespective of the collateral security." The case declines, as a controlling one, the following equitable rule from Judge Story's Equity Jurisprudence (section 638): That where the creditor has two funds of his debtor, to which he can resort for payment, and another creditor has a lien only on one fund, equity will compel a resort by the first creditor to that fund to which the lien of the other does not extend, on the ground that the rule is based on a reason that, by its application, no injustice is done to the first creditor in point of security or payment, and that its application in that case would have that effect. It seems that the rule in bankruptcy cases is that the creditor can only prove up after realizing upon or valuing his securities. The case distinguishes that rule because of the provisions of the bankrupt law. In reaching a conclusion, it gives effect to the general rule that a creditor is not bound to apply his collateral securities before enforcing his direct remedies against the debtor. In *Amory v. Francis*, 16 Mass. 308, the court had under consideration the rights of a creditor against the estate of an insolvent debtor, under a statute requiring an equal *pro rata* distribution where the creditor had security; and the syllabus is as follows: "If a creditor to an insolvent estate have a mortgage, as security for his debt, he can claim from the commissioners only for the difference between his debt and the value of the property mortgaged." The case likens the rule to that obtaining in bankruptcy proceedings, and it is said in the opinion: "The practice in cases of bankruptcy is not the effect of a statute provision, but the result of general principles of equity, which are equally applicable in cases of insolvency, like the present." *Bank v. Lanahan*, 66 Md. 461 (7 Atl. Rep. 615), is a case quite in point, and a syllabus is as follows: "Under an assignment for the benefit of creditors, the obligation of the trustee to pay a debt owing by the assignor does not depend on the state of the account between the creditor and the assignor at the time of the assignment, but at the time when payment is made." The case fully sustains the syllabus, and, on principle, we discover no distinguishing facts from the case at bar. The authorities on both sides are quite fully collected in 3 Am. & Eng. Enc. Law (2d ed.).

We have noticed these cases to show the different views entertained by courts as to the equitable considerations that control in such cases, and that there is no general rule of jurisprudence to be violated by our conclusion. It may be conceded that other courts have announced different views and conclusions on the same subject. We may say that if the estate of the insolvent, in the hands of the assignee, is to be treated as a security for all the creditors, as some of the cases treat it,— and it is appellant's theory also,—we see no way to escape the application of the general rule that where a creditor has security on two funds, and another creditor has it on but one of them, equity will require the first creditor to first exhaust his security not pledged to the other, so that both creditors may be protected. Treating the estate as property pledged by the law for the payment of all the creditors *pro rata*, it seems to us the relation of the appellant to the other creditors is exactly that of the one with security on two funds, on one of which the other creditors have security. In fact, it seems to us the rule has express recognition in this state, in *Wurtz v. Hart*, 13 Iowa, 515. It is thought by

appellant that the case is not in point, that case being
in equity, and this a proceeding at law; that the *Wurtz
Case* is by one creditor against another creditor, while
in this case the question is raised by the assignee. An
examination of that case will show that the question is
directly involved whether, in assignment proceedings,
a creditor with special security may be required to
resort to such security, and can only claim a dividend
upon the amount remaining unpaid after exhausting
the property on which he has the special lien. The case
answers the question in the affirmative, and, in the
interest of precision, re-states the rule in this way: "Or
this same rule may be stated thus: that, if a creditor has
two funds out of which he may make his debt, he may
be required to resort to that fund upon which another
creditor has no lien." This is precisely in accord with
what we have before stated in this case. The only
doubtful feature of that case, as authority in this, is the
difference in the proceedings; but the case states the
equitable rule, and, by the general current of authority,
the equitable rule obtains even where the question is
presented in the assignment proceedings. See *Amory
v. Francis, supra.* The *Wurtz Case* refers to *Dickson v.
Chorn*, 6 Iowa, 19. So far as the character of the proceeding is concerned, it is to be said that, while the
issues present the question fairly as to the rule applicable to such facts, no question was made, nor is one now,
as to this being a proper proceeding in which to settle
the rule. We, of course, determine no question broader
than the one involved: That, because of the payment
from the proceeds of the collateral security, the claim,
as a basis for a dividend, was reduced to the extent of
the payment. The judgment is AFFIRMED.

NELS L. WEIGEN v. THE COUNCIL BLUFFS INSURANCE COMPANY, Appellant.

Insurance: FORFEITURE: *Ineffective mortgage.* A chattel mortgage covering property insured is not such an authorized incumbrance
2 . as will avoid the policy, when it was given to obtain money to take up a prior mortgage and discharged eight days later, upon the mortgagee's failure to raise the amount of the loan it was intended to secure.

Action: AFTER APPOINTMENT OF RECEIVER. An action may be maintained against an insolvent incorporation notwithstanding the appointment of a receiver, when it has not been enjoined by the
1 court from the exercise of its corporate powers, and the receiver is not a necessary party to the action, and when no relief is asked against him.

Appeal from Howard District Court.—HON. L. E. FELLOWS, Judge.

FRIDAY, JANUARY 21, 1898.

ACTION on insurance policy. Trial to court. Judgment for plaintiff, and defendant appeals.—*Affirmed.*

Flickinger Bros. and *John McCook* for appellant.

H. T. Reed for appellee.

LADD, J.—This action was begun November 9, 1895, on an insurance policy issued by the defendant November 6, 1894, covering furniture, fixtures, and merchandise which were destroyed by fire May 13, 1895. The contract of limitations had not run. *Reed v. Insurance Co.*, 103 Iowa, 307. In the view taken, it becomes immaterial whether Nason was an adjusting agent for defendant, or what he said or did; for, if the existence of the mortgage was not a violation of the conditions of the policy, the failure to disclose it in the proof of loss, if shown, would not amount to fraudulent concealment forfeiting all claims against the company. Only the remaining errors assigned will be considered.

II. In the second count of the answer the defend-ant alleged that on June 5, 1895, W. W. Loomis was appointed receiver and took possession of all the prop-erty and papers of the defendant company, and has since continued in the exercise of his duties as such; that said receiver is a necessary party to the determina-tion of this controversy; that the court entered
1   an order requiring all claims against the defend-ant to be filed with the receiver before October 5, 1895, and that of plaintiff has never been so filed. To this count the plaintiff demurred on two grounds: (1) This action is against the company, and the appoint-ment of a receiver is no defense; (2) the failure to file the claim with the receiver is not a defence against the company. The appellant complains of the action of the court in sustaining this demurrer. It will be observed that there is no allegation that the corporation had been dissolved, or that the court, in appointing the receiver, enjoined it from exercising any of its corporate powers. No statute of this state limits the powers of a corporation upon the appointment of a receiver, and those of the defendant were restrained only by depriv-ing it of its property. The right to sue and be sued, conferred by the statute, was retained. No relief was asked against the receiver, and he was not a necessary party, though he might, in the discretion of the court, be permitted, by intervening, to interpose any proper defense to the action. The authorities seem in entire harmony on these propositions. See 20 Am. & Eng. Enc. Law, 253; *Allen v. Railroad Co.*, 42 Iowa, 683.

III. The policy contains this clause: "If there be now or hereafter any mortgage, judgment, lien, or

incumbrance on or against the whole or a part of the property hereby insured," then the policy shall
2   be void. The plaintiff executed to his brother, A. O. Weigen, a chattel mortgage, February 20, 1895, covering the goods insured and destroyed by fire, securing the payment of eight hundred and ninety-nine dollars and twenty-five cents, which was duly recorded. Eight days thereafter the mortgagee satisfied the same on the margin of the records, and returned the instrument to the mortgagor. The defendant insists that this transaction rendered the policy void. To meet this contention the plaintiff was permitted to show that, when the mortgage was executed, by agreement of the brothers, the mortgagee was to furnish money to take up a prior mortgage given by the plaintiff to the Powers Dry Goods Company, and in event of failure to do so he would cancel this mortgage, and that, having found it impossible to raise the necessary means, he satisfied and returned it in pursuance of such agreement, though given to secure the exact amount owing him. The mortgage was not to be effective between the brothers unless the mortgagee fulfilled his promise to pay off that to the Powers Dry Goods Company. The evidence of this was competent, because it went to the very consideration which induced the giving of the security. The plaintiff, while bound to pay his debt, was not required, under the law, to pledge any property for its payment; and, having done so, the consideration therefor may be inquired into. The condition against liability in event of incumbrances was undoubtedly inserted in the policy in order to guard against any increased moral hazard. This court has held that a provision against subsequent insurance is not violated when such insurance is not effective. *Hubbard v. Insurance Co.,* 33 Iowa, 325; *Behrens v. Insurance Co.,* 64 Iowa, 19. In *Forward v. Insurance Co.,* 142 N. Y. App. 381 (37 N. E. Rep. 615), a bill of sale executed by the insured

without consideration, and with intent to defraud creditors, was held not to be a breach of a contract against
change of ownership or incumbrances. A deed absolute
on its face, though intended only as a mortgage, was held
not to be in violation of a condition in a policy against
any change of title in *German Insurance Co. v. Gibe*, 162
Ill. Sup. 251 (44 N. E. Rep. 490). The mortgage did not
affect any interest the plaintiff had in the property, and
could not have been enforced by his brother. The moral
hazard was not increased by it. The incumbrance to
avoid a policy must be valid, not merely nominal, and
such as would have a tendency to create or increase
temptation or motive for the destruction of the property, or decrease the owner's interest in guarding and
preserving it. The execution of this mortgage had no
such tendency. It was, at most, merely a technical, not
a real, violation of the terms of the policy, and did not
work a forfeiture.—AFFIRMED.

AUGUST MUECKE, Appellant, v. JOEL BARRETT.

Judgments: EFFECT: *Boundaries.* Surveyors were commissioned to
locate the corner and boundary line common to four sections,
which were the only issue raised by the pleadings. The report
located, not only the corner and lines stated, but also the quarter
sections. The court found the report correct and confirmed it as
to the line and corner in dispute, and rendered judgment establishing the latter as shown by the report. *Held,* that such judgment did not affect a quarter section corner in one of the four
sections which had been established by the general government
survey, and recognized by all parties interested.

Appeal from Plymouth District Court.—HON. F. R. GAY-
NOR, Judge.

FRIDAY, JANUARY 21, 1898.

ACTION at law to recover the possession of real
estate and damages for its detention. There was a trial
by the court, without jury, and a judgment in favor of
the defendant. The plaintiff appeals.—*Affirmed.*

Ira T. Martin for appellant.

Sammis & Scott for appellee.

ROBINSON, J.—The plaintiff is the owner of the
northwest one-fourth of section numbered 14, in township numbered 90 north, of range numbered 45 west of
fifth P. M.; and the defendant owns the northeast one-
fourth of the same section. The plaintiff claims that
the defendant wrongfully holds possession of a strip
of land on the east side of said northwest one-fourth,
which is a part thereof, and is seventeen rods wide at
the north end, and eight rods wide at the south end,
containing about twelve and one-half acres. Judgment
is demanded for the possession of that land, and for the
sum of forty-five dollars for each year of the time plaintiff claims to have been entitled to possess and use it.
The district court dismissed the petition. There is no
material conflict in the evidence in this case. The land
which belongs to the plaintiff was a part of the Agricul-
tural College grant, and was leased to Frederick
Muecke in May, 1874. Ten years later it was patented
to him, and in May, 1891, he conveyed it to the plaintiff.
The defendant has owned the north one-half of his
quarter section since the year 1869, and the south one-
half for nine years preceding the trial in the district
court. In August, 1884, one W. S. Fisher commenced
a proceeding in the district court of Plymouth county
against the plaintiff and the defendant in this action,
and other persons, to have established the corner which

was common to sections 10, 11, 14, and 15, in the township specified, and the boundary line between the sections. There was an appearance in that proceeding by
some of the defendants. Commissioners were appointed
to locate the corner and boundary lines specified, and
judgment was rendered establishing them. The controversy in this case is in regard to the scope and effect
of that judgment. The interest held at that time by the
plaintiff in the land he now owns does not appear, but
it was conceded that he was bound by the judgment
rendered. It is also admitted that prior to the year
1885 the respective owners of the two quarter sections
described believed the boundary line common to them
was where the defendant now claims it to be, and that
the occupation of both tracts had been fixed by that
line. But it is claimed by the appellant, and denied by
the appellee, that the effect of the proceeding and judgment referred to was to establish the boundary line
now in dispute where the appellant claims it to be.

The petition of Fisher in the case referred to is as
follows: "Plaintiff states that the corner common to the
four following sections of land in said county, to-wit,
sections 10, 11, 14, and 15, in township 90, range 45, and
the boundary lines between said sections, are in dispute,
and the plaintiff is desirous of having said corner and
boundaries permanently established; that the plaintiff
and the defendants are the proprietors of the lands
adjoining said corner, and lying along said boundaries,
and are all of such proprietors, and will not enter into
an agreement to abide by the survey of some surveyor
to establish said corner and boundaries. Wherefore
plaintiff prays that the court will appoint a commission
of one or more disinterested surveyors to survey said
sections, as provided by law, and to permanently establish said corner and the boundaries of and between
said sections, to-wit, the corner lying and being the

common corner of sections 10, 11, 14, and 15, in township 90, range 45, and the section line boundary running
north and south between sections 10 and 11, and
between sections 14 and 15, and the section line running
east and west between sections 10 and 15 and sections
11 and 14, and to apportion the costs of said survey and
this suit among the parties according to their respective
interests." The answer to that petition, filed by the
plaintiff in this case and one other, denied that the common corner of the section specified and the boundary
lines between them were in dispute, and alleged that
they were where they should be, and where they were
located by the government survey. A judgment establishing the "said corner and boundary lines where they
now are" was asked. The commission which was issued
to the surveyors directed them to survey the sections
specified, "and locate and establish the corner common
to said sections; to also locate and establish the north
and south boundary lines between said sections 10 and
11, and between said sections 14 and 15, and the
boundary line running east and west between said
sections 10 and 15 and, said sections 11 and 14, as provided by law." In executing the commission, the surveyors located not only the section corners in the
boundary lines they were directed to fix, but also the
quarter section corners; and their report showed that
fact. The district court found that the report and sur-
veys were correct, and the report "of the lines and
corners in dispute" was approved and confirmed, and it
was ordered "that the lines and boundaries in dispute,
to-wit, the corner common to sections 10, 11, 14, and 15,
township 90, range 45, in said county, and the section
lines between said sections, be, and the same are fixed
and established as shown in said report and in the plat
attached thereto, and are declared to be the legal and
permanent corner and boundaries therein shown forever." After that judgment was rendered, the plaintiff

caused a stone to be located at what he claimed to be
the southeast corner of his land. It is agreed that the
stone thus placed correctly marks the center of the section as ascertained from the survey which was made by
the commissioners appointed by the court in the *Fisher
Case;* but the stone is eight rods east of the south end
of the boundary line to which defendant claims, and the
quarter corner established by the commissioners in the
north boundary line of the section is seventeen rods east
of the north end of the boundary line to which defendant claims. We are required to determine whether
the judgment rendered in the *Fisher Case* established
the boundary line in controversy in this action. The
survey made in that case was involved in *Fisher v.
Muecke,* 82 Iowa, 547, but that case involved the true
location of the boundary line between the northwest
one-fourth of section 14 and the northeast one-fourth of
section 15, and as that boundary was an exterior one,
common to the two sections, the question decided in
that case is not the one which is controlling in this case.

A careful examination of the record in the *Fisher
Case,* submitted to us, fails to show that it involved any
controversy whatever in regard to the boundary line
now in question. The petition only asked that the
corner common to the four sections specified, and the
boundary lines between those sections, be established,
and the judgment rendered granted that relief only.
It is true, the surveyors had located some corners which
were not in dispute, but their action in that respect was
not confirmed by the judgment, which was limited to
the corner and boundaries in dispute. The petition
did not allege that the quarter corner in the north
boundary line of section 14 was in dispute, nor ask that
it be established. Therefore, it was not within the purview of the judgment rendered, unless it was necessary
to establish that corner in order to locate and establish the north boundary line of the section. It is true,

VOL. 104 Ia—27

the location of that line was necessarily governed by
the location of the corner; but, as none of those were
alleged to be lost excepting the one common to the four
sections specified, it was fair to presume that the location of the lines, so far as they were not dependent upon
the lost corner, would be fixed by the corners which were
not lost. Moreover, the location of the north boundary
line of section 14 would not be affected by the location
of the north quarter corner, whether it be at the point
at which the plaintiff claims it should have been
located, or at a point seventeen rods further west, so
long as it occupied the same relative position with
respect to distance north and south.

It is to be observed in this connection that although
both the plaintiff and the defendant were parties to the
proceeding by Fisher, the defendant did not appear
thereto, and no attempt was made to have adjudicated
any controversy between the several defendants. The
original notice served on Barrett only notified him that
Fisher sought to have established one lost corner, and
to have fixed the boundaries between the sections to
which the lost corner was common. The petition followed the notice, and, as the relief demanded did not
require the location of the corner in controversy in this
action, the court was not authorized to establish it, and,
as we have seen, did not attempt to do so.

The appellant has called our attention to several
authorities in regard to the effect of an adjudication
upon all matters which were necessarily involved in
the litigation, or which might have been determined by
it; but, in our opinion, none of the authorities cited are
applicable to the undisputed facts of this case. The
north quarter corner in question appears to have been
established by the survey of the general government, at
the point for which the appellant contends, and to have
been recognized by all parties in interest as the true
corner, until the judgment in the *Fisher Case* was

rendered. The district court was authorized and required by the evidence to find that the corner so recognized was not affected by the judgment rendered in that case, and we find no ground upon which its judgment in this case can be disturbed. It is therefore AFFIRMED.

W. J. PRATT, Appellant, v. C. C. PROUTY.

104 41
111

Interpretation of Contracts: EVIDENCE The testimony of parties as
2 to how they understood an unambiguous instrument, is inadmissi-
8 ble.

SAME. The acts of the parties to a contract, illustrating their under-
2 standing of it, may be shown to aid the court in arriving at a
proper interpretation.

SAME. The proviso in an option for the purchase of enough of the
2 stock of one of the parties in a corporation to reduce his holding
to one-third of the whole capital stock, that the stock shall be
purchased at par in amounts of ten thousand dollars at the end
8 of each business year, after a dividend has been declared and paid
on the stock, will be construed merely to fix that sum as the
greatest amount of stock that can be demanded in any one year,
especially where the parties have practically so construed it

Joint Contracts. The consent of all the persons to whom an option
for the purchase of stock of a corporation, in which they are all
interested, is given by an agreement to sell and deliver to them a
1 specified amount of stock, in the number of shares to each that
4 they may agree upon. is necessary to the exercise of the option by
any one of them, although one or more of them has disposed of
his interest in the corporation.

Appeal from Polk District Court.—HON. C. P. HOLMES, Judge.

SATURDAY, JANUARY 22, 1898.

Action for damages for failure to sell and deliver certain shares of stock. Trial to jury. Verdict and judgment for defendant. Plaintiff appeals.— *Affirmed.*

Earle & Prouty for appellant.

Cummins, Hewitt & Wright for appellee. ·

WATERMAN, J.—As to many of the facts presented by appellant, there is no dispute. We may state the case in this way: In November, 1888, plaintiff and defendant, together with Isaac W. Aikin and P. H. Skinner, incorporated as the Prouty & Pratt Company, for the purpose of carrying on a whole sale grocery business in Des Moines, Iowa. The capital stock of the corporation was one hundred and sixty-two thousand dollars, divided into three hundred and twenty-four shares, of five hundred dollars each, which were held by the different parties in the following amounts: Defendant, one hundred and sixty-four shares; plaintiff, one hundred and eight shares; Isaac W. Aikin, fifty shares; P. H. Skinner, two shares. At or about the time of the incorporation of said company, an agreement was entered into by defendant, a copy of which is as follows: "Des Moines, Iowa, Nov. 24, 1888. In consideration of one dollar in hand paid, I hereby agree to sell to W. J. Pratt, Isaac W. Aikin, and P. H. Skinner, my associate partners in the Prouty & Pratt Co., enough of the capital stock that I may hold in said Co. to reduce my capital stock to one-third of the whole capital stock in said Co.: provided, said stock is to be purchased by said W. J. Pratt, Isaac W. Aikin and P. H. Skinner at par, in amounts of ten thousand dollars, at the end of each business year of said Co., after a dividend has been declared and paid on said stock; and I further agree to sell and deliver to the above parties the ten thousand dollars stock in the number of shares to each that they may agree upon. C. C. Prouty."

It is claimed by the appellant that the trial court erroneously construed this contract as providing that

plaintiff and his associates, Aikin and Skinner, could call
each year for exactly the amount of ten thousand dollars of said stock,—no more and no less. We are by no
means sure that the record shows the lower court to
have so construed the contract. We are called upon,
however, to give our interpretation of it. It must be
admitted that the ten thousand dollars mentioned in
the contract was a limitation of some kind. Was it
meant to limit the purchaser's rights to exactly ten
thousand dollars worth of said stock, or did it mean
that no less, or that no more, than ten thousand dollars
in amount was to be taken in any one year? Appellant
says it could not have been a restriction to the exact
amount stated, because defendant held twenty-eight
thousand dollars more than one-third of the stock, and
to say that the purchaser could demand only the particular sum of ten thousand dollars, would be to deprive
him or his associates of the ability to get the whole of the
surplus offered them in this agreement; for, after two
calls, there would remain a sum of but eight thousand
dollars in defendant's hands. He insists that the agreement meant that no less than ten thousand dollars
should be demanded at any one time. But we think this
leaves him in the same dilemma he has stated as arising
from the construction which he says was given by the
lower court. Plaintiff claims to have demanded ten
thousand the first year, and a like sum the second year.
This would leave, under his construction, a remainder of
eight thousand dollars, which could never be obtained.
We suggest that the ten thousand dollars mentioned
was an amount that could not be exceeded; that it was
fixed as the largest sum that could be demanded in any
one year. Let us look at the contract in the light of
this suggestion. One of the first provisions governing

the construction of a written instrument is that it should be interpreted, if possible, so as to effectu-
2 ate the intention of the parties. When it is ascertained what the parties intended, the contract will be construed so as to carry out that intent, as far as the language employed will admit. To discover the intent, we can consider, not only the written instrument and its subject-matter, but the situation of the parties, and the circumstances surrounding them, at the time the contract was made. *Field v. Schricher*, 14 Iowa, 119; *Jacobs v. Jacobs*, 42 Iowa, 600. This was a unilateral agreement. The defendant was bound to sell. The plaintiff was under no obligation to buy. The price fixed for the stock was its face, or par, value. Plaintiff, of course, would not exercise his option to purchase unless the stock should be worth more than this. The greater the value of the stock, the more of it the plaintiff would naturally want; and, for like reason, the less of it defendant would care to dispose of. Viewing the matter in this light, it is but reasonable to think that defendant would fix a limit to the amount that he was willing to part with in any one year. This construction, we think the evidence shows, is in accord with the understanding of the parties. The best evidence of how the parties to an agreement understand its terms is afforded by their acts under it, and these may be shown in order to aid the court in arriving at a proper interpretation. *Thompson v. Locke*, 65 Iowa, 429. Plaintiff claims that this stock, when he made his first demand, had earned for that year eleven and one-half per cent., net, making it worth a considerable sum above the price he was to pay, and at the end of the second year it had earned net twenty-three per cent.; yet he demanded each time just ten thousand dollars in amount. It is difficult to believe that plaintiff did not try to get all that he considered he was entitled to of the stock that was yielding such handsome returns,

As we have already said, we do not find in the record that the lower court gave the contract the construction alleged by plaintiff. There is nothing in the instructions to indicate that it interpreted the agreement differently from what we do. The instrument does not appear ambiguous in its terms. The rulings of the trial judge excluding the statements of the parties as to how they understood the words they had used, were correct.

3

We have devoted this much attention to the construction of this agreement because we think, notwithstanding the special verdict which was rendered by the jury, that the plaintiff might have been prejudiced by an erroneous interpretation of the option given by defendant; but we are quite clear that every other question in the case is disposed of by the findings of the jury. In response to special interrogatories submitted, the jury found that plaintiff made no demand for stock at the end of the first year, and that he did not have the consent of Aikin and Skinner to take the stock at the end of the second year. While Aiken had disposed of his stock during the second year, he was still a party to this agreement, and his consent was necessary to give validity to plaintiff's demand. There was testimony to sustain these findings and we have no disposition to interfere with them. For the reasons given, the judgment below will be AFFIRMED.

4

J. T. WILLIAMS v. B. C. HAMILTON AND MAGGIE HAMILTON, Appellants.

Contract: REFORMATION. A unilateral mistake, unaccompanied by 1-2 fraud of the other party, as to the contents or legal effect of an 8-4 instrument does not justify its reformation. Such mistake must be mutual to warrant reformation.

SAME. A unilateral mistake of law, accompanied by fraud on the
1-2 part of the other party, may, under some circumstances, author-
8 ize the reformation of a contract.

SAME. An illiterate party, who, with the knowledge of the other
1 party, relied upon the latter to embody their oral agreement in a
2 written instrument, is not precluded from having the written
8 instrument reformed to conform to their understanding, because
4 it was read over to him before it was executed, and he mentioned
5 certain omissions, but was assured by the other party that he had
embodied everything they had agreed on.

RATIFICATION. To preclude a party from obtaining a reformation of
a written contract, on the ground that he ratified it after its execu-
6 tion, it must appear that he knew of and understood the contents
of the instrument at the time he is claimed to have ratified it.

Innocent Purchaser: REFORMATION. A wife was not a *bona fide*
purchaser of land from her husband, where she was conversant
7 with the terms on which he bought the land, and the conveyance
to her was in furtherance of an attempt to procure the property
for an inadequate consideration.

*Appeal from Greene District Court.—*HON. S. M.
ELWOOD, Judge.

SATURDAY, JANUARY, 22, 1898.

SUIT in equity to rescind and set aside a contract for
the exchange of real estate because of fraud, or to
reform the contract because of mistake, and to recover
the remainder of the consideration due on the instrument as reformed. The trial court decreed reformation
and awarded damages as prayed, and defendants
appeal.—*Affirmed.*

Bishop, Bowen & Fleming for appellants.

B. O. Clark, Russell & Toliver, and *M. W. Beach*
for appellee.

DEEMER, C. J.—After some negotiations between
plaintiff and defendant B. C. Hamilton with reference

to the exchange of real estate, they entered into a written contract, of which the following is a copy:

"To Whom It May Concern: This is to certify that we have this day entered an agreement whereby J. T. Williams will sell and convey unto Dr. B. C. Hamilton one hundred and seventy-six acres of land, 1. described as follows, to-wit: The northeast fraction of the northwest quarter of section 2, of Glidden township, Carroll county, Iowa, containing fifty-eight acres; also, south half of northeast quarter; also, north half of north half of southeast quarter of section 2, in Glidden township, Carroll county, Iowa. The said Dr. B. C. Hamilton agreeing to give me, in payment for same, one house and four lots situated in S. & S. addition of Scranton, Iowa; also, sixteen head of shoats,—the above valued at one thousand seven hundred dollars; also, two thousand five hundred dollars worth of accounts and notes; the said J. T. Williams agreeing to return to the said B. C. Hamilton all money or accounts left after collecting the one thousand nine hundred dollars, the sum total being three thousand five hundred dollars; the said B. C. Hamilton guaranteeing the said amounts to be true and correct in all respects, and giving two years for collection, but not guaranteeing the payment of same.

B. C. HAMILMON,

his

J. T.   X   WILLIAMS,
mark.

"Witnesses: Charles Rowley, Nellie Rowley.

"Dated at Scranton City, Iowa, 2, 21, 1891."

Plaintiff claims that the contract was induced by fraud, in that defendant represented that the town lots were worth one thousand six hundred dollars, and had cost him that amount, whereas, in truth and in fact, they were worth and had cost but nine hundred dollars;

and that the accounts and notes referred to in the contract were correct, and were against persons of good credit and financial standing, and would be paid within one year, whereas, in truth, the said accounts and notes were incorrect and untrue, and were against persons of poor credit and standing. Plaintiff further alleged that defendant agreed to assign the notes and accounts to him as security for the payment of one thousand eight hundred dollars, inducing him to believe that such security would be better than a mortgage upon the property, and that, when the contract was reduced to writing by defendant, he (defendant) pretended to embody this condition therein, and stated to plaintiff (who is illiterate, and unable to either read or write) that the contract, as so written, contained all of the oral contracts previously made, whereas, in truth, it did not set forth the true agreement, but contained a clause absolving defendant from future liability on account of the notes and accounts; that defendant intentionally omitted from the written contract his oral promise to pay one thousand eight hundred dollars in cash within two years from the date of the contract, and his further promise to assign two thousand five hundred dollars worth of accounts and notes as security for this payment; and, taking advantage of plaintiff's ignorance, fraudulently and intentionally wrote the contract as it now appears; that plaintiff believed from defendant's statements that the written contract contained the oral agreement theretofore made, and was thereby induced to sign the same. Plaintiff further charges that he conveyed the land called for by the contract to B. C. Hamilton, who in turn conveyed the same to Maggie Hamilton, but that this last-named conveyance was made with intent to wrong and cheat him out of the purchase price. He further alleges that he received a conveyance of the town lots, the personal property called for by the contract, and an assignment of notes

and accounts, but that said notes and accounts were
not worth to exceed seven hundred and twenty dollars
and fifty cents, which was the amount actually collected
thereon. He further pleaded a rescission of the contract, and asked that defendants be ordered to reconvey,
or that the written contract be reformed to express the
true agreement of the parties, and that he have judg-
men for the remainder of the one thousand eight hundred dollars agreed to be paid. The trial court denied
the prayer for rescission, but decreed a reformation of
the contract, and awarded plaintiff the balance of the
one thousand eight hundred dollars. As plaintiff is content with this conclusion, and does not appeal, we have
only to consider the correctness of the decree reforming
the contract. If the decree is right as to the reformation, then it should be affirmed, for there is no doubt
that the award of compensation thereunder is correct.

It appears from the evidence that plaintiff is an
ignorant man, unable to read or write, and that defendant gained his confidence through a claim of religious
brotherhood. True, plaintiff had theretofore managed
a farm, in rather a small way, and had accumulated
sufficient to satisfy the necessities of life, with enough
remaining to induce him to seek life in town. He was
introduced to defendant as one who had town property
to exchange for land. After some negotiations, the
parties each viewed the lands and lots of the other, and
propositions pro and con were made, resulting in an
agreement for exchange. Plaintiff valued his lands at
twenty dollars per acre; and defendant, his lots, at one
thousand six hundred dollars. Finally it was agreed
that plaintiff's property was to be taken at three thousand five hundred, and defendant's at one thousand six hundred dollars. Defendant was also to give
plaintiff personal property valued at one hundred dollars, and was also to assign to him notes and accounts
to the amount of two thousand five hundred dollars,

Whether this assignment was absolute, or was intended as security for the remainder of the purchase price, is one of the questions in dispute. We are constrained to believe that plaintiff's version of the matter is correct—as it is the more reasonable—and that the assignment was to be as security for one thousand eight hundred dollars which defendant agreed to pay as the remainder of the consideration for the land. But this does not determine the controversy, for the reason that the oral contract was presumptively merged into the written one, which is set out at the beginning of this opinion, and, unless it was made under such circumstances as to justify its reformation, plaintiff must fail.

We are well satisfied that plaintiff was mistaken
2   as to the contents or legal effect of the instrument when he signed it. But this, in itself, is not sufficient to justify reformation. Defendant must also have been mistaken as to its contents or legal effect, or must, with knowledge of plaintiff's erroneous conclusion, have been guilty of such fraud or inequitable conduct as will justify reformation. After
3   Hamilton had reduced the contract to writing, he read it to Williams, and Williams thereupon remarked that he did not just understand it; that there was one thing mentioned that it did not say anything about, as he understood it, and that was that, if he did not get his money in two years, he did not see anything about what Hamilton would do. To which Hamilton said, "Brother Williams, I guarantee it covers everything we have agreed on." Williams then remarked, "If that is so, it is all right," and thereupon signed the contract. This may have been a mistake of law,
4   taken advantage of by Hamilton. But it is well settled that a mistake of law may, under certain circumstances, afford ground for relief in equity. *Lee v. Percival*, 85 Iowa, 639; *Winans v. Huyck*, 71 Iowa, 459; *Stafford v. Fetters*, 55 Iowa, 484, and cases cited.

Appellants contend, however, that appellee was negligent in signing the contract without informing himself as to its contents or legal effect, and that he cannot have relief. It must be remembered that appellee could neither read nor write, and that he was compelled to rely upon the appellant for a correct reading of the instrument. Had he signed it without informing himself of its contents, or had he signed after hearing it read, and without more, there is no doubt that his negligence would have barred him of recovery, under the rule announced in *Glenn v. Statler*, 42 Iowa, 107, and *McCormack v. Molburg*, 43 Iowa, 561, and other like cases. But the appellee did not do this. On the contrary, he called attention to what he supposed was an omission in the contract, and was assured by appellant that it covered everything agreed upon. Here, then, was a mutual mistake as to the legal effect of the terms used, or mistake on the part of appellee coupled with fraud or inequitable conduct on the part of appellant. Appellant knew that appellee was relying upon him to properly express the terms of the oral agreement in the writing, and it was his duty, under the circumstances disclosed, to correctly represent the condition and effect of the written instrument. In relying upon this representation, appellee was not negligent, and the instrument should be reformed to express the agreement as represented.

Appellants further contend that appellee afterwards ratified the agreement as written. A few days after the making of the agreement, the parties met to carry it out. Present at this meeting, besides the parties, was a notary public, and a minister of the denomination to which both belonged. Deeds and bills of sale were made out in execution of the contract, and the contract was read over to the parties. Just how Myers, the minister, came to be there, is not definitely shown, although we incline to the belief

that it was at the request of Williams to witness some
of the papers. In any event, he signed one of the deeds
as a witness. Just prior to the execution of the papers
in consummation of the agreement, Williams and Myers
withdrew to one side, and had some conversation about
them. Myers did not, however, read the contract to
Williams, nor is there any evidence that he explained,
or attempted to explain, it to him. That he did look
over the deeds and other instruments seems clear, but
there is no evidence that he understood the purport of
the written instrument, or that he in any way or manner
indicated to Williams its effect. Before there could be
any ratification on the part of Williams, it must appear
that he knew and understood the contents of the paper
which it is claimed he ratified. As there is no showing
of any such knowledge, there was, of course, no ratification.

Appellant Maggie Hamilton contends that the
decree, which established a lien upon the property for
the amount of the judgment, is erroneous, for the reason
that she is a *bona fide* purchaser for value, and without
notice. An examination of the evidence leads us
7   to believe that she was conversant with the
terms of the oral agreement, and that the conveyance to her was in furtherance of an attempt to procure the property without paying an adequate consideration therefor.

We have gone to the transcript for a better understanding of the record, and, while we have not
attempted to set out the evidence upon which we base
our conclusions, we have given the case careful consideration, and find the ultimate facts to be as stated.
There are many circumstances, small in themselves,
which point to the correctness of the conclusion
reached. And, as the decree of the district court is
manifestly equitable and just, it is AFFIRMED.

FRANK SIGMOND, *et al.*, Appellants, v. MARY M. BEB-   104
    BER, *et al.*, Appellees.   121

Appeal: HARMLESS ERROR. Plaintiffs could not be harmed by an
    order requiring their petition to be made more specific, but not
1   changing the effect of the original averments, where a demurrer
    was sustained to the petition as amended, because not stating a
    cause of action.

Executors and Administrators: JURISDICTION TO ORDER SALE. An
    order directing an administrator to sell the real property, includ-
2   ing the homestead, to pay claims against the estate, though erro-
    neous, is not void for want of jurisdiction.

Appeal from Linn District Court.—HON. WILLIAM G.
    THOMPSON, Judge.

SATURDAY, JANUARY 22, 1898.

THE following are the material averments of the
petition as amended: The plaintiffs are the children
and heirs of Christopher Sigmond, deceased, who died
testate December 10, 1894, seized of about one hundred
and seventy-two acres of land, which included a homestead of forty acres. By his will he devised to his
widow, now defendant Mary M. Bebber, the control
and possession of all his property, real and personal,
as long as she should live and remain his widow, with a
right of disposal, except as to the real estate, which
under no circumstances was to be sold or mortgaged,
except that, in the event of the marriage of his widow,
then all the property was to be sold, real and personal,
the widow to take one-third, and the balance to go to
his children in a manner specified. It further appears
from the petition that the widow was duly appointed
administratrix of the estate; that she did not elect to
take according to the law, and waive the provisions of

the will in her favor; that in October, 1887, as administratrix, she applied to the court for an order to mortgage all of said real estate for the payment of the debts
of the estate; that plaintiffs were duly notified of such
application, and a guardian *ad litem* appointed for
the minors, and upon the hearing the order was made
to mortgage it for the sum of one thousand, three hundred and fifty dollars, which was done; that in October,
1888, the administratrix presented an application to
the district court to sell all of said land for the purpose
of paying the claims against it, of which application
plaintiffs had notice, and a guardian *ad litem* was
appointed for the minors, who answered, and, upon the
hearing, the order for a sale was made, and all of the
land was sold for the sum of three thousand, two hundred dollars, and the sale was approved by the court;
that defendant James Bruce was the purchaser of the
land, and the title has passed from one to another of the
defendants, until it rests in defendant Spottswood, all
of the purchasers being parties defendant. The relief
asked is that the sale of the land be set aside so far as
the homestead forty is concerned, and canceling the
record thereof. To the petition there was a general
demurrer, which the court sustained, and, the plaintiffs
electing to stand on their petition, a judgment was
entered, from which they appealed.—*Affirmed.*

Moses & Burr for appellants.

Griffen & Voris and *W. F. Fitzgerald* for appellees.

GRANGER, J.—I. The defendants, aside from Mary
M. Bebber, who was the widow of Christopher Sigmond,
deceased, are the respective purchasers of the land, in
pursuance of the sale by her as administratrix, and one
Mary Holub, a daughter of the testator, who had received
her proportion of the estate as an advancement, and

she filed a disclaimer of any interest in the land, and
hence has no further interest in the suit. During the
adjustment of the pleadings, the court required the
plaintiffs to make the petition more specific in certain
particulars, on motion of defendants, and com-
1   plaint is now made of such rulings. The effect
of the rulings was to add to and not take from the
petition, so that all remains upon which plaintiffs rely
to state a cause of action. Nothing added in pursuance of the motions in any way changes the legal effect
of the averments relied on by plaintiffs, and as the petition, when amended, was tested, as to its sufficiency,
by ˙demurrer, there could have been no prejudice
because of the rulings on the motions. The objection
to the petition is, as shown by arguments, that it does
not state facts sufficient to show a cause of action, and,
as we have said, the rulings on the motions took nothing
from the petition.

II. This is a direct, and not a collateral, proceeding. It may be conceded that, if the judgment of the
court, ordering the sale of the land to pay the mortgage
debt, is open to attack in a proceeding other than the
one in which it was rendered, this is a proper
2   one. The relief sought is based on a claim that
the order of sale made by the district court is
void, so far as the homestead is concerned, because of
the provisions of the law that the homestead descends
to the heirs, and is not liable for the payment of debts
of the estate. That rule may be conceded, but we do
not understand its operation to defeat the jurisdiction
of the court to determine the question, if such an order
is sought. In determining the jurisdiction of the court,
as to subject-matter, we do not inquire what the law is
on the subject, or what the holding should be, but the
inquiry is, has the court authority to hear and determine the question? "Jurisdiction" is thus defined:
"Jurisdiction is the authorty by which judicial officers

take cognizance of a'nd decide causes, or, as it has been
most frequently defined, the power to hear and determine the cause.   The definition, thus limited, implies
that, if a court having power to hear and determine a
cause enters a judgment therein, the validity of
such a judgment is not affected by the power of
the court to enter the judgment in question." 12 Am.
& Eng. Euc. Law, 244. No modification of this general
rule in any way affects the case before us. Great stress
is placed on the claim that the law gives no authority
for the court to make an order to mortgage real estate
for the payment of the debts of an estate, and it is said
that, because of such want of authority, the action of
the court in making such an order is void, and, as we
understand, because such order was void, the making of
the order to sell the land to pay the mortgage is void,
and especially so as to a homestead. We cannot understand how the order for the mortgaging of the land can
in any way affect the jurisdiction of the district court to
order the sale. The application for the order of sale
stated the purpose of the sale, and the whole question
was before the court. Nothing more can be said than
that the administatrix asked an order of sale for a purpose not authorized by the law. If so, it was the duty
of the court to have denied the order, but not to dismiss the application, because without jurisdiction to
determine the question. The determination of the
question is precisely what the court should have done,
and, had it denied the order, no one would say that it
had not jurisdiction to do so. The jurisdiction is as
complete for a decision one way as the other, but a
decision one way would not be legal, while the other it
would. Such an illegality would merely involve error
in an authorized proceeding, while an absence of jurisdiction as to subject-matter would nullify the proceeding for any purpose. Appellant cites us to such cases
as *Deery v. Hamilton,* 41 Iowa, 16; *McMannis v. Rice*

48 Iowa, 361; *Wetherill v. Harris*, 67 Ind. 452. A reference to the cases will show they do not bear on the
question of jurisdiction, as involved here. In the
McMannis Case, the court held that an application for
an order to sell real estate by a guardian did not give
the court jurisdiction to make an order to mortgage the
land. That was because no proceeding was pending for
such a purpose, and the parties were not in court on
such an issue. It is not a holding that the court would
not have had jurisdiction of the subject-matter had its
action, in that respect, been invoked. That the district
court had jurisdiction in the matter of the application
to sell the real estate, with the parties in court, we
have no doubt. If so, the remedy of those not satisfied
was by appeal. The facts, now claimed, as ousting the
court of jurisdiction, if available at all, could have been
pleaded in defense, or presented in the way of objections
to the granting of such an order. In Freeman, Judgments (2d ed.) 249, it is said: "An adjudication is final
and conclusive, not only as to the matter actually
determined, but as to every other matter which the
parties might have litigated and have had decided, as
incident to, or essentially connected with, the subject-
matter of the litigation, and every matter coming
within the legitimate purview of the original action,
both in respect to matters of claim and defense." We
cited this rule in *Donahue v. McCosh*, 81 Iowa, 296. See,
also, *Lamb v. McConkey*, 76 Iowa, 47, and *Phillips v.
Gephart*, 53 Iowa, 396. As to the homestead feature,
the order would be no more void, because without
authority to make it, than would a judgment declaring
a lien on a homestead that the law exempted it from.
In *Collins v. Chantland*, 48 Iowa, 241, it is held that,
where such a lien was established, and the party was
in court and failed to make the defense, he could not
resist the enforcement of the judgment upon the ground
that the property was exempt from the lien. It is said

in that case: "Any defense which he had to the claim for a lien made against him should have been made in that action. * * * The question of the lien is *res judicata*. His ignorance of his rights at the time the judgment was rendered is no ground for setting it aside." There is no claim of fraud in obtaining the order of sale. With jurisdiction of the parties and the subject-matter the remedy of plaintiff was by appeal in that action. *Central Iowa Railway Co. v. Piersol*, 65 Iowa, 498. The rule is universal, we think. The judgment will stand AFFIRMED.

G. F. VAN VECHTEN v. ELIAS F. JONES AND P. D. JONES, Appellants.

Payment: EXTENSION. Where the payment of an interest coupon note is extended more than thirty days in all, from time to time, pending negotiation for a new loan from the holder of the note, which is finally refused, and the holder notifies the payee that the

1   note must be paid by the first of April, the time of extension expires with the thirty-first day in March; and under a clause, contained in the principal note, that upon a failure to pay any of said interest within thirty days after due, the holder may elect and consider the whole note due, the holder may, on April 1, if the extended note is unpaid, declare the principal note and all the interest coupon notes due, and sue thereon.

SAME. Payment of an interest coupon, which will prevent the holder from foreclosing under the provision of his mortgage giving him the right to foreclose if any interest coupon remains unpaid

8   thirty days after maturity, is not effected by depositing the amount thereof in bank other than that at which the principal note is payable, subject to the holder's order, and instructing the bank to notify him of the deposit and request him to forward the coupon.

Principal and Agent. An agent to collect an interest coupon has no

2   implied authority to extend the time of payment or to negotiate a new loan.

Appeal from Palo Alto District Court.—HON. W. B. QUARTON, Judge.

SATURDAY, JANUARY 22, 1898.

ON April 18, 1895, the plaintiff filed his petition for judgment on a promissory note, and three interest coupons attached thereto, and for foreclosure of a mortgage on real estate given to secure said notes, which notes are, in substance, as follows: The principal note was executed July 31, 1891, by Elias T. Jones, for eight hundred dollars, with interest as per coupons attached, payable to T. W. Harrison, or order, on the first day of November, 1896, "at the Palo Alto County Bank, Emmetsburg, Iowa, * * * and upon a failure to pay any of said interest within thirty days after due the holder may elect to consider the whole note due, and it may be collected at once, with reasonable attorney's fees." The mortgage contains a similar provision. The three coupon notes attached bear the same date, are for sixty-four dollars each,—one payable on the first day of November, 1894, one on the first day of November, 1895, and one on the first day of November, 1896, each "at Emmetsburg, Iowa." Plaintiff alleges that he is the owner of said note, coupons, and mortgage by assignment from T. W. Harrison before maturity; that the same were past due and unpaid; and that "plaintiff elected, and does hereby elect and declare, the whole indebtedness on said note due and payable." P. D. Jones, having been made a defendant as claiming some interest in the mortgaged lands, filed his substituted answer, in substance as follows: He admits the execution of the notes and mortgage sued upon, denies for want of knowledge that plaintiff is the owner thereof, and specifically denies that said note and coupon notes are past due, or that there is any sum due and owing

thereon, and denies that plaintiff had a right to or did
declare said indebtedness due and payable. For defense
he alleges: That he is the owner in fee simple of the
mortgaged lands. That, the coupons attached to said
note being payable at Emmetsburg, Iowa, it had been
the custom of the owners of said mortgage, including
the plaintiff, to deposit the coupons as they matured in
the First National Bank of Emmetsburg, Iowa, and
with J. J. Watson, at his office in Emmetsburg, Iowa,
for payment and collection. That, in accordance therewith, plaintiff forwarded to Watson the coupon matur-
ing November 1, 1894, for payment and collection as
aforesaid. That this defendant negotiated with plaintiff personally and through his agent, Watson, for a
new loan on said premises whereby to pay the loan represented by the notes in suit. That plaintiff continued
the negotiations until in March, 1895, when he
announced, through Watson, his refusal to make the
loan. That on or about March 1, 1895, and while said
coupon was in the possession of Watson for collection,
this defendant offered Watson the amount thereof, and
that by reason of said negotiations for a loan Watson
waived the payment thereof. That on the sixteenth
day of March, 1895, plaintiff wrote this defendant as
follows: "Unless the E. F. Jones coupon of $64.00 and
interest on it since Nov. 1 last is paid by the first of
April, I shall be compelled to commence foreclosure
proceedings." That on the first day of April, 1895,
defendant called at the office of Watson for the purpose
of paying said coupon. That without knowledge of this
defendant, plaintiff had withdrawn said coupon from
the possession of Watson, for which reason defendant
could not pay the same to him. That defendant then
went to the First National Bank, to pay the same, but
that the coupon was not in the possession of said bank.
That he thereupon gave notice to Watson, the bank,
and the plaintiff of his desire to pay said coupon when

the same should be surrendered. That plaintiff knew that defendant had on deposit in said bank sufficient funds for the payment of said coupons, and that he has at all times since March sixteenth been ready and willing to pay the same, but has been prevented by accident, mistake, and the inequitable conduct of the plaintiff as aforesaid. Defendant avers that plaintiff waived his right to declare said indebtedness due, wherefore he prays that he be permitted to pay the plaintiff the amount due upon said interest coupon, and that this suit be dismissed, at the plaintiff's cost. The defendant Elias F. Jones answered, making the allegations of the answer of P. D. Jones, his answer to the petition. Plaintiff replied at length, which reply seems to have been addressed to the original, rather than to the substituted, answer of P. D. Jones. It denies that Watson was the agent of the plaintiff, that the plaintiff extended the time of payment of said first coupon, that defendant stood ready and willing to pay the same, that Watson had any authority to extend the time of payment, and, in effect, denies all the allegations tending to show that plaintiff did not have the right to declare said mortgage indebtedness due. Judgment was entered in favor of the plaintiff upon the principal notes and for the interest matured thereon as per coupon notes, and decree foreclosing the mortgage. Defendants appeal.— *Affirmed.*

E. A. Morling and *Jones & Jones* for appellants.

A. T. Cooper and *McCarty & Linderman* for appellee.

Given, J.—The defendant P. D. Jones purchased the mortgaged land, and as part of the consideration agreed to pay this mortgage indebtedness. It is not questioned but that, under the terms of the note and

mortgage, plaintiff had the right to declare the whole
indebtedness due because of the failure to pay the
interest coupon due November 1, 1894, were it not for
the matters set up as constituting a waiver of that
right, and an extension of the time of payment. See
Swearingen v. Lahner. 93 Iowa, 152. We now inquire
whether there was a waiver or extension of the time of
payment of said first coupon. It appears that on
November 3, 1895, the plaintiff sent said coupon to J. J.
Watson at Emmetsburg, for collection; that defendants were informed of that fact; and that, the coupon
not being paid, Mr. Watson returned it to the plaintiff
on March 15, 1895. Defendants contend that payment
was tendered to Mr. Watson within thirty days, and
while the coupon was in his possession; that payment
was declined, Watson agreeing to extend the time until
it was ascertained whether the loan which defendant
solicited from plaintiff would be made. There is no
doubt but that the defendant P. D. Jones did seek to
secure a loan from the plaintiff through Mr. Watson,
and that plaintiff declined to make the loan. We do not
think that the claim that payment was tendered to
Watson is sustained. We are satisfied that the defendants relied upon effecting a loan from the plaintiff for
the means with which to pay that coupon. Nor
1   do we think that the claim that Watson agreed
to an extension of the time of payment is sustained. Whether or not Watson so agreed is immaterial, as it is entirely clear that his only authority from
plaintiff was to collect the coupon, and that he had no
authority to extend the time of payment or to negotiate
a new loan. In view of these conclusions, it is clear that
up to March 15 the plaintiff had not done, or authorized
the doing of, anything that waived his right to declare
the entire indebtedness due because of the failure to

pay said interest coupon within thirty days after its
maturity. On March 16, 1895, the plaintiff wrote
2   to defendant P. D. Jones that, unless the coupon
due November 1, 1894, "is paid by the first of
April, I shall be compelled to commence foreclosure
proceedings." Let it be conceded that this was an
extension of the time of payment to April 1, yet the
right remained to plaintiff to declare the whole debt due
if payment was not made by that date. Notwithstanding this notice to defendant, it does not appear that
any attempt was made to ascertain the whereabouts of
the coupon, or to make payment thereof, until the first
day of April, 1895. On that day, defendant P. D. Jones
called upon Watson, as he says, for the purpose of
paying the coupon. Watson not having it, he went to
the First National Bank, and failed to find it there. He
says that he had on deposit in that bank funds for the
paying of the coupon, and that the plaintiff knew that
fact. Defendant does not explain why he did not
inquire for the coupon at the Palo Alto County Bank,
where the principal note is payable, and why his
deposit was not made in that bank. Under the circumstances, plaintiff was not bound to keep the coupon at
Emmetsburg indefinitely, and the defendants should
have availed themselves of the time between March 16
and April 1, in which to learn where payment
3   might be made. The defendant P. D. Jones
testifies that on the eleventh, twelfth, or
thirteenth of April, 1895, he again inquired at the bank
for the coupon, but, not finding it, deposited sixty-six
dollars and fifteen cents subject to plaintiff's order, and
told the bank to notify him of the deposit, and to send
up the coupon. Under the facts, such a deposit was not
a payment of the coupon, and it was only payment at
maturity, or within any extension that may have been
granted, that would have deprived the plaintiff of the
. right to declare the whole debt due. We are satisfied.

from all the evidence that the defendant P. D. Jones, relying upon securing a loan from the plaintiff, failed to pay or tender payment of this coupon as by the terms of the notes and mortgage he was bound to do, and therefore the plaintiff had a right to and did declare the whole debt due. It follows from these conclusions that the judgment of the district court must be AFFIRMED.

E. H. CLARK, Administrator, v. EUGENE A. S. ELLS-
WORTH, Appellant.

Evidence: DISCRETION OF COURT: *Attorney and client.* The court may in its discretion, to show the character of the contest between the husband and wife, admit her depositions taken by his attorney
10   for use in resisting her application to set aside a decree of divorce in an action by her attorney to recover the value of his services from the husband on the ground that they were necessary for her protection, notwithstanding that the defendant offered to agree not to contradict any testimony which should be given as to the nature of the depositions, or as to the time spent, or character of the labor required on plaintiff's part, to meet them.

SAME. Where the length of time spent is made an important element of recovery in an action for legal services, and the various ques-
13   tions examined by the attorney, and the several papers which he drew, together with the facts involved, have been detailed by him at length, evidence that a much less time than that which he claimed to have spent therein was reasonably necessary for the performance of the services, is admissible.

OF VALUE. The value of legal services rendered in a certain county
8   is to be determined with reference to the practice there, so far as it has established the value of such services.

DESTRUCTION OF EVIDENCE: *Witness.* The mere fact that a witness for defendant had destroyed letters, does not render her testimony
11   as to their contents incompetent, it not being shown that they were destroyed by defendant's procurement or for a fraudulent purpose.

Attorney's Fees: EXPERT EVIDENCE. Attorneys who show general
2   knowledge of the customary and reasonable charges for attorney's
3   services in a certain county, though not having as great knowl-
9   edge thereof as others, may give their opinion as to the value of certain services rendered there.

SAME. The opinions of expert witnesses are competent to show the
2-3 value of the services of an attorney, though not conclusive upon
9 that question.

SAME. Expert testimony as to the time necessary to prepare for the
2 trial of a case, is admissible on the question as to the value of
legal services, where the length of time spent by plaintiff in the
13 preparation of the case is made prominent as an element of
recovery

SAME. A question of an expert as to what professional services
2 were necessary in preparing for the trial of a case, is properly
12 excluded.

HYPOTHETICAL QUESTIONS: *Competency.* The failure to expressly,
2 restrict hypothetical questions as to the value of an attorney's
services, to their value in the county in which they were performed,
4 does not render it immaterial or incompetent where it shows that
the services were performed in such county.

VALUE OF: *Elements.* In determining value of legal services, not
5 only the amount and character thereof and the results obtained.
but also the professional ability and standing of the attorney, his
learning, skill, and proficiency in his profession. and experience,
may be considered.

SAME The importance of a litigation, success attained, and the benefit
5-6 which it procured, may be considered in estimating the value of
7 the services rendered by an attorney.

SAME: *Husband and wife.* The wealth of the husband, though not
5 admissible as an independent factor, in determining the value of
6 an attorney's services rendered to a wife in litigation with her
7 husband. may be considered in connection with the husband's
disposition to make a severe contest in such litigation, as tending
to show the importance of the service, in an action by an attorney
to recover the value thereof from the husband, on the ground that
they were necessary for the protection of the wife.

EXPENSE OF PREPARATION. The liability of a husband for services
and disbursements rendered to and made in behalf of his wife in
14 a suit for divorce, which were necessary for her protection, includes
costs paid by her attorney, and expenses reasonably necessary in
procuring information upon which to act, in preparing for trial
an application for the wife to have decree against her set aside.

ATTORNEY OUTSIDE OF COUNTY. Where a wife, in divorce proceed-
14 ings, hires an attorney from outside the county, he cannot recover
against her husband for expenses for traveling outside the county,
it not being shown that services of competent attorneys within
the county could not have been procured, and it appearing that
several of them were not employed by the husband.

SAME: *Usage*. Whether an attorney from outside the county,
16 employed to render services therein, can recover for hotel bills
and other expenses in the county, depends on the usage therein.

Appeal: ABSTRACTS. Appellee's additional abstract will not be
stricken from the files because it was not filed within the time
fixed by the rules where it does not appear that the submission of
the cause had been delayed or that any prejudice had been caused
by the non-compliance with the rules in that respect.

Appeal from Kossuth District Court.—HON. LOT
THOMAS, Judge.

SATURDAY, JANUARY 22, 1898.

ACTION at law to recover for professional services
rendered by an attorney. There was a trial by jury,
and a verdict and judgment for the plaintiff. The
defendant appeals.—*Reversed.*

R. M. Wright and *J. C. Cook* for appellant.

George H. Carr and *George E. Clarke* for appellee.

ROBINSON, J.—In the year 1891, and during the first
part of the year 1892, the defendant and his wife resided
in Hardin county. On the fifteenth day of December,
1891, the district court of that county rendered a decree
which divorced the defendant from his wife, and gave
him the custody and control of their two minor children.
No allowance to her for alimony was made. In January, 1892, she applied to have the decree set aside.
The application was resisted, and a trial thereon was
commenced; but before it was concluded Ellsworth
withdrew all objections to the application, and asked
that it be granted. Thereupon the decree was set aside,
and Ellsworth dismissed his action without prejudice.
Mrs. Ellsworth then commenced an action against her
husband for a divorce, but before it was reached for
trial a reconciliation was effected, the parties again

cohabited, and the action of the wife was discontinued. In the proceedings mentioned she was represented by Attorneys Charles A. Clark and F. C. Hormel, both of whom resided in Cedar Rapids. Clark not having been paid for his services and disbursements, assigned his claim therefor to William C. Stevens, by whom this action was brought, to recover the sum of five thousand dollars for services rendered, and ninety-five dollars for money paid for costs and other expenses caused by the litigation. The plaintiff seeks to hold the defendant liable for the amounts in question, on the ground that the services and expenses were necessary to enable Mrs. Ellsworth to prosecute her litigation and secure and protect her rights; that she was without financial means to pay for them; and that by her agreement with Clark she made the defendant liable for them. The defendant denies that Clark was employed by Mrs. Ellsworth, denies that he is liable on account of the services and expenses in controversy in any sum, and denies that the services rendered were of the value claimed. A trial was had on the issue joined, and a judgment rendered, from which the defendant appealed to this court. The judgment of the district court was reversed, and the cause was remanded for further proceedings. See *Stevens v. Ellsworth*, 95 Iowa, 231. The death of Stevens was then suggested in the district court, and the administrator of his estate was substituted as plaintiff. A second trial was had, which resulted in a second judgment against the defendant, and he again appeals.

I. The appellant presents a motion to strike from the files an additional abstract of the appellee, on the ground that it was not served and filed within the time fixed by the rules for that purpose, and on the 1 further ground that it does not comply with the rules, and is unnecessary. It does not appear that the submission of this cause has been delayed, nor any prejudice caused, by not serving the additional

abstract within the time fixed by the rules; and it is not
our practice, when that is the case, to strike the additional abstract from the files. The one in question contains some material matter, and, although it may set
out some parts of the record with unnecessary fullness,
yet it cannot be said that it is not an abstract, within
the meaning of the rules. The motion to strike it from
the files is therefore overruled.

II. The evidence in regard to the employment of
Clark, by Mrs. Ellsworth, is conflicting, but the jury was
authorized to find that he was employed to render the
services for which a recovery is sought, and that question need not be further considered on this appeal. The
question of chief importance is, what amount should
the defendant pay for the services rendered and the
disbursements made by Clark? The jury allowed the
plaintiff three thousand dollars for the services of Clark,
ninety-five dollars on account of his disbursements, and
interest in the sum of seven hundred and fifty-seven dollars and eighty cents, and judgment was rendered for
the aggregate amount of these sums. We held on the
former appeal that where, as in this case, the compensation of an attorney is to be paid, not by the person who
employed him, but by a third person, on the ground
that it was a necessary expense, the amount allowed
should be no more than what the service was reasonably
worth where it was rendered, to be fixed by the practice
at that place, and, in effect, that expert witnesses, to be
qualified to testify in regard to the compensation to
which Clark was entitled in this case, should know the
value in Hardin county of services rendered there, and
that the wealth of the defendant cannot be considered
in estimating the amount of the compensation to which
Clark is entitled. On the second trial the testimony of
numerous attorneys, who resided in different parts of

the state, was submitted by the plaintiff to show the
value of the services rendered by Clark. Those

2   witnesses were asked a hypothetical question,
which covers nearly twelve printed pages. That
assumed to be true, numerous alleged facts which the
evidence tended to establish, which were designed to
show that the duties Clark was required to perform
involved much labor and professional knowledge and
judgment; that he was required to investigate many
facts, to examine many authorities and records, to draw
numerous pleadings, motions, and other papers, and to
make oral arguments; that he appeared in the district
court of Hardin county on several occasions, and
assisted in the trial of the application to vacate the
decree of divorce; that the trial lasted four days, and
that his efforts were successful; and that he devoted
a full month to the discharge of the duties which he was
required to perform. The statements contained in the
hypothetical question, if true, showed that the defendant was worth five hundred thousand dollars when he
obtained the decree of divorce; that the original grounds
upon which the divorce was sought were that the wife
had for years been guilty of improper conduct with
different men, receiving visits from them at unusual
and improper hours, in the night-time, and by her conduct had disgraced herself and family; that knowledge
of such conduct had reached him with such effect as to
make him nearly distracted, and greatly impair his
health, and that the conduct of his wife had been so
cruel and inhuman as to endanger his life; and that
when the application to set aside the decree was made
it was resisted, and to support the resistance he took
the depositions of two witnesses to prove that his wife
had been guilty of adultery. The interrogative part of
the hypothetical question, answered by nine of the
attorneys who testified for the plaintiff, was as follows:

"What, in your judgment, is fair and reasonable compensation in gross for the services rendered by the said
Clark on behalf of Mrs. Ellsworth in the litigation
aforesaid, taking into consideration all the facts and
circumstances above set forth, and the importance of
the interests involved and the success attained?" The
question, as answered by five of the witnesses for the
plaintiff, contained the words, "in Hardin county,
Iowa," inserted immediately after the words, "compensation in gross." Objections to the interrogatory in
both its original and modified forms were made on
various grounds, and motions to suppress depositions
upon such objections were made and overruled. The
objections thus made were chiefly that the witnesses
had not shown themselves qualified to testify in regard
to the value in Hardin county of the services rendered,
and that they had included in their estimates of the
value of such services improper elements, as, the wealth
of the defendant and the ultimate benefit to his wife
of the litigation in which the services were rendered.
Each witness who answered the hypothetical question
showed before he answered it that he had practiced law
in different counties of the state, and that he knew
generally the value of the professional services of attorneys throughout the state, or in Hardin county and
vicinity, in the year 1892, when the services in question
were rendered. There was nothing in the hypothetical
question which required the answers thereto to be
based, in whole or in part, upon improper considerations,
and we are of the opinion that each witness who
answered the question showed such knowledge and
qualifications as made his testimony competent and
admissible. The value of his testimony, if not shown by
his direct examination, could have been and was disclosed by his cross-examination. Some showed greater
knowledge than did others of the customary and reasonable charges made in Hardin county, but each one

showed such general knowledge of the subject that his
__stimony should not have been suppressed, although
it might not have been of much value. The gen-
3   eral rules which regulate the admission of expert
testimony in regard to tangible property, and
services other than those rendered by an attorney,
apply to the testimony of attorneys respecting the value
of legal services; and it is well settled that evidence as
to the value of such property is admissible, even though
it be not of the highest degree of competency. *Leek v.
Chesley*, 98 Iowa, 593; *Carruthers v. Towne*, 86 Iowa,
323; *Latham v. Shipley*, 86 Iowa, 543; *St te v. Finch*,
70 Iowa, 317; *Tubbs v. Garrison*, 68 Iowa, 48; *Lanning
v. Railroad Co.*, 68 Iowa, 503; *Gere v. Insurance Co.*, 67
Iowa, 275; *State v. Maynes*, 61 Iowa, 120; *Smalley v.
Railroad Co.*, 36 Iowa, 574; *Vilas v. Downer*, 21 Vt. 423;
Lawson, Expert Evidence, 236. The hypothet-
4   ical question showed that the services for which
a recovery is sought were rendered in connection
with litigation in Hardin county, and the answers were
necessarily based upon that fact. Therefore, we think
the omission of the interrogative part of the question,
as asked some witnesses, to refer specially to Hardin
county, did not render the answers immaterial nor
incompetent.

III.   Several witnesses for the plaintiff testified, in
effect, that in answering the hypothetical question,
they considered to some extent the wealth of the defendant, and some of them stated that the benefit to the wife
which resulted from the litigation was considered. It
is a well-settled rule that the importance of the
5   litigation, the success attained, and the benefit
which it secured may be considered in estimating
the compensation to which the attorney who conducted
it is entitled for the services he rendered. The responsibility of an attorney may be, and usually is, much
greater where large interests are involved than it is

where the interests are of but little importance. *Smith v. Railroad Co.,* 60 Iowa, 522; *Berry v. Davis,* 34 Iowa, 594. And where the subject-matter of the litiga-

6   tion is of great importance to the litigants, and of a character to lead them to use every legiti-mate effort to succeed, the wealth of a party, and his consequent ability to make a severe contest, may be considered in connection with his disposition to do so, as tending to show the importance and value of the ser-vices which the attorney, for whose compensation he was responsible, was required to render. The hypo-thetical question asked on the second trial differed from that asked on the first, in that it did not require the witnesses to consider the wealth of the defendant in estimating the compensation in question. The district court, by its charge, required the jury not to take into consideration the wealth of the defendant, nor his ability to pay for the services rendered by Clark to enhance the value of the services, but permitted the jury to consider it as an incident in ascertaining the importance and gravity of the interests involved in the litigation in which the services were rendered. We think this was correct, and not in conflict with what we

7   decided on the former appeal. The jury was also instructed that it should not take into considera-tion the ultimate benefits to Mrs. Ellsworth of the litigation as a distinct element to enhance the value of the services in question, but the success or non-success of the litigation. That portion of the charge was in the interest of the defendant, and we are of the opinion that the effect of the evidence admitted which may be regarded as objectionable, was so far modified by the charge as to prevent prejudice to the defendant. See *Shepard v. Railway Co.,* 77 Iowa, 56, and cases therein cited. Not only the amount and character of the services and the results attained, but also the pro-fessional ability and standing of the attorney, his

learning, skill, and proficiency in his profession, and his
experience, may be considered in estimating the reasonable value of his services. *Stanton v. Embrey*, 93 U. S.
548 (23 L. Ed. 985); *Randall v. Packard*, 142 N. Y. 56;
Allis v. Day, 14 Minn. 516 (Gil. 388); *Vilas v. Downer*,
21 Vt. 419; *Eggleston v. Boardman*, 37 Mich. 16; 1 Lawson, Rights, Remedies, Practice, section 198; Weeks,
Attorneys (2d ed.), 687. These elements of value are to
be considered in this case in connection with other facts
in order to ascertain the value of the services rendered in
Hardin county, and not their value had they been rendered elsewhere. The value to be determined is
8   the reasonable value of the services in Hardin
county, as fixed by the practice in that county.
This does not mean that it is necessary to show what
charges have been made in that county in cases like those
in which the compensation in question was earned. It
rarely happens that two contested cases, involving not
only different parties, but different interests, are so
nearly alike that the compensation of the attorneys
should be precisely the same in one as in the other. But
the value is to be determined with reference to the
practice in Hardin county, so far as it has established
the value of such services as those in controversy.

IV.   It is claimed that the opinions of expert witnesses are not competent to show the value of the services of an attorney, but that it is to be determined by
the jury, from all the testimony which tends to show
what the value is. It is true that such value is to
9   be determined by the jury, and that the testimony
of experts is not conclusive; but that their opinions are competent is, we think, well established by the
authorities, and the admission of such opinions in evidence is sanctioned by reason and usage. *Head v. Hargrave*, 105 U. S. 45; *Allis v. Day*, 14 Minn. 518 (Gil. 388);
Thompson v. Boyle, 85 Pa. St. 477; *Blizzard v. Applegate*, 61 Ind. 317; *Williams v. Brown*, 28 Ohio St. 551;

Lawson, Expert Evidence 61, 63; Rogers, Expert Evidence, section 157; 1 Wharton, Evidence, sections 442, 446; Weeks, Attorneys, sections 126, 340; Bradner, Evidence, 477; Underhill, Evidence, 291.

V. The defendant objected to the introduction in evidence in this case of the depositions of two witnesses taken by him for use in resisting the application of his wife to set aside the decree in the action for divorce, and offered to agree not to contradict any testimony which had been or should be given as to the nature of the depositions, or as to the time spent or character of the labor required on the part of Mrs. Ellsworth's attorneys to meet them. The objection was overruled, and the depositions were read in evidence.

10

In that, we think, there was no error. The depositions were introduced to show something of the character of the contest in which the services in question were rendered, and the nature of those services, and were competent for that purpose. It was certainly within the discretion of the court to permit the evidence to be read, and to refuse to accept the offer of the defendant. The appellant also complains of the refusal of the court to permit the wife of the defendant to testify as to the contents of letters which were written to her by Mr. Hormel, but which she had destroyed. The fact that she had destroyed the letters did not alone render her testimony as to their contents incompetent. It is not shown that they were destroyed by the procurement of the defendant, nor for a fraudulent purpose; but it is not shown that the rejected testimony was material to any issue on the case, and the court did not err in rejecting it.

11

VI. The defendant sought to show by two witnesses that Clark had spent an unnecessary number of days in preparing for the trial of the cases in which he was employed by Mrs. Ellsworth, but was not permitted to do so. Some of the questions asked those witnesses

sought to elicit their opinions respecting matters of
law, and the court rightly refused to receive the answers
to them. Others inquired as to what services
12   were necessary, and for that reason were objectionable, under the rule announced in *Kelly v.
Inc. Town of West Bend*, 101 Iowa, 669. But Col. Clark
testified as to the number of days he spent out of court
in preparing the cases, and the number of days he spent
in court, and it is claimed that it was competent to
show that he spent more time than was needed in preparation. It was said in the case last cited, which involved
the necessity and value of services performed by an
attorney who had represented the town in an action
against it, that whether the work performed by the
attorney was necessary was a question for the jury, and
that witnesses could not be permitted to usurp the
functions of that body. It was also said of the case in
which the services there in dispute were rendered: "The
proper method of procedure in such a case, and the
amount of labor and time that a lawyer of the average
degree of skill and learning would expend, might be
the subject of expert testimony. But the ultimate fact
as to what was necessary was not." We think it was
proper to consider the services of Clark as a whole, and
not to split them up, and show what time was required
for the consideration of each question involved in the
litigation in which he was employed. But he testified
at considerable length in regard to the questions he
considered and the time he spent in investigating them,
and he also testified in regard to the time he spent in
court, and showed that he had spent about one month
in the course of his employment. The hypothetical
question stated that he "devoted at least a full month's
time" to said divorce proceedings, and his said client's
interests therein, outside of court. The defend-
13   ant offered, and attempted to show, by witnesses
he introduced, that the time required by an
attorney of fair qualification, ability, and experience in

the district court to perform the services which Clark
states that he rendered out of court, would not be more
than four days, but the court sustained an objection to
the offer. In that, we think, it erred. The length of
time spent by Clark was made prominent as an element
of recovery; and while the value of legal services rendered does not bear any fixed ratio to the length of time
required to perform them, yet time is usually, if not
always, an important consideration. The various legal
questions which Clark examined, and the several papers
which he drew, together with the facts involved, were
detailed by him at length, and a competent, experienced
lawyer could readily form a reasonably accurate opinion
as to the number of days which would be required to do
what was done. The plaintiff very properly showed the
time which he claimed to have been necessary to perform the work for which he seeks a recovery, and we
do not know any rule of law which would prevent the
defendant from showing that the work performed could
have been done in less time than that for which the
plaintiff claims. We do not overlook the fact that some
attorneys spend more time in the preparation of a cause
for trial than do others, but it does not follow that
inquiry cannot be made as to the time necessarily spent.
The character of the work performed by Clark is such
that an estimate of the time necessarily required to do
it can be very readily made. It cannot be true that an
attorney is entitled to compensation for all the time he
spends in the interest of his client, even though an
unreasonable length of time be spent, and that the
client cannot inquire into the fact, but is compelled to
compensate the attorney on the basis of the time
actually spent. Where the length of time spent is made
an important element of recovery, as it is in this case,
evidence may be received to show what time was, and
what was not, reasonably necessary for the performance of the services rendered. If it be true that the

preparatory work for which the plaintiff seeks a recovery could have been thoroughly and well done in four days, the amount of his recovery should be less than as though thirty days had been required for such work.

VII. Some question is made as to the amount of the disbursements of Clark for which the plaintiff is entitled to recover. It is our opinion that, if the defendant is liable in this action, the plaintiff is entitled

14   to recover for costs which he paid, and for expenses which were reasonably necessary in procuring information upon which to act in preparing the application of Mrs. Ellsworth for trial. We do not think he is entitled to recover for expenses for traveling outside of Hardin county, since it is not shown

15   that the services of competent attorneys in Hardin county could not have been procured, while it does appear that several of them were not employed by Ellsworth. Whether the plaintiff is entitled to recover for hotel bills and other expenses within

16   Hardin county depends upon the usage in that county.

VIII. Questions which we have not mentioned are presented in argument, but are disposed of by what we have already said, or are unimportant, or are not likely to arise on another trial, and therefore do not need further consideration. For the error pointed out the judgment of the district court is REVERSED.

PATRICK HAYS v. J. J. BERRY, Defendant, and J. J. PORTER AND HAINES & LYMAN, Interveners, Appellants.

Landlord's Lien: EXEMPTION: *Burden of proof.* Though the burden of proof is upon the landlord to show that property distrained was owned by the lessee, and used in the demised premises, under

1   Code, 1873, section 2017, the one who asserts that the lien does not

attach, by reason of the property being exempt, must prove such fact.

INNOCENT PURCHASERS. Want of notice on behalf of the vendee of property sold by a lessee, that it was subject to a landlord's lien
2 does not divest the lien, nor afford the purchaser protection against it.

Appeal from Poweshiek District Court.—HON. D. RYAN, Judge.

SATURDAY, JANUARY 22, 1898.

Affirmed.

Haines & Lyman for appellants.

No appearance for appellee.

LADD, J.—As the value of the horse in controversy is under one hundred dollars, the questions involved are presented in the certificate of the trial judge. These may be stated rather than set out in detail. It appears that the plaintiff executed a lease of his farm for three years, beginning March 1, 1894, to Berry, who took possession thereunder, and used six or eight horses on the premises. In 1895 he traded one of these to Simmons for the black horse in controversy, which he also kept and used on the farm. In 1896 Berry exchanged it with Frost for another. Frost traded this black horse to the intervener Porter, who used it on the farm he had leased from Haines & Lyman. Berry absconded in August, 1896, owing the plaintiff rent to the amount of several hundred dollars, for the recovery of which this action was begun, and a landlord's writ of attachment issued therein, and levied on said horse while in the possession of Porter, and on the farm of Haines & Lyman, to whom Porter was indebted for rent. Porter intervened, claiming the horse was not subject to the landlord's lien of plaintiff, while Haines & Lyman

averred that their lien was superior. Porter, when he
received the horse from Frost, had no actual notice that
it had ever been owned by Berry, or that it had ever
been used on plaintiff's farm. It was not shown that
Berry did not claim the horse as exempt to him under
the statute.

I. In such a case, is the burden of proof on the
landlord, in order to establish his lien, not only to
show that the property was owned by the lessee and
used on the demised premises, but also that it
1   was not exempt from execution? The statute
gives the landlord "a lien for his rent upon all
crops grown upon the demised premises, and upon any
other property of.the tenant which has been used on
the premises during the term and not exempt from
execution." Code 1873, section 2017. The authorities
seem to agree that the purpose of exemption is to protect the family of the debtor from want, by not permitting his creditors to strip from him the necessities
of life and the means of support, and that the right to
the exemption is a personal privilege, to be asserted by
the debtor. His wife may do so if he absconds. Code
1897, section 4016. *Nix v. Goodhile*, 95 Iowa, 282, does
not announce a different rule. It has been adjudged
by this court that the burden is on the defendant or garnishee to show that the money owing by the
latter is exempt as personal earnings. *Oaks v. Marquardt*, 49 Iowa, 643. No exemptions were allowed at
common law, and, as the great mass of property is subject to the satisfaction of debts, these are exceptions to
the general rule. If, then, it was made to appear that
the horse levied on was owned by Berry, and used on
the leased premises, the burden was upon him who
asserted that the lien did not attach by reason of the
property being exempt, to so prove. Section 4017 of the
Code was enacted to obviate any waiver by reason of
the surrender of the property to the sheriff, or failure

to object to the levy by the debtor, in ignorance of his rights, in supposed obedience to one in authority. The question of proof was not involved in *Bank v. Honnold*, 85 Iowa, 352, the court simply holding, in that case, that the lease was, in effect, a mortgage, and the property, being exempt to the lessee, was not subject to the land-lord's lien. In *Richardson v. Peterson*, 58 Iowa, 724, the defendant did not allege that the property was exempt, nor argue that, by reason thereof, the lien did not attach, but rested his defense solely upon the propo-sition that a sale of the property to the intervener, Kurz, without actual notice thereof, divested the landlord's lien. The facts in this case illustrate the necessity of the rule placing the burden of proof upon the party alleging the exemption. Berry had six or eight horses, any two of which he might have held as exempt under the law; but because of his failure to make an election which he would claim, and having absconded, so that he could not be required to do so, it was utterly impossible to establish the plaintiff's lien on any of them, if appel-lant's position were adopted. The same would be true with reference to other property. The question must be answered in the negative.

II. The other two questions are involved in that already stated. Haines & Lyman acquired no better right to the horse than Porter, and the case of *Richardson v. Peterson*, *supra*, adjudges that the purchase by Porter without notice would afford him no protection. See, also, *Blake v. Counsel-man*, 95 Iowa, 219.—AFFIRMED.

2

JENNIE L. PHILLIPS v. F. H. GIFFORD, *et al.*, Appel-lants.

Contracts: PUBLIC POLICY: *Consideration.* Two persons were engaged in selling intoxicating liquors under acts Twenty-fifth

General Assembly, chapter 62, known as the "mulct law." A note for the price of the interest of one of them contained the clause "if payor is obliged to abandon his present business on account of change in the liquor law by the next legislature of the state, then this note to be void; otherwise to be full of force." *Held*, that the words "present business" meant the business he then had, and that, said business being a legal business, the note was not invalid, as being a "gambling, wagering contract," and that it was supported by a valid consideration.

Appeal from Marshall District Court.—HON. O. CASWELL, Judge.

MONDAY, JANUARY 24, 1898.

ACTION on a promissory note. Judgment for plaintiff, and the defendant appeals.—*Affirmed.*

Anthony C. Daly, Theo. F. Bradford, and *W. E. Bradford* for appellants.

J. L. Carney for appellee.

GRANGER, J.—The action is upon a note in words as follows: "$500.00. Marshalltown, Iowa, July 8, 1895. June 1, 1896, after date, we promise to pay F. S. Rockafellow, or order, five hundred dollars, with seven per cent. (payable annually) interest per annum from date (overdue interest and principal draws seven per cent. per annum), and reasonable attorney's fees for collection if action is commenced hereon. Payable at Marshalltown, Iowa. This note is conditional. If payor is obliged to abandon his present business on account of a change of the liquor law by the next legislature of the state, then this note to be void; otherwise in full force. F. H. Gifford. I. B. Capron." The note was indorsed to plaintiff. After much contention over the pleadings, each party moved for judgment in his favor; each party presenting as a ground therefor, that there were no disputed questions of fact, so that we may properly state the facts as we find them from the pleadings. It appears that the defendant Gifford and the payee in the note, Rockafellow, were, prior to the execution of the note engaged in the saloon business in Marshalltown, Iowa, under the provisions of chapter 62, Acts Twenty-fifth General Assembly, known as the "Mulct Law;" that the consideration for the note was Rockafellow's undivided interest in the saloon, and the stock of liquor on hand, including whisky, beer, wine, and other intox-icating liquors kept for the purposes of sale by the drink. If it should be thought that a finding of fact that Gifford and Rockafellow were operating the saloon in Marshalltown *under the provisions of the mulct law* is not supported by the record, we may say that such is our conclusion from the admission of para-graph 4 of the reply. The averment in that paragraph that the firm was engaged in the sale of liquor under that law must be considered in connection with the averments in the preceding paragraph, to know what was meant. The admission of the facts stated in the paragraph carries with it the right to consider other facts essential to know its meaning, and from the reply it clearly appears that the intent of the pleading was to state the conclusion we have expressed. The legal sit-uation may be summarized as follows: Where two per-sons are engaged in the sale of intoxicating liquors under the provisions of the mulct law, is a note for the interest of one of them supported by a valid considera-tion, and enforcible?

II. The legal contention arises largely over the words of the note, that: "This note is conditional. If the payor is obliged to abandon his present business on account of a change of the liquor law by the next legislature of the state, then this note is to be void; otherwise in full force." It is thought that it does not appear that the consideration of the note was the par-ticular saloon in which Gifford and Rockafellow were

engaged, but we have no doubt of that being the proper
understanding from the pleadings. It is true, it is not
said in so many words, but it is the natural and the legal
inference. We think, also, that the "present business"
spoken of in the condition of the note, meant the business he had, and was taken from Rockafellow for the
note. Because of a claim that it does not appear that
the note was given for a saloon business, nor that
it was to be void if the payor had to abandon the
identical saloon for which the note was given, it is urged
that the giving of the note was a "gambling, wagering
contract." Our theory as to the facts puts at rest such
a contention; for, if the business was being carried on
under the mulct law, it was a legal business, under our
holding in *McKeever v. Beacom,* 101 Iowa, 173. If a
legal business, we know of no reason why it may not
be sold, if in so doing the provisions of the law against
sales are not violated. It is apparent that the condition in the note was intended to render the note void
if the consideration of the note should fail because of
a change in the law in a particular time. Such a transaction has none of the elements of a wagering or
gambling contract. It is no more such a contract than
would be an agreement that a note given for a horse
should be void if the horse should die within a month.
There is, of course, a contingency, a chance, involved in
the transaction, but it is no more than an undertaking
by the seller that the horse will live for a certain time.
In both cases the consideration that supports the note
is property actually delivered. It is in no sense a speculation on the chances for or against the happening of
an event, or on a contingency.

III. It is said "that the condition of the note is
against public policy and void; that it contemplates a
violation of the liquor laws of the state." If it does
contemplate that result, it is void; but we do not so
understand the facts, as we have said. We understand

the transaction to refer to a business done under the provisions of the mulct law, which, as we held in *McKeever v. Beacom, supra,* is a legal business. It is said that the presumptions of the law are that it was illegal. Concede the rule, and we look to the pleadings for the facts, and find it admitted that the business was done under the mulct law, and the presumption is thus overcome. With the facts as we understand them, and the case of *McKeever v. Beacom,* there is no room for any of the legal contentions made in the case. It is simply a sale of a legal business, with a stipulation that the consideration need not be paid, if from certain causes, the business shall become illegal within a certain time, and the consideration thus be lost. No good reasons have been suggested why such a contract should not be sustained.

A motion to reverse the judgment, made by appellant, presents only questions otherwise presented, and need not be considered. The judgment of the district court is AFFIRMED.

T. W. HARRISON v. J. P. STEBBINS, E. P. BARRINGER, JAMES HAND, W. H. HARRISON, and MYLES McNALLY, Members of the Board of Supervisors of Palo Alto County, Iowa, Appellants.

APPEAL: COUNTY: *Supersedeas.* An appeal from a judgment against a county does not operate as a stay of proceedings thereon without the filing of a supersedeas bond, as Code. section 4126. providing that no proceedings under a judgment shall be stayed by an appeal unless the appellant executes and files a bond makes no exceptions, and the only exemptions from furnishing security is that made by section 8175 in favor of the state. Citing *People v. Clingan,* 5 Cal. 389; *McClay v. Lincoln,* 32 Neb. 412 (49 N. W. Rep. 282).

Appeal from Palo Alto District Court. — HON. W. B. QUARTON, Judge.

MONDAY, JANUARY 24, 1898.

ACTION to compel the board of supervisors of Palo Alto county to levy a tax from which to pay plaintiff's judgment against said county. The defendants interposed the defense that an appeal had been taken to the supreme court, though no supersedeas bond had been filed. A motion for judgment having been sustained, and judgment entered as prayed, the defendant's appeal. —*Affirmed.*

John Menzies, county attorney, and *Soper, Allen & Morling* for appellants.

T. W. Harrison and *McCarty & Linderman* for appellee.

LADD, J.—Does an appeal from a judgment against a county operate as a stay of proceedings thereon without the filing of a supersedeas bond? Section 4128 of the Code provides that "no proceedings under a judgment or order, nor any part thereof, shall be stayed by an appeal, unless, the appellant executes a bond with one or more sureties, to be filed with and approved by the clerk, of the court in which the judgment or order was rendered or made," and conditioned as therein set out. No exception is made of any litigant, and the only exemption from furnishing security is that of section 3475, providing: "The state may maintain actions in the same manner as natural persons, but no security shall be required in such cases." The fact that the state is excepted would indicate that others are not. The sections relating to stay of proceedings are a part of chapter 2 of title 20, which includes the procedure in the supreme court in all cases, and it seems that municipalities might, with as much reason, claim exemption from some of the other provisions as this. The bond is purely statutory, as the writ of error at common law operated as a stay of proceedings by implication, and its purpose is quite as much to protect the appellee against vexatious litigation as the expenses incident to the appeal. While it has been held that the state is not within the contemplation of such statutes, our attention has not been called to any authority extending this exemption to counties and municipal corporations. See *People v. Clingan*, 5 Cal. 389. In *McClay v. City of Lincoln*, 32 Neb. 412 (49 N. W. Rep. 282), the supreme court of Nebraska holds that statutes exempting political corporations from the requirement of giving appeal bonds do not violate the constitutional provisions prohibiting special legislation, and Cobb, C. J., in delivering the opinion of the court, remarks: "The rule is that, in order to bind cities by law like the one under consideration, the city or any branch of the sovereignty shall be specially named; otherwise it is exempt." Then some very good reasons are given for not requiring bonds in such cases. A similar decision will be found in *Holmes v. Mattoon*, 111 Ill. 28 (53 Am. Rep. 602). In so far as these opinions refer to the rule as applied to the state or government, they cannot be doubted, but, as before remarked, our attention has not been called to any authority extending it to counties or municipalities. In many of the states public corporations, and persons acting in a trust capacity, are exempt from giving appeal bonds, by the express provisions of the statute; and the tendency of judicial construction has been not to extend these by implication, as they are exceptions to the general policy of the law protecting the appellee. *Von Schmidt v. Widber*, 99 Cal. 511 (32 Pac. Rep. 532); *State v. Judge of Third Dist.*, 18 La. 444; 1 Enc. Pl. & Prac. 968. The entity of the county is distinct from that of the state, though included in it, and existing for the purpose of carrying out its powers; and while the reasons for exempting the former from giving supersedeas bonds in order to stay proceedings on judgments, pending appeal, are cogent, and possibly unanswerable, they appeal to the lawmakers for appropriate legislation, rather than to the courts for the ingrafting of exceptions not intended. The very wording of our statute precludes any exception, and the provision exempting the state excludes all others.—AFFIRMED.

DONALD C. McGREGOR, Appellant, v. JOHN CONE.

Constitutional Law: INTERSTATE COMMERCE. Under Const. U. S. article 1, section 8, conferring on congress the exclusive right to regulate commerce between the several states, Acts Twenty-sixth General Assembly, chapter 96, prohibiting the sale of cigarettes within the state by all persons save jobbers doing an inter-state business, is unconstitutional and void, in so far as it amounts to a regulation of inter-state commerce.

ORIGINAL PACKAGES. An original package is that which is delivered by the importer to the carrier at the initial point of shipment in the exact condition in which it was shipped. *Collins v. Hill*, 77 Iowa, 181, and *State v. Coonan*, 82 Iowa, 400, disapproved, citing *State v. Board of Assessors*, 46 La. 146 (15 So. Rep. 10); *Keith v. State*, 91 Ala. 2 (8 So. Rep. 853); *United States v. 132 Packages*, 22 C. C. A. 228 (76 Fed. Rep. 864); *State v. Winters*, 44 Kan. Sup. 723 (25 Pac. Rep. 287).

SAME: *Cigarettes.* A pine box in which are packed for convenience in shipment packages of cigarettes, each of which contains ten cigarettes and sealed with an internal revenue stamp, without any other packing or inclosure around or about them except the box itself, is the original package of commerce, and when that is opened the packages of cigarettes are subject to the police power of the state as a part of the common mass of property therein.

DECISION OF REVENUE OFFICERS. The fact that the internal revenue department has recognized a package containing ten cigarettes as an "original package," for the purpose of taxation, is not conclusive, as the repacking of such packages in additional coverings is optional with the manufacturer. Disapproving, *State v. Goetze,* (W. Va.) 27 S. E. Rep. 225.

Appeal from Cedar Rapids Superior Court.—Hon. T. M. GIBERSON, Judge.

MONDAY, JANUARY 24, 1898.

THIS is a *habeas corpus* proceeding in which plain-tiff and appellant alleges that he was unlawfully restrained of his liberty by defendant, who is sheriff of Linn county, under a warrant of commitment issued by one Rall, a justice of the peace in and for said county, in pursuance of a judgment of conviction for violation of what is familiarly known as the "Anti-Cigarette Law." Plaintiff says that his commitment was and is illegal, for the reason that while he sold cigarettes, yet that the same were sold in the "original package" in which imported, and that the law under which he was convicted is unconstitutional in so far as it applies to such sales. The trial court remanded the petitioner, and from the order and judgment so entered he appeals. —*Affirmed.*

W. W. Fuller and *John W. Redmond* for appellant.

J. W. Grimm, county attorney, and *Milton Rem-ley,* attorney general, for the state.

DEEMER, C. J.—The case was tried upon the follow-ing agreed statement of facts: "The defendant pur-chased in Illinois from the American Tobacco Company,

1
a corporation organized under the laws of the state of New Jersey, and having a factory for the manufacture of cigarettes in the city of New York and state of New York, a number of packages of cigarettes, manufactured at its said factory in New York by said company. Each said package so pur-chased contained ten cigarettes, and had upon it the

label bearing the name or brand of the cigarettes con·
tained in it, the caution notice, the number of the fac·
tory and of the revenue district in which the factory
was located, the name of the state in which such fac·
tory was, the name of the manufacturer, and the inter·
nal revenue stamp for ten cigarettes, duly canceled,
pasted across the end of each of said packages so as to
seal the same (which said stamp had to be broken and
destroyed in opening said package), and all other
requirements of the acts of congress and of the internal
revenue laws governing the packing, shipment, and
sale of cigarettes. The packages of cigarettes so purchased by said defendant of said company were placed
in a common pine box, for convenience of shipment,
without any other packing or inclosure around or about
said packages of ten cigarettes each, and were so
shipped by said company to said defendant by a common carrier, from the factory of said company in the
city of New York, in the state of New York, to the ware-
house and offices of said company in the city of Chicago,
in the state of Illinois, and from Chicago, in the state of
Illinois, shipped by said company in the same package,
without opening the same, to the defendant, in Cedar
Rapids, in the state of Iowa, by common carrier. Upon
the arrival of such pine box at the place of business of
defendant in Cedar Rapids, in the state of Iowa, he
opened said pine box, by taking the lid therefrom, and
sold one of the packages, containing ten cigarettes, in
Cedar Rapids, Linn county, Iowa, on July 10, 1896, to
Andrew Harmon. The remaining packages of cigarettes
were not removed from said pine box, and are still
therein as they were received. The one package, of ten
cigarettes, sold to said Andrew Harmon, was of like
kind in every respect with the other packages in the
same box, and said Andrew Harmon was not a cus-

tomer outside of the state, but resided in the state of
Iowa." It further appears that the American
2   Tobacco Company submitted to the department
of internal revenue of the general government a
sample package of cigarettes similar to the one for the
selling of which appellant was convicted, and received
the following letter in response: "American Tobacco
Company, No. 45 Broadway, New York, N. Y.—Gentlemen: In reply to your inquiry of April 3d, submitting
a sample package of cigarettes bearing thereon the
internal revenue stamp and the printed marks and
caution label, and inquiring as to the necessity for a
reinclosing, in an additional covering of paper, wood,
or other material in placing the same upon the market,
you are notified that said package being a statutory
quantity, and properly stamped and canceled, and bearing thereon the caution label and the number of the
manufactory, the district and state, and the number of
cigarettes contained therein, meets with the approval
of this bureau, being a proper and original package, as
contemplated by existing laws and regulations. Therefore, the repacking of said packages in additional coverings of wood, paper, etc., is optional with the manufacturer, and does not concern this bureau. The option is
permissible, under existing regulations (series 7, No. 8,
Revised, page 46, and Internal Revenue Record, Vol. 32,
page 365, dated November 22, 1886). Respectfully yours,
"[Signed.]   John W. Mason, Commissioner."

The so-called "Anti-Cigarette Law," being chapter
96, Acts Twenty-sixth General Assembly, prohibits the
sale of cigarettes within this state by all persons whomsoever, save jobbers doing an interstate business with
customers outside of the state. Appellant contends
that this law is unconstitutional, in so far as it interferes with commerce among the several states; that the

package which he sold was an "original package;" and
that his detention was and is illegal. This statute
3   was enacted in virtue of the police power of the
state, and, unless it infringes upon some constitutional provision, it is undoubtedly valid. The contention is, however, that the statute is invalid in so far
as it interferes with, interrupts, or embarrasses interstate commerce; on the theory that the federal constitution (article 1, section 8) confers upon congress the
exclusive right to regulate commerce among the several
states. It seems to be well settled by the later decisions
of the United States court that, while the states have
the undoubted right to control their purely internal
affairs, yet whenever the law enacted in the exercise of
this power amounts to a regulation of commerce among
the states, as it does when it directly or indirectly
inhibits the receipt of an imported commodity, or its
disposition, before it has ceased to become an article of
trade between one state and another, it comes in conflict with a power which has been invested in the general government, and is therefore void. That the use of
the article is deleterious to the inhabitants of the state
is not regarded as material, so long as it is recognized
by the commercial world, by the laws of congress, and
by the decisions of the courts as a commodity in which
a right of traffic exists. *Brown v. Maryland*, 12 Wheat.
419; *Leisy v. Hardin*, 135 U. S. 100 (10 Sup. Ct. Rep. 681);
In re Rahrer, 140 U. S. 559 (11 Sup. Ct. Rep. 865); *Bowman v. Railway Co.*, 125 U. S. 465 (8 Sup. Ct. Rep. 689).
That cigarettes are a recognized commercial commodity
must be conceded, and it follows that, in so far as the
law in question amounts to a regulation of commerce,
it is unconstitutional and void. There must of necessity
be a time, however, when an article which is the subject of interstate commerce becomes subject to the taxing power and police regulations of the state; a time
when the article loses its character as an import, and

its owner becomes subject to local regulations. In the
case of *Brown v. Maryland* it is said that the point of
time when the prohibition ceases, and the power of the
state to tax commences, is not the instant when the
article enters the country, but when the importer has
so acted upon it that it has become incorporated
4   and mixed up with the mass of property in the
country, which happens when the original package is no longer such in his hands; that the distinction
is obvious between a tax which intercepts the import
as an import on its way to become incorporated with the
general mass of property, and a tax which finds the
article already incorporated with that mass by the act
of the importer; and that the right to sell any imported
article is an inseparable incident to the right to import
it. In another case (*Bowman v. Railway Co., supra*), it
is said in the dissenting opinion that while the question
involved did not require a decision, yet the argument
of the majority conducts to the conclusion that the
right of transportation included by necessary implication the right of the consignee to sell in unbroken packages at the place where the transportation terminated.
This language was subsequently approved by a majority
of the court in the case of *Leisy v. Hardin*. Again, in
the *License Cases*, 5 How. 504, Chief Justice Taney said:
"These state laws act altogether upon the retail or
domestic traffic within their respective borders. They
act upon the article after it has passed the line of foreign commerce, and become a part of the general mass
of property in the state." Chief Justice Waite declared
in the *Bowman Case* that "it is only after the importation is completed, and the property incorporated is
mingled with and becomes a part of the general property of the state, that its regulations can act upon it,
except in so far as it may be necessary to insure safety
in the disposition of the import until thus mingled." In
the case of *Leisy v. Hardin* the beer was held for sale in

the original barrels and cases in which it was imported,
and none of it was broken or opened upon the premises.
Chief Justice Fuller said, referring to these facts, that
the brewers who brewed and owned the beer had the
right to import it into this state, and also had the right
to sell it, by which act alone it would become mingled
in the common mass of property within the state, and
that up to that time the state had no power to interfere,
by seizure or otherwise. All the cases agree that, when
the article is once sold by the importer, it then becomes
subject to the taxing and police power of the state;
and it is quite generally held that the same result follows when the original package in which it is imported
is broken, and the several parcels are so mingled with
other property, or so exposed for sale, as to destroy the
identity of the package as imported. See *Brown v.
Maryland, supra; Robbins v. Taxing, Dis.*, 120 U. S.
489 (7 Sup. Ct. Rep. 592).

As the law is confessedly valid, except in so far as
it interferes with or impedes commerce between the
states, it follows that the constitutional provision has
reference to and protects that which is the subject of
commerce, and only so long as it preserves the form and
remains the exact subject of importation. It is
5   the "original package" which is protected. The
question then arises, what is an "original package?" The definition commonly accepted, and believed
by us to be correct, is that "it is a bundle put up for
transportation or commercial handling, and usually
consists of a number of things bound together, con-
venient for handling and conveyance." See *State v.
Board of Assessors*, 46 La. 146 (15 South. Rep. 10);
Keith v. State, 91 Ala. 2 (8 South. Rep. 353); *U. S. v.
One Hundred and Thirty-Two Packages*, 22 C. C. A. 228
(76 Fed. Rep. 364). In the case of *State v. Winters*, 44
Kan. Sup. 723 (25 Pac. Rep. 237), it is said: "The original
package was and is the package as it existed at the time

of its transportation from one state to another." It is quite apparent, we think, that the words "original package" have reference to the unit which the carrier receives, transports, and delivers as an article of commerce. The importer decides for himself the size of the package which he desires to import, and when he delivers it to the carrier for transportation he gives it the initial step, and from that time until sold in that form or broken, and transformed, it is the subject of interstate commerce. But when sold or broken, or when it changes form, it ceases to be an article of interstate commerce, and no longer enjoys this protection. The original package, then, is that package which is delivered by the importer to the carrier at the initial point of shipment, in the exact condition in which it was shipped. If sold, it must be in the form as shipped or received; for, if the package be broken after such delivery, it, by that act alone, becomes a part of the common mass of property within the state, and is subject to the laws of that state enacted in virtue of its police power.

Appellant contends that the internal revenue department has declared the small package sold by him to be "an original package," and that this is conclusive. We do not so regard it. The package

6 referred to in the letter from the internal revenue department is the one recognized by that department for the purposes of taxation, and has no reference to the unit of commerce which is protected by the federal constitution. The commissioner of internal revenue, in his letter heretofore set forth, says that "the repacking of said packages in additional coverings is optional with the manufacturer, and does not concern this bureau." In the case at bar the "original package," the unit of commerce, was broken, the contents exposed to sale, and one of the small packages was sold. Such sale was, as it seems to us, of an article which had lost its distinctive character

as an import, and was therefore in violation of law.
In this respect it differs from most of the cases to which
our attention has been called, for in all but one of them
it appears that the sales were of original and unbroken
packages. See *In re Minor*, 69 Fed. Rep. 235; *State v.
McGregor*, 76 Fed. Rep. 957; *Sawrie v. Tennessee* (U. S.
Cir. Ct. Tenn.), 82 Fed. Rep. 615. The one case, and
the only one, which we have been able to find holding
to a contrary doctrine, *State v. Goetz*, (W. Va.) (27 S. E.
Rep. 225), fails to recognize the distinction between the
original package of commerce and that recognized by
the internal revenue department of the general government for the purposes of taxation. There are a number
of liquor cases in line with our holding as to what constitutes an original package. *State v. Winters, Keith v.
State,* and *State v. Board of Assessors, supra.* See, also,
State v. Chapman, 1 S. D. 414 (47 N. W. Rep. 411);
Haley v. State, 42 Neb. 566 (60 N. W. Rep. 962);
Commonwealth v. Zelt, 138 Pa. St. 615 (21 Atl. Rep.
7); *Commonwealth v. Bishman,* 138 Pa. St. 639 (21
Atl. Rep. 12); *Commonwealth v. Paul,* 170 Pa. St. 284
(33 Atl. Rep. 82); *Commonwealth v. Schollenberger.*
156 Pa. St. 201 (27 Atl. Rep. 30). *In re Beine,* 42 Fed,
Rep. 545; *Smith v. State,* 54 Ark. 248 (15 S. W. Rep.
882). *In re Harmen,* 43 Fed. Rep. 372; *U. S. v. One Hun-
dre l and Thirty-two Packages, supra; Tinker v. State,*
96 Ala. 115 (11 South. Rep. 383). We find no cases in the
federal courts holding to a contrary doctrine. On the
contrary, it is said specifically in the case of *Brown v.
Maryland, supra,* that, "if the importer breaks
7   up the original packages for sale or for use, or
changes the form in which they were imported, or
they pass into second hands, the goods will lose their
distinctive character as imports, and become subject
to the taxing power of the state; and in such cases
nothing that has been said will protect an article so
acted upon by the importer." *Welton v. Missouri,* 61

U. S. 275. See, also, *State v. Shapleigh*, 27 Mo. 344;
State v. North, 27 Mo. 464.

The question as to what constitutes an original
package of liquor, was considered in the following cases, heretofore decided by this court: *Collins v. Hills*, 77 Iowa, 181; *State v. Coonan*, 82
Iowa, 400; *State v. Miller*, 86 Iowa, 639; *Hopkins
v. Lewis*, 84 Iowa, 691. The matter was also referred to in *Wind v. Iler*, 93 Iowa, 324. What was
said in *Collins v. Hills, supra*, must be regarded as
dictum, for it was not essential to the determination
of the question involved. Moreover, the decision of the
controlling point in that case was overruled by the
supreme court of the United States. Reference to the
point in *Wind v. Iler* was purely arguendo, and *Hopkins v. Lewis* contains nothing in conflict with the
views here expressed. Moreover, the rule of the *Collins
Case* was questioned. *State v. Miller* simply follows
State v. Coonan. In the *Coonan Case* it appeared that
Coonan was the agent of non-resident importers; that
he kept an "original package house," which was leased
by his principals; that the liquor was shipped by the
importers, consigned to themselves; that the beer was
put into bottles and sealed and labeled at the brewery,
and for convenience of shipment was placed in open
frame boxes, with twenty-four separate compartments;
that the whisky was sealed and labeled, and packed in
barrels, and that Coonan removed the bottles from
boxes and barrels, and sold them as sealed and labeled.
It was held, under this state of facts, citing the *Collins*
and the *Beine Cases*, that the separate bottles were the
original packages. We have already seen that the *Collins Case* should not be regarded as authority upon the
proposition involved, and an examination of the *Beine
Case* will disclose that it does not hold to any such rule.
The contrary seems to be the holding in that case.

Aside from this, however, the facts are essentially different from those in the case at bar. Here the appellant is
a resident of the state, engaged in the business of selling cigarettes at retail, and as such is amenable to all
its laws which do not deprive him of some constitutional
right. When he received the package which had been
made up by the manufacturer, and started upon its
journey, he opened it and displayed its contents, not the
package, for sale; and it affirmatively appears that he
sold one of the small parcels from the original package
to a customer who applied for the same. We think
these distinguishing features are quite important; for if
it be the rule that all imported goods, no matter
how treated or sold, are exempt from state taxation or
regulation, it is apparent that the state must forego
the exercise of the power of taxation and regulation, in
cases where the right has never heretofore been questioned. See *State v. Wheelock*, 95 Iowa, 577. But,
aside from these distinctions, we are abidingly convinced that the *Coonan Case*, if it holds to the doctrine
contended for by the appellant, is wrong, and ought to
be overruled; and in so far as it may be said to be out
of harmony with this opinion, and the great weight of
reason and authority, it is overruled. The order of the
district court remanding the appellant is right, and it is
AFFIRMED.

YOUNIE, BROWN & MARTIN V. R. P. WALROD, Appellant.

Land Sale; WARRANTY. Contract for sale of land which the purchaser knew the vendor had no patent to, though he was the
owner of the land and entitled to patent, requires the purchaser
to accept deed and abstract when tendered, if the abstract shows
1 a perfect title, except as to the issuing of the patent; it being pro-
3 vided that he is to make payments at certain times, and that
"good abstract and warranty deed" is to be furnished by the

vendor. Under such circumstances the seller cannot be compelled to furnish patent, but the purchaser must rely on the covenant of warranty.

EVIDENCE: *Parol variance.* A contemporaneous verbal agreement that the vendor will procure and have recorded a patent for the 2 unpatented portion of the land, within sixty days from the date of the contract, is inadmissible, where the written contract simply requires the vendor to furnish a good abstract and warranty deed.

Appeal from Ida District Court.—HON. S. M. ELWOOD, Judge.

MONDAY, JANUARY 24, 1898.

ACTION at law to recover an amount alleged to be due on a contract for the sale of real estate. When evidence had been fully submitted, a verdict for the plaintiff was returned by direction of the court, and a judgment was rendered thereon. The defendant appeals.— *Affirmed.*

Charles C. Warren and *Will E. Johnston* for appellant.

Carr & Parker for appellees.

ROBINSON, J.—On the eighth day of May, 1893, the defendant signed the contract upon which this action is brought, a copy of which is as follows: "Armour, S. D., May 8, 1893. I certify that I have pur-
1   chased, subject to approval of the owner, the south half of section 6, Tp. 99, Rg. 63, for $4,160, as follows: Mortgage to be assumed, $1,300; on or before March 1, '94, at not over eight per cent., $1,360; cash, $1,500,—and have paid down $100 to bind bargain. Good abstract warranty deed to be furnished. Papers to be delivered at the office of Johnson Bros., Armour, S. D. R. P. Walrod." The contract was procured in behalf of the plaintiff by Johnson Bros., of Armour,

S. D., and was approved by the plaintiff. In the latter part of the month the defendant requested Johnson Bros. to forward the "deed and papers," when received, to John T. Hallam, at Ida Grove, Iowa. On the twenty-sixth day of June, the defendant wrote to one of the members of the firm of Johnson Bros., and offered him the one hundred dollars paid, and twenty-five dollars in addition, to secure a cancellation of the contract, but the offer was not accepted. In June, 1893, a deed for the land and an abstract were forwarded to Ida Grove for delivery, and on the tenth day of July the defendant wrote to Johnson Bros. that he would have them examined, and, if found correct, would send a draft in payment on the next day. The land described in the contract included two tracts known as lots 6 and 7, and the abstracts furnished did not show that a patent had issued for those tracts, nor for the east one-half of the southwest one-fourth of the section. The defendant objected to paying the amount for which his contract provided, and accepting the deed, until a patent for the unpatented land should be issued. Considerable correspondence followed between Johnson Bros., on one side, and the defendant and his attorneys, on the other. On the seventeenth day of August, 1893, the defendant informed the plaintiff that he was anxious to have the land, but would not close the transaction, in consequence of the alleged defect in the title. On the thirteenth day of February, 1894, the defendant informed the plaintiff that, on account of its failure to perfect the title within a reasonable time, he did not desire the land. The facts in regard to the title to which objection was made are as follows: The land had been taken as a tree claim, but the entry had been "commuted to cash," payment had been made, and a final receiver's receipt was issued in December, 1892. On the twentieth day of April, 1893, the title acquired by the person who entered the land was transferred to the plaintiff by a

warranty deed. The entry of the land was approved
for patent on the second day of March, 1894, and a
patent was issued on the twenty-seventh day of the
same month, and was recorded in the proper county in
South Dakota on the fourteenth day of the next month.
On the ninth day of March, 1894, the plaintiff notified
the defendant that the land had been approved for
patent, and on the thirtieth day of April, notified him
that the patent had been received, and that his contract
would be enforced. He failed to perform his part of it,
and this action was commenced to recover the unpaid
portión of the contract price, and taxes paid on the land
since the contract was made.

   I.   The defendant alleges that the writing we have
set out did not contain the entire contract of the parties;
that when the writing was signed it was verbally agreed
that the plaintiff should procure, and have prop-
1   erly recorded, a patent for the unpatented portion
of the land within sixty days of that date, and
should send it, with the deed and an abstract of title,
showing the patent, to the defendant; that the defendant
refused to sign the writing until the verbal agreement
was made, and relied upon that agreement in signing
the writing; also, that after the writing was signed and
the payment therein mentioned was made, and in consideration thereof, the plaintiff orally agreed to obtain
the patent within sixty days, and send it to the defendant. The defendant submitted evidence which tended
to support the alleged verbal agreement, but on motion
of the plaintiff it was stricken from the record, and of
that ruling the appellant complains. We think it was
correct. The alleged verbal agreement was contemporaneous with the writing, and was in conflict with it.
That was an absolute undertaking to pay the amounts
of money specified at the times designated, and the
undertaking of the plaintiff was to furnish, at the office
of Johnson Bros., "good abstract and warranty deed."

The alleged verbal agreement sought to make the performance of the written contract depend upon a condition not contained in, and which was in conflict with the terms of, the writing. Therefore, proof of the verbal agreement was incompetent, and properly stricken from the record.

II. The chief controversy in this case is in regard to the title to the unpatented land, which the plaintiff held at and prior to the time the defendant attempted to rescind the contract. It is contended by him that the contract required the plaintiff to transfer a marketable title, and that, until the patent issued, the one it possessed was not marketable. It is the general

3   rule that a contract to convey land by warranty deed, or by good and sufficient deed,—especially where the price to be paid is a fair equivalent for the property,—requires the conveyance of a good title. *Shreck v. Pierce*, 3 Iowa, 360; *Fitch v. Casey*, 2 G Greene, 300; *Corbett v. Berryhill*, 29 Iowa, 157; *Bartle v. Curtis*, 68 Iowa, 202; *Easton v. Montgomery*, 90 Cal. 307 (27 Pac. Rep. 280; 25 Am. St. 123); Rawle, Covenants, section 32. That rule is not denied by the appellee, but it insists that it does not apply where the circumstances under which the contract is made show that the parties to it could not have contemplated the transfer of a perfect title, and that appears to be the law. In *Shreck v. Pierce, supra*, it was said that the rule does not apply to cases "where the vendee appears to be purchasing the vendor's title, such as it may be." It is said in 1 Warvelle, Vendors, 325, that "it has been held that where a purchaser knows when he makes his contract that there is a defect in the title, and it will take considerable time to remove it, or acquires his knowledge after the purchase, and acquiesces in the delay, or proceeds with knowledge of the defects in the

execution of the contract, he cannot thereafter complain." See, also, *Rader v. Neal*, 13 W. Va. 373; Godderis' Executors, 14 Grat. 102; *Golding v. Decker*, 3 Colo. 198 (32 Pac. Rep. 832); Warvelle, Vendors, 321. The defendant, by his own testimony, shows that he knew that the patent had not issued when he signed the contract. He states that he said at the time that, if the patent came within thirty or sixty days, he would be satisfied; but he was to pay one thousand five hundred dollars in cash, presumably when the deed and abstract were delivered, and not at the end of thirty or sixty days, when the patent should have been procured. One hundred dollars of the cash payment were paid when the contract was signed. It cannot be said that under these circumstances the obtaining of the patent was to be a condition precedent to the performance of the contract. No objection to taking a deed before the patent issued was made by the defendant, until after he had expressed a desire to be released from his contract, and had submitted the abstract to attorneys for examination. We are of the opinion, in view of the circumstances under which the contract was signed, and the language used in it, that, in legal effect, it required the defendant to accept the deed and abstract when tendered, if the abstract showed a perfect title, excepting as to the issue of the patent, and that the defendant was to rely upon the covenants of warranty contained in the deed, to indemnify himself against loss by reason of the non-issuance of the patent. The plaintiff was in fact the owner of the land, and entitled to the patent title. The general government, at most, held the legal title as trustee, and that title was duly transferred by patent in the ordinary course of the business of the general land office. The title of the plaintiff was perfected within a reasonable time, and the defendant should be held to the performance of his agreement. Since there was no conflict in the evidence which showed the facts we have set out, the district court rightly directed a verdict for the plaintiff, and no objection is made to the amount for which it was rendered.

The appellee insists that its title was marketable when the contract was made, and before the patent was issued, but the conclusion already reached makes it unnecessary to determine that question. The judgment of the district court appears to be fully sustained by the evidence, and is AFFIRMED.

T. F. GREENLEE, *et al.,* v. THE HANOVER INSURANCE COMPANY, Appellant.

Insurance: FORFEITURE: *Concealment.* To avoid liability under a policy of insurance providing that it shall be void if the insured has concealed or misrepresented in writing or otherwise any material fact or circumstance concerning the insurance or the subject thereof, or if he has not truly stated his interest in the property, it is not sufficient to show that there were mechanic's liens on the property at the time the policy issued; it must also appear that there was some independent concealment in respect thereto.

SERVICE OF PROOF OF LOSS: *Recording agent.* The service of proofs of loss upon the recording agent of the insurer, who issued the policy in suit, is sufficient. Citing *McCullough v. Ins. Co.* (Mo.) 21 S. W. Rep. 207.

Appeal from Benton District Court.—HON. G. W. BURNHAM, Judge.

TUESDAY, JANUARY 25, 1898.

ACTION on a policy of fire insurance. Judgment for plaintiffs, and the defendant appealed.—*Affirmed.*

McVey & McVey for appellant.

J. J. Mosnat for appellees.

GRANGER, J.—I. The court, at the close of the evidence, on motion of plaintiffs, directed a verdict for them. The issues involved the question of whether proofs of loss had been served, and, for the court to direct a verdict, the evidence must show that fact without substantial conflict. It is urged here that the record does not show such a service, but we think it does. Appellant's conclusion is based on a partial abstract and consideration of the evidence. It appears conclusively that Milner & Decker were the recording agents of defendant, and issued the policy in suit. It also appears that service of proofs of loss was made on Milner & Decker, agents, at Belle Plaine, Iowa. Such a service is sufficient. *McCullough v. Insurance Co.*, 113 Mo. Sup. 606 (21 S. W. Rep. 207); 2 Beach, Insurance, section 1203.

II. The policy contained this provision: "This policy shall be void if the insured has concealed or misrepresented, in writing or otherwise, any material fact or circumstance concerning this insurance, or the subject thereof, or if the interest of the insured in the property be not truly stated herein." At the time the policy issued there were certain mechanics' liens that had been put in judgment, as to which, it is claimed, there was a concealment by plaintiffs, that avoids the policy. To avoid the policy because of such concealment, the fact must be shown in some manner. The policy is in the record, but not the application, and we do not find a word of evidence on the subject of concealment, nor anything to sustain such an inference. So far as the record shows, the policy issued with full knowledge of all the facts. The judgment will stand AFFIRMED.

Henry Agne v. J. T. Seitsinger, Appellant.

Highways: RESERVATION IN GRANT. A reservation in a grant of land for a highway, of the right to attach fences to a bridge to be

8   erected over a ravine, implies the right to have a cattle way under the bridge, where the highway and bridge divide a pasture, and

without such a way, would cut off the access of the cattle to a supply of water.

Same. One who gave a right of way for a highway, reserving to him-
1 self certain privileges, may recover for a denial of such privileges, whether his act of giving was a grant or a dedication.

Same. A person has a right to have his cattle pass under a new
5 bridge erected in the place of one that had been washed away, where he had had such a right as to the old bridge.

Damages: obstruction. The rule that one cannot recover dam ges for obstruction of his right of way. if by the use of ordinary dili-
6 gence and effort he could have removed the obstruction at a moderate expense, does not apply where the obstruction to right of way is a low bridge in a county highway, as any attempt to remove the obstruction in such a case would constitute a trespass.

Evidence: jury question: *Dedication.* Evidence of the execution of an instrument giving, or offering to give, a right of way for a
2 highway, that it was received and filed by the county judge, and that thereafter a highway was established over the *locus in quo* at
8 a time when the jurisdiction to establish highways was in the county court, is sufficient to require the submission to the jury of the question as to the grant of the highway and the acceptance thereof by the public.

Appeal: harmless error. Error in striking out matter in special
4 denial is not prejudicial where the defendant has the b nefit of the latter under his general denial.

Law of case. It is proper to strike out a special denial attempting
4 to put in issue a proposition which had been determined, on an appeal, after a former trial.

Appeal from Cedar District Court.—Hon. W. P. Wolf,
Judge.

Tuesday, January 25, 1898.

Action at law to recover damages for maliciously destroying a cattleway claimed by plaintiff under a highway bridge in Cedar county, Iowa. There was a trial to jury. Verdict and judgment for plaintiff. Defendant appeals.—*Affirmed.*

E. M. Brink and *S. H. Fairall* for appellant.

Isaac Landt and *Preston, Wheeler & Moffet* for appellee.

WATERMAN, J.—This is the fourth time this case has been in this court. An opinion deciding it on demurrer will be found in 85 Iowa, 305. On the second appeal, an opinion affirming the judgment below, appears in 60 N. W. Rep. 483. Upon re-hearing, we reconsidered the case, and reversed the lower court, and this opinion is in 96 Iowa, 181. The facts will be found fully stated in the former opinions, and need not again be set out. The controversy here grows out of the fact that one Sem. Simmons, who was the owner of certain real estate in Cedar county, executed a written instrument giving, or offering to give, a right of way for a highway, and reserving to himself certain privileges. This instrument was received and filed by the county judge, and the highway thereafter opened. Much

1   of appellant's argument is devoted to showing that the act of Simmons was not a grant, but a dedication. We do not think it necessary to determine this technical question. It may have been a "grant;" it may have been a "dedication;" it might very well be both. A reference to the former decisions of this court, referred to above, will disclose that both terms have been used interchangeably in referring to this instrument. Many of the assignments of error are so indefinite that we cannot consider them; many more are not argued by counsel. We can, perhaps, do no better than take the argument for appellant, and consider the objections there made, so far as they are good in form.

It is first urged that the lower court erred in the first instruction in stating the issues to the jury. We are referred to assignments of error 26 to 31, inclusive.

Only the first of these has any reference to the statement of the issues; the others relate to a different part
of the charge. We can only say that we find the issues
as set out in the pleadings to have been fairly presented to the jury.

Considerable attention is devoted to the question
whether there was evidence tending to show a pre-
scriptive right in plaintiff to have his cattle pass under
the bridge in question. It is asserted that this
issue should not have been given to the jury,
because there was no evidence to support the
claim. This, we think, is disposed of by paragraph
3 of the opinion in this case, reported in 96 Iowa, 181.
There is the same evidence now as then.

The next error discussed is that there was no evidence tending to prove a grant of the right of way and
an acceptance thereof. The execution of the instrument
by Simmons is undisputed. So is the fact that it
was received and filed by the county judge, and
that thereafter a highway was opened and established over said land. This was done in 1858, when the
jurisdiction to establish highways was in the county
court. Code 1851, section 514. We think this was
clearly enough to take these matters to the jury. It is
said, too, in this connection, that it was an error for the
trial court to assume that the right reserved by Simmons to attach his fences to said bridge included the
right to have a cattle way thereunder. This, we think,
is disposed of in the second paragraph of the opinion
in 96 Iowa, 181. What is there said on this subject
is the law of this case.

The next error that is not disposed of by what we
have already said is as to a ruling of the lower court in
striking out matter in special denial contained in the
answer. If erroneous, this action was not prejudicial, for the defendant had the benefit of it
under his general denial. It might also be said in
this connection that by the denial in question the

defendant attempted to put in issue a proposition which
had been announced as the law of this case on a former
appeal, and for this reason the action of the court in
striking it was correct.

The objections urged to the seventh instruction we
can dispose of briefly by saying that they are without
merit. That instruction presents only a single phase
of the case. It does not pretend to, nor, indeed, would
it be possible for it to, include all the issues and at the
same time be intelligible.

Objection is made to the eighth instruction. It is
said that it announces a theory not in conformity to
the claim of defendant. It seems that the bridge originally built was washed away, and that a new
5   one was erected, and this instruction, in effect,
says that plaintiff's rights, as to the new bridge,
are the same as to the old one. This must be so. In this
connection we may say that there was no prejudicial
error in the ninth instruction. It is practically the
same as an instruction asked by appellant.

Error is assigned on the lower court's refusal to
give the fifth instruction asked by defendant. This
instruction was with relation to defendant's right to
use piling owned by the plaintiff to make repairs on the
bridge. We cannot see how this matter was material,
and think the trial judge was right in refusing to give it.

Passing certain rulings on evidence that are complained of, as we find, without just cause, and we reach
the last error assigned and argued. The lower court
refused to give instruction No. 12 asked by
6   defendant, which is as follows: "If you find that
the obstruction complained of could have been,
by the use of ordinary diligence and effort, removed by
plaintiff at a moderate expense, it was his duty to have
removed the same, and, not having done so, he cannot
recover in this action, and your verdict should be for
the defendant." This instruction announces a correct

rule of law for some cases, but we do not think it applies to the case at bar. The obstruction here was a low bridge in a county highway. Plaintiff had no right to remove it, or work about it. Any such an act on his part would have been a trespass. The instruction was rightly refused. *City of McGregor v. Boyle,* 34 Iowa, 268. This disposes of every question which is properly presented. Our conclusion is that the judgment below should be AFFIRMED.

C. R. METCALF v. W. M. KENT, Appellant.

Land Sale Commissions: EXCLUSIVE BROKERAGE. A contract for sale of land giving the agent "exclusive right to sell" the farm described, on certain terms, and agreeing to a commission "in
1   case the above described property is sold during the pendency of this contract, or to person whom second party finds, or secures as a customer, after the expiration of this contract, or if second party secures a purchaser who will purchase it on the above-mentioned terms," which is indorsed, "good until December 1, 1895," is a contract for exclusive right to sell, which gives a right to commission on any sale made within the time, and the question of whether or not the agent was instrumental in the sale actually made, is wholly immaterial.

Release: CONSIDERATION. The release of an existing indebtedness for commissions due under a mutual contract for sale of land is a new contract, and must be based on a consideration and an oral
2   statement by the agent that he claims no commission is not, therefore, sufficient to show release.

Appeal from Sac District Court.—HON. Z. A. CHURCH, Judge.

TUESDAY, JANUARY 25, 1898.

ACTION upon a written contract to recover commissions for the sale of real estate. Defendant answered, admitting the execution of the contract, and alleging that it was without consideration; that plaintiff failed to perform his part, and that a full settlement had been made with plaintiff. At the conclusion of the evidence, the court, on a motion of the plaintiff, directed a verdict for plaintiff, for the amount claimed, and rendered judgment thereon. Defendant appeals.—*Affirmed.*

M. R. McCrary and *Brown McCrary* for appellant.

C. R. Metcalf and *I. S. Struble* for appellee.

GIVEN, J.—I. The written contract sued upon is as follows: Contract good until Dec. 1, '95. Contract to Sell Land. This agreement, made and entered into this eighth day of June, A. D., 1895, between W. M. Kent, party of the first part, and C. R. Metcalf, party of the second part, witnesseth: First party hereby gives second party the exclusive right to sell his farm, situated as follows: N. E. quarter of Sec. 26, and east one-half of the N. W. quarter of Sec. 26—87—35, Sac county, Iowa, and upon the following terms and conditions: Two thousand, five hundred dollars or three thousand dollars cash, balance in yearly payments on reasonable terms; and consisting of two hundred and forty acres, more or less; said land to be sold at $35.00 per acre, or a less price, or different terms, if first party shall take it; and the first party agrees to and with second party to pay him a commission at Sac City, Iowa, of 2½ per cent. commission in case the above-described property is sold during the pendency of this contract, or to a person whom second party finds, shows the property to, or directs such person to said property or secures such person as a customer after the expiration of this contract, or if second party secures a purchaser who will purchase it on the above-mentioned terms. (Signed) C. R. Metcalf. W. M. Kent."

1   There is no dispute but that the plaintiff was engaged in finding purchasers for lands in Sac county, and that he included defendant's farm in cir-

culars and advertisement as among the lands in his
hands for sale, and otherwise sought to find a purchaser
therefor. It is also undisputed that between the eighth
day of June and the first day of December, 1895, the
defendant sold said farm to one J. M. Gregory for eight
thousand, four hundred dollars. There is a dispute as
to whether plaintiff was instrumental in procuring said
Gregory as a purchaser, but, in the view we take of the
contract and the time of the sale, this contention is
immaterial. If the sale had not been made until after
December 1, 1895, it would be otherwise. It was for the
court to construe this contract, and it correctly construed it as giving to the plaintiff the exclusive right to
sell the farm between its date and December 1, 1895,
and as entitling plaintiff to the commission named on
any sale that might be made of it between those dates.
Thus construed, the plaintiff was entitled to recover on
the undisputed facts, unless a settlement had been
had. The consideration for the contract was that
plaintiff would endeavor, as he did, to find a purchaser.
By his efforts to find a purchaser, plaintiff performed
his part of the contract, as applied to the sale made,
whether he was instrumental in procuring Mr. Gregory
to purchase or not.

II. As to the alleged settlement, the defendant
testifies as follows: "I met Mr. Metcalf the day that I
sold the farm after the contract was drawed up; met
him in front of the First National Bank in Sac City;
and I told him that I had sold my farm. 'Now,'
2   I says, you had better come up, and give me up
my contract.' He says: 'That don't amount to
anything. I don't charge you any commission.' I says,
'All right, I will set up the cigars and call it square.'
He says, 'That is all right, sir.' Mr. Tom Riddinough
was present at this conversation. Since that time there
has been no conversation between Mr. Metcalf and
myself concerning this matter; nothing more than I

spoke to him here some time ago, after he had sued me, and I asked him what he had done it for, was all the con- versation we had." Riddinough testifies: "Mr. Kent says to Mr. Metcalf, 'I sold my farm.' Mr. Metcalf says, 'Is that so?' and he says, 'Yes, and I thought I would get my contract.' Mr. Metcalf says: 'That contract is no account. I don't charge anything for it.' Mr. Kent pulled out a cigar, 'If that is all you charge, I will treat you and call it square.' Mr. Metcalf says, 'That is all right.'" We have seen that under the contract and the fact of the sale to Gregory defendant was liable to plaintiff for the commission named on the eight thou- sand four hundred dollars. Defendant's counsel con- tend that a consideration is not necessary to a release from the liability, citing *Stensgaard v. Smith*, 43 Minn. 11 (44 N. W. Rep. 669). Plaintiff's counsel contend that a consideration is necessary to sustain a release, citing *Whitehill v. Wilson*, 3 Pen. & W. 405, and *Shaw v. Pratt*, 22 Pick, 308. In the case of *Stensgaard v. Smith*, in the writing, signed by Smith alone, in consideration of plaintiff's agreeing to act as agent for the sale of the property, Smith gave him the exclusive sale of the prop- erty for three months, and agreed to pay a commission "for his services rendered in selling," etc. The court held that this was not a contract, for want of mutuality, but conferred a present authority to sell, revocable at any time before a sale was effected by plaintiff. In this case there was a mutuality, and hence a contract, irre- vocable, except by consent of the parties. The cases cited by plaintiff's counsel sustain the claim that the release of an existing indebtedness is a new contract, and, to be binding, must be based upon a consideration. It is not seriously contended that the cigar was given or received as a consideration for the claimed release. Surely, such a trifle as that could not have been so intended. In determining whether the court erred in ordering a verdict, we do not consider plaintiff's evidence denying that there was any settlement or release. Accepting the evidence for defendant as true, it fails to show any consideration for the alleged release. Therefore, though made as claimed, it is not binding, and is no bar to plaintiff's right to recover. There was no error in sustaining plaintiff's motion for a verdict, and the judgment is therefore AFFIRMED.

A. J. McCoy, Appellant, v. John W. Clark,

Injunction: INTOXICATING LIQUORS. A temporary injunction may be granted against a person holding a permit to sell intoxicating liquors, if he keeps or sells the same in his pharmacy contrary to

1   law, under Acts Twenty-third General Assembly, chapter 85, section 2, providing that every permit holder shall be subject to all the proceedings and actions, criminal or civil, whether at law or in equity, authorized by the laws "now" or "hereafter" in force for any violation of "this" act, and the acts for the suppression of intemperance, and any law regulating the sale of intoxicating liquors, and in case of conviction in any proceeding, civil or criminal, all the liquors in his possession may, by order of the court, be destroyed.

Intoxicating Liquors: PERMIT IS NOT PROPERTY. An order under the Iowa statutes granting a permit to sell intoxicating liquor confers

2   no property right, and amounts to no more than the mere privilege to sell, under certain conditions, granted in the exercise of the police power of the state.

Appeal from Appanoose District Court.—HON. F. W. EICHELBERGER, Judge.

TUESDAY, JANUARY 25, 1898.

APPLICATION for temporary writ of injunction, which was denied, and plaintiff appeals.—*Reversed.*

Baker & Moore and *J. A. Elliott* for appellant.

Mabry & Payne for appellee.

LADD, J.—The question involved in this case is whether a temporary writ of injunction may be granted against a person holding a permit to sell intoxicating liquors, if he keeps for sale or sells the same in his pharmacy contrary to law. Section 7, chapter 35, Acts Twenty-third General Assembly prohibits the sale by permit holders for any purpose other than therein specified. The permit is a trust reposed in the holder, granted after being shown worthy, and may be revoked by the court or judge, on the complaint of three citizens, "if it shall appear upon such hearing, that the accused has in any way abused the trust, or that liquors are sold by the accused or his employes in violation of law or if it shall appear that any liquor has been sold or dispensed unlawfully or has been unlawfully obtained at said place from the holder of the permit or any employe assisting therein, or that he has in any proceedings, civil or criminal, since receiving his permit, been adjudged guilty of violating any of the provisions of this act for the suppression of intemperance." Section 12 is in part as follows: "Every permit holder or his clerk, under this act, shall be subject to all the penalties, forfeitures and judgments and may be prosecuted by all the proceedings and actions, criminal and civil, and whether at law or in equity, provided for or authorized by the laws now or hereinafter in force for any violation of this act, and the acts for the suppression of intemperance, and any law regulating the sale of intoxicating liquors and by any or all of such proceedings applicable to complaints against such permit holder; and the permit shall not shield any person who abuses the trust imposed by it or violates the laws aforesaid, and in case of conviction in any proceeding, civil or criminal, all the liquors in possession of the permit holder may by the order of the court be destroyed." This language seems very explicit.

1

It provides for the prosecution of the permit holder, "whether at law or in equity," and an action to enjoin is the only one maintainable in equity. The last clause expressly subjects him to actions for injunction, as these are the only civil proceedings in which orders for the destruction of liquors may be entered. The provision for the destruction of all liquors in possession obviates the objection, which might otherwise be urged, that a portion were kept for lawful sale, and indicates a revocation may have been intended, as none are to be left with him for sale under the permit. The remedy mentioned in section 7 is not exclusive in terms, and not so intended. The permit may be revoked on complaint of three citizens, without resorting to the more drastic remedies by indictment or injunction, or these may be insisted upon under the plain provisions of section 12 of the act. In no other way may all the provisions of this chapter be given force and effect, which must be done, if possible, under the rules of construction. The abatement and destruction of the liquors would as inevitably revoke a permit for the time being as might be done in a direct proceeding for that purpose, and whether permanently we are not called upon to determine. The order granting the permit conferred no property right, and amounted to no more than the mere privilege to sell, under certain conditions, granted in the exercise of the police power of the state (*State v. Schmidtz*, 65 Iowa, 556; *State v. Mullenhoff*, 74 Iowa, 271; *Hurber v. Baugh* 43 Iowa, 514); and was taken subject to all the conditions and provisions of the act, and no good reason appears for not giving to all of these effect. If the permit holder not only violates the law, but also the trust reposed in him, there is the greater cause for subjecting him to all the penalties of the law. The temporary writ of injunction ought to have been granted. The appeal was from rulings excluding evidence and refusing such writ. The appellee had no occasion to put in his defense. The appellant is not, therefore, entitled to final decree, and attorney's fees can only be taxed, under the statute, on hearing to make the injunction perpetual.—REVERSED.

THE FREY-SHECKLER COMPANY v. THE IOWA BRICK COMPANY, Appellant.

Contracts: ACCEPTANCE: *Sale on refusal.* The refusal of a party to a contract for the construction and installment of a brick-making
1 plant to allow the other party to remove it, in accordance with a
2 provision of the contract to that effect, if it is proved unsatis-
5 factory after the test contemplated by the contract, constitutes an acceptance thereof, and a subsequent direction for its removal is ineffectual to defeat an action for the purchase price

SAME. A corporation cannot avoid liability for the contract price of a brick-making plant installed on its property under an agreement
6 by the other party to remove it and cancel all obligations against the corporation, if it proves unsatisfactory, where it appropriates to its own use the material of which the plant is composed.

INCONSISTENT CLAIMS. The appropriation to defendant's use of machinery sold on approval, after an expression of dissatisfaction
7 therewith, was inconsistent with defendant's claim that the title to such property never passed under such contract, and rendered it liable for the price thereof.

Principal and Agent: CORPORATION. The power conferred upon an
2 officer of a corporation to object to a plant constructed for the
8 corporation if he is not satisfied therewith, necessarily includes the power to accept, if he is satisfied.

Fixtures: REAL AND CHATTEL PROPERTY: *Contracts.* Machinery of such character that, when installed in a building prepared for it, it
4 would become a part of such structure, remained a chattel until accepted by the purchaser, where sold on approval.

Appeal from Polk District Court.—HON. T. F. STEVENSON, Judge.

WEDNESDAY, JANUARY 26, 1898.

ACTION in equity to establish and enforce a mechanic's lien. There was a decree below for plaintiff.

Defendant appeals.   The facts will be found in the opinion.—*Affirmed.*

Gatch, Connor & Weaver for appellant.

Wesley Martin and *George W. Seevers* for appellee.

Waterman, J.—The plaintiff corporation agreed to make, and place in the brickmaking plant of defendant, at Des Moines, what is called a "Bucyrus dryer,"—a somewhat complicated machine, consisting of steam pipes, valves, tracks, and cars, and which, when set up in the building that was erected by defendant, was so attached and connected with it as to become a part of the structure.   The material provisions of the contract between the parties are as follows: "Bucyrus, Ohio, U. S. A., Feb. 23, 1892.   Iowa Brick-Paving Company, Des Moines, Iowa—Gentlemen: We propose to construct a Bucyrus dryer, in fifteen tunnels, capable of accommodating ten cars each, each car capable of carrying five hundred green brick, of standard size, or, in other words, a dry house capable of holding seventy-five thousand brick at one filling.   You are to furnish the building * * * Said dryer is capable of drying standard size green brick in from twenty-four to thirty-six hours, according to the character and condition of the clay, and the effect of heat upon the quality of the product.   It will contain at one filling seventy-five thousand standard size green brick, for which the price is eighty-five dollars per thousand; total six thousand three hundred and seventy-five dollars.   Our representatives will dry for you two turns of brick, and afterwards you shall have the privilege of using it for thirty days; and if, at the end of that time, it is not satisfactory to you, we will remove our property, and cancel all obligations held against you on account of the dry house."   This offer was signed by plaintiff, and accepted by defendant. The dryer was duly constructed in a building provided for it by defendant. But defendant claims that, after three trials made under the supervision of plaintiff's agents, it developed that said dryer would not do the work agreed; that defendant was not satisfied with it, and refused to accept it, and is therefore not liable in any sum to plaintiff.

A great many of the legal propositions argued by counsel can be disposed of by two findings of fact, which, when considered in connection with an allegation of defendant's answer are decisive of the case. Walker, the president of the defendant company, being dissatisfied with the work of the dryer, testifies that at one time he told Batley, the agent of plaintiff, to remove it from defendant's premises. This is denied by Batley. But, admitting the fact to be so, the time when this was said is not fixed definitely or clearly, further than that it was prior to the occurrence of which we are about

2   to speak. Immediately after the third trial of the dryer, which was had by mutual consent, when Jackson, the defendant's secretary and general manager, expressed dissatisfaction with the result of its work, Batley told him, in effect, that plaintiff must have the dryer, or its price; and the answer he received from Jackson was, in substance, that it could have neither. Appellant asserts that Jackson had no authority to speak for defendant, or to bind it by any thing he might say. This contention is easily settled by a reference to the record. The president of defendant corporation testifies: "Don't know whether any of the objections I now claim appear on the books of defendant company. There was no objection made by the full board of directors. We never paid any attention to that. The directors talked it over together, and then left it to Jackson and myself." At the time of the last test, the president was absent. Jackson was on the ground, and had charge for defendant. Altogether, it

appears that he had full power to act for his company.
Indeed, the defendant seems in no position to
3   question Jackson's authority. It relies for its
defense upon the rejection of this machinery by
Walker, the president, and his request, by letter to
plaintiff, for its removal. Jackson had equal authority
with Walker. The power to object included, necessarily, the power to not object, or, in other words, to
accept. When Jackson refused to permit Batley to
remove the machinery, he accepted it for defendant,
and this was done before any letter was written by
Walker on this subject. The construction of the dryer
was completed July 14, 1893. The first test was in that
month, the second was in October, and the last in
November of the same year. Defendant, in its answer,
admits the contract as stated; admits that the dryer
was constructed by plaintiff, but alleges that it did
not work satisfactorily; and the second division of this
pleading concludes as follows: "And notwithstanding
it thereupon became its [plaintiff's] duty, by the terms
of said contract, to at once remove its said property
composing said dryer, and notwithstanding it was
notified by defendant, as it avers the fact to have been,
that, unless it did so, defendant would treat its failure
so to do as an abandonment of its said property, plaintiff neglected and refused to remove the same, or any
part thereof, but abandoned the same. Wherefore
defendant denies that there is anything due from it to
plaintiff for or on account of said dryer." Some time
after the third test spoken of, defendant remodeled the
dryer, appropriating some of the materials of which it
was originally composed, taking out and selling other
of the material, and ever since has used said
4   machine in its business. Counsel for appellant
devote much attention in their argument to a
discussion of the question whether the dryer was a
chattel or a fixture. So long as defendant had not

accepted it, and plaintiff retained a right of removal, the machine was certainly a chattel. Further than this we need not pursue the inquiry. Nor do we deem it necessary to say what the right of the parties would have been, had defendant refused to accept the machine, and plaintiff failed to remove it. That is not the case we have here. The defendant, as we have seen, refused

5   to permit plaintiff to remove the dryer in November, 1893. This fixed the rights of the parties. The letters afterwards written, in which plaintiff was asked to take the dryer out, could not affect the status of the parties, as established by Jackson's refusal, after the third test, to surrender it. This action of defendant, alone, we think, would have bound it to take and pay for the property under the contract.

But this is not all. The defendant has since that

6   time appropriated to its own use the material of which the dryer was composed, and in its answer herein it claims title thereto by abandonment. The general rule is that one who seeks to reject an article, as not in accordance with the contract, must do nothing after he discovers its true condition inconsistent with the vendor's ownership of the property. We see no reason why this rule does not govern the contract in question. Appellant cites authorities to show that there is a distinction to be taken between the duties of the buyer in a case of sale or return, and a sale on approval, in the latter of which classes this case falls. This may be granted. But in no case cited is it held that in sales on approval the buyer can appropriate the property, and not be liable for its price. We do not hold defendant liable here because it did not return the property to plaintiff. It could have done nothing, and been safe, as was the case in *Exhaust Ventilator Co. v. Chicago, M. & St. P. Ry. Co.*, 69 Wis. 454 (34 N.

7   W. Rep. 509), and similar decisions cited by appellant. It is liable in this case because it did something, and something that is entirely at war with

its claim now made, that the title to the property never
passed to it under the contract. It came into possesion
of this property by reason of the agreement. It has con·
verted it to its own use. In effect, it claims title thereto.
How did it get this right of possession and authority to
use, if not under the contract, and' how can it claim
these rights without assuming the corresponding
liability to pay? We see no need to review the cases
cited. They do not seem to be in point. The doctrine
upon which we rest our decision is elementary. The
decree below is AFFIRMED.

F. D. STOUT AND M. E. McHENRY, Appellants, v. F. M.
HUBBELL.

104
111
111

Corporations: STOCKHOLDERS: Creditors. Creditors of a corporation
   are not estopped to hold stockholders liable for the difference
1 between the real value of the property transferred in payment of
   the stock and the face value of the stock, because they were
   chargeable with constructive notice that the stock was issued in
   exchange for property, where there was nothing to indicate to
   them the value of the property received in exchange for the stock.

RULE APPLIED. The promoters of a corporation agreed to purchase
   at a grossly excessive valuation. and pay therefor by issuing
   paid-up stock. The articles of incorporation recited the contract,
1 and that the directors should pay for the land by issuing "stock
   at par for (the agreed valuation). Said stock, when so issued, to
   be held and regarded as fully paid for by the conveyance of" such
   land. Held, that the record of the articles did not impart knowledge to creditors of the corporation, of the fraudulent valuation.

SAME. Property received by a corporation at an excessive valuation,
2 in payment for shares of its capital stock, is only a payment to
   the extent of its value as to the corporation's creditors, and the
   owners of the stock are liable to creditors for the difference
   between the actual value of the property and the face value of the
   stock.

Appeal from Polk District Court.—HON. T. F. STEVEN-
SON, Judge.

WEDNESDAY, JANUARY 26, 1898.

THIS appeal is by the plaintiffs from a judgment overruling their demurrer to the second count of defendant's answer. The averments in the pleadings and the grounds of demurrer, will appear in the opinion.— *Reversed.*

Hubbard & Dawley for appellants.

Cummins, Hewitt & Wright for appellee.

GIVEN, J.—I.   Plaintiffs, owners of a judgment for six thousand one hundred and sixty-two dollars against the Des Moines Driving Park, an insolvent corporation organized under the laws of Iowa for pecuniary profit, bring this action to charge the defendant, as the owner of unpaid stock in said corporation, to the extent of their said judgment. They allege that the defendant is, and at all times since the organization of said corporation has been, a stockholder therein, and the owner of five hundred and forty-eight shares of its capital stock, of the par value of fifty- four thousand eight hundred dollars;. that said corporation "has received for said stock nothing but ninety-one (91) acres of land, of only the value of eight thousand dollars, and there is still unpaid upon said shares of stock the sum of forty-six thousand eight hundred dollars, by reason of which defendant has become, and is now, liable to plaintiffs to the amount of six thousand one hundred and sixty-two dollars, with interest and costs." In the second count of his answer the defendant avers, in substance, as follows: That prior to the organization of said corporation the projectors thereof determined that the land owned by defendant, together with two smaller adjoining tracts owned by other parties, would be suitable for the purposes of the proposed corporation; that he proposed to take six hundred dollars per acre for his land, in the capital stock of the corporation to be organized, and at

the same time said other owners agreed to convey their
tracts of land to said corporation, when organized, upon
the same terms; that thereupon said corporation was
organized, and adopted articles of incorporation.
wherein said agreement was substantially set forth as
shown by the copy attached; that thereafter, and in pursuance of said articles, and under a resolution of the
board of directors, the defendant conveyed said lands
to the corporation, in consideration whereof, and in payment of said agreed price he received from the corporation said five hundred and forty-eight shares of its
capital stock. He alleges that said articles of incorporation were duly filed for record, and recorded, as
required by law, and that the notice of incorporation
provided by law was duly published. Copies of said
articles and notice are set out as exhibits. "The defendant further alleges that through the said articles of
incorporation and notice so filed and recorded, and so
published, the plaintiffs, and each of them, had notice
of the agreement so entered into between the said Des
Moines Driving Park and this defendant, and of the
fact that said land so owned by this defendant,
and conveyed by him to the Des Moines Driving
Park, had been accepted by the said Des Moines
Driving Park in full payment of the said five
hundred and forty-eight (548) shares of its capital
stock, and therefore the plaintiffs cannot now be heard
to allege that the said stock has not been fully paid for."
The articles of incorporation set out show that F. M.
Hubbell, R. G. Scott, J. N. Neiman, Elmer Jackaway,
and F. C. Hubbell were the incorporators, and that F. M.
Hubbell was selected as president and one of the board
of directors, of said corporation. Article 3, after providing that the capital stock should be one hundred
thousand dollars, divided into shares of one hundred
dollars each, to be subscribed for and paid under the

direction of the board of directors, and that the directors were not authorized to incur any indebtedness until sixty thousand dollars of stock were actually subscribed and paid, contains the following: "The directors of the corporation, however, shall be authorized, and it is hereby declared to be the purpose and intent of these incorporators that the said directors shall purchase of F. M. Hubbell, the West End Syndicate, and the National Real-Estate Investment Company, the real estate hereinafter described, as follows, to-wit: [Here the 91 acres and the two other tracts are described.] And the directors shall pay therefor the sum of sixty-four thousand four hundred and thirty-seven dollars ($64,-437.00), which sum shall be paid by issuing to the said F. M. Hubbell stock at par for the said sum of fifty-four thousand and eight hundred dollars ($54,800.00), and to the West End Syndicate stock at par for four thousand seven hundred and sixty-eight ($4,768.00), and to the National Real Estate Investment Company stock at par for four thousand, eight hundred and sixty-nine dollars ($4,869.00). Said stock, when so issued, to be held and regarded as fully paid for by the conveyance of the real estate hereinbefore described to this association." The notice published contains the following: "The capital stock shall be one hundred thousand dollars, divided into shares of one hundred dollars each. Stock, fully paid up and non-assessable, for the sum of sixty-four thousand, four hundred and thirty-seven dollars, shall be issued to pay for the real estate purchased by said corporation to be used as its park or ground inclosure." Plaintiffs demurred to the second count of the answer "upon the ground that the facts stated in said count 2 do not constitute any defense to plaintiff's petition, for the following reasons." The reasons set out need not be here stated, but will hereafter be considered. The demurrer being overruled, and plaintiffs electing to stand thereon, judgment was entered against them.

II. Section 1082 of the Code of 1873 is as follows: "Neither anything in this chapter contained, nor any provision in the articles of incorporation, shall exempt the stockholders from individual liability to the amount of unpaid installment on the stock owned by them, or transferred by them for the purpose of defrauding creditors, and execution against the company may, to that extent, be levied upon the private property of any such individual." It will be observed that it is averred in the petition that said corporation "has received for said stock nothing but ninety-one (91) acres of land, of only the value of eight thousand dollars. This allegation is not denied in said second count of the answer. Therefore, it stands as admitted that the only payment made for this fifty-four thousand eight hundred dollars of stock, was this tract of land, of the value of eight thousand dollars. It is alleged in said second count that the land was given and received under an agreement that it was a full payment for said stock. This, alone, would be no defense; for this court has held, as to creditors of a corporation, that when property is received by the corporation, at an excessive valuation, in payment for shares of its capital stock, it is only a payment to the extent of the value of the property received, and that owners of such stock are liable to creditors for the difference between the actual value of the property and the face value of the stock. See *Osgood v. King*, 42 Iowa, 478; *Chisholm v. Forny*, 65 Iowa, 333; *Carbon Co. v. Mills*, 78 Iowa, 460; Defendant's counsel do not contend that an agreement by which the stock was received as fully paid up, in consideration of land at an excessive valuation, would alone constitute a defense. They concede that it is a fraud upon creditors for the corporation to agree to accept either less than par value in money, or property worth

less than par." Their contention is that "it is impossible,
however, that such an agreement upon the part of the
corporation shall be a fraud upon a creditor whose debt
is created with full knowledge of the manner in which,
as between the corporation and the stockholder, the
stock has been fully paid." Relying upon the
2   rule that those dealing with the corporation
must be held to have knowledge of the provisions of its articles of incorporation, they insist that the
further allegation of said second count, as to the contents and recording of the articles of incorporation,
and publication of the notice of incorporation, show
actual or constructive notice to the plaintiffs of the
terms upon which this stock was issued, and that,
having extended credit with that knowledge, they are
not entitled to recover. Let it be conceded that the
plaintiffs are chargeable with all the knowledge which
the record of the articles of incorporation imparted. It
remains to inquire what that knowledge is. That
record told that the directors were authorized and
required to purchase of the defendant his said tract of
land, and to pay therefor by issuing to him "stock at
par for the said sum of fifty-four thousand eight hundred dollars. * * * Said stock, when so issued, to
be held and regarded as fully paid for by the conveyance of the real estate described to this association."
A person examining these articles with a view to determining whether or not to extend credit to the corporation, would know therefrom that the corporation had
given, as fully paid up, fifty-four thousand eight hundred
dollars of its capital stock in payment for these ninety-
one acres of land. He would have a right to presume
that the transaction was fair and free from fraud, and
therefore to understand that the land was substantially
equal in value to the par value of the stock. There is
nothing in this record to indicate otherwise, and these
plaintiffs, in extending credit to the corporation, had a

right to assume from this record that, instead of said
stock, the corporation had ninety-one acres of land of
the value of fifty-four thousand eight hundred dollars.
The fraud upon creditors in this transaction is not in
the fact that land was taken in payment for stock, but
that, according to these pleadings, land was taken at an
excessive valuation of forty-six thousand eight hundred
dollars,—a fact of which these articles imparted no
information. Charging these plaintiffs with all knowledge which the record of the articles imparted, it is
clear that that record did not impart the very information that was necessary to a knowledge of the fraud.
Therefore, they dealt with the corporation without
knowledge that the land had been taken at an excessive
valuation. It is said that no fraud is alleged, but facts
are alleged which constitute a fraud as to the creditors.
In *Carbon Co. v. Mills, supra,* fraud was not pleaded in
the petition, and this court said, "But, under the facts
of the case, this was not necessary." The cases are so
alike in their facts that there is no greater reason for
pleading fraud in this than in that case. The statement
in the published notice gave no information additional
to that contained in the articles, and therefore need not
be further noticed. Our conclusion is that matters
alleged in the second count of the answer do not constitute any defense to plaintiff's petition, and that the
demurrer should have been sustained.—REVERSED.

B. G. WALKER v. C. A. WALKER, Appellant, and   104
Another Case.   140

Contracts: AGREEMENT TO SUPPORT: *Evidence.* Where a father, who
   has made advancement to his other children, gave to his son with
 1 whom he was then living, a deed of the land on which they lived,
   remarking that there was a deed of the property he intended for
   his son, and that he wanted to make his home with his son, as he
   had always lived there, and it seemed like home, and his son

replied that he was welcome, if he could put up with his son's manner of living, and. in response, the father said he guessed that would be all right, such statements amounted to an agreement to support, as consideration for the deed.

CONSIDERATION.   A deed, the consideration of which is an agreement
8   by the grantee to support the grantor during his life, may be set aside for breach of such agreement, notwithstanding that the only consideration expressed in the deed is love and affection and one dollar.

BREACH.   An agreement by grantee to support the grantor, constituting the consideration for the conveyance, is broken by the grantee's
2   denial of his obligation to support the grantor in pursuance thereof, although he offers, as a charity or filial duty, to allow the grantor to live with him during his life.

EXECUTION: *Lease*. A lease which has never been effectually exe-
4   cuted is absolutely null *ab initio*, and the parties thereto must be
5   left to adjust any claims arising from the occupancy of the land, without reference to the lease.

MEETING OF MINDS.   A written lease will be set aside on the ground
5   that the minds of the parties never met, where parts of the oral agreement were omitted, and the lease, having been signed, was
4   delivered to the other party for inspection, by him to be recorded, if satisfactory, and he never recorded it.

SAME.   A lease is not effectual as such, though signed by the lessor,
4   where he signed it with the understanding that it would not be
5   effective unless recorded, and under the impression that if it did not conform to the oral understanding of the parties he would destroy it, and he subsequently told the lessee that it did not contain their understanding, and he would never record it.

Appeal from Decatur District Court.—HON. W. H. TEDFORD, Judge.

WEDNESDAY, JANUARY 26, 1898.

THE plaintiff and defendant are father and son; the plaintiff being father. Two cases are consolidated for trial, and the parties (the plaintiff and defendant) are the same in each case. Prior to August 18, 1891, plaintiff was the owner of one hundred and ninety acres of land, and about that time he made to defendant a deed for one hundred and thirty acres, and to a daughter a deed for sixty acres. As we gather from the record, there was one hundred and sixty acres in one tract, and thirty acres outlying. The deed to the defendant was of the east one hundred acres of the one hundred and sixty-acre tract, and the outlying thirty acres, and the deed to the daughter was of the west sixty acres of the one hundred and sixty-acre tract. The deed to each expressed, as a consideration, "love and affection, and one dollar." Each deed contained the following: "Reserving to myself the possession of said premises, and the use, rents, and profits thereof, during my natural life." On September 24, 1894, the plaintiff and defendant signed a written agreement or lease of all the land mentioned, to defendant, for "ninety-nine years, or during the life of party of the first part, commencing March first, 1895;" the party of the first part being the plaintiff. The annual rental to be paid for the use of the land was two hundred and twenty-five dollars, and the payment of taxes and assessments, and keeping the premises in repair. The lease also contained certain reservations to the plaintiff. The action entitled above is to set aside and annul the deed on the ground that the actual consideration therefor was the promise of the defendant to support and care for plaintiff during his natural life, and the petition shows a breach of the agreement. The other action is to set aside the lease, on the ground that it was obtained by fraud and collusion, and was never legally consummated. Issues were taken upon the petitions, and the causes, as consolidated, were tried; and the district court, as to the first action, adjudged the consideration for the deed to be a promise to support the plaintiff during his life, and sustained the deed, but gave plaintiff a judgment for one hundred and fifty-six dollars annually during life, and made the payment thereof a lien on the land deeded. It decreed the lease of no force and effect after March 1, 1896, and adjudged certain amounts to be due for support up to July 1, 1895, and one hundred dollars due on the lease at the date of the judgment. The defendant appealed.—*Modified.*

Marion F. Stookey and *C. W. Hoffman* for appellant.

V. R. McGinnis and *Harvey & Parrish* for appellee.

GRANGER, J.—I. We will give the cases separate consideration. We should first determine the dispute as to the consideration for the deed. As we have said, on the face of the deed it was love and affection, and one dollar. The evidence bearing directly on this question is not extended, and the question is not difficult of solution. As to how the deed came to be made, the parties are in dispute; the plaintiff claiming that the defendant and his wife solicited the deed under promises to take care of him while he lived, and that he need not work. On the other hand, defendant says that the first he knew that the deed was made, or thought of its being made, was through the papers announcing the transfers of real estate, and that the deed came to him in an envelope a week or ten days after it was recorded, and denies explicitly any agreement whatever as to the support of plaintiff. At the time the case was tried the plaintiff was a man seventy-five years old, and he was about seventy when the deed was executed. The deed was made in August, 1891, and his wife had died the April previous. He had five children, of whom defendant was the youngest,—then some thirty-eight years old. Prior to August, 1891, when the deed was made, he had made advancements to his children other than the defendant and the daughter. The value of the property deeded to the daughter was about one thousand five hundred dollars, and that to defendant about six thousand dollars. Of course, these are estimates of value. As we understand, the deeds to the defendant and the daughter were a practical closing out of plaintiff's property to his children, except the life estate reserved. After the death of his wife, in April, 1891, he lived with defendant, except when traveling or temporarily away, till about December, 1893. It was really his home. Defendant had long lived on the land as a renter prior to the execution of the deed. We now notice what, to us, is the controlling evidence as to the agreement to support the plaintiff. Plaintiff's evidence is directly to that effect. We may pass over some particulars as to which there is a conflict. The following is a brief extract from defendant's testimony: "There was no agreement, contract, or anything else made in regard to the land prior to the time the deed was made. After the deed had been made and delivered, he said something about living with us. He handed it to me, and said, 'There is a deed;' that was my portion of the property he intended for me; that he wanted to make his home with us; that he always lived there; and that it seemed more like home than any place else. And I told him he could, if he could put up with the way we done, or with what we had to eat." Defendant's wife was present when the deed was delivered, and the following is a part of her testimony: "When father gave the deed to Caleb, he handed it to him and said that was his part that he had deeded to him, and he says, 'I want you to farm this place as long as I live, and I also want to stay here, and make my home here with you.' My husband said he was welcome to, if he could put up with the way we done. My father-in-law replied, and said he guessed that would be all right; that we had always set a good table, and he guessed he could live if we did." Both also testified that nothing was said about clothing or boarding him as a consideration for the land. There are other facts favorable to our conclusion, but, without

doubt, we think plaintiff understood, in delivering the
deed, that he was providing for a home; and we also
think that defendant so understood, or, at least, should
have. Under date of February 15, after the deed was
made, the defendant, in a letter to a brother and sister,
in which he was stating what disposition his father had
made of the property, and what had been deeded to
him, and that some of them wanted him to give up a
part, said: "I don't think that we have got any too
much, and have got to take care of him." Later in the
same letter, as we understand, referring to the property
deeded: "We don't know how much will be left. It
might take it all for doctor bills before he dies, for all
we know. He holds the place as long as he lives." The
situation, to us, is conclusive that the actual consideration for the deed was, in part, his support while
he lived. This construction harmonizes with the testimony of both parties, and with fair dealing. With the
contract settled as to the obligation for support, we
need not give extended consideration to the question of
its breach, for it is practically conceded. The district
court filed in the case an opinion in which the facts
are quite minutely found and considered. The court
found a breach of the agreement on the part of defendant and his wife, as to their treatment of the plaintiff,
that we are unable to concur in, as to some particulars.
There is evidence showing neglect in some particulars,
but we think most of the matters as to which plaintiff
complains resulted from the change he was compelled
to experience in losing his former home, and taking
another, in which other methods and practices obtained,
and with his age, and want of adaptability, he was led
to regard as ill treatment or neglect things that, under
other conditions, he would not. His complaints reach
to matters of privilege about the house; to the way he
was spoken to and looked at. Harshness in word or deed
is nowhere claimed. The district court speaks of it as

"the smooth, velvet stroke of indifference, ingeniously
exercised, in a way more cruel and exasperating than
blows." The district court saw and heard the witnesses. They are not before us. The record, as presented here, does not justify such a conclusion. With
every concession against defendant, warranted by the
record, as to the treatment of plaintiff, we do not escape
the conclusion that much of which plaintiff complains
is of matters to have been anticipated in the change he
was compelled to make as a result of his family mis-
fortune. His age may have unfitted him to duly appreci-
ate the loss he must sustain as to those little matters
that make one's home different and better to him than
all other places. He did not have his former home. It was
not to be expected. In December, 1893, plaintiff again
married, since which he has resided in another house on
the place, but has not been supported by defendant.
This act on his part was not satisfactory to the defendant. With it established that the consideration for the
deed was the agreement to support the plaintiff, there
is a clear breach of the agreement, in the denial of the
obligation by defendant, and his continued refusal to so
support him in pursuance of the agreement since
2   it was made. It is true that plaintiff did live
with defendant up to about December, 1893, just
prior to his marriage; and it is also true that defendant
now says that he is welcome to come and live with him
during his life, but not to bring his wife. The offer is
not made in fulfillment of his duty under the agreement, but as charity or filial duty. If this deed is to be
sustained without other relief, the situation is this:
That the plaintiff must accept a mere proffered support,
while it may be granted, or forfeit the legal right to
support that he has under the agreement to deed the
land. No claim is made, or would be, that he should do
that. While we have spoken of the consideration for
the deed being the promise of support, it should not

be understood that such was the only inducement in making it. It was undoubtedly the intention that a part of the grant should be as defendant's share of the estate; that is, plaintiff intended the land to be equal to defendant's share, and his support. The district court declined to set aside the deed, and, to secure plaintiff's support, gave judgment for one hundred and fifty-six dollars per year, being an allowance of $3 per week, and adjusted some other matters. Of this the plaintiff does not complain, and we do not understand appellant

3 to, as between such a judgment and one setting aside the deed. That a deed, the consideration of which is an agreement for such support, may be set aside where a different consideration is expressed in the deed, see *Gardner v. Lightfoot*, 71 Iowa, 577; *Saville v. Chalmers*, 76 Iowa, 325; *Puttman v. Haltey*, 24 Iowa, 425; *Harper v. Perry*, 28 Iowa, 57. We conclude that the action of the court, in its conclusion and judgment on this branch of the case, is fully authorized.

II. As we have said, the lease executed September 24, 1894, of the land conveyed in the deed, and also the sixty acres deeded to the daughter, with the one hundred-acre tract deeded to defendant, make a quarter section of land, which had constituted the home of the plaintiff. It will be remembered that the plaintiff, after the making of the deeds to defendant and his sister, had, by the terms of the deeds, a life estate in this quarter section. And he signed the lease in question for ninety-nine years, or during his life, at an annual rental of two hundred and twenty-five dollars; the defendant to pay taxes and keep the place in

4 repair. It is now asked that the lease be set aside, for the reason that it does not contain the entire contract of the parties; that there is omitted therefrom the right of plaintiff to remove and occupy certain buildings, and to take wood therefrom; and

that the term of the lease was to be for one year, or to
continue from year to year, to be terminated by notice.
It is also averred that there was no such agreement of
minds as that the lease became valid. It is averred that
these defects as to the lease were caused by the fraud
of the defendant; and the district court so found, and set
aside the lease. It is conceded by the defendant, in his
answer that some matters were omitted from the
written lease by mistake. This action was commenced
in January after the lease was made, in September. The
plaintiff and defendant went to Van Wert, and the
lease was written by one Pearl Hall. It was signed and
acknowledged before Hall, as a notary public. After
it was completed it was handed to plaintiff, as he says,
to take it and read it, and he says that he was told by
Hall that it was of no account if not recorded; and,
while the thought is not clearly expressed, we
5   understand the plaintiff to mean this: That he
signed the lease and took it for examination, and,
if he put it on record, it would be valid, and, if not, it
would not be; that, if not satisfactory (that is, according to the agreement), he could destroy it. He said in
his testimony: "When the contract was written, he
handed it to me, and told me to take it and read it. He
told me that if the contract was not put on record, that
it would be of no account; that it wouldn't stand in
law. I looked at it, and thought, if that was the case,
I could sign it and take it home, and, if it didn't suit me,
I could stick it in the fire and burn it." He further
stated that afterwards defendant asked him if he had
the lease recorded, and he told him he had not, and
never would record it; that it did not contain half that
was agreed upon. It appears from defendant's testimony, that the next morning after the lease was written
and signed, he had a talk with plaintiff, in which plaintiff was objecting to the lease as written, and that he
(defendant) told him that, as to the omitted parts, he

would perform as if they were included; that the lease
was to run for but one year. In the preparation of the
lease there was a wide departure from the agreement of
the parties. It appears that it was thought that it would
take too much paper to write it all out. It is strange
that ninety-nine years, or during life, should be put in
the lease, when, as defendant says, it should run but
one year. Certain it is that, when plaintiff took the
lease from the office of Hall, he had not agreed to it,
and defendant did not think he had. Defendant's evidence, in effect, corroborates plaintiff's as to that; for,
when told of its omissions, he did not then claim the
lease to contain what it should. It is true, defendant
testifies that the omissions were by plaintiff's assent,
but in his answer he states that they were omitted by
oversight. He also denies, in his answer, that the lease
was to run from year to year, and avers that it was to
be during the lifetime of the plaintiff, while in his testimony he says that he said to plaintiff, after the lease
was written, that it was for but one year. We need not
pass directly on the question of fraud. The petition
pleaded the facts as to the agreement, that parts thereof
were omitted from the written lease, that it was signed
and delivered to plaintiff for inspection, and that there
was never any binding contract between the parties, as
the minds of the parties never met on any common
ground. We think that claim has full suppport in the
evidence. It is to be said that this written lease was
never agreed to. Certainly it had not been when taken
from Hall's office, and both parties then understood that
it was subject to further examination, and to be placed
of record if found correct. It was not found correct, and
never afterwards assented to. Plaintiff expressly
refused to place it of record, because not in accord with
the agreement. There has never been a moment that
it met the assent of both parties, nor has it been

delivered, or treated as binding. It is true that this dis
position of the question is not in line with the argument,
but it is in line with the pleadings, and with the facts,
without practical dispute. The district court annulled
the lease, but gave it validity to March 1, 1896, and gave
judgment for rentals for the year 1895. We think that
the lease should be absolutely annulled, and the parties
left to adjust any claims arising from the occupancy of
the land as their rights may be in view of such a judgment. Thus MODIFIED, the decree of the district court
will stand AFFIRMED.

J. W. GARNER, *et al.*, Appellants, v. JOHN W. FRY, *et al.*

General Assignment: FILING CLAIMS. A verified notice filed with an
　assignee in insolvency, that one is the owner of a chattel mort-
7 gage on the property assigned, giving date, amount, and rate of
　interest, describing the notes secured by the mortgage, and stat-
　ing that the entire amount is due and upaid, amounts to a claim,
　under Code 1873, section 2120, requiring the facts to be fully stated
　and verified.

OPTIONAL CLAIM BY MORTGAGEE The court having power to protect
　all liens and priorities by appropriate orders in the distribution of
8 money derived from the sale of an assignee's property, it is
　optional with the mortgagee whether he will accept such protec-
　tion or enforce his lien

SAME: *Waiver*. A chattel mortgagee who presents her claim to an
　assignee for creditors of a mortgagor, and allows the mortgaged
　property to remain with the assignee for over two years, and a
8 portion of it to be sold by him under the direction of the court
　waives her right to foreclose, and must look to the assignee and
　the courts to protect her preference by virtue of the lien of her
　mortgage.

Fraudulent Conveyance: SALE OF DOWER: *Gifts.* An indebtedness
1 from a husband to his wife, will sustain a chattel mortgage by the
　former to the latter, as against his creditors, notwithstanding
4 that the indebtedness arose from a loan to him of money which
5 she exacted from him as a condition of her executing a convey-
　ance of their homestead, and which he consented to allow her at a
　time when he could make a valid gift to her.

Failure to record. The withholding a chattel mortgage from the
2 record in pursuance of an agreement to that effect, does not affect
3 its validity as to pre-existing creditors.

Appeal. Where an appeal is taken from a judgment sustaining a
6 mortgage, and also from a subsequent order denying an injunction restraining foreclosure of such mortgage, a motion to strike
out the latter appeal, as in no way connected with the main case,
will be overruled, as there is nothing in the rules prohibiting printing two appeals under one cover.

Appeal from Van Buren District Court.—Hon. F. W.
Eichelberger and Hon. M. A. Roberts, Judges.

Wednesday, January 26, 1898.

The plaintiffs are creditors of John W. Fry, who
made an assignment, February 3, 1894. He executed
a mortgage to his wife, January 1, previous, securing
the payment of three thousand dollars, and this action
was brought to set aside such mortgage as fraudulent.
Decree for defendants, and plaintiffs appeal. Thereafter the plaintiffs applied for an order restraining
Mrs. Fry from foreclosing her mortgage, and they also
appeal from an order denying such relief. Judgment
sustaining mortgage *affirmed.* Order denying injunction *reversed.*

Mitchell & Sloan, Work & Lewis, and *Wherry &
Walker* for appellants.

McCoid & McCoid for appellees.

Ladd, J.—The important question presented
relates to the execution of a mortgage by Fry to his
wife, securing the payment of two notes of one thousand, five hundred dollars each. The facts are somewhat peculiar. When married, in 1876, both were without means other than necessary to begin housekeeping.
In 1888 there was owing her one hundred and ten dollars

for millinery and household goods sold in Kansas, for which he gave her a due bill. In 1890 he sold thirty acres of land, the title to which was in her name, and executed to her a note of six hundred dollars in payment therefor. In 1892 he had arranged to exchange their homestead and some other property to one Stuart for a farm, which he had in turn sold to Pearson.

1 She refused to sign the deed without having first been paid one-half of the proceeds derived from the sale. This was finally agreed to, the deed signed, and left with a justice of the peace, who was to retain the amount, but, upon its receipt, handed it to Fry, who paid it over to his wife. Thereafter Fry traded for a store building, residence, and stock of goods in Leando, paying therefor in horses and money. He borrowed one thousand, eight hundred dollars of his wife, with which to purchase goods and use in his business, and as security, agreed that the deed of the real estate be made to her. A few days after the deed was so drawn, however, the commercial agencies at Keokuk and Burlington wrote to a notary, Morrison, inquiring if Fry had conveyed his property to his wife. Morrison showed these communications to Fry, and informed him that having the real estate in his wife's name would injure his credit. He then advised Fry and wife that, instead of the deed, he execute to her a mortgage on the stock of goods, and that, by withholding this from record, his credit would not be injured, and she would be fully secured. The deed was made to him and he agreed to give her a mortgage on the merchandise. But there is no evidence of an

2 understanding that the mortgage should be withheld from record, nor is there any that its execution be delayed till the store was filled up with goods bought on credit. True, she said she would not have taken a mortgage at that time. Then there were few goods in the store, as she explains, and she might well wait till those for the purchase of which he borrowed

the money were placed on the shelves. That she repeatedly demanded the execution of the mortgage, and was put off by him, cannot be doubted, if their undisputed testimony is to be credited. In August she loaned him seventy dollars, and in October three hundred and seventy-five dollars, received from the sale of land in her name, and he owed her one hundred and thirty-two dollars for produce taken by her on sales of millinery goods, as she conducted a shop in one part of the store. These amounts make up a little more than the three thousand dollars, for which the two notes were given, and to secure which, he executed the mortgage in con-

3　　　troversy, January 1, 1894. This was not placed on record till February 2, following, but the indebtedness to plaintiffs had been contracted prior to its execution. For this reason the case does not come within the rule announced in *Goll & Frank Co. v. Miller*, 87 Iowa, 426, and *Falker v. Linehan*, 88 Iowa, 641. Besides, no agreement not to record is shown. It is insisted the mortgage was dated back. This is only a suspicion, and the evidence is to the contrary. Before this Fry had been paying considerable amounts on his indebtedness, and, if it be conceded that he did not act in good faith, there is nothing in the record to indicate that his wife participated in any fraudulent purpose or was put on inquiry with reference thereto. It does show, however, that she was keen in the care and protection of her own interests, and inclined to overreach her husband in their business transactions.

II. It might well be urged that the one thousand, eight hundred dollars was obtained from Fry by his wife without consideration. This is true. While the

4　　　statutes of this state confer on married women the largest freedom in contracting, they stop short of that interest in the husband's property with which the wife is endowed for the protection and well-being of the family. She cannot convey it, as a seprate and independent interest, to a third party. *McKee v. Reynolds,* 26 Iowa, 578; *Dunlap v. Thomas,* 69 Iowa, 358. Nor can she convey it to her husband. *Linton v. Crosby,* 54 Iowa, 478; *In re Lennon's Estate,* 58 Iowa, 760; *Shane v. McNeill,* 76 Iowa, 459. The inchoate dower interest may be released, but not bargained and sold. *Reiff v. Horst,* 55 Md. 42. The statute is not limited to conveyances, but is extended to all contracts. "When property is owned by either the husband or wife, the other has no interest therein which can be the subject of contract between them. * * *" Code, section 3154. This evidently refers to the interest arising from the marriage relation, such as dower, or homestead, and not that derived from some other source. *Baxter v. Hecht,* 98 Iowa, 531. It is the policy of the law to foster and protect family unity and harmony, and for this purpose the contingent interest of the husband or wife in the other's property is created, though not such as may, in any event, become the subject of barter and sale between them. In all their dealings each must treat the property of the other as his own, and never pervert the inchoate interest therein as a means of private gain. Either may elect whether he will join in a conveyance, but is precluded from using the right for the purposes of speculation or oppression. The statute is intended to serve the double purpose of shielding the contingent rights of the one against the fraud or imposition of the other, and guarding against the possibility of selfish calculation and unjust exactions and interferences of the one in the management and control of the other's estate. See *Miller v. Miller,* 104 Iowa, 186.

III. But Fry paid this money voluntarily. While his wife took advantage of the situation, he was not compelled to convey the property. It seems well settled

that, where money is voluntarily paid, with full knowledge and without duress, no recovery can be had.
1 Parsons, Contracts (6th ed.), 489; *Forbes v. Appleton*, 5 Cuch. 117; *Rutherford v. McIvor*, 21 Ala.
750; 2 Greenleaf, Evidence, section 123, and notes. The
transaction was in the nature of a gift, and, after its
completion, in the absence of fraud or mistake, Mrs.
Fry became as absolutely the owner of the money as
though received for a consideration the law recognized
as valid. This being true, she could loan it or use it for
any lawful purpose. It appears all the indebtedness of
Fry existing at that time has been paid, and the transaction was not had in view of creating any other.
Undoubtedly the circumstances are to be considered, in
connection with others, as bearing on the charge of
fraud, but we think the evidence fully warrants the conclusion that the money was paid Mrs. Fry in good
faith, and without any thought of acting with the purpose of defeating future creditors. The conclusion of
the district court is supported by the evidence, and is
affirmed.

IV.   After the action just considered had been
determined, and an appeal perfected, Mrs. Fry proceeded
to foreclose her mortgage, and the plaintiffs presented
a petition to Hon. M. A. Roberts, one of the judges of
that district, praying that she be enjoined from so
doing. From an order denying such relief they
6   appeal. The appellee moves to strike this portion
of the abstract, because in no way connected
with the main case. It is an independent action, but
the rules do not prohibit printing two appeals under
one cover. The parties were practically the same, and
the cases separately abstracted and argued. No prejudice has resulted. The motion is overruled. This petition sets out all the proceedings and orders in the matter
of the assignment of Fry for the benefit of his creditors,
and based the prayers for relief on the ground that the

right of Mrs. Fry, to foreclose her mortgage, had been
waived and adjudicated. On May 1, 1894, she
7   filed a paper, in these words, with the assignee:
"To James Elerick, assignee of J. W. Fry: You
are hereby notified that I, Sadie H. Fry, have a chattel
mortgage on the entire stock of merchandise included
in the assignment of J. W. Fry, for the sum of three
thousand dollars, at six per cent. interest from Jan. 1,
1894.   I hold two promissory notes, for $1,500 each,
drawing six per cent. interest, secured by chattel mortgage, and the entire amount is due and unpaid. Sadie
H. Fry." This was duly verified, and reported by the
assignee among the claims filed. Objections to the
report of the assignee having been made, hearing was
set for the November term, 1895, and the assignee and
Mrs. Fry cited to appear for examination. Both
appeared personally and by attorneys, and the court, on
the twenty-ninth of the month, entered an order adjusting the assignee's accounts, and that he proceed "to dispose of all the property remaining in his hands as
assignee, and will advertise the same for sale, and proceed at once to sell and dispose of the same at either
public or private sale, in bulk or by retail, as will best
subserve the interests of the estate," and provided for
the approval of the court or judge. Mrs. Fry excepted,
but took no appeal from this order. On December 12
following, the assignee called the court's attention to a
notice received from her December 2, saying the paper
heretofore referred to was not filed as a claim, but as a
notice of the existence of the mortgage. The decree in
The action begun July 18, 1894, declaring the mortgage
valid, was entered March 11, 1896, and on June 14, Mrs.
Fry began the foreclosure of her mortgage. The facts
have been somewhat fully set out, because they clearly
indicate Mrs. Fry had no right to enforce her lien on
the merchandise by advertisement and sale. The
assignee took the stock subject to her mortgage, and

charged with notice of its existence. No other notice was required. The paper filed could serve no purpose other than that of a claim against the estate, and it was so treated by the assignee. The particular form was not material. It is sufficient that the facts were fully stated and verified. Code 1873, section 2119.

8 She allowed the property to remain with the assignee two years and four months, and nearly one-half to be sold under the direction of the court. The assignee was ordered to sell the balance of the merchandise at a hearing to which she was a party. This order was absolutely inconsistent with the right to foreclose, and she cannot be permitted to ignore it. The court has ample power to protect all liens and priorities by appropriate orders in the distribution of moneys derived from the sale of the assignor's property, and it is optional with the mortgagee whether he will enforce his lien against the property or rely on the protection thus afforded. If he choose the latter remedy, he may not thereafter foreclose, because, in doing so he waives such right. By filing her claim, and alleging her right to preference, and allowing the assignee to retain possession, and manage and control the property, under the direction of the court, Mrs. Fry elected to look to the assignee for the satisfaction of the debt owing her. This was doubtless the ground on which the court proceeded in making the order of sale. The plaintiffs are creditors interested in the estate, and entitled to maintain the action. The only question determined in the main case was the validity of the mortgage. Here the right to foreclose is the issue. We conclude the temporary writ of injunction should have been granted, and the order denying it REVERSED.

JOHNSTON & SON, JOSEPH JOHNSTON, and O. P. JOHNSTON, Appellants, v. WILLIAM ROBUCK AND J. M. AMOS, Defendants, and HARRY WATKINS. Intervener.

Chattel Mortgage: FORECLOSURE. A chattel mortgage executed to 6 secure a debt past due, may be foreclosed *eo instante*, on delivery.

PRIVATE SALE. A chattel mortgagee of a stock of goods may, if he acts in good faith and with ordinary prudence, sell the property 7 at retail, under a provision of the mortgage authorizing to sell at private sale. Citing *Wygal v Bigelow* (Kan. Sup.) 24 Am. St. 495; *Hanna v. Harrington*, 18 Ark. 85; *Stromberg v. Lindberg*, 25 Minn. 58; *Hungate v. Reynolds*, 72 Ill. 425.

CONVERSION. A chattel mortgagee who takes possession of the prop-8 erty before the happening of any of the contingencies which give him the right to take possession, is guilty of conversion.

CONSIDERATION. An existing indebtedness is ample consideration, as 4 between the debtor and creditor, for the execution of a mortgage securing its payment. Citing *Kranery v. Simon*, 65 Ill. 844; *Louthain v. Miller*, 85 Ind. 161; *McMurtrie v. Riddell*, 9 Colo. 497; *Smith v. Worman*, 19 Ohio St. 145; *Shufeldt v. Pease*, 16 Wis. 659; *Cromelin v. McCauley*, 67 Ala. 562; *Hettman v. Griffith*, 48 Kan. 53; *Corning v. Medicine Co.*, 46 Mo App. 16; *Henry v. Vliet* (Neb.) 49 N. W. Rep. 1107; *Gassen v. Hendrick*, 74 Cal. 444; *Bank v. Carrington*, 5 R. I. 515; *Fair v. Howard*, 6 Nev 804

SAME A corporation may secure the payment of the individual 4 indebtedness of one member of the firm, where it is solvent, and 5 there is no intention to defraud subsequent creditors.

Partnership. Existing indebtedness is ample consideration for the 4 execution of a mortgage by a firm, of which the debtor is a mem-5 ber, securing its payment, as between the mortgagee and the members of the firm.

Transfer to Equity. The court did not err in transferring a cause 1 from the law to the equity side of the calendar on its own motion, 8 where the petition did not state a cause of action.

WAIVER OF ERROR IN. Going to trial does not waive the error of the 2 court in transferring a law case to the equity side of the calendar.

SAME. Issues cognizable in equity may be transferred to the equity
8   side, under Code, section 3433, but not issues at law, and no motion
is required to have those tried separately in the proper forum

Trial: LAW AND EQUITY. The ordinary rule is to hear the equitable
1   issues first; but where a trial at law will practically settle all matters in controversy, it ought to be first had.

Appeal from Marion District Court.—HON. A. W. WIL-
KINSON, Judge.

THURSDAY, JANUARY 27, 1898.

ACTION against defendants for the value of a stock
of goods alleged to have been converted. Decree for
defendants, and plaintiffs appeal.—*Affirmed.*

Earle & Prouty and *S. C. Johnston* for appellants.

L. N. Hayes for appellees.

LADD, J.—The firm of Johnston & Son, consisting
of Joseph and O. P. Johnston, were engaged in the general mercantile business at Knoxville, and on June 14,
1895, executed a chattel mortgage on their stock of
goods to Henry Watkins and William Robuck, securing
the payment of a note of five thousand, four hundred
dollars, to the former, payable June 14, 1896, and a note
to the latter of three thousand, two hundred dollars,
due September 14, 1896. Thereafter, though on the
same day, the firm executed a second mortgage to Wil-
·liam Robuck, securing the payment of a note of three
hundred and thirty-two dollars, due September 14,
1896, and another note of four thousand, five hundred
and fifty-nine dollars and thirty-six cents, signed by
Johnston & Frush, which had matured January 6, 1894,
The notes referred to represented debts of Johnston &
Son, except the last, which Joseph Johnston, a member
of the firm of Johnston & Frush, had assumed and
agreed to pay. On the following day, Johnston & Son

gave a third mortgage to other creditors, securing the payment of divers sums, aggregating one thousand, seven hundred and forty dollars and forty-nine cents. On June 19, 1895, Robuck, with the consent of Watkins, placed the second mortgage in the hands of his co-defendant Amos, sheriff of Marion county, with instructions to foreclose. Amos, theretofore, took possession of the entire stock of goods, and advertised it for sale July 8. Two days before the day fixed for the sale, he was served with a written notice by Johnston & Son and O. P. Johnston, warning him not to sell, and not to pay the Johnston & Frush note out of the proceeds, if he did sell, and demanding immediate possession of the goods. The property, however, was offered for sale at public auction; but, as there were no bidders, the sheriff proceeded to sell at retail. This action was brought for the value of the stock of goods, basing the claim for damages on two grounds: (1) That, as the Johnston & Frush note did not represent an indebtedness of Johnston & Son, the mortgage securing its payment was without consideration and void, and, the three hundred and thirty-two-dollar note not being due, the foreclosure proceedings were premature; (2) the mortgage, by its terms, conferred no authority to sell at retail. The defendants justified their action in foreclosing on several grounds, and asked, in their counter-claim, that a decree of foreclosure be entered. Watkins and the creditors of the third mortgage intervened, praying that the money held by or due from defendants be applied on their mortgages. After a jury had been impaneled for the trial of the case, the court, on its own motion, discharged it, and transferred the cause to the equity side of the calendar, and there heard it.

I. It may be conceded that, unless the petition failed to state a cause of action, the court erred in

ordering the issues at law to be tried in equity. Under
section 3435 of the Code, on motion, issues
1   cognizable in equity may be transferred to the
equity side, but not the issues at law, and no
motion is required to have these tried separately in the
proper forum. It is said in *Byers v. Rodabaugh*, 17 Iowa,
53, "that the right to have an action transferred from
one docket to another arises only where the plaintiff has
brought his action by the wrong proceedings; that is,
where he has brought his action by ordinary, when he
should have adopted equitable, proceedings, and *e con-
verso*." *Morris v. Merrit*, 52 Iowa, 496, is in point.
Referring to this section, Beck, J., says, "that issues
exclusively cognizable in equity shall be tried as
equitable proceedings; *i. e.* by the court without a jury.
Other issues, not cognizable in equity, are to be tried
as issues at law; *i. e.* by a jury. This is the obvious
meaning of the section. In actions at law, therefore,
when equitable issues are presented, they are triable
as in chancery. Pure issues at law, which are not
cognizable as in equity, are to be tried to a jury." Where
the issues are mixed, the procedure seems to be somewhat controlled by statute. For this reason, defenses
at law to an equitable action must be determined by the
chancellor. *Ryman v. Lynch*, 76 Iowa, 587; *Frost v.
Clark*, 82 Iowa, 298; *Wilkinson v. Pritchard*, 93 Iowa,
308; *Leach v. Kundson*, 97 Iowa, 643; *Gatch v. Garretson*, 100 Iowa, 252; *Evans v. McConnell*, 99 Iowa, 326.
Going to trial does not waive the error of the
2   court in changing the form of action. *Rabb v.
Albright*, 93 Iowa, 50. Undoubtedly, the ordinary rule is to hear the equitable issues first. But,
where a trial at law will practically settle all matters
in controversy, it ought to be first had. *Morris v. Merritt, supra*.

II. We inquire, then, whether a cause of action is
stated in the petition. Each mortgage is set out, and

contains this clause: "And I, the said Johnston & Son,
do hereby covenant and agree to and with the said Wm.
H. Robuck that in case of default made in the payment
of the above-mentioned promissory note, or in case of
my attempting to dispose of the same, other than in the
ordinary course of trade, or remove from said county of
Marion, the aforesaid goods and chattels, or any part
thereof, then, in that case, it shall be lawful for the
said mortgagee or his assigns, by himself or agent, to
take immediate possession of said goods and chattels,
wherever found,—the possession of these presents
being his sufficient authority therefor,—and to sell the
same at private sale or public auction, or so much
thereof as shall be sufficient to pay the amount due or to
become due, as the case may be, with all reasonable
costs and attorney's fees pertaining to the taking, keeping, advertising, and selling of said property."

3   So that, on the happening of one of the three contingencies, the mortgagee might proceed to foreclose, but until then he acquired no such right, and the
taking of possession, and sale, prior to that time would
amount to a conversion. *Edwards v. Cottrell*, 43 Iowa,
194; *Howery v. Hoover*, 97 Iowa, 581; *Gravel v. Clough*,
81 Iowa, 272; *Colby v. W. W. Kimball Co.*, 99 Iowa, 321;
Eslow v. Mitchell, 26 Mich, 500.

III.   The second mortgage was signed by Johnston & Son and O. P. Johnston. The note of Johnston
& Frush represented the individual debt of Joseph
Johnston, and not that of the firm, or of the other
4   member thereof. Time for payment of the note
was not extended. Appellants argue that it was
to be, and, for this reason, the mortgage was invalid.
That issue is not raised by the pleadings. An existing
indebtedness is ample consideration, as between the
parties, for the execution of a mortgage securing its
payment. Jones, Chattel Mortgages, section 81;
Kranert v. Simon, 65 Ill. 344; 15 Am. & Eng. Enc. Law,

758; *Louthian v. Miller*, 85 Ind. 161; *McMurtrie v.
Riddell*, 9 Colo. 497 (13 Pac. Rep. 181); *Smith v.
Worman*, 19 Ohio St. 145; *Shufeldt v. Pease*, 16 Wis.
659; *Cromelin v. McCauley*, 67 Ala. 542; *Heitman v.
Griffith*, 43 Kan. 553 (23 Pac. Rep. 589); *Corning v.
Medicine Co.*, 46 Mo. App. 16; *Henry v. Vliet*, 33 Neb.
130 (49 N. W. Rep. 1107); *Gassen v. Hendrick*, 74 Cal.
444 (16 Pac. Rep. 242); *Bank v. Carrington*, 5 R. I. 515;
Fair v. Howard, 6 Nev. 304; *Smith v. Smith*, 87 Iowa,
93; *Koon v. Tramel*, 71 Iowa, 137; *Clark v. Barnes*, 72
Iowa, 563. And a co-partnership may secure the payment of the individual indebtedness of one mem-
5   ber of the firm. *Poole v. Seney*, 66 Iowa, 502;
Smith v. Smith, supra; Jones, Chattel Mortgages,
section 44. In joining in the execution of the mortgage
securing the payment of the indidvidual indebtedness
of Joseph Johnston, the other member of the firm simply
waived his right to have the firm property applied to
the satisfaction of its debts. This right was for his
benefit, and it was his privilege to allow the individual debts of Joseph to be first paid. The order in which
the assets of the firm were to be disposed of was
for the determination of the partners. They were
supposed to know their respective interests therein,
and, having agreed that the property might be appropriated by Joseph Johnston, in securing his indebtedness, they are not in a situation to complain. It simply
amounted to an understanding, in the absence of any
showing to the contrary, that Joseph had an interest in
the assets equal, at least, to the debt secured, and
consent that he might withdraw therefrom to this
amount. The agreement that this might be done was
certainly valid, as between the partners; and, the consideration as to Joseph Johnston being sufficient, the
validity of the mortgage will be upheld. *Smith v.
Smith, supra.*

IV. The mortgage was executed to secure a debt. past due, and the mortgagee had the right to foreclose it, upon delivery, *eo instante.*   Jones, Chattel
6 .   Mortgages, section 770; *Farrell v. Bean*, 10 Md. 217. See, also, *Bearss v. Preston*, 66 Mich. 11 (32 N. W. Rep. 912); *Phelps v. Fockler*, 61 Iowa, 340.

V. By the terms of the mortgage, the mortgagee was authorized to sell at private sale. This meant in the manner that property of the kind is usually disposed of, for cash, other than at public auction.
7   It cannot be said that the sale must be invariably made at retail, or so made in bulk. The mortgagee, in such cases, is the trustee for the mortgagor, and is required to act in entire good faith, and conduct the sale fairly. The manner of doing this necessarily depends largely upon the character of the property and the opportunities presented. He must sell the articles separately, in lots, or all together, as may best suit the convenience of buyers, and insure the largest returns. If, in doing this, he acts in good faith, and with ordinary prudence, the law exacts no more. See *Wygal v. Bigelow*, 42 Kan. 477 (24 Am. St. Rep. 495, and notes; 22 Pac. Rep. 612); *Hannah v. Carrington*, 18 Ark. 85; *Stromburg v. Lindberg*, 25 Minn. 513; *Hungate v. Reynolds*, 72 Ill. 425. There is no allegation of bad faith or negligence, and, in the absence of both, it cannot be said that sale at retail was not authorized.

VI. It thus appears that the petition did not state a cause of action, as the mortgage, by its terms, was mature, and Robuck had the right to foreclose it. Sale of the goods at retail was not necessarily unlawful.
The counter-claim and the petitions of inter-
8   vention raised the only issue to be determined, and the court rightly heard them in the proper forum. No motion was made to so hear them, but none was required. No prejudice can result to anyone in

having a trial where the law requires it. In view of our conclusion, the other errors alleged are not considered. —AFFIRMED.

FLORENCE C. FIELDING, for the Use of, Etc., v. TUNIS J. LA GRANGE, A. VANSLIKE, JAMES W. RIDENOUR, and RICHARD JOHNSON, Appellants.

Intoxicating Liquor: SALES TO MINORS. The honest belief of defendant, justified by appearances, is not a defense to an action under
1 Code 1873, section 1539, to recover a penalty for selling intoxicating liquor to a minor.

Evidence: DECLARATIONS: *Impeachment.* Declarations of one not a party to a suit can only be used to impeach his credibility as a wit-
3 nesses, and not as substantive proof of matters in issue.

RULE APPLIED. Statements by the alleged minor when he purchased
3 the liquor that he was not a minor, are admissible to impeach him as a witness in an action by a third person, under Code, 1873, sec-
4 tion 1539, to recover a penalty for selling intoxicating liquors to a minor, but are not substantive evidence on that question, and do not authorize its submission to the jury in the absence of other evidence thereon.

EXCLUSION: *Harmless error.* The exclusion of a question asked plaintiff in an action under Code 1873, section 1539, to recover a
2 penalty for selling intoxicating liquor to a minor, whether she had not stated that she intended to get after defendant for some money, or that she expected "to pull his leg," is not prejudicial, even if erroneous.

DIRECTED VERDICT. It is not error to direct a verdict for plaintiff in an action for the statutory penalty for selling liquor to a minor,
3 where the minority of the purchaser, which was the only question in issue, was testified to by two unimpeached witnesses, and the
4 only evidence that he was not a minor was the statements he signed when he purchased the liquor, in which he claimed he was of age.

Appeal from Benton District Court.—HON. G. W. BURNHAM, Judge.

THURSDAY, JANUARY 27, 1898.

ACTION at law to recover the statutory penalty for selling intoxicating liquor to one Otto H. Fielding, a minor. Defendant La Grange pleads that he is a registered pharmacist, holding a permit, and denies that he made sales as claimed. The case was tried to a jury, and at the conclusion of the evidence, plaintiff moved for a verdict in the sum of seven hundred dollars. This motion was sustained and judgment entered upon the verdict. Defendants appeal.—*Affirmed.*

Cato Sells, Matt Gaasch, and *T. H. Milner* for appellants

Whipple & Zollinger and *W. C. Connell* for appellee.

DEEMER, C. J.—Appellant attempted to show that from inquiries made; and from the general appearance of Otto Fielding he was justified in believing that he
(Fielding) was of age. The statute upon which
1   the action is predicated (Code 1873, section 1539)
absolutely inhibits the sale of liquor to a minor for any purpose whatever, and we have frequently held that the seller is bound, at his peril, to know whether the person to whom he sells is within the prohibited class. Good faith is no defense. *Dudley v. Sautbine,* 49 Iowa, 650; *State v. Ward,* 75 Iowa, 641; *Jamison v. Burton,* 43 Iowa, 282; *State v. Thompson,* 74 Iowa, 119.

II. Mrs. Fielding was asked, on cross-examination, if she had not stated that she expected to get after La Grange for some money, or that she expected to
"pull his leg." Objection to the question was
2   sustained. We think the ruling was correct. It
is apparent that she has attempted to "get after" La Grange for some money. In any event, the ruling was without prejudice.

III. Complaint is made of the court's ruling on the motion to direct a verdict. It is argued that there was a conflict in the evidence, and that the case should have been submitted to the jury. The sales were admitted by the defendant, and the only question remaining was as to the age of the buyer. He, his father, and his mother testified that he was a minor, and there was no substantive evidence to contradict this positive testimony. True, Otto signed statements, when he purchased the liquor, to the effect that he was not a minor. But these statements were admissible for impeaching purposes alone. Declarations of one not a party to a suit can only be used for that purpose. They go to the credibility of the witness, and do not, of themselves, furnish substantive proof of the matter in issue. If we discard Otto's evidence entirely, there yet remains the uncontradicted evidence of two witnesses, who were unimpeached, that the buyer was a minor when he purchased the liquor. With nothing to contradict this evidence, the trial judge was justified in sustaining the motion and directing the verdict.—AFFIRMED.

3

4

THE FIDELITY LOAN AND TRUST COMPANY, as Trustee
v. HARRY E. DOUGLAS, Appellant.

Judgments: RAILROADS: *Street railways.* A street "railway corporation" is not within Code 1873, section 130), providing that a judgment against any "railway corporation" for any injury to any person or property shall be a lien within the county where recovered, on its property, prior to the lien of any mortgage or trust deed executed since July 4, 1862, in view of the fact that there were no street railways in the state when the original act from which this section was taken was passed, and that the context apparently excludes street railways.

1

SAME The fact that the franchise of a corporation denominated as a street railway company does not limit its operation to the city, but includes the territory adjacent to the city, and that it is

2 authorized to carry freight, baggage and express matter, does not make it a commercial railway company as distinguished from a street railway company, and so bring it within the scope of Code 1878, section 1809, giving judgments for personal injuries against commercial railway corporations preference over prior mortgages. where there is nothing to indicate that it has done or intended to do any business except that usually and properly done by street railway corporations.

LADD, J., took no part.

WATERMAN, J., dissenting.

*Appeal from Woodbury District Court.—*HON. SCOTT M. LADD, Judge.

THURSDAY, JANUARY 27, 1898.

· ACTION in equity to foreclose a mortgage, and for other equitable relief. A demurrer to the petition was filed and overruled, and from that ruling the defendant, Douglas, appeals.—*Affirmed.*

Argo, McDuffie & Argo, Kennedy & Kennedy, J. S. Lathrop, and *Kennedy, Jackson & Kennedy* for appellant.

Charles A. Clark & Son and *S. E. Hostetter* for appellee.

ROBINSON, J.—I. On the first day of August, 1890, the Sioux City Street Railway Company executed the mortgage in suit to the plaintiff as trustee, to secure bonds of the street railway company, the issuance of which, to the amount of one million dollars, it had authorized. The mortgage was recorded on the second day of September, 1890, and bonds which it was designed to secure, to the amount of five hundred and twenty-five thousand dollars, were issued. Of that amount, bonds for three hundred and fifty thousand dollars have been sold, and are owned by good-faith purchasers, and the remainder have been pledged to secure outstanding indebtedness of the street railway

company. The property mortgaged included the franchise of the street railway company, its roadbed and
street railway and appurtenances, including both real
and personal property. On the fourth day of June, 1892,
the defendant, Douglas, obtained judgment against the
street railway company for personal injuries inflicted
upon him, in the sum of three thousand five hundred dollars, with interest and costs. That judgment is unpaid,
and the controlling question presented by the demurrer,
and to to be determined by us is, which one of the two
      liens, created by the mortgage and the judgment,
1   is senior to the other. It is not denied
      that the lien of plaintiff is first in point
of time, but it is claimed by the appellant that
the lien of his judgment is made superior to that
of the plaintiff by section 1309 of the Code of
1873, which is as follows: "A judgment against
any railway corporation for any injury to any person   •
or property, shall be a lien within the county where
recovered, on the property of such corporation, and
such lien shall be prior and superior to the lien of any
mortgage or trust deed executed since the fourth day
of July, A. D. 1862." The Sioux City Street Railway
Company is a corporation organized under the laws of
this state, with power "to locate, construct, maintain,
and operate street railways within and adjacent to the
city of Sioux City," and has constructed, maintained,
and operated street railways within that city. Is it a
"railway corporation," within the meaning of the statute quoted? So far as its provisions are material in this
case, they were first enacted as a part of section 9 of
chapter 169 of the Acts of the Ninth General Assembly.
That act was entitled, "An act in relation to the duties
of railroad companies." An examination of it shows
that but two of the ten sections, exclusive of the repeal-
ing clause which it contained, could have had any reference to street railways. Eight sections refer clearly to

commercial railroads. Sections 7 and 9 use the term "every railroad company," and, had the context justified such an interpretation, might be held to refer to street railway companies. But those sections must be construed in connection with the remaining one of the chapter, and, when that is done, the most evident and satisfactory conclusion is that nothing contained in the chapter was designed to apply to street railway corporations. That conclusion is supported to some extent by the conceded fact that, when the statute was enacted, there were no street railways in this state, and, therefore, there was no occasion to legislate in regard to them. It is said in Sutherland, Statutory Construction, section 241, in reference to statutes, that: "The application of particular provisions is not to be extended beyond the general scope of a statute, unless such extension is manifestly designed. Legislatures, like courts, must be considered as using expressions concerning the thing they have in hand; and it would not be a fair method of interpretation to apply their words to subjects not within their consideration, and which, if thought of, would have been more particularly and carefully disposed of. The mere literal construction ought not to prevail, if it is opposed to the intention of the legislature apparent from the statute. * * * The intention of an act involves a consideration of its subject-matter, and the change in, or an addition to, the law which it proposes; hence the supreme importance of the rule that a statute should be construed with reference to its general purpose and aim." When the Code of 1873 was enacted, the most important of the provisions of chapter 169 of the Acts of the Ninth General Assembly were included, with numerous other provisions, in the chapter relating to railways. Section 9 of chapter 169, with some modifications, not material to any question involved in this case, appears as section

1309 of the new chapter. Street railways were in existence in this state when the Code of 1873 took effect,
and it is urged, if it be true that section 9 of the chapter
169, aforesaid, did not apply to street-railway corporations, the re-enactment of the section gave it that effect.
We are of the opinion, however, that the terms "railway" and "railways," where used in the chapter of the
Code of 1873 referred to, are always intended to desig-
nate one or more of the commercial railways,—that is,
railways designed for the transportation of passengers
and freight from place to place within the state, or from
state to state, or both, and upon which, as a rule, the
transportation is effected by means of trains of cars
moved by locomotive engines,—and not railways which
are designed chiefly for the carriage of passengers from
point to point in a single city or town. And we are of
the opinion that the term, "railway corporations," as
used in that chapter, refers only to corporations which
own or operate such commercial railways. · Certainly
such corporations are intended in every instance where
the context makes clear the character of the corporation intended, and we are not authorized to presume
that the term is used in a different sense when its meaning is not so definitely expressed. The words "railroad"
and "railway" may undoubtedly be so used as to mean
a street railway, but by popular usage, when used without qualifying words, they are understood to refer to
commercial railways, the word "street" being almost
invariably used in connection with "railway" to desig-
nate a street railway. See *Sears v. Railway Co.*, 65
Iowa, 744; *Funk v. Railway Co.*, 61 Minn. 435 (63 N. W.
Rep. 1099). And the history of legislation in this state
shows that it has conformed in great measure to popular usage, and that, as a rule, in statutes designed to
apply to street railways, they have been designated by
that name. Nothing contained in the chapter under
consideration makes it at all probable that any part of

it was intended to apply to street railways or to street railway corporations.

Our attention has been called to various decisions of this court and of other courts, but we do not find anything in any of them which is in conflict with the views we have expressed. It must be remembered that the true application of the statute in question depends upon the legislative intent, which is to be ascertained by means of well-known rules of interpretation, and not alone from the abstract and permissible definitions of terms used. The case of *City of Clinton v. Clinton & L. H. Ry. Co.*, 37 Iowa, 61, especially relied upon by appellant, did not arise under the statute in controversy, and, although some language was used in the opinion which tends logically to support the claim made by the appellant, yet nothing was actually decided in that case which is in conflict with the conclusion we reach in this. It will be understood that the interpretation of the statute we have adopted applies only to section 1309 of the Code of 1873, and the statute of which that was a revision, and not to the corresponding provision of the existing law which is found in section 2075 of the Code (1897). That applies in terms to street railway corporations.

Some claim is made in argument that the Sioux City Street Railway Company is a commercial, and not a street, railway company, for the reason that its franchise does not limit its operation to the city of Sioux City, and for the further reason that it is authorized to carry freight, baggage, and express matter. But we do not find anything in the record to justify the conclusion that it has done, or intends to do, any business excepting that which is usually and properly done by street railway corporations. We conclude that the demurrer to the petition was properly sustained.

II. It is shown that Belinda Marshall and William T. Parmely appeared in this action, and demurred to the petition, that their demurrers were overruled, and that they have appealed. They are the owners of judgments for personal injuries, rendered against the street railway company which are unpaid. A stipulation signed by the parties and filed in this case shows that their legal rights are the same as those of Douglas, and are to be adjudicated at this time. Therefore, what we have said applies to their respective claims. The orders of the district court as to all of the appellants are AFFIRMED.

LADD, J., took no part.

WATERMAN, J. (dissenting).—I cannot yield my assent to the construction given by the majority of the court to section 1309, Code 1873. Whatever may be said of the other portions of the act in which this section first appeared, or of its context in the Code of 1873, it must be admitted that there is nothing in the language of this particular section to restrict its meaning to any class or kind of railways. It may be conceded that when this statute was first enacted there were no street railways in Iowa, and that urban railways, as they now exist, were not within the contemplation of the most speculative member of the Ninth General Assembly. But this is not the only, or, indeed, the best test to apply in order to ascertain the legislative intent as embodied in this section. By its enactment the general assembly sought to correct an evil caused, not by a particular kind of railways, but by a certain class of mortgages, and these instruments are the same in character, whether executed by commercial or street railways. They are always for very large amounts. They cover all species of railway property, including money on hand and future earnings or profits. If they can be set

up as a bar to the satisfaction of a judgment in favor
of one who has suffered injury to person or property
through the negligence of the railway company, then
such involuntary creditor is practically denied all
relief. To say that the judgment creditor can sell, subject to the mortgage, or redeem from it, would be to
add ridicule to wrong. In this case, the mortgage debt
exceeds five hundred thousand dollars, and the judgment amounts to but three thousand five hundred dollars. This was the evil, as I view it, that the general
assembly sought to remedy by the adoption of this provision. Being remedial in its character, the section
should receive a broad and liberal construction. In
interpreting such statutes, it is said: "The old law,
the mischief, and the remedy, must be kept in mind.
That which is within the mischief intended to be remedied is considered within the statute, though not
within the letter; and that which is not within the mischief is not within the statute, though within the
letter." *Stephens v. Railroad Co.*, 36 Iowa, 327; *Haskel
v. City of Burlington*, 30 Iowa, 232; *The "Kentucky" v.
Brooks*, 1 G. Greene, 398; *Kaiser v. Seaton*, 62 Iowa,
463; 23 Am. & Eng. Enc. Law, p. 414, and cases collected. Here the railway mortgage is clearly within
the mischief, and just as clearly within the letter of this
remedial section. To restrict the statute to a particular
class of "mischief makers," rather than apply it to the
"mischief," by whomsoever done, is to adopt a narrow
and illiberal rule of construction. The fact that this
section is found in the statutes among the provisions
that relate admittedly to commercial railways only, or
that the other sections of the chapter in which it was
originally enacted could apply only to railways operated
with steam as a motive power, ought not to control us.
Cook v. Association, 74 Iowa, 746. In this case an act
of three sections was considered. The first and second
sections were general in terms. The third section, by

its language, was confined to fire insurance companies
only. But, because section 2 was remedial in character,
we held it to apply to life insurance companies also. In
Iowa Union Tel. Co. v. Board of Equalization, 67 Iowa,
250, it was held that telephone companies could be
taxed under the statutes providing for the taxation of
telegraph companies. Neither should it make any
difference, in our interpretation of the statute, that
the section has been amended by the Code so as
expressly to include mortgages-made by street railways,
for it was not the province of the Twenty-sixth General
Assembly to give a construction to existing laws that
should in any way bind this court, or even influence its
action.

II. Another thought that we may well conceive
to have been in the legislative mind when section 1309
was originally adopted is that, if these mortgages could
be used as shields to protect the railways from the consequences of their own negligence, it would take away
one of the strongest incentives such carriers have for
the exercise of diligence and care in the operation of
their roads. This consideration applies with equal force
to street railways.

We are not called upon here, in giving priority to
the judgment, to go as far as was done in the case of
City of Clinton v. Clinton & L. H. Ry. Co., *supra*, cited
by the majority. In that case a horse railway was given
the benefit of the provisions of the general right of way
act (article 3, chapter 55, Revision 1860), which according to its literal reading, seems to apply only to commercial railways. The court in that case adopted a
more liberal construction in order to confer a right than
we are willing to do in order to afford a remedy. Keeping in mind the character of this section, and the fact
that the mortgage in controversy is within both its
letter and spirit, and it seems to me impossible to

invoke any rule of law that will sustain the conclusion
of the majority. I think the judgment below should
have been REVERSED.

Augusta T. Vorse v. The Des Moines Marble and
Mantel Company, Appellant.

Landlord and Tenant: TAXES. Acts Twenty-first General Assembly,
chapter 168, sections 17, 18, provide that when the owner of any
lot, the assessments against which are embraced in a certificate
1 for street improvements, shall promise in writing on the certificates that, in consideration of the right to pay in installments, he
will waive any illegality, and will pay the same with interest, he
shall be subject to the provisions of the act authorizing such payments in installments *Held,* that where a lease of a lot provided
that the lessee would pay all assessments for street improvements
levied during the term, the lessee could not, as between him and
the lessor, extend the time of payment by executing such writing.

Same: *Maturity.* Where the assessments were made during the last
1 year of the lessee's term, it could not, by executing such promise,
evade liability for such installments after the first.

Principal and Surety. The payment by the lessor of the amount of
a street paving assessment levied against the property during the
2 term is not a condition precedent to an action by him to recover
the amount thereof from the lessee, under a provision of the lease
requiring the latter to pay such assessments, as the rule that a
surety has no right of action against his principal until he has paid
the debt, does not apply.

Same. It is not a valid objection to the right of the lessor to main-
3 tain a suit for the amount of assessments not paid by the lessee
that the lessor is not the real party in interest, because not primarily liable.

Removal of Improvements. A lease for a certain term, expiring
March 1, 1894, provided that the lessor, at the expiration of the
lease, should pay for improvements placed on the lot, what they
were reasonably worth to tear down, and for arbitration if the
parties could not agree, or the lessee might remove the improve-
4 ments. On February 1, 1894, the lessee attempted to agree with
the lessor as to the amount to be paid, and failed On February
10 the lessee asked for an arbitration. An attempt to arbitrate
extended to April 10, when, without the lessee's fault, it failed.
The lessee vacated the premises in February, and notified the
lessor of such fact, March 1, and removed such improvements

within a reasonable time after April 10, 1894. *Held*, that the lessee was not liable for rent from March 1, 1894, to the time of his removal.

Appeal from Polk District Court.—HON. W. F. CONRAD, Judge.

THURSDAY, JANUARY 27, 1898.

JANUARY 22, 1884, other parties executed a lease to a certain lot in the city of Des Moines, Iowa, to which lease the parties to this suit have succeeded in interest, the plaintiff as lessor, or party of the first part, and the defendant as lessee, or party of the second part, and a consideration of the case does not require a reference to other parties. The lease provided that the lessee should pay, aside from the annual rental, all taxes and assessments of every kind and nature, that might be assessed against said lot, including street paving and curbing, during the continuance of the lease. The term of the lease was from March 1, 1884, to March 1, 1894. During the year 1893 four assessments were made against the lot, two for curbing and two for paving. For all of such, paving certificates were issued, and on the back of each the defendant signed a written waiver and agreement, under the law for making such assessments payable in installments instead of all at one time. The first installment of the assessment was paid by defendant, March 3, 1894, but it denies any liability for the payment of the balance of the assessments, and this action is, in part, to recover such amount. Plaintiff also seeks to recover for rent after the expiration of the lease, the facts as to which can better be stated in connection with the consideration of the question. The district court gave judgment for plaintiff on both claims, and the defendant appealed.—*Modified and affirmed.*

McVey & McVey for appellant.

Davis & Davis for appellee.

GRANGER, J.—I. We notice first the question as to defendant's liability for the unpaid balance of the assessments. The facts in the case are so far stipulated that there is really no question of fact at issue. As much importance, in argument, is attached to the fact of the assessments being payable in installments, it may be well to at once consider the law on that subject, and ascertain how the assessments are affected by it. It is appellee's claim that as to her, at least, there is no such right, because she is the owner of the lot, and only the owner can, under the law, make the waiver and agreement by which such right is obtained. The following are sections 17, 18, chapter 168, Acts Twenty-first General Assembly.

"Sec. 17. Whenever the owner or owners of any lot or lots, the assessment or assessments against which is or are embraced in any such certificate, shall severally promise and agree in writing endorsed on such certificate that, in consideration of having the right to pay his or their assessment or respective assessments in installments, they will not make any objection of illegality or irregularity as to their respective assessments, and will pay the same with interest thereon, * * * he or they shall have the benefit and be subject to all the provisions of this act authorizing the payment of assessments in annual installments relating to the lien and collection and payment of assessments so far as applicable.

"Sec. 18. Any owner of any lot or lots assessed for payment of the cost of any such improvements, who will not promise and agree in writing as provided by section seventeen hereof, shall be required to pay his assessment in full, when made, and the same shall be collectible by or through any of the methods provided by law for the collection of assessments for local improvements, including the provisions of this act."

It will be seen that the right of payment by installments is not primary or absolute, but conditional, and based on an undertaking in writing to waive legal objections and pay absolutely the principal and interest. The form of agreement on the back of each certificate is as follows: "I, ————, in consideration of having the right to pay the assessment mentioned in the within certificate in installments, as provided by law, do hereby agree that I will not make any objections of illegality or irregularity as to said assessment, and that I will pay the same, with interest thereon at the rate of six per cent. per annum, and all penalties, as provided by law, from the date of said assessment." The defendant signed this agreement on each certificate, because of which a payment in full at one time was avoided and annual payments permitted. The law says the owner of the lot may make this agreement. Technically, at least, the plaintiff is the owner. It is not necessary that we should say that only the fee title owner is within the meaning of the statute, and could make such agreement and waiver. Certain it is that none other is such owner, and can make the agreement, if only the fee title owner is obligated for the payment. The effect of the agreement made by defendant was to postpone payments for which it asserts, in this suit, it is in no way liable. Because of its own act, in making the assessment payable in installments, instead of at once, it argues that the lease only contemplates payments of taxes within the years of occupancy, and not future years. The difficulty is that this assessment was all for one of the years of occupancy, and must have been paid as such, had defendant not engaged, in writing to pay it later.   If it was an assessment for 1893, payable at one time, it was, confessedly, the defendant's obligation.   That it was so, independent of defendant's agreement, admits of no doubt.   Could defendant shift the obligation by such agreement?   We do not argue the proposition.

Thus far we have considered defendant's liability without determining the significance of the word "owner" in connection with its right to make the agreement and secure the right of payment by installments. Another proposition in the case is as to the validity of the judgment for the full amount; for, in fact, when the suit was commenced, no other installment was due, and, if defendant's agreement is valid as to the plaintiff, there could be no right of recovery.   As between a lessee, liable for such assessments, and the public or a certificate holder, there are considerations that suggest a construction of the law favorable to the lessee.   There are not the same considerations as between the lessee and lessor.   This payment of assessments and taxes is in the nature of rental for the use of the lot, and we are not to assume that the amount actually to be paid is not what the parties contemplated; that is, they contracted with reference to what might or might not be done, and the amounts to be paid would be greater or less, according to the facts as to which they contracted.   There is nothing to indicate that, as between the parties to the lease, all liabilities were not to be paid, as plaintiff would have to pay them to protect her property, under the law, independent of any agreement she might make for further time.   We think a construction of the lease fixes the rights of these parties in this respect.   If this agreement of defendant's must bind plaintiff, then her property must stand subject to the lien for seven years, and her security must be the personal responsibility of defendant during that time.   We adhere to the rule

that defendant's liability for payment of assessments
was when they became due under the law, for the law
becomes a part of the lease, and all is to be considered
in reaching a conclusion. As we have said, these assessments were primarily all due and payable at one time.
Without the provision as to the agreement to waive
objection and secure time, there would be no question
that the payment must be so made. When the lease was
made, the act giving the right of payment in installments had not been enacted; but, of course, the parties
contracted with reference to the law as it would be in
relation to such assessments. We think it is not to be
properly said that the intent of the law was, in the use
of the word "owner," to give such a lessee the right to
extend the time of payments that would otherwise be
due under the terms of the lease.

II. It is urged that plaintiff cannot recover
because she has not paid the assessments. The claim
is made relying on the rule, as to principal and surety,
that a surety has no right of action against his
2   principal in respect to a debt for which he is
surety until he has paid the debt for his principal.
A different rule is applicable here; that, wherein one
party agrees not to be surety for, but to absolutely pay
the debt of, another, so that, as between the two, such
party is primarily liable. We said in *Stout v. Folger*,
34 Iowa, 71, that "the authorities agree that, upon an
undertaking to pay a debt due a third person, the plaintiff may maintain an action without showing that he
has paid the debt." See· *Bacon v. Marshall*, 37 Iowa,
581; *Lyon v. Aiken*, 70 Iowa, 16.

III. It is thought that plaintiff is not the real
party in interest, so as to maintain the suit, because
she is not the one primarily liable. The assess-
3   ment is a lien on the lot, and, if the assessment
is not paid, the lot may be sold to pay it, and it is
to protect her property that she brings the suit based

on defendant's breach of contract. Her interest is direct and enforceable.

IV. The lease contemplated that the lessee should make improvements on the lot, and at the expiration of the lease, the same should be paid for or removed. The lease expired March 1, 1894. The following is a

4   provision of the lease: "It is also herein further mutually agreed that, at the expiration of this lease, the party of the first part shall pay, for the improvements placed on said lot by the party of the second part, an amount equal to what said building or buildings shall be reasonably worth to tear down and use in the construction of a new building. If the parties hereto cannot agree as to said amount, each party shall choose a competent person, and these two a third party, the three to fix the amount to be paid, or the party of the second part may remove the said improvement from the said premises." The defendant ceased to occupy the lot in February, 1894, and on the first of March gave written notice to that effect. Its buildings, however, were not removed till June 1, 1894, and a part of the judgment is for rental from March 1 to June 1. Appellant thinks such judgment erroneous. The following facts are stipulated: "(6) That prior to the first day of February, A. D. 1894, these defendants attempted to agree with the plaintiff as to the value and reasonable worth of the buildings upon said premises, but were unable so to agree; whereupon, on the tenth day of February, 1894, these defendants gave notice to plaintiff that they wished to submit the question of reasonable worth of said buildings to competent persons for determination, as provided in said contract (Exhibit A), and further notified said plaintiff at said time that these defendants were ready and willing to name a competent person to act for them. That on the twentieth day of February these defendants and the plaintiff appointed two persons to act for them. The plaintiff

named Samuel Saucerman and the defendants Charles
Cross. That said persons could not agree upon the
worth of said building, and proceeded to choose an
umpire, or third person, and that said Saucerman
refused to consider any person other than three, to-wit,
George Garver, David Ewing, and L. M. Mann, and
said to Charles Cross that he would not consider any
other person or persons to act as umpire except these
three. That said Charles Cross submitted many names
of competent persons, and made every effort to agree
with said Saucerman on some competent person, but
was unable to do so, and finally it was agreed on the
twenty-eighth day of March that George Garver should
act as umpire, and said parties proceeded to appraise
the worth of said buildings, but did not make any report
until the tenth day of April, and, the parties hereto then
being unable to agree, these defendants determined to
remove said buildings and at once proceeded to let the
contract for the removal of said building, and said
building was removed from said premises by the first
day of June, 1894, and that said lot was entirely cleared
of said building on said last-named date. The defendants say that they vacated said premises and removed
their business therefrom prior to the fifteenth day of
February, 1894, and notified said plaintiff on the first
day of March, 1894, that they had vacated said premises." Some evidence shows the diligence used to
remove the buildings. The lease contemplates that, as
to the buildings, the parties may, first, agree as to their
value; second, they may select persons to fix the value;
and, third, the defendant might remove them. As we
understand, the time to commence this adjustment was
"at the expiration of the lease." There could be no
payment until the amount was known, and two ways
are provided for knowing it. The time of ascertainment was when payment could be required. Defendant
was no more to anticipate a failure of adjustment as to

price than was plaintiff. However, as early as February 1, it attempted to agree with plaintiff and failed. Defendant then, February 10, asked for a determination by the other method, which failed. This attempt was extended to April 10, when it proved unsuccessful, and with no fault on the part of defendant. Thus far defendant had been guilty of no breach of the terms of the lease. Beyond this, it was entitled to a reasonable time to remove the improvements. Without the provisions as to paying for the improvements, defendant would have been entitled to a reasonable time after the expiration of the lease to remove them. See *Smith v. Park*, 31 Minn. 70 (16 N. W. Rep. 490); *Sullivan v. Carberry*, 67 Me. 531. The rule is a familiar one. Because of the provisions as to agreeing upon the amount to be paid, if defendant was not in fault because of delays in trying to agree, he would be entitled to a reasonable time for removal after there was a failure to agree. The lease does not provide that such things should be done before the expiration of the lease, nor does it provide for rent after such expiration, and the law does not fix such a right, unless the delay is unreasonable. The rule stated in section 22, 1 Taylor, Landlords and Tenants, is not in point. There the tenant was holding over because his improvements were not paid for. Here there was no holding over in such a sense, but merely an occupancy for the removal of improvements, under the terms of the lease. The judgment will be modified to conform to this holding, and, thus modified, it will stand affirmed. The plaintiff will pay her own costs in this court and the cost of defendant's witnesses in the court below.— AFFIRMED.

John McWhirter, Appellant, v. John Crawford.

Sales on Contract: FORFEITURE. A vendor in a contract to convey land subject to the dower interest of his wife, cannot insist upon a forfeiture for non-payment of the purchase price, where, before the date of payment, he had put it out of his power to comply on his part with the terms of the contract by conveying an undivided one-third interest in fee to his wife.

Tender: SPECIFIC PERFORMANCE. An offer by a purchaser in his cross-petition praying the specific performance of the contract, to pay the amount found due, is sufficient, where the vendor, at the time the tender was due, was insisting that the contract was forfeited, and had put it out of his power to perform by conveying an interest in the property to another.

SAME. The failure of the vendor to object to the amount tendered by a purchaser at the time thereof, does not prevent him from subsequently making the objection, under Code 1873, section 2107, providing that the person to whom a tender is made must, at the time, make any objections which he may have to the money tendered or he will be deemed to have waived them, as the phrase "objection to money" refers to the character or kind of money, and not to the amount.

Estoppels: SALES: *Fraud.* A vendor is estopped to claim fraud in the inception of the contract where, with full knowledge of all the facts relied on to constitute the fraud, he accepted the note secured by mortgage as part of the purchase price and received the payment of interest and principal.

SAME. A vendor's acceptance of payments on the price, long after the contract was made, and with full knowledge of all the facts, estops him from urging fraud on the vendee's part in procuring the contract.

Costs: ESTOPPEL. The appellee is taxable with the costs of his amendment to appellant's abstract, although the judgment is affirmed, where the abstract prepared and filed by the appellant contained everything necessary to the full understanding of the questions raised, and the amendment did not aim to correct it or made it complete, but is an independent abstract of all the evidence, about one-half being devoted to questions and answers printed in full.

Appeal: RELIEF. The relief granted on appeal will not be more favorable to a party who does not appeal than the judgment below.

Appeal from Jefferson District Court.—Hon. W. D. Tisdale, Judge.

Wednesday, October 13, 1897.

The plaintiff entered into a written contract for the sale of one hundred and forty-eight and two-thirds acres of land to the defendant at the price of twelve dollars and fifty cents per acre. The purchase price was to draw interest at the rate of six per cent. per annum, payable annually, and two-thirds of it was to be paid within five years. The remaining one-third was to be paid on the death of plaintiff's wife in the event she died before he did. Time was of the essence of the contract. The defendant having failed to pay the annual interest, this action was begun April 8, 1890, to declare a forfeiture. Thereafter the defendand filed an amendment to his cross-petition, asking that specific performance be decreed. On the same day the plaintiff amended his petition by alleging that the contract was procured through fraud, and asking its cancellation on that ground. Decree was entered ordering that the contract be performed, and plaintiff appeals. —*Affirmed.*

Leggett & McKemey for appellant.

Raney & Simmons for appellee.

Ladd, J.—As the contract of sale was fully ratified and confirmed after its execution, inquiry as to whether there was fraud in its inception is unnecessary. The plaintiff accepted a note of five hundred dollars, secured by mortgage, as part of the purchase price, nearly three months after the date of the contract; and payment of this note a year later. He also received the annual interest in February, 1889.

These payments were received without objection,
and there is no showing that the alleged fraud was
undiscovered. The plaintiff will not be permitted to
avail himself of the benefits of the contract, and at the
same time insist that he is not bound thereby because
procured through fraud. The receipt of the payments
with full knowledge of all the facts estops him from
urging its invalidity.

II. The tender of sixty-nine dollars and fifty cents
in payment of the interest due February 20, 1890, is
now conceded to have been insufficient in amount. The

2   three dollars claimed on account of road tax
was not chargeable to the plaintiff; and this,—
without entering into the controversy with reference to the nine dollars retained on the claim that
plaintiff took growing timber, instead of that upon the
ground,—rendered the tender inadequate. It is not a
case of mistake in computation, but the deliberate
retention of a part of the payment due, on a groundless
claim.

III. The plaintiff, however, has put it beyond
his power to comply on his part with the terms of the
tract, and is not in a situation to insist upon a forfeiture. He executed a quit-claim deed conveying an
undivided one-third of the land to his wife, November 6,
1889. By the terms of the agreement the land "is sold
subject to the dower interest of Catherine M.
McWhirter, and it is agreed that one-third of said purchase money shall not be due until the death of the said
Catherine M. McWhirter; and in case of the death of
John McWhirter, the grantor herein, prior to the death
of his said wife, then she can claim one-third of the said
purchase price as her one-third interest in said land, at
her option." The deed to his wife places it beyond his
power to give defendant title to one-third of the land in
the event of her death before his demise. This was a
part of the contract; and, having deprived himself of the

power to carry out its terms, he is not in a situation to
complain of the breach thereof on the part of the
defendant. If the wife should die first, without conveying the land, the plaintiff would inherit but one-
third of the one-third in event she left children, and one-
half of the one-third in event there were none. The law
presumes that every person leaves heirs, until the contrary appears. In the case of any vendor conveying
land there is a possibility of his again procuring title
so as to be able to comply with his contract, but this
does no obviate the rule that in such cases he will not
be permitted to insist on strict performance of the contract by the vendee.

IV.   Is the defendant entitled to specific performance of the contract as prayed in the amendment to his
petition filed January 25, 1894? He tendered seven hundred and fifty-one dollars and eight-four cents as the
amount due on the contract February 4, 1890,
4   and this was inadequate. Why he did not tender
the full amount, does not clearly appear, and no
excuse is offered for failing to do so. It is insisted that
for this reason he is not entitled to an order of specific
performance. At the time of the tender no objection
was made. Under the Revision of 1860, this would
prove fatal to any objection now. *Hayward v. Munger*,
14 Iowa, 516; *Guengerich v. Smith*, 36 Iowa, 587; *Sheriff
v. Hull*, 37 Iowa, 174. But under the Code of 1873 this
sentence contained in section 1818 of the Revision is
omitted: "And if the objection be to the amount of
money, the terms of the instrument, or the amount or
kind of property, he must specify the amount, terms or
kind which he requires, or be precluded from objecting
afterward." The section, as it now stands, reads: "The
person to whom a tender is made, must, at the time,
make any objection which he may have to the money,
instrument, or property tendered, or he will be deemed
to have waived it." Section 2107, Code 1873. The

clause "objection to money" was construed in *Chicago & S. W. R. Co. v. Northwestern Union Packet Co.*, 38 Iowa, 377, to refer to the character or kind of money, and not to the amount. The tender must, therefore, be held insufficient upon which to base a demand for the deed.

V. The cross-petition, however, offers to pay the amount found to be due. The plaintiff was at that time insisting that the contract be forfeited; and upon its cancellation. Under such circumstances, it is not reasonable to suppose that a tender, if made, would have been of any efficacy. The law will not indulge in idle formalities. It has been repeatedly held that, where a vendor of real property has conveyed to another after entering into a contract of sale, the purchaser may maintain his action without first tendering the purchase price. *Watson v. White*, 152 Ill. Sup. 364 (38 N. E. Rep. 902; *Collins v. Vandever*, 1 Iowa, 573; *Laverty v. Hall's Adm'x*, 19 Iowa, 526; *Auxier v. Taylor*, 102 Iowa, 673. In *Sheplar v. Green*, 95 Cal. 218 (31 Pac. Rep. 42), it was held that, where the vendor brought an action to quiet title without first tendering the deed, the purchaser may maintain an action on his cross-petition for specific performance, without having previously tendered the purchase price. See Pomeroy, Specific Performance, section 361. The plaintiff, in asking that the contract be forfeited, is presumed to have done so in good faith, and, if so, a tender of the purchase price would have been useless. Every purpose was fully subserved by offering performance in the pleading. Decree will be entered ordering the plaintiff to file with the clerk of the district court a good and sufficient warranty deed conveying an undivided two-thirds of this land to the defendant within sixty days from the filing of this opinion, and that the defendant pay into the hands of such clerk, for the use of the plaintiff, the sum of seven hundred and thirty-two dollars and twenty-two cents, with interest at the rate of six per cent. per annum from February 20, 1889, within thirty days thereafter; and, in event of his failure to do so, the contract shall stand canceled. Should plaintiff fail to deposit the deed as herein directed, then drawing of interest shall cease until thirty days after he has done so, and has notified the defendant in writing.

VI. The appellant prepared and filed an abstract of twenty-six pages, in strict accord with the rules of this court,—a model in point of brevity and concise-ness, and yet containing everything essential to a full understanding of the questions raised. Thereupon, the defendant filed what he is pleased to call an "amendment to the abstract" of seventy-seven pages, but which does not aim to correct or make complete that of the appellant. It is an independent abstract of all the evidence, about one-half of which is devoted to questions and answers printed in full. There may be something in this volume necessary to be set out, but very little. Heed must be given by litigants to the rules of this court. The motion to tax the costs of the amendment to the abstract to the appellee is sustained.—AFFIRMED.

SUPPLEMENTAL OPINION ON REHEARING.

THURSDAY, JANUARY 27, 1898.

PER CURIAM.—The appellant has called our attention to the fact that by the decree of the district court the appellee was required to pay, in order to obtain a deed, the balance of the purchase price of two-thirds of the land, being seven hundred and thirty-eight dollars

and eighty-eight cents, together with the interest
thereon, and on the contract price of the remain-
7   ing one-third, being six hundred and nineteen dollars and forty-five cents, at the rate of six per
cent. per annum, with annual rests from February 20,
1889. As the defendant did not appeal, the relief granted
here will not be more favorable to him. Without inquiring what the rule would be, had the correctness of the
result been questioned, the opinion heretofore filed will
be so far modified as to require the defendant to pay
seven hundred and thirty-eight dollars and eighty-eight
cents, together with interest on one thousand three hundred and fifty-eight dollars and thirty-three cents, at
the rate of six per cent. per annum, with annual rests,
from February 20, 1889, instead of the amount therein
named.

LEONARD MARSH v. NETTIE CHOWN AND O. D. CHOWN,
Appellants.

Advancements: CONSIDERATION. An advancement made by a parent
1   to his child constitutes no consideration for a promissory note
subsequently executed by the latter to the former.

PAROL EVIDENCE. Parol evidence is admissible to show that a note
from a child to his father, which is still held by the latter, and
given as a mere receipt for an advancement previously made to
2   the maker, under Code 1873, section 2114, providing that the want
of consideration for the written contract may be shown as a
defense, except as to negotiable paper transferred in good faith
and for a valuable consideration before maturity. *Distinguishing
Bank v. Felt,* 100 Iowa, 680; 69 N. W. Rep. 1057; *Dickinson v. Harris,* 60 Iowa, 727; *Atherton v. Dearmond,* 33 Iowa, 853; *Barhydt v.
Benney,* 55 Iowa, 717; *Mason v. Mason,* 72 Iowa, 457.

Pleading: STRIKING OFF: *Discretion.* Where at the close of the evidence, defendant filed a fourth amendment to his answer, largely
3   repeating what he had previously alleged, it was not an abuse of
discretion to strke it out.

Appeal from Tama District Court.—HON. G. W. BURN-HAM, Judge.

THURSDAY, JANUARY 27, 1898.

THIS is an action at law for judgment on six promissory notes executed by the defendants to the plaintiff. Defendants filed an answer in two counts, an "amended answer" in three counts, an "amendment to amended answer" in three counts, an "additional amendment to amended answer" in four counts, and at the close of the evidence an "amendment to their answer" in four paragraphs, which last amendment the court struck from the files. These several pleadings are of great length, covering about fourteen closely printed pages, and so abound in repetition that it is difficult to gather therefrom the precise defense relied upon. The court might very properly have required the defendants to file a substituted answer, and thereby avoid the confusion that arises from these numerous amendments. The defendants admit the execution of the promissory notes sued upon, and, as we gather from their answer and amendments, allege the following defenses: That the defendant Nettie Chown is the daughter of the plaintiff, and wife of the defendant O. D. Chown, and that the amounts represented by said notes were given to the defendants as advancements made by the plaintiff to his daughter under an agreement that the same were to stand as an advancement to her out of the estate of plaintiff; that said promissory notes were executed long after said advancements were made, and under an agreement that they were to stand as mere receipts to show the amount of said advancements. As another defense it is alleged that, in consideration of said advancements, and that the said amounts should stand

as such, and said notes as mere receipts therefor, defendants agreed to take and keep the plaintiff during his
life, and make a home for him, and that in pursuance of
said agreement defendants moved from their home in
Western Iowa, to West Irving, Tama county, at the
request of the plaintiff, and at great expense to defendants, and did keep and care for the plaintiff, and are
now, and always since have been, willing to do so, but
that shortly before the commencement of this suit,
plaintiff, without cause, left the home of defendants;
that defendants are willing to carry out their part of
said conract. As a defense to the note for one thousand
dollars, identified as Exhibit B, defendants allege that
in October, 1889, the plaintiff purchased certain real
estate in Tama county, and had the title made to his
said daughter; that he paid part of the purchase money
for said land, which was intended as an advancement
to his said daughter, and that long after, at plaintiff's
request, defendants executed said note simply to show
the amount of said advancements, and that defendants
took and retained possession of said land. Defendants
alleged that said several agreements were partly oral
and partly in writing, the written portion consisting of
letters, which letters are lost or destroyed, or in the
hands and under the control of the plaintiff. Defendants, by way of counter-claim, ask to recover one thousand dollars for board, lodging and washing furnished
to the plaintiff during the years 1889 to 1893, inclusive.
Plaintiff's demurrer "to first and second counts of
defendant's amendment to amended answer as
amended, and to original answer, and to the first, second, and third counts of amended answer," was sustained. Plaintiff, in reply, denies every allegation of
said answer as amended, except expressly admitted.
He admits that defendant furnished him with board,
and did part of his washing during a part of the year
1889, and all of the years 1890 to 1893, inclusive. He

avers that the board and washing done in 1889 was for
him as a member of defendants' family, and in consideration of the use of plaintiff's house, in which the family resided, and labor and services performed by the
plaintiff for defendants. Also, that the board, lodging, and washing done during 1890 to 1893, inclusive,
was by virtue of a special written contract set out. The
case was tried to a jury, and a verdict returned for the
defendants upon their counter-claim in the sum of
five hundred dollars, and in favor of the plaintiff for
one thousand seven hundred and twenty-five dollars.
Defendants' motion for a new trial being overruled,
judgment was entered upon the verdict, from which the
defendants appeal.—*Reversed.*

J. J. Mosnat for appellants.

Struble & Stiger for appellee.

GIVEN, J.—I. Appellants' first complaint is of the
ruling of the court sustaining appellee's demurrer to
the answer and amendments. The answer and amendments demurred to alleged that the several amounts
shown in the notice were given to and received by appellant Nettie Chown, from the plaintiff, her father, under
an agreement that the same was an advancement to her,
by her father, in anticipation of her share in his estate.
Also, that said notes were executed long after said
advancements had been made and received, and as mere
receipts to show the amounts advanced, and that said
agreements were partly in parol and partly in writing,
by letters, which have been lost, or are in the possession
of the plaintiff. The question raised by the demurrer is
whether these allegations showed a defense, or, in

other words, whether evidence thereof is admissible to
defeat a recovery upon the notes. Appellee con-
1   tends that the promise contained in the notes
cannot be varied by prior, or contemporaneous
arrangements in parol, or partly in parol and partly
in writing. He contends that, as the answer shows that
the alleged agreements that these sums should stand as
advancements, and that the notes should be as mere
receipts, was partly in parol and partly in writing, the
plea is as if the agreements were all in parol, and constitute no defense. Appellants contend that an
advancement is an irrevocable gift in anticipation of
the share of the heir in the estate; that it becomes the
absolute property of the one to whom it is given; that
it does not create an indebtedness, cannot be recovered
back, and, therefore, did not constitute a consideration
for the execution of the promissory notes. *In re Miller's
Will*, 73 Iowa, 123, this court says as follows: "An
advancement is an irrevocable gift in anticipation of
the share of the heir in the estate. *In re Lyon's Estate*
70 Iowa, 375. What is given as an advancement
becomes the absolute property of the child to whom the
advancement is made. The father has no claim upon it,
and cannot recover it. Neither has he any claim against
the child in the nature of a debt. He can bring no
action against the child on account of the gift and
advancement." The authorities are uniformly to the
same effect, and it is, therefore, clear that an advancement previously given and received constitutes no consideration for a promissory note subsequently executed.
Now, while it is the law that an express promise in writing, such as these promissory notes contain, cannot be
varied by prior or contemporaneous agreements in
parol, or partly in parol, yet the consideration of such

notes in the hands of the payee may be questioned.
Section 2114 of the Code of 1873 is as follows:
2   "The want or failure, in whole or in part, of the
consideration of a written contract, may be
shown as a defense, total or partial, as the case may be,
except to negotiable paper transferred in good faith,
and for a valuable consideration, before maturity."
Section 3070, present Code. See, also, *Bank v. Felt*, 100
Iowa, 680. *Dickson v. Harris,* 60 Iowa, 727, cited by
appellee, is not in point, inasmuch as in that case the
promissory note sued upon was executed at the time
the money was received, and the defense set up was
that the money was to be carried to Iowa, and applied in
satisfaction of a judgment against the plaintiff's son,
and that it was so applied. The defense was not a
want of consideration, but of a contemporaneous agreement as to the application of the money received. *Atherton v. Dearmond*, 33 Iowa, 353, and *Barhydt v. Bonney*,
55 Iowa, 717, also cited, are not applicable, or in point.
Mason v. Mason, 72 Iowa, 457, was an action upon a
promissory note, to which defendant pleaded want of
consideration, based upon this state of facts: That his
father was having a public sale, and was about to sell
a cow that defendant claimed; that the father said to
defendant to buy all the stock he wanted at the sale; to
give his note for it; that he had not given him any
money to make him equal with the rest, and that he
wanted to show that defendant had had that much
money advanced. Defendant bid in property, and, at the
time, and as a part of the transaction, executed the notes
sued upon. It was held that evidence of a parol agreement that the notes should be held as a mere receipt was
not admissible, citing *Dickson v. Harris, supra.* The
court says: "It may be, if a parent should make an
advancement to a child, and actually deliver the money
or property advanced, and, after thus fully executing
the gift, he should take a promissory note, the note

would be void, as being wholly without consideration. It would be a transaction independent of the gift, in that the gift was fully executed. But that is not the question presented in this case. The defendant bid upon the property and it was sold to him, the same as it was to other bidders, and he gave his note the same as other purchasers, and all that was done was, in effect, one transaction. He gave the note when the property was delivered to him." It will be observed that in that case the agreement alleged was in advance of the purchase at the sale, and was a promise to make an advancement, while in this the advancements are alleged to have been made and received prior and independent of the execution of these notes. It is argued that what we have quoted last above was not involved in *Mason's Case*, and, therefore, is mere dicta. It is, nevertheless, the announcement of a rule grounded in equity and reason. *In re Lyon's Estate, supra*, is not in point, for the reason that the question of consideration was not involved, as in this case. Accepting the allegation of the answer that these several amounts were given and received as advancements prior to the execution of the notes, it seems to us clear that they did not constitute a consideration for the giving of the notes, and that, the notes still being in the hands of the original payee, the defendants may, under the statute quoted above, plead and prove a want of consideration, in whole, or in part, by agreements in parol as alleged. Our conclusion is that the parts of the answer and amendments demurred to show a valid defense, and that the demurrer should have been overruled.

II. Appellants complain that the court struck their amendment to their answer filed after the close of the evidence. Whether or not said amendment should be allowed was discretionary with the court, and

3   we do not think the court abused its discretion.

The proposed amendment was largely a repetition of matters that had already been repeated, and, in view of the complication of answers, the court might very well refuse this additional amendment.

Appellants' further complaints are as to instructions with reference to the amounts to be considered. As, for the reasons already given, the judgment of the district court must be reversed, and as the matters complained of as to these instructions need not occur upon a re-trial, we do not consider them. For the error in sustaining appellee's demurrer to the answer and amendments, the judgment of the district court is REVERSED.

A. B. Beem, Administrator, Appellant, v. The Tama AND Toledo Electric Railway and Light Company.

104
106
10
11
1
104
129
104
132
104
d143

Contributory Negligence: EVIDENCE: *Railroads.* Decedent was seventy-one years old, and quite deaf. A few minutes before the

1 accident occurred, he was walking along the street, parallel to, and a short distance from, a railway track. He turned to cross

2 the track, and was struck by the cars, and was killed He did not look toward the approaching train, although he could have seen it for a distance of five hundred and fifty feet. The train was running at a higher rate of speed than allowed by the city. *Held* not to warrant a finding that the decedent was free from contributory negligence.

SAME. Contributory negligence by a person killed by a street car is sufficiently established by evidence that he was deaf and that he

1 could not have failed to discover the approaching car if he had looked in the direction from which it came, before attempting to cross the track.

CARE OF EMPLOYE: *Presumption* One in charge of a street car has the right to presume that one walking along the side of a track

2 will exercise the caution which a person of ordinary prudence

would exercise and will not attempt to cross the track immediately in front of a car, until there is reasonable ground for concluding that he may do so

Appeal from Tama District Court.—HON. G. W. BURN-HAM, Judge.

FRIDAY, JANUARY 28, 1898.

ACTION at law to recover for injuries to the plaintiff's intestate, which caused his death, and which are alleged to have been the result of negligence on the part of the defendant. When the evidence on the part of the plaintiff had been fully submitted, the jury, by direction of the court, returned a verdict for the defendant, and judgment was rendered in its favor for costs. The plaintiff appeals.—*Affirmed.*

T. Brown for appellant.

Struble & Stiger for appellee.

ROBINSON, J.—In September of the year 1895, the defendant was engaged in operating an electric railway between points in Toledo and Tama. The railway passed through a portion of McClellan street, which extends from north to south, over a ridge. At a point from four hundred to five hundred feet south of the crest of the ridge, McClellan street is intersected by Brice street, which extends from east to west. On the twelfth day of the month named, A. B. Beem, the decedent, was struck by a train of the defendant in McClellan street, at a point north of, but near Brice street, and received injuries which caused his death within a short time. The train in question was composed of a freight car and an electric motor behind it. The plaintiff alleges that the defendant was negligent in operating its train with the freight car in front of the motor, in not having a person on the car to keep a

lookout for persons on the track, in not having the car
supplied with a brake, in running the train at a higher
rate of speed than was permitted by the ordinance of the
city of Tama, in which the accident occurred, and in
not stopping the train after the peril of the decedent
was known, and before he was struck. The evi-
1   dence for the plaintiff shows the following facts:
At the time of the accident the decedent was
seventy-one years of age and quite deaf. A few moments
before the collision, he was seen to be walking southward on McClellan street, parallel to, and a short distance east of, the railway track. Just before the collision occurred, he turned, and walked in a southwest-
erly direction, to cross the track, and was then struck.
He is not shown to have looked towards the approaching train, although he could have seen it for a distance
of five hundred and fifty feet before it reached the
place of the accident. He resides west of the railway
track, and not far from the place where he was hurt.
The grade of the railway descended from the crest of
the ridge southward, and, although the evidence as to
the speed of the train is not satisfactory, it may be conceded that the jury would have been justified in finding that it was greater than the city ordinance permitted, and that the accident was due in part to negligence on the part of the defendant. It remains to be
determined whether the jury would have been authorized to find that the decedent was free from negligence
which contributd to the accident. It is true, as contended by the appellant, that it is the duty of persons
in charge of a street car to be watchful and diligent to
avoid doing injury to others, but persons who cross
street railway tracks also have duties to perform. They
cannot assume that, without care on their part, they
will be seen, and protected from harm, and the car
stopped, if necessary, to avoid a collision. They are not,
as a rule, required to use the same degree of care as

would be required if they were about to cross an ordinary commercial railway track. *Orr v. Railway Co.*, 94 Iowa, 426. But street cars are usually operated according to established time schedules, and their efficiency and value to the public demand that they be so operated. To require, whenever a person approach the track, that they be stopped, or the speed slackened, until it is evident that the person will not be endangered by the running of the cars, would be to impose a serious, and, in many cases, an intolerable burden upon the railway corporation, and subject its patrons to annoying and injurious delays, without any substantial reason for so doing, or benefit of importance to any one. Ordinarily, a pedestrian who approaches a street railway track may, and does, without appreciable effort or loss of time, ascertain if a car be near, and it is his duty to do so. *Fenton v. Railroad Co.*, 126 N. Y. 625 (26 N. E. Rep. 967); *Fleckstein v. Railway*, 105 N. Y. 655 (11 N. E. Rep. 951); *Adolph v. Railroad Co.*, 76 N. Y. 530; *Schwartz v. Railway Co.*, 30 La. Ann. 16; *Buzby v. Traction Co.*, 126 Pa. St. 559 (17 Atl. Rep. 895.)

The only conclusion which can reasonably be drawn from the evidence in this case, is that the decedent did not take any precaution to avoid the accident. Although he was unable to hear readily, and therefore should have been more diligent to discover the approach of the train by the sense of sight, he could not have looked in the direction of the car when about to cross the track. There is no room for the presumption which arises in some cases, that the natural instincts of the decedent led him to use reasonable care to avoid the accident. The evidence clearly shows that he could not have done so without avoiding it. It may be (although it is not shown) that the employe in charge of the train, saw the deceased while he was walking southward, near the track; but, if so, the employe had no reason to suppose that the decedent would turn towards, and attempt to cross, the track, without looking for and avoiding the train. Until there was reasonable ground for concluding that he might do so, the employe had the right to rely upon the presumption that he would exercise the caution which a person of ordinary prudence would have exercised. It is not shown that when the decedent turned toward the railroad track, to cross it, the car could have been stopped in time to avoid the collision. On the contrary, it is clear that the car could not then have been stopped before it occurred. We conclude that the evidence would not have authorized a recovery by the plaintiff, and the verdict was, therefore, properly directed for the defendant. The judgment of the district court is AFFIRMED.

JULIA A. POLK v. FRED McCARTNEY, *et al.*, Appellants.

Public Improvements: HIGHWAYS: *Notice.* A public notice for bids for a street improvement is fatally defective where it fails to state when the work is to be done and the proposals acted upon, as
8   required by Acts Twenty-third General Assembly, chapter 14, section 8, and does not specify the "extent of the work," as required by the section, except that it states that the work is to be done on certain "alleys" in a block, it appearing that the municipal authorities did not correctly understand what was included in the terms "alleys."

Limitation of Actions: CERTIORARI. The limitation prescribed by Code 1873, section 3224, providing that no writ of *certiorari* shall be granted after twelve months have elapsed from the time the
1   board has, as alleged, exceeded its proper jurisdiction, does not commence to run against the writ complaining of a street paving assessment until the assessment is made, although the objections to the assessment are based on the irregularities in the preliminary proceedings.

Appeal: REVIEW. The finding of the district court that a so-called
2   street was actually a street, and did not come within the term "alley" in a street paving resolution, is conclusive upon the supreme court on appeal, at law, on conflicting evidence.

Appeal from Polk District Court.—HON. W. F. CONRAD,
Judge.

FRIDAY, JANUARY 28, 1898.

THE defendants, except the treasurer of Polk
county, constitute the city council of Des Moines,
Iowa. The petition shows that the plaintiff is
the owner of lots 7 and 8 in block 3, in the original
town of Fort Des Moines, now a part of the city of
Des Moines; "that said council exceeded its jurisdiction in this: that on the tenth day of October, 1893,
at a session of said council, an order was made
by said council assessing against said lot seven (7),
the sum of three hundred and seventy-two dollars and
thirty-two cents ($372.32), and against said lot eight
(8) the sum of ninety-nine dollars and twenty-eight
cents ($99.28), as a special assessment against said
property, as its proportionate share of the cost of paving Plum street, in said city, which abuts on said lot
seven (7), and the cost of paving the alley running
north and south through said block three (3);" that the
paving on said street and alley, and for which the
assessment was made, was done under a pretended contract between the city of Des Moines and M. H. King;
that said contract did not embrace Plum street, and
there was no contract, or pretended contract, with said
city, for the paving of Plum street, and the same was
paved without authority; that there never was any
resolution of the council of said city that said Plum
street should be paved; that, by the terms of said pretended contract, the cost of keeping said paving in
repair for five years was included in the contract price,
and was assessed against the abutting property; and
that there was no advertisement for bids, as required by
law, for said improvement. The petition asks that a

writ of *certorairi* issue, and that, upon the hearing, the proceedings as to the levy and assessments be annulled and held for nought, and that a writ of injunction issue to restrain the collection of the tax. The return to the writ shows the proceedings of the council in the premises, the particulars of which may be noticed in the opinion. The issues were upon the petition and return, and additional evidence was taken. At the conclusion of the hearing, the court gave judgment for plaintiff, and the defendants appealed.—*Affirmed.*

J. K. Macomber for appellants.

J. S. Polk and *St. John & Stevenson* for appellee.

GRANGER, J.—I. The point is first presented that this case is barred by the statute of limitation. The chapter of the Code of 1873 providing for the proceedings by writ of *certiorari* contains a section as follows:

1   "Sec. 3224. No writ shall be granted after twelve months have elapsed from the time the inferior court, tribunal, board, or officer has, as alleged, exceeded his proper jurisdiction, or has otherwise acted illegally." The resolution ordering the pavement in question was passed by the city council April 7, 1893, and the petition in this action was filed August 11, 1894, being more than twelve months after the passage of the resolution. It is, however, said by appellee, that the act of which she complains is the act by which the assessment was made, and not the passage of the resolution authorizing the paving. *Shepard v. Supervisors*, 72 Iowa, 258, is a like case in principle. In that case, the board of supervisors had ordered a ditch dug, under the provisions of the statute, to be paid for by an assessment on real estate benefited thereby. The action was to annul the

assessment and levy because of defects in the proceeding, by which the making of the ditch was authorized.
The question of the statute of limitation arose in that
case, and it is held that as the action was to set aside
the assessment and levy, and not the order for making
the ditch, the action was commenced in time, it not
being one year from the date of the assessment and levy,
although more than one year from the making of the
order for constructing the ditch. Looking to the petition in this case, we find it is the same,—that the court
is asked to set aside the proceedings as to the assessment. While it is true, that such a result must be based
on the invalidity of the former acts, it is no more so
than it was in the cited case; and it seems to be a
conclusive authority against appellants' claim in this
case. The cases seem to be alike in every essential
particular for the purposes of this question.

II. The court made, among others, the following
findings: "(2) That the street running east and west
through said block three (3), and on which said lot seven
(7) abuts, is Plum street, and is not properly
2   designated as an alley. (3) That there was never
any resolution of the city council that Plum
street be paved, and the resolution of date April 17,
1893, of the city council, does not refer to or embrace
said Plum street; and the same was not contained in any
notice to bidders, nor in any contract therefor, and the
same was paved wholly without authority." The resolution passed by the council was for paving alleys in
block 3, of the original town of Ft. Des Moines. The
record contains a plat of said block, showing streets
and alleys, and the strip in controversy is designated
"Plum street," and appears to be thirty-three feet
wide; while streets around the block are sixty-six feet
wide, and alleys are marked sixteen and one-half feet
wide. Evidence was taken as to the condition and use
of the strip, how it was kept, and the kind of property

located along it. It was from this evidence that the court found that it was not an alley, but a street. The finding, numbered 3, that Plum street was not included in the resolution for paving, nor contained in the notice to bidders, nor in any contract, is, as we understand, based on the facts found, that it was actually a street, and so recognized, and did not come within the term, "alleys in block 3, town of Fort Des Moines," that being the term used in the resolution, notice, and contract. The evidence is in decided conflict, and the finding of the district court is conclusive upon us. It stands as the verdict of a jury. *Remey v. Board,* 80 Iowa, 470; Code, 1873, section 3223.

III. The court made the following finding: "(4) That the notice to bidders contained in the return herein, and shown in the evidence, is not such notice as is contemplated by law, in that it does not 3 · invite bids for the paving of Plum street, and does not state as nearly as practicable or otherwise the extent of the work, when the work shall be done, or what time the proposals shall be acted upon." The following is section 3, chapter 14, Acts Twenty-third General Assmbly: "Sec. 3. All such contracts shall be made by the council or the board of public works when such board shall exist, in the name of the city, and shall be made with the lowest bidder or bidders, upon sealed proposals, after public notice for not less than ten days, in at least two newspapers of said city, which notice shall state as nearly as practicable the extent of the work, the kind of materials to be furnished, when the work shall be done, and at what time the proposals shall be acted upon." The only language in the notice that could be construed as an attempt at compliance with the prescribed notice is the following: "Brick paving, consisting of two courses of brick on sand foundation, with top filling as described on pages 9 and 10 of specifications." In another part of the notice it appears that plans and specifications are on file in the office of the board of public works. The provisions of the law quoted are mandatory, and their observance is a condition precedent to the right of the council to make contracts in pursuance of them. The notice is fatally defective. The requirements as to "when the work shall be done," and "what time the proposals shall be acted upon," are absolutely disregarded. There is not a reference to either in the notice, and, if the notice could be aided by the plans and specifications, it is to be said there is no reference to either of them. The same is true as to the "extent of the work," except the words in the notice, "alleys in block three (3), town of Fort Des Moines." The plans and specifications contain no reference to the place, nor to the extent of the work. Even an inspection of the block itself would not disclose it, for, as we have seen in another division of the opinion, the fact of what were, and what were not, alleys, was not understood by the council. See *Coggeshall v. City of Des Moines*, 78 Iowa, 235. See, also, *Osburn v. City of Lyons*, 104 Iowa, 160. These holdings render it unimportant to consider some other questions argued, for they seem conclusive of the case. The judgment of the district court will stand AFFIRMED.

572|
466|
MARY E. CARRIER v. BERNSTEIN BROTHERS, ADOLPH BERNSTEIN, and CHARLES BERNSTEIN, Appellants.

Intoxicating Liquors: MISJOINDER OF CAUSES. Under Code 1873, section 2630, providing that "causes of action of whatever kind, where each may be prosecuted by the same kind of proceedings, provided that they be by the same party, and against the same party, in the same rights, and if suit on all may be brought and tried in that county, may be joined in the same petition," in an
1   action for damages for the sale of intoxicating liquors, where the wife, in one count of the petition, sues as such, under section 1557, allowing her to recover actual damages and exemplary

damages for injury to her person, property, and means of support, caused by sales of intoxicating liquors, to her husband, whereby he was rendered intoxicated, and where in another count, she sues as a citizen of the county and an informer, under section 1539, which provided that persons who sell intoxicating liquors to intoxicated persons or habitual drunkards, shall be liable to a certain forfeit for each offense, to be collected in an action brought by any citizen in the county, one-half of said amount to go to the informer, there was a misjoinder of causes of action, since they v ere not in the same right nor to be brought by the same plaintiff.

ACTION FOR PENALTY: *Venue*   Under Code 1873, section 1539, providing that persons who sell intoxicating liquors to intoxicated persons or habitual drunkards, shall forfeit a certain sum for each offense, to the school fund of the county, to be collected in an action brought by any citizen in the county, one-half of said amount to go to the informer, such action need not be brought in the county where the liquor was sold

MULCT LAW: *Bar.*   Under section 19 of such law, providing that "whenever any of the conditions of this act shall be violated * * * the bar to proceedings as provided in section 17 hereof
2   shall cease to operate as a bar," where defendant sold intoxicating liquors to plaintiff's husband' causing him to become intoxicated, idle, profligate, and neglectful of his business, and so as to impair him in body and mind, and render him unable to obtain remunerative employment, to plaintiff's damage, there was a violation of the mulct law, and the bar ceased to operate.

SAME.   Compliance with Act Twenty-fifth General Assembly, chapter 62, known as the mulct law, is not a defense to an action by a a wife, under Code 1873, section 1557, for damages for injury to her means of support caused by means of the illegal sale of intoxicating liquor to her husband, or to an action under section 1539 for the penalty for selling intoxicating liquor to an intoxicated person, or to one in the habit of becoming intoxicated.

PURCHASE BY THIRD PERSON.   In an action by a wife, under Code 1873, section 1557, for damages for the sale of intoxicating liquors
5   to her husband, the fact that the liquor drank by the husband was bought by other persons, does not preclude a recovery

PLEA AND PROOF.   The averment in a petition in an action to recover damages for the statutory penalty for illegal sales of intoxicating
8   liquor, that the sales were made in the spring and summer of a certain year, is sufficiently definite as to time.

SAME.   Evidence that sales were made by the defendant's employes is
4   admissible under the averment in a petition for damages, or for the statutory penalty prescribed for the illegal sale of liquor, that the defendant sold the liquor.

Appeal from Marshall District Court.—Hon. S. M. Weaver, Judge.

FRIDAY, JANUARY 28, 1898.

THE plaintiff, a citizen and resident of Marshall county, Iowa, and wife of John Carrier, filed her petition, in two counts, to recover from the defendants for alleged sales of intoxicating liquors made by them in said county, in a place described, to her said husband. In the first count, she asks to recover, under section 1557 of the Code of 1873, for damages to her person, property, and means of support, caused by illegal sales of intoxicating liquors to her husband by the defendants, whereby he was rendered drunken, intoxicated, idle, profligate, and wholly neglected his business, and was broken down in body and mind. In the second count she asks to recover for herself and the school fund of the state, under section 1539 of said Code, for alleged sales of intoxicating liquors by the defendants to said John Carrier when intoxicated and in the habit of becoming intoxicated. Defendants moved to strike said first count, or that the plaintiff be required to elect upon which count she would proceed, upon the grounds that there was a misjoinder of parties and of causes of action. This motion being overruled, the defendants moved for more specific statement as to the time and place of the sales, by which defendant sales were made, and the kind and quantity of liquors sold. This motion was overruled, and the defendants answered, admitting that they were conducting a wholesale and retail liquor store at the place described, in said county, and denying every other allegation in the petition. They further answered that their said place and business were conducted in accordance with chapter 62, Laws Twenty-ffth General Assembly, and that, therefore, the plaintiff has no right of action against them. A verdict was returned upon the first count in favor of the plaintiff for five hundred dollars, and judgment rendered thereon against the defendants, "in favor of plaintiff, in her own right, in the sum of $500, and for costs of action." A verdict was also rendered as follows: "We, the jury, find for the plaintiff, for the use of the school fund, upon the second count of the petition, in the sum of four hundred dollars ($400)." Judgment was rendered thereon as follows: "Judgment is also entered against all of said defendants in the further sum of $400, for the use of the school fund." To these judgments the defendants excepted, and from them they appealed.—*Reversed.*

Anthony C. Daly and *Theodore F. Bradford* for appellants.

Meeker & Meeker for appellee.

GIVEN, J.—Appellants' first contention is that the court erred in overruling defendants' motion to strike the first count, or to require the plaintiff to elect upon which count she would proceed, insisting that there is a misjoinder of parties, and of causes of action. Section 2630 of the Code of 1873 provides as follows:

1 "Causes of action of whatever kind, where each may be prosecuted by the same kind of proceedings, provided that they be by the same party, and against the same party in the same rights, and if suit on all may be brought and tried in that county, may be joined in the same petition." Said section 1557 (Code, 1873), upon which the first count is based, gives to every wife who shall be injured, in person, or property, or means of support, by any intoxicated person, or in consequence of the intoxication, habitual or otherwise, of any person, the right of action in her own name

against any person who shall, by selling intoxicating liquors, cause the intoxication of such person, for all damages actually sustained, as well as
exemplary damages, to be recovered by civil action
in any court having jurisdiction thereof. It will be
observed that the wife thus injured is the only proper
person plaintiff in such an action, and that the right of
recovery is to her, and to her alone, and for her own
exclusive benefit. Section 1539 (Code, 1873), upon which
the second count is based, declares it unlawful for any
person to sell intoxicating liquors to any intoxicated
person, or to any person who is in the habit of becoming
intoxicated. It provides that any person violating this
provision shall forfeit and pay to the school fund the
sum of one hundred dollars for each offense, to be collected by action against him by any citizen in the
county. "One-half of the amount so recovered shall go
to the informer, and the other half shall go to the
school fund of the county." While it may be said that
these causes of action may be prosecuted by the same
kind of proceedings, we think that they are not by the
same party as plaintiff, nor in the same right. In the
first count the plaintiff sues in her own name, and no
other person could properly be joined with her as plaintiff. The second count is not to recover an amount due
to her, but a forfeiture payable to the school fund. The
language of section 1539 is: "Any person violating
the provisions of this section shall forfeit and pay to the
school fund the sum of one hundred dollars for each
offense." In the second count plaintiff does not sue as
wife, but as "citizen in the county," and as informer.
Such an action might be properly entitled in the name
of the citizen, as informer, for the use of the school fund
of the county, naming it, as plaintiff. If it may be said
that, because of plaintiff's right as citizen to bring the
action as in the second count, the two actions are by the
same party, surely it cannot be said that they are in the

same right. The first is in the right as wife for dam
ages to her person, property, and means of support, and
is a right existing solely and exclusively in favor of the
plaintiff, for injuries actually suffered by her. The
second is in the right of the county, not to damages, but
to the forfeiture to its school fund. The citizen prosecuting such an action as informer has no personal right
of recovery. He cannot recover anything in his own
right, and it is only when recovery is had in favor of the
school fund that the informer is compensated by receiving one-half the amount recovered. The judgment
rendered on the verdict returned upon this second
count is not in favor of the plaintiff, Mary E. Carrier,
but is against the defendants, "for the use of the school
fund." Mrs. Carrier is not even named in that judgment, nor does it even provide that she shall receive one-
half the recovery as informer. It seems to us quite
clear that these two causes of action are not in the same
right. It is suggested that this case is not unlike those
wherein judgment may be rendered in favor of the state
for the use of the school fund of the county, when
it is ascertained that the contract sued upon is
usurious. Section 2080 of the Code of 1873 expressly
authorized the court to render such a judgment in the
suit on the usurious contract, and no action is required
to be brought for the use of the school fund. The cases
would be similar if the statute provided that judgment
for forfeitures, under section 1539, might be recovered
in an action under section 1557. It is only when all the
suits may be brought and tried in the same county that
they may be joined in the same petition. Now, it is
true, because of the citizenship of the plaintiff and the
residence of the defendants being Marshall county,
these cases were properly brought and tried in that
county. Appellants insist that an action under section
1557 must be brought in the county where some of the
defendants reside, and that an action under section

1539 must be brought in the county where the liquor was sold, and that, it being possible that such actions could not be brought and tried in the same county, therefore they cannot be joined, even when the parties all reside in the same county. The fault of this contention is in assuming that an action under section 1539 must be brought and tried in the county where the liquor is alleged to have been sold. Said section provides that the action may be "by any citizen in the county," but does not provide that it must be brought and tried in the county where the liquor is alleged to have been sold. So far as the place of bringing and trying this action is concerned, there was no misjoinder, but holding, as we do, that the two actions are not in the same right, it follows that there was a misjoinder of these causes of action, and that defendants' motion to require plaintiff to elect upon which count she would proceed should have been sustained.

II. As already stated, the defendants pleaded compliance with chapter 62, Acts Twenty-fifth General Assembly, known as the "Mulct Law," as a defense. This plea the court disregarded throughout the trial, and instructed to the effect that the mulct law does not have the effect to repeal or supersede said sections 1539 and 1557, and does not release any person violating said section from the liabilities therein mentioned. Of this action of the court appellants complain, and insist that the mulct law is a license law, and that, as against one who has complied therewith, "there is no civil action for damages, unless the sale is to some prohibited person." It is argued that sales made under the mulct law, except to prohibited persons, are legalized, and that there is no liability under section 1557, except for illegal sales. The right of action given in section 1557 is grounded upon the fact that injury has been sustained by reason of the intoxication of some person, and the remedy is against the

person, who, by selling the liquor, caused the intoxication. It is not questioned but that sales to minors,
intoxicated persons, persons in the habit of becoming
intoxicated, and knowingly to those who have taken
any of the recognized cures for drunkenness, are unlawful. Prior to the enactment of the mulct law, only
those holding permits could sell at all, and they only to
others than the prohibited classes, and for specified
purposes, which did not include use as a beverage. The
statute prohibits the business of keeping a place for the
unlawful sale, or keeping for unlawful sale, of intoxicating liquors, and provides for proceedings to abate
such a place and business as a nuisance. Section 17 of
the mulct law provides that compliance therewith shall
"be a bar to proceedings under the statute prohibiting
such business." Such "proceedings" are the "certain
penalties" that section 16 says may be suspended.
Whether this bar may be pleaded to any other proceeding than for nuisance we do not determine, but it is
certainly clear that it is no bar to the recovery of damages under section 1557. Section 19 of the mulct law
provides that "whenever any of the conditions of this act
shall be violated * * * the bar to proceedings as
provided in section 17 hereof shall cease to operate as a
bar." If it be true, as alleged, and as found by the jury,
that defendants sold intoxicating liquors to plaintiff's
husband, causing him to become intoxicated, idle, profli
gate, and neglectful of his business, and so as to impair
him in body and mind, and to render him unable to
obtain remunerative employment, to the damage of
the plaintiff, they surely violated the conditions of the
mulct law, wherefore the bar ceased to operate. Plaintiff, in an amendment, alleged that said sales were made
to her husband by the defendants, "who knew at the
time he had taken one of the recognized cures for drunkenness." There was no evidence to show knowledge as
alleged, and therefore this allegation of the petition

was not presented to the jury. We do not understand
appellants to contend that compliance with the mulct
law would bar a recovery, in a proper case, under said
section 1539, as in that case the sale must be to a minor,
intoxicated person, or person who is in the habit of
becoming intoxicated, which it is conceded would be
unlawful. We think there was no error in disregarding
the plaintiff's plea of the mulct law as a defense, nor in
giving the instructions mentioned above.

III. There was no error in overruling defendant's
motion for more specific statement as to the time of the
sales complained of. They were alleged to have been
made in the spring and summer of 1895, which
3   was sufficiently definite. Appellants complain
that, under the allegation that the defendants
sold the liquors, plaintiff was permitted to prove that
sales were made by their employes. This evidence was
admissible, under the pleadings, and the provisions of
the statute. The evidence shows that some of
4   the liquors drank by the plaintiff's husband were
bought by other persons, and it is contended
that this was not selling beer to Jack Carrier. There is
no merit in this contention, as is shown by the
5   familiar provisions of our statute and the
repeated decisions of this court. Other errors
assigned need not be considered, in view of the conclusions we have reached, as they will not occur upon a
re-trial. For the error pointed out in the first paragraph of this opinion, the judgment of the district court
is REVERSED.

A. KIBURZ v. JOHN JACOBS, Appellant.

Contracts. The fact that a contract for services in training race
horses was made upon the erroneous supposition that one of the
8 horses possessed speed qualities, and that upon learning the error

the employer terminated the contract, does not affect his liability thereon.

Transfer to Different County. Defendant is not entitled to a transfer 2 of the case to the county to which he has changed his residence, since the service of the notice upon him.

BILL OF EXCEPTIONS: *Filing.* Appellee's motion to strike from the appellant's abstract all that portion of it which must be preserved 1 by a bill of exceptions will be granted where the appellant failed to prepare and submit to the judge for approval a bill of exceptions in time to reach the clerk's office for filing within the time allowed for that purpose.

AMENDED ABSTRACT: *Costs.* Appellant's motion to tax the costs of the transcript on appeal against the appellee, on the ground that 4 his own abstract was full, fair and complete, will be denied where his abstract omitted to give the date of the judgment or the fact that time was allowed for filing a bill of exceptions, and was defective in other important particulars.

Appeal from Jones District Court.—HON. W. P. WOLF, Judge.

SATURDAY, JANUARY 29, 1898.

ACTION to recover for services rendered and expenses incurred under a written contract set out. Defendant answered, joining issues, and setting up a counter-claim, which counter-claim plaintiff denied. Verdict and judgment were rendered in favor of the plaintiff. Defendant appeals.—*Affirmed.*

Welch & Welch for appellant.

Hicks & Ellison for appellee.

GIVEN, J.—I. Appellee moves to strike from appellant's abstract all that part purporting to set forth the evidence, and objections and rulings thereon, and

also instructions, upon the ground that said matters
have not been identified and preserved by bill of
1   exceptions filed within the time fixed by the
court. Appellant's abstract does not show when
the judgment was rendered, nor that any time was
allowed for filing a bill of exceptions; but appellee's
additional abstract shows that the judgment was
rendered on March 19, 1896; that, by consent, thirty
days were allowed to settle and file a bill of exceptions;
and that on the first day of May, 1896, defendant filed
his bill of exceptions. Appellant files the affidavit of
one of his counsel to the effect that within the thirty
days he prepared the bill of exceptions, and forwarded
the same from Monticello, Iowa, to Judge Wolf, at Tip-
ton, for signature and allowance; that same was duly
sent by mail by Judge Wolf to F. O. Ellison, attorney for
appellee, at Anamosa, within the thirty days, for his
approval. Affiant says: "And the delay in filing said
bill was occasioned by said Ellison retaining said bill
in his possession, or by being detained or delayed in
the mail beyond the said thirty days." He says that
Ellison, some time thereafter mailed the bill, without
objections, to the clerk, to be filed. Appellant also
produces a statement from Judge Wolf, entitled as in
the case, June 3, 1896, but which does not appear to
have been filed in the district court, in substance as follows: That the bill was prepared and sent to him, was
allowed and signed by him, and mailed to F. O. Ellison,
attorney for the plaintiff, at Anamosa, within the thirty
days, with instructions to notify the judge if the bill
was not satisfactory, and, if objected to, to return it,
with his objections, and that it was not returned. It is
not contended that the bill was filed within the thirty
days, nor, indeed, until May 1, 1896; but appellant contends that it was because of the detention of the bill
beyond that time by attorney Ellison. Mr. Ellison

makes affidavit that he did not receive the bill of exceptions until the twenty-third day of April, 1896, when he
received what purported to be a bill of exceptions,
accompanied by a letter from Judge Wolf, which is
set'out, and which is dated April 21, 1896, and in which
Judge Wolf says as follows: "Welch & Welch have
sent bill of exceptions for my signature in case of
Kiburz vs. Jacobs. I do not remember what entries
were made on the docket. I see there is no exception to
the judgment of the court or the verdict. As they did
not submit the bill to you, I send it, to be delivered to
them if you find no objection, and have so written
them." Mr. Ellison further says that he had no knowledge that a bill of exceptions had been made until it
was received, April 23; that he then observed that the
time had expired for filing the same; that, in accordance
with the request in the judge's letter, he forwarded the
bill to Welch & Welch on the twenty-fourth of April;
and that the letter set out is the only communication
that he received concerning the bill. It is evident from
the date and statements of Judge Wolf's letter that he
is mistaken in saying in his statement of June 3, 1896,
that the bill of exceptions was allowed and signed by
him, and forwarded to Mr. Ellison, within the thirty
days; and therefore we must conclude that the failure
to file the bill in time was not because of its detention
by Mr. Ellison, but because it was not prepared and
submitted to the judge for approval in time to reach
the clerk's office for filing within the thirty days. Under
this state of the record, appellee's motion to strike from
the abstract must be sustained.

II. Before answering, the defendant moved to
transfer the case to Blackhawk county, on the ground
that he was a resident of that county. This motion
was overruled, and of this the appellant complains. The affidavits show that on September
20, 1895, when the original notice was served,
defendant's residence was in Jones county, and that

2

he did not become a resident of Blackhawk county until
September 24 or 25, 1895. The motion was properly
overruled.

III. The contract sued upon is for services to be
rendered by the plaintiff in training, taking care of, and
driving certain race horses belonging to the defendant,
and for the furnishing of certain assistance and outfit.
Defendant filed an amendment to his answer, alleging
that, at the time of making the contract, it was mutually supposed by said parties that one of the horses
(Cola M.) possessed certain qualities of speed;
3   that the contract was made upon that supposition, and that the mare did not possess said
qualities, "and, upon learning the same, defendant
terminated said contract." This amendment was
stricken, on plaintiff's motion, and of this the appellant
complains. We see no reason for the complaint. The
amendment was irrelevant and immaterial, and presented no defense to the action upon the contract. All
other errors assigned are grounded upon the evidence,
instructions, and rulings in taking the evidence; and,
as these were not preserved by a bill of exceptions filed
in time, the errors cannot be considered.

IV. Appellant moves to tax the costs of the
transcript herein to the appellee, on the ground that
appellant's abstract was full, fair, and complete, and
that appellee's additional abstract contains no matters
necessary or material to the determination of the
4   case. As we have seen, appellant's abstract
omitted to give the date of the judgment, or the
fact that time was allowed for filing a bill of exceptions.
An examination of the transcript in connection with
this motion discovers that the abstract was defective in
other important particulars, and that appellee's denial
of its sufficiency is correct. Our examination of the
abstracts and transcript leads us to conclude that this
motion to tax the costs of the transcript to appellee

should be overruled, and, for the reasons heretofore
given, that the judgment of the district court should
be AFFIRMED.

C. M. KELLER v. R. B. STRONG, Appellant.

104
114
104
136

Compromise and Settlement: CONSIDERATION. An agreement to
8 accept less than the amount due is without consideration,

Evidence: TRUSTS: *Parol variance.* An express trust in real prop-
2 erty cannot be established by oral evidence.

Pleading: MOTION TO STRIKE: *Waiver.* The remedy for the addition to a petition by amendment, of a count which is inconsistent
1 with a count already set up in the petition, is by motion to strike,
and the objection is waived by answering.

Appeal from Decatur District Court. — HON. H. M.
TOWNER, Judge.

SATURDAY, JANUARY 29, 1898.

THE plaintiff conveyed to the defendant one hundred and forty acres of land August 28, 1893, and this
action is brought to recover the balance of the consideration. Judgment for plaintiff, and defendant appeals.
—*Affirmed.*

Marion F. Stookey for appellant.

C..W. Hoffman and *V. R. McGinnis* for appellee.

LADD, J.—The amended and substituted petition
alleges a sale of the land to defendant for four thousand
two hundred dollars, of which two thousand six hundred and thirty-one dollars had been paid, and asks
judgment for the balance. The original petition, as an
amendment, was thereafter filed, averring that the conveyance was made to Strong, with the oral understanding that he control the premises, exercise reasonable
diligence to sell the same, and, out of the proceeds, pay

certain indebtedness of the plaintiff, and account for
the balance; that he had sold it for three thousand
five hundred dollars, appropriated the crops growing
thereon to his own use, paid two thousand six hundred
and thirty-one dollars of plaintiff's debts, and asking
that he account for anything remaining in his hands.
The defendant insists that, by filing the amendment
alleging an express trust, inconsistent with the averments of sale, the plaintiff elected to rely thereon.

1   But it neither withdrew nor modified any of the
        allegations of the amended and substituted peti-
tion.   It was in the nature of a separate count or cause
of action for the same indebtedness, and, if so inconsistent that it could not be properly joined (a point
not decided), the remedy was by motion to strike, and
the objection waived was by filing the answer.   Code,
        section 3548; *Kimball v. Bryan*, 56 Iowa, 632. The
2   amendment did not state a cause of action which
        could be maintained, as an express trust cannot
be established by oral evidence.   Code, section 2818;
Andrew v. Concannon, 76 Iowa, 251; *McGinness v.
Barton*, 71 Iowa, 644; *McClain v. McClain*, 57 Iowa, 167;
Shaffer v. McCrackin, 90 Iowa, 578; *Brown v. Barngrover*, 82 Iowa, 204; *Dunn v. Zwilling*, 94 Iowa, 233;
Maroney v. Maroney, 97 Iowa, 711. And a party will
be presumed to rely upon a cause of action which may
be sustained by proof, rather than upon another, to
support which the evidence offered is incompetent.

II. The defendant answered by pleading a general denial, alleged that he bought the land at the
agreed price of three thousand dollars, and that the
conveyance was made to defraud creditors. There was
some evidence of statements made by each party, to the
effect that the conveyance was fraudulent, but neither
so testified, and this defense is not proven.

III.   If the sale of the land was for specific amount, which the defendant orally agreed to pay in consideration of the conveyance, the indebtedness may be enforced like any other.   The defendant insists that he bought the land at the price of three thousand dollars, out of which he agreed to, and did, discharge the indebtedness of plaintiff, and paid him the balance in cash. The plaintiff says it was a sale on similar terms, but the price fixed was four thousand two hundred dollars, and this was the consideration named in the deed.   The plaintiff testified that it was orally understood that Strong was to do the best he could with the land, and, if he could not sell it, he (plaintiff)was to take it back. This was mere talk at the time of the sale, and does not show that Strong took the land to hold for Keller, nor does it show that a price was not agreed upon.   The sale may have been absolute, and yet plaintiff have agreed to take it back on a contingency, which in this case did not arise.   The evidence shows that a written memorandum of the sale was made about a month after the delivery of the deed, but this is not controlling as to price or terms.   An agreement to accept less than the amount due is without consideration.

3

Bender v. Been, 78 Iowa, 283; *Murray v. Walker,* 83 Iowa, 202.   And the evidence shows it was not made in settlement, but for defendant's use in some attachment suit.   Strong paid Keller on his indebtedness more than the amount claimed by him to have been agreed upon, and admitted in words and by his conduct a large sum still due.   He claimed to have paid one debt of Keller, at least, not owing by him, and which he had not in fact paid.   Several witnesses testify that Keller admitted having sold the land at twenty dollars per acre.   Without reviewing the evidence in detail, it is enough to say we are fully satisfied with the conclusion reached by the district court. The plaintiff only asked for the amount received by the defendant, and no exception is taken to that allowed.—AFFIRMED.

PAULINE FISHER, Administratrix of the Estate of WILLIAM A. FISHER, Deceased, v. THE BURLINGTON, CEDAR RAPIDS & NORTHERN RAILWAY COMPANY, Appellant.

Retaxation of Costs. Where a party makes a motion to retax the costs in the trial court, it is not governed by Code, 1873. section 3154. relating to proceedings to reverse, vacate, or modify judg-
1 ments in the court in which rendered. but by section 2944, relating to retaxing costs, as the claim is not that the judgment should be reversed or modified, but that the costs were improperly taxed by the clerk, and this applies to costs adjudged upon dismissal of an action by plaintiff

TIME FOR APPLICATION. A motion to retax costs under Code 1878,
2 section 2944, may be made at any time before laches or equitable limitation has intervened since no limit has been placed by statute upon the time for such a motion

RULE APPLIED. A motion to retax costs, made the second term of
2 court after judgment was rendered, does not show laches.

Witness: FEES. Witnesses who are not subpœnaed or sworn are not
3 entitled to fees for attendance, under the statute, although they attend at the request of one of the parties

SAME. Witnesses who are not subpœnaed are not entitled to mileage
3 under the statute, although they testify in a case.

Appeal from Linn District Court.—HON. WILLIAM G. THOMPSON, Judge.

MONDAY, JANUARY 31, 1898.

APPEAL from an order sustaining plaintiff's motion to retax costs.—*Modified.*

S. K. Tracy and *J. C. Leonard* for appellant.

Rickel & Crocker, Clemens & Steele, and *Jamison & Smythe* for appellee.

DEEMER, C. J.—Plaintiff's action was to recover damages from defendant for negligence resulting in the death of William H. Fisher. The case was tried to a jury, and at the conclusion of plaintiff's evidence the defendant moved for a verdict. While this motion was pending, plaintiff dismissed her cause of action without prejudice, and on the fourth day of February, 1896, the lower court rendered judgment against the plaintiff for the sum of two hundred and ninety-three dollars and fifty-five cents taxed as costs, and ordered execution to issue. On the ninth day of September, 1896, and after one term of court had intervened, plaintiff filed a motion to retax all costs of defendant's witnesses, for the reason that none of them were subpoenaed or used upon the trial of the case. The motion was sustained, and the appeal is from this ruling. It appears from the record that none of the defendant's witnesses whose fees and mileage were taxed were subpoenaed; and that none of them were sworn or used upon the trial, save five, who were used by plaintiff in attempting to make out her case. It also appears that they were each and all in attendance at the request of the defendant, but were not used upon the trial.

Appellant's first contention is that the original judgment is a finality, and that it cannot be modified except under the provisions of section 3154, Code 1873, relating to proceedings to reverse, vacate or modify judgments in the courts in which rendered. Were this an application to set aside, reverse, or modify the judgment,—if, for example, it was to set aside the judgment for costs,—there would

be much force in the contention. Such is not the
motion, however. The judgment in a case is rendered,
or ordered, by the court. Primarily, it has nothing to
do with the taxation of costs. This duty devolves upon
the clerk. Code 1873, section 2942. Section 2944 of the
same Code is as follows: "Any person aggrieved by the
taxation of a bill of costs may, upon application, have
the same retaxed * * * by the court * * * in
which the proceeding was had, and in such retaxation
all errors shall be corrected." The motion was bottomed upon this section, and was, as we think, in proper
form. The plaintiff is not seeking a reversal or modification of the judgment. His claim is that the costs
were improperly taxed by the clerk. The distinction
here attempted to be drawn is quite fully pointed out in
the case of *Fairburn v. Dana*, 68 Iowa, 231. See, also,
Allen v. Seward, 86 Iowa, 718. Manifestly, section 3154
has no application.

II. Claim is also made that the motion was not
filed in time. The judgment was rendered at the January term of the district court, and the motion was not
filed until the second term thereafter. The con-
2   tention is based upon the proposition that this is
a motion or petition to modify a judgment, and
that it should have been made on the second day of the
term immediately succeeding the one at which the
judgment was rendered, as provided in section 3156 of
the Code of 1873. We have already determined that
this is not such a motion or petition, and we find, upon
an examination of the statutes, that no time has been
fixed within which a motion to retax shall be filed. As
the legislature has not seen fit to place a limit upon the
time within which such motions shall be filed, nothing
but the doctrine of laches or equitable limitation
seems to apply. No "hard and fast rule" should therefore be adopted, but each case should be determined
upon its own peculiar facts. In the case of *Solomon v.*

McLennan, 81 Iowa, 406, we held that a petition and motion to tax attorney's fees in an attachment suit, filed more than a year after the judgment was rendered, and after it had been paid, should not be allowed. In that case it was said, however, that the clerk could not, on his own motion, have taxed the fees, and that they were not taxed because of oversight of the person who was entitled to them. There is no showing of laches in this case, and no equitable reason is presented as a ground for denying the motion.

III.   As none of defendant's witnesses were subpoenaed, they were clearly not entitled to mileage. *State v. Willis*, 79 Iowa, 326. It also appears that none

3   of them, except the five already referred to, were sworn or used upon the trial. Are these witnesses entitled to fees for attendance? We have held that when a witness is called and sworn, and has thus placed himself under and subject to the order and direction of the court, he is entitled to fees for attendance. *State v. Willis, supra.* The witnesses in this case were not sworn, and did not subject themselves to the order of the court. They were not required to attend, and could have departed at pleasure. They were present solely at the defendant's request, and defendant alone is responsible to them. The statute (Code 1873, section 3814) fixes the compensation of witnesses at so much for each day's attendance upon a court of record. Generally speaking, a witness is one who gives evidence in a court. A person who is neither subpoenaed nor called nor used upon a trial is not a witness, even though he be present by request of one of the parties. If one who has not been subpoenaed cannot have mileage taxed, surely such a one, who has neither been called nor sworn, is not entitled to fees for attendance. Five of the witnesses whose fees are asked to be re-taxed were used by the plaintiff, and their fees for attendance were paid by defendant. Plaintiff should

be taxed with these fees, amounting to thirty-seven dollars and fifty cents, and in all other respects the order should be affirmed.—MODIFIED AND AFFIRMED.

THE CHANCY PARK LAND COMPANY v. B. B. HART, Appellant.

Contracts: LOTTERIES. That the subscribers for lots, which were to be divided or apportioned among them in such manner as they should decide, made the apportionment by drawing lots, does not prevent the promoters, who did not participate in or suggest the manner of the apportionment, from enforcing the contract entered into by a subscriber, for the lot drawn by him.

RULE APPLIED. Certain lots contracted for by the promoter of a packing house plant, were subscribed for under an agreement to take the number set opposite the name of each subscriber, if the packing house was secured. The lots were to be apportioned in such manner (as subscribers) may decide. At a meeting called by the promoters to divide the lots by "method * * * to be decided upon by a vote of the subscribers," the plan of one of the promoters was adopted; the other promoters taking no actual part, and all having announced that they left the method of the apportionment to the subscribers. The subscribers' names were drawn out of one box, and the numbers of the lots to correspond were drawn out of the other, by two of the subscribers agreed upon. None of the lots were worth more than the price paid. *Held*, that the apportionment of the lots was by the subscribers alone, and the method was not a lottery, within the meaning of Code 1873, section 4043, constitution, article 3, section 28, prohibiting lotteries

Appeal from Clinton District Court. — HON. P. B. WOLFE, Judge.

MONDAY, JANUARY 31, 1898.

ACTION to foreclose a contract for the sale of a city lot. Decree as prayed, and defendant appeals.— *Affirmed.*

Frank W. Ellis and *L. A. Ellis* for appellant.

A. P. Barker for appellee.

LADD, J.—In the early part of 1892, W. H. Pearce, J. H. Dunham, and A. P. Barker engaged in the enter-prise of inducing the Iowa Packing Company to erect a pork-packing and beef-killing plant at Clinton, Iowa, and in order to obtain a site therefor, and to pay a bonus, entered into a contract with C. H. and Mary M. Aller and Lura M. Hall for the purchase of ninety-six acres of land, with the condition that the grantors should plat the west sixty acres into lots and streets, and execute an agreement for the conveyance of lots therein, at the price of three hundred dollars each, to purchasers, as directed by the grantees, in the event that two hundred and twenty-five were sold. These agreements, or contracts, were to be held as security for the payment of the consideration. The grantors agreed to take sixteen lots at the price named, and indorse the amount upon the contract of sale, and, when two hundred and twenty-five lots were sold, to convey to the promoters the east thirty-six acres, and, upon the pay-ment of the entire balance, to assign all contracts, and deed all unconveyed lots, to the said promoters, Pearce, Dunham, and Barker. Subscribers for the purchase of 211 lots were procured, on the condition that "the under-signed, in consideration of the securing of such plant, and the agreements of others whose names are sub-scribed hereto, agree to take the number of lots in such proposed sub-division set opposite our names; * * * said lots to be divided or apportioned among the sub-scribers hereto in such manner as they may decide; each subscriber to have one vote for each lot purchased by him; and this agreement not to be binding unless a con-tract is closed with said Iowa Packing Company for the erection of said plant substantially in accordance with the terms of said written proposition." A meeting of the subscribers was called by the promoters, for the purpose of dividing or apportioning among them the lots; and it was stated in the notice that, "according to the terms of subscription, the method of division of said lots will be decided upon by vote of subscribers." Barker called the meeting to order, and stated its object. Thereupon a president and secretary were selected. Methods of apportioning the lots were discussed generally, but finally that suggested by Barker was adopted. Dunham answered a few questions asked by persons present, and Pearce said nothing. It was announced, however, that the promoters wanted nothing to do with the meeting, and left it entirely in the hands of the subscribers; and the evidence warrants the conclusion that the method of apportioning the lots, and the apportionment thereof, were determined upon and carried out by the subscribers alone. A drawing committee was selected, and the names of all subscribers placed in a box, and the number of the lots, with the blocks, put into another. The two oldest men present were then required to lay aside their spectacles, that they might not see, and one drew names, and the other the lots to correspond. The result was kept by the secretary, and a contract of sale executed by the Allers and Hall accordingly. The lots varied in value, though none appear to have been worth more than the price paid. The defendant was so unfortunate as to secure one with a ravine passing through it. He paid the first installment of one hundred dollars, and, failing to pay the remaining two hundred dollars, this action was brought to foreclose the contract. The defenses interposed are that the methods employed in distributing the lots constituted a lottery, and that the contract was obtained by fraud.

I. It is conceded that the defendant's contract for
the purchase of the lot, if in pursuance of, or in promo-
tion of, a lottery scheme, is against public policy, and
cannot be enforced. *Guenther v. Dewien,* 11 Iowa, 133;
Seidenbender v. Charles, 8 Am. Dec. 682, and notes; 13
Am. & Eng. Enc. Law, 1187. For, if a transaction is
prohibited by the statute, a contract based thereon is
void. It is important, then, to determine what is a lottery, such as is prohibited by the statute and constitution. Section 28, article 3, Constitution Iowa; Code,
1873, section 4043. The word has not acquired a technical or legal significance differing from that of
approved usage in the language. The lexicographers
are agreed that a distribution of prizes by lot or chance
may constitute a lottery. •Worcester and the American
Cyclopedia include payment of a consideration for the
chance, while nearly all refer to it as a scheme. See
U. S. v. Olney, 1 Deady, 461. To bring the transaction
within the meaning of the statute prohibiting lotteries,
something of value must be parted with, directly or
indirectly, by him who has the chance. *Yellowstone
Kit v. State,* 88 Ala. 196 (7 South. Rep. 338; 16 Ann. St.
Rep. 38, and extended note); *Cross v. People,* 18 Colo.
321 (32 Pac. Rep. 821). The authorities uniformly refer
to a lottery as a scheme. Bishop defines it as "a scheme
by which, on one's paying money, or some other thing
of value, he obtains the contingent right to have something of greater value, if an appeal to chance, by lot
or otherwise, under the direction of the manager of the
scheme, should decide in his favor." Bishop, Statutory
Crimes, section 952. The accepted definition of the
court of appeals of New York is found in *Hull v.
Ruggles,* 56 N. Y. 424, approved in *Wilkinson v. Gill,*
74 N. Y. 63 (30 Am. Rep. 264): "Where a pecuniary consideration is paid, and it is to be determined by lot or
chance, according to some scheme held out to the public,
what and how much he who pays the money is to receive

for it, that is a lottery." In *Rothrock v. Perkinson*, 61 Ind. 39, the court says: "It is well settled in this state that every scheme for the division or disposition of property or money by chance, or any game of hazard, is prohibited by law, and that every contract or agreement in aid of such a scheme is void." The supreme court of Michigan defines a lottery as a "scheme by which a result is reached by some action or means taken, and in which the result of man's choice or will has no part, nor can human reason, foresight, sagacity, or design enable him to know or determine such results until the same has been accomplished." *People v. Elliott*, 74 Mich. 264 (16 Am. St. 644). So, in *State v. Clarke*, 33 N. H. 329 (66 Am. Dec. 723): "Where a pecuniary condition is paid, and it is determined by lot or chance, according to some scheme held out to the public, what the party who pays the money is to have for it, or whether he is to have anything, it is a lottery, within the meaning of the statute." See, also, *Lynch v. Rosenthal*, 144 Ind Sup. 86 (42 N. E. Rep. 1103); 13 Am. & Eng. Enc. Law, 1164. It thus appears that there must be some plan or scheme, on the part of the promoters of the enterprise alleged to be unlawful, for the sale or disposition of property by lot or chance, before it can be said to have the character of a lottery. If the sale is without the purpose that the property, or any part of it, shall be obtained by the purchaser through chance, and this does not result from the nature of the transaction, then it is not so tainted. The sale of the lots to the subscribers in this case was not in pursuance of any design to promote a lottery, or in evasion of the law. Each subscriber contracted,—as he had the right to do,—for the purchase of one or more of the lots, with the understanding that they should be apportioned as the subscribers themselves might determine. Having agreed to buy before the land was platted,—induced by a desire to aid an enterprise of anticipated advantage to the

city,—they concluded, after much discussion, and the
proposal of other plans, to make the selection by draw·
ing the number of a lot and name from different boxes,
at the same time. We know of no good reason why
these purchasers did not have the right to divide their
property or that contracted for, according to their own
notions and agreement. We have discovered no authority denying them that right, but, on the contrary, it is
recognized in *Commonwealth v. Manderfield*, 8 Phila.
457; 2 Wharton, Criminal Law, section 1891; *Yellowstone Kit v. State, supra.* Joshua so apportioned the
promised land among seven tribes of the children of
Israel. The disciples of Christ chose Matthias to succeed Judas by casting lots. Under the laws of this
state, the right to an office is determined, when there is
a tie vote, by the same method. Code, section 1169.
There was nothing in the transaction opposed to good
morals, and it was not a lottery, within the meaning of
the law. Without a scheme or plan to distribute by
chance, on the part of the promoters, the vital part of a
lottery was lacking. The evidence fails to show that
any fraud was practiced as to this defendant. The
judgment and decree of the district court is AFFIRMED.

J. A. YOUNG, Appellant, v. F. STUART. |104
|127

Justice of the Peace: APPEAL: *Remittitur.* Plaintiff in an action in
a justice's court may at any time before judgment reduce his
claim below the amount essential to the appellate jurisdiction of
the district court, and the error of the justice in rendering judgment for a larger amount does not confer appellate jurisdiction
upon the district court.

Appeal from Linn District Court.—HON. W. G. THOMP-
SON, Judge.

MONDAY, JANUARY 31, 1898

THIS appeal is by the plaintiff upon a certificate of the trial judge.—*Reversed.*

John A. Reed for appellant.

Heims & Heims for appellee.

GIVEN, J.—I. The certificate of the trial judge is, in substance, as follows: Plaintiff brought the action claiming of the defendant the sum of thirty-eight dollars. The trial was had before the justice, and after he heard the evidence the defendant gave notice of appeal to the district court, and filed his appeal bond, which was approved by the justice. Thereupon plaintiff filed a remittitur of all demands sued on in excess of twenty-four dollars and ninety-nine cents. Thereupon the justice rendered judgment in favor of plaintiff, and against the defendant, for twenty-eight dollars and sixty cents and costs. The justice allowed an appeal to the district court. In the district court the plaintiff filed a motion to dismiss the appeal, upon the ground that the amount in controversy was less than twenty-five dollars, which motion was overruled; and the defendant demanding a trial, and plaintiff refusing to introduce any testimony, but electing to stand upon his motion to dismiss, the court rendered judgment for the defendant, and against the plaintiff for the costs. The questions of law certified are as follows: "(1) The defendant having given notice of appeal and filed his appeal bond before the justice, and the defendant having filed a remititur of all of his claim in excess of the sum of twenty-four dollars and ninety-nine cents, all before judgment was rendered in said action, there being no counter-claim, and the justice having subsequently rendered judgment in favor of the plaintiff for twenty-eight dollars and sixty cents and costs, did the amount in controversy exceed the sum of twenty-five dollars, and has this court jurisdiction to entertain said appeal? (2) Was the action of the district court of Linn county, Iowa, in entertaining the appeal and over-ruling plaintiff's motion to dismiss, erroneous?" It will be observed that the defendant's notice of appeal and approval of his bond to the district court, though after the justice had heard the evidence, was before any judgment had been rendered in the case; also that the plaintiff filed a remittitur before judgment was rendered. The remittitur was in time, and by it the amount demanded was reduced to twenty-four dollars and ninety-nine cents, and therefore the case was not appealable to the district court. In view of the remittitur, the justice had no authority to render a judgment for more than the amount claimed. That the justice erroneously rendered a judgment for more than the amount claimed, does not change the fact that twenty-four dollars and ninety-nine cents was all that was being claimed in the action; therefore was the full amount in controversy. We think plaintiff's motion to dismiss the appeal to the district court should have been sustained, and that the first question certified must be answered in the negative, and the second in the affirmative.—Reversed.

M. Gensburg v. Marshall Field & Company, Appellant.

Conversion: DAMAGES. The measure of damages in an action for property converted is, in the absence of special circumstances
1 requiring a different rule, their fair market value at the time and place of conversion, with interest, and not their cost at a distant locality, with or without transportation charges added.

SAME. If it appears that personal property converted has no market
1 value at the place of conversion, the actual value may be shown.

EVIDENCE OF PARTNERSHIP. The firm of B. & G. was in business at N., and, several months before its failure, bought merchandise and shipped considerable quantities thereof to plaintiff, at several different places where they were sold at less than cost. A part of the goods were shipped to other addresses, although all were received by him. At one place he sold under an assumed name, and was assisted by a member of the firm. A portion of the

2 money derived from such sales was used in purchasing the goods in controversy. The firm had a store at D. in which plaintiff took a great interest. When asked the reason of the sales, he said that trade was dull, and they were closing out their stock at M., and, when applying for a license with B , a member of the firm, to sell at auction, stated that he was in partnership with B. in selling out the goods. *Held*, that an inference of a partnership relation between plaintiff and B. and G. might be drawn from such circumstances, and the question should properly have been submitted to the jury

OF MALICE. In an action for wrongful seizure of goods under an execution against another firm, testimony by plaintiff that, at the

8 time he brought part of the goods from defendant, he told its credit man that he was starting business at N., was admissible as tending to show defendant's knowledge that the purchase was made for the plaintiff, rather than the firm of B. & G , and was material as bearing on the question of malice in making the levy.

Pleading: MALICE. An allegation in a petition in an action for the conversion of property levied upon, which avers that the acts of the sheriff and defendant "were done for the purpose of oppress-

4 ing plaintiff, and compelling him to surrender his property without receiving compensation therefor," sufficiently charges "malice," although the word is not expressly used.

Appeal from Dubuque District Court. — HON. J. L. HUSTED, Judge.

TUESDAY, FEBRUARY 1, 1898.

THE defendant obtained judgment against A. Goldberg and Blumenthal & Goldberg, and, on November 13, 1894, caused execution to be issued thereon; later levied on the goods in controversy. Though duly served with notice of plaintiff's ownership, the sheriff sold the goods, and this action is brought for damages resulting from their conversion. Trial to jury. Judgment for plaintiffs, and defendant appeals.—*Reversed.*

Powers, Lacey & Brown for appellant.

Henderson, Hurd & Kiesel and *Longueville & McCarthy* for appellee.

LADD, J.—In actions for the conversion of personal property, where no special circumstances require a different rule, the measure of damages is the fair market value of the property at the place and time of conversion, with interest. *Brown v. Allen*, 35 Iowa, 306; *Gravel v. Clough*, 81 Iowa, 274; *Thew v. Miller*, 73 Iowa, 742; 5 Am. & Eng. Enc. Law, 40; *Ripley v. Davis*, 90 Am. Dec. 262, and note. If it appears that the property has no market value at that place, then the actual value may be allowed instead. *Gere v. Insurance Co.*, 67 Iowa, 275; *Clements v. Railway Co.*, 74 Iowa, 442. In the last case such value was adjudged established by proof of the price for which goods were sold; and it has been held that, where there is no home market for goods, the measure of value is the foreign market price, less transportation charges. *U. P. Railway Co. v. Williams*, 3 Colo. App. 526 (34 Pac. Rep. 731). No special circumstances, however, take this case out of the general rule. The only question is whether proof of the cost of the goods, alleged to have been converted, in Dubuque and Chicago, and of freight, without more, furnishes a proper basis for the estimate of value at New Hampton, the place of conversion. Some authorities hold that evidence of the price paid for merchandise, shortly before or after, and when in substantially the same condition, without purpose of fixing a criterion, is competent as tending to show the market value. *Hoffman v. Conner*, 76 N. Y. 121; *Hangen v. Hachemeister*, 114 N. Y. 566 (21 N. E. Rep. 1046); *Parmenter v. Fitzpatrick*, 135 N. Y. 190 (31 N. E. Rep. 1032); *Crampton v. Marble Co.*, 60 Vt.

291 (15 Atl. Rep. 153). Whether such evidence of price at or in the vicinity of the place of conversion is admissible for such purpose has not been determined by this court; but, if it be conceded that it is, it would not follow that such cost in a locality several hundred miles distant, and beyond the state, would alone establish the market value. At the most, the cost of the goods in controversy would only have a tendency to show the market value at the places where purchased, and would not indicate in any way what the market might be at New Hampton. Indeed, it often occurs that goods are readily saleable in one locality which cannot be disposed of at another. There may be a demand for many articles in a large city for which the people in the smaller places have no use, and *rice versa*. The district court instructed the jury that the market value at New Hampton was the cost of the goods in Chicago and Dubuque, with freight added. Why not with freight subtracted? No market for the goods at New Hampton being shown, as well conclude the value thereof would be that in Chicago and Dubuque, less transportation for their return. There was no evidence that the goods were staple articles, such as are in use everywhere, nor that there was or was not any market at New Hampton, nor that values at the latter place were in any way controlled by the markets of Dubuque and Chicago. As well say the cost price of any other distant city, with transportation charges. The measure of damages cannot be left to mere conjecture. There is no basis for the claim that value would be the cost in Chicago, with transportation charges added, or with them subtracted. Recovery cannot be had for the value of goods at one place on proof of what they are worth at another. Many circumstances which need not here be enumerated render such a criterion utterly fallacious. No excuse appears of record for not establishing the market value at New Hampton. If such

value were the cost of the goods, with freight added,
this could have been readily shown; but the mere cost
at a distant locality, with or without transportation
charges, does not furnish a proper basis for estimating
the market value at the place of conversion.

II. The court held the evidence insufficient to
warrant a finding that plaintiff was a member of the
firm of Blumenthal & Goldberg. That issue ought to have
been submitted to the jury. The evidence, without giving it in detail, tended to show that said
firm was in business at New Hampton, and, during several months before its failure, had bought large
quantities of merchandise from many different wholesale houses, and re-shipped considerable quantities
thereof from New Hampton to the plaintiff, at Goldfield, Dows, Thrall, and other places, where he had sold
for less than cost; that a portion of the goods was
shipped to other addresses, though all were received by
the plaintiff; that he made the sales at Goldfield, under
an assumed name, and was assisted there a part of the
time by Goldberg, a member of the firm, and used a
portion of the money derived therefrom in purchasing
the goods in controversy; that at Dows the firm had a
store, in which plaintiff took a great deal of interest,
and at which he passed the most of his time when there;
that, when asked the reason for the sales, he remarked
that trade was dull, and they were closing their stock
at New Hampton; and, when he and Blumenthal
applied to the mayor for license to sell at auction, Blum-
enthall, in plaintiff's presence, said the goods belonged
to the firm of Blumenthal & Goldberg, which they were
selling there, and at other places; and thereupon the
plaintiff stated that he was in partnership with Blumenthal in selling out said stock of goods. The inference
of a partnership relation is not inevitable, but might
be drawn from such a state of facts if established by
the evidence. If he was in partnership, the nature of

the transactions in which the firm was engaged furnished a controlling motive for concealing it. The goods were purchased under circumstances indicating an intention never to make payment therefor. Large quantities were unpacked, put in other boxes, and immediately re-shipped to the plaintiff. He assumed charge of the sales, assisted at one time by Goldberg, and at another by Blumenthal. Goods recently purchased were sold at much below their cost. He certainly knew the nature of the transactions in which the firm was engaged, and he spoke of its business as though he had a direct interest therein. He admitted that he was a partner of one member of the firm in handling goods shown at that time to be the firm property. If the jury found the plaintiff a member of that firm, we think the finding would have such support in the evidence, as not to call for any interference by the court.

III.   Gensburg testified, when about to buy a part of the goods in controversy from the defendant, that he told the credit man of the firm he "was starting business at New Hampton, and wanted to look at some goods, and would pay cash for them." This was admissible as tending to show knowledge of defendant that the purchase was made for the plaintiff, rather than for the firm of Blumenthal & Goldberg, and was material as bearing on the question of malice in making the levy. The information was imparted to the employe of the defendant, acting within the scope of his employment; and, under such circumstances, knowledge of the agent is that of the principal. *Warburton v. Lauman*, 2 G. Greene, 420; *Jones v. Bamford*, 21 Iowa, 217; *Thompson v. Merrill*, 58 Iowa, 419; *Huff v. Farwell*, 67 Iowa, 298. The goods were still in the original packages at the railroad depot when levied on, so that defendant was advised of the identity with those purchased.

IV.   It is said malice is not alleged in the petition, nor established by the evidence. The use of the word "malice" is not essential in charging it, but language defining or describing it, under the rules of pleading, is quite enough. Even if it be conceded that malice cannot be inferred as a conclusion from the defendant's knowledge of plaintiff's ownership of the property prior to the levy, the petition also alleges that the acts of the sheriff and defendant "were done for the purpose of oppressing plaintiff and compelling him to surrender his property, without receiving compensation therefor." This is a very good description of that evil motive termed "malice." Without reviewing the evidence in detail, it will be sufficient to say that this issue was properly left to the determination of the jury. The instructions announced the rules of law familiar in such cases. The other error argued will not be likely to arise on another trial.—REVERSED.

4

ELIZABETH B. HIGGINS, Appellant, v. M. E. DENNIS, *et al.*

Mortgage Priority: RECORDING: *Notice.* Where the vendee of land, on the day on which it was conveyed to her, executed a mortgage thereon to a loan company for a part of the price and also a mortgage to her vendor for the balance, and such deed and both mortgages were filed for record on the same day; first, the mortgage to the loan company; next, the deed to the mortgagor; and last, the mortgage to her vendor, such mortgage to the loan company was entitled to priority, in the absence of notice otherwise, over that of the vendor, the holder of which was chargeable with all the knowledge the record imparted. *Distinguishing Trust Co. v. Malby*, 8 Paige, 361, *Turk v. Funk*, 68 Me. 18; *Calder v. Chapean*, 52 Penn. St. 359.

Appeal from Polk District Court.—HON. W. F. CONRAD, Judge.

TUESDAY, FEBRUARY 1, 1898.

Action for judgment on a promissory note, and for decree foreclosing a mortgage on certain real estate given to secure said note. The Iowa Loan & Trust Company was made defendant, as claiming some interest in the property under a mortgage which plaintiff alleges is junior to her mortgage. Said defendant company answered, setting out its mortgage, denying that the plaintiff's mortgage is superior thereto, and alleging that it is junior to the mortgage of the defendant, and asking decree accordingly. Decree was rendered in favor of said defendant company as prayed. Plaintiff appeals.—*Affirmed.*

Earle & Prouty for appellant.

D. F. Witter, John H. Blair, and *Dudley & Coffin* for appellee.

Given, J.—I. The sole question involved in this appeal is as to which of said mortgages is entitled to priority. There is no dispute as to the facts, and they are substantially as follows: One A. J. Reashaw owned the mortgaged property, with an unsatisfied mortgage thereon to the New England Loan & Trust Company for three hundred and fifty dollars, and a mortgage to J. K. and W. H. Gilcrest for seventy-two dollars. On the tenth day of August, 1886, Reashaw sold the property to the defendant Dennis for nine hundred and fifty dollars, six hundred dollars to be paid in cash, sufficient of which was to be applied to the satisfaction of said mortgages to the New England Loan & Trust Company and to J. K. and W. H. Gilcrest. For the balance of the purchase price, namely three hundred and fifty dollars, M. E. Dennis was to execute to Reashaw her promissory note secured by mortgage on the premises. To procure the amount with which to make the cash payment, M.

E. Dennis applied to the Iowa Loan & Trust Company for a loan, stating in her application that, "to secure the same, I will give first mortgage on the following property," describing that in controversy. On the said tenth day of August, 1886, Reashaw executed a deed for said property to M. E. Dennis, subject to said two mortgages to the New England Company and to the Gilcrests, "which the said M. E. Dennis is to assume and agrees to pay." This deed was deposited with the Iowa Loan & Trust Company, to be delivered when said two existing mortgages were satisfied. On that day M. E. Dennis executed to Reashaw the promissory note and mortgage sued upon. She also, on that day, executed and delivered to the Iowa Loan & Trust Company the mortgage set up in its answer, to secure the loan to her of six hundred dollars. The six hundred dollars were applied in satisfaction of said two prior mortgages, and the balance thereof paid to Reashaw. Reashaw knew of the execution of the mortgage to the defendant company, and consented that it should be a first mortgage. There is no evidence, however, that said defendant company knew of the execution of the mortgage to Reashaw. These three instruments, thus executed and delivered on the same day, were each filed for record on that day and in the following order: The mortgage from M. E. Dennis to the Iowa Loan & Trust Company was filed for record at 4 o'clock and fifty minutes P. M.; the deed from Mr. Reashaw to M. E. Dennis was filed for record at 4 o'clock and fifty-five minutes P. M.; and the mortgage from M. E. Dennis to A. J. Reashaw was filed for record at 5 o'clock and twenty-five minutes P. M. Mr. Heighton, of the Iowa Loan & Trust Company, who transacted the business on behalf of the company in the loan to M. E. Dennis, took said deed and the mortgage to the company to have the proper transfer made, and to file the same for record. He first stopped at the auditor's office and left the deed

to have the transfer made. He then proceeded to the
recorder's office, filed said mortgage to the company
for record, returned to the auditor's office, obtained the
deed, and immediately went to the recorder's office,
and had it filed for record. It was in this manner that
the mortgage came to be filed for record five minutes
before the deed was filed. The promissory note sued
upon is an ordinary, negotiable promissory note, dated
August 10, 1886, and due on or before two years from
date. The mortgage securing said note is in the usual
form. Before maturity Reashaw assigned said note
and mortgage to H. T. Harriett, who thereafter, and
before maturity, assigned the same to Benjamin Higgins, now deceased, and through whom the plaintiff
became and now is the owner of said note and mortgage.

II. Plaintiff's first contention is that, as holder of
the negotiable note sued upon, and of the mortgage as
an incident thereto, she is, in the absence of proof,
assumed to have obtained them in good faith, for value,
before maturity, and that she is, therefore, not chargeable with the knowledge of Reashaw, nor his agreements, with respect to the defendant's mortgage. This
claim may, for the purpose of this suit be conceded; and,
being conceded, the question of priority cannot be
determined by the knowledge or agreements of Reashaw. The two mortgages were executed and delivered
on th same day, but it does not appear in what order;
therefore, the question of priority cannot be determined
by the order of their execution and delivery. No reference is made in either mortgage to the other; therefore,
the question of priority cannot be determined from anything appearing in the mortgages. The mortgage to
the defendant was executed to secure a loan of borrowed money, to be paid, and which was paid, as a part
of the purchase price, and the plaintiff's mortgage was
executed to secure the balance of the purchase price.
There is conflict in the authorities as to whether each

may be regarded as given for purchase money, but we
think that each is in such a sense for the purchase price
that neither can be said to have priority on that ground.
See 1 Jones, Mortgages, section 472; *Laidley v. Aiken*,
80 Iowa, 112. We will not pursue these propositions
further, as they are not really contentions in the case.
We have referred to them to show that, as stated by
plaintiff's counsel, "the only question in this case is
whether plaintiff is charged with the knowledge
imparted by the recording of the Iowa Loan & Trust
Company's mortgage prior to the recording of the deed
placing title in the mortgagor." It is plaintiff's contention that she is not chargeable with knowledge of
anything appearing upon the record prior to the time
the deed to Miss Dennis was filed for record, namely
4:55 P. M., August 10, 1886. It is argued that, if the
searcher of the record must go back of that time, he
must go back indefinitely, even to the beginning of the
record, and that this would be impractible, if not impossible. In support of this contention, cases are cited
wherein a party not having legal title executed a mortgage which was placed on record before the deed by
which the mortgagor subsequently acquired the legal
title. In these cases it was held that one purchasing
subsequent to the deed conferring the legal title was
not charged by the record with knowledge of the mortgage previously recorded. Of these cases we note *Trust
Co. v. Maltby*, 8 Paige, 361; *Turk v. Funk*, 68 Mo. 18;
Calder v. Chapman, 52 Pa. St. 359; Jones, Mortgages,
section 471; 20 Am. & Eng.. Enc. Law, 597. These cases
are not in point, for the reason that, in this, Miss Dennis
had the legal title at the time she executed and delivered
these mortgages. She had the legal title for the reason
that the deed to her was either executed and delivered
prior to the execution and delivery of the mortgages or
contemporaneous therewith. The rights of a mortgagee
to after-acquired by title is not involved in this case. The

question before us is simply whether the plaintiff is chargeable with knowledge of what appeared upon the record in the chain of title, only from the hour and minute at which Miss Dennis' deed was filed for record, or from the day of its execution. Authorities are cited in which it is said that the searcher need only go back to the time that evidence of title was filed for record, but surely such a rule should not apply to these facts. Suppose that Miss Dennis had withheld her deed from record for several days, and executed a third mortgage, surely that mortgage would not be entitled to priority over these, based, as they are, upon the legal title, and recorded after that title had been acquired. Miss Dennis was not required to file her deed within any specified time, nor were these mortgagees required to withhold their mortgages from record until her deed was recorded. Appellant quotes from 20 Am. & Eng. Enc. Law, 597, as follows: "The rule that a recorded instruments imparts constructive notice must be limited to these instruments recorded after the grantor therein acquires the title to the property thereby conveyed. To hold otherwise, by imposing upon a subsequent purchaser the duty of examining the records indefinitely, would militate against the practical advantage of the recording system." This statement of the rule is in harmony with our recording acts, and under it the plaintiff is charged with whatever knowledge the record imparted back to the time the title was acquired, and not to the hour and minute at which the evidence of the title was filed for record. By recording the deed, it was shown that Miss Dennis acquired title on the tenth day of August, 1886. Now, as Miss Dennis might incumber the property after acquiring title, and before filing her deed for record, a diligent searcher would inquire back to the date of the deed. If this deed had not been filed for several days after its date, a searcher, advised by the record of its date, would surely have examined back to that date for the incumbrances from her. Such transactions as those under consideration are of common occurrence, and it is not requiring too much of searchers for the chain of title that they shall not stop at the day and hour at which the evidence of title was filed for record, but go back to the date of that title as shown by the record. Such a rule is in harmony with reason. The recording act has support in the authorities, and does not require anything that is impracticable or impossible.

Applying this rule to the case under consideration, the plaintiff is chargeable with all the knowledge that the record imparted with respect to this claim of title, back to the time that the title was acquired by the deed to Miss Dennis. The deed was filed for record on the day of its date, and, while the hour of its filing appears, there is nothing to show at what hour of that day it was executed and delivered. While it may be said that the law takes notice of fractions of days as to the time of filing instruments for record, the general rule that the law takes no notice of fractions of days applies to the execution of deeds and mortgages, where the hour of their execution does not appear. The rule requiring a searcher to go back to the time of the execution of this deed, and it not appearing at what hour of the tenth day of August, 1886, it was executed, diligence required that he should examine as to all the hours of that day. In other words, under the facts of this case, the plaintiff is chargeable with all the knowledge with respect to this chain of title that the records of August 10, 1886, imparted, for that day as well as thereafter. Thus charged, the plaintiff must be held to have had knowledge of defendant's mortgage. Our conclusion is that the decree of the district court is correct, and it is therefore AFFIRMED.

L. W. NAMES V. THE UNION INSURANCE COMPANY, Appellant. .

Concurrent Insurance: FRAUD: An insurance company cannot complain in an action upon a policy issued by it, that one whose
8 property has been destroyed by fire, placed additional insurance upon it with another company, and at the time of his application therefor, stated that the property was not insured, where there was no limitation in defendant's policy as to concurrent insurance, since such misrepresentation was not a fraud upon the defendant.

Evidence: OFFER OF PROOF OF LOSS. That the proof of loss was offered in evidence in an action upon an insurance policy, both
2 for the purpose of showing that it was made and as tending to show what articles were lost, and their value, is not prejudicial to the defendant company.

SAME. A witness who testifies that he was at a certain house on the evening before it was destroyed by fire, may state that he had
4 heard that it was said that he burned the property, where in an action on the policy the insurance company alleged that the plaintiff had burned the house, or caused it to be burned.

SAME. A witness who visited a house some days before, and also on the evening it was destroyed by fire, may testify whether she saw
8 anything to indicate that there was less property in the house on that evening than on her former visit, when the insurance company alleged that the plaintiff removed some of his property from the house, before the fire.

WITNESS: *Competency.* One formerly in the mercantile business, although for some years retired, may testify in an action upon an
7 insurance policy as to the value of articles destroyed, and the fact that he is not actually engaged in trade, while affecting the weight of his evidence, is not ground for excluding it.

PLEA AND PROOF: *Amendment.* Testimony may be given of the value of an article destroyed by fire, but not included in the proof of
6 loss, in an action on the policy, since the plaintiff has the right to amend to conform to the proof.

REMOTENESS. Evidence that it was more expensive to ship law books by mail than by express, and that plaintiff had received no law
7 books by express, is too remote to show that plaintiff had not received law books by mail.

New Trial: NEWLY DISCOVERED EVIDENCE   Testimony of plaintiff
   that he had bought books in the fall of 1890 is not such a surprise
   to defendant as to allow him a new trial to present newly discov-
1   ered evidence contradicting such statement, where on a previous
   trial plaintiff had testified that he purchased books after the
   spring of 1890, and counsel for defendant had, before the trial,
   read depositions to that effect, and defendant had presented evidence on the trial as to the purchase of such books.

Appeal: CONFLICTING EVIDENCE. A verdict based upon conflicting
9   testimony will not be disturbed on appeal, when it has evidence to
   support it.

Appeal from Wright District Court.—HON. P. B. BIRD-
SALL, Judge.

WEDNESDAY, FEBRUARY 2, 1898.

ACTION to recover on a policy of insurance issued
by the defendant to the plaintiff, insuring personal
property contained in a certain dwelling house in the
city of Fort Dodge against loss or damage by fire in
the sum of one thousand dollars. Plaintiff alleges
a total loss of said property by fire on the night of February 15, 1892; that he made proofs of loss, and otherwise complied with the terms of the policy; that the
property was of the value of three thousand five hundred dollars; and that defendant has paid no part of
said loss. He asks judgment for one thousand dollars,
with interest. Defendant answered, admitting the execution of the policy, that no part of the alleged loss had
been paid by it, and pleading in defense, in substance,
as follows: That the policy was procured by fraud, and
by concealment of the amount of insurance which plaintiff had upon his property at the time of taking out his
policy; that the plaintiff made a false and fraudulent
schedule of the pretended property destroyed; that the
property had been removed before the fire; and that
the building was set on fire, or procured to be set on

fire, by the plaintiff. Verdict and judgment were rendered in favor of the plaintiff for the amount claimed. Defendant appeals.—*Affirmed.*

Yeoman & Kenyon and *McVey & Cheshire* for appellant.

R. M. Wright and *T. M. Healy* for appellee.

GIVEN, J.—I. Defendant moved for a new trial upon the ground, among others, of newly discovered evidence, and now complains of the overruling of its motion as to that ground. Among the property insured is "printed books." Plaintiff asks to recover for books claimed to have been destroyed, including twenty-four volumes and index, Encyclopedia Britannica, two hundred and forty dollars, and a large number of law books. In support of its motion the defendant filed the affidavit of two of its counsel to the effect that on the trial of the case of *Names ,. Dwelling-House Ins. Co.*, 95 Iowa, 642, previously had, based upon the same loss, plaintiff testified that he bought no law books after the spring of 1890, and that they were surprised by his testimony on this trial that he had bought thirty or thirty-two law books of Callaghan & Co., of Chicago, in the fall if 1890. They produced the affidavits of Willis R. Thomas and of W. H. Woodward, of Callaghan & Co., and of Frederick B. Smith, of A. C. McClurg & Co., book dealers in Chicago, tending to show that plaintiff did not buy books of either of said houses in the fall of 1890. On said former trial it was shown that some of the books claimed to have been destroyed were not published until after the spring of 1890. On this trial plaintiff testified to having purchased the Encyclopedia Britannica, with the index, and thirty or thirty-two volumes of law books, from said dealers, in the fall of 1890, and that he had them sent to his lodgings in the city, from whence he brought them to his home. In resistance of the motion, plaintiff shows by his own affidavit, into which he copies from the record of the former trial extracts of his testimony, to the effect, that he testified that he did purchase "quite a good many books in Chicago after the spring of 1890." He further shows, by the affidavit of one of his counsel that, about ten days before the commencement of the trial of this case, counsel for defendant read the depositions of Mrs. Hayes and her daughter, taken and filed in this case by the plaintiff, in which they testified, in substance, that a brother of the plaintiff roomed with them in Chicago; that plaintiff lodged with them for a time in 1890, and that while there a lot of books were brought to their house and placed in the parlor; that plaintiff opened said books; that they saw twenty-five volumes of the Encyclopedia Britannica among them, and about thirty law books. It appears that defendant took and used on this trial a deposition of said Smith, of McClurg & Co., as to the value of the Encyclopedia Britannica; and of said Thompson, of Callaghan & Co., that plaintiff purchased McClain's Code and Digest, May 7, 1890, and that their books did not show any later purchases by him. In view of said extracts from plaintiff's former testimony, we think the conclusion warranted that he testified on that trial to the purchase of books after the spring of 1890. This conclusion is strengthened by the fact that the defendant took the deposition of said Smith and Thompson. For this reason, and the further fact that defendant's counsel had read the deposition of Mrs. Hayes and her daughter ten days prior to this trial, they should not have been surprised that the plaintiff testified as he did concerning the purchase of the books in the fall of 1890. With this state of the record, we think the district court might properly hold that the newly-discovered evidence was merely cumulative, and that the defendant had not shown reason for surprise, or the exercise of diligence, and that, therefore, a new trial should not be granted on the ground of newly-discovered evidence.

II. The record shows that plaintiff offered in evidence the proof of loss, identified as furnished to the defendant, to which is attached a list of the articles claimed to have been lost, with the value of each, aggregating three thousand four hundred and fifty-four dollars. Upon inquiry by defendant's counsel as to the purpose for which this offer was made, counsel for plaintiff answered as follows: "I offer this for several purposes, one of which is that the several items contained in this exhibit have been identified as the items of goods, etc., that were destroyed in the fire, and the reasonable market value of the same at the time, and as enumerating and describing the several articles lost in the fire. That is one of the purposes. The other is, of course, to show that such proof was given."

2   Defendant objected as incompetent, immaterial, and irrelevant, which objection was overruled, the court remarking: "It is not to be taken by the jury as establishing a distinct fact in relation to the cause or origin of the fire." Thereupon the proof of loss was read to the jury. Defendant's counsel contend, upon the authority of numerous cases cited, that the proof of loss was only admissible for the purpose of showing that it was furnished to the defendant, and that it was not competent evidence to establish any of the matters stated therein. This statement of the law is not disputed, and therefore we do not refer to the authorities. It appears that a copy of the proof of loss, including the schedule of articles, and the value of each, was set out in the petition, and that, previous to this offer, plaintiff had been examined at length with reference to the items and values shown in that schedule. Now, if plaintiff had produced and identified a copy of this schedule as a correct statement of the articles lost, and of the value

of each,—the articles being numerous,—that copy, thus verified, would have been admissible, as tending to show what articles were destroyed, and their value. Now, according to the statement of plaintiff's counsel, this exhibit (the schedule) was offered because it had been identified as to the items of goods destroyed, and as giving the value thereof. While it would have avoided confusion to have offered the proof of loss, to show that such proof was given, and to have separately offered the schedule as identified by the plaintiff in his evidence, yet we think no prejudice could have resulted from the offer being made as it was. The proof of loss was, as stated, offered "to show that such proof was given," and the schedule attached was offered to show what property had been destroyed, and its value, for the reason that it had been testified to by the plaintiff as a correct schedule of the lost property, and its value, and not as proof, independent of his testimony, of the property lost, and of its value. If defendant desired that the purposes of the offer should have been more clearly presented to the jury, an instruction to that effect should have been asked. We think the defendant was not prejudiced by the offer as made.

III.   Defendant assigns and discusses several rulings of the court in taking testimony, as erroneous. A Miss Griffin, having testified that she was in plaintiff's house two or three weeks before the fire, and 3   also on the evening of the fire, was asked to say whether on that evening she saw anything to indicate that there was less property in the house than there was at the time of her former visit. This was objected to, and the objection overruled; and it is urged that the evidence was incompetent and immaterial, because there was no claim that plaintiff had changed the contents of his house between the two visits. It was claimed that Names had removed some of his property from the

house before the fire. This evidence was competent to
rebut that contention. One McCaffrey, witness for the
plaintiff, who had been at the house with the others on
the evening before the fire, was asked if he had heard
that it had been said in this case that he burned the

4   property, to which he answered that he had. In
view of his testimony as to how he came to be
at the house, and the claim of the defendant that
plaintiff had burned, or caused to be burned, we think
there was no prejudice to defendant in permitting this
answer. Mrs. Sherman, who had testified as to the
articles destroyed, stated that there were "three feather
beds,—only two in the proof of loss." She was asked
what the one not in the proof of loss was worth, to

5   which she answered, "About ten dollars."
Defendant's objection that the question was
immaterial was properly overruled, as plaintiff
had a right to amend to conform to the proofs. One
Julius was examined as to the value of articles claimed
to have been lost. It is contended that, as he said he
had not been in the mercantile business for about eleven
years, he was not competent to testify to values, and

6   that the court erred in not sustaining defendant's
motion to strike his evidence. While that statement would go to the weight to be given to his
evidence, it was no ground for excluding it. Defendant
offered in evidence certain sections of the United States
statutes, as to the weight of books receivable for carriage in the mails, and the rate of postage chargeable
thereon. This evidence was offered, in connection with

7   certain other evidence introduced as to the
weight of law books, and the rate of express
charges thereon, for the purpose of showing that
their shipment by mail would be more expensive than
by express. Evidence was also introdudced tending
to show that plaintiff did not receive books by express.
This evidence was offered to show that plaintiff did not

receive law books through the mail. It was too remote for that purpose, and there was no error in excluding it. Other errors assigned upon rulings in taking the testimony are not argued, and therefore will not be considered. We discover no prejudicial errors in the rulings on evidence.

IV.   We next notice defendant's contention that this policy was procured by fraud. This contention rests upon the following facts: On the thirty-first day of December, 1891, this policy was issued for one thousand dollars, plaintiff then having insurance in another company for one thousand dollars. In January following he took out an additional one thousand dollars on the same property, in the Home Insurance Company. The agent through whom that policy was taken testifies that plaintiff told him that he had no other insurance
8   on the property. If this false statement was fraudulent, it was against the Home Insurance Company, and not this defendant. There is no provision in defendant's policy limiting as to concurrent insurance. The only provisions are that in case of loss the plaintiff shall state "all other insurance covering any of said property;" also, that this company shall not, "under any circumstances whatever, be liable for a greater portion of any loss upon the property described in this policy than the sum hereby insured bears to the whole sum insured thereon, whether such other insurance be by specific or by general or by floating policies, or whether such other insurance be valid or not, and without reference to the solvency of other insurance companies." In view of the terms of this policy, we do not think that the additional insurance, though procured by misrepresentation, was a fraud upon this defendant.

V.   The defendant's further contention is that the verdict is contrary to the evidence, and was the result

of passion and prejudice. Defendant's contention as to
the origin of the fire, the removal of the furniture
9   from the building, that furniture claimed to be
lost was never in the building, that the building
would not contain the furniture and library claimed to
have been lost, and that plaintiff did not have all the
books claimed in the schedule, are all involved in the
inquiry as to the sufficiency of the evidence to sustain
the verdict. The evidence is voluminous, covering more
than two hundred and fifty closely printed pages of
abstract. We will not consume the space necessary to
set out or discuss this evidence, but rest our conclusion
upon the careful examination which we have given it.
There is certainly much warrant in the evidence for the
argument that defendant's counsel make against the
justness of this verdict, especially as to the amount of
property claimed to have been in the house at the time
of the fire. There is force in the argument that the
dimensions of the house were not sufficient to contain
all the furniture claimed to have been therein, and that
the library room was too small to contain the "over
one hundred volumes of miscellaneous books" and the
two hundred and fifty or more volumes of law books."
It is not contended in argument that the matters alleged
as defense were not properly submitted to the jury, and,
while we might find differently as to the amount of
property lost, we cannot say that the verdict of the
jury is without evidence to sustain it. The evidence
as to the amount of property in the building at the time
of the fire was conflicting. It was the province of the
jury to settle this conflict, and this they have done by
finding with the plaintiff. Under the oft-repeated decisions of this court, we cannot say that the verdict is contrary to the evidence. Our conclusions upon the whole
record is that the judgment of the district court should
be AFFIRMED.

HELEN FARRAR, Appellant, v. T. S. FARRAR, Defendant, FRED STUART, Appellant.

Attorney and Client: ALIMONY. Defendant was desirous of procuring a divorce from his wife (an appellant herein), but was advised
by appellant S an attorney, that he could not get it He then
induced his wife to apply for a divorce, on the promise that
she should have one thousand dollars alimony. Appellant S. was
acting as her attorney, but was to be paid for his services by
defendant A divorce was granted appellant, and one thousand
dollars alimony was awarded her as agreed upon On the same
day appellant S. procured a marriage license for defendant and
one M. F., who was to pay the alimony, which was paid, when the
marriage was consummated, by M. F. indorsing a draft for the
amount, and turning it over to appellant S. *Held*, that appellant
S. was liable to appellant for the whole amount of the one thousand dollars, less court costs, and could not pay any part of it on
defendant's order, or retain any part as attorney's fees. None of
such money can be diverted to the use of the husband, or the
payment of his creditors, although he has assigned certain
accounts to his second wife to secure the payment of money
advanced.

Appeal from Linn District Court.—HON. WILLIAM G.
THOMPSON, Judge.

WEDNESDAY, FEBRUARY 2, 1898.

HELEN FARRAR began an action for divorce against
her husband, T. S. Farrar, December 28, 1894, and
decree was entered as prayed, February 5, 1895, allowing her one thousand dollars as alimony. Thereafter
the plaintiff moved the court for an order on her
attorney, requiring him to pay over such amount, which
she alleged he had collected. The attorney was directed
to pay into court, within thirty days, the sum of five
hundred and eighty-eight dollars, with interest at six
per cent. per annum from February 5, 1895. Both

parties appeal, that of the attorney being perfected
first.—*Modified.*

Smith & Son and *Lewis Heins* for appellant Stuart.

Preston, Wheeler & Moffit for defendant appellee.

LADD, J.—The decree of divorce, allowing one thousand dollars as alimony, was entered February 5, 1895,
and on the same day the defendant married Martha
Foss. After this marriage, a draft of one thousand dollars, in favor of the latter, was delivered to her by the
Cedar Rapids Savings Bank, in pursuance of instructions so to do upon the happening of that event. This
she at once indorsed and delivered to Stuart, who paid
the plaintiff two hundred and fifty dollars. This motion
seeks to compel him to pay the balance into court for
her use and benefit.

I. Farrar first contemplated obtaining a divorce,
but, being advised no just cause existed, induced his
wife to begin proceedings. They called at Stuart's office
together, and, in his words, "it was then agreed that
she would bring the action, and he talked about turning
over a certain one thousand dollars. That was the talk,
and was the talk for some time, in connection with this
certain one thousand dollars, which was the interest of
a certain Miss Martha Foss, with whom Dr. Farrar was
then intimate, and who was subsequently to be his wife.
That certain one thousand dollars was spoken of, but
at no time was it talked that it should be the identical
one thousand dollars. That thousand was mentioned to
induce Mrs. Farrar,—to show her that there was something,—that there was a one thousand dollars to get
somehow; that there could be a one thousand dollars
put in the pot. She then began proceedings." The
plaintiff, up to the time of divorce, was led to believe,
not only that she would be allowed, but would receive

one thousand dollars alimony. At that time Stuart
paid her two hundred and fifty dollars only, and advised
her that the remainder was in notes not due, deposited
at the bank. She was not informed of the receipt of the
money. Prior to this, he had made one trip to Iowa
county with Farrar, and another with Miss Foss, to
induce the latter's brother to pay a note of one thousand
dollars, owing her, before maturity, and to assure him
of Farrar's good faith in proposing marriage in event
a divorce were procured. While doing this, at the
instance of Farrar, it was with the understanding that
the money to be obtained was for the payment of alimony to the plaintiff. The brother was informed of the
purpose for which it was being obtained, and caused it
to be sent, as heretofore stated. The draft was in favor
of Martha Foss, and was indorsed by her, and delivered
to Stuart for the purpose of paying the judgment, in
pursuance of an understanding had by her with Stuart
and Farrar. If Stuart and Farrar had a different
arrangement, it was not made known to Martha Foss,
nor to the plaintiff. Certain it is, that Foss had the
right to have the money applied as she wished. It is
said that, as Farrar assigned certain accounts to Miss
Foss to secure the payment of this money, he became
the owner thereof, and entitled to direct its disburse-
ment. But the money was procured for a specific purpose, and the security given to indemnify, in the event
of the payment of the defendant's obligation. This
Stuart fully understood, and that it was not to be paid
to Farrar, but to the plaintiff. Farrar never acquired
any interest in it, save that of having it applied on the
judgment. Stuart's action in going to Iowa county, and
assisting in procuring the money, cannot be justified on
any other ground than that of obtaining for his client,
the plaintiff, the amount to be allowed her. On any
other hypothesis, he was simply conniving in the

arrangement for a marriage of a party before any lawful right existed for making such an arrangement. Though employed by the defendant, he appeared in the action for the plaintiff, and was bound to act with perfect fidelity in the care and protection of all her interests pertaining to the suit. The testimony of Reed and Gale shows that, even after receiving the draft, he understood it to be for the appellee. If he entered into any secret arrangement with Farrar to divert this money from the purpose for which it was paid, this did not affect the right of Foss to have the money applied as agreed, or of the plaintiff to have it appropriated for the purpose intended by Foss. It is incredible that the attorney, after arranging for the payment and assuring his client that it would be paid, and after indicating to the brother its purpose, and understanding the application Foss desired, should yet enter into an agreement for the appropriation of the money, when received, for the benefit of one to whom he owed no duty, legal or moral. If true, however, it conferred upon him no authority to pay Farrar or his creditors any portion of the money received for the appellee, and he must restore to her that which fidelity and the dictates of common honesty require.

II. The district court allowed the attorney the costs paid, twelve dollars, one hundred dollars paid to Farrar, and fifty dollars for services rendered in procuring the decree of divorce. As the plaintiff was liable for the costs, these were properly credited. Stuart, however, made no claim that the plaintiff was indebted to him for attorney's fees. On the contrary, he says, "it was expressly understood I should not charge her a cent." This being true, he ought not to have been allowed anything therefor. As already stated, he was not authorized to pay Farrar the one hundred dollars, or any of his debts. We think he ought to have been required to pay into the court seven hundred and sixty-three dollars, with interest at six per cent. from February 5, 1895, instead of the amount fixed by the district court; and the cause will be remanded, with instructions to modify its order accordingly.—Affirmed on Stuart's appeal.   Reversed on plaintiff's appeal.

Bleik Peters, Appellant, v. The City of Davenport.

Contracts: fees: *Public policy.* A contract whereby an officer agrees to accept a different compensation than that provided by statute
3 for his official acts, or whereby he agrees not to avail himself of the statutory method of enforcing a collection of his fees, is contrary to public policy, and void

Same. An illegal contract, fully executed, cannot be relied upon as
5 the basis of a claim for additional compensation for services rendered thereunder

Statutory fees: *When collectible.* An officer who performs services
2 in his official capacity, at the request of another, is entitled to statutory fees therefor.

Same. Where a justice of the peace has no authority to bring an
3 action, he cannot recover his costs taxed therein, from the party in whose name the action was brought.

Same. The statutory fees allowed to a justice of the peace for per-
4 forming judicial services, cannot be claimed by a magistrate employed to collect delinquent poll taxes, when he institutes the action under a specific agreement as to compensation.

Contracts. A justice of the peace autorized to "collect delinquent poll tax lists on the same terms as last year," cannot, after receiving twenty-five per cent. of the amount collected, which the city alleges was the agreed compensation therefor, assert that he is
1 entitled, as an officer, to the statutory fees for such services, and that the contract to take less is void as against public policy where it is not shown that the tax lists were delivered to him in his official capacity, and since the resolution employing him does not, in itself, empower him to collect the taxes by suit.

Evidence. In an action by a justice of the peace against the city to recover fees alleged to be due him arising from the collection of a delinquent poll tax list, it is immaterial whether the city officers
6 ratify the bringing of the suits, when his services were performed under a specific agreement as to compensation.

SAME. Testimony as to statements made to a justice of the peace by
    city officials, is inadmissible in an action by the magistrate to
7 recover for fees alleged to be due him, when none of the officers
    or agents making the statements had power to bind the city.

SAME. Evidence as to the value of services rendered by a justice of
1 the peace in sending out notices to delinquents and publishing
2 demands in the city newspapers in connection with the collection
3 of the delinquent poll tax list placed in his hands, is inadmissible
    in an action by him to receive fees for services rendered therein as
    a justice of the peace.

Appeal from Scott District Court.—HON. WILLIAM F.
BRANNAN, Judge.

THURSDAY, FEBRUARY 3, 1898.

ACTION at law to recover fees taxed by plaintiff—a
justice of the peace—in certain actions, wherein the
defendant was plaintiff, and certain poll-tax delinquents
were defendants. The trial court directed a verdict for
defendant, and plaintiff appeals.—*Affirmed.*

D. B. Nash and *J. N. Helmick* for appellant.

E. M. Sharon for appellee.

DEEMER, C. J.—Appellant claims that appellee
requested him, in his official capacity as justice of the
peace, to collect the delinquent poll taxes appearing
upon its lists, by a resolution as follows: "That the
1   city collector be authorized to deliver to Justice
Peters for collection, the delinquent poll tax lists,
on the same terms as last year;" that he brought suit for
the collection of these taxes, with knowledge of
defendant; and that his fees for so doing amounted to
three thousand two hundred and sixty dollars, which
amount he sought to recover from defendant. Defendant pleaded that, prior to the year 1888, it had entered
into contracts with various persons for the collection
of like taxes, and had agreed to give the persons so

employed twenty-five per cent. of the amount actually collected, in full compensation for their services; that, when passing the resolution relied upon by appellant, it had in mind and referred to this arrangement, and appellant so understood it in accepting the lists for collection; that the collections made by him were under and by virtue of this contract, as an agent of the city, and not in his capacity as justice of the peace; that appellee paid him the agreed compensation from time to time as earned; and that appellant accepted the same as full compensation, and never made any claim to the contrary until many years after the services were performed. The appellant offered evidence tending to show that he was a justice of the peace when the lists were turned over to him, and that fees to the amount claimed were taxed against appellee, and that the tax lists were turned over to him by the city collector. He also offered the resolution of the city council hereinbefore referred to, and stated that he did not know what the words "on the same terms as last year" referred to, except that "the city council used to pay twenty-five per cent. on delinquent poll tax collection." He further proved that the city council took action with reference to the relief of certain parties who were made defendants to the suits. Evidence was also adduced to the effect that the appellant was allowed twenty-five per cent. of the collections made. It was also proven that the mayor of the city, during the years 1890 and 1891, knew that suits were instituted for the collection of poll taxes. This was the showing made by appellant. Appellee's motion to direct a verdict was based upon the ground that appellant's services were rendered under contract, and that, by his own showing, he had been fully paid; and for the further reason that he has shown the services were performed under contract, but has failed to show what the contract in fact was.

The issues upon which the case was tried are somewhat peculiar. Appellant seeks to recover, upon the
theory that the tax lists were turned over to him for collection in his official capacity as justice of the peace.
True, he also pleads that appellee's officers and agents
had knowledge that actions were being brought, and
judgments obtained, and that it accepted the pro-
          ceeds collected through judicial proceedings,
2   But he makes this allegation as evidence of the
          fact that he was requested to collect these taxes
as justice of the peace, and not by way of estoppel. To
recover upon this theory, he must show that the tax
lists were delivered to him in his official capacity; that
he was authorized and empowered to commence suits
against those who failed to pay, and was to receive his
fees as part compensation. For this purpose he introduced the evidence heretofore set out. It also appears
that he received from time to time twenty-five per cent.
of the amount collected for his compensation, and
never made any claim to the contrary until the commencement of this suit, which was some four years
after the services were performed. The trial court evidently found that the lists were delivered to appellant
for collection as an agent for appellee, and not in his
official capacity as justice of the peace. It is conceded
that appellant might act in either capacity, and counsel
agree that if he acted simply as agent of the city, for an
agreed compensation, he is only entitled, under the
issues as stated, to the sum agreed to be paid.

Suggestion is made in argument that a contract
whereby an officer agrees to accept a less or greater
compensation than is prescribed by statute, or whereby
          he agrees not to avail himself of the statutory
3   mode of enforcing the collection of his fees, is
          contrary to public policy, and void, and that an
officer performing service at the request of another is
entitled to the fees provided by statute. That these are

correct rules must be conceded, but the difficulty lies in
their application. Appellant has failed to show that
the tax lists were delivered to him for collection in his
official capacity. Moreover, the resolution offered does
not in itself authorize the ·collection of the taxes by
suit, and there is nothing to show that the "terms of the
last year" justified the bringing of actions against the
delinquents. Appellee cannot be made liable for costs
without authority, either express or implied, in him
who instituted the actions. Just what appellant's
authority was is not shown, and for that reason, if for
no other, he cannot recover.

One theory of appellant seems to be, that as he was
employed to collect the delinquent taxes, and instituted
the suits with knowledge of the defendant's officers, he
is entitled to the fees taxed in those actions, without
reference to the fact that he has received full compensation under his contract. No doubt this would have
been true had he instituted suits under authority simply
to collect. But as he instituted the actions under
4   a specific agreement as to compensation, and as he
has received the amount agreed to be paid, he
is in no position to say that he is also entitled to fees as
justice of the peace for performing judicial service.
See *Willemin v. Bateson,* **63** Mich. 309 (29 N. W. Rep.
734). It is familiar doctrine that, when an illegal or
immoral contract is executed, the parties will be left as
they are found, and neither can predicate any rights
thereon. Concede, then, that the contract con-
5   templated services by the appellant as justice of
the peace, and that the agreement was illegal;
as it has been fully executed, the appellant cannot rely
thereon as a basis for his claim for additional compensation. *Harvey v. Tama County,* 53 Iowa, 228. If it
should turn out, therefore, that appellant had authority
to institute suits by reason of his contract of employment, it does not follow that he is entitled to the fees

taxed in these actions. He cannot make an illegal contract the basis for the recovery of his fees. Had there been no contract except that he should collect as justice of the peace, he would then be entitled to statutory compensation, and no other. Here was a contract, however, and appellant has received his compensation thereunder. At least, he has not shown that anything is due him thereon. If this were a suit to collect fees, probably a different rule would obtain, and the question in such an action would relate simply to the authority of the justice to institute the proceedings, or to ratification by the city of the appellant's conduct in bringing the suits.

Claim is made that various officers of the city, and the council itself, ratified the bringing of the suits, and for that reason is liable for the fees. If the case turned upon the authority of appellant to bring the suits, there might be some force in this position, for there was evidence from which a jury might have found ratification. But such is not the point of inquiry. The ultimate question for determination is: Is plaintiff entitled to his fees, as part compensation for services performed under the contract? In this respect the case differs from *Hawkeye Ins. Co. v. Brainard*, 72 Iowa, 130, and *Gilman v. Railroad Co.*, 40 Iowa, 200.

I. Complaint is made of the rulings of the court in the admission and rejection of evidence. For instance, appellant attempted to introduce certain statements made to him by a member of the finance committee of the city council, before he entered into the contract. He also offered to prove certain statements said to have been made to him by the city collector. He further offered evidence as to what his duties were in the collection of the taxes, and also offered to show what he did in the matter of sending out notices to delinquents, and publishing demands in the city newspapers. All this evidence was clearly inadmissible under the issues presented. None of these officers or agents had authority to make any statements which would be binding upon the city; and, as plaintiff was seeking to recover fees for services rendered, as justice of the peace, evidence as to the value of other services was clearly improper. We have examined all questions presented, and find no error.—AFFIRMED.

J. L. SUTTON, Appellant, v. CHARLES E. RISSER, et al.

Reformation: EVIDENCE: *Laches* A self constituted agent falsely represented that the managing member of a defendant firm had read and pronounced satisfactory a written contract of sale with
1 plaintiff, the terms of which had previously been agreed on, and thereby induced the other member of the firm to sign it without reading the contents The contract signed did not express the actual agreement, as it contained a clause of which the defendants were ignorant. It was not shown that plaintiffs authorized
2 the agent to insert the clause, or to make the false representations *Held*, that the negligence of defendant in signing the contract was not so gross as to bar them of the right of reformation of the contract on the ground of fraud and mistake *Distinguishing Wallace v. Railway Co.*, 67 Iowa, 547; *Glenn v. Statler*, 42 Iowa, 107; *McCormack v. Molburg*, 43 Iowa, 561; *McKinney v. Herrick*, 66 Iowa, 414; *Jenkins v. Coal Co*, 82 Iowa, 613.

Sales: REFUSAL TO ACCEPT. Where a buyer refused to accept goods
8 on account of their quality, he cannot thereafter justify such refusal by alleging a shortage which the seller offered to correct.

EVIDENCE OF SHORTAGE. The evidence is insufficient to establish a claim of shortage, in the quantity of goods sent to a purchaser,
4 where the contract was for an exchange of land in consideration of six thousand dollars' worth of goods, shelf-worn and out of style, taken at wholesale or cost prices, since such mode of computation places a higher price upon the property than its actual value, and does not furnish any information from which that value can be determined.

Appeal from Polk District Court.—HON. THOMAS F. STEVENSON, Judge.

THURSDAY, FEBRUARY 3, 1898.

ACTION to recover upon an agreement in writing for the delivery of merchandise. The defendants allege a mistake in the agreement, and ask that it be corrected. The action was tried as in equity, and a decree was rendered in favor of the defendants. The plaintiff appeals.—*Affirmed.*

Carr & Parker for appellant.

Bishop, Bowen & Fleming for appellees.

ROBINSON, J.—The agreement in suit was made by the plaintiff and the defendants under the firm name of C. E. Risser & Bro., and as signed contains the following: "C. E. Risser & Bro. have this day bar-

1   gained and sold to J. L. Sutton six thousand dollars worth of goods, of which five thousand dollars is ladies' cloaks, of various sizes and styles, which is now in stock in store, and one thousand dollars in dress trimmings, fancy goods, and notions, and one hundred and ninety-seven dollars in cash. No damaged goods to be taken. Said goods to be invoiced at wholesale or cost price. And take in payment for same six hundred acres of land in Juneau county, Wisconsin. * * * Consideration, ten dollars per acre or six thousand dollars, said land to be free and clear of all incumbrance. Said J. L. Sutton to give warranty deed and furnish abstract for same. Said sale to be closed within thirty days from this date." A description of the land to be conveyed was inserted in the agreement. The plaintiff delivered to the defendants a warranty deed and abstract for the land within the required time, and the defendants, to perform their part of the agreement, boxed and shipped to the plaintiff, at Algona, merchandise which was invoiced at the valuation of six thousand dollars. The plaintiff refused to accept it, for the alleged reason that it consisted in

large part of old, decayed, burned, and worn-out clothing, and that it was not of the quality required by the
agreement. The defendants admit that much of the
merchandise was not new, and that some of it was damaged, but insist that it was of the kind which the agreement which the parties actually made contemplated,
and that much of it was selected and agreed upon by
the parties about the time the agreement was signed,
and that the words, "no damaged goods to be taken,"
were inserted in the agreement by mistake and fraudulently. The defendant asks that the contract be
reformed, and made to express the true agreement. The
district court granted that relief, and adjudged that the
agreement had been performed by the defendants. During the first part of the year 1894, and for some time
prior to that year, the defendants carried on, in East
Des Moines, a department store, and in West Des Moines
a dry goods store. Ladies' cloaks, dress goods, and
other articles were kept for sale in each store. In January of the year specified, a resident of Des Moines
named Griffith, asked the defendants if they had any
goods they would exchange for land, and said, in explanation, that other merchants of the city found it desirable to trade off old stock for land. The defendants said
they would consider the matter, and afterwards told
Griffith they might make an exchange of the character
indicated. Griffith said he thought he could negotiate
a trade, and from time to time made different propositions to the defendants, none of which were accepted.
Finally Griffith and a real estate agent of Des Moines,
named McClure, brought to the defendants one Nicoulin, a resident of Algona, with whom negotiations were
had. He returned to Algona, and a short time thereafter received from McClure, for execution, a contract
drawn by McClure, and signed by the defendants. It
was in all respects like the contract in suit, excepting
that the name "Bradley & Nicoulin" appeared therein,

instead of Sutton's, and no provision was made for the payment of money. The writing was given to Sutton, who changed it by inserting his own name in lieu of that of Bradley and Nicoulin, and by inserting the clause in regard to the payment of one hundred and ninety-seven dollars in money. As we understand the facts, he then signed the writing, and returned it to McClure. About that time a fire occurred in the east side store of the defendants, which damaged some of their goods; and, when the altered agreement was presented to them, they declined to approve it, on the ground that by reason of the fire they could not furnish the goods it required. It appears to have been retained by McClure, and was marked by him, "Canceled on account of fire." It appears, however, that Griffith and McClure continued their efforts to effect a trade. The plaintiff went to Des Moines, and the writing in suit was signed, and the merchandise was shipped to the plaintiff, and refused by him, as already stated. There is some conflict in the evidence in regard to the making of the contract; but we are satisfied that the facts are substantially as follows: Neither Griffith nor McClure was authorized to act as agent for the defendants, and neither was authorized to do more for them than to submit offers, although the defendants knew before the transaction was closed that a commission was to be paid to Griffith and McClure from the money payment for which the contract provided. After signing the contract, the plaintiff examined a large quantity of goods in the basement of the west-side store, which the defendants proposed to use in filling the contract. Those goods included some that had been damaged by the fire on the east side, and which had been transferred to the west side. A part of the goods were shopworn and out of style, and were not salable in Des Moines at cost prices; but the plaintiff knew what they were, and his most serious objections are made to them. It was

fully understood and agreed that the goods thus examined were to be included in those to be sent to the
plaintiff.

The writing in controversy seems to have been prepared and signed substantially as follows: After the
terms of the agreement with the plaintiff had been
settled, McClure copied the first agreement, as it
2 had been changed by the plaintiff, including the
provision that no damaged goods should be
taken, and gave the copy to Griffith. He took it to W.
H. Risser, a member of the defendant firm, and told
him that his brother, C. E. Risser, had examined the
writing, and was satisfied with it, and had sent it to
him to attach to it the firm name. Griffith represented
that he was in a hurry, and W. H. Risser, relying upon
his statements respecting C. E. Risser, and supposing
that it expressed the agreement which had actually
been made, affixed to it the firm signature, without
reading it. His brother had not in fact seen it, nor in
any manner approved it. Neither of them knew at the
time that it provided that no damaged goods were to be
taken, and in that particular it did not represent the
agreement of the parties. That the plaintiff knew that
he was to have damaged and unsalable goods is clearly
established. He knew that the defendants refused to
ratify the first agreement as changed, because they
were unable to comply with its terms on account of the
fire. We are satisfied that the goods sent to the plaintiff
were in all respects of as good quality and as valuable
as were those for which he contracted, and the larger
part of them were the same goods. After the defendants had boxed the goods and delivered them at the
railway station for shipment, they discovered that the
land which the plaintiff was to convey to them was
practically worthless, and there was some delay in
shipping the goods; but the plaintiff insisted that the
defendants should fulfill their part of the agreement,

and the goods were shipped, and the money required by
the contract was paid. It is not shown that the plaintiff authorized McClure to insert in the contract the provision in question, nor that he directed Griffith to make
to W. H. Risser the representations which induced
him to sign the writing without reading it; but he is
endeavoring to take all the advantage to himself possible from what they did and said. When the writing
was presented to him for his signature, he must have
known that it did not embody the contract which had
been made, and was chargeable with knowledge of
what had been done to secure it; or, if that be not true,
he did not understand its contents, and signed it under
a mistake of fact. If he knew what it contained, he
was constructively, at least, a party to the fraud which
had been perpetrated upon the defendants; and, if he
did not know its contents, the mistake as to what it
provided for was mutual. In view of all the circumstances of the case, we do not regard the fact that he
signed the contract before he examined the goods as
material.

We are of the opinion that, whether the contract
was procured by fraud or mistake, the defendants are
entitled to its reformation, unless they are estopped
by their own laches from obtaining that relief. See
2 Pomeroy, Equity Jurisprudence, sections 852, 853.
It is said in 3 Pomeroy, Equity Jurisprudence, section
1376, that "equity has jurisdiction to reform written
instruments in but two well-defined cases: (1) Where
there is a mutual mistake,—that is, where there has
been a meeting of the minds, an agreement actually
entered into, but the contract, deed, settlement, or other
instrument, in its written form, does not express what
was really intended by the parties thereto; and (2)
where there has been a mistake of one party, accompanied by fraud or other inequitable conduct of the
remaining parties. In such cases the instrument may

be made to conform to the agreement or transaction entered into, according to the intention of the parties."

It is insisted by the appellant that the transaction in question is within the rule of numerous cases in which relief has been denied to parties who sought to be relieved from contracts they had entered into under a mistake respecting their scope and effect, and among the cases cited to support the claim thus made are *Wallace v. Railway Co.*, 67 Iowa, 547; *Glenn v. Statler*, .42 Iowa, 107; *McCormack v. Molburg*, 43 Iowa, 561; *McKinney v. Herrick*, 66 Iowa, 414, and *Jenkins v. Coal Co.*, 82 Iowa, 618. But an examination of these cases will show that none of them involved facts which, in principle, were the same as those which must control in this case. Had the defendants not been influenced not to read the contract by artifice or false statement on the part of others interested in it, the rule of the cases cited would have applied. But the contract was signed by the defendants in consequence of the false statements of Griffith to W. H. Risser, that his brother had seen and approved it. C. E. Risser was the member of the firm who negotiated its contracts, and W. H. Risser attended to the office work. It was, therefore, natural that he should rely upon the conclusions of his brother. He did not exercise the highest degree of care and diligence which prudent men would be apt to exercise in matters of such importance, but it does not appear that he knew of any reason for questioning the truthfulness of Griffith; and since the plaintiff has not been misled by what was done, and will have all the rights to which he was entitled under the agreement actually made, we do not think it should be held that the negligence of the defendants in signing the contract was so gross as to debar them from relief. 2 Pomeroy Equity Jurisprudence, section 856. To enforce the writing as signed,

would perpetrate a great wrong, and be so unconscion-
able that a court of equity should not hesitate to
prevent it.

II. It is claimed that the invoice price of the goods
sent to the plaintiff lacked six hundred and forty-nine
dollars and ten cents of six thousand dollars, and it is
insisted that he had the right to reject all of the
3   goods sent because of the shortage. The evidence shows that the plaintiff did not reject the
goods for that reason, but because of their quality.
The defendants offered to correct "any error or discrep-
ancy," but the plaintiff refused to accept the offer, and
would not receive the goods. His refusal to accept any
of the goods cannot now be justified by the alleged failure of the defendants to furnish a small quantity which
he refused to receive.

III. Whether there was, in fact, any shortage in
the goods sent, is a question which has not received
much attention in argument. The evidence respecting
it is conflicting, and the plaintiff does not com-
4   plain because he was not permitted to recover
for shortage, although he refers to it in argument, in connection with his alleged right to reject all
of the goods, because all required by the contract were
not sent. The contract required the defendants to
furnish "six thousand dollars' worth of goods," but
that amount was to be made up with goods taken "at
wholesale or cost prices." The evidence shows that
to have been much greater than the actual value of the
goods, but does not furnish any information from which
that value can be determined. The evidence does not
satisfy us that there was any shortage, nor show what
the recovery should have been had the shortage existed,
and we conclude that we are not authorized to allow
anything on account of it. The judgment of the district
court is AFFIRMED.

IN THE MATTER OF THE ESTATE OF B. F. KAUFFMAN, Deceased. POLK COUNTY, Appellant, v. ANNA O. KAUFFMAN, Administratrix.

Taxation. The omission by the assessor to inform the person assessed, in writing, of the valuation placed upon his property as provided
1 by Code, section 1356, does not invalidate the assessment nor prejudice the owner, unless the valuation is excessive or property is erroneously included, and it will be presumed that the assessment was properly made.

SAME. Property must be assessed in the name of the owner, on Jan-
2 uary 1, previous to the time of making it under Code 1873, section 312, even though he has since died.

EXECUTORS AND ADMINISTRATORS. An administrator may, under
3 Code, section 831, seek redress from an excessive or erroneous assessment, before the board of equalization or on appeal to the courts.

Appeal from Polk District Court.—HON. T. F. STEVENSON, Judge.

THURSDAY, FEBRUARY 3, 1898.

POLK county filed with the administratrix of B. F. Kauffman, deceased, a claim for the sum of one thousand one hundred and thirty-three dollars and forty-four cents, for taxes alleged to have been levied on the personal property of the decedent. Judgment in favor of administratrix, and the county appeals.—*Reversed.*

W. G. Harvison for appellant.

N. T. Guernsey for appellee.

LADD, J.—B. F. Kauffman died May 19, 1893; and, on the following day, D. S. Calkins, an assistant of one of the assessors of the city of Des Moines, called on the wife of the deceased, for the purpose of assessing the property left by him. He did so, fixing the value of the personal property at one thousand and ten dollars, including "corporate stocks, $600.00," and gave the wife a copy of the assessment, appearing on page 123 of the assessor's book. The taxes levied on this valuation have been paid. On page 259 of such book is this entry:

Owner's Name.	Corporation Stocks.	Total of all Property.
Kauffman, B. F............	16,800 800	17,600

The taxes levied on this assessment are in controversy. No copy thereof was given Mrs. Kauffman, and she was not advised of this assessment until January, 1895. The time of the additional entry does not appear. Calkins explains that the assessors met every Saturday, and that, from information derived from one of them, the assessment was made, and, as was customary in such cases, placed in the back part of the book.

1   Whether Kauffman was owner of any stock, or of more than first assessed, is not shown; but the assessment, in the absence of evidence to the contrary, will be presumed to have been properly made. *Silcott v. McCarty*, 62 Iowa, 161. And it may be conceded that, if illegal, the taxes levied thereon cannot be collected. *Tackaberry v. City of Keokuk*, 32 Iowa, 155; *Wangler v. Black Hawk County*, 56 Iowa, 384; *Farmers' Loan & Trust Co. v. City of Newton*, 97 Iowa, 502. The failure to notify Mrs. Kauffman of the assessment did not render it void. *Powers v. Bowman*, 53 Iowa, 359. It is true, that section 1356 of the Code provides that the person assessed shall be informed in writing of the valuation placed upon his property, and that he may appear before the board of review if aggrieved. This imposes a duty on the assessor. Its

omission, however, will not invalidate the assessment. The owner is not prejudiced unless the valuation is excessive, or property is erroneously included. Mere irregularities, not resulting in injury, will not be permitted to defeat the collection of taxes justly due. *Conway v. Younkin,* 28 Iowa, 295; *Meyer v. City of Dubuque,* 49 Iowa, 193; *Litchfield v. Hamilton County,* 40 Iowa, 66; *Robbins v. Magoun,* 101 Iowa, 580. The theory of the law is that all property not exempt therefrom shall be subject to taxation; and in order to accomplish this result, and at the same time avoid the imposition of this burden more than once, a specific date must be fixed when property shall be assessed, because of the many changes of ownership constantly occurring. For this reason the assessments of

2   personal property in this state relate back to the first of January previous, under the provision of section 812 of the Code, 1873, that "all taxable property shall be taxed each year, and personal property shall be listed and assessed each year in the name of the owner thereof on the first day of January. * * *" Section 803 relates only to the duty of persons to assist the assessor in listing property. Sections 805 and 806 relate to the manner of listing. Now, on January 1, 1893, Kauffman was the owner of certain property; and, under the statute quoted, it was assessable in his name, for the assessment must be to the owner at that time, rather than when made. See *Shippen v. Hardin,* 34 N. J. Law, 79. Had he departed this life prior to that date, it might not have been properly assessed in his name, though, even under such circumstances, it is doubtful, in the absence of prejudice, whether such an assessment would not be valid. See *City of New Orleans v. Ferguson,* 28 La. Ann. 240; *State v. Platt,* 24 N. J. Law, 108. It is said that, in event the valuation be raised by the board of equalization, no notice could be given, under section 3, chapter 109, of the Acts of the

Eighteenth General Assembly. The notice there provided is by posting, and those interested in the estate are as fully advised by the publication of the name of the owner of January 1, previous, as of that of his administrator or heirs. Secton 831 (Code 1873) permits the owner of the property assessed to seek redress before the board of equalization, and, on appeal, in the courts. It has reference to the owner to whom the property was assessed, or his representatives and is broad enough to include the administrator. In *Burns v. McNally*, 90 Iowa, 432, the executors were such, January 1 prvious to the assessment, and were therefore owners, in the meaning of the law; and the contrary does not appear in *Cameron v. City of Burlington*, 56 Iowa, 320. Unless the statute is given an interpretation antagonistic to its plain language and evident meaning, property must be assessed in the name of the owner, January 1 previous to the time of making it, even though he has died since. Such a ruling tends to uniformity, and enables every person to guard his interests. Some authorities are called to our attention to the effect that under certain circumstances an assessment cannot be made in the name of a dead man; but a careful examination of these discloses that they are not in point, or construe statutes differing essentially from those of this state. Such provisions seem to be uniformly upheld. See authorities collected in 25 Am. & Eng. Enc. Law, 213. That valuation of stock cannot be offset by indebtedness, is settled in *Bridgman v. City of Keokuk*, 72 Iowa, 42. It follows that the amount of taxes, with penalties, ought to have been established as a claim against the estate of the deceased.—REVERSED.

THE J. MILLER COMPANY, Appellant, v. J. L. BRACKEN, Garnishee.

Mortgages: CREDITORS: *Fraud.* A creditor whose claim is directed to be paid from the proceeds of a stock of goods, by the erms of a mortgage on the property, executed to a trustee for that pur. pose, is entitled to the fund as against general creditors, although a previous chattel mortgage alleged to be fraudulent had been executed in her favor, which was left unfiled for about two years. but under which she made no claim.

Appeal from Tama District Court.—HON. G. W. BURN-HAM, Judge.

FRIDAY, FEBRUARY 4, 1898.

ISSUES were joined between the plaintiff, a creditor of W. A. Inscho, and J. L. Bracken, garnished as a supposed debtor to said Inscho. The garnishee moved for a verdict, which motion was sustained, and a verdict return for the defendant, and judgment for costs rendered against plaintiff. Plaintiff appeals.—*Affirmed.*

Struble & Stiger for appellant.

W. H. Stivers and *J. W. Willett* for appellee.

GIVEN, J.—Plaintiff commenced this action, to recover one hundred and sixty-three dollars and forty cents, against W. A. Inscho. An attachment was issued, and J. L. Bracken garnished, as a supposed debtor of said Inscho. Inscho had been engaged in the mercantile business at Tama, Iowa, for a number of years, and at that time owned a stock of merchandise worth about four thousand dollars. On October 31, 1892, Inscho executed to Diana Salsbury, his wife's mother, a chattel mortgage on said goods, to secure two

notes aggregating two thousand five hundred and forty
dollars. On November 5, 1894, about 8 o'clock P. M.,
said mortgage was filed for record by one Johnson, at
the instance of the mortgagor. Soon thereafter the
First National Bank of Tama brought an action, aided
by attachment, against said Inscho, to recover an
indebtedness of about two thousand dollars, and caused
the attachment to be levied upon said stock of merchandise. On the seventh day of November, 1894, W. A.
Inscho executed to James L. Bracken, as trustee, a mortgage upon said stock of goods to secure the indebtedness
to said bank and to Diana Salsbury; priority being
given to the indebtedness to the bank. Mr. Bracken,
as such trustee, took possession and disposed of the
goods; and it is agreed that he has in his hands, funds
sufficient, realized from the sale of the goods, after paying the claim of the bank, to pay the amount of plaintiff's claim and the costs herein. The contention is
whether that balance remaining in the hands of the
garnishee shall go to Mrs. Salsbury, or to the plaintiff
company. Appellant's contention is that the mortgage
of October 31, 1892, to Mrs. Salsbury, was never delivered, or, if delivered, was withheld from record, in pursuance of an understanding between the parties thereto,
and was, therefore, fraudulent, as to the plaintiff, who
extended credit to Inscho upon the faith of his being
the owner of said stock of goods free from incumbrance.
This contention may be conceded, yet the question
remains whether Mrs. Salsbury is not entitled to the balance remaining in the hands of the garnishee under the
mortgage made to him as trustee, November 7, 1894.
That mortgage appears to have been executed in pursuance of an arrangement between the attorney for the
bank, and the attorney for Mrs. Salsbury. There is no
question but that Inscho was indebted to Mrs. Salsbury in the amount secured by the mortgage, and no
reason appears why her attorney might not, for her,

have taken this last mortgage. The fact that the mortgage of October 31, 1892, was fraudulent as to creditors of Inscho, was no reason why a valid mortgage might not be taken to secure the same idebtedness. Nothing is claimed for Mrs. Salsbury under that first mortgage, but only under the second, the validity of which is not questioned. Nothing occurred in connection with this second mortgage to deceive the plaintiff into extending credit to Inscho. As we view the case, it stands as though the first mortgage had never been given, and Mrs. Salsbury is entitled to the amount in the hands of the garnishee under the mortgage executed to him as trustee. This conclusion finds support in *Letts-Fletcher Co. v. McMaster*, 83 Iowa, 450, and *Everingham v. Harris*, 99 Iowa, 447. There was no error in sustaining the garnishee's motion to strike said mortgage of October 31, 1892, from the evidence, nor in directing a verdict for the garnishee.—AFFIRMED.

CHARLES A. WESCOTT, *et al.*, Appellants, v. T. BINFORD, *et al.*

Wills: INTENTION: *Rule in Shelley's Case.* The rule in *Shelley's Case*, if it be in force in the state of Iowa, cannot defeat the intent of a testator as expr ssed by the language of the will.

SAME In a devise of land to one "to hold the s me during the term of his natural life," and giving him the use, rents, and profits of it during such time, but providing that he should "have no power to convey or dispose of the same" for a period longer than his life, and that at his death it should descend to his heirs, the word "heirs" will not be given its technical effect, and the rule in *Shelley's Case* will not apply, as it was testator's clear intention to create a life estate only.

SAME. In such devise, the fact that testator is presumed to have intended a devise of all his interest in the property, and that the heirs of the devisee could not be definite y known until his death, would not create in him a larger estate than the testator intended him to have.

Appeal from Marshall District Court.—HON. B. P. BIRD-SALL, Judge.

SATURDAY, FEBRUARY 5, 1898.

ACTION at law to recover the possession of real property and damages for its detention. A demurrer to the petition was sustained, and, the plaintiffs refusing to plead further, judgment was rendered in favor of the defendants for costs. The plaintiffs appeal.—*Reversed.*

R. W. Hargrave and *Struble & Stiger* for appellants.

Binford & Snelling and *J. H. Preston* for appellees.

ROBINSON, J.—The material facts admitted by the demurrer are substantially as follows: In October, 1865, John Wescott, a resident of Marshall county, died testate, seized, in fee simple, of real property in the town of Marshall, in Marshall county. The will of the decedent was admitted to probate, and contains the following provisions: "* * * I do give, devise, and bequeath unto my wife, Hannah Westcott, the real estate situated in said county of Marshall and state of Iowa, described as follows, to-wit: Lots numbered four and five, block numbered nineteen, and lots numbered seven and nine in block numbered six, all in the town of Marshall; * * * to have and to hold said real estate in her own right. I do further give and bequeath unto my wife, Hannah Westcott, the real estate situated in said county of Marshall and state of Iowa described as follows: Lots numbered seven and eight, in block eleven, in the town of Marshall; to have and to hold the same during the term of her natural life, and at her decease to be divided among my children as follows: * * * The east one-third of said lot [seven, in block eleven] I do give and bequeath to my son William Edwin Westcott, to have and to become possessed of the same at the death of my said wife, and to hold the same during the term of his natural life." The west one-third of the same lot was devised to Mrs. Scott, the middle one-third to Mrs. Gibson, and separate parts of lot 8, in block 11, were devised to Mrs. Hardenberg, Joseph Leander Westcott, and Charles Alfred Westcott, on the same terms and conditions as those which applied to the devise to William Edwin Wescott. All of the devisees named, excepting the wife, were children of the testator. The last paragraph of the will is as follows: "My said children are to have the use, rents, and profits of their portion of said lots number seven and eight, in block numbered eleven, in the town of Marshall, respectively, during the term of their natural lives. They are to have no power to convey or dispose of the same, their respective portions, for a longer period than during their natural lives, respectively. At the death of my children aforesaid, their respective portions of said lots numbered seven and eight descend to their heirs, respectively, said heirs to have absolute title to their respective portions." In August, 1875, William Edwin Wescott and his wife executed to Thaddeus Binford a deed of special warranty, which purported to convey the interest of Wescott in the east one-third of lot 7, in block 11, in words as follows: "conveying hereby all the right and title I have in the above property by virtue of the last will and testament of John Wescott, deceased." William Edwin Wescott died in January, 1892. The plaintiffs are his children, and the husbands and wives of the children who are married. The children claim to own, and in this action seek to recover, the part of the lot conveyed by their father to Binford. The defendants are Binford and W. E. Snelling and their wives. Binford and Snelling claim the property in question through the deed of Wescott

to Binford, and are in possession of it. The grounds of
the demurrer are, in substance, that the petition does
not state facts which show that the plaintiffs are
entitled to relief, for the reason that it shows that William Edwin Wescott obtained a title in fee simple to
the property in question through the will of his father,
and that his title was transferred by his deed to Binford.

    I. The question we are required to determine
involves the consideration of the rule in *Shelley's Case.*
A statement of that rule, found in 4 Kent, Commentaries, 215, and several times quoted by this court, is

2
as follows: "When a person takes an estate of
freehold, legally or equitably, under a deed, will,
or other writing, and in the same instrument
there is a limitation by way of remainder, either with
or without the interposition of another estate, of an
interest of the same legal or equitable quality, to his
heirs, or heirs of his body, as a class of persons to take
in succession, from generation to generation, the limitation to the heirs entitles the ancestor to the whole
estate." See *Pierno v.s Lane*, 60 Iowa, 61; *Zaritz v.
Preston*, 96 Iowa, 52. The rule is of common-law origin,
and has been the subject of much controversy. Where
the rule is enforced in all its rigor, it is held to be a rule
of property, and not of construction, and a grant or
devise to a person named, "and his heirs," would be
subject to the rule, and no declaration, however une-
quivocal, that the ancestor should have the estate for
life only, or that his heirs should take as purchasers,
would be effective. The particular intent thus clearly
stated would be compelled to yield to the intent
expressed by the use of words havng a technical meaning. *Trumbull v. Trumbull*, 149 Mass. 200. It was said
in *Daniel v. Whartenby*, 17 Wall. 639, that where the
rule is in force, "if the testator has used technical
language which brings the case within the rule, a
declaration, however positive, that the rule shall not

apply, or that the estate of the ancestors shall not continue beyond the primary express limitation, or that
his heirs shall take by purchase, and not by descent, will
be unavailing to exclude the rule, and cannot affect the
result." In *Silva v. Hopkinson*, 158 Ill. 386 (41
N. E. Rep 1013), it is said, with reference to the application of the rule: "No principle of law is better established than that, although the testator did intend the
first taker to have but a life estate, yet, if the technical
words are used, that intention, be it ever so clearly
expressed, will be defeated, and the first devisee allowed
to take the whole estate. * * * The only method
in which an instrument employing the word 'heirs' can
be shown not to be within the rule is by showing that
the word was not employed in its strict legal sense.
* * * It is well settled that the words must be given
their legal effect, even though the subsequent words are
inconsistent therewith, unless they make it clear that
they were not so used." See, also, *Conger v. Lowe*, 124
Ind. 368 (24 N. E. Rep. 889); *Kleppner v. Laverty*, 70 Pa.
St. 73; 2 Washburn, Real Property, *272; 1 Jones, Real
Property, section 601 *et seq.*; Hay's Principles for
Express Disposition of Real Property, 96; 22 Am. &
Eng. Enc. Law, 495, and note.

The rule was not designed to defeat the intention
of the grantor or testator, but gave to certain words,
as "heirs," such force and effect that when used they
were conclusively presumed to show an intent to vest
the estate in the ancestor, in fee. Theoretically, the
rule was not applied to ascertain the intent of the
grantor or testator, but to declare its effect when ascertained. *Smith v. Collins*, 90 Ga. 411 (17 S. E. Rep. 1013);
Allen v. Craft, 109 Ind. 476 (58 Am. Rep. 425; 9 N. E.
Rep. 919); 22 Am. & Eng. Enc. Law, 495. The practical
operation of the rule has been such, however, that it has
not met with general favor in this country. It has never
been adopted in some states, and in others, where it was

once in force, it has been abolished by statute. At the
present time it is in force in but few of the states. 1
Jones, Real Property, 602, and notes. *Daniel v. Whartenby, supra.* It has been recognized to some extent in
this state, but has never been formally adopted or
declared to be in force. It was referred to in *Zuver
v. Lyons,* 40 Iowa, 513, but held not to apply to the
matter there in controversy. In *Hanna v. Hawes,* 45
Iowa, 441, it was said: "Conceding the rule in *Shelley's
Case* to be the law in this state, it is not applicable. It is
evident that the concession stated was for the purposes
of that case only, and was not intended to be of general
application. In *Slemmer v. Crampton,* 50 Iowa, 302, the
rule was again referred to, but this court held, in effect,
that the devise involved in that case was not within the
rule. In *Kiene v. Gmehle,* 85 Iowa, 313, the rule was
discussed, but not found to apply in that case. In
Zavitz v. Preston, 96 Iowa, 52,—the latest case decided
by this court, in which the rule was considered,—it was
said: "Whether the rule in *Shelley's Case* is in force in
this state we need not determine." Two cases have
been decided by this court, in which the rule was
applied. In the first of these (*Pierson v. Lane,* 60 Iowa,
60), it was held that a conveyance of real estate to
"Minerva Pierson, and the heirs of her body, begotten
by her present husband," vested in Mrs. Pierson the
title in fee. Whether the rule in *Shelley's Case* was in
force in this state was a mooted question, but the discussion turned upon the statute *de donis* (13 Edwards,
I Chancery, 1), with the conclusion that it was not in
force as a part of the common law of this state. It was
held that the conveyance to Mrs. Pierson vested in her
the title in fee simple, and it is fair to say that the
holding was based upon the rule in *Shelley's Case,*
although no statement to that effect was made. The
second case in which that rule was applied is *Broliar
v. Marquis,* 80 Iowa, 49, which involved a conveyance

by John Marquis to "Annie Marquis and her children and joint heirs with her and myself and Mercelly Marquis and Ella Marquis." It was conceded by the parties in that case that under the holding in *Pierson v. Lane, supra,* and *Case v. Dwire,* 60 Iowa, 442, the children of Annie Marquis took nothing by the conveyance. Whether the concession thus made was well founded, or whether the rule in *Shelley's Case* was in force in this state, was not discussed nor decided.

The decisions of this court to which we have referred comprise all the cases, so far as we are advised, in which this court has considered the rule in question, and it cannot be said that they show that it has been adopted or should be enforced in this state. The most that can be said of the recognition of the rule by this court is that in the cases of *Pierson v. Lane* and *Broliar v. Marquis, supra,* it was assumed to be in force. Whether the decisions in those cases might not well have been placed on other grounds than the rule in *Shelley's Case,* and whether the concession made in the case last named was well founded, we need not determine. It should be noticed, however, that both cases involved deeds of conveyance of real property, and not wills.

A material distinction between wills and deeds of conveyance, in the application of the rule, has been observed by the authorities. It is said of the rule in 4 Kent, Commentaries, *216, that "there is more latitude of construction allowed in the case of wills, in furtherance of the testator's intention; and the rule seems to have been considered as of more absolute control in its application to deeds." In *Ridgeway v. Lanphere,* 99 Ind. 253, it was said: "The rule in *Shelley's Case,* 1 Coke, 88, is the law in this state, and, in all cases where the facts make it applicable, we must enforce it, although we may think there was not much reason for it at the time of its adoption and none at all under the existing system of tenures and conveyances. But in accepting the rule we take it as construed and enforced by the courts which formulated and proclaimed it. Pressed by the evils wrought by the rule, and shocked by the great number of instances in which it operated to utterly overthrow the intention of the testator, these courts, centuries ago, affirmed that there existed an important difference between wills and deeds, and that the rule should not be so strictly enforced in the case of a will as in the case of a deed. It has long stood as the law that there is a material distinction between wills and deeds, and that the rule in *Shelley's Case* will not be allowed to override the manifest and clearly expressed intention of the testator, but that the intention will always be carried into effect if it can be ascertained. It is true, that, where the words used are such as to bring the case within the rule, it will be given full force and effect; but, where the context clearly shows that the testator annexed a different meaning, that meaning will be adopted, and the rule will not be allowed to frustrate his intention." See, also, *McIlhinny v. McIlhinny*, 137 Ind. 411 (37 N. E. Rep. 147). It was said in Jones Real Property, section 606, that, "as applied to wills, the rule is not allowed to override the manifest and clearly expressed intention of the testator, but the intention will always be carried into effect if it can be ascertained. * * * This distinction between deeds and wills in the application of the rule is in accordance with the general rule applicable to the construction of wills, that the intention of the testator shall, so far as possible, be observed."

The rule of interpretation of general application, which this court has invariably followed, is that the intention of the testator, when ascertained, and not in violation of law, must control. *Hopkins v. Grimes*, 14 Iowa, 77; *Benkert v. Jacoby*, 36 Iowa, 275; *Hanna v. Hawes*, 45 Iowa, 439; *Meek v. Briggs*, 87 Iowa, 616;

Kiene v. Gmehle, 85 Iowa, 316; *Zavitz v. Preston*, 96 Iowa, 52. In *Kiene v. Gmehle* it was said: "There are some respectable authorities that hold that the rule in *Shelley's Case* is independent of the intention of the donor or devisor; that it is absolute and imperative. Such application of the rule is not sanctioned by reason or the current of adjudicated cases in this country." The devise considered in that case was to the daughter of the testator, "for and during her lifetime, * * * and on her demise the said estate, both real and personal, shall descend to and vest in such heirs of her body begotten, in fee simple;" and it was held to give the daughter only a life estate in the real property of the testator. In *Zavitz v. Preston, supra,* a devise of real estate to a grandson "during his natural life," and at his death "to go to and be equally divided between, his lawful heirs and next of kin," was held to vest in the grandson a life estate, only. The rule in *Shelley's Case* was referred to, but, without determining that it was in force in this state, we said that "it certainly cannot be invoked to defeat the intent of the testator." In *Slemmer v. Crampton, supra,* a devise of land to Maria A. Avery, "to be used, occupied, and enjoyed by her after she becomes of the age of legal majority, during her natural life only," and, after her death, "to the heirs of her body," was held to vest in Maria A. Avery a life estate, only, notwithstanding the rule in *Shelley's Case.*

It is well know that wills are frequently drawn hurriedly, by persons not skilled in the use of technical terms, and words are often used in them in a sense not technically accurate. That is true of the word 4 "heirs." *Furenes v. Severtson,* 102 Iowa, 322. To hold that when used it must be given a technical effect; that it must be taken as a word of limitation, and not of purchase, notwithstanding the fact that the context shows clearly that it was not used in a technical sense,—does not seem to us to be in harmony with the best rules of interpretation, nor with the weight of authority, nor to be founded in reason, nor to be demanded by anything in the letter or spirit of the laws of this state, or the condition and policy of its people and their institutions. The conditions which the rule was originally designed to meet do not exist here, and to hold that it applies to the will under consideration would be to go counter to the rules of interpretation which this court has always applied to wills, to overrule in effect many cases which we have decided, and to some of which we have referred, and to establish a rule which has been so unjust in its operation as to be abandoned or modified by nearly all of the states in which it was once in force.

The will under consideration gave to William Edwin Wescott the property in controversy, "to hold the same during the term of his natural life," and provided that he should have the use, rents, and profits of it during that time. The will also provided that he should "have no power to convey or dispose of the same" for a longer period than during his natural life, and that at his death it should descend to his heirs. That the will was intended to create in the ancestor a life estate only, is too clear for controversy, and the fact that the testator will be presumed to have intended a devise of all his interest in the property, and the further fact that the heirs of the devisee could not be definitely known until his death, would not create in him a larger estate than the testator intended him to have. Upon his death the absolute title to the property vested in his heirs. The language of the will brings it within the rule of the cases of *Slemmer v. Crampton, Kiene v. Gmehle*, and *Zavitz v. Preston, supra*, to which we 5   have referred. We do not find it necessary to determine whether the rule in *Shelley's Case* is in force, in this state, but hold that, if it be in force, it cannot defeat the intent of a testator, as expressed by the language of his will. It follows from what we have said that the demurrer to the petition should have been overruled, and the judgment of the district court is REVERSED.

THE VALLEY NATIONAL BANK v. W. C. GARRETSON; *et al.*, Appellants.

104
f 111

104
d124

Attorneys: SURETIES ON APPEAL. An attorney cannot, under Code 1873, section 2931, become a surety upon a bond given on appeal from a justice's court to the district court, and the giving of such bond do s not perfect the appeal Citing *Noble v. Bradley*, 50 N. W. Rep. (S. D.) 1057; *Cilbank v. Stephenson*, 30 Wis. 155; *Cothren v. Connaughton*, 24 Wis. 187; *Schuck v. Hager*, 24 Minn. 341.

Appeal from Polk District Court.—HON. C. P. HOLMES, Judge.

MONDAY, FEBRUARY 7, 1898.

ACTION at law upon a promissory note, commenced in justice's court. In the district court a motion to dismiss the cause on the ground that a sufficient appeal bond had not been filed was overruled, the cause was tried by the court, and a judgment was rendered in favor of the plaintiff. The defendants appeal.— REVERSED.

J. A. Merritt for appellants.

Powell & Paschal for appellee.

ROBINSON, J.—In justice's court there was a trial by jury, a verdict in favor of the defendants, and a judgment in favor of the plaintiff for certain sums which the defendants had tendered to him, and paid into court. Thereafter a notice of appeal to the district court was served by the plaintiff upon the defendants, and an appeal bond, signed by F. W. Paschal as surety, was filed. The motion to dismiss, which the district court

overruled, was based upon the ground that the bond
was not sufficient, because Paschal, the only surety
who signed it, was a practicing attorney, and one of the
attorneys for the plaintiff. It is admitted that the
ground stated was true, and we are to determine
whether the bond was sufficient to give the district court
jurisdiction to try the cause.

Section 3576 of the Code of 1873 required appeals
from the judgments of justices' courts to be taken and
perfected within twenty days after the rendition of the
judgments. Section 3580 provided that an appeal
should not be allowed in any case until a bond in the
form given in this section, or its equivalent, should be
taken and filed in the office of the justice, or clerk of the
district court, in certain cases. The form given required
one surety. The bond given in this case was in the statutory form. The surety, by affidavit, showed that he was a
resident of this state, and had the requisite property
qualifications, and the bond was approved by the
justice. It appears the bond was sufficient, unless
Paschal was disqualified to sign it as surety. Section
2931 of the Code of 1873, in force when the bond was
given, was as follows: "No attorney or other officer of
the court shall be received as security in any proceeding
in court." It was said in *Massie v. Mann*, 17 Iowa, 131,
of this provision, as it appeared in the Revision of 1860,
that, although it was found in the chapter regulating
security for costs, it was not limited to such cases, but
was intended to prohibit attorneys from becoming sureties in any proceedings pending in court. It was further
said that "the language is general, is imperative, and
the reason for the law applies to injunctions, attachments, and similar bonds as fully as to those for securing costs." See, also, *Cuppy v. Coffman*, 82 Iowa, 214.
It was held in *Wright v. Schmidt*, 47 Iowa, 233, that
an attorney who had become surety on a bond to which
the section applied could not escape liability where the

bond had been accepted and treated as valid; but the legal effect of such a bond, excepting as to the liability of the surety, was not determined. In *Towle v. Bradley*, 2 S. D. 472 (50 N. W. Rep. 1057) a statute was considered which was as follows: "No practicing attorney and counselor shall be a surety in any suit or proceeding which may be instituted in any of the courts of this state;" and it was held to deprive an attorney of the legal power or ability to become a surety on an undertaking, in any action pending in the courts of that state; that the statute was not a personal privilege, which the attorney could waive, but was based upon public policy; and that the appeal from justice's court, which was there under consideration, should have been dismissed, because the appeal bond was not sufficient. Similar decisions have been rendered by the supreme courts of Wisconsin and Minnesota. See *Gilbank v. Stephenson*, 30 Wis. 155; *Cothren v. Connaughton*, 24 Wis. 137; *Schuek v. Hagar*, 24 Minn. 341.

It is claimed, however, that the statute in question does no apply to proceedings in justices' courts; and the case of *Smith v. Humphrey*, 15 Iowa, 428, is relied upon as supporting the claim thus made. It was said in that case that chapter 136 of the Revision of 1860, which corresponds with the chapter of the Code of 1873, in which is found the section in controversy, did not authorize justice's courts to require the plaintiffs to give security for costs. The provision in question, although contained in the chapter of the Revision referred to, was not in controversy. The question really involved in the case was whether so much of chapter 136 of the Revision as provided for the giving of security for costs applied to cases in justice's court, and it was answered in the negative. It is true, the opinion stated that the question presented was whether the chapter applied exclusively to proceedings in the district court, but the question thus stated was not presented, and it was not decided. Every section of that chapter but one, and every section but one of the corresponding chapter of the Code of 1873, referred, in terms, to security for costs. The two sections which did not refer specially to such security were section 3446 of the Revision and section 2931 of the Code of 1873, now in question, and these sections are in language and legal effect precisely the same. That the general assembly did not intend to limit the application of either to security for costs is shown by the fact that the words which showed such an intent in the other section were omitted from these, and language of a much broader and more comprehensive scope was used. They provided that no attorney should be received "as security in any proceeding in court." As we have stated, this court has held that the section was not limited to security for costs, but was general, and we are of the opinion that the same is true of the reference to courts. The language of the section is sufficiently broad to include all courts over which the legislative authority extends, and the same reasons exist for applying it to justices' courts as to courts of record.

We conclude that the justice was not authorized to accept the appeal bond in controversy; that the plain-tiff failed to comply with the law in regard to appeal bonds; and that the district court did not have jurisdiction to try the case on its merits. It follows that the motion to dismiss the case should have been sustained by the district court, and for the error in overruling the motion its judgment is REVERSED.

JOHN GRIEVE v. THE ILLINOIS CENTRAL RAILWAY COM-
PANY, Appellant.

Contract: CARRIERS: *Public policy.* A railroad company cannot,
under Code 2074, preventing any limitation of the liability of a
common carrier, relieve itself from care of live stock by a contract
8 providing that the cars shall be in charge of the shipper, who
assumes the duty of loading and unloading, attending a and feeding the stock at his own expense and risk.

RULE APPLIED. Notwithstanding the invalidity of a provision of a
3 contract for the shipment of live stock requiring the shipper to
4 care for the same, a shipper who is furnished transportation and
5 actually undertakes to care for his stock, cannot recover from the
6 carrier for injuries occasioned by his neglect to exercise such care.
Citing *Railroad Co. v. McRue* (Texas) 27 Am. St Rep. 926; *Johnson v. Railroad Co.* (Miss.) 11 So. Rep 104; *Clark v. Railroad Co.*,
67 Am. Dec. 205.

SAME. Valid conditions in a shipping contract, which cannot be
5 separated from those which are understood by both parties to be
invalid, can be enforced.

SAME. The fact that no notice of damage was given a railroad company, as required in a shipping contract, does not relieve the company of liability, since the condition is a limitation of the carrier's
6 liability, and therefore void, under Code, section 2074, providing
no contract shall exempt any railroad corporation engaged in
transporting property from the liability of a common carrier,
which would exist had no contract been made or entered into.

EVIDENCE. Injury to property in transit being shown, the burden is
7-8 cast upon the carrier to exculpate itself from blame.

Same. A shipper who has undertaken to care for his own stock while
7 in transit, has the burden of showing that injury thereto did not
result from his own negligence, and, if occasioned by failure to
8 do what he has undertaken then, that such failure resulted from
omission on the part of the carrier to do some duty devolving
upon it.

Appeal: CONDUCT BELOW. Where a defendant, by answer, meets
1 issues indefinitely stated in the petition, he cannot afterwards
complain that they are not properly tendered.

RULE APPLIED. The petition alleged that stock was damaged by
delay in delivery, and by "their long confinement, * * * exposure, and lack of proper care and attention " The answer denied

lack of care, and set up matter in justification of the delay. *Held*, that the answer put in issue the question of negligence in the delay and failure to exercise care.

HARMLESS ERROR. Error in overruling a motion to direct a verdict for defendant is cured so far as possible by setting aside the 2 verdict returned and granting a new trial; and the refusal to direct will not be reviewed, on appeal.

Appeal from Buena Vista District Court.—HON. W. B. QUARTON, Judge.

MONDAY, FEBRUARY 7, 1898.

ACTION for damages on shipment of stock. Trial to jury, and verdict for the plaintiff. The motion of the defendant for new trial was sustained, and that for judgment on the answers to special interrogatories overruled. The defendant appeals.—*Affirmed*.

Duncombe & Kenyon and *T. D. Higgs* for appellant.

Mack & De Land for appellee.

LADD, J.—The plaintiff shipped thirty-nine head of fat cattle and some hogs over the defendant's railway, June 26, 1894, from Storm Lake to Chicago. These were loaded at about 9 o'clock P. M., and reached Chicago at 5 o'clock A. M., of June 28th, but were not delivered to the consignee at the stock yards till eight minutes after 2 o'clock P. M. The plaintiff alleged in his petition that "during all the time from 5 o'clock A M. to 3 o'clock P. M. of the said twenty-eighth day of June, 1894, the said cattle and hogs were kept confined in the cars within which they were shipped, and upon the tracks of the defendant, at different points of the city of Chicago, exposed constantly and continuously during all such time to the heat of the sun, which was excessive; that when said cattle and hogs were delivered to the

consignee at about 3 o'clock P. M. of said twenty-eighth
day of June, 1894, they were in a badly-damaged condition, having shrunken considerably in weight, and
showing in other ways their long confinement in the
cars, exposure, and lack of proper care and attention,
by reason of which this plaintiff has been damaged in
the sum of six hundred dollars." It is asserted

1   that no allegation of failure to properly care for
the stock is contained in the portion of the petition set out. The statement is not as specific as might
have been required, had timely obejection been made.
The answer, however, clearly puts in issue the negligence charged in delay and the failure to exercise care,
as it, in terms, denies lack of care, and alleges the delay
was occasioned by the intimidation, violence, and interference of strikers and mobs in Chicago, and that the
stock was delivered as soon as possible. Having met
the issues, indefinitely stated in the petition, the defendant is not in a position to say they were not tendered.

II.   The alleged error in overruling the motion to
direct a verdict for the defendant ought not to be determined. If it be conceded, the court corrected it,

2   in so far as possible, by setting aside the verdict
returned, and granting a new trial. The evidence may be different on another trial, and, in any
event, we cannot anticipate what the court's ruling will
be when the question is again presented.

III. The jury found, in answer to special interrogatories, that the transportation of the stock was
unreasonably delayed, but that this was not occasioned
by any negligence on the part of the defendant. It will
be observed that no finding was returned with respect
to the care given the stock. The assertion that this is
not within the issues has been disposed of. It is said,

however, that no notice of the claim for damages was
given, as required by the shipping contract. This
3   contains the condition that "no claim for loss or
damage to stock shall be valid against said railroad company unless it shall be made in writing, verified by affidavit, and delivered to the general freight
agent of the railroad company at Chicago, or to agent
of the company at the station from which the stock is
shipped, or to the agent of the company at the point of
destination, within ten days from the time said stock is
removed from said cars." Such limitations have been
regarded as reasonable and binding, in the absence of
statutory regulations, as tending to prevent fraud. *Dawson v. Railway Co.*, 76 Mo. 514; *Coggin v. Railway Co.*,
12 Kan. 416. But they are limitations of the liability of
the common carrier, and cannot be upheld, because
against the prohibition of section 2074 of the Code: "No
contract, receipt, rule or regulation shall exempt any
railroad corporation engaged in transporting persons or
property, from the liability of a common carrier, or
carrier of passengers, which would exist had no contract, receipt, rule or regulation been made or entered
into." See *Missouri P. R'y Co. v. Vandeventer*, 26 Neb. 222
(41 N. W. Rep. 998); *Ohio & M. R'y Co. v. Tabor*, 98 Ky.
503 (32 S. W. Rep. 168; 36 S. W. Rep. 18); *Brown v. Railroad Co.*(Ky.) 38 S. W. Rep. 862.

IV. The defendant insists it was relieved from the
care of the stock by the terms of the contract, in the
words following: "(2) The cars containing the stock are
to be in charge of the shipper or his agents, while in
transit, free transportation for such persons being furnished by the railroad company, upon the conditions,
and in accordance with the rules printed at the head of
this contract, and the shipper assumes the duty of loading and unloading said stock, and of attending to, feeding and watering the same, at his own expense, and risk,
The railroad company shall not be liable for any injury

the animals may do to each other or themselves, nor for any loss or damage caused by theft, cold, heat, or suffocation. * * *" The plaintiff accompanied

4   the stock, but insists that all provisions of the contract relieving the defendant of liability are void, under the section of the statute already quoted. That a railroad company is not permitted to limit its liability in such cases has been too often determined by this court to call for further elaboration. *McCoy v. Railroad Co.*, 44 Iowa, 424; *McDaniel v. Railway Co.*, 24 Iowa, 412; *Kinnick v. Railroad Co.*, 69 Iowa, 665;

5   *McCune v. Railroad Co.*, 52 Iowa, 600. Such conditions are readily severable from those relating to the transportation of the stock, which the parties had the right to make, and the plaintiff may insist on those which are valid, without being bound by those understood by both parties to be void. See *Casady v. Woodbury County*, 13 Iowa, 113; *Osgood v. Bauder*, 75 Iowa, 550; *Smith v. Smith*, 87 Iowa, 93; 2 Parsons, Contract, 517; 3 Am. & Eng. Enc. Law, 886. But the company had the right to employ the plaintiff by furnishing him transportation to accompany the stock, load and unload, water and feed it, and,

6   if he actually undertook to do this, and injury was occasioned by his negligence, it is not perceived on what theory the carrier may be held responsible. In such a case, damages result, not from any lack of care on the part of the carrier, but from that of the owner. See *Hart v. Railroad Co.*, 69 Iowa, 485; *McCoy v. Railroad Co., supra.* Now, if the owner undertakes to oversee the transportation of his stock and attend to loading and unloading it, feeding and watering it, whether by contract or voluntarily, and it suffers injury through his fault, he cannot recover, though the contract in no way relieves the company from liability. Hence the section of the statute is not applicable in such a case. From his familiarity with the animals he

is presumed to know what care is required, better than
a stranger, and, having undertaken to bestow this,
the company is not liable for his omission to do so,
unless resulting from its failure to furnish proper facilities therefor, or reasonable opportunity for so doing.
In other words, the carrier is liable for such losses only
as result from its failure to discharge the duties not
assumed and undertaken by the shipper. *Railway Co.
v. McRae*, 82 Tex. Sup. 614 (27 Am. St. Rep. 926 (18
S. W. Rep. 672); *Johnson v. Railway Co.*, 69 Miss. 191
(11 South. Rep. 104); *Clarke v. Railway Co.*, 67 Am. Dec.
205, and note; 5 Am. & Eng. Enc. Law (2d ed.), 440.
The right to require the shipper to accompany the stock,
it will be noticed, is not involved, as Grieve, in fact, did

7

so.   As a general rule, injury to property trans-
ported being shown, the burden is cast upon the
carrier to exculpate itself from blame.   This is
because of its exclusive control of the property, and
of the instrumentalities of transportation, and of its
superior means of information.   But is this true where
the shipper assumes to and actually does take charge of
his stock during its transportation?   In such a case the
animals are not in the exclusive custody of the carrier,
nor are its means of information superior to those of the
shipper, who is in a position to know what has been
done or omitted, as well, if not better, than the carrier.
Now, the cattle were kept in the cars, without unloading, or feeding, or watering, in Chicago, for about nine
hours, and the injury, if any, was occasioned thereby.
All this, however, the plaintiff had assumed to do, and,
if his failure therein was caused by any act of the
defendant, he knew what it was as well as the company.
If he demanded facilities for unloading the cattle, or for
feeding and watering them, and these were not pro-

·vided, or were refused, then the burden was cast upon the defendant to excuse itself for not furnishing
8   them. But the burden is certainly on the shipper, in the first instance, to show that the injury did not result from his own negligence, and if occasioned by failure to do what he has undertaken, then that such failure resulted from an omission on the part of the company to perform some duty devolving upon it. This conclusion has ample support in the authorities. 4 Elliott, Railroads, sections 1549, 1552; *Terre Haute Ry. Co. v. Sherwood,* 132 Ind. 129 (31 N. E. Rep. 781); *St. Louis Ry. Co. v. Weakly,* 50 Ark. 397 (8 S. W. Rep. 134; 7 Am. St. 104); *Louisville, Etc., Ry. Co. v. Hedger,* 9 Bush, 645 (15 Am. Rep. 740); *Railway Co. v. Reynolds.* 8 Kan. 623. See *Faust v. Railway Co.,* 104 Iowa, 241. We have called attention to these rules in view of another trial, because not recognized in the instructions given.—AFFIRMED.

URIAH TRIMBLE v. JOHN TANTLINGER, Appellant.

Libel. PLEA AND PROOF. Special damages need not be alleged nor
8   proved in an action for slanderous words alleged to have been
5   spoken which are actionable *per se.*

Evidence: PRACTICE. Evidence of a conversation between the parties to the action is properly stricken out where the witness fails
2   to fix the time and shows by his evidence that the conversation related to another matter than that involved in the suit.

SAME. In an action for slander, evidence that the witness was present
7   at a conversation between the plaintiff and defendant, but did not hear the actionable words alleged to have been spoken, is inadmis-
9   sible as not amounting to a statement that the defendant did not speak the words charged

SAME   Testimony that one of the witnesses for the plaintiff in an action for slander stated that the plaintiff could thank him for
8   information concerning the slanderous words is immaterial, since it does not tend necessarily to show bias or prejudice on the part
.   of the witness.

New Trial: NEWLY DISCOVERED EVIDENCE: *Discretion.* It is not error to deny a new trial on the ground of newly discovered evi-
6 dence showing that witnesses for the successful party made statements out of court at variance with their testimony, where such testimony is cumulative.

SAME. A motion for a new trial on the ground of newly discovered evidence, contained affidavits of two persons, one of whom was present at the trial, that a witness for the plaintiff, who had testified to hearing defendant speak the slanderous words sued on, had stated before the trial that he could do defendant no harm nor
10 plaintiff any good, and that he never heard defendant assail plaintiff's character or his business, and that the suit was brought for spite The statements were all specifically denied by counter affidavit, and the witness' testimony at the trial was corroborated. *Held,* that the discretion of the trial court was not abused by the refusal of a new trial, and that the matter asserted amounted to no more than an impeachment

Appeal: PRESUMPTIONS On a trial for slander, where the jury is charged to estimate the amount of "actual injury" plaintiff would
4 naturally sustain, the supreme court cannot presume, from the amount of the verdict, that exemplary damages were allowed.

HARMLESS ERROR. Error in sustaining an objection to certain ques-
1 tions is harmless, where the answer thereto is subsequently given.

Appeal from Johnson District Court.—HON. M. J. WADE, Judge.

WEDNESDAY, JANUARY 27, 1897.

ACTION to recover damages for the alleged speaking of certain false, malicious, and defamatory words, in March, 1894, in the presence of Thomas Jordan, James Evans, J. W. White, and others. Defendant answered, denying generally. The case was tried to a jury, and a verdict of one thousand three hundred dollars rendered in favor of the plaintiff. Defendant moved for a new trial, upon the ground, among others, that the damages were excessive. The court overruled said motion as to all said other grounds, and, finding that the verdict was excessive, reduced the same to eight hundred dollars, giving the plaintiff the right to elect to accept judgment for eight hundred dollars or to submit to a new trial. Plaintiff elected to accept judgment for eight hundred dollars, and the motion for new trial was overruled as to all the grounds thereof, and judgment entered against the defendant for eight hundred dollars, from which he appeals.—*Affirmed.*

Ranck & Bradley and *Joe A. Edwards* for appellant.

Ewing & Hart for appellee.

GIVEN, J.—I. Appellant's first complaints are as to certain rulings in taking the testimony. There is evidence tending to show two conversations in which the defendant spoke concerning the plaintiff,—one in Leonard's store, and one in the street near the store. Plaintiff was asked, on cross-examination, how long he stayed in the store, and whether he went in to inquire if the township trustees had been there. These questions were objected to and objection sustained, as not proper cross-examination. Conceding that the ruling was erroneous, yet there was no prejudice, as the witness proceeded to state that he did not go there to inquire about the township trustees. Appellant complains that plaintiff's objection to two questions asked the witness, Horace Page, was sustained, and that plaintiff's motion to strike out all of his testimony was also sustained. Page testified to a conversation between the parties to this suit in Leonard's store, but failed to fix the time, and showed by his evidence that the conversation was in relation to another matter than that involved in this suit. The testimony was properly stricken out, and, therefore, there was no prejudice in sustaining plaintiff's objection to the question asked.

II. Plaintiff does not allege any damages in his petition, but, after setting out the speaking of the words, concludes his petition as follows: "Wherefore, plaintiff asks judgment against defendant for two thou-

3　　　sand dollars and costs." Appellant contends, that, no damages being alleged, the court erred in instructing the jury that, if they found for the plaintiff, they should allow him such damages as they believed he suffered by the use of such language. He also contends that, from the amount returned by the jury, they must have found exemplary damages, and that no

4　　　such damages could be recovered under the pleaa· ings. By the instructions, the jury were directed to inquire as to actual damages only. They were told to, "estimate as near as you can, the amount of actual injury that the plaintiff would naturally sustain by reason of the statement made by the defendant." We may not presume, under these instructions, from

5　　　the amount returned, that the jury allowed exemplary damages. The slanderous words alleged to have been spoken being actionable *per se*, special damages need not be alleged nor proven. *Parker v. Lewis.* 2 G. Greene, 311; *Hicks v. Walker,* 2 G. Greene, 440. There was no error in the instructions in the respect complained of.

III. Appellant's motion for a new trial was based upon the grounds already considered, and upon the further ground of newly-discovered evidence, as to

6　　　which a number of affidavits were filed. We will not set out nor discuss these affidavits at length. It is sufficient to say that their general tenor is to show that witnesses for plaintiff, particularly one J. L. Evans, made statements out of court at variance with the testimony given on the trial. While the purpose of such testimony is impeaching, it may not be within the rule that refuses a new trial upon the ground

of newly discovered evidence as to the character or general reputation of a witness. We think, however, that
this alleged newly-discovered evidence was so far cumulative that the court was warranted in refusing a new
trial on that ground. We find no error in the record
prejudicial to appellant, and the judgment of the district court is therefore AFFIRMED.

SUPPLEMENTAL OPINION ON REHEARING.

MONDAY, FEBRUARY 7, 1898.

Ranck & Bradley, Remley, Ney & Remley, and *Joe
A. Edwards* for appellant.

Ewing & Hart and *S. H. Fairall* for appellee.

WATERMAN, J.—A re-hearing having been granted
in this case, we have again considered the questions
involved, and have to say that we are quite satisfied
with what was said in the preceding opinion, upon
all the issues presented, save as to the matter
of newly-discovered evidence, and upon this branch
of the case, in view of appellant's earnest and
insistent claims, we desire to add something to what is
there stated. In support of his application for a new
trial on the ground of newly discovered evidence, the
defendant presented certain affidavits. The first is an
affidavit of George Miller, who avers that one James
Evans, who was a witness for plaintiff on the trial
below, and there testified to having heard the words
complained of spoken, stated to affiant before said trial,
"that he could not do Tantlinger any harm, nor Trimble
any good, in the case, and that he never heard Tantlinger say anything against the character of Mr.
Trimble." Thomas Jordan also makes affidavit that he
was present during a conversation between plaintiff and

defendant, in the store of Leonard & Ritter, in the spring of 1894, and he adds: "I did not hear

7   Tantlinger say that Trimble kept a house of ill fame, or a whore house, or a place where girls resort for prostitution, at this time or any other time." John White swears that he never heard defendant say that Trimble kept a house of ill fame, or that he kept a piano to entice girls there for bad purposes. W. S. Stout, in his affidavit, says that, after the verdict was rendered in the court below, he heard James Evans say to another person: "Trimble may thank me for this. I am

8   the man that put him onto it." Henry C. Lane testifies that James Evans, in a conversation with affiant, said, in substance, that he never heard Tantlinger say that Trimble was keeping a house of ill fame, or whore house, or a place where girls or women resorted, and that he never heard defendant say anything about Trimble, or about the kind of house he was keeping; that Evans did say: "The suit was brought for spite, on account of liquor prosecutions, or for intimidation." In resistance to the application for a new trial, plaintiff filed, among others, the affidavits of James Evans, who denies specifically the statements attributed to him in the above-mentioned affidavits. The negative matter testified to by Jordan and White would be inadmissible, if offered in evidence. It

9   will be noticed that they do not say that Tantlinger did not speak the words charged, but only that affiants did not hear him speak them. So, too, the statement of Evans, if made as averred by Stout, would be inadmissible because of immateriality. It does not even tend, necessarily, to show bias or prejudice on the part of Evans. There is left, then, only the testimony of Miller and Lane, relating to asserted statements made by Evans out of court, which are inconsistent with his

testimony on the trial. It is shown that Lane is a son-
in-law of defendant; that he was present at the trial
below and heard the witness Evans testify. We
think it was proper for the trial court to consider
this fact, and also the further fact that Evans
denies flatly that he ever made any of the statements
charged. A considerable discretion is vested in the
lower court in passing upon an application for a new
trial, on the ground of newly-discovered evidence, and
we will not interfere with the exercise of that discretion,
unless it appears to us to have been abused. *Searcy v.
Martin Woods Co.*, 93 Iowa, 420; *Moore v. Railroad Co.*,
94 Iowa, 736. Viewed in the most favorable light for
defendant, this evidence must be regarded as merely of
an impeaching character. It tended only to show that
the witness Evans had made statement, out of court,
inconsistent with his testimony as given on the trial
But there were other witnesses who corroborated
Evans, and we think it was for the court below to say
whether a different result could be reasonably expected
if a new trial was granted, and this evidence received.
Too much, we think, is claimed by appellant's counsel
for the case of *Murray v. Weber*, 92 Iowa, 757. A new
trial was granted by the lower court in that case, and
we affirmed its action; but it by no means follows that
we should have interfered if the court had refused to set
aside the verdict. Much that is said in that case as to
the new evidence was unnecessary. The motion for a
new trial contained other grounds, and there is nothing
in the record to show what particular matter influenced
the trial court in its ruling. We might well have rested
our affirmance of its judgment upon the well-established
rule that this court will be slow to interfere with the
action of the trial court when a new trial is awarded.
For the reasons stated we think the former opinion
must be adhered to, and the judgment below AFFIRMED.

JAMES CALLANAN, Appellant, v. M. VOTRUBA.

Judgment: RENDITION: *Lien.* A judgment is not rendered so as to constitute a lien from the "time of such rendition," within the meaning of Code, section 880', until it is entered on the records of the court as required by section 3784, although a form of judgment has been signed by the judge and indorsed "Filed" by the clerk.

Appeal from Polk District Court.—HON. W. F. CONRAD, Judge.

TUESDAY, FEBRUARY 8, 1898.

ACTION to quiet title against two judgments in favor of the defendant. Decree was entered on the cross-petition of the defendant, establishing such judgments as liens on the plaintiff's lot, and he appeals.—*Reversed.*

J. J. & E. A. Davis for appellant.

Day & Corry for appellee.

LADD, J.—In September, 1895, McClure was the owner of a lot in the city of Des Moines, and conveyed it by warranty deed, delivered to plaintiff September 27, of the same year, in pursuance of an oral contract so to do made September 3, previous. The agreed consideration was eight hundred dollars, of which four hundred and sixteen dollars was credited on an antecedent indebtedness, and three hundred and eighty-four dollars, a mortgage on the lot, subject to which Callanan took the deed. Two judgments by default were ordered in favor of the defendant and against McClure September 24, 1895, and entries therefor were signed by the trial judge and indorsed "Filed" by the clerk, on the

same day, but were not recorded in the record book or
entered until the twenty-eighth or thirtieth of the same
month, and after the conveyance to Callanan.   Are
these judgments liens on the land?   Section 3801 of the
Code provides that "judgments in the supreme or district courts of this state or in the circuit or district courts of the United States, within this state, are
liens upon the real estate owned by the defendant at
the time of such rendition, and also upon all he may
subsequently acquire, for the period of ten years from
the date of the judgment."   What is meant by the
"time of such rendition?"   Rendering a judgment is the
judicial act of the court in pronouncing the sentence of
the law upon the facts in controversy, as ascertained
from the pleadings and the evidence; and, technically,
the ministerial act of spreading upon the record a statement of the final conclusion reached by the court is not
included therein.   Black, Judgments, section 106;
Shuster v. Rader, 13 Colo. 329 (22 Pac. Rep. 505); *Blatchford v. Newberry*, 100 Ill. 489; *Conwell v. Kuykendall*,
29 Kan. 707; *Hall v. Tuttle*, 40 Am. Dec. 382, and note;
Stephens v. Santee, 49 N Y., 39; *Durant v. Comegys*, 2
Idaho, 809 (35 Am. St. 267; 26 Pac. Rep. 755); *In re
Cook's Estate*, 77 Cal. 220 (11 Am. St. 276; 17 Pac.
Rep. 923, and 19 Pac. Rep. 431).   But, in construing this statute, its relation to others on the
same subject, and the sense in which the words
are used, as determined by this court, must be
considered.   Every final adjudication of the rights
of the parties in an action is a judgment.   Code, section
3769.   All judgments and orders must be entered on
the record of the court, and must specify clearly the
relief granted or order made in the action.   Code, section
3784.   It will be noticed that the definition of a "judgment" in the Code differs somewhat from that of some of
the lexicographers, in that it is a final adjudication.
Zeigler v. Vance, 3 Iowa, 528; *Taylor v. Runyon*, 3 Iowa,

474. See definitions by authorities collected in 12 Am.
& Eng. Enc. Law. In *Humphrey v. Havens*, 9 Minn.
318 (Gil. 301), it was held that, where a writ of error
must be issued within a year after the "rendition of
judgment," the time began to run from the entry of
judgment or order, on the record. The question was
first suggested in this court in *Brown v. Scott*, 2 G.
Greene, 454; Kinney, J., remarking: "We are at a loss
to know how the justice could have rendered a judgment that would have any force or virtue without
rendering that judgment in proper form in the docket
which he is required by law to keep for that purpose. It
is true, he might, in his mind, resolve upon entering the
judgment; but, unless put into shape and form, it would
be as though no judgment at all had existed in the
mind." In *Case v. Plato*, 54 Iowa, 64, the court, through
Day, J., after quoting the statutes, said: "It is apparent from the foregoing provisions that it is essential to
the validity of a judgment that it should be entered
upon the record book. This is the book in which a statement of the proceedings of the court is kept, and to
which appeal must always be made to determine what
has been done. The theory of the law is that it is kept
under the direction and supervision of the judge, is
approved by him, and constitutes the only proof of his
acts." In *Balm v. Nunn*, 63 Iowa, 641, the opinion is by
Beck, J., who said: "There can be no judgment until
it is entered in the proper record of the court. It cannot
exist in the memory of the officers of the court, nor in
the memoranda entered upon the books not intended to
preserve the record of judgments. * * * It is not
competent to prove a judgment in any other way than
by the production of the proper record thereof." *Insurance Co. v. Hesser*, 77 Iowa, 381, seems to be decisive.
In that case, the judgment was erroneously indexed,
and the court, in holding it was not a lien superior
to a subsequent mortgage, bases its conclusion

on three grounds: (1) No constructive notice was imparted owing to the failure to index; (2) the judgment, before it becomes a lien, must be of record, *i e.*, entered in the record book required by the statute; (3) a judgment is not rendered, so as to be effective and capable of enforcement, until it is "made up, finished, stated or delivered" in the form and manner, and entered of record as required by the statutes. Appellee insists the last two grounds amount to no more than dicta, but these are not stated in the way of argument, but as conclusions of law. In *Winter v. Coulthard*, 94 Iowa, 312, the court had announced its decisions; but these had not been entered of record, and the executions were held invalid because no judgments existed. The judge's calendar is not a record of the court, but entries therein announce his conclusions, and are intended for the guidance of the clerk. *Traer v. Whitman*, 56 Iowa, 443; *Miller v. Wolf*, 63 Iowa, 233; *State v. Manley*, 63 Iowa, 344; *Burroughs v. Ellis*, 76 Iowa, 649. While not proof of a decree or judgment, such minutes may tend to show a decree or judgment has been ordered. *In re Edwards' Estate*, 58 Iowa, 431. If the record is the only proof of a judgment, as has been repeatedly held by this court, then how can a judgment be said to have been rendered before spread on the records, when its very existence prior to that time cannot be established? If the statute making the judgment a lien "at the time of such rendition" refers to the time of announcement by the judge, rather than when entered on the proper books, it would certainly be capable of enforcement by execution. Section 3954 of the Code. But it was adjudged otherwise in *Winter v. Coulthard, supra*. If the court has announced judgment, the clerk may complete the record after the term. Code, section 242. But until the record is prepared no evidence exists of the rendition of the judgment. These records are under the control of the court (section 248 of the Code), and through them it speaks the final adjudication defined by the statute as a judgment. Until so rendered, there is no judgment. The Code contains no provisions relating to judgment forms signed by the judge, and these amounted to no more than directions for judgments. Until recorded, they were not such, but merely evidence that the court had ordered judgments, and approved their form This view finds support in *Babcock v. Wolf*, 70 Iowa, 676, and *Guthrie v. Guthrie*, 71 Iowa, 744. In these cases decisions were, by agreement, to be made in vacation, and were written and signed by the judges before the expiration of their terms of office, though not delivered in the clerk's office until afterwards. In the former it is said: "Now, we think the decision was made when it was deposited in the express office at Afton. Under the agreement of the parties, it was as complete then as if there had been no agreement, and the judge had entered a decision in his minutes in open court, because the parties agreed that the decision was not to be made at Clarinda." But it did not have the force of a judgment until spread upon the records as required by law.—Reversed.

A. E. Giddings and F. H. Giddings v. The Iowa Savings Bank of Ruthven, Appellant.

Duress. A threat to imprison one for an offense of which he is in fact innocent, is as to him a threat of unlawful imprisonment
8 and will constitute duress, although the one making it had reasonable ground to believe that such person was guilty as charged.

Action: joint rights A husband intending to join with his wife in the execution of a mortgage on her separate property, who signs
4 the instrument freely, while her signature is obtained by compulsion exerted by others, may properly join with her in the claim, when she sets up the invalidity of the instrument as against her, since it is not the instrument he intended to execute

Husband and wife. A mortgage given upon a homestead and signed by the wife is executed under duress, where her fear or affections

are worked upon through threats made against her husband and
2 she is induced thereby against her will to convey her property to
secure his debt, although the liability was valid and the threat
was of a lawful prosecution of a crime which he had in fact committed. Citing *Beindoif v. Cohegan* (Neb) 60 N. W Rep. 101;
Meech v. Lee (Mich.) 46 N. W. Rep. 338.

INSTRUCTIONS.   In an action by a husband and wife to secure possession of a promissory note and the mo'tgage securing it, on the
ground that the wife executed the instrument upon her homestead under duress to secure the debt of her husband by reason of
5 the threats of a creditor that he would otherwise institute a prosecution against the husband for an alleged crime the jury should
take into consideration whether the crime had in fact been committed as charged and whether the debt was a valid existing
obligation against the husband, and it is error to charge that such
matters are immaterial, for, among other things, they bear on the
question whether there was coercion

Evidence: COMMUNICATIONS BETWEEN HUSBAND AND WIFE.   Where
defendant demanded of a husband a mortgage on his wife's
homestead, which was in his wife's name, claiming that he was a
1 defaulter, and threatening criminal prosecution unless he gave
the mortgage, evidence of the conversation between husband and
wife, when he told her of such interview was admissible, in an
action by them for possession of the mortgage, on the ground of
duress, and admission of such evidence did not contravene Code
1873, section 3642, forbidding husband and wife divulging confidential communications made by one to the other.

Appeal from Palo Alto District Court.—HON. W. B.
QUARTON, Judge.

THURSDAY, FEBRUARY 10, 1898.

ACTION to recover possession of a promissory note
and the mortgage securing it. There was a trial by
jury. Verdict and judgment for plaintiffs. Defendant
appeals.—*Reversed.*

Soper, Allen & Morling and *George E. Clarke* for
appellant.

Carr & Parker and *B. E. Kelly* for appellees

WATERMAN, J.—I. The record before us discloses
these facts: The plaintiffs are husband and wife. F.
H. Giddings, the husband, was for some years the
cashier of defendant bank, which is located at Ruthven,
in this state. During the time he occupied this position
he made loans of the bank's funds to himself, and to the
firm of Calkins & Giddings, of which he was a member,
and also to F. W. Calkins, the senior member of said
firm. Some of the loans were without security, and in
other cases the security was insufficient. Early in January, 1894, Giddings resigned as cashier, and the
president of the bank, with two of the directors, undertook to look over the accounts and make a settlement
with him. It is claimed by plaintiff that said bank
officers, finding the loans mentioned standing as an
existing indebtedness to the bank, wrongfully insisted
that he was a defaulter or embezzler, and that he had
violated a criminal statute of the state; that they threatened him with criminal prosecution, and put him in
fear, and that like threats were made to his wife, and
that by such duress the plaintiffs were coerced into
giving the promissory note in question, and also the
mortgage securing it, which covers plaintiff's homestead in Ruthven, title to which is in the wife. Some
months thereafter, to correct a misdescription of the
real estate in the mortgage, plaintiffs gave another
mortgage, in which the homestead was correctly
described. This action was begun January 21, 1896,
to recover possession of the note and mortgage, on the
ground that they were obtained by duress. We are
not attempting in what we say to set out the facts,
further than to give an outline of plaintiff's case, sufficient to an understanding of our rulings on certain legal
propositions presented for determination. The errors
assigned by appellant are numerous, but we shall

endeavor in what we say to give consideration to all
such as are material.

II. The wife was not present at the interview
between the bank officers and Giddings, when the
alleged threats were made, but plaintiffs claim that she
was told by him what had occurred when he came home
in the evening. Both husband and wife were permitted,
over defendant's objection, to testify to what was said
by the husband to the wife on this occasion. The
1   bank officers, in the interview with Giddings,
were demanding a mortgage on his homestead.
They knew that this instrument must be signed by the
wife. If they unlawfully threatened Giddings in order
to procure the mortgage and note, they must have
known that to comply with their demands he would be
compelled to disclose the facts to his wife. In principle,
it is the same as though defendant's officers had
requested Giddings to inform his wife of their desire
and purpose. The evidence, we think, was rightfully
admitted. *Schultz v. Catlin,* 78 Wis. 611 (47 N. W. Rep.
946); *Taylor v. Jaques,* 106 Mass. 291. The gist of this
testimony was simply that the husband told his wife
what had been said to him by defendant's officers. Its
admission did not contravene section 3642, Code 1873,
which forbids husband or wife divulging confidential
communications made by one to the other.

III. It is contended by appellant that a claim of
duress cannot properly be predicated upon a threat of
lawful prosecution or imprisonment; that, if Giddings
was in fact guilty of the crime charged, a threat by
defendant to prosecute him therefor, unless he secured
the bank against loss, would not amount to duress.
This states the rule very broadly, but we may, for
present purposes, concede it to be true as to Giddings.

The instructions of the trial court recognize this
2   rule. But we think a different doctrine prevails
in case of the wife. Where the fears or affection
of a wife are worked upon through threats made against

her husband, and she is induced thereby against her
will, to convey her property to secure his debt, there
is duress as to her, even though the debt was valid, and
the threat was of lawful prosecution for a crime that
had in fact been committed by the husband. *Gohegan
v. Leach*, 24 Iowa, 509; *Beindorff v. Kaufman*, 41 Neb.
824 (60 N. W. Rep. 101); *Meech v. Lee*, 87 Mich. 274 (46
N. W. Rep. 383), and cases cited. Appellant insists that
the case of *Green v. Scranage*, 19 Iowa, 461, lays down
a different rule; but we think not. Speaking upon the
matter, the court says in that case: "On the other hand,
if the wife was induced to execute the mortgage from
fear excited by threats made to her, by the plaintiffs, of
an illegal criminal prosecution against her husband,
the instrument thus obtained would not be binding
upon her. * * * But if the debt were just, and the
criminal accusation was well founded, or, upon reasonable grounds, believed to be so by the plaintiffs, *and the
wife freely, upon her own deliberate conviction of what
was best, and without undue influence exercised by the
plaintiffs, executed the security, it would be valid,*" etc.
We have italicized the qualification in this opinion
which we deem important. At a glance, it will appear
that what is there said begs the question at issue here,
for it is assumed that the act of the wife was vol-
3   untary and deliberate. Another claim made by
appellant is, in substance, that, if Giddings was
not, in fact, guilty of a crime, the threats of prosecution
or imprisonment would not amount to duress, if defendant's officers at the time had reasonable ground to
believe that he was so guilty. We think this contention is based upon a casual remark in the passage just
quoted from *Green v. Scranage, supra*. No such issue
was involved in that case. We are not inclined to sanction any such rule. Whatever may have been the belief
of the bank officials, a threat to imprison Giddings for

an offense of which he was in fact innocent would be, as to him, a threat of unlawful imprisonment.

IV. The trial court, in its instructions, told the jury, in effect, that, if the note was voluntarily signed by the husband, it could not be recovered in this action, although the wife's signature thereto was procured by duress, but that a different rule obtained in case of the mortgage, and that it might be recovered if signed under coercion by the wife, though voluntarily executed by the husband. Defendant's contention is that, this being a joint action, a recovery can be had only on a showing of joint right in both plaintiffs. That, generally, is the correct rule; but, in this case, if the husband, intending to join his wife in the execution of a mortgage on her separate property, signed the instrument freely, while her signature was obtained by compulsion, exerted by others, then, when she sets up the invalidity of the instrument, as against her, he may properly join with her in the claim, for it is not the instrument he intended to execute.

V. Exception is taken to the eleventh instruction, which is as follows: "And, in determining whether the mortgage was executed by Mrs. Giddings under duress, it is wholly immaterial whether or not F. H. Giddings had, in fact, committed the crime of embezzlement, and it is wholly immaterial whether or not the several claims secured by said mortgage were valid existing obligations of the plaintiff F. H. Giddings." And in the fourteenth instruction this thought is repeated in a more extended form, for the jury is there told that they need not consider these matters in determining whether either Giddings or his wife executed the mortgage under duress. These instructions are clearly erroneous. It is impossible to see how the jury could fairly pass upon the rights of the parties without having in mind all of the facts and circumstances of the transaction. It is true that, if there

was, in fact, duress of the wife, it is immaterial whether
her husband owed the debt or was guilty of the charged
crime. *Beindorff v. Kaufman, supra.* But these are
important matters, to be considered in determining
whether there was any coercion. The defendant's
theory was that Giddings had unlawfully made the
loans in question, and that he was liable, both civilly
and criminally, therefor, and that, because he was so
liable, he and his wife voluntarily executed the note
and mortgage in question. It was its right to have the
jury consider these matters in determining how it came
that said instruments were executed. For the error
pointed out in the last instruction considered, the judgment below is REVERSED.

THE METROPOLITAN NATIONAL BANK, *et al.*, v. THE COM-
MERCIAL STATE BANK, Appellant.

Receivers; ADJUDICATION: *Collateral attack.* The defendant in an
1 action upon a promissory note brought by a receiver cannot ques-
2 tion the appointment of the plaintiff on the ground that, as
3 clerk of the court, he had approved his own bond, when it was
adjudged sufficient at the time of his appointment.

SAME. The approval by the court of a bond given by a receiver who
1 was at the same time clerk of the court, is an adjudication in the
2 receivership proceedings that the bond was sufficient, and cannot
3 be collaterally attacked

SAME. Although a receiver has given no bond, he may be a receiver
1 *de facto,* so that his authority to sue in such capacity cannot be
2-3 questioned collaterally.

SAME In an action upon a promissory note in which the receiver is
plaintiff, it cannot be objected that he was disqualified to accept
1 the appointment because as clerk of the court it was necessary for
2 him to approve his own bond as receiver, since such contention is
3 in the nature of a collateral attack upon proceedings had and an
order made in another action. Citing *Whittlesey v. Frantz,* 74 N.
Y. 459; *Attorney General v. Insurance Co.,* 77 N. Y. 274; *Bangs v.
Duckinfield,* 18 N. Y. 595; *Jones v. Blum* (N. Y. App.) 39 N. E.
Rep. 954; *Davis v. Shearer* (Wis.) 62 N. W. Rep. 1050; *Cadle v.
Baker,* 20 Wall., 650.

OFFICER DE FACTO. That the clerk of the district court in his capacity
as receiver of an insolvent bank has instituted an action to recover
1 a debt due it, does not vacate the office of clerk and invalidate
2 his acts in docketing the case, filing papers and making entries,
8 thus preventing the court from acquiring jurisdiction of the
action, since he acted as clerk *de facto*, and third persons dealing
with him had the right to rely upon his acts so performed as being
legal. *People v. Nelson*, 27 N. E. Rep. (Ill Sup) 226; *People v
Payment*, 67 N. W. Rep. (Mich.) 689; *Clark v. Easton*, 14 N. E. Rep
(Mass) 795; *Petersilea v. Stone*, 119 Mass. 465.

AUTHORITY TO SUE A receiver who was directed by the court to
2 make a settlement with reference to defendant company, and to
8 collect the claim due the insolvent debtor by litigation, if neces-
4 sary, and who was as receiver an officer of the court in which he
was allowed to intervene as a plaintiff in the suit at bar, is authorized to prosecute the suit.

Evidence: COMPETENCY: *Conclusions.* Testimony that the cashier
of a bank stated "that he felt he was somewhat negligent or
5 careless in the matter," is inadmissible in an action wherein it is
6 sought to charge the bank with liability by reason of its alleged
7 negligence in failing to apply funds on deposit with it in payment
of a note sent it for collection, before such funds were withdrawn.
Such statements are incompetent, for they are merely his conclusions as to what constitutes negligence.

RES GESTÆ. A statement by an agent that his principal had been
6 negligent, made after the settlement had been effected which con-
7 stituted the alleged negligence, is not a part of the *res gestœ.*

TENDER. Where plaintiff sued defendant for negligence in collecting
a note intrusted to it, and defendant tendered a part payment it
11 had collected, which was refused, plaintiff was entitled to the
amount of the tender without evidence, as it was an admission of
the liability to that extent.

INTEREST. Where money is tendered in part payment of an over due
12 debt, without condition, and the tender is kept good, interest on
the amount tendered ceases from the time of the tender.

Appeal: EXCEPTIONS: *Waiver.* An exception to the erroneous
8 admission of evidence is not waived by failure to object to the
9 subsequent introduction of evidence of the same kind. Citing
Church v. Howerd, 79 N. Y. 421; *In re Eysman*, 113 N. Y. 71;
Sharon v. Sharon, 79 Cal. 674; *Whitney v. Traynor*, 74 Wis. 289; *Gilpin v. Gilpin*, 12 Colo. 516; *Railroad Co. v. Gower*, 8 S. W. Rep.
(Tenn. Sup.) 824.

SAME The mere silence of a party when incompetent evidence is
offered, should be treated as a waiver of the objection to the par-
10 ticular evidence offered only, and will not preclude him from

objecting to similar testimony offered subsequently. **Citing**
McLane v. Paschal, 11 S. W. Rep (Tex. Sup.) 839.

RULE APPLIED. Where a question asked plaintiff by his counsel was
8   not objected to, and defendant offered evidence in contradiction
9   of the answer, defendant did not waive his right to object to the
 · evidence given by another witness, to the same effect, in rebuttal.
    Citing *McLane v. Paschal,* 11 S. W. Rep. (Tex. Sup.) 839.

Appeal from Buena Vista District Court.—HON. LOT
·   THOMAS, Judge.

THURSDAY, FEBRUARY 10, 1898.

ACTION at law to recover the amount due on a
promissory note. There was a trial by jury, and a judgment against the Commercial State Bank, from which
it appeals.—*Reversed.*

M. J. Sweeley and *T. D. Higgs* for appellant.

F. H. Helsell for appellee.

ROBINSON, J.—In May, 1895, the defendant H. H.
Bridge made to the Buena Vista State Bank of Storm
Lake, Iowa, a banking corporation of this state, his
promissory note for the sum of two hundred and ninety-
nine dollars and twelve cents, payable on the twelfth
day of October, 1895. That note, with other notes, was
transferred by the payee to the Metropolitan National
Bank of Chicago, to be held by it as security for a loan
it had made to the Buena Vista State Bank. On the
third day of September, 1895, in a suit instituted by
the attorney general, the district court of Buena Vista
county, adjudged the bank last named to be insolvent,
and appointed as receiver S. C. Bradford, who was the
clerk of that court. He executed a bond for the amount
fixed by the court, which was approved by himself as
clerk, and by the court. About the twenty-fifth day of
September, 1895, the Metropolitan National Bank sent

to the defendant the Commercial State Bank the Bridge note for collection. On the tenth day of October, 1895, Bridge, who was a resident of Buena Vista county, had a public sale of property, at which sale notes were taken, and proceeds of those notes, to the amount of more than one thousand eight hundred dollars, were received by the Commercial State Bank on account of Bridge, nearly all of which were paid out to him, or on his checks. On the twenty-fifth day of October, 1895, this action was commenced by the Metropolitan National Bank against Bridge to recover the amount of the note, and against the Commercial State Bank, to recover the same amount, on the ground that it had failed to collect the note by reason of negligence on its part. The note had been indorsed by the Buena Vista State Bank, and after the action was commenced, Bradford, as receiver, paid to the Metropolitan National Bank the amount due on the note; and that bank and Bradford, by an amendment to the petition, set out that fact, and asked that Bradford, as receiver, be substituted as party plaintiff, and that he have the relief which had been asked by the original plaintiff. Thereafter, by another amendment, they asked that they be joined as parties plaintiff. The verdict and judgment against the Commercial State Bank were for the full amount due on the note.

I. The first complaint made by the appellant is that the court erred in sustaining a demurrer to the second division of its answer. The defense alleged in that division was, in substance, as follows: That

1   Bradford is not the receiver of the Buena Vista State Bank, and is not authorized to maintain this action, for the reason that, as he was clerk of the district court in and for Buena Vista county at the time the order purporting to appoint him receiver was made, he was disqualified to accept the appointment, because he was the only person authorized by law to approve

the bonds of receivers appointed by the court and keep
possession thereof, and the only person authorized to
keep the records and entries of the appointment of such
receivers, and to preserve the pleadings, papers, reports,
bonds, records, and other proceedings connected therewith and arising therefrom; that his appointment as
receiver was void, and that he is wholly without right
or power to maintain this action. It is urged by the
appellee that, even if it be true that the duties of clerk
and receiver are such that one person should not hold
both offices, yet that question cannot be considered on
its merits in this action, for the reason that the second
division of the answer is in the nature of a collateral
attack upon proceedings had and an order made in
another action, and that, we think, is true. The eligibil-
ity of Bradford was necessarily involved in the proceedings which were instituted to close the insolvent bank,
and distribute its assets through the medium of a
receiver. The court has jurisdiction of the subject-
matter of the proceedings and of the parties, and its
order appointing Bradford receiver involved a finding
that he was eligible to the office. It may be that, if
proper objection has been made, the order would have
been set aside or reversed on appeal; but, if the bank
and its stockholders and other persons interested in its
assets are satisfied with the appointment, other persons
should not be heard to complain, especially by a collateral attack, as attempted in this case. Van Fleet,
Collateral Attack, section 3; *Whittlesey v. Frantz*, 74
N. Y. 459; *Attorney General v. Insurance Co.*, 77 N. Y.
274; *Bangs v. Duckenfield*, 18 N. Y. 595; *Jones v. Blun*,
145 N. Y. App. 333 (39 N. E. Rep. 954); *Davis v. Shearer*,
90 Wis. 250 (62 N. W. Rep. 1050); *Cadle v. Baker*, 20
Wall. 650. See, also, *Pursley v. Hayes*, 22 Iowa, 11;
McCandless v. Hazen, 98 Iowa, 321. But it is
2   said, if it be conceded that the appointment of
the clerk as receiver cannot be questioned in this
action, yet the appellant may show that he never qual-

ified as receiver, for the reason that he could not approve
his own bond, and the court was not authorized to
approve it. We think this objection is shown to be
unsound by what has already been said, and by the
fact that the approval by the court of the bond given
by the receiver was, in effect, an ajudication in that proceeding that the bond was sufficient. Moreover, Bradford may have been a receiver *de facto*, although he had
not given any bond. *Manufacturing Co. v. Sterrett*, 94
Iowa, 158. We conclude that the demurrer to the second division of the answer was properly sustained.

II. It is contended that, if the appointment of
Bradford as receiver be sustained, his acceptance of
that office had the effect to vacate the office of clerk of
the district court, because the offices are so incompat-
ible that they cannot be held by the same person at
one time; hence that the acts of Bradford as clerk, after
his qualification as receiver, were void; that his docketing of this case, the noting of papers filed, and the
making of other entries were void; and that, as a result,

3   the district court did not acquire jurisdiction to
       hear and determine this action. In what Brad-
       ford did as clerk after he qualified as receiver he
acted as clerk *de facto*, and third persons dealing with
him had the right to rely upon his acts so performed as
being legal. It is the well-settled general rule that the
acts of officers *de facto* are as valid and effectual, where
they concern the public or the rights of third persons, as
though they were officers *de jure*, and that their authority to act cannot be questioned in collateral proceedings. *People v. Nelson*, 133 Ill. 565 (27 N. E. Rep.
217); *People v. Payment* (Mich.), 67 N. W. Rep. 689;
Clark v. Town of Easton, 146 Mass. 43 (14 N. E. Rep.
795); *Petersilea v. Stone*, 119 Mass. 465. See, also, *Lufkin v. Preston*, 52 Iowa, 238; *Desmond v. McCarthy*, 17
Iowa, 526. We do not think the fact that Bradford, in
his capacity as receiver, is seeking to recover in this

action, affects the application of the general rule, since his acts as clerk, and not his acts as receiver, are questioned by the objection now under consideration. It follows that the alleged fact that the office of clerk was vacated when Bradford qualified as receiver is not available as a defense in this action, since he continued to act as clerk.

III.   It is said that Bradford, as receiver, cannot maintain this action, for the reason that the court has not authorized him to do so. It is not shown that he was authorized in express terms to prosecute this action. or to assist in doing so, but he was directed by the court to effect a settlement with the Metropolitan National Bank. The directions given to him also contemplated the collection of claims due the Buena Vista State Bank, and litigation to enforce collection. This action was brought in the court which had jurisdiction of the receiver. He was an officer of that court, and asked permission to be substituted, or to join as party plaintiff, in this action, and was permitted by the court to do so. We think the authority thus shown to prosecute this action was ample.

4

IV.   It is claimed that a verbal agreement was made to which the receiver, the Commercial State Bank, and Bridge were parties, by virtue of which a sufficient amount of the proceeds of the sale notes deposited by Bridge should be used by the bank in paying the receiver the amount due on the note in suit, and that the bank, through its cashier, Tiede, negligently omitted to perform its part of the agreement, and permitted Bridge to withdraw the proceeds of the sale notes, or use them for other purposes. Testimony was given in behalf of the plaintiff which tended strongly to support the claim thus made. That claim was denied by the bank, and testimony of Tiede and Bridge tended strongly to sustain that denial. After the evidence for the bank had been submittted, the receiver placed upon

the stand A. C. Smith, who was permitted, notwithstanding objections made by the bank, to state that,
during the fall of the year 1895, he heard a conversation
between the receiver and Tiede in regard to the
5   Bridge note, in which Tiede said "that he felt he
was somewhat negligent or careless in the
matter," and that there was not enough money to pay
the note.   There can be no doubt that the testimony
thus given was important to the plaintiff, and that it
must have been prejudicial, if erroneously admitted.
The question to which the bank objected was, "What, if
anything, was said in that connection by Mr. Tiede to
Mr. Bradford in regard to any negligence on the part of
Mr. Tiede or the Commercial State Bank in the collection of this note of H. H. Bridge?"   The objection made
and overruled, was that the question was "incompetent,
immaterial, and irrelevant, and called for the admission of a conclusion."   The admissions and rep-
6   resentations of an agent are not competent
evidence against his principal, unless made with
respect to a matter within the scope of his authority, in
reference to the subject-matter of his agency, and at
the time of the transaction to which they refer, and
while engaged in it, or so soon thereafter as to be vir-
tually a part of it.   Mechem, Agency, section 714; 1
Am. & Eng. Enc. Law (2d ed.), 691 et seq.; Phelps v.
James, 86 Iowa, 398; Verry v. Railroad Co., 47 Iowa,
549; Treadway v. Railway Co., 40 Iowa, 526; Osgood v.
Bringolf, 32 Iowa, 265.   Statements which are mere
narration of a past event are not competent.   Yordy
v. Marshall County, 86 Iowa, 340; Sherman v. Railroad
Co., 106 N. Y. 542 (13 N. E. Rep. 616).

The appellee, Bradford, contends that the testimony in question was only designed to show that there
was an agreement which required the defendant bank
to apply enough of the proceeds of the sale to pay the
note in suit, not to show negligence.   But we do not

think the record shows that such was the case. Neither
the question nor the answer objected to referred to any
agreement, but the question did refer specifically to
negligence. It is said that the conversation in question
related to a part of the transaction in question which
had not been closed, and, therefore, that the statement
made by Tiede was a part of the *res gestæ*. The conversation in which the statement in question is alleged
to have been made, took place on the day Tiebe settled
with Bridge, but after the settlement had been effected.
At that time only thirty-five dollars subject to the control of Bridge remained in the bank, and the payments
from the proceeds of the sale of which the receiver complains were chiefly, if not wholly, made before that time.
Certainly there was not a sufficient amount of the proceeds of the sale remaining with the bank to pay the
note when the settlement was made. Therefore, the
statement of Tiede in controversy, if made, related to
past transactions. It may be that, had he merely stated
the amount of the proceeds received, the payments
made from them, and similar facts, in view of the circumstances of the case, his statements would have been
within the scope of his employment, and therefore
binding upon his principal. But the statement
7   he is alleged to have made was his opinion or conclusion, based upon facts known to him, and not
a statement of facts. It was in the nature of an admission of liability, which is the gist of the plaintiff's cause
of action, and cannot be regarded as a mere declaration
of a fact which he was authorized to make. Whether
the bank had been negligent depended upon what agreement, if any, the bank had made, its knowledge of the
proceeds of the sale, the payments therefrom which it
made, and its right and ability to appropriate enough
of the proceeds to pay the note in question. It is urged
that the business of the bank was transacted by Tiede;
that he was its chief officer, and more than a mere agent.

It is true that he was active in the management of the affairs of the bank, and was invested with large powers and a large discretion in the discharge of his duties. He was not, however, the bank, but its agent, subject to the rules which govern agents, and it is not shown that he was authorized to confess liability on the part of the bank. His opinion as to what constituted negligence was inadmissible. *Brant v. City of Lyons*, 60 Iowa, 174; 16 Am. & Eng. Enc. Law, 462, and note.

It is said, however, that if the answer in question was erroneously admitted, the error was waived, for the reason that in response to the next question, to which there was no objection, the answer was, in substance and effect, repeated. It is not true, however, that a party waives an objection by merely failing to object to evidence of the same character subsequently offered. On the contrary, it is the general rule that an exception to the erroneous admission of evidence is not waived by the failure to object to the subsequent introduction of evidence of the same kind. If an objection to improper evidence is once duly stated to the court, and overruled, an exception is taken, and the evidence is admitted, the exception is as effectual to preserve the objection as though it were many times repeated. If the court, upon due consideration, has once overruled an objection to evidence, there is ordinarily no good reason for again presenting it for further consideration. It was said in *Jordan v. Kavanaugh*, 63 Iowa, 155, that "when a party has once properly made his exception to an adverse ruling, he does not waive it by failing to except to some other decision which involves the same question." In *Oppenheimer v. Barr*, 71 Iowa, 529, several witnesses gave incompetent evidence in regard to the character of one Oppenheimer. Objections were made to some of the testimony when it was given, but no objection was made to other portions of it as it was offered: This court said: "It was the class of evidence which was objected to, and we do not think that it should be required that the defendants should object to every question and answer, and that, if there was any omission in this regard, they should be held to have waived objections. If that course had been pursued in this case, the time of the court would have been taken up in unseemly interruptions, and in rendering and repeating rulings, which would have the appearance of repetitions." In *Dilleber v. Insurance Co.*, 69 N. Y. 260, it was said: "When, upon a trial, an objection has once been distinctly made and overruled, it need not be repeated to the same class of evidence. The rule in such cases has been laid down, and should be observed in the further progress of the trial, without further vexing the court with useless objections and exceptions. Nothing is waived by conforming to the rule laid down." In *McKinnon v. Gates*, 102 Mich. 618 (61 N. W. Rep. 74), the court held that certain evidence for the plaintiff was erroneously admitted, and then said: "It is, however, insisted that other evidence of this character was afterwards introduced without objection; that the defendant introduced evidence to controvert it; and that this cured the error. This is not the law. One ruling upon the point by the court was sufficient, and the defendant had the right to rest upon such ruling, and to meet the evidence by counter proof, without waiving the error." The rule we have stated finds ample support in other authorities See *Church v. Howard*, 79 N. Y. 421; *In re Eysaman*, 113 N. Y. 71; *Sharon v. Sharon*, 79 Cal. 633 (22 Pac. Rep. 36, 131); *Whitney v. Traynor*, 74 Wis. 289 (42 N. W. Rep. 269); *Gilpin v. Gilpin*, 12 Colo. 516 (21 Pac. Rep. 612); *Railroad Co. v. Gower*, 1 Pickle (Tenn.), 465 (3 S. W. Rep. 824); 3 Jones, Evidence, section 897; Underhill, Evidnce, section 367; Bradner, Evidence, page 499, section 11; 1 Thompson, Trials, section 705.

It is said, however, that the appellant waived his right to complain of the evidence in question, for the reason that similar testimony had been erroneously given by another witness. The facts appear to 9   be that Bradford had testified that Tiede, during the conversation concerning which Smith testified, said to him: "Scott, I do feel that I have been negligent in that matter, and that the note ought to have been paid." No objection whatever was made to that testimony. Tiede was afterwards called as a witness by the defendant, and denied that he had made the statement to which Bradford testified. After the defendant rested, Smith was examined in rebuttal and testified as already shown. The question presented for our consideration, on the facts stated is, Did the defendant waive its right to object to the incompetent evidence which Smith gave by failing to object to Bradford's evidence to the same effect. There are numerous authorities which hold that a party waives his right to object to improper evidence by consenting that it be introduced, or by introducing similar evidence in his own behalf. But where a party objects to incompetent testimony, which is, nevertheless received, he does not waive his objection by cross-examining the witness respecting the objectionable testimony, nor by introducing evidence to rebut it. *Laver v. Hotaling*, 115 Cal. 613 (46 Pac. Rep. 1070; 47 Pac. Rep. 593); *Scarbrough v. Blackman*, 108 Ala. 656 (18 South. Rep. 735); *Martin v. Railroad Co.*, 103 N. Y. App. 626 (9 N. E. Rep. 505); *Railroad Co. v. Crocker*, 95 Ala. 412 (11 South. Rep. 262); *Lyon v. Lenon*, 106 Ind. 567 (7 N. E. Rep. 311); *Barker v. Railway Co.*, 126 Mo. 143 (28 S. W. Rep. 866); *Marsh v. Snyder*, 14 Neb. 237 (15 N. W. Rep. 341). There are also numerous cases which hold that the introduction of improper evidence will not constitute reversible error, where other evidence of the same character is admitted without objection. *State v.*

Eifert, 102 Iowa, 188; *Butler v. Railroad Co.*, 87 Iowa, 207; *Baltimore & O. R. Co. v. State*, 81 Md. 371 (32 Atl. Rep. 202); *Railway Co. v. Huffman* (Tex Civ. App.), 32 S. W. Rep. 30; *Washington Bridge Co. v. Land & River Imp. Co.* 12 Wash, 272 (40 Pac. Rep. 982); *Hickman v. Layne*, 47 Neb. 177 (66 N. W. Rep. 298); *Railway Co. v. Garteiser*, 9 Tex. Civ. App. 456 (29 S. W. Rep. 941); *Railway Co. v. John*, 9 Tex. Civ. App. 342 (29 S. W. Rep. 558). In none of the cases of that character to which our attention has been called does it appear that any attempt was made to disprove what the evidence, admitted without objection, tended to establish; therefore, the exclusion of other evidence to prove what was not disputed could not have been prejudicial. This case is not within the rule which controls in such cases. It does not appear that the defendant agreed to or was in any manner responsible for the introduction of the evidence in question. It had not offered evidence of that kind, and the mere fact that it did not object to the testimony of Bradford did not estop it to object to similar testimony offered subsequently. It may have been willing to waive objections, as it did to Bradford's testimony, and unwilling to have any other of the same character admitted. In view of the fact that Bradford alone had testified to the alleged statement of Tiede, and that the latter denied having made it, the natural and probable effect of Smith's testimony was prejudicial to the defendant. We are of the opinion that it waived objection to Bradford's testimony only; that it did not waive the right to object to the testimony of Smith; and that the objection thereto should have been sustained. The authorities which can be regarded as applicable to the rule under consideration do not appear to be numerous. In *McLane v. Paschal*, 14 Tex. 20 (11 S. W. Rep. 837), it was held that the introduction of immaterial evidence, without objection, to prove a certain fact, "furnished no reason for the admission of

such evidence when properly objected to," and that,
we think, should be the general rule.   The mere
10   silence of a party, when incompetent evidence is
offered, should be treated as a waiver of objection to the particular evidence offered only, and not as
a waiver of objections to all evidence of the same kind
or character, which may be offered subsequently.

V.   On the final settlement made by the defendant
bank with Bridge, thirty-five dollars were left by him
with the bank, and he paid to it thereafter a small
amount, making fifty-three dollars and five cents in the
aggregate, which he directed the bank to apply in part
payment of the note in suit. Tiede states that the amount
was offered to the receiver, but that he declined to
accept it.   The answer pleads a tender of that amount,
and a readiness on the part of the bank to pay it to the
        receiver, but the receiver has not accepted the
11   tender thus made.   The court charged the jury
that the plaintiff was entitled to recover the
amount of the tender without evidence.   The appellant
complains of that ruling, on the ground that the receiver
seeks to recover on account of its alleged negligence,
and that, as it had not been negligent with respect to
the amount it had collected, no recovery for such
amount is authorized.   The receiver demands a recovery
for the full amount of the note, and the statement of the defendant bank that it has collected and is
ready to pay on the note the amount stated, should be
given the effect of an admission of liability to that
extent, and the court properly charged the jury that
the receiver was entitled to recover that amount.   The
        court also charged the jury to allow interest on
12   the amount under consideration from the date it
was paid to the bank to the time of the trial.   In
view of the disposition we find it necessary to make of
this case, it is only necessary to say, in regard to this,
that, if the bank tendered, without condition, the

.imount as claimed, and has kept that tender good, it should not be required to pay interest upon the amount so tendered. The liability of the receiver and of the defendant bank for costs on account of the amount tendered is not involved in this appeal. For the error of the district court in admitting objectionable testi mony, to which objection was made, its judgment is REVERSED.

S. C. SLOSS, Appellant, v. SIMPSON BAILEY AND AMOS BAILEY,

Tender. A transcript of the record of a case tried before a justice of the peace, which recites an offer of judgment made by the defend-
2 ant to the plaintiff, need not show that the plaintiff was in court when the offer was made, since it might be given to an attorney or agent acting for the plaintiff in the prosecution of the suit

Record: PAROL VARIANCE. A record of the proceedings before a
1 justice of the peace, which shows an offer by the defendant, made in writing, to confess judgment in favor of the plaintiff for a certain sum, can neither be supported or contradicted by affidavit

RULE APPLIED Under Code section 3818, requiring the offer to con-
fess judgment, after action is brought before a justice, to be made in the presence of plaintiff, or after notice to him that it will be made, the transcript of the justice need not expressly show that
2 the plaintiff was present when such offer was made. If it appears from the record that an offer was made as contemplated or this is the necessary inference from the language employed, it is suffi cient; and, if the record is silent, parol evidence is admissible to show the offer.

Appeal Certificate. A question certified to the supreme court, which involves an examination of the record and the proceedings of the
3 lower court, will not be considered, as the certificate must set out the very point to be dertermined.

Appeal from Appanoose District Court.—HON. M. A. ROBERTS, Judge.

THURSDAY, FEBRUARY 10, 1898.

C. F. Howell for appellant.

Mabry & Payne for appellees.

LADD, J.—This action was brought to recover seventy-six dollars and thirty-four cents on certain promissory notes, and judgment was rendered in the
. justice court for fifty-six dollars and fifty-five cents. On appeal, in the district court, the jury returned a verdict in favor of the plaintiff for ninety-three cents, for which amount judgment was entered; and afterwards, on motion of the defendants, all costs were taxed against the plaintiff. This ruling was based on an alleged offer to confess judgment for one dollar and costs in the justice court. The motion was resisted by affidavits tending to show that the plaintiff was not present when any offer was made, had no notice thereof, and that none was in fact made. It was supported by affidavits to the contrary.

After stating these facts, we are asked the question, in the certificate of the trial judge: "Where the record of the justice before whom the case was tried

1   below shows that the defendants in the justice court made an offer in writing to confess judgment in favor of the plaintiff for one dollar and costs prior to entering upon the trial of the case below, are affidavits tending to show that no offer to confess judgment was in fact made by defendants in the court below, competent; that is, can the record of the justice of the peace as to such offer be contradicted or supported by affidavits?" The statute requires the offer to confess judgment, after an action is brought, to be made in the presence of the plaintiff, or after notice to him that it will be made. Code, section 3818. It is not a matter of pleading, may be oral, and, where the record is silent, may be shown by parol testimony. *City*

of Davenport v. C., R. I. & P. R. Co., 38 Iowa, 633; *Barlow v. Buckingham*, 68 Iowa, 169. But the making of the offer is a part of the court proceedings, and it was appropriate for the justice to determine whether made as contemplated by law. Though it might be shown when omitted, this did not relieve the court of the duty of passing upon the question, and entering his conclusion of record. The manner of making it is not raised by the inquiry, though it may fairly be inferred therefrom that this was done as required. That such a record is a verity is conceded, and, if so, it may not be varied or contradicted. *Farley v. Budd*, 14 Iowa, 289; *Maynes v. Brockway*, 55 Iowa, 457. It is said, however, that the authorities allow parol testimony to prove a fact on which the record is silent,—to supply an omission. That point is not raised by the question. The record being a verity, evidence *aliunde* to support or contradict it would be unnecessary, and therefore not admissible. Whether it might be received to supply an omission, no intimation of which is found in the question, we are not called upon to determine.

The second inquiry is: "Must the transcript of the justice in such a case expressly show that the plaintiff was present in court when such offer to confess judgment was made?" The statute provides that the offer

2 shall be effectual, if in pursuance of notice to the plaintiff. Undoubtedly, the offer might be made to an attorney or agent acting for the plaintiff in the prosecution of the suit. If it appears from the record that the offer was made as contemplated, or this is the necessary inference from the language employed, then enough is shown. If the record is silent, then parol evidence is admissible to establish the offer.

The third question involves an examination of the record and the proceedings of the justice. This cannot

be done. *Stern v. Sample,* 96 Iowa, 341; *Buchanan
County Bank v. Cedar Rapids, I. F. & N. W. R'y
3   Co.,* 62 Iowa, 494; *Long v. Railway Co.,* 64 Iowa,
541. The certificate must set out the very point
to be determined. *McLenon v. Railroad Co.,* 69 Iowa,
320; *Bennett v. Parker,* 67 Iowa, 451; *Cooker Co. v.
Olive,* 82 Iowa, 122. The fact that the certificate contains the transcript and the proceedings on the motion
does not obviate the rule. Under the law as interpreted
by this court, the question itself must raise the desired
point, without resort to the record.—AFFIRMED.

HENRY WILLENBURG V. CAROLINE C. HERSEY, Appellant.

Decree: IMPEACHMENT. A recital in a decree of foreclosure that
defendant appeared by attorney, who was her husband, is conclusive as to such appearance where the only evidence to show
2   the recital erroneous is testimony by the husband, who is also a
party, that she did not appear or answer, and that he knew she did
not, because she told him so. and he filed the answer himself,
where it is not alleged that he had no authority to do so.

EVIDENCE   A contention that a party defendant in a foreclosure
proceeding was not served and did not appear in the action, although
1   the decree rendered recites such appearance, is not established by
a paragraph therein providing that the cause be "continued as to
4   the other defendants for service," where there were other defendants than the party whose appearance is denied.

SAME. The recitals of a decree cannot be contradicted by extrinsic
3   evidence which is not clear and positive.

SAME. No inference will be drawn or presumptions indulged in in ref
3   erence to the recitals in a decree, except such as support the decree,

Appeal from Carroll District Court.—HON. S. M.
ELWOOD, Judge.

SATURDAY, FEBRUARY 12, 1898.

ACTION to quiet title to certain real estate.   There
was a cross-petition by defendant.   Upon the hearing,
there was a decree for plaintiff.   Defendant appeals.—
Reversed.

F. M. Powers for appellant.

F. M. Davenport for appellee.

WATERMAN, J.—This action was originally brought
in the name of H. B. Barbee, as plaintiff.   Subsequently,
Henry Willenburg having purchased the land of H. B.
Barbee, he was substituted as plaintiff.   The land in
question is the northeast, northwest, 16—82—34, in
Carroll county.   The petition is in the ordinary form for
actions of this nature.   The defendant answers by general
denial and in a cross-petition, claims title to the land,
and asks that the same be quieted as against plaintiff.
Both parties claim through one Henry J. Cooley, who
obtained title to the forty acres in question October 18,
1882.   Plaintiff's title was derived through a sale under
general execution issued on a judgment of a justice of
the peace against Cooley, in favor of one Arts, a transcript of which was filed in the office of the clerk of the
court March 10, 1879.   The sheriff's deed to H. B. Barbee, executed on said sale, was dated February 14, 1887,
and duly recorded.   So much for plaintiff's title.   While
the abstract is not very full or clear, it is safe to say as
to defendant's title that she held a mortgage on the
land which was executed by said Henry J. Cooley.   This
mortgage was duly foreclosed, and the land sold, and
conveyed by sheriff's deed to defendant.   This deed was
dated September 8, 1890, and filed for record the following day.   It appears that Cooley, on September 29, 1889,
by quit-claim deed, conveyed his interest in the land
to Thomas F. Barbee, the husband of H. B. Barbee.
The proceedings in the action for foreclosure are not set

out entire in the record, but the decree appears in full. The material portions of this decree will be stated, for its construction is important in view of the claims of the respective parties. It is entitled: "Caroline C. Hersey vs. Thomas F. Barbee and Henrietta B. Barbee, His Wife, Henry J. Cooley, Joel V. Cole, George W. Paine and Francis B. Paine, His Wife." Among other recitals are these: "Plaintiff appeared by George W. Paine, her attorney, and defendants Thomas F. Barbee and H. B. Barbee, his wife, appeared by Thomas F. Barbee, attorney; * * * whereupon the plaintiff offers her evidence and proofs, and the same are duly considered by the court, and thereupon the court finds that the allegations of the plaintiff's petition are true, and that there is justly due the plaintiff on the promissory note of Henry J. Cooley, sued on herein, the sum of one thousand two hundred and one dollars and forty cents, and for attorney's fees, as stipulated in the mortgage, the sum of fifty-two dollars. * * * It is therefore considered and adjudged by the court that the plaintiff, Caroline Hersey, have and recover of the defendant Thomas F. Barbee the said sum of one thousand two hundred and one dollars and forty cents, etc. * * * And it is further adjudged and decreed that the liens, interest, and estate of the defendants in and to the mortgaged premises [describing them] are inferior and junior to the lien of plaintiff's mortgage thereon; that the equity of redemption of each and all of the defendants in and to said real estate be, and the same are, forever barred and foreclosed. * * * And this cause is hereby continued as to the other defendants for service."

Thomas F. Barbee testified on the trial that his wife told him that she was never served with notice of

this foreclosure proceeding. This evidence was objected
to, and it was clearly incompetent. He also testi-
2   fied that his wife did not appear in said action.
His testimony on this point is very brief. It is
as follows: "She did not appear in that action. She
did not answer." Cross-examination: "I know that
she did not answer or appear in that case, because I
filed answer myself. * * * I know she did not
appear in that suit, because she told me so." He also
says that he was attorney for his wife in all cases.
Nowhere does he assert that he did not, with authority,
appear for her. It may be claimed that, by inference,
his testimony excludes the idea of an appearance for
his wife; but the difficulty about this is that, if presumptions are to be indulged in, they must all be held to support the recitals of the decree. *Emigrant Co. v. Fuller*,
83 Iowa, 599; *Toliver v. Morgan*, 75 Iowa, 619; *Suiter v.
Turner*, 10 Iowa, 517; *State v. Elgin*, 11 Iowa, 216;
Campbell v. Ayres, 6 Iowa, 339. As stated in
3   these cases, the presumptions are in favor of
the jurisdiction of the district court and the
verity of its judgment. If extrinsic evidence can be
received to contradict its recitals, such evidence must
be clear and positive. The testimony in this case is by
no means of that character. It leaves too much to
inference. We think the decree must be held good for
what it says. This decree, in terms, establishes defendant's mortgage lien as prior and superior to any claim
of said H. B. Barbee. Inasmuch as it was rendered
long after the interest of the latter had been acquired
by execution sale under the Arts judgment, it deter-
mines in favor of defendant her claim to a paramount
title.

Plaintiff lays much stress upon the closing paragraph of the decree, in which it is said that the cause is

"continued as to the other defendants for service," and
seems to insist that this expression is incon-
4   sistent with the idea that any defendant-
other than Thomas F. Barbee was before
the court. But there were other defendants than
Barbee and his wife, and, to give all of the recitals
of the decree effect we must construe this last
clause as referring to those who were not served
with notice, and who did not appear. To meet the
argument of appellee's counsel, we will say that it
makes no difference that Mrs. Barbee was not served
with notice of the action in foreclosure if she appeared
in court in that proceeding; and this, the decree recites,
she did. We think defendant should have had a decree
in her favor on her cross-bill. If she so elects, she may
have a decree in this court. For the present, the
entry here will be simply that the decree of the district
court is REVERSED.

MICHAEL KINNEY, Appellant, v. PATRICK KINNEY.

Partition Fence: HEDGES. Neglect of an adjoining owner to trim a
hedge fence standing on part of the division line, is not, within
Code 1873, section 1490, providing that if any party neglect to
2   "repair or rebuild" a partition fence, the aggrieved party may
appeal to the fence viewers, and if they determine the fence is
"insufficient," they shall signify it in writing to the delinquent
owner and direct him to repair or rebuild

FENCE VIEWER.   Under Code 1873, section 1490, authorizing hedges
as partition fences, but making no provision as to trimming them,
1   the owner thereof is not liable to the adjoining owner for allowing them to grow so that his land is shaded and encroached on
thereby. It is a clear case of *damnum absque injuria.*[*]

Appeal from Lucas District Court.—HON. M. A.
ROBERTS, Judge.

WEDNESDAY, APRIL 6, 1898.

[*] See Chapter 4, Title XII, Code of 1897.—REPORTER.

ACTION at law to recover damages for the use and occupation of a part of plaintiff's land. The trial court sustained a demurrer to the plaintiff's petition, and he appeals.—*Affirmed.*

Stuart & Bartholomew for appellant.

Will B. Barger and *J. A. Penick* for appellee.

DEEMER, C. J.—From the petition, we gather the following facts material to the determination of the question presented: The parties are owners of adjoining tracts of land, plaintiff owing the north one-half of the southwest one-fourth of section 22, and the defendant the south one-half of the northwest quarter of section 36, in the same township and range. The lands are inclosed, and the parties maintain a partition fence between their tracts. This fence was built about fifteen years ago, by agreement between the parties. It was the duty of plaintiff to maintain the east half of the fence, and of defendant to build and repair the west half. In recognition of this duty, defendant planted and cultivated an osage orange and willow hedge fence upon his part of the division line. It is claimed that, while this hedge fence is sufficient as a lawful fence, yet defendant has failed to trim and cut down said fence to a proper height, and has permitted the limbs to grow out over plaintiff's land to the distance of from ten to twenty feet, thus depriving him of the use of that much of his land. Plaintiff also charged that defendant has allowed the fence to grow to the height of from thirty to forty feet, creating a dense shade upon plaintiff's land for a distance of from thirty to forty feet, effectually hindering and preventing the growth of products thereon. These acts are said to have been done willfully and maliciously, and *to*

plaintiff's great damage. The demurrer raises the question as to the obligation of the defendant to
1   trim the hedge. Appellee insists in argument that the fence viewers have exclusive jurisdiction of the matter at issue. This point was not made by the demurrer, and does not seem to have been presented to the trial court; but, as it goes to the jurisdiction of the court, we are required to consider it. Section 1490 of the Code of 1873 is as follows: "If any party neglect to repair or rebuild a partition fence, or a portion thereof, which he ought to maintain, the aggrieved party may complain to the fence viewers, who, after due notice to each party, shall examine the same; and if they determine the fence is insufficient shall signify it in writing to the delinquent occupant of the land, and direct him to repair or rebuild the same, within such time as they may deem reasonable." Section 1492 provides for the settlement of a controversy between the respective owners about the obligation to erect or maintain partition fences, by the fence viewers. The argument is that this case involves the maintenance or repair of a partition fence, and that the fence viewers have exclusive jurisdiction of the controversy. The fault with the argument lies in the assumption that the issue is over the neglect of one of the parties to repair or maintain his part of the fence. Such is not the point in dispute. There is no question that the fence is sufficient for the purpose intended. The complaint is that the fence, as constructed, is an invasion of plaintiff's property rights. The fence viewers have no jurisdiction of such a controversy.

II. The Code of 1873 provides, in substance, that the respective owners of land inclosed with fences shall keep up and maintain partition fences between their own and the next adjoining inclosure. It also provides that a person building a fence may lay the same upon the line between him and the adjacent owners, and

that he shall have the same right to remove it as if it were upon his own land. It further provides that a certain fence, built of rails, or boards and posts, or its equivalent, shall be a lawful fence. This same Code also recognizes a hedge fence as lawful, and provides for its cultivation, by allowing the owner to enter upon his neighbor's land for this purpose. There is no
2 statute, prior to the enactment of the present Code, regulating the height of such a fence, nor any provision requiring the owner or other person to trim the same. Appellant contends that the owner of the hedge has no right to use more of his neighbor's land than is essential for the purpose of making a lawful fence, or its equivalent, and that when he does this, he is liable to respond in damages. The right to plant the hedge upon the line is unquestioned, and defendant is not in fault, unless it be in failing to trim and cut down the hedge to such a height that it will answer the purpose of a lawful fence. As the statute authorizes the growth of such a fence upon the division line, and as there is no express requirement upon the owner to trim it, such duty arises, if at all, in virtue of some implied obligation. The rights and duties of adjacent owners of land with respect to partition fences is purely statutory, and as the statute expressly provides for and recognizes hedge fences, and does not undertake to specify their height, or as to how they shall be trimmed, it follows, we think, that neither party can hold the other responsible for damages incident to the natural growth of the hedge. See *Musch v. Burkhart*, 83 Iowa, 301. It is a clear case of *damnum absque injuria*. The new Code (section 2355) remedies this mischief by requiring the owner to trim division fences. The demurrer was properly sustained, and the judgment is AFFIRMED.

E. J. CHRISTE, Administrator, Appellant, v. THE CHI-CAGO, ROCK ISLAND & PACIFIC RAILWAY COMPANY.

Release: ESTATES OF DECEDENTS. The parents of an intestate, who was killed while employed on a railroad, settled with the company and released all claims to damages There were no debts against the deceased, and his parents were his sole heirs. *Held*, that the settlement and release by the parents, though made without intervention of an administrator, was .valid, and precluded a recovery for the intes ate death, by an administrator who was appointed after the settlement.

Appeal from Johnson District Court.—HON. M. J. WADE, Judge.

WEDNESDAY, APRIL 6, 1898.

PLAINTIFF is administrator of the estate of one Lloyd P. Connor, deceased, and brings this action to recover of defendant damages for the death of said intestate, caused, it is charged, by the negligence of said railway company. Among other defenses set up was that defendant had fully settled and paid the claim for the death of said Connor. The cause was brought on for trial before a jury. After the testimony was all in, on motion, the court instructed the jury to return a verdidct for defendant, on the ground that the damages sued for had been fully satisfied, and defendant released from all claims. A verdict was returned in accordance with the instruction, and from the judg-ment rendered thereon the plaintiff appeals.—*Affirmed.*

Rickel, Crocker & Christie and *Ranck & Bradley* for appellant.

A. E. Swisher, John T. Scott, Geo. E. McCaughan, and *Carroll Wright* for appellee.

WATERMAN, J.—Lloyd P. Connor, while in the employ of defendant company, was killed in its yards at Brooklyn, Iowa, May 11, 1893. At the time of his death he was unmarried, and he left, surviving, his father and mother, who were his sole heirs at law. On September 20, 1893, defendant made a settlement with the father and mother of said Connor, and took from them the following instrument:

"For the consideration of $250.00, received of the Chicago, Rock Island & Pacific Railway Company, I hereby release and discharge said company from all claims and demands against it, and especially from all liability for loss or damages to us, or either of us, or to the estate of the said Lloyd Connor, deceased, of which estate we are the sole distributees; the said Lloyd Connor having died from injuries received at Brooklyn, Iowa, having been run over by a car while in the employ of said railway company as a switchman. And the said Lloyd Connor being our minor son, and having died intestate, unmarried, and without issue, we, his surviving parents, for the consideration above named, do hereby release and discharge said railway company from all liability to us, or to the estate of said Lloyd Connor, whether on account of damages by reason of his death, for money due him, or for or on any other account whatsoever. Said accident having occurred on or about the eleventh day of May, A. D. 1893. Received payment September 20th, 1893. Mrs. J. E. Connor. John Connor.

"The above was read to and signed by the said Mrs.
J. E. Connor and John Connor in our presence, at Brook-
lyn, Iowa, on the twentieth day of September, 1893.
J. H. Tucker. Lewis Clark."

The fairness or good faith of this settlement is not
questioned, nor is it claimed that Lloyd Connor had any
creditors. On August 1, 1894, plaintiff procured himself to be appointed administrator of the estate of said
Connor, and on the fourteenth of that month he began
this action. The sole question for determination is
whether the settlement with the heirs precludes a
recovery by the administrator; or, putting it in another
way, is administration of the estate of an intestate a
necessity in this state, or is it only a matter of legal
convenience? Counsel for appellant insist that the
heirs had no title to or ownership of the claim against
the defendant, and that, therefore, the settlement with
them was of no validity, and their receipt cannot bar
the administrator in this action.

II. By section 2526, Code 1873, it is provided:
"When a wrongful act produces death, the damages
shall be disposed of as personal property, belonging to
the estate of the deceased, except that if the deceased
leaves a husband, wife, child or parent, it shall not be
liable for the payment of debts." Under our law the
right to a distributive share of personalty in the
estate of an intestate vests *instanter* in the heir upon
the death of the owner, and not from the time of distribution made. Distribution gives to the distributee no
new title, but only ascertains the property to which
title attaches. *Moore v. Gordon*, 24 Iowa, 158. 2 Williams, Personal Property, 277, gives this as the common
rule. It has been held in this state that heirs cannot
maintain an action upon notes due the estate during
the period allotted for administration. The ground
upon which this holding is based is, not that they have
no title, but that the extent of their interest has not

been determined. Creditors have a first right to such of the personal assets as are not exempt, and it is only through administration that their rights can properly be made known and determined. After the time limited for administration has expired, the heirs may maintain such an action in their own names. *Phinny v. Warren*, 52 Iowa, 332. As bearing upon this question of the rights of the heirs, see *Adkinson v. Breeding*, 56 Iowa, 26; *Kelley v. Mann*, 56 Iowa, 625, 628; *Stewart v. Phenice*, 65 Iowa, 475 (481); *Jordan v. Hunnell*, 96 Iowa, 334. To hold that the heirs of an intestate have no property right in the personal estate until after distribution would cut off the estate of an heir who died before administration was closed, from an interest in such property. This, we take it, no one will claim to be the law. In *Phinny v. Warren, supra*, it is said, speaking of a note which was part of the assets of an estate upon which no administration had been taken out: "Upon the death of the payee of the note, it may be conceded that the note became the property of the administrator, if there was one. But, if no administrator is appointed, it will not do to say the note ceased to be property. Property cannot be thus blotted out. There is no statute which requires that letters of administration should be taken out, or that imposes a penalty for not so doing."

Section 2367 of the Code of 1873 provides that original administration cannot be had after a lapse of five years from the death of the intestate. This does not mean that letters must be taken out within that time, whether desired or not, but is intended as a bar to creditors. If, in the case of an intestate estate, there are no debts, and the property is such as can be divided, and the heirs agree upon a division, we know of nothing, either in law or reason, to prevent them from settling the estate without the intervention of an administrator. In the case at bar, the only property

of the estate was the claim against defendant railway.
There were no creditors, and the money received from
the railway was not subject to their claims, had there
been any. The father and mother were sole heirs, and,
as such, they received this money, and receipted in full
for all demands of the estate against the company.
To say that they cannot do this,—that there must be an
administrator, whether they wish or not, through whose
hands this money must pass to them,—is to establish
a rule that we are not inclined to sanction. In *Walworth v. Abel*, 52 Pa. St. 370, it is said: "No doubt
the personal estate of a decedent vests in the administrator, but in trust for the creditors and heirs or legatees. The mere legal estate passes to the administrator. The equitable descends upon the parties entitled
to distribution. If there be no creditors, the heirs have
a complete equity in the property; and if they choose,
instead of taking letters of administration, to distribute it by arrangement made and executed among themselves, where is the principle which forbids it?   *   *   *
And why shall the arrangement be broken up by a mere
intermeddler? Family arrangements are favorites of
the law, and when fairly made are never allowed to be
disturbed by the parties, or any other for them." In
a case in Minnesota identical in principle with the case
at bar, it was held that a settlement with the next of
kin of a claim for damages for the death of the intestate
would bar a recovery by an administrator, afterwards
appointed. *Sykora v. Machine Co.*, 59 Minn. 130 (60
N. W. Rep. 1008). See, also, *Needham v. Gillett*, 39
Mich. 574; *Schmidt v. Deegan*, 69 Wis. 300 (34 N. W.
Rep. 83); *Vail v. Anderson*, 61 Minn. 552 (64 N. W.
Rep. 47).

The administrator is a mere trustee for the creditors and the heirs. If he received the money from
defendant, he could but do with it what has already
been done. It would seem both useless and expensive

to re-open this matter, in which he has no interest, save as he represents the heirs, and with the present status of which the heirs are entirely satisfied. In *Dowell v. Railway Co.*, 62 Iowa, 632, in a suit by the administrator to recover damages for the death of his intestate, the defendant pleaded satisfaction by payment to the widow; and it was held that she could release the claim, so far as her interest was concerned, but that the satisfaction could extend no further. This case is cited by appellant in support of his contention. We regard it as conclusive against him. Our attention has been called to no decision in conflict with the views here expressed. In *Wymore v. Mahaska County*, 78 Iowa, 396, cited by appellant, the holding was that, when the negligence of parents could not be directly urged as a defense, it could not be set up indirectly; or, stating it more specifically, that one liable to an administrator for negligence which caused the death of a child of tender years, could not set up as a reason for not responding in damages, that the parents, who were also negligent, would get the benefit of what might be paid. In *Stahl v. Brown*, 72 Iowa, 720, the only question decided was that the heirs could not bind the administrator by agreeing in advance upon the amount in which he should allow a claim. The opinion contains this express qualification. "It will be observed, also, that it was not stipulated that the estate should not be administered upon, nor that it was entered into for the purpose of avoiding the cost of administration; and we do not determine the question whether the heirs could have precluded administration by an agreement to that effect, for no such question arises in the case." The statement in the opinion, that "the heirs take no title to or ownership of the personal property of the estate while it is subject to administration," is, as we have already indicated, inaccurate. The trial court was entirely justified in taking the case from the jury, and its judgment in defendant's favor is AFFIRMED.

[HENRY L. B. LANGFORD BROOKE, Intervener, v. MATHEW KING, Assignee, Appellant.

Banks: TRUSTS: *Preferences.* A claim against an insolvent bank for
1   money paid to the proprietor of such bank, as agent for the sale of land, and deposited by him in such bank, is entitled to prefer-
2   ence over the claims of general creditors.

SAME. A vendor of land is not entitled to a preference in the funds of an insolvent bank, the proprietor of which was an agent for the sale of the land, on the ground that the purchase money was deposited in such bank without authority, where the purchaser
2   had an account at the bank and the payments were made by merely charging him with the amount of each payment and giving the vendor credit for the amount, unless there were actually in the bank funds of such purchaser to be applied on such payments.

EVIDENCE. A vendor of land, who claims a preference over general creditors in the funds of an insolvent bank, on the ground that
2   the purchase money had been deposited in such bank without authority by the proprietor of the bank, who was agent for the sale of the land, has the burden of showing that the money was actually received by the bank.

Appeal: NOTICE OF MOTION. A motion to affirm a judgment on
2   appeal will be discharged if there is no evidence of service in the record.

Appeal from Crawford District Court.—HON. S. M. ELWOOD, Judge.

WEDNESDAY, APRIL 6, 1898.

PRIOR to August 10, 1893, John H. DeWolf was engaged in business at Vail, Iowa, a part of which business was the operation of a private bank, known as the Citizens' Bank. August 10, 1893, he made an assignment for the benefit of creditors, both as to himself and the bank. The petition shows that prior to June 5,

1891, the intervener was the owner of the undivided nine-twenty-fourths of section 17, township 84, range 37 west, in Crawford county; that a Mrs. White was the owner of the balance of said section before her death in May, 1885; that by her will, which was duly probated in Crawford county, Iowa, in January, 1887, intervener was duly appointed as agent, and, as such, had charge of the part of said land belonging to his estate; that in 1890, John H. De Wolf, as intervener's agent, collected the rents of said land amounting to nine hundred dollars, of which amount five hundred and thirty-three dollars was never paid over by him; that in 1891, De Wolf, as such agent, sold said land for the sum of fourteen thousand dollars, receiving four thousand dollars in cash, and the balance in annual payments of two thousand dollars each; that, of the four thousand dollars paid, eight hundred and eighty-two dollars and twenty-five cents remained in the hands of said agent; that July 1, 1892, he received a payment on said land of two thousand six hundred dollars, and July 1, 1893, another payment of two thousand four hundred and eight dollars, which he failed to turn over to intervener. The petition asks that said claims be allowed and made preferred claims against the estate. The answer denies the averments except as to the assignment and that the property came into the hands of the assignee. Upon a trial of the issues the district court established the claims, and gave them preference over the general creditors. The assignee appealed.—*Modified and affirmed.*

P. E. C. Lally and *J. P. Conner* for appellant.

Swan, Lawrence & Swan and *Shaw & Kuehnle* for appellee.

GRANGER, J.—Some questions of fact are controverted, and it will be well to first determine them. We
find that the intervener was owner of a part of the land,
and as to the remainder a trustee, so that his authority
is complete for the purpose of creating the agency of De
Wolf for the sale of the land and the collection of
deferred payments therefor. We also find that all the
money paid to De Wolf as rent, and on the purchase
price, were paid to him as such agent. We may sum-
marize by saying that we find the facts to be such as to
sustain a preference of the claims over general conditions for all moneys actually paid to De Wolf, and by
him retained, whether in the bank or otherwise. The
controversy is mainly as to facts. The rules as to
preference are so well settled that there is little
or no contention as to the law. The ground upon
which such preferences have been sustained
heretofore is that, when trust money was paid into a
bank for deposit, it was impressed with a trust character, the deposit being unauthorized; and, hence, that
the estate, when the bank afterwards assigned, was
enhanced to the amount of the deposit by the worngful
act of the trustee or agent, and that it was no prejudice
to general creditors to take from the fund what should
not have been placed there. See *Independent Dist. v.
King.* 80 Iowa, 498; *Plow Co. v. Lamp*, 80 Iowa, 723. It
appears in this case that the payment of two thousand
four hundred and eighty dollars, being the second
annual payment of two thousand dollars, and the interest on deferred payments, was paid by draft, and we
think that payment is clearly within the rule of the
cases cited. One Wells was the purchaser of the land,
and the payments were made by him. As to the
four thousand dollars payment, at the time of the
purchase, and the first annual payment of two
thousand dollars, with the interest on deferred pay-

ments, making two thousand six hundred dollars, it appears that Wells had an account at the bank, and the payments were made by merely charging Wells with the amount of each payment, and giving the White estate,—which meant the previous owner of the land,— credit for the amount. A question is, does this difference as to facts, change the rule as to preference? It is thought that, until the money was actually paid to De Wolf, there was nothing to impress with the trust character. We are not disposed to state a rule so broadly, but we incline to the view that it cannot be said, in this case, as to the two payments thus made, that the estate was benefited by the changes made on the books; in other words, that any money was deposited in the bank as a result of the transaction. To be better understood, let us suppose the changes had not been made on the books, and the assignment had followed. We cannot say that precisely the same funds would not have been there for the general creditors as are there now. It appears that the charges were made against Wells without reference to the state of his account. He may have had either a debit or credit balance at the time. The burden is with the intervener to show that the money was actually received by the bank. If Wells had not the credit balance, so that, after the change on the books he was no longer a debtor as to that particular transaction, there would be a serious doubt of the change on the books amounting to a payment, conceding that he authorized it. One Haskins was the renter, and paid the rent claimed for, and the payments of rent were made in the same way, by merely charging Haskins on the books of the bank, and giving the White estate credit; and it is quite manifest that Haskins was, at all times, a debtor to the bank, and that no rent was really paid by him. The result was that De Wolf made himself a debtor to intervener for the rent, and Haskins a debtor to him. The same would be true as to the Wells payments, if there was no money, so as to make an actual payment by the change on the books. Whether or not an actual payment made in that way would bring the case within the rule, as to preferences, we do not decide; for, because of the failure to show that there were funds of the debtor to be applied in payment, we think the right to a preference does not exist. It follows that the

3　judgment should be so modified that the preference should apply only to the two thousand four hundred and eighty dollars payment. There is a motion by appellee to affirm the judgment, but there is no evidence of record of any service, and hence we disregard it. With the modification suggested, the judgment will stand AFFIRMED.

The German State Bank v. The Northwestern Water and Light Company, Appellant.

Contracts: DEBT OF ANOTHER. A promise by a stockholder of a corporation to a purchaser of his stock to pay an indebtedness of the corporation, so as to make its earnings available to payment of dividends and subsequent obligations, cannot be enforced by the corporation.

Pledge. A stockholder in a corporation who pledges his stock to another person to secure the payment of a debt due by the corporation may, with the consent of the pledgee, withdraw the stock pledged, although the corporation objects thereto.

Same: *Rights of debtor.* A debtor cannot complain of a decree that its property be first exhausted to satisfy the judgment before proceeding against property of another voluntarily pledged for the debt

Appeal from Plymouth District Court.—Hon. F. R. Gaynor, Judge.

WEDNESDAY, APRIL 6, 1898.

PLAINTIFFS bring this action upon two promissory notes, executed by the defendant the Northwestern Water & Light Company. These notes were secured by certain shares of stock of said water and light company, which were deposited with plaintiff. The shares were owned by J. H. Winchell, who, as president of the water and light company, executed the notes, and were by him transferred to plaintiff, as collateral security for the payment of the notes. The first answer of the water and light company denies a part of the indebtedness claimed. By an amendment to its petition, plaintiff states that said Winchell deposited, as collateral security for the payment of said notes, eighty shares of stock in said defendant company; that thereafter Winchell, by written contract, sold and transferred to one J. F. Rogers, four hundred and thirty-nine shares of stock in the defendant company, and, as a part consideration for said transaction, Winchell agreed in writing with Rogers to pay all indebtedness of defendant company except its mortgage debt of sixty thousand dollars. Plaintiff alleges that it has accepted the benefit of such contract, and asks that Winchell be made a defendant, and that it have judgment against him, as well as against the water and light company. The water and light company filed a cross-petition, making plaintiff, Winchell, and one M. W. Richey, defendants. It recites the agreement of Winchell with Rogers, whereby the former agreed to pay the water and light company's indebtedness. It states further the pledge by Winchell of his shares of stock to plaintiff, to secure the notes of the water and light company. It claims that it has accepted and is entitled to the benefit of Winchell's promise to Rogers; and it is then alleged that, with the consent of Winchell, plaintiff has transferred the shares of stock it held to said M. W. Richey. It prays that Winchell may be considered the principal debtor to plaintiff, and that it be held only a surety, and that Winchell's property, including said shares of stock, be first exhausted before plaintiff be allowed to proceed against the property of cross-petitioner. Said Richey answers also, claiming that he gave a valuable consideration for the stock, and says, in effect, that he took the same subject to plaintiff's claim thereto. He pleads also an estoppel, the details of which we need not consider. There was a reply by the water and light company to Richey's answer, and then was made this stipulation: "It is hereby stipulated between the parties to the above-entitled cause that judgment may be entered in said cause on the first and second counts of the petition herein filed in favor of the German State Bank, and against the Northwestern Water & Light Company, for the sum of four thousand nine hundred and fifty dollars, costs and attorney's fees, to be paid by the plaintiff. It is further stipulated that execution in said cause shall be stayed, without bond or further proceedings, until the trial and termination of the issues joined in the amendment to the petition in said cause and the cross-petition and answer thereto; and that in case it is adjudged and ordered by the court that plaintiff first exhaust certain eighty shares of stock of the Northwestern Water & Light Company, held by plaintiff as collateral security of the idebtedness sued on in this action, that said stock shall be first sold, and the proceeds of said sale applied on said indebtedness, before levy shall be made upon the property of the defendant Northwestern Water & Light Company. Dated this twentieth day of May, 1896. German State Bank, by John Zurawrki, Vice Pres. Sammis & Scott, Attorneys for Defendant Northwestern Water & Light Company." The judgment below awarded plaintiff a recovery for the stipulated amount, dismissed the cross-petition of the water and light company, and

ordered that plaintiff exhaust the property of defendant water and light company before proceeding against
the shares of stock assigned to Richey. From this
judgment the water and light company appeals.—
Affirmed.

Sammis & Scott for appellant.

Zink & Roseberry for appellee Richey.

P. Farrell for appellee Winchell.

WATERMAN, J.—The question to be determined, as
we have extracted it from this volume of pleadings and
multiplicity of claims, is, in its statement at least, a
very simple one. It is this: How far, if at all, is the liability of the water and light company affected by the
contract between Winchell and Rogers? The provisions of this contract, so far as are material here,
1   are as follows: "This agreement, made and
entered into and executed in duplicate this
seventeenth day of May, A. D. 1894, by and between J.
H. Winchell and J. F. Rogers, both of Le Mars, Iowa,
witnesseth: *First.* That the said J. H. Winchell
agrees to sell and transfer to the said J. F. Rogers four
hundred thirty-nine and one-half shares of the stock of
the Northwestern Water & Light Company, of Le Mars,
Iowa, at and for the sum of thirty thousand dollars,
which stock is to be transferred to the said Rogers upon
the execution and delivery of this contract; and the
transfer of the same shall carry with it the right to have
and receive from the said company the full amount of
all dividends to be paid thereon by the company from
and after the first day of May, 1894. * * * *Fifth.*
And the said Winchell also agrees and covenants that
he will pay or cause to be paid all indebtedness of the
said company except the sum of sixty thousand dollars,

its present mortgage debt, so that all earnings of the said company from and after the first day of May, 1894, will be available to pay its obligations and dividends to accrue thereafter."

II. The claim of the company is that, by reason of this contract, its status towards plaintiff was changed; that it has ceased to be the principal debtor, and is now only a surety for Winchell. We know of no principle of law by which the relation of defendant company to plaintiff could be changed without the latter's assent. *James v. Day*, 37 Iowa, 166. The cases cited by appellant to establish its claim that it now occupies the position of a surety only, are not in point. They are all instances of sales by a mortgagor of mortgaged real estate to one who either takes subject to the mortgage or expressly assumes to pay it. The general rule in such cases is that the real estate is the primary fund for the payment of the debt; that the original mortgagor, if he pays, is entitled to subrogation; and that, because of these facts, he occupies, after the sale of the premises, the position of a surety to the extent of the value of the mortgaged property. This rule, however, it would seem, has once been refused recognition in this state. *Corbett v. Waterman*, 11 Iowa, 87. But, even if it be conceded that the doctrine of which we have spoken should be held to prevail here, it would afford no support to appellant's claim. We shall attempt to show that it had no interest in or connection with the contract between Winchell and Rogers.

III. It is said that the agreement between Winchell and Rogers was made for appellant's benefit, and therefore it can take advantage of it. We think

2   Winchell's promise to pay the debts of the water and light company was made for Roger's benefit, and not for that of appellant or any other person.

It was nothing more than an agreement to protect the stocks sold, in Rogers' hands. As bearing somewhat on

the mattter, we cite *Peacock v. Williams*, 98 N. C. 324
(4 S. E. Rep. 550). If Winchell had owned all of the
stock, and had transferred the whole of it to Rogers
under this agreement, we hardly think it would be
claimed that the water and light company, which would
then have no interest distinct from that of its sole
owner, could assert rights under Winchell's promise,
especially if Rogers made no complaint, and Rogers is
not a party to this action. The trial court held that
plaintiff could sue upon Winchell's promise as made for
its benefit, and it was given a judgment against him.
Winchell does not appeal; so this action of the court
must stand. In what we have to say further, if this
holding of the trial court is questioned, it is done only
as necessarily incident to a discussion of the extent of
Winchell's liability on his promise. It is true that if a
person, upon lawful consideration, received from
another, promise to pay money to a third person, the
latter may, under ordinary circumstances, maintain
an action upon the promise, as made for his benefit.
But it does not follow that, if two persons agree that
one of them shall pay to a third a debt owing by a
fourth, the latter would have any right under such an
agreement; and that is the case we have here. If it be
accepted that the bank could take advantage of
Winchell's promise, it is by no means a necessary
sequence that the water and light company could do
so; for, though it might derive advantage from the
performance of the contract, that is not enough. The
promise is not made to it, either directly or indirectly.
Originally, the rule was that, in order to maintain
assumpsit, the consideration must move from the party
seeking to enforce the promise. In time this was modified so that privity of promise was sufficient, even if
there was no privity of consideration. But this rule
has some qualifications. No man will be held liable
in law to different parties for the same cause of action.

The principle is, therefore, confined to cases where the person for whose benefit the promise is made has the sole exclusive interest in its performance. *Treat v. Stanton*, 14 Conn. 452; *Blymire v. Boitle*, 6 Watts, 182. In the case at bar it is claimed that appellant, plaintiff, and Rogers, are interested in the performance of Winchell's promise; and, to give effect to the argument made here, we should have to hold that each in his own right has a cause of action against Winchell on this ground. Another qualification, it has been said is this: If A. promise B. to pay C. a sum of money, C. can sue upon the promise only in the event that B. was indebted to him. *Farlow v. Kemp*, 7 Blackford, 544. In other words, Rogers owed nothing to either the bank or appellant. When Winchell promised to pay something to or for them, it being a gratuity on Rogers' part, he alone would have a right of action on such promise. This rule, doubtless, would not prevail in a case where the doctrine of trust was applicable; as where money or property is given another for delivery to a third person. A very full and exhaustive consideration of this whole subject will be found in the note to *Vadakin v. Soper*, 2 Am. Lead. Cas. 163 *et seq.* As tending to show that something more is necessary to give a right of action on a promise than the mere fact that one would be benefited by its performance, we cite *Davis v. Waterworks Co.*, 54 Iowa, 59; *Lorillard v. Clyde*, 122 N. Y. 498; *Chung Kee v. Davidson*, 73 Cal. 522 (15 Pac. Rep. 100). Let us suppose that Rogers did not see fit to claim any rights under the agreement with Winchell, but was willing to let his interest in defendant company stand good for its debts; on what principle could appellant complain? This, so far as the record discloses, is the exact situation in the case.

IV. Appellant cannot complain of the provision in the decree that plaintiff shall first exhaust its property before proceeding against the stock assigned to Richey. So far as appears, Winchell voluntarily

3   pledged his stock to secure appellant's debt. He had a right, with the consent of the pledgee, to withdraw it if he chose, or to make any other disposition of it that he thought fit. The bank consenting, he pledged it to Richey, subject, however, to the bank's claim. This was his right. As between the bank and Richey, it was proper enough to hold that the former, having a claim upon two funds, should first exhaust that one which the latter could not take. The judgment of the trial court is AFFIRMED.

<hr />

STATE OF IOWA v. THOMAS SHEA, Appellant.

Assault: INSTRUCTIONS. An instruction on a trial for assault with intent to murder that whoever assaults another with the intent to inflict upon him some injury of a greater or more serious charac-

2 ter than an ordinary battery, is guilty of an assault with intent to inflict great bodily injury, is erroneous as omitting reference to the unlawfulness of the assault

EVIDENCE. The state has the burden of proving beyond reasonable

8 doubt, on a trial for assault with intent to murder, that defendant was not acting in self defense.

RIGHT OF A SALOON KEEPER. A saloon keeper has the right to repel an

4 assault made upon him by one whom he has ordered off his premises, if such order was not given for the purpose of provoking a difficulty.

Appeal: REVIEW. The verdict of the jury will not be disturbed

1 where there is evidence justifying its finding.

Appeal from Wapello District Court.—HON. T. M. FEE, Judge.

WEDNESDAY, APRIL 6, 1898.

DEFENDANT was indicted for the crime of an assault with intent to commit murder. He was convicted of an assault with intent to do a great bodily injury, and from the sentence imposed appeals.—*Reversed.*

Steck & Smith for appellant.

Milton Remley, attorney general, and *Jesse A. Miller* for the state.

DEEMER, C. J.—Appellant and one Adams engaged in a quarrel upon one of the streets in the city of Ottumwa, resulting in the exchange of several shots between them, one of which took effect upon Adams'
arm. The shooting is admitted, but appellant
1　　claims that his act in so doing was in defense of
his person against the attack of Adams. There is evidence which justified the jury in finding that defendant was the aggressor, and appellant's claim that the verdict is without support is of no merit.

II. In the seventh instruction to the jury the court said: "(7) Whoever assaults another person with the intent to inflict upon such person some injury of a
more grave and serious character than an ordi-　.
2　　nary battery, is guilty of an assault with intent
to inflict a great bodily injury." This instruction is clearly erroneous. It overlooks a material ingredient of the offense, to-wit: the unlawfulness of the assault. *State v. Wyatt*, 76 Iowa, 328; *State v. Smith*, 102 Iowa, 656. The attorney general contends that the error, if any, is without prejudice, for the reason that the instructions as a whole required a finding by the jury that the assault was unlawful before they would be justified in finding a verdict of guilty. To this proposition we cannot agree, for the reason that some of the other instructions relating to the question of self-defense are erroneous.

III. Appellant asked the court to instruct that if, after considering the whole evidence, the jury entertained a reasonable doubt as to whether or not the shooting was in self-defense, they should acquit him. This instruction was refused, and none was given covering the point, save the general ones relating to reasonable doubt. The law seems to be well settled

3   that the burden is upon the state to show that the defendant was not acting in self-defense, and this it must do so by evidence sufficiently strong to remove all reasonable doubt. *State v. Morphy,* 33 Iowa, 270; *State v. Porter,* 34 Iowa, 131; *State v. Fowler,* 52 Iowa, 103; *State v. Cross,* 68 Iowa, 180; *State v. Dillon,* 74 Iowa, 653; *State v. Donahoe,* 78 Iowa, 486. No instruction to this effect was given. Such omission, in view of the instruction asked, was prejudicial error. Contention is made that, as no evidence was adduced by the state tending to show that the act was in self-defense, the burden was upon the defendant to establish the claim that his act was so done. This proposition is mooted, but not decided, in *State v. Cross, supra.* The court, as now constituted, cannot see any good reason for incorporating such qualification into the rule. As said in *State v. Porter, supra:* "The defendant is entitled to an acquittal if he shows by the facts attending the commission of the offense, proved either by himself or the state, that there is a reasonable doubt that his act was willful." If the evidence introduced by the state negatives the idea of self-defense, this, in itself, is affirmative proof that the act was not justifiable. But such evidence, whether direct or circumstantial, does not change the rule as to the burden of proof. Aside from this, however, there was some evidence adduced by the state which tended to show that Adams was the aggressor; and it was the duty of the court, under all of the authorities, to place the burden upon the state of proving beyond a reasonable doubt that the shooting was unjustifiable,

IV. Adams was in defendant's saloon just prior to the time the shooting occurred, and defendant ordered him out of the place and off the premises. The defendant asked an instruction to the effect that 4   he had a right to do this, and that if Adams, after leaving the place, made an assault upon defendant, defendant was justified in repelling the assault. No such instruction was given, and error is predicated upon the omission. We think that this proposition, limited by the thought that defendant's act in so doing was not for the purpose of provoking a difficulty with Adams, should have been given. Some other errors are complained of, but, as the questions presented are not likely to arise upon a re-trial, we do not consider them. For the errors pointed out, the judgment is REVERSED.

STATE OF IOWA V. CHARLES L. KING, Appellant.

Conspiracy to Assault: SUFFICIENCY OF EVIDENCE. Accused told D¹ that if he would lick W. his fine would be paid, to which D. replied that he did not want anybody to pay his fine, but that he would punch and whip W., whereupon accused advised D. not to do so, but to slap him. D. afterwards stated to others that he would whip W.. and that accused and another would pay his fine; and later he did severely beat W., rendering him unconscious for several days. As D. withdrew from the assault, accused approached and indicated his satisfaction with what had been done, but did not strike W. or assist D. *Held,* that accused was not guilty of conspiring with D. to commit the assault.

Appeal from Buchanan District Court.—HON. A. S. BLAIR, Judge.

WEDNESDAY, APRIL 6, 1898.

THE defendant was accused and convicted of the crime of conspiracy. From judgment of imprisonment in the penitentiary, he appeals.—*Reversed.*

No arguments for either party.

LADD, J.—The indictment charged the defendant and one De Wald with the crime of conspiring and confederating together with malicious intent wrong fully to injure the person of J. H. Willey, and that they did, in pursuance thereof, inflict on him great bodily injury. It appears that just after noon of September 22, 1896, De Wald met Willey near Littell's store, in Independence, knocked him down, and so beat him that he was unconscious for several days. King did not touch Willey, but the theory of the state at the trial was that the assault and battery was the result of a criminal conspiracy between him and De Wald. The evidence shows that Raymond, DeWald, King, and others were in Reisner's saloon. Raymond asked King about the scar on his nose, and the latter responded that Willey had struck him with his cane. De Wald then remarked he had a grievance against Willey, and intended to whip him at the first opportunity; that Willey had published an article in his paper to the effect that, if his (De Wald's) circulation was cut short, it would be a good thing for the community. Something was then said about the payment of the fine, and King stated that, if he licked Willey, his fine would be paid, and related that Farwell, a partner of Willey, had said he would pay it, if some one would whip him. This state of facts is testified to by Raymond, De Wald, and King, but Mullick says King told De Wald that he would pay his fine. This witness, however, is unable to recall anything else in the conversation. De Wald and King are uncontradicted in the statement that the former answered that he did not want anybody to pay his fine. De Wald repeated that he would punch Willey in the face, and whip him in good shape. Both Raymond and King advised him not to punch or kick

Willey, but that he might as well slap his mouth, or
something of that kind. De Wald, after leaving the
saloon, said to several that he was going to whip Willey,
and that Raymond and King were to pay the fine.
King left the saloon, and was on his way to order a
team at the livery stable, with which to take a political
orator to Winthrop, when he saw people gathering
as he approached. One Tapper called to De Wald not
to strike a man when he was down, and King replied
to this remark, "No interfering," and spoke of Willey's
assault on him, and mentioned the fact that he was a
cripple. We have set out this evidence with particu-
larity, because of the ruling on the motion to direct a
verdict for defendant at the conclusion of the state's
evidence, and also after both parties had rested. The
evidence does not establish the conclusion that the
defendant was guilty of the offense charged. The usual
definition of "conspiracy" is "a combination of two or
more persons by concerted action to accomplish a criminal or unlawful purpose, or some purpose not in itself
criminal by criminal or unlawful means." 2 McClain,
Criminal Law, 953; 2 Bishop, Criminal Law, 592; *State
v. Jones*, 13 Iowa, 269; *State v. Potter*, 28 Iowa, 554;
State v. Stevens, 30 Iowa, 391; Code, section 5059.
There is no proof of any concert of action, or of any
understanding or agreement therefor. The mere knowledge, acquiesence, or approval of an act, without
co-operation or agreement to co-operate, is not enough
to constitute the crime of conspiracy. 2 McClain, Criminal Law, 968; *Evans v. People*, 90 Ill. 384; *Miles v.
State*, 58 Ala. 390; 2 Bishop, Criminal Law, 181, 183;
State v. Cox, 65 Mo. 29; 2 Wharton, Criminal Law, 1341.
The combination must contemplate the accomplish-
ment of the purpose by the united energy of the accused,
or active participation must be shown. The testimony,
at most, shows King not superior to the ordinary
instincts of human nature. He was smarting under an

assault from Willey, and was willing the latter should be humiliated by a stroke on the mouth from the palm of the hand; but he entered into no arrangement that this should be done, and suggested it only, instead of the beating De Wald was insisting he would inflict. His suggestion was not acted upon. King neither agreed to do nor did anything to aid in carrying out the unlawful purpose of De Wald. The payment of the fine, if promised, as stated, by Mullick, constituted no part of the offense. The statement was made to Tapper just as De Wald withdrew from beating Willey, and indicated his satisfaction with what was done, rather than any intention of affording aid or comfort. It was not made until the encounter was ended. The court, in the twelfth instruction, correctely stated the law, in language which ought not to have been misunderstood. After cautioning the jurors not to confuse the crime charged with that of assault and battery, or one of a similar nature, they are told not to convict the defendant unless "he agreed to participate in the commission of such offense in concert and combination with the said Bert De Wald, or that he aided in it by advising and counseling the act, and promising De Wald immunity from punishment therefor, and in any manner aided in its commission at the time and place where it was committed. A mere passive cognizance or consent to an illegal act or commission of an unlawful offense is not sufficient to sustain the charge of conspiracy." Under the evidence and the law as given in this instruction the defendant was entitled to an acquittal.— REVERSED.

STATE OF IOWA v. WILLIAM YOUNG, Appellant.

Murder: INSTRUCTIONS. An accused, relying on self defense as jus-
1 tification, complained that the court's charge presenting the issue,

was not sufficiently specific. *Held*, that he should have requested a specific instruction.

SAME. It appearing from the evidence and admissions that the
1 accused was guilty of murder in the first or second degree, or manslaughter, the jury were instructed that to convict of either
2 offense it must be found that the killing was not in self defense. *Held*, sufficient to cover an omitted instruction on burden of proof.

SAME. An instruction, after giving the rules of self defense, that courts and juries must "exercise due caution in applying these
2 principles," is not objectionable as nullifying the instructions relating to self defense.

SAME. The court may properly call the attention of the jury, on a trial for murder, to the fact that defendant is directly interested
4 in the result. without referring to other witnesses, individually, where none of such other witnesses are directly interested.

EVIDENCE: *Dying declarations.* Declarations of the deceased, for whose murder defendant is on trial, made the day after the injury was inflicted and the day before his death and after he had
3 been advised by a physician that he could not recover to which he replied that he expected to die, are admissible as dying declarations, although he stated to another person that he was not a "quitter."

Challenge: JUROR. Under Code, section 5360, requiring a challenge of a juror for cause, to distinctly specify the facts constituting
5 such cause, a challenge which does not distinctly specify such cause, is properly overruled.

SAME One will not be excluded from sitting as a juror on a trial for murder because he has formed an opinion solely on what he has read in the papers, and such opinion simply is, that the defendant
6 killed the deceased, where there is no dispute as to that fact and he states that he can listen to the evidence and base his verdict on that alone, and that he knows nothing to prevent him from rendering a fair and impartial verdict.

Attorney Fees: DEFENSE OF CRIMINAL: *Courts.* A motion for an order on the county treasurer to compensate attorneys for defend-
7 ant charged with murder, for services rendered on appeal, will be refused, as the statutes do not authorize such an order.

Appeal from Woodbury District Court.—HON. GEORGE W. WAKEFIELD, Judge.

WEDNESDAY, APRIL 6, 1898,

THE defendant was indicted and convicted of the crime of murder in the first degree, and from judgment of imprisonment for life he appeals.—*Affirmed*.

H. A. McManus and *C. S. Argo* for appellant.

Milton Remley, attorney general and *Jesse A. Miller,* for the state.

LADD, J.—The defendant admitted on the trial that he shot and killed George Elliott in the afternoon on December 16, 1896, and sought to justify the act on the plea of self-defense. It appears that, while playing cards in a gambling room with Robinson, a dispute arose, and the latter threw Young to the floor and took his money. Young, who had been drinking, then left, and, after obtaining a revolver by pawning his overcoat, returned, and fired once or twice into the wall, with the purpose, he says, of so frightening Robinson that he would give back the money taken. Thereupon Young went into the hall and was followed by Elliott, then in charge of the rooms, who ordered him to go down stairs. Young promised to go, but fired at Elliott, the bullet entering his abdomen and causing death. There is a conflict in the evidence as to who shot first. That of the state tended to show Young first shot Elliott, and the latter then entered the room and procured a revolver, with which he returned and shot Young in the arm. That of the defendant tended to show that Elliott followed Young into the hall in a threatening manner, and shot him in the arm, before the latter fired at the deceased. The determination of which was the aggressor was fairly for the jury, and their conclusion has ample support in the evidence.

II. The defendant complains that the instruction submitting the plea of self-defense, while correctly stat-

ing rules applicable thereto, was not as specific as it
should have been. The main issue for the jury
1   to determine was which was the aggressor, and
this was clearly indicated in the instruction
given. If the defendant had desired the attention of
the jury to be more particularly called to the circumstances of the transaction, he ought to have requested
an instruction to that effect. It is also said that the
court did not indicate upon whom was the burden of
proof on this issue. Under the evidence and admissions,
Young was guilty of murder in the first or second
degree, or of manslaughter, and, if not of one of these,
was entitled to an acquittal. The jury was told, in the
eleventh, twelfth, and thirteenth instructions, that, in
order to convict of one of these offenses, it must be found
beyond a reasonable doubt that the killing was not in
self-defense.

III. After stating the rules relating to self-
defense, the court added, "Courts and jurors, however,
must exercise due caution in applying these principles,"
and said that the jury must determine from all
2   the evidence whether the defendant acted in self-
defense. It is said this caution nullified that
which preceded. It is certainly the duty of the jury
to exercise care and caution in passing upon the issues
in every case, and it was not error for the court to
admonish them of that duty. In what way it detracted
from other portions of the instruction does not appear,
and is not pointed out.

IV. The court admitted testimony of the dying
declarations of Elliott. It is asserted that this was
done without proof that he was under the solemn belief
of impending death. It appears from the evidence, however, that Dr. Knott advised the deceased, on
3   the morning after the injury, that he could not
recover, and that the deceased replied he knew
it, and expected to die. The testimony of Coon was to

the effect that he tried to encourage deceased, and that the latter said he was not a "quitter," and complained of being in great pain, but, except in the expression used, did not indicate any hope of recovery. He died two days after being shot. The evidence justified the court in the conclusion that the declarations of Elliott were made with the understanding that he was in *extremis*.

V. In stating the rules for weighing the evidence, the court called the attention of the jury to the fact that the defendant was directly interested in 4 the result of the case, and did not refer to other witnesses individually. He was the only witness who appeared to be directly interested, and for this reason others could not well have been included. *State v. Mecum*, 95 Iowa, 433.

VI. The challenge to the juror Bacon was properly overruled, as it did not distinctly specify the facts constituting the causes thereof. Code, section 5360; *State v. Munchrath*, 78 Iowa, 268. But in any 5 event, the juror based his opinion solely on what he had read in the papers, and indicated that it was confined to the belief that the defendant had killed Elliott,—a fact not in dispute. He stated that he could listen to the evidence, and found his verdict upon that alone, and knew nothing to prevent 6 him from rendering a fair and impartial verdict. The newspaper reports of such transactions are based on information hurriedly obtained, and are generally understood not to be accurate in detail. They are necessarily subject to much infirmity. Should a juror be excluded because of reading these, the public would be deprived of the benefit of its most intelligent citizens in this important service. There appears no good reason for not adhering to the rule approved in *State v. Munchrath*, *supra*, and *State v. Brady*, 100 Iowa, 191.

7   The statutes do not authorize an order on the treasurer of the county for the compensation of defendant's attorneys for services rendered on this appeal, and the motion for such order, therefore, is overruled.   The judgment is AFFIRMED.

JOHN J. MAHONEY, *et al.*, Appellants, v. F. M. McCREA.

Sales: FORFEITURE: *Election.* Where a contract for sale of real estate provided, that if the purchaser should fail to make any payments when due, he should forfeit all right to the property,
1   and also any money paid by him, unless the vendor should elect otherwise, it was the vendor's duty to give the vendee notice, within a reasonable time after default, that he elected not to treat the contract as forfeited; and his failure so to do, worked a forfeiture, and barred him recovering the price.

SAME. Where a contract for sale of real estate provides that on the purchaser's failure to make payments when due, he shall forfeit all right to the property and to "any money paid by him," and the forfeiture occurs, a subsequent acceptance of part of the
2   amount due, while it was a waiver of the forfeiture, gave the vendor no right to recover the balance due and unpaid at the time of such acceptance, after a forfeiture had again occurred by reason of a subsequent default.

Appeal from Wapello District Court.—HON. ROBERT SLOAN, Judge.

WEDNESDAY, APRIL 6, 1898.

THE following statements of the issues and facts made by appellants' counsel are conceded to be substantially correct, and are sufficiently so for the purposes of the questions to be considered: "This action was commenced in the district court of Wapello county to recover on five promissory notes, each dated January 24, 1887, one for one hundred and fifty dollars, due two years after date, one for one hundred and fifty dollars, due three years after date, and three for one hundred and thirty-one dollars and twenty-five cents each, due, respectively, one, two, and three years after date. Each note drew interest at the rate of eight per cent. per annum, payable annually. The answer admitted the making of the notes sued on, but set up as a defense that these five notes were part of a series of six notes given by the defendant for a part of the purchase price of two lots in an addition to the city of South Omaha, Nebraska; that at the time of making these notes two land contracts were signed between the parties, and that, among other things, the contracts provided that, if the defendant should fail to make any payments when due, he should forfeit all right to the real estate, and also any money paid by him, unless the plaintiffs should elect otherwise; that he did fail to make payments as they became due; that the plaintiffs did not elect not to forfeit the contracts; and that thereby he became released of liability on the notes. The plaintiffs, in their reply to the answer, admit the making of land contracts, deny that they elected to forfeit the defendant's right to the land, and deny that they did not elect to require payment of the notes. The proof showed that on the twenty-fourth of January, 1887, plaintiffs sold the defendant two lots in Mahoney & Minnahan's addition to South Omaha,—one for six hundred dollars, and one for five hundred and twenty-five dollars,—on each of which the defendant at the time paid one-fourth of the purchase price; that the defendant at the same time gave to the plaintiffs the three notes for one hundred and thirty-one dollars and twenty-five cents sued on in this action, and the three notes for one hundred and fifty dollars each, two of which are included in this suit. The land contracts contain, among other things, these provisions: 'In case the said party of the second part shall fail, refuse or neglect to pay such purchase money, interest, and taxes, as herein agreed, he shall forfeit any rights he may have to said real estate, and also shall forfeit any money

paid by him to purchase the same, which shall be
retained and applied in payment and satisfaction of
rent for the use and occupation of said real estate,
unless the said parties of the first part shall elect otherwise.' 'The said party of the second part shall be
entitled to the possession of said real estate so long as
he shall comply with the foregoing terms of agreement,
but upon a failure to comply with same his right to possession shall terminate, and he shall surrender the
possession of said real estate, and improvements
thereon, if any, to said parties of the first part.' By the
terms of the contracts and notes, there fell due on the
twenty-fourth of January, 1888, one note of one hundred and fifty dollars, and interest on three notes of one
hundred and fifty dollars each, amounting to thirty-six
dollars; also, one note of one hundred and thirty-one
dollars and twenty-five cents, and interest on three
notes of one hundred and thirty-one dollars and twenty-
five cents each, amounting to thirty-one dollars and fifty
cents. None of this money was paid on the twenty-
fourth of January, 1888, but on the twelfth of July,
1888, the defendant paid two hundred and thirty-nine
dollars and fifty cents. The payment, as shown by the
surrender of the first one hundred and fifty dollar note,
and indorsements made upon some of the notes in suit,
seems to have been applied,—first, in the taking up of
the one hundred and fifty dollar note which matured on
the twenty-fourth of January, 1888; second, in paying
the interest on the other two one hundred and fifty dollar notes up to January 24, 1888; and, third, in an
endorsement of forty-eight dollars and fifty cents on the
note for one hundred and thirty-one dollars and twenty-
five cents, which matured on the twenty-fourth of January, 1888. When the twenty-fourth of January, 1889,
was reached, nothing was paid; but afterwards, on
the twenty-fourth of June, 1889. the defendant paid
one hundred and fifty dollars, which does not appear to

have been specifically applied on any particular note or
interest. Subsequent to June 24, 1889, no payments
whatever were made. There was testimony put in by
plaintiffs tending to show that after the twenty-fourth
of June, 1889, they made repeated demands for payments. This was denied by the defendant, and thus was
made the issue of fact, which, under the ruling of the
court below, was submitted to the jury. By means of
instructions 2, 3, 4, 5, and 6, the court charged the jury
that, when defendant made default in payments, it
became the duty of the plaintiffs, within a reasonable
time, to elect that they would not claim a forfeiture of
the land, and if they failed to so elect, and to notify the
defendant of their election, they could not recover on
the notes. By instruction 7, the court charged that
the acceptance of payments after they were due would
not be a waiver of forfeiture on account of any failure
on the part of the defendant to pay installments there
after accruing. Under these instructions the jury
returned a general verdict for the defendant, and judgment was rendered upon that verdict." Plaintiffs
appeal.—*Affirmed.*

Work & Lewis and *R. W. Boyd* for appellants.

McNett & Tisdale for appellee.

GIVEN, J.—I. The court instructed that a failure
to pay any installment of the purchase money evidenced
by these notes would operate as a forfeiture of all the
defendant's interest in the real estate, and the money
paid by him to purchase the same, unless the plaintiffs
elected otherwise; that it was the duty of the plaintiffs
to elect not to treat the contract as forfeited, within a
reasonable time after the default was made in payment,
and to notify the defendant thereof; and that unless the
plaintiffs did so notify him within a reasonable time the

defendant had the right to assume that the plaintiffs
claimed a forfeiture; and that under such circumstances the plaintiffs would have no right to enforce collection of the notes. The only question submitted to
the jury was whether or not the plaintiffs, within a
reasonable time after the defendant made default in
payments of said notes, elected not to treat the contract
as forfeited, and notified the defendant thereof. Appellants contend that this is an erroneous construction of
those parts of the written contract set out above, providing for forfeiture. They contend, on the
1   authority of *Barrett v. Dean*, 21 Iowa, 423, and
Sigler v. Wick, 45 Iowa, 690, that the defendant
could not work a forfeiture by defaulting in payments;
that the right of forfeiture is for the benefit of the plaintiffs, and at their election; and that no forfeiture could
exist until so elected by them. In *Barrett v. Dean*, the
contract provided that a failure to make payments
when due should render the agreement utterly void,
and all payments made thereon forfeited. It also provided that the purchaser should hold possession subject
to removal if he failed to perform any condition or
covenant of the contract. It was held that, taking the
whole contract together, it was intended that Barrett's
agreement to convey should not be binding upon him,
and Dean should forfeit all money paid if he did not
fully comply with his contract, and that this provision
was intended for Barrett's benefit, not Dean's. In
Sigler v. Wick, the contract provided that, if the purchaser should fail to make payments when due, the
land should be considered forfeited, and the vendor
should have the right to enter upon the possession of
the same, and should be held under no obligation to the
vendee. It was held that the forfeiture should be at
the option of the vendor. It is said, "The general rule
is that a stipulation that the contract for the sale of
the land shall become void upon non-payment is for

the benefit of the vendor." A noticeable difference
between those contracts and the ones under consideration is that in these the forfeiture is expressly made to
follow a failure to pay, "unless the said parties of the
first part shall elect otherwise." Here we have an
affirmative duty imposed upon appellants,—to elect
in case of default in payment, whether or not that
default shall work a forfeiture. In this respect these
contracts are unusual, but it is conceded that in construing them we should give effect to the intention of
the parties. We think it was clearly the intention of
the parties that in case of default of payment the appellants should elect within a reasonable time whether
they would insist upon forfeiture or performance, and
notify the defendant thereof. The instructions are in
harmony with this view of the contract. See *Steel v.
Long*, 104 Iowa, 39.

II. The court instructed that acceptance of payment after the same was due would not be a waiver of
the right to forfeit by reason of a default in any install-

2   ment falling due after such acceptance. The correctness of this instruction is not questioned,
but appellants insist that, at the time forfeiture
was waived by receiving payment, there were three
hundred and seventeen dollars and nineteen cents due
more than was paid, and that, notwithstanding forfeiture resulted from subsequent defaults in payment,
they are entitled to recover the said sum of three hundred and seventeen dollars and nineteen cents, with
interest. Turning to the contracts, we see that it is
"any money paid by him" that the defendant forfeited,
and not money which, in the absence of forfeiture he
might be liable to pay. Our conclusion is that the
judgment of the district court should be AFFIRMED.

STATE OF IOWA V. JOHN S. DIXON, Appellant.

Indictment: INTOXICATING LIQUORS   An indictment under Code,
section 2384, providing that whoever erects, estab ishes, or uses
any building erected or place for specified purposes shall be
guilty of a nuisance, alleging that defendant did unlawfully
1 establish and use a certain building "or" plac in a designated
city, with the intention of unlawfully keeping, selling and giving
away intoxicating liquors in such building, is not equivocal,
uncertain and doubtful because of the use of the word "or."

SAME. An indictment alleging that defendant unlawfully sold and
gave away intoxicating liquors "at" a specified building or place
2 within the county, is not indefinite or uncertain because of the
use of the word "at" instead of "in "

Appeal from Cerro Gordo District Court.—HON. JOHN
C. SHERWIN, Judge.

WEDNESDAY, APRIL 6, 1898.

INDICTMENT for maintaining a nuisance.   Verdict
of guilty, and judgment thereon, from which the
defendant appealed.—*Affirmed.*

Cliggitt & Rule, for appellant.

Milton Remley, attorney general, for the state.

GRANGER, J.—The following is the charging part
of the indictment: "The said John S. Dixon on the
first of February in the year of our Lord one thousand
eight hundred and ninety-seven, in the county aforesaid, did unlawfully establish, keep, use, maintain, and
continue a certain building or place in the city of
Mason City, Cerro Gordo county, state of Iowa, for the
purpose and with the intention of unlawfully keeping,
selling, and giving away in said building or place
aforesaid, in said county and state, intoxicating liquors,

to-wit, whisky, beer, gin, brandy, and other intoxicating liquors to the grand jury unknown, aud did then,
and at said building or place in said county, unlawfully keep, 'sell, and give away the said intoxicating
liquors, contrary to the form of the statutes in such
cases made and provided, and against the peace and
dignity of the state of Iowa." It is said that the indictment is so equivocal, uncertain, and doubtful that a
conviction under it cannot be sustained, because of the
use of the word "or," so that the *locus* is expressed
as "a certain building or place," "in said building
or place," and "at said building or place." These
several expressions occur in the indictment. The
language of the statute is, "And whoever shall
erect or establish, or continue or use any building,
erection or place for the purposes prohibited in this
section, shall be guilty of a nuisance." Code, section
2384. Appellant relies on the rule stated in 1 Bishop,
Criminal Procedure (3d ed.), section 586, as follows: "If
a statute makes it a crime to do this, or that, men-
tioning several things disjunctively, all may, indeed,
in general, be charged in a single count; but it must
use the conjunctive 'and' where 'or' occurs in the
statute, else it will be defective as being uncertain. All are but one offense, laid or committed in
different ways." The section has reference, not to the
place of committing an offense, but to the manner of
its commission. The following, being a part of the
preceding section (585), seems to us to be more applicable to the question under consideration: "Whenever the conjunction 'or' would leave it uncertain
which of two things is meant, it is inadmissible, and
in its stead 'and' may be employed, if it makes the
required sense." To us there is no uncertainty in the
use of the word "or." It is true that in many cases
its meaning would be to denote one of two places, and
leave it uncertain which was the right one; but it is

also many times used to make certain a designation
or place named, because of doubts as to accuracy of
name or description. A building is always a place,
but all places are not buildings; hence, if the term
"building" was thought to be of doubtful accuracy,
the term "place," being more comprehensive, might
cure or make certain what might otherwise be uncertain or defective. To us the phrase "building or
place" is not of uncertain meaning. The indictment
need not charge the commission of the offense as
having been committed at any particular place in the
county, but may charge it as having been committed
in the county. *State v. Waltz,* 74 Iowa, 610. We are
not saying that this indictment would not be good if
the language was construed as meaning that the
offense was committed in a building or other place in
the county. We do not decide that question.

II. It is said in the indictment that the defendant
"did then and there, at said building or place in said
county, lawfully keep, sell," etc. It is thought the
word "at" is fatal to the indictment, and that
the word "in" should have been used to make
it sufficiently certain. Reliance is placed on a
holding in *Helgers v. Quinney,* 51 Wis. 62 (8 N. W.
Rep. 17). The validity of a treasurer's deed was in
question, which depended on an observance of a
statute requiring a notice to be published in four
public places in the county, one of which should be in
some conspicuous place in the treasurer's office.
The affidavit to show the fact of such posting
stated that the notices were posted "at four
places," instead of in such places. The holding
is that there is a difference between at a village,
and in a village, at a drug store and in a drug
store, and at the treasurer's office, and in a conspicuous place in the treasurer's office. The ruling is
placed on the statutory requirements to sustain a

deed, and the departure was held fatal. The maintaining of a nuisance is not made to depend on any
such distinction. If the building or place is established, erected, continued or used for selling, or keeping with intent to sell, it is what constitutes the
offense. The keeping at the building or place may be
as clear a violation of the law as keeping in the building or place. The question is, what was the building
or place kept or used for? The judgment is AFFIRMED.

APPENDIX

Notes of Cases Not Otherwise Reported.

THOMAS WATSON v. NELSON T. BURROUGHS AND N. S. BURROUGHS,
et al, and BELLE BALDWIN, Appellant.

APPEAL. Where appellant's abstract does not purport to show all the
evidence, and the appellee denies that it is all in the record, the
case cannot be tried *de novo*

Same An amendment to an abstract, made after the case has been
submitted on appeal, will not be considered unless filed on permission of the court, where the party has ample time to file it
before submission, after discovering the necessity therefor.

Appeal from Cherokee District Court.—HON. GEORGE W. WAKEFIELD,
Judge.

THURSDAY, JANUARY 20, 1898.

THE defendant (appellant) Belle Baldwin filed her cross-petition
against Nelson T. Burroughs and others, asking an accounting
between her and N. T. Burroughs; that a conveyance of the real
estate described, by Byron H. Evers to Byron C. Evers, be declared
fraudulent and void; that a certain judgment claimed to be owned
by her be declared a first lien on said real estate; and that the same
be subjected to the payment of said judgment. The petition of the
plaintiff, Watson, was dismissed, and issues were joined upon said
cross-petition; and after a trial a decree was rendered dismissing
the same, from which said defendant Belle Baldwin appeals.—
Affirmed.

Cavanaugh & Thomas, E. R. Duffie, and *A. R. Molyneux* for appellant.

E. C Herrick and *W. L. Joy* for appellees.

GIVEN, J.—It is not questioned but that this case, if triable at all
on this appeal, is triable *de novo* Appellees insist that all the evi-

(761)

dence is not before this court, and that, therefore, the case cannot be tried *de novo*, but that the appeal must be dismissed. The case was submitted October 14, 1897, at which time the state of the record was as follows: September 15, 1896, appellant filed what is entitled "Appellant's Abstract of Record," but which is neither certified nor signed by either the appellant or her counsel, and does not purport to be an abstract of all the evidence offered and introduced. On April 15, 1897, appellees filed an additional abstract, making certain corrections to appellant's abstract, and in which they deny that the appellant's abstract and said additional abstract of the appellees together contain all the evidence offered or introduced on the trial. On May 27, 1897, appellant filed what is entitled "Appellant's Amendment to Abstract of Record;" setting out several pages of evidence, and stating that it is to correct an oversight in the preparation of her abstract. At the conclusion the following appears: "The above and foregoing, together with appellant's original abstract filed herein, is all the evidence introduced or offered by the parties on the trial of the cause, and constitutes all the evidence in the case." This abstract and certificate do not purport to be signed by either appellant or her attorneys. On August 18, 1897, appellees filed their "second additional abstract," in which they reaffirm their former denial, and deny that the abstract on file showed all the evidence introduced or offered on the trial. It was upon this state of the record that the case was submitted October 14, 1894, and it will be observed therefrom that it does not appear that we have all the evidence offered and introduced on the trial. It is not questioned that, to try the case *de novo*, we must have all the evidence offered and introduced before us, and that, where it is made to appear that all the evidence is not before us, the appeal must be dismissed. After the submission of the cause, namely, October 15, 1897, appellant filed what is entitled "Amendment to Appellant's Abstract of Record," which was served on appellees October 16th. It is said in this amendment that it embraced certain exhibits which appellant considered wholly immaterial, and which she did not, therefore, set forth in her former abstract. This amendment contains some seventeen printed pages of evidence, in the form of exhibits, and concludes as follows: "The above and foregoing, together with the original abstract of the record and the appellant's first amendment thereto, contains all the evidence offered or received on the trial of the cause, and constitutes all the evidence in the case. [Signed.] E. G. Thomas, Attorney for Appellant." If this amendment be considered for any purpose, it certainly shows that at the time the cause was submitted we did not have all the evidence before us. Surely, in a case triable *de novo*, it is not for the appellant to withhold abstracting any part of the evidence because he may consider it immaterial. That is a question for the court to determine, and it is only upon all the evidence offered and introduced that this court can properly consider the case *de novo*

It has been the uniform practice in this court not to consider matters filed after the submission of the cause, unless filed in pursuance of express permission of the court. Appellees' last denial was filed August 18th, thus affording to appellant ample time to have filed her amendment prior to the submission of the cause. As this amendment was not filed until after the submission, it cannot be considered, and therefore the case stands upon appellees' denial of August 18th, which shows that we did not have all the evidence before us at the time the cause was submitted. With this state of the record, we cannot consider the case *de novo*, and the appeal is therefore AFFIRMED.

OLE L. ODDEN, Guardian v. SETH LEWIS, *et al* , Appellants.

APPEAL. A judgment will be affirmed when the record fails to present sufficient information to enable the court to intelligently consider the assignments of error

Appeal from Mitchell District Court.—HON. P. W. BURR, Judge.

THURSDAY, JANUARY 20, 1898.

L. M. Ryce for appellant.

Sweney & Lovejoy for appellee.

GRANGER, J.—The question is presented as to the condition of the record being such as to permit us to consider this case on its merits. The petition shows it to be a case for malicious trespass on the lands of plaintiff, by the defendants, by cutting trees, destroying fences, and plowing and scraping the earth. The trespass is alleged to have been done in pursuance of a mutual understanding and agreement by the defendants. While we may presume, from the arguments and some parts of the record, that an answer was filed, and an issue presented and tried, there is no way of knowing from the record what the issue is, for the abstract neither sets out the answer, nor, in fact, any pleading other than the petition. Looking to the instructions for the court's statement of the issue, and there is simply the statement that the first and second instructions correctly stated the issues, and the two instructions are omitted; all the others appearing. From the instructions in the record and the evidence it appears that the issues involved a conroversy about a public highway that had once been established, and then vacated, and there seems to be a claim of an establishment by prescription, that is in issue. Nothing whatever as to a highway appears in the petition, so that we have no way of knowing what the issues are. The assignments of error and the arguments are with reference to instructions given and refused and the admission and exclusion of evidence. We cannot, without knowledge of the issues, know whether the instructions were applicable thereto or not, nor can we know whether the rulings on evidence are correct or not. As to the instructions, they are not erroneous as abstract propositions of law, and, being abstractly correct, we must assume them as pertinent to the issues being tried, till the contrary appears, which cannot be with the condition of the record. The same is true of the rulings on evidence. We assume them to be correct till it is made to appear otherwise. As, with the condition of the record, none of the assignments argued can be considered, the judgment must stand AFFIRMED.

CLAY, ROBINSON & COMPANY, Appellants, v THE MAYNARD SAVINGS BANK, *et al.*

OPINION ON APPEAL. Where the facts are undisputed, and no questions of law are presented rendering an opinion necessary, the judgment, under Code, section 198, will be affirmed without opinion.

Appeal from Fayette District Court.—HON. L. E. FELLOWS, Judge.

SATURDAY, JANUARY 22, 1898.

ACTION in replevin for certain cattle mortgaged to the plaintiff. A writ issued, and the cattle were seized by virtue thereof. The answer put in issue plaintiff's right to recover because the cattle seized were not those mortgaged to the plaintiff, because some of the cattle were not owned by plaintiff's mortgagor when the mortgage to plaintiff was made, and because the description in the mortgage was not sufficient to impart notice. The defendant bank also claimed the property by virtue of a chattel mortgage thereon in its favor. At the close of plaintiff's evidence the court sustained a motion by defendants for judgment in their favor, and from such judgment the plaintiff appealed.—*Affirmed*

W. E. Fuller and *E. E. Hasner* for appellant.

Ainsworth & Ainsworth and *D. W. Clements & Son* for appellees.

PER CURIAM.—The facts are not in dispute, and there are no law questions that render an opinion necessary, and, under section 198 of the Code, none need be filed. The judgment will stand AFFIRMED

,V. F. PIERCE v. R. R. DUNHAM, Administratrix, Appellant.

OPINION ON APPEAL.

Appeal from Pottawattamie District Court.—HON. W. R. GREEN, Judge

SATURDAY, JANUARY 22, 1898.

THIS is a proceeding in probate to establish a claim on two promis sory notes against the estate of W. E. Durham, deceased Issues were formed, and a trial had thereon; and, at the conclusio i of the evidence, the court, on motion of plaintiff directed a verdict in his favor, from which the defendant appealed.—*Affirmed.*

C. H. Converse for appellant.

Benjamin & Preston for appellee.

PER CURIAM.—Most of the errors assigned and argued are as to the rulings on the admission and exclusion of evidence. Of the questions that could be considered, in view of the assignments, none are of sufficient importance to justify an opinion, and the judgment will stand AFFIRMED

JACOB A PAYNE, Appellant, v. SARAH MARTHA CRESAP.

TRIAL DE NOVO. Where all the questions to be considered in a trial *de novo* in equity, by the appellate court, involve a consideration of the evidence, and the abstract of record shows that all the evidence is not contained therein, the decree of the lower court must be affirmed.

Appeal from Fremont District Court.—HON. W. R. GREEN, Judge.

MONDAY, JANUARY 24, 1898.

No appearance for appellant.

W. E. Mitchell and *William Eaton* for appellee.

PER CURIAM.—Action in equity to determine and to quiet th title to certain lands described, to which each party claims title Decree was rendered in favor of the defendant, from which plaintiff appeals. On January 5, 1897, appellee filed an amendment to appellant's abstract, and a denial as follows: "Appellee denies that the 'abstract of record' filed by appellant herein contains all the evidence introduced, or offered to be introduced, in the trial of this cause, and of record herein, and denies that said abstract is a full, complete, or fair abstract of the evidence and testimony of record in said case. And appellee avers that the 'abstract of record' of appellant, with 'amendment to abstract' of appellee, does not present all the evidence, nor all the material evidence, introduced in the trial of the cause, and of record herein. W. E. Mitchell and William Eaton, Attorneys for Appellee." With this state of the record, it is not made to appear that all the evidence is before us. As each of the questions presented involves a consideration of the evidence, and as the case is before us for trial *de novo*, we cannot consider it without all the evidence being presented. Under this state of the record, the decree must be affirmed. We may add that we are better satis^fed with this result, as an examination of the case, as it is presented in the record we have, leads to the conclusion that the decree is correct.—AFFIRMED.

JOHN BRODERICK, Appellant, v. ALLAMAKEE COUNTY, GEORGE J. HELMING, Treasurer

I JUNCTION. An injunction to restrain the sale of town lots for taxes will not be granted although the plaintiff claims to have paid assessments upon the property, where the location of the town plat cannot be exactly fixed, except that it was laid out on the southwest quarter section claimed by the plaintiff, and third persons are in possession of some parts of the village plat, but the character of their possession does not appear.

E *idence.* In an action to enjoin defendants from selling property at tax sale, when the land is shown to be occupied by others in conjunction with the plaintiff, the latter is put upon proof of his legal title.

Appeal from Allamakee District Court.—HON L. E. FELLOWS, Judge,

MONDAY, JANUARY 24, 1898

ACTION in equity to enjoin defendants from selling certain real estate at tax sale. Decree for defendants. Plaintiff appeals.— *Affirmed.*

J. H *Trewin* for appellant

E. M *Woodward* and M B. *Hendricks* for appellees

WATERMAN, J.—Plaintiff claims to be the owner of the S. W. fractional quarter of section 33 township north, 90 range, west of 3 P. M., in Allamakee county, and that as such owner he has paid taxes upon it for many years past by its description according to government survey. He also alleges that the defendants are about to sell for taxes certain lots and blocks in the town plat of Capoli, or Columbus, which they claim are included in, and located on, the land of plaintiff, upon which, as already said, the tax has been paid. It seems clear that plaintiff's right to the relief sought must rest upon his ownership of the southwest quarter of the section named. If he has no title thereto, then his payment of taxes assessed against it would give him no right to enjoin the sale for taxes on the town lots. It is difficult, f not impossible, to fix the exact location of the town plat in question. About all that can be definitely said is that it was laid out on the fractional quarter section claimed by plaintiff. Some lots in this plat—how many, it is not shown—are in the possession of other persons. Nor does the character of their possession appear. It is enough to say that, when the land is shown to be so occupied by others in conjunction with plaintiff, the latter, in order to maintain a standing in court, is put upon proof of his legal title; and this is the showing he makes: September 2, 1890, he received a tax deed for lot No. 3 in said section. This is the northeast quarter of the southwest quarter. It was sold for taxes October 6, 1879. He obtained a tax deed January 11, 1830 to certain lots and blocks in Capoli, but not including any of those the sale of which he seeks to enjoin, and also the northwest quarter southwest quarter of section 33. October 14, 1889, he received a tax deed for the southwest quarter of the southwest quarter of section 33, except that portion situated in the town of Capoli. Sale held December 1, 1879. He received from one Strong and wife a warranty deed to the undivided one-half of the southwest quarter of the southwest quarter of section 33, excepting that portion that is included in the village of Capoli. Deed dated June 5, 1875. He took title by warranty deed to the southeast quarter of southwest quarter of section 33 from one Charles Gadsby; the conveyance being dated April 21, 1881. But, in showing chain of title to Gadsby, it appears that in Exhibit "R," as shown in the abstract of record (being a deed record introduced by plaintiff, setting out conveyances to Gadsby), there is a complete break in the chain of title; the description there being the southeast quarter of section 33. We have, then, this condition of things: Plaintiff has no legal title to the southeast of the southwest. He has no such title to any part of the southwest of the southwest as is located in the town plat. He avers, and we think correctly, that the location of the town plat cannot be definitely or exactly fixed; and by his own evidence it is established that third persons are in possession of some parts of the land included in the village plat,—what part, or how much, as we have said, does not appear. Under these circumstances, we are not inclined to interfere wjth the holding of the lower court. It is true that a plat was introduced by defendant tending to show in what portions of the government subdivisions of the southwest quarter of section 33 the town plat of Capoli lies, but it was objected to by plaintiff, and its correctness questioned; and as it is somewhat indefinite in its outlines, and dubious in character, we shall give it no consideration. Decree below AFFIRMED.

INDEX.

ACCEPTANCE—See CONTRACTS, [1], [2], [3]; FIXTURES; SALES, [1].

ACCESSORIES—See CRIM. LAW, [11], [29]; CONSTRUCTION, [1].

ACCRETIONS—See WATERS, [1], [2].

ACKNOWLEDGMENTS—See DEEDS.

ADEMPTION—See WILLS, [1].

ADJUDICATION—See PRACT. [3], [4], [5], [6].

1. ESTOPPEL—*Parties*—One not made a party defendant to an action is not concluded by the decree rendered therein.—Sherod v. Ewell, 253.

2. SUIT BY ADMINISTRATOR FOR CREDITORS.—A creditor in whose behalf an administrator brought suit to set aside a conveyance as fraudulent, and to obtain a decree that the grantee held the property in trust for the payment of debts due from the estate, is concluded, by an adverse determination of such suit, from thereafter asserting that the land should be sold to pay his claim as one of the creditors of the estate.—Hansen's Fur Fact. v Teabout, 360.

ADMINISTRATORS—See ADJUDICATION, [2]; NEW TRIAL, [1]; PRACT. [17]; PRACT. SUP. CT. [6], [7], [33].

ADVANCEMENTS—See EVID. [16].

Consideration--An advancement made by a parent to his child constitutes no consideration for a promissory note subsequently executed by the latter to the former.—Marsh v. Chown, 556.

ADVERSE POSSESSION—See HIGHWAYS, [3].

ALIMONY—See ATTYS. [1].

APPEAL—See ATTYS. [16]; INTOX. LIQUORS, [1]; PRACT. SUP. CT.

Under Code, section 3818, requiring the offer to confess judgment after action is brought before a justice, to be made in the presence of plaintiff, or after notice to him that it will be made, the transcript of the justice need not expressly show that the plaintiff was present when such offer was made. If it appears from the record that an offer was made as contemplated, or this is

Small figures refer to subdivisions of Index. The others to page of report.

VOL. 104 Ia—48   (753)

the necessary inference from the language employed, it is sufficient; and, if the record is silent, parol evidence is admissible
to show the offer —Sloss v Bailey, 698

ASSAULT—See CRIM LAW, ¹, ², ³, ⁴; EVID. ⁷a; INSTRUCTION, ⁵, ⁶; PLEA AND PROOF, ².

1. *Exemplary Damages*—In a joint malicious assault if one of the
    participants was actuated by malice, each will be liable for
    damages, both actual and exemplary, resulting from the
    assault.—Reizenstein v. Clark, 237.

2. EVIDENCE—Plaintiff in an action for wanton, malicious assault
    committed by two persons need not show that either defend-
    ant expressly directed the other to make the assault, or that
    they struck him at the same moment of time or that one
    struck him after the other.—*Idem.*

3. *Same*—Evidence that plaintiff, in an action for malicious
    assault, had been assaulted at another time, before the assault
    in question, is inadmissible in the absence of any contention
    that any of the disorders from which the plaintiff claims to
    be suffering were due to the prior assault.—*Idem.*

ASSESSMENTS—See INS. ⁴, ⁶, ⁷, ⁸, ⁹; PRACT ⁸³a

ASSIGNMENT—See INS ¹⁰; MECHANIC'S LIEN, ¹.

JUDGMENT—An assignee of a judgment acquires no greater
rights as against the judgment debtor than his assignor has.—
Fred Miller Brewing Co. v. Hansen, 307.

ASSUMPSIT—See WARRANTY.
ATTACHMENT—See LAND. AND TENANT, ³.

ATTORNEY AND CLIENT—See CRIM. LAW, ⁴; ESTOPPEL, ³; EVID. ², ³; PRACT SUP. CT. ³⁶.

1. Alimony—Defendant was desirous of procuring a divorce from
    his wife (an appellant herein), but was advised by appellant S.,
    an attorney, that he could not get it He then induced his wife
    to apply for a divorce, on the promise that she should have one
    thousand dollars alimony. Appellant S was acting as her
    attorney, but was to be paid for his services by defendant A
    divorce was granted appellant, and one thousand dollars ali-
    mony was awarded her as agreed upon On the same day
    appellant S. procured a marriage license for defendant and one
    M. F , who was to pay the alimony, which was paid, when the
    marriage was consummated, by M. F indorsing a draft for the
    amount, and turning it over to appellant S. *Held*, that appellant
    S. was liable to appellant for the whole amount of the one
    thousand dollars, less court costs, and could not pay any part

ATTORNEY AND CLIENT Continued

of it on defendant's order, or retain any part as attorney's fees. None of such money can be diverted to the use of the husband, or to the payment of his creditors, although he has assigned certain accounts to his second wife to secure the payment of money advanced —Farrar v. Farrar, 691.

2. Authority—An attorney who has no other authority than to collect a debt, cannot ratify the acceptance by an agent of the creditor of a bill of sale from the debtor, as a payment.—Hartman Steel Co. v. Hoag & Son, 269.

3. Fees—RECOVERY—*Elements Of*—In determining value of legal services, not only the amount and character thereof and the results obtained, but also the professional ability and standing of the attorney, his learning, skill, and proficiency in his profession, and experience, may be considered.—Clark v. Ellsworth, 442.

4. *Same*—The importance of a litigation, success attained, and the benefit which it procured, may be considered in estimating the value of the services rendered by an attorney.—*Idem.*

5. *Expense of Preparation*—The liability of a husband for services and disbursements rendered to and made in behalf of his wife in a suit for divorce, which were necessary for her protection, includes costs paid by her attorney, and expenses reasonably necessary in procuring information upon which to act, in preparing for trial an application for the wife to have decree against her set aside.—*Idem.*

6. *Attorney Outside of County*—Where a wife, in divorce proceedings, hires an attorney from outside the county, he cannot recover against her husband for expenses for traveling outside the county, it not being shown that services of competent attorneys within the county could not have been procured, and it appearing that several of them were not employed by the husband.—*Idem.*

7. SAME--*Usage*—Whether an attorney from outside the county, employed to render services therein, can recover for hotel bills and other expenses in the county, depends on the usage therein.—*Idem.*

8. *Wealth of Husband*—The wealth of the husband, though not admissible as an independent factor, in determining the value of an attorney's services rendered to a wife in litigation with the husband, may be considered in connection with the husband's disposition to make a severe contest in such litigation, as tending to show the importance of the service, in an action by an attorney to recover the value thereof from

the husband, on the ground that they were necessary for the protection of the wife —*Idem*.

9.   EVIDENCE—*Of Value*—The value of legal services rendered in a certain county is to be determined with reference to the practice there, so far as it has established the value of such services.—*Idem*.

10.   *Hypothetical Questions*— The failure to expressly restrict hypothetical questions as to the value of an attorney's services, to their value in the county in which they were performed, does not render it immaterial or incompetent where it shows that the services were performed in such county —*Idem*

11.   *Expert Evidence*—Attorneys who show general knowledge of the customary and reasonable charges for attorneys' services in a certain county, though not having as great knowledge thereof as others, may give their opinion as to the value of certain services rendered there.—*Idem*.

12.   *Same*—A question of an expert as to what professional services were necessary in preparing for the trial of a case. is properly excluded —*Idem*

13.   *Same*- Expert testimony as to the time necessary to prepare for the trial of a case. is admissible on the question as to the value of legal services, where the length of time spent by plaintiff in the preparation of the case is made prominent as an element of recovery.—*Idem*.

14.   *Same* - The opinions of expert witnesses are competent to show the value of the services of an attorney. though not conclusive upon that question.—*Idem*.

15.   **Sureties on Appeal**—An attorney cannot, under Code 1873, section 2931, become a surety upon a bond given on appeal from a justice's court to the district court, and the giving of such bond does not perfect the appeal.—Valley Nat. Bank v. Garretson, 655.

BANKS—See PARTNERSHIP, ¹, ².

1.   **Trusts**—PREFERENCES—A claim against an insolvent bank for money paid to the proprietor of such bank, as agent for the sale of land, and deposited by him in such bank, is entitled to preference over the claims of general creditors.—Brooke v. King, 713.

2.   **Evidence**—A vendor of land, who claims a preference over general creditors in the funds of an insolvent bank, on the ground that the purchase money had been deposited in such bank without authority by the proprietor of the bank, who

was agent for the sale of the land. has the burden of showing that the money was actually received by the bank.— *Idem.*

8. SAME. A vendor of land is not entitled to a preference in the funds of an insolvent bank, the proprietor of which was an agent for the sale of the land, on the ground that the purchase money was deposited in such bank without authority, where the purchaser had an account at the bank and the payments were made by merely charging him with the amount of each payment and giving the vendor credit for the amount, unless there were actually in the bank funds of such purchaser to be applied on such payments. —*Idem.*

BEES—See CRIM. LAW, [33], [33].

BILL OF EXCEPTIONS—See PRACT. SUP. CT. [10].

BLACKMAIL—See CRIM. LAW, [15], [16]; EVID, [25]; INSTR. [1].

1. Action—JOINT RIGHTS—A husband intending to join with his wife in the execution of a mortgage on her separate property, who signs the instrument freely. while her signature is obtained by compulsion exerted by others may properly join with her in the claim when she sets up the invalidity of the instrument as against her. since it is not the instrument he intended to execute.—Giddings v Iowa Savings Bank. 676.

2. Duress —A threat to imprison one for an offense of which he is in fact innocent, is as to him a threat of unlawful imprisonment and will constitute duress, although the one making it had reasonable ground to believe that such person was guilty as charged.—*Idem.*

3. HUSBAND AND WIFE—A mortgage given upon a homestead and signed by the wife is executed under duress, where her fear or affections are worked upon through threats made against her husband, and she is induced thereby against her will to convey her 'property to secure his debt. although the liability was valid and the threat was of a lawful prosecution of a crime which he had in fact committed.—*Idem.*

4. *Instructions*—In an action by a husband and wife to secure possession of a promissory note and the mortgage securing it, on the ground that the wife executed the instrument upon her homestead under duress to secure the debt of her husband, by reason of the threats of a creditor that he would otherwise institute a prosecution against the husband, for an alleged crime. the jury should take into consideration whether the crime had in fact been committed as charged, and whether the debt was a valid existing

obligation against the husband and it is error to charge that such matters are immaterial, for, among other things, they bear on the question whether there was coercion.—*Idem.*

BONA FIDE PURCHASER—See LAND. AND TENANT, [1].

Reformation.—A wife was not a *bona fide* purchaser of land from her husband, where she was conversant with the terms on which he bought the land, and the conveyance to her was in furtherance of an attempt to procure the property for an inadequate consideration.—Williams v. Hamilton, 433.

BONDS—See ATT'YS, [15]; PRACT. SUP. CT. [63].

DEATH OF OBLIGOR—*Estates* —The liability of a surety on a bond of an insurance agent, conditioned that such agent will perform all duties as such, and at the termination of the agency, by resignation, removal or otherwise, faithfully account with the company, and pay over all money due, is not terminated by the death of the surety, but continues against his estate and its distributees, where the bond provides that such surety binds himself, his "heirs, executors and administrators "—Security Fire Insurance Co. v. Hansen, 264.

BOUNDARIES—See JUDGMENTS, [2].

Deeds — Plaintiff's and defendant's common grantor, in conveying plaintiff's land, reserved land west of it, "commencing nineteen rods west of the southwest corner of out lot six" (evidently an error, as lot five is the only one adjoining), and, in conveying the reserved land to defendant, defined its eastern boundary as commencing "nineteen rods west from the southwest corner of out lot five," which corner is one rod east of the section. *Held*, that plaintiff's western boundary was eighteen rods west of the section line —Hyatt v. Clever, 388.

BOUNTIES.—See COUNTIES, [1].

BRIDGES—See COUNTIES, [2]; HIGHWAYS.

BROKERS—See SALES, [2].

BURDEN OF PROOF—See BANKS, [1]; CRIM. LAW, [1]; ELECTION CONTEST, [1], [2]; HOMESTEADS, [5]; INJUNCTIONS, [2]; LAND. AND TENANT, [1]; RAILROADS, [28].

CERTIFICATION—See JUSTICES, [2]; PRACT. SUP. Cr. [12], [13], [67].

CERTIORARI—See LIM. OF ACT. [1].

CHALLENGE—See CRIM. LAW, [5], [6].

CHANGE OF VENUE—See CRIM. LAW, [7]; PRACT. [7].

CLAIMS—See ESTATES, [2]; GENL. ASSIGN [1], [3].

CIGARETTES—See CONST. LAW.

CIRCUMSTANTIAL EVIDENCE—See INST. [1].

CITIES AND TOWNS—See HIGHWAYS, [2], [3], [4], [5].

COLLATERAL ATTACK—See PRACT [3], [4], [5], [6], [8], [20], [22].

COMMISSIONS—See SALES, [2]; RELEASES.

CONSIDERATION—See ADVANCEMENT; CONTRACTS, [4], [5], [6], [7], [18], [22];
EVID [16]; FRAUD. CONV. [2]; MORTGS. [1], [2]; RELEASE.

CONSPIRACY—See CRIM. LAW, [8].

CONSTITUTIONAL LAW.

1. **Interstate Commerce**—Under Const. U. S. article 1, section 8, conferring on congress the exclusive right to regulate commerce between the several states, Acts Twenty-sixth General Assembly, chapter 96, prohibiting the sale of cigarettes within the state by all persons save jobbers doing an inter-state business, is unconstitutional and void, in so far as it amounts to a regulation of inter state commerce.—McGregor v. Cone. 465.

2. **Original Packages** — An original package is that which is delivered by the importer to the carrier at the initial point of shipment in the exact condition in which it was shipped.— *Idem.*

3. CIGARETTES —A pine box in which are packed for convenience in shipment packages of cigarettes, each of which contains ten cigarettes, and sealed with an internal revenue stamp without any other packing or inclosure around or about them except the box itself, is the original package of commerce, and when that is opened the packages of cigarettes are subject to the police power of the state as a part of the common mass of property therein.—*Idem.*

4. DECISION OF REVENUE OFFICERS—The fact that the internal revenue department has recognized a package containing ten cigarettes as an "original package," for the purpose of taxation, is not conclusive, as the repacking of such packages in additional coverings is optional with the manufacturer.— *Idem.*

CONSTRUCTION—See CONTRACTS, [19], [21]; FRAUD. CONV. [4]; PRACT.
SUP CT [20]; WILLS, [8], [9], [10].

1. **Information**—An information which charges one with embezzlement by aiding and abetting another in the commission of such offense, does not charge defendant as an accessory before the fact.—State v. Rowe, 323.

2. **Mortgage**—RELEASE—An instrument acknowledging "full and entire satisfaction for a mortgage" on specified land, does not operate as an entire satisfaction of the mortgage debt, but only as the release of the land described in such instrument, where

the mortgage covered other land, and had not in fact been paid.—Wood v. Brown, 124.

CONTEMPT—See New Trial, ², ⁴; Pract. Sup. Ct. ⁴⁰

CONTINUANCES—See Crim. Law, ⁹; Pract. ¹¹.

CONTRACTS—See Counties, ²; Corporations, ³, ⁴; Evid. ¹³,¹⁶; Railways, ¹,², ³, ⁴, ¹⁰; Reformation, ³, ³, ⁴; Release, Sales, ⁵,⁶.

1. **Acceptance**—*Sale on refusal*—The refusal of a party to a contract for the construction and installment of a brick-making plant to allow the other party to remove it, in accordance with a provision of the contract to that effect, if it is proved unsatisfactory after the test contemplated by the contract, constitutes an acceptance thereof, and a subsequent direction for its removal is ineffectual to defeat an action for the purchase price.—Frey-Sheckler Co. v. Iowa Brick Co., 494.

2. **Same**—A corporation cannot avoid liability for the contract price of a brick-making plant installed on its property under an agreement by the other party to remove it and cancel all obligations against the corporation, if it proves unsatisfactory, where it appropriates to its own use the material of which the plant is composed.—*Idem.*

3. *Inconsistent Claims*—The appropriation to defendant's use of machinery sold on approval, after an expression of dissatisfaction therewith, was inconsistent with defendant's claim that the title to such property never passed under such contract, and rendered it liable for the price thereof.—*Idem.*

4. **Agreement to Support**—*Evidence*—Where a father, who has made advancements to his other children, gave to his son with whom he was then living, a deed of the land on which they lived, remarking that there was a deed of the property he intended for his son, and that he wanted to make his home with his son, as he had always lived there, and it seemed like home, and his son replied that he was welcome, if he could put up with his son's manner of living, and, in response, the father said he guessed that would be all right, such statements amounted to an agreement to support, as consideration for the deed.—Walker v. Walker, 505.

5. **Consideration**—A deed, the consideration of which is an agreement by the grantee to support the grantor during his life, may be set aside for breach of such agreement, notwithstanding that the only consideration expressed in the deed is love and affection and one dollar.—*Idem.*

6. **Breach**—An agreement by grantee to support the grantor constituting the consideration for the conveyance, is broken

CONTRACTS Continued

by the grantee's denial of his obligation to support the grantor in pursuance thereof, although he offers, as a charity or filial duty, to allow the grantor to live with him during his life.—*Idem*.

Breach - See *ante*, °; *post*, ¹⁵.

7. **Compromise and Settlement** —*Consideration*—An agreement to accept less than the amount due is without consideration — Keller v. Strong, 585.

8. **Debt of Another** —A promise by a stockholder of a corporation to a purchaser of his stock to pay an indebtedness of the corporation, so as tó make its earnings available to payment of dividends and subsequent obligations, cannot be enforced by the corporation. -German Savings Bank v N. W. Water & Light Co , 717.

9. **Error**—The fact that a contract for services in training race horses was made upon the erroneous supposition that one of the horses possessed speed qualities, and that upon learning the error the employer terminated the contract, does not affect his liability thereon —Kiburz v. Jacobs 580.

10. **Execution**—*Lease*—A lease which has never been effectually executed is absolutely null *ab initio*, and the parties thereto must be left to adjust any claims arising from the. occupancy of the land, without reference to the lease —Walker v. Walker, 505.

11. **MEETING OF MINDS** -A written lease will be set aside on the ground that the minds of the parties never met, where parts of the oral agreement were omitted, and the lease, having been signed, was delivered to the other party for inspection, by him to be recorded, if satisfactory, and he never recorded it —*Idem*.

12. **Same**—A lease is not effectual as such though signed by the lessor, where he signed it with the understanding that it would not be effective unless recorded, and under the impression that if it did not conform to the oral understanding of the parties he would destroy it and he subsequently told the lessee that it did not contain their understanding, and he would never record it —*Idem*.

13. **Forfeiture**—A failure to make a payment at the time agreed does not of itself work a forfeiture of contract but forfeiture for such cause is optional with the payee the contract having, after reciting the agreement of S to sell to J certain land, and. after receipt of full payment to make a deed to J, and of J to make the payments in certain installments provided that till said payments are fully and promptly paid no title shall pass; that

CONTRACTS Continued

time is of the essence of the contract and if there be any default
in any of the payments, then all rights of J, except as hereinafter provided, shall, because thereof and thereby, be immediately forfeited without notice from S and that, unless S shall,
in writing, expressly waive such forfeiture, J shall thereafter
simply be a tenant in common at sufferance, and shall surrender possession on demand; and that, in case of forfeiture, all
improvements may be retained by S as liquidated damages for
breach of the contract and for rent; or S, waiving such forfeiture may at any time before such surrender proceed to require
the fulfillment of J's obligations, or may treat any amount
unpaid as overdue.—Steel v. Long, 39.

14. **Husband and Wife** –A written obligation for the payment of
money given by a husband to a wife in consideration of her
joining in a deed and conveying her contingent interest in the
husband's land, is an unenforcable contract, under Code 1873,
section 2203. Miller v. Miller, 186.

15. **Conveyance of Homestead**—Where a husband agrees to convey a homestead, and receives the full consideration therefor,
without his wife's concurrence, and failed to make such conveyance, such consideration may be recovered back, though
such contract was void because not concurred in and signed by
the wife, as a judgment therefor is for the return of the money
obtained by a false pretense, rather than for damages for the
breach of a contract to convey a homestead. –De Kalb v.
Hingston, 23.

16. **Joint Contracts**—The consent of all the persons to whom an
option for the purchase of stock of a corporation, in which
they are all interested, is given by an agreement to sell and
deliver to them a specified amount of stock, in the number of
shares to each that they may agree upon, is necessary to the
exercise of the option by any one of them, although one or
more of them has disposed of his interest in the corporation.—
Pratt v. Prouty, 419.

17. **Lotteries**—That the subscribers for lots, which were to be
divided or apportioned among them in such manner as they
should decide, made the apportionment by drawing lots, does
not prevent the promoters, who did not participate in or suggest the manner of the apportionment, from enforcing the
contract entered into by a subscriber, for the lot drawn by
him.—Chancy Park Land Co. v. Hart, 592.

18. RULE APPLIED—Certain lots contracted for by the promoter
of a packing house plant, were subscribed for under an
agreement to take the number set opposite the name of each

subscriber, if the packing house was secured. The lots were to be apportioned in such manner (as subscribers) may decide. At a meeting called by the promoters to divide the lots by "method ⁎ ⁎ ⁎ to be decided upon by a vote of the subscribers," the plan of one of the promoters was adopted; the other promoters taking no actual part, and all having announced that they left the method of the apportionment to the subscribers. The subscribers' names were drawn out of one box, and the numbers of the lots to correspond were drawn out of the other, by two of the subscribers agreed upon. None of the lots were worth more than the price paid. *Held*, that the apportionment of the lots was by the subscribers alone, and the method was not a lottery, within the meaning of Code 1873, section 4043, constitution, article 3, section 28, prohibiting lotteries.—*Idem*.

19. **Municipal Corporations** –PUBLIC IMPROVEMENTS—*Guaranty* —A provision in a contract for grading, curbing, guttering and paving a street, that the contractor shall, without further compensation, keep in continuous good repair all pavements laid under the contract for a period of five years, except as to defects or repairs required by excavations or disturbances of the street not caused by the contractor, and requiring the pavement to remain during such time a good, substantial, reliable and durable pavement in all its parts "except ordinary wear," does not invalidate the contract, although Code 1873, section 465, requires the city to pay the expense of repairs,—as such provision is a mere guaranty of the proper construction of the pavement.—Osburn v City of Lyons, 160.

20. NOTICE — *Validity of Contract* — Acts Twenty-third General Assembly, chapter 14, section 3, as amended by Acts Twenty-fourth General Assembly, chapter 12, provides that all contracts for public improvements shall be made after public notice of the extent of the work, the kind of materials used, and the time when the work shall be completed A notice provided for sealed proposals for paving, and referred to an ordinance of the city fixing November 1, 1893, as the time for completion of the work Four months after notice was published, two bids were received, and six months before either of them was accepted, the council changed the time for completing the work to August 1, 1894 The bid of the contractor was not accepted until May 1, 1894 *Held*, that as the bid of the company was originally made under the proposition that the work should be completed November 1, 1893, and as no bid had been secured to do the work to be completed at the second date fixed, the contract, as finally made, was entered into without

CONTRACTS Continued

notice and without the competition required by the statute.—
Idem.

21. Option—The proviso in an option for the purchase of enough
of the stock of one of the parties in a corporation to reduce
his holding to one-third of the whole capital stock that the
stock shall be purchased at par in amounts of ten thousand
dollars at the end of each business year, after a dividend has
been declared and paid on the stock, will be construed merely
to fix that sum as the greatest amount of stock that can be
demanded in any one year, especially where the parties have
practically so construed it —Pratt v Prouty, 419

22. Public Policy—*Consideration*—Two persons were engaged in
selling intoxicating liquors under Acts Twenty fifth General
Assembly, chapter 62, kno vn as the "mulct law " A note for
the price of the interest of one of them contained the clause
"if payor is obliged to abandon his present business on account
of change in the liquor law by the next legislature of the
state then this note to be void, otherwise to be of full force"
Held, that the words "present business" meant the business he
then had, and that, said business being a legal business. the
note was not invalid, as being a "gambling, wagering contract," and that it was supported by a valid consideration.—
Phillips v. Gifford, 458.

23. Fees—A contract whereby an officer agrees to accept a different compensation than that provided by statute for his official acts or whereby he agrees not to avail himself of the
statutory method of enforcing a collection of his fees. is contrary to public policy, and void —Peters v City of Davenport,
625.

24. *Same*—An illegal contract. fully executed cannot be relied
upon as the basis of a claim for additional compensation for
services rendered thereunder —*Idem*

25. *When Collectible*—An officer who performs services in his official capacity. at the request of another, is entitled to statutory fees therefor —*Idem.*

26. *Same*—Where a justice of the peace has no authority to bring
an action he cannot recover his costs taxed therein, from the
party in whose name the action was brought.—*Idem.*

27. *Same*—The statutory fees allowed to a justice of the peace for
performing judicial services cannot be claimed by a magistrate employed to collect delinquent poll taxes, when he
institutes the action under a specific agreement as to compensation. —*Idem.*

28. *Same*—A justice of the peace authorized to "collect delinquent poll tax lists on the same terms as last year," cannot, after receiving twenty-five per cent. of the amount collected, which the city alleges was the agreed compensation therefor. assert that he is entitled, as an officer, to the statutory fees for such services, and that the contract to take less is void as against public policy where it is not shown that the tax lists were delivered to him in his official capacity, and since the resolution employing him does not, in itself, empower him to collect the taxes by suit.—*Idem.*

29. *Evidence*—In an action by a justice of the peace against the city to recover fees alleged to be due him arising from the collection of a delinquent poll tax list, it is immaterial whether the city officers ratify the bringing of the suits, when his services were performed under a specific agreement as to compensation.—*Idem.*

80. *Same*—Testimony as to statements made to a justice of the peace by city officials, is inadmissible in an action by the magistrate to recover for fees alleged to be due him, when none of the officers or agents making the statements had power to bind the city.—*Idem.*

81. *Same*—Evidence as to the value of services rendered by a justice of the peace in sending out notices to delinquents, and publishing demands in the city newspapers in connection with the collection of the delinquent poll tax list placed in his hands, is inadmissible in an action by him to receive fees for services rendered therein as a justice of the peace.—*Idem.*

CONTRIBUTORY NEGLIGENCE—See RAILWAYS, [15], [17].
CONVERSION—See DAMAGES, [1], [2]; MORTGS. [3]; PRACT. SUP. CT. [5].

CORPORATIONS—See CONTR. [8], [16]; PRINCIPAL AND AGT. [8]; PRACT. [1].

1. Debt of Member—A corporation may secure the payment of the individual indebtedness of one member of the firm, where it is solvent, and there is no intention to defraud subsequent creditors—Johnston & Son v. Robuck, 528.

2. Directors—*Who deemed*—One who, though not a stockholder in a corporation, acted as a director for two years, was treated by the officers of the company—all of whom were non-residents —as such director and gave advice concerning the affairs of the company in his city, comes within the rule applicable to dealings between a director in his own interest and his corporation.—Stetson v. Northern Inv. Co., 898.

Corp. Continued

8. Contract with—One occupying the relation of local director of a corporation whose stockholders were non-residents,sold property to the corporation. His valuation of the property, and his representations as to its probable rental value, were in excess of the real values, but were mere expressions of opinion. The deal was not consummated until after deliberations by the stockholders, and until after one director familiar with real estate values in the city had visited the property and made a report. The owner of the property was not present at the meeting at which it was decided to make the purchase. *Held,* that since the owner had not acquired his information as to the values by reason of his position as director of the corporation, and the corporation had not relied solely upon his representation the sale would not be set aside on the ground of fraud or bad faith.—*Idem.*

4. Ratification—A corporation which has purchased property of a director, had paid off incumbrances assumed by it, and had possession, management, and control for nearly three years, will be presumed to have ratified the contract, and cannot assert for the first time, as a defense in an action for the price, that the director had acted in bad faith in his representations regarding its value.—*Idem*

5. *President of Corporation*—A creditor of a corporation cannot ratify the unauthorized act of the president of such corporation in executing a bill of sale of corporate property for payment of a debt.—Hartman Steel Co. v. Hoag & Son, 269.

6. Pledge—A stockholder in a corporation who pledges his stock to another person to secure the payment of a debt due by the corporation may, with the consent of the pledgee, withdraw the stock pledged, although the corporation objects thereto.—German S. Bank v. N. W. Water & L. Co., 717.

7. *Rights of Debtor*—A debtor cannot complain of a decree that its property be first exhausted to satisfy the judgment before proceeding against property of another, voluntarily pledged for the debt.—*Idem.*

8. Stockholders—*Creditors*—Creditors of a corporation are not estopped to hold stockholders liable for the difference between the real value of the property transferred in payment of the stock and the face value of the stock, because they were chargeable with constructive notice that the stock was issued in exchange for property, where there was nothing to indicate to them the value of the property received in exchange for the stock.—Stout v. Hubbell, 499.

Small figures refer to subdivisions of Index. The others to page of report.

CORP. Continued   TO   COUNTIES

9. RULE APPLIED—The promoters of a corporation agreed to purchase at a grossly excessive valuation, and pay therefor by issuing paid-up stock. The articles of incorporation recited the contract, and that the directors should pay for the land by issuing "stock at par for (the agreed valuation). Said stock, when so issued, to be held and regarded as fully paid for by the conveyance of" such land. *Held*, that the record of the articles did not impart knowledge to creditors of the corporation, of the fraudulent valuation.—*Idem.*

10. SAME—Property received by a corporation at an excessive valuation, in payment for shares of its capital stock, is only a payment to the extent of its value as to the corporation's creditors, and the owners of the stock are liable to creditors for the difference between the actual value of the property and the face value of the stock.—*Idem.*

COSTS—See PRACT. ¹²; PRACT PUP. CT. ⁴.

1. Retaxation—Where a party makes a motion to retax the costs in the trial court, it is not governed by Code, 1873, section 3154, relating to proceedings to reverse, vacate, or modify judgments in the court in which rendered, but by section 2944, relating to retaxing costs, as the claim is not that the judgment should be reversed or modified, but that the costs were improperly taxed by the clerk, and this applies to costs adjudged upon dismissal of an action by plaintiff.—Fisher v. B., C. R. & N. R'y Co., 588.

2. TIME FOR APPLICATION—A motion to retax costs under Code 1873, section 2944, may be made at any time before laches or equitable limitation has intervened, since no limit has been placed by statute upon the time for such a motion.—*Idem.*

8. WITNESS FEES—Witnesses who are not subpœnaed or sworn are not entitled to fees for attendance, under the statute, although they attend at the request of one of the parties.—*Idem.*

4. *Same*—Witnesses who are not subpœnaed are not entitled to mileage under the statute, although they testify in a case.—*Idem.*

5. *Rule applied*—A motion to retax costs, made the second term of court after judgment was rendered, does no show laches.—*Idem.*

COUNTIES—See PRACT. SUP. CT. ⁶²; WARRANTY.

1. POWERS OF BOARD—*Bounties*—The board of supervisors has no discretion to refuse a bounty for a wolf skin, if the complainant has fully complied with the law, and the facts are undisputed, under Acts Twenty-fourth General Assembly, chapter 87, providing for the allowance for such a bounty upon a certified

statement of the facts, together with such other evidence as the board may demand, showing the claimant to be entitled thereto, and if they so refuse, the bounty may be recovered in a court of law.—Bourrett v. Palo Alto County, 850.

2.   BRIDGES—It being the duty of a county to keep its bridges and the approaches thereto in repair, where sand and gravel were taken from plaintiff's land, with his consent, by direction of the board of supervisors of the defendant county, for the construction and repair of the approach to a county bridge, defendant was liable for the value thereof, as on an implied contract, and not for what it would cost to restore the land from which it was taken to its former condition.— *Idem.*

3.   DEED WITH WARRANTY—A county has no authority to execute a deed with covenants of warranty, as no statute confers such power, and it cannot be implied; being neither necessary in order to make such conveyance available, or essential to the purpose of such corporation.—*Idem.*

4.   *Frauds in Sale by*—Where the grantee in a deed made by a county in settlement of litigation pending between the parties had knowledge respecting the title, equal to that possessed by the agents of the county, who concealed nothing from him, and were guilty of no other fraud, the mere failure of the title to the land conveyed did not render the county liable to him as for money had and received. —*Idem.*

5.   *Same*—An action for fraud will not lie against a county upon failure of title to land deeded by it in compromise of a pending litigation, when no fact was withheld from the record, or any statement made to the grantee, except such as could be inferred from the fact that the land was offered and deeded as part consideration for a compromise.— *Idem.*

COURTS—See COUNTIES, 1.
COURT AND JURY—See CRIM. LAW, 17.
CREDITORS—See CORP. 1, 5, 8, 9, 10. FRAUD CONV. 1; MORTGS. 2.

CRIMINAL LAW—CONSTR. 1; INTOX. LIQ.; EXTRADITION, 1; NEW TRIAL, 2; PRACT. 15; PRACT. SUP. CT. 64.

Accessories—See *post*, 11, 30.

1.   Assault—See *post*, 8, 24, 30—INSTRUCTIONS—An instruction on a trial for assault with intent to murder that whoever assaults another with the intent to inflict upon him some injury of a greater or more serious character than an ordinary battery, is

---

guilty of an assault with intent to inflict great bodily injury, is erroneous as omitting reference to the unlawfulness of the assault.—State of Iowa v. Shea, 724.

2. EVIDENCE— The state has the burden of proving beyond reason ble doubt, on a trial for assault with intent to murder, that defendant was not acting in self-defense.—*Idem.*

3. RIGHT OF A SALOON KEEPER—A saloon keeper has the right to repel an assault made upon him by one whom he has ordered off his premises, if such order was not given for the purpose of provoking a difficulty.—*Idem.*

4. **Attorney Fees** · DEFENSE OF CRIMINALS—*Courts*—A motion for an order on the county treasurer to compensate attorneys for defendant charged with murder, for services rendered on appeal, will be refused, as the statutes do not authorize such an order.—State of Iowa v. Young 730.

Demurrer—See *post*, ⁴⁸.

5. **Challenge**—*Juror*—Under Code, section 5360, requiring a challenge of a juror for cause to distinctly specify the facts constituting such cause, a challenge which does not distinctly specify such cause is properly overruled.—*Idem.*

6. SAME—One will not be excluded from sitting as a juror on a trial for murder because he has formed an opinion solely on what he has read in the papers, and such opinion simply is that the defendant killed the deceased. where there is no dispute as to that fact, and he states that he can listen to the evidence and base his verdict on that alone, and that he knows nothing to prevent him from rendering a fair and impartial verdict.—*Idem.*

7. **Change of Venue**—A change of venue need not be granted in a trial for rape, by reason of sensational newspaper articles in reference to the crime, which allege that the organization of a vigilance committee is seriously contemplated, and that it might take a hand in the proceedings if the preliminary trial is unduly prolonged, when no feeling against the defendant pervades the county, although some exists in the vicinity where the crime was committed.—State of Iowa v. McDonough, 6.

8. **Conspiracy to Assault**—*Sufficiency of Evidence*—Accused told D. that if he would lick W. his fine would be paid, to which D. replied that he did not want anybody to pay his fine, but that he would punch and whip W., whereupon accused advised D. not to do so, but to slap him. D. afterwards stated to others that he would whip W., and [that accused and another would pay his fine; and later he did severely beat W., rendering him unconscious for several days. As D. withdrew from the, assault.

Small figures refer to subdivisions of Index   The others to page of report.

VOL. 104 Ia—49

CRIM. LAW Continued

accused approached and indicated his satisfaction with what had been done, but did not strike W. or assist D. *Held*, that accused was not guilty of conspiring with D. to commit the assault.—State of Iowa v. King, 737.

9. **Continuance**—A motion made by defendant, in a trial for rape, for a continuance, based upon the absence of two witnesses, will not be granted where no excuse is made for the delay in making the application, nor any facts constituting diligence in endeavoring to procure the attendance of the witnesses set forth, and when most of the facts expected to be proved by them are immaterial and irrelevant.—*Idem*.

10. **Dying Declarations**—Declarations of the deceased, for whose murder defendant is on trial, made the day after the injury was inflicted and the day before his death and after he had been advised by a physician that he could not recover to which he replied that he expected to die, are admissible as dying declarations, although he stated to another person that he was not a "quitter."—State of Iowa v. Young, 730.

Evidence—See *ante*, ³.

11. **Embezzlement**—*Accessories*—One may, independently of statute, be an accessory by procuring a crime, although he is incompetent to commit the crime in person —State of Iowa v. Rowe, 323.

12. **Evidence**—See *post*, ¹⁶, ³⁸, ⁴³—*Reputation*—In a prosecution for rape the character of the prosecutrix may be proved by evidence of general reputation, but testimony as to particular acts or specific facts is not admissible.—State of Iowa v. McDonough, 6.

13. PLEA AND PROOF—Evidence of the mental weakness of the prosecutrix was admissible as bearing on the question of consent, though it was not alleged in the indictment that she was feeble minded —*Idem*.

14. VENUE--An allegation in an indictment that a crime was committed within the county is sufficiently established by evidence as to the places where certain persons reside, and as to where the defendant went, from which the alleged fact may be inferred.--State of Iowa v. Bailor, 1.

15. **Extortion by Accusation**—*Indictment*—An indictment under Code section 3871, providing for the punishment of one who "maliciously threatens to accuse another of crime " with intent to extort money, need not allege that the person threatened was not guilty of the crime; and his guilt or innocence *is immaterial* —State of Iowa v. Debolt, 105.

16. EVIDENCE—*Intent*—In the case of malicious threats to accuse another of an offense with intent thereby to extort money or pecuniary advantage, the intent to extort is of the essence of the crime, and proof of the threats, even though conclusive, is not proof of that specific intent or that it accompanied the act.—*Idem*.

False Pretenses—See *post*, ²⁵.

17. Former Jeopardy—*Court and Jury*—When, under the law, or for want of evidence, a plea of former conviction is not sustained the court may so charge the jury.—State of Iowa v. Jamison, 843.

18. PLEADING—The state may defeat a former conviction by showing that the court in which the defendant was convicted had no jurisdiction. without alleging that fact in the replication, as the rules in civil cases have no application to criminal procedure and Code, section 4349, expressly provides that no replication or further pleading is necessary to a plea of former adjudication.—*Idem*.

19. Harmless Error—In a trial for rape where the prosecutrix was enticed from a dance hall by one of the defendants and taken to a stone quarry, where drunken men were carousing, by several of whom she was ravished evidence of the presence of such defendant and the complaining witness at the dance hall and as to what occurred at the quarry prior to their arrival there, is not prejudicial to the defendant on the trial, when the jury was instructed not to consider any acts or statements of other defendants not made in the presence and hearing of the accused.—State of Iowa v. McDonough, 6.

20. SAME—In a trial for rape, testimony offered to show certain acts of the prosecutrix in wrestling with persons other than the defendant in an unbecoming manner, is inadmissible when it is not shown that such improper conduct occurred before the commission of the alleged offense, and as being evidence of specific acts —*Idem*.

21. SAME—A defendant accused of seduction cannot complain of a refusal to permit the prosecutrix to answer, on cross-examination, whether she ever thought, from his words and conduct prior to her alleged seduction, that he desired to have connection with her, where he was permitted to inquire of her what his object and purpose were in going with her.— State of Iowa v. Reilly, 13.

22. *Same*—In a prosecution for seduction the error of permitting prosecutrix's doctor to testify that the prosecutrix had stated

CRIM. LAW Continued

that she was unmarried was cured by prosecutrix's testimony
to that effect.—*Idem*.

23. STRIKING OUT—*Curing Error*—In a prosecution for seduction. a
certain witness testified that the neighbors, three strange ladies,
prosecutrix and a lady named O. had told her that prosecutrix
and defendant were engaged to be married. Thereafter, the
court struck out the evidence of said witness as to what the
neighbors said and charged that all evidence of other witnesses
as to talk among neighbors about such engagement was withdrawn　*Held* that the statements of the thr--e strange ladies,
the prosecutrix, and O were not withdrawn, and the error of
their admission was not cured —*Idem*.

Incest—See *post*, ²⁶.

24. Included Offenses –Assault with the intent to commit great
bodily injury is not necessarily included in a charge of rape.
and the court need not instruct respecting it —State of Iowa v.
McDonough, 6.

Indictment -See *ante* ¹²; *post*, ⁴⁰, ⁴¹.

25. FALSE PRETENSES—An indictment for "obtaining property under
false pretenses" charged that defendant did designedly and
with intent to defraud, feloniously and falsely represent to L
that he was solvent, and worth ten thousand dollars, whereas,
he was not worth that sum, or any other; that L believed and
relied on such representations, which were made knowingly,
designedly and feloniously, to obtain L's signature as security
for defendant to a note; that the note so obtained was signed
by L, and delivered to the payee; and that the facts that the
defendant was not worth ten thousand dollars, nor any other
sum, and that he was insolvent, were at the time unknown to
L. *H-ld*, sufficient. under Code 1873, section 4073, providing
that if one designedly, and by false pretense, and with intent
to defraud, obtains the signature of any person to any writing.
the false making of which would be punished as forgery, he
shall be punished, though the intent to defraud L was not
specifically alleged.—State of Iowa v. Hazen, 16.

26. INCEST—Indictment for incest, charging carnal knowledge on
part of accused only, is sufficient.—State of Iowa v. Kimble, 19.

27. INTOXICATING LIQUORS –An indictment under Code. section
2384, providing that whoever erects. establishes, or uses any
building erected or place for specified purposes, shall be guilty
of a nuisance, alleging that defendant did unlawfully establish
and use a certain building "or" place in a-designated city, with
the intention of unlawfully keeping, selling and giving away
intoxicating liquors in such building, is not equivocal, uncertain

CRIM. LAW Continued

and doubtful because of the use of the word ' or."—State of Iowa v. Dixon, 741.

28. SAME—An indictment alleging that defendant unlawfully sold and gave away intoxicating liquors "at" a specified building or place within the county, is not indefinite or uncertain because of the use of the word "at" instead of "in "—*Idem.*

29. Instructions — See *ante,* ¹; *post,* ²⁴, ³⁵, ³⁶, ³⁷—*Conflict*—An instruction that, in determining whether or not a rape had been committed the jury should consider the prosecutrix's demeanor, condition, and declarations, immediately after the alleged commission, does not conflict with an instruction that in case they found the crime had been committed, they should not consider the prosecutrix's conduct, declarations, nor condition, in determining whether or not she was corroborated in charging the defendant with it.—State of Iowa v. Bailor, 1.

30. SAME—It was not necessary to instruct respecting a simple assault, where the evidence showed that, if defendant was guilty of an assault, he also committed a battery —*Idem.*

31. SAME—The court in a trial for rape need not instruct, the defendant may be found guilty of a simple assault, although evidence of such an assault, made by the defendant upon the prosecutrix after he was placed under arrest, was given, where he was not tried for that offense, but for an assault included in the crime charged.—*Idem.*

Intoxicating Liquors—See *ante,* ²⁷.

Jurors—See *ante,* ⁵, ⁶.

32. Larceny—A trespasser, who finds bees on the land of another, and hives them, but is not the owner of the hive in which he puts them, has no interest in them which is the subject of larceny.—State of Iowa v. Repp, 305.

33. SAME—The mere finding of bees in a tree on the land of another person, gives the finder no right to the bees or to the tree.—*Idem.*

Law of Case –See *post,* ⁴⁵.

34. Murder –INSTRUCTIONS—An accused, relying on self defense as justification, complained that the court's charge presenting the issue, was not sufficiently specific. *Held,* that he should have requested a specific instruction —State of Iowa v. Young, 780.

35. SAME—It appearing from the evidence and admissions that the accused was guilty of murder in the first or second degree, or manslaughter, the jury were instructed that to convict of either offense it must be found that the killing

was not in self defense. *Held*, sufficient to cover an omitted instruction on burden of proof.—*Idem*.

86. SAME—An instruction, after giving the rules of self defense, that courts and juries must "exercise due caution in applying these principles," is not objectionable as nullifying the instructions relating to self defense.—*Idem*.

87. SAME—The court may properly call the attention of the jury, on a trial for murder, to the fact that defendant is directly interested in the result, without referring to other witnesses, individually, where none of such other witnesses are directly interested.—*Idem*.

88. **Newly Discovered Evidence** — Two witnesses, in affidavits filed in support of a motion for a new trial on the ground of newly discovered evidence, after defendant was convicted of rape. testified that the prosecutrix told them the defendant "had never done anything to her," but upon being cited before the court, and examined orally, with the prosecutrix, it appeared that her statements referred to her being pregnant only. *Held*, not ground for a new trial.—State of Iowa *v.* Bailor, 1.

Pleading—See *ante*, ¹⁸.

Plea and Proof— See *ante*, ¹⁸.

89. **Principal and Accessory**—The declaration of Code 1873, section 4314, that one aiding or abetting the commission of a public offense is a principal, enlarges the scope of section 3908, providing that public officers who shall convert to their own use money entrusted to their care and keeping shall be guilty of embezzlement; and therefore, one not a public officer, and who therefore, would not violate section 3908 if he took the money himself, may commit the crime of aiding and abetting another, who is such officer.— State of Iowa v. Rose, 328.

40. **Practice**—*Defective Indictment*— Upon the discharge of a jury, and the termination of a criminal trial by reason of a defective indictment, the court may, in its discretion re-submit the case to the grand jury, under Code 1873, section 4450, when it will tend to prevent the failure of justice.—State of Iowa *v.* Kimble, 19.

41. SAME—The court may in a criminal trial, when by an objection to the offering of testimony it is pointed out that the indictment does not charge a crime punishable by law, discharge the jury and end the trial, under Code 1873, section 4444.—*Idem*.

---

42. DEMURRER—Defendant should demur to indictment on the ground that it does not charge a crime (Code 1873, sections 4345, 4352), this not being one of the grounds for which section 4337 authorized the indictment to be set aside on motion.—*Idem.*

43. Rape—See *ante,* [7], [10], [13], [24], [29], [31].—MENTAL CAPACITY—*Evidence*— It was competent to show the appearance, condition, and actions of the prosecutrix at and for some time prior to the time of the commission of the offense, to prove mental capacity, by non-expert witnesses —State of Iowa v McDonough. 6.

44. AGE OF CONSENT—In a prosecution for rape upon a female child under the age of fifteen years, under Code 1873, section 3861, as amended by Laws Twenty-sixth General Assembly, chapter 70, fixing the age of consent at fifteen years, it is immaterial that the prosecutrix is large of her age, physically strong, and of a romping disposition, as the defendant was guilty of rape whether the sexual intercouse was against her will or not —State of Iowa v. Ed. Bailor, 1.

45. Seduction—See *ante,* [21], [22], [23]—*Law of the Case*—A conviction of the crime of seduction will not be sustained, when the court instructed the jury that the case rested entirely on an alleged promise of marriage, and that if the prosecutrix assented to the intercourse upon the defendant's promise to marry her should pregnancy result therefrom, they should find for the defendant, where the testimony of the prosecutrix was that the promise of marriage was conditioned upon her getting in a family way.—State of Iowa v. Reilly, 13.

Venue—See *ante.* [14].

CROSS-EXAMINATION—See EVID. [5], [6].
CROSS-PETITION—See PRACT. [13], [14].

DAMAGES—See ASSAULT, [1]; HIGHWAY, [1]; INSTRUCTIONS, [4]; PRACT. SUP. CT. [60]; RAILWAYS, [8], [21].

1. Conversion—The measure of damages in an action for property converted is, in the absence of special circumstances requiring a different rule, their fair market value at the time and place of conversion, with interest, and not their cost at a distant locality, with or without transportation charges added.— Gensburg v. Marshall Field & Co , 599.

2. SAME—If it appears that personal property converted has no market value at the place of conversion, the actual value may be shown —*Idem.*

DEATH—See BONDS, [1]; EVIDENCE, [21].
DECEDENTS—See EVID. [19].

DECREE—See Pract. [21].

DEDICATION—See Highways, [1], [2], [4], [5], [6], [8]; Railways, [6].

1. **Platting**—The platting of land as a public square amounts to a dedication thereof to public use.—Moore v. Klepdish, 319.

2. **Vacation of**—An owner of lots abutting on a public square is not estopped to attack the validity of an attempted vacation by another owner, of the dedication of the square to public use, by subsequently occupying a portion of the square, where he supposed that the attempted vacation was valid.—*Idem.*

3. **Revocation**—A dedication of a square to the public cannot be revoked without the joint act of all parties interested, including owners of abutting lots.—*Idem.*

4. *Rule Applied*—Where land has been platted as a public square, an instrument executed by the party who made the plat, and others whose interests do not clearly appear, in which some of the abutting property owners did not join, is ineffectual as a vacation of such square.—*Idem.*

DEEDS—See Boundaries; Counties, [3], [4], [6]; Fraud; Fraud. Conv.[1].

Acknowledgment of—Forged Deed—*Recording*—The fact that a deed to which the signature of a wife was forged was recorded, does not give one the right to rely upon her execution of the instrument when there is no pretense that she acknowledged it, for an unacknowledged deed is not entitled to record. Code (McClain's) section 3118.—Sherod v. Ewell, 253.

DE FACTO OFFICER—See Pract. [5], [6], [26].

DELIVERY—See Contr. [11], [12].

DEMURRER—See Pract., [4], [42].

DEPUTY MARSHAL—See Officers.

DIRECTED VERDICT—See Intox. Liq., [23]; Pract., [16], [19]; Pract. Sup Ct., [21].

DIRECTORS—See Corporations, [2].

DISMISSAL—See Pract., [20]; Pract. Sup, Ct., [5], [16]; Remittitur.

DIVORCE—See Attys., [1].

DOWER—See Fraud. Conv., [1].

DURESS—See Blackmail, [1], [2], [3], [4].

DYING DECLARATIONS—See Crim. Law, [10].

ELECTION CONTEST.

1. **Burden of Proof**—Where an official count has been made, it is better evidence of who was elected than the ballots. unless he who discredits the count shows affirmatively that the ballots have been preserved with a care which precludes the opportunity

---

of tampering and all suspicion of change, abstraction or substitution.—Davenport v. Olerich, 194.

2. RULE APPLIED—Ballots cast were placed in the custody of the auditor until removed to that of the clerk under the order of court. They were properly protected, except those from two precincts, which were wrapped in paper and placed on the floor under the table in the vault in the auditor s office, where, the inmates of the office did not at all times have them in sight. Some of these packages were unsealed, and the seals of others were broken. At one time three of the packages were mislaid; the vault in which they were placed was left open, and many people had access thereto Held, that the ballots had not been so preserved as to be competent as evidence for the purpose of overthrowing the official count.— *Idem.*

EMBEZZLEMENT—See CRIM. LAW, [11], [39].

ERROR—See HARMLESS ERROR.

ESTATES—See ADJUDICATION, [3]; BONDS; EVID. [19]; EXECUTIONS, [1]; LIM. OF ACT. [3], [4]; NEW TRIAL, [1]; PRACT. SUP. CT. [6]; REFORMATION, [1]; SETTLEMENTS; TAXATION, [3].

1. Filing Claims—LIMITATION OF ACTION—Filing and allowance of a claim of a judgment creditor against the debtor's estate gives the former no additional right against the real estate of the decedent, when the lien of his judgment thereon has expired by statutory limitation.—Hansen's Empire Fur Fact. v. Teabout, 360.

2. SAME—Code 1873, section 2421, fixing a period in which claims against the estate of a deceased person shall be filed, does not apply to contingent and undetermined claims growing out of a bond given by decedent to stand good for the business conduct of an insurance agent, such claims arising after that period has expired.—Security Fire Insurance Co. v. Hansen, 265.

3. EXECUTORS AND ADMINISTRATORS—A judgment creditor who has filed his claim with the debtor's administrator cannot, after the expiration of the lien of his judgment upon the lands of the decedent, proceed, independently of the administrator, to subject the property to the payment of his judgment.— *Idem*

4. Insurance—*Action by Administrator*—The administrator of insured cannot maintain an action on a certificate of insurance payable to the legal heirs of insured, but the action must be brought by such heirs.—Schoep v. Bankers Alliance Ins. Co., 854.

Small figures refer to subdivisions of Index. The others to page of report.

5.   *Same*—The provisions of Code 1873, sections 2371, 2372, do not
     apply to the avails of life insurance which do not belong to
     the estate of the decedent, and are not designed to authorize
     the administrator to collect an amount due on a policy which
     is not a part of the estate but which belong to the beneficiaries
     named therein, who are not the legal representatives of the
     decedent.—*Idem*

6.   **Jurisdiction to Order Sale**—An order directing an adminis-
     trator to sell the real property, including the homestead, to pay
     claims against the estate, though erroneous, is not void for want
     of jurisdiction.—Sigmond v. Bebber, 431.

ESTOPPEL—See ADJUDICATION, ¹; DEDICATION, ²; CORP., ¹, ²; INS., ²; MECHANICS' LIENS. ²; PLEADING, ¹, ²; PRACT. SUP. CT., ⁴, ¹¹; RAILWAYS, ²⁰; SALES, ⁷.

1.   DITCHES—The owner of a city lot below grade does not by acqui-
     escing in the construction by a city of ditch conveying surface
     water over his premises estop himself to obstruct the flow of
     the water in such ditch by raising his lot to grade.—City of
     Cedar Falls v. Hansen, 189.

2.   Laches—One who attacks a defective sheriff's sale more than
     ten years after it was made is guilty of such laches as will pre-
     vent him from being heard, in the absence of any excuse for
     not sooner bringing his suit.—Hansen's Fur Fact. v. Teabout,
     360.

3.   Representations—Reliance by a debtor on the advice of an
     attorney for the creditor, that a bill of sale of personal prop-
     erty by the debtor to the creditor was sufficient to fully and
     legally transfer the property to the creditor, does not estop the
     creditor to subsequently set up that the title to the property
     did not pass by such bill of sale, and that the debt was there
     fore unpaid, as the debtor has no right to rely on the advice of
     the creditor's attorney in such matter.—Hartman v. Hoag, 269.

4.   By Testifying—The court instructed that if, on the trial of
     another cause, plaintiff in this cause, *for the purpose of enabling
     another to recover against the defendant for personal injuries*,
     gave testimony that he was the physician in attendance, and
     performed the services, and of their value, thus enabling that
     other to recover of the defendant for such services, he was
     esstopped to recover in this suit. It was also charged that if,
     when plaintiff testified in the prior case as to the value of his
     services, he added that he had a suit pending against the
     defendant for the services, and that he expected to collect for
     the services from the defendant, then there would be no *estoppel.*

Held, that both instructions were proper.—Smith v. C. & N. W. R'y Co., 147.

5. *Same*—Failure of a physician who attended an employe of a railway company to state, while testifying as a witness for such employe in an action against the company, that he has a suit pending against the company for his services, does not estop him from subsequently recovering from the company for such services, on the ground that the employe was enabled by his testimony to recover therefor from the company. It was not the duty of the witness to decline to answer nor to inform the court that he had a suit pending for such services.—*Idem*.

EVIDENCE—See ASSAULT, ², ³; ATTYS. ¹⁰; BANKS, ²; CONTR. ²⁰, ³⁰, ³¹; CRIM. LAW, ¹⁰. ¹². ¹³, ¹⁶, ¹⁹, ²⁰, ²¹, ²², ⁴⁸; ELECT. CONTEST, ¹, ²; INST. ¹; INS. ¹², ¹³, ¹⁴, ¹⁵, ¹⁹, ²⁰; LAND. AND TENANT, ¹; LIBEL, ¹, ²; PLEA AND PROOF, ²; PRACT. ¹², ²², ³⁰; RAILWAYS, ⁶, ⁷, ¹⁶; SALES, ²; WILLS, ⁶.

1. **Admission by Pleadings**—Evidence that the claim of plaintiff was, from its inception, a debt of a corporation, in which defendants had an interest, instead of a debt of the defendants themselves, is properly excluded where defendants admit in their answer that it was their debt from its inception.—Hartman Steel Co. v. Hoag & Son, 269.

Advancements—See *post*, ¹⁶.

2. **Attorney and Client**—*Discretion*—The court may, in its discretion, to show the character of the contest between husband and wife, admit her depositions taken by his attorney for use in resisting her application to set aside a decree of divorce, in an action by her attorney to recover the value of his services from the husband, on the ground that they were necessary for her protection, notwithstanding that the defendant offered to agree not to contradict any testimony which should be given as to the nature of the depositions, or as to the time spent, or character of the labor required on plaintiff's part, to meet them.—Clark v. Ellsworth, 442.

8. *Same*—Where the length of time spent is made an important element of recovery in an action for legal services, and the various questions examined by the attorney, and the several papers which he drew, together with the facts involved, have been detailed by him at length, evidence that a much less time than that which he claimed to have spent therein was reasonably necessary for the performance of the services, is admissible.—*Idem*.

EVID. Continued

. 4. **Competency**—See *post*, [17]—*Conclusions*—Testimony that the
cashier of a bank stated "that he felt he was somewhat negligent or careless in the matter," is inadmissible in an action
wherein it is sought to charge the bank with liability by reason
of its alleged negligence in failing to apply funds on deposit
with it in payment of a note sent it for collection, before such
funds were withdrawn. Such statements are incompetent, for
they are merely his conclusions as to what constitutes negligence.—Metropolitan N. Bk. v. Commerc. S. Bak., 682.

Consideration—See *post*, [16].

Contracts—See *post*, [13], [14], [17].

Declarations—See *ante*, [4]; *post*, [10], [11].

5. **Cross-Examination**—A witness, having testified to a conver-
tion had with plaintiff's attorney relative to the mortgage
in question, stated that he had told them what he thought
about it. On cross-examination, it was proper to ask him "what"
he told them.—Hartman Steel Co. v. Hoag & Son, 269.

6. SAME—A question asked on cross-examination which has already
been answered may be properly objected to on that account.—
Waterbury v. C., M. & St. P. R'y Co., 82.

Death—See *post*, [11].

7. **Exclusion**—*Harmless error*—The exclusion of a question asked
plaintiff in an action under Code 1873, section 1539, to recover
a penalty for selling intoxicating liquor to a minor, whether
she had not stated that she intended to get after defendant for
some money, or that she expected to "pull his leg," is not preja-
dicial, even if erroneous.—Fielding v. La Grange, 530.

Harmless Error—See *ante*, [7].

Husband and Wife—See *post*, [26].

7a. **Harmless Error**—In an action for damages resulting from an
assault, the exclusion, on cross-examination of plaintiff, of evidence that plaintiff was suffering from the injury complained
of before the alleged assault, is harmless error, where such
facts are subsequently testified to by other witnesses.—Reizenstein v. Clark, 287.

8. **Impeachment of Witness**—Evidence of the reputation of a
witness for veracity in a place where he lived about a year
before he testified is competent, in the absence of proof of a
subsequent permanent residence at any particular place.—
Schoep v. Bankers Alliance Insurance Co., 854.

9. SAME—Plaintiff, in an action for malicious assault, who testified on his cross-examination that on the trial of a criminal
case against defendant, growing out of the assault, he had

EVID. Continued

not refused to answer a question of defendant's attorney as to whether he was ruptured at the time of the alleged assault, but that an objection to the question was sustained, and that he does not remember all the questions that were asked on the criminal trial, cannot be impeached by reading the answers made by him on such trial.—Reizenstein v. Clark, 287.

10. DECLARATIONS—Declarations of one not a party to a suit can only be used to impeach his credibility as a witness, and not as to substantive proof of matters in issue.—Fielding v. LaGrange, 580.

11. *Rule Applied*—Statements by the alleged minor when he purchased the liquor that he was not a minor, are admissible to impeach him as a witness in an action by a third person, under Code, 1873, section 1539, to recover a penalty for selling intoxicating liquors to a minor, but are not substantive evidence on that question, and do not authorize its submission to the jury in the absence of other evidence thereon. —*Idem.*

12. DESTRUCTION OF EVIDENCE—The mere fact that a witness for defendant had destroyed letters, does not render her testimony as to their contents incompetent, it not being shown that they were destroyed by defendant's procurement, or for a fraudulent purpose.—Clark v. Ellsworth, 442.

13. Interpretation of Contracts—The testimony of parties as to how they understood an unambiguous instrument, is inadmissible.—Pratt v. Prouty, 419.

14. SAME—The acts of the parties to a contract, illustrating their understanding of it, may be shown to aid the court in arriving at a proper interpretation.—*Idem.*

Intoxicating Liquors—See *ante*, [11].

15. Malice—In an action for wrongful seizure of goods under an execution against another firm, testimony by plaintiff that, at the time he bought part of the goods from defendant, he told its credit man that he was starting business at N., was admissible as tending to show that defendant's knowledge that the purchase was made for the plaintiff, rather than the firm of B. & G., and was material as bearing on the question of malice in making the levy.—Gensburg v. Marshall Field & Co., 599.

Parent and Child—See *post*. [16].

16. Parol Evidence—Parol evidence is admissible to show that a note from a child to his father, which is still held by the latter, was given as a mere receipt for an advancement previously made to the maker, under Code 1873, section 2114, providing

EVID. Continued

that the want of consideration for the written contract may be
shown as a defense, except as to negotiable paper transferred
in good faith and for a valuable consideration before maturity.—
Marsh v. Chown, 556.

17. **Parol Variance**—A contemporaneous verbal agreement that
the vendor will procure and have recorded a patent for the
unpatented portion of the land, within sixty days from the date
of the contract, is inadmissible, where the written contract
simply requires the vendor to furnish a good abstract and warranty deed.—Younie, Brown & Martin v. Walrod, 475.

18. TRUSTS—An express trust in real [property cannot be established by oral evidence.—Keller v. Strong. 585.

19. **Personal Transaction**—Under Code 1873, section 8639, providing that no party to any action shall be examined as a witness
in regard to any communication between him and a person
who is dead at the commencement of the examination, against
the survivor of such deceased person, the plaintiff in an action
for personal injuries against the members of a partnership is
incompetent to testify to a conversation with one of the partners who dies before the trial, although his personal representative is not substituted as a party to the action —Salyers v
Monroe, 74.

    Pleading—See *ante,* [1].

20. **Practice**—Evidence of a conversation between the parties to
the action is properly stricken out where the witness fails to
fix the time and shows by his evidence that the conversation
related to another matter than that involved in the suit —
Trimble v. Tantlinger, 665.

21. **Presumption of Death**—Undisputed evidence that a man has
been absent from home and unheard from for seventeen years,
although his family have continued to reside in the same place,
will warrant the conclusion that he is dead; and his wife is
entitled to dower in his lands.—Sherod v. Ewell, 253

22. **Principal and Agent**—See *ante,* [4]; *post,* [27]—Letters in reference
to the transfer of a policy of fire insurance written by an agent
to the company, which notify it of the facts and form the
basis of its communications to him, are admissible in evidence. —
Medearis v. Anchor Mut. F. Ins. Co , 88.

23. SAME—Evidence of a conversation between the insured and an
agent who acted as the medium of communication between
the insurance company and the insured, is admissible,
although he was only a soliciting agent with authority to
organize certain counties and look after local agents —*Idem.*

24. SAME—Testimony given by the insured in an action brought upon a fire insurance policy, that after a conversation with the company's agent he believed that he was insured in defendant company, is harmless error where the liability is fixed by an estoppel, resting upon undisputed testimony.— *Idem.*

25. Privileged Communication — *Husband and Wife* — Where defendant demanded of a husband a mortgage on his wife's homestead, which was in his wife's name, claiming that he was a defaulter, and threatening criminal prosecution unless he gave the mortgage, evidence of the conversation between husband and wife, when he told her of such interview, was admissible, in an action by them for possession of the mortgage, on the ground of duress, and admission of such evidence did not contravene Code 1873, section 3642, forbidding husband and wife divulging confidential communications made by one to the other.—Giddings v. Iowa Savings Bank, 676.

26. Remoteness –Evidence that it was more expensive to ship law books by mail than by express, and that plaintiff had received no law books by express, is too remote to show that plaintiff had not received law books by mail —Names v. Union Ins. Co., 612.

Reputation—See *ante,* [8].

27. Res Gestæ –A statement by an agent that his principal had been negligent, made after the settlement had been effected which constituted the alleged negligence is not a part of the *res gestæ.* –Metropolitan National Bank v. Commercial Savings Bank, 682.

Trusts—See *ante,* [18].

Witness –See *ante.* [8], [10], [11], [12], [19].

EXCEPTIONS – See PRACT. SUP CT [17], [18], [19], [60].

EXECUTIONS—See JUDGMENTS, [6].

1. AGAINST DECEDENT—*Jurisdiction*—Since under McClain's Code section 4321, none but the court which rendered a judgment can award execution against one deceased after its rendition, the judgment creditor cannot enforce payment of the judgment out of the deceased's real estate in a county other than that in which the judgment was rendered.—Hansen's Empire Fur Fact. v Teabout, 360.

2. ATTACK ON SALE—*Expired Judgment Lien*—Since a junior judgment creditor has no right to redeem from an execution sale after ten years from the date of his judgment, an action by him, after ten years have expired, to subject real estate to the payment of his judgment, and to redeem from execution sales because of defects therein, is barred.—*Idem.*

EXECUTORS—See ESTATES; TAXATION, *.

EXEMPTIONS—See LAND. AND TENANT, ¹, ¹a

EXPERTS—See ATTYS. ¹¹, ¹², ¹³, ¹⁴; CRIM. LAW, ⁴³.

EXTENSION—See PAYMENT, ¹, ². ·

EXTORTION—See CRIM LAW, ¹⁵, ¹⁶; INSTR ¹.

EXTRADITION.

1. One extradited under an information containing a single count may be prosecuted under an indictment charging the same offenses in different counts, presenting different ways in which the offense was committed.—State of Iowa v. Rowe, 323.

2. INFORMATION AND INDICTMENT—The treaty of the United States with Mexico provides for the surrender of persons "to justice * * * who being accused of the crimes enumerated," etc. *Held*, that such provision means that he is to be accused in due form of law, and hence it applies to one who is accused on information, as well as one charged by indictment, since an information is one of the forms of accusation prescribed by statute.—*Idem.*

FALSE PRETENSES—See CONTR. ¹⁵; CRIM. LAW, ²⁵.

FALSE REPRESENTATIONS—See ESTOPPEL, ².

FEDERAL COURTS—See REMOVAL OF CAUSES.

FEES—See CONTR ²⁴, ²⁵, ²⁶, ²⁷, ²⁸, ²⁹, ³⁰, ³¹.

FENCES.

1. FENCE VIEWERS—Under Code 1873, section 1490, authorizing hedges as partition fences, but making no provision as to trimming them, the owner thereof is not liable to the adjoining owner for allowing them to grow so that his land is shaded and encroached on thereby. It is a clear case of *damnum absque injuria.*—Kinney v. Kinney, 708.

2. PARTITION FENCE—*Hedges*—Neglect of an adjoining owner to trim a hedge fence standing on part of the division line, is not, within Code 1873, section 1490, providing that if any party neglect to 'repair or rebuild" a partition fence, the aggrieved party may, appeal to the fence viewers, and if they determine the fence is "insufficient," they shall signify it in writing to the delinquent owner and direct him to repair or rebuild.—*Idem.*

FILING—See GEN'L. ASSIGNMENT, ¹, ².

FIXTURES.

REAL AND CHATTEL PROPERTY—*Contracts*—Machinery of such character that, when installed in a building prepared for it, it would become a part of such structure, remained a chattel until accepted by the purchaser, where sold on approval.— Frey-Sheckler Co. v. Iowa Brick Co , 494.

FORECLOSURE—See MTGS ³, ⁴, ⁵, ⁷.

FORFEITURE—See CONTR. ¹²; INS. ¹⁶; RELEASE; SALES, ⁴, ⁵, ⁶. TENDER, ¹.

FORMER ADJUDICATION—See ADJUDICATION, ¹.

FORGERY—See DEEDS.

FORMER JEOPARDY—See CRIM. LAW, ¹⁷, ¹⁸.

FRAUD—CORP. ¹; COUNTIES, ⁴, ⁵; LIM. OF ACT. ²; MTGS. ⁹; PRACT. SUP. CT. ⁵; SALES, ⁷; WARRANTY.

SETTING DEED ASIDE—A widow made deed to F. Part of the land belonged to a minor and a bond was given that the minor should deed upon attaining majority. The land passed to M and the bond was acquired by plaintiff. When the minor attained majority she desired not only to relieve the makers of the bond from liability, but, as well. to perfect the title of M, to whom the land had passed. Plaintiff fraudulently induced her to make deed to him, representing that by so doing she would quiet the title of M. *Held*, the deed should be set aside —Spurrier v. McClintock. 79.

FRAUDULENT CONVEYANCE—See MTGS. ⁶; PRACT. ¹³, ¹⁴.

1. DOWER—*Gifts*—An indebtedness from a husband to his wife, will sustain a chattel mortgage by the former to the latter, as against his creditors, notwithstanding that the indebtedness arose from a loan to him of money which she exacted from him as a condition of her executing a conveyance of her home-stead, and which he consented to allow her at a time when he could make a valid gift to her.—Garner v. Fry, 515.

2. Deeds as Mortgage—*Consideration*—Inadequacy of consideration for a deed is not material on the question of fraud as against the grantor's creditors where the deed, though absolute on its face, was intended as a mortgage.—Cathcart v. Grieve, 830.

3. Evidence—Shortly before judgment was obtained against him, an insolvent debtor deeded land to his uncle, who lived at a remote distance, for an adequate consideration, and at the same time he leased the land of his uncle at a fair rental, and the deed and lease were recorded together. The grantor occupied the land under the lease the succeeding year. The deed, though absolute in form, was in fact a mortgage, and the rent reserved in the lease was intended as additional security. At about the same time, the grantor mortgaged all his property to other creditors, including a chattel mortgage to his uncle.

Small figures refer to subdivisions of Index. The others to page of report.

The uncle knew only of the indebtedness to others, recited in the instruments made to him. No concealment was made of the deed's being a mortgage, and, when questioned, the parties declared it to be a mortgage *Held*, that the conveyance was not fraudulent as to the judgment creditor.—*Idem*.

4. BADGES—Mere relationship between the parties to a transfer is not a badge of fraud as against creditors, which calls for explanation.—*Idem*.

5. FAILURE TO RECORD—The withholding a chattel mortgage from the record in pursuance of an agreement to that effect, does not affect its validity as to pre existing creditors.—Garner v. Fry, 515.

6. Rights of Creditors—A creditor has the right to secure himself, though he knows that in so doing he will delay other creditors in the collection of their claims, unless he participates in a fraudulent intent by the debtor —*Idem*.

7. Secret Trust—*Rental*—The execution of a lease, by a grantee to the grantor, is not a badge of fraud as against the grantor's creditors, when the lease containing such reservation is duly recorded.—*Idem*.

GENERAL ASSIGNMENT—See PRACT. [10].

1. Filing Claims — A verified notice filed with an assignee in insolvency, that one is the owner of a chattel mortgage on the property assigned, giving date, amount, and rate of interest, describing the notes secured by the mortgage, and stating that the entire amount is due and unpaid, amounts to a claim, under Code 1873, section 2120, requiring the facts to be fully stated and verified —Garner v. Fry, 515.

2. OPTIONAL CLAIM BY MORTGAGEE —The court having power to protect all liens and priorities by appropriate orders in the distribution of money derived from the sale of an assignee's property it is optional with the mortgagee whether he will accept such protection or enforce his lien —*Idem*

3. *Waiver*—A chattel mortgagee who presents her claim to an assignee for creditors of a mortgagor, and allows the mortgaged property to remain with the assignee for over two years, and a portion of it to be sold by him under the direction of the court waives her right to foreclose, and must look to the assignee and the courts to protect her preference by virtue of the lien of her mortgage.—*Idem*.

GIFTS—See FRAUD. CONV. [1].

GRADES—ESTOPPEL, [1]; WATERS, [2].

GRAND JURY—See PRACT. SUP. CT. [40].

GUARANTY—See CONTR. [19].

HARMLESS ERROR—See CRIM. LAW, [19], [21], [23]; EVID. [7], ['a]; PRACT. SUP. CT. [21], [22], [23], [24], [25], [26]; Salyers v. Monroe, at pp. 78, 79.

HEIRS—See ESTATES, [4], [5].

HIGHWAYS—See MUNIC. CORP; RAILWAYS, [25], [26], [28].

1. **Damages**—*Obstruction*—The rule that one cannot recover damages for obstruction of his right of way, if by the use of ordinary diligence and effort he could have removed the obstruction at a moderate expense, does not apply where the obstruction to right of way is a low bridge in a county highway, as any attempt to remove the obstruction in such a case would constitute a trespass.—Agne v. Seitsinger, 482.

2. **Dedication**—*Cities and Towns*—Land uninclosed by a railroad company and made use of for over twenty years with adjacent land for a public highway upon which a town has expended money and labor, will be held to have been dedicated to, and accepted by it, unless a formal acceptance of the strip is required by law.—B., C. R. & N. R'y Co. v. Columbus Junction, 110.

3. PRESCRIPTION AND ADVERSE POSSESSION—A town will acquire title by prescription and adverse possession to a strip of land forming part of the right of way of a railroad company, but left uninclosed for many years, and which has been taken into a public highway and used and improved as such, where the property was originally entered upon under agreement with one purporting to represent the company, that it would dedicate the strip for road purposes.—*Idem.*

4. SAME—Such statutes, being intended to protect cities from liability being imposed upon them from land owners in dedicating streets irrespective of necessity therefor, does not prohibit the city from acquiring title to streets in some other way than by a dedication, and an acceptance by ordinance, as by purchase or prescription.—*Idem.*

5. *Construction of Statute*—The provision of Code 1873, section 527, which requires that a dedication of land to public use can be acquired and confirmed only by special ordinances passed for the purpose, does not apply to towns, but to cities, only.—*Idem.*

6. **Evidence**—JURY QUESTION—*Dedication*—Evidence of the execution of an instrument giving, or offering to give, a right of way for a highway, that it was received and filed by the county judge, and that thereafter a highway was established over the *locus in quo* at a time when the jurisdiction to establish highways

was in the county court, is sufficient to require the submission to the jury of the question as to the grant of the highway and the acceptance thereof by the public.—Agne v. Seitsinger, 483.

7. **Reservation in Grant**—A reservation in a grant of land for a highway, of the right to attach fences to a bridge to be erected over a ravine, implies the right to have a cattle-way under the bridge, where the highway and bridge divide a pasture, and without such a way would cut off the access of the cattle to a supply of water.—*Idem.*

8. SAME—One who gave a right of way for a highway, reserving to himself certain privileges, may recover for a denial of such privileges, whether his act of giving was a grant or a dedication.—*Idem.*

9. SAME—A person has a right to have his cattle pass under a new bridge erected in the place of one that had been washed away, where he had had such right as to the old bridge.—*Idem.*

HOMESTEADS—See CONTR. [14]; ESTATES, [4].

1. **Abandonment**—The formation of a purpose by the owner of a homestead to sell the land and invest the proceeds in another home, does not operate as an abandoment of the homestead, under Code, section 2000, permitting the owner to do so, and also entitling him to a reasonable time within which to accomplish such object.—Robinson v. Charleton, 296.

2. RULE APPLIED—In an action to set aside a sheriff's sale on the ground that the land sold was a homestead and exempt, the evidence showed that plaintiff purchased the land in 1887, and occupied it as a home until December 10, 1890, when he moved to another place to educate his children, intending to return to the homestead, which intention he retained until the death of his son, in September, 1893. Thereafter he thought it desirable to sell the homestead and invest the proceeds in another home, though it is doubtful whether this conclusion was reached before or after the sheriff's sale, December 29, 1893. *Held,* that under Code, section 2000, plaintiff was entitled to a reasonable time, after concluding to sell the homestead, to accomplish it, and that in this case such reasonable time had not elapsed, and the sheriff's sale was void.—*Idem.*

3. SAME—That the owner of a farm, which has been occupied as a homestead, talked about exchanging the farm, or said he was not built for farming, or told what he considered the

land worth, does not of itself show a purpose to abandon the homestead.—*Idem*.

4. SAME—The mere fact that the owner of a homestead, who is temporarily absent therefrom, with the intention of returning, votes at the place where he temporarily resides, is not of itself conclusive of an intention to abandon the homestead, though it is strong evidence of abandonment.—*Idem*.

5. *Burden of Proof*—The burden of showing the abandonment of a homestead after the homestead character has once been established, rests upon the one who seeks to subject land to a judgment in his favor, and where the debt for which the judgment is rendered is contracted while the land was occupied as a homestead, so that no credit was extended on the faith of its being subject to the payment of debts, the evidence of abandonment should be more satisfactory —*Idem*.

HUSBAND AND WIFE–See ATT'YS, [5], [6], [7]; BLACKMAIL, [1], [2], [3]; BONA FIDE; CONTR. [14], [15]; FRAUD. CONV. [1]; INTOX. LIQ. [20]; SALES, [4].

HYPOTHETICAL QUESTIONS—See ATT'YS, [10].

ICE—See RAILWAYS, [11], [15].

IMPEACHMENT—See EVID. [8], [9], [10], [11]; JUDGMENTS, [3], [4], [5]; PRACT. SUP. CT. [45].

IMPROVEMENTS—See LAND. AND TENANT, [4].

INCEST—See PRACT. SUP. CT. [20].

INCLUDED OFFENSES–See CRIM. LAW, [24], [30], [31].

INCONSISTENT CLAIMS—See CONTR [8].

INDICTMENT—See CRIM. LAW, [16], [25], [26], [27], [28], [40], [41], [42]; EXTRADITION, [2].

INDORSEMENT—See INS. [1], [2].

INFORMATION—See CONSTR. [1]; EXTRADITION, [1], [2].

INJUNCTIONS—See INTOX. LIQ. [3], [4], [5]; PRACT. [10].

1. **After Appeal**—Under Code 1873, section 3389, providing that an injunction affecting the subject-matter of an action can be granted only by the court before which it is pending, an injunction restraining the taking possession of land in dispute, after an appeal has been taken, can be granted only by the appellate court.—Hyatt v. Clever, 338.

2. **Tax Sale**—An injunction to restrain the sale of town lots for taxes will not be granted although the plaintiff claims to have paid assessments upon the property, where the location of the town plat cannot be exactly fixed, except that it was laid out on the southwest quarter section claimed by the plaintiff, and third persons are in possession of some parts of the village

plat, but the character of their possession does not appear.—
Broderick v. Allamakee County, 750.

8. *Evidence*—In an action to enjoin defendants from selling property at tax sale, when the land is shown to be occupied by others in conjunction with the plaintiff, the latter is put upon proof of his legal title.—*Idem.*

INSTRUCTIONS—See BLACKMAIL, [4]; CRIM. LAW, [1], [19], [24], [29], [30], [31], [34], [35], [36], [37], [46]; INTOX. LIQS. [6], [7], [8], [9], [10], [13]; PRACT. [21]; PRACT. SUP. CT. [27], [30]; RAILWAYS, [21], [30].

1. **Character and Degree of Evidence**—It is improper to charge the jury that the intent with which an act was committed "must be strictly proven." It is misleading, since circumstantial evidence is often sufficient for the purpose.—State of Iowa v. Debolt, 105.

2. **Collating Facts**—An instruction is not objectionable for collating facts instead of charging separately on each point and stating the rule of law applicable thereto, when the method adopted is calculated to better bring the case within the comprehension of the jury.—Medearis v. Anchor Mut. F. Ins. Co., 68.

8. **Conflict**—An instruction authorizing the jury to consider, for the purpose of determining whether a physician employed by defendants to attend an injured employe had apparent authority to employ plaintiff to assist him, the facts that the physician said to plaintiff that the company would pay him for his services and that he was only to assist the company's physician, who was to remain in charge of the case, and that plaintiff was to report the condition of the patient to the company's physician, and to make such reports and have the free use of the telegraph service of the company, is improper and irreconcilable with another instruction correctly stating as the law that, "none of the declarations or statements" of, the company's physician to plaintiff can be considered by the jury as any evidence that he had any authority to employ plaintiff.—Smith v. C. & N. W. R'y Co., 147.

4. **Construed**—In a proceeding for the probate of a will an instruction to the jury that if the testator did not adopt the signature to the instrument as his own after his name was signed for him, it will be "proper" to find that it is not his will, is not objectionable as leaving the nature of the finding upon such facts discretionary with the jury, where, in view of preceding instructions, the word could only have been understood in *the* sense that it was the right or duty of the jury, under such facts, to find there was no will.—In re Estate of Allison, 130.

5. **Exemplary Damages**—An instruction in an action for assault that the jury may award exemplary damages if they find the assault was malicious, and that the amount thereof rested solely in the discretion of the jury, is proper, although the verdict might be reversed as excessive.—Reizenstein v. Clark, 287.

6. **Requesting Instructions**—In an action for malicious assault, failure, in an instruction, to define "malice," or to state that the burden of proving it is on plaintiff, is not error, where no such instruction was asked by defendant.—Reizenstein v. Clark, 287.

INSURANCE—See ESTATES,[4],[5]; EVID. [22], [23], [24], [26]; PRACT. [27].

1. **Additional Premium**—An insurance company is liable upon a policy of fire insurance forwarded to it by its agent, to be indorsed with its consent to a transfer of the policy, when an additional premium was demanded and paid to the agent, although the following day the property was destroyed by fire, and before an indorsement by the company.—Medearis v. Anchor Mut. F. Ins. Co. 88.

2. ESTOPPEL—Where an insurer had written its agent that it could not approve an assignment of a policy to the purchaser of the insured property, unless he agreed to an advanced rate, and instructed him to secure a new note for the rate as advanced, return same, together with policy, when, if found satisfactory, consent to the assignment of the policy would be indorsed thereon, and the agent had procured the advanced rate and followed such instructions, it is estopped to take advantage of the provisions of a policy rendering it void where the legal title to the property was changed, and that an agent could not waive any of the conditions of the policy.—*Idem.*

3. **Appraisement**—See *post*,[22]—*Condition Precedent*—An appraisement and award is a prerequisite to the maintenance of an action on an insurance policy unless such appraisement is waived or submission and award prevented by the company, where the policy provides that the ascertainments and estimates shall be made by the parties, or if they differ, by the appraisers, and that the loss shall not be payable until sixty days after the award of the appraisers has been rendered.—Dee & Sons v. Key City Fire Ins. Co., 167.

4. SAME—*Right of Assured to Appraisement*—An insured has the right to insist that if an appraisement of the amount of damages provided for by the policy is made it shall embrace all property claimed by him to be covered by the policy, although the company denies that it is so covered.—*Idem.*

Small figures refer to subdivisions of Index. The others to page of report.

Ins. Continued

Assessment—See *post*, ⁵, ⁹.

5. NOTICE OF—A mutual insurance company organized under Acts
Sixteenth General Assembly, chapter 108, expressly prohibiting
such companies from receiving premiums or making dividends,
is not within Acts Eighteenth General Assembly, chapter 210,
section 1, providing that in every instance where a fire insurance company takes a note for the "premium" of any policy,
such company shall not declare the policy forfeited or suspended for non-payment of the note, without first giving a prescribed notice. Hence, the failure on part of such mutual
company to give notice which conforms to such statutes is not
material.—Beeman v. Farmers P. Mut. Ins. Asso. 83.

6. NEW CONTRACT—Notice of assessments not having been mailed
within the time after their date required by by-laws, and not
having allowed the insured the full time he was entitled to
in which to make payment, and the payments made after the
time they were due having been retained, the provision in
the receipts that they were given and accepted on condition
that assured was in as good health as when received as a
member of the association (which conditional receipt was not
authorized by the by-laws or otherwise, except that it was
examined and approved by the board of directors, but without record of their action), cannot be asserted to defeat recovery on the certificate of insurance.—Pray v. Life Indemnity
and Security Co., 114.

7. PAYMENT OF INTEREST—A life insurance company will not be
required to collect and pay over interest on a death claim where
the contract of insurance entitles the beneficiary to "the net
proceeds of one full assessment at schedule rates" and there is
no provision in the schedule for assessment for the payment of
interest, but simply for a specific sum for each death, according
to the age of the person assessed.—*Idem.*

8. WAIVER—The reception by a mutual insurance company, after
a loss of part of the property insured, of an assessment which
had become payable before the loss occurred, does not waive a
forfeiture of the policy for non-payment of such assessment,
under a provision of the policy that it shall be null and void in
case of non-payment within a specified time "until" the assessment is paid; as the insured had the right to make the payment
at any time, and the company was bound to accept it, to revive
the policy for the remaining time, as to the other property.—
Beeman v. Farmers P. Mut. Ins. Asso., 83.

9. *Same*—A second assessment by a mutual insurance company
after a failure of a member to pay a prior assessment within
the time required by a provision of the policy, that if any

INS. Continued

member fails to pay his assessment within a specified time after receiving notice thereof his insurance shall be null and void until such assessments are paid, does not estop it to claim that it is not liable on the policy because of the failure to pay the prior assessment.—*Idem.*

10. **Assignment**—*Practice*—A life insurance association against which a beneficiary has recovered judgment cannot ask to be protected against an assignment of a portion of the claim made by the plaintiff when the assignee, although testifying as a witness, did not claim an interest in the case and it does not appear that the company is liable to him, though it is notified by the beneficiary that she has borrowed of the assignee and is directed by her to charge the amount against the policy and retain it for the lender.—Pray v. Life Indemnity & Security Co., 114.

11. **Concurrent**—FRAUD—An insurance company cannot complain in an action upon a policy issued by it, that one whose property has been destroyed by fire, placed additional insurance upon it with another company, and at the time of his application therefor, stated that the property was not insured, where there was no limitation in defendant' policy as to concurrent insurance, since such misrepresentation was not a fraud upon the defendant.—Names v. Union Ins Co , 612.

Declarations—See *post*, [19], [20].

Estoppel—See *ante*, [2].

12. **Evidence**—OFFER OF PROOF OF LOSS—That the proof of loss was offered in evidence in an action upon an insurance policy, both for the purpose of showing that it was made and as tending to show what articles were lost, and their value, is not prejudicial to the defendant company.—*Idem.*

13. *Same*—A witness who testifies that he was at a certain house on the evening before is was destroyed by fire, may state that he had heard that it was said that he burned the property, where in an action on the policy the insurance company alleged that the plaintiff had burned the house, or caused it to be burned.—*Idem.*

14. *Same*—A witness who visited a house some days before, and also on the evening it was destroyed by fire, may testify whether she saw anything to indicate that there was less property in the house on that evening than on her former visit, when the insurance company alleged that the plaintiff removed some of his property from the house, before the fire.—*Idem.*

15. WITNESS—*Competency*—One formerly in the mercantile business, although for some years retired, may testify in an action upon

INS. Continued

an insurance policy as to the value of articles destroyed, and the fact that he is not actually engaged in trade, while affecting the weight of his evidence, is not ground for excluding it.— *Idem.*

16. Forfeiture—*Concealment*—To avoid liability under a policy of insurance providing that it shall be void if the insured has concealed or misrepresented in writing or otherwise any material fact or circumstance concerning the insurance or the subject thereof, or if he has not truly stated his interest in the property, it is not sufficient to show that there were mechanic's liens on the property at the time the policy issued; it must also appear that there was some independent concealment in respect thereto—Greenlee v. Hanover Ins. Co. 481.

17. *Ineffective Mortgage*—A chattel mortgage covering property insured is not such an authorized incumbrance as will avoid the policy, when it was given to obtain money to take up a prior mortgage and discharged eight days later, upon the mortgagee's failure to raise the amount of the loan it was intended to secure.—Weigen v. Council Bluffs Ins. Co. 410.

Fraud—See *ante*, [11].

Mortgages—See *ante*, [17].

Notice—See *ante*, [5], [6].

18. Plea and Proof—*Amendment*—Testimony may be given of the value of an article destroyed by fire, but not included in the proof of loss, in an action on the policy, since the plaintiff has the right to amend to conform to the proof.—Names v. Union Ins. Co., 612.

Practice—See *ante*, [10].

19. Principal and Agent—See *post*, [21]—*Declarations of Agent*—A soliciting agent of an insurance company who has power to take and forward application, receive money, and to reserve fund notes in certain cases, when the certificate of insurance is delivered, has no authority to bind the company by declarations as to the validity of the certificate or as to the rights and liabilities of the company, when not made in the discharge of his duty, as agent in the transaction in question, though he had the policy in his possession when he made the statements.— Schoep v. Bankers Alliance Ins. Co., 354.

20. *Rule Applied*—In an action on a life policy which had been sent to a bank for delivery, but was not delivered before insured died, defendant claimed that it never became a valid

contract. It recited payment by insured of ten dollars, but defendant's soliciting agent testified that the money had never been paid, and that the policy was not to be delivered until the money was paid. *Held*, that it was error to admit evidence of statements by such agent, after insured's death, that insured "had fully supplied the company," that the policy was all right, that the ten dollars payment for which it provided belonged to him, and that whether he received it was none of the company's business.—*Idem.*

Proof of Loss—See *ante*, [12]; *post*, [21], [23], [24].

21. Service of Proof of Loss—*Recording Agent*—The service of proofs of loss upon the recording agent of the insurer, who issued the policy in suit, is sufficient.—Greenlee v. Hanover Ins. Co., 481.

Witness—See *ante*, [16].

22. Waiver—A condition in an insurance policy making an appraisement a prerequisite to the bringing of a suit on the policy is waived where the company refuses to permit an agreement of submission to appraisements to be so changed as to embrace certain property claimed by the insured to be covered by the policy, although the company denies that such property is within the policy.—Dee & Sons v. Key City Fire Insurance Co., 167.

23. Proof of Loss—An action upon a life insurance certificate is not barred for failure to furnish proofs of death of a prescribed form, where the beneficiary applied to the company for blank forms to be filled out, and which were refused on the sole ground that the certificate had been forfeited.—Pray v. Life Indemnity and Security Co., 114.

24. Same—Proofs of loss are waived by an insurance company where the secretary of the company, empowered to waive such proofs, leads the insured to believe that he has done all in that respect that is required, and promises an early payment of the loss.—Dee & Sons v. Key City Fire Ins. Co., 167.

INTENT—See Crim. Law, [16]; Instr. [1].

INTEREST—See Pract. [24].

Judgments—Interest may be allowed on a judgment for costs and attorney's fees from the date of the entry of the judgment (Code 1873), section 2078.—Hoyt v. Beach, 257.

INTERSTATE COMMERCE—See Const. Law.

Small figures refer to subdivisions of Index. The others to page of report.

INTERVENTION—See LAND. AND TENANT, ²; MTGS. ⁸.

INTOXICATING LIQUORS—See CONTR. ²²; CRIM. LAW, ²·³; EVID. ¹⁰, ¹¹; PLEADINGS, ⁶; PLEA AND PROOF, ⁸; PRACT. ², ²⁴.

Applications—See *post*, ¹¹.

Bondsmen—See *post*, ⁴.

Collusion—See *post*, ⁶.

1. **Evidence**—*Sufficiency*—In a prosecution for maintaining a liquor nuisance, the evidence was sufficient to sustain the verdict where it warranted the jury to find that several of the purchasers were persons in the habit of using intoxicating liquors as a beverage, and that their purchases were for such purposes, and that, as to some of them, defendant had reason for so believing, though they represented in each instance that they wanted the liquor for medical purposes.—State of Iowa v. Skillicorn, 97.

2. **SAME**—Intoxicating liquors were sold upon leased premises during the summer and fall of 1895, and during all the years of 1895 and 1896 the place had the reputation of being a place where intoxicating liquors were sold in violation of law. The lessor, who had leased the premises to be lawfully used as a pharmacy, had no actual notice of the sale of liquor until December, 1895, when she canceled the lease, and re-leased the property to another for lawful purposes. She was in the store where the liquors were sold from three to six times per week, but testified that she did not see or hear of liquors being sold therein. *Held*, she "might have known of the sale of intoxicating liquors," within Acts Twenty-fifth General Assembly, chapter 62, section 6, so as to render the property liable for the tax.—David v. Hardin County, 204.

Husband and Wife—See *post*, ¹⁴, ¹⁵.

8. **Injunctions**—A temporary injunction may be granted against a person holding a permit to sell intoxicating liquors, if he keeps or sells the same in his pharmacy contrary to law, under Acts Twenty-third General Assembly, chapter 35, section 2, providing that every permit holder shall be subject to all the proceedings and actions, criminal or civil, whether at law or in equity, authorized by the laws "now" or "hereafter" in force for any violation of "this" act, and the acts for the suppression of intemperance, and any law regulating the sale of intoxicating liquors, and in case of conviction in any proceedings, civil or criminal, all the liquors in his possession, may by order of the court, be destroyed.—McCoy v. Clark, 491.

INTOX. LIQUORS Continued

4. PARTIES—The granting of an injunction against the sale of intoxicating liquors will not prevent the granting of a subsequent injunction against the sale of intoxicating liquors by the sureties on the bond of the person enjoined in the prior action, where the first injunction was not directed against said bondsmen.—Cameron v. Tucker, 211.

5. *Collusion*—An injunction to restrain the sale of intoxicating liquors will not be refused on the ground that an injunction against such sale has previously been obtained by another person, where the prior injunction was fraudulently obtained for the purpose of shielding the liquor seller.—*Idem*.

6. Instructions—*Applicability*—Where the jury were instructed in a prosecution for maintaining a liquor nuisance, that if they found that a person commonly, or frequently, or whenever the opportunity offers, uses intoxicating liquors as a beverage, they would have the right to infer that he was in the habit of so doing, and the evidence showed that several persons purchasing were in the habit of using intoxicating liquors as a beverage, the jury were warranted in so finding, though it did not appear that any of them made such use thereof "whenever the opportunity offers."—State of Iowa v. Skillicorn, 97.

7. *Same*—In a trial for the illegal sale of intoxicating liquors, a reference in the charge to sales to minors is not prejudicial although there is no evidence that any of the purchasers were minors, when such reference was necessary to a full statement of the law, and the question was plainly stated to the jury to be whether purchasers habitually used liquor as a beverage.—*Idem*.

8. CONSTRUCTION—The expression "to use as a beverage is to use as a drink," followed by the statement, "It will be seen, therefore, that, when liquor is not used with intent to either treat, cure, or alleviate some bodily disorder or disease, it is not used for medical purposes," could not have been understood to mean that such liquor was used as a beverage merely because it was taken into the system through the process of "drinking."—*Idem*.

9. *Same*—In a trial for the illegal sale of intoxicating liquors an instruction to the jury that whoever uses any building as a place for selling, or keeping for sale, intoxicating liquors in violation of law, is guilty of the crime of nuisance, and proof of a single sale in a building so used will warrant a conviction, is not objectionable as a charge that a single sale, whether lawful or unlawful, will warrant conviction. The words "single sale" have reference to a sale "in violation of law."—*Idem*.

Small figures refer to subdivisions of Index. The others to page of report.

INTOX. LIQUORS Continued

10. *Same*—An instruction to the jury in a trial for the illegal sale of intoxicating liquors that they should so construe the law as to prevent its evasion, and that no devise, art, or contrivance can avail the defendant if they find there was a substantial violation of the law, is in harmony with Code, section 1554, and not objectionable as leaving the jury to place their own construction upon the law as given in the instructions, and allowing them to hold the law to be other than that given in the instruction.—*Idem.*

11. *Liquor applications*—An instruction to the jury in a trial for the illegal sale of intoxicating liquors, which directs it to take into consideration the applications for the sale of liquor, the habits of the purchaser with reference to the use of ardent spirits, the frequency of the applications, and the amount purchased, in determining whether the law had been violated, sufficiently gives the defendant the full benefit of the proposition that applications made to him are evidence tending to show that the sales were legal.—*Idem.*

12. *Medicinal use*—An instruction given to the jury in a trial for the illegal sale of intoxicating liquors, that "to use as a medicine is to use as a remedy for some disease, or as a medical agent in the treatment thereof" is not objectionable as a charge that if an ailment does not in fact exist, a purchase is unlawful, however honest the belief and purchase of the purchaser. It merely requires that purchases should be in good faith, for medical purposes.—*Idem.*

13. ENUMERATION—An instruction in a trial for the illegal sale of intoxicating liquors, which, without purporting to enumerate all, enumerates certain facts to be taken into consideration in determining whether any of the sales were unlawful to which is added, "and all other matters throwing light thereon," is not objectionable as authorizing the jury to go outside of the testimony.—*Idem.*

Lessor and Lessee—See *ante,* [2].
Medicinal Use—See *ante,* [12].
Minors—See *ante,* [7]; *post,* [27], [28].

14. **Mulct Law**—See *ante,* [2]—BAR—Under section 19 of such law, providing that "whenever any of the conditions of this act shall be violated * * * the bar to proceedings as provided in section 17 hereof shall cease to operate as a bar," where defendant sold intoxicating liquors to plaintiff's husband, causing him to become intoxicated, idle, profligate, and neglectful of his business, and so as to impair him in body and mind, and render him unable to obtain remunerative employment, to plaintiff's damage, there was a violation of the mulct

Small figures refer to subdivisions of Index. The others to page of report.

INTOX. LIQUORS Continued

law, and the bar ceased to operate.—Carrier v. Bernstein Brothers, 572.

15. SAME—Compliance with act Twenty-fifth General Assembly, chapter 62, known as the mulct law, is not a defense to an action by a wife, under Code, 1873, section 1557, for damages for injury to her means of support caused by means of the illegal sale of intoxicating liquor to her husband, or to an action under section 1539 for the penalty for selling intoxicating liquor to an intoxicated person, or to one in the habit of becoming intoxicated.—*Idem.*

16. PHARMACIST'S PERMIT—Under Acts Twenty-fifth General Assembly, chapter 62, section 1, which provide for the assessing of a tax for the selling of liquors against persons, other than registered pharmacists holding permits, such a pharmacist is not liable for the tax, although selling liquor in violation of his permit. A statute which is clearly expressed must be given the effect of the legislative intent as thus expressed.—In re Shonkwiler's Assignment, 67.

17. LESSOR AND LESSEE—See *ante*, ²—A lessor of premises under a lease expressly providing that they shall be used for hotel purposes only, cannot escape liability for a tax for the sale of intoxicating liquors on such premises under an act passed after the execution of the lease, on the ground that the lease was in existence at the passage of such act, where he knew of the sale of liquors on such premises before the tax was levied and took no steps to terminate the lease for violation of its terms.—In re Application of Smith, 199.

18. Mulct Tax—That one who sells intoxicating liquors does not obtain a consent or comply with other provisions of Acts Twenty-fifth General Assembly, chapter 62, imposing a tax against all persons selling intoxicating liquors does not relieve him from liability for such tax, although section 17 provides that after obtaining a written statement of consent the payment of such tax shall on certain conditions bar proceedings under the statute prohibiting the business.—*Idem.*

19. ASSESSMENT OF—Section 1, of Acts Twenty-fifth General Assembly, chapter 62, provides for a tax of six hundred dollars per annum for selling liquor. Section 7, that if on a trial to rebate the tax it appears that sales were not continued for more than six months in the "year" for which the tax was assessed, the total tax for the year may be reduced *pro rata*, and section 9 provides that the board shall at the September meeting levy an annual tax of six hundred dollars, payable semi-annually and that it shall at each regular meeting

INTOX. LIQUORS Continued

     examine the assessment books and levy a tax against such
persons as have not previously been taxed, but that there
shall be "only a *pro rata* tax for the *remainder of the year*,'
depending on the time of the assessment.   The board made
an assessment December 27, in a case where sales had not
continued for six months. *Held*, in view of section 45, Code
1873, providing that, where not repugnant to the context, the
word "year" means the year of our Lord, the said annual
tax assessed should have been rebated to six dollars and
sixty cents, or enough to pay for the time between December
27, 1895, and the end of the year 1895.—David v. Hardin
County, 204.

20.   *Notice of*—No notice of the assessment and levying of a tax on
premises in which intoxicating liquors are sold by a lessee
thereof need be given to the owner under Acts Twenty-fifth
General Assembly, section 11, which contemplates that the
person liable to the tax shall appear and pay the same without notice.—In re Application of Smith, 199.

21.   REBATE—Under Acts Twenty-fifth General Assembly. chapter
62, section 7, providing that in case sales of intoxicating liquors
have not continued for more than six months of the year for
which the taxes are assessed, the total tax for the year may be
reduced *pro rata*, the year referred to is the calendar year, and
therefore it is immaterial that sales have not continued for
more than six months before levy of the tax. If, therefore, a
party sells liquors for more than six months of the calendar
year 1895, and a mulct tax is levied on him at the September
meeting of that year, he can have no rebate from the payment
of six hundred dollars for the year 1895.—Engelthaler v. Linn
County, 293.

22.   *Jurisdiction*—The district court has no jurisdiction to determine priorities of liens on appeal from a decision of the
board of supervisors in proceedings under Acts Twenty-
fifth General Assembly, chapter 62, section 8, to assess property on the ground that intoxicating liquors were sold on
the premises, as the board of supervisors had no such authority.—David v. Hardin County, 204.

23.   *Same*—The board of supervisors has no jurisdiction to determine priority of liens on property listed for assessment, on
the ground that intoxicating liquors are sold on the premises
under the provisions of Acts Twenty-fifth General Assembly,
chapter 62, section 3—*Idem*.

24.   *Same*—Acts Twenty-fifth General Assembly, chapter 62, section 9, providing that, if a tax for selling intoxicating

liquors on premises be not levied at the September meeting of the board of supervisors, it shall be levied for a *pro rata* amount of tax for the remainder of the year, does not authorize the board to levy a *pro rata* tax at a September meeting.—Engelthaler v. Linn County, 293.

Parties—See *ante*, [4].

Pharmacists—See *ante*, [5], [16].

25. **Permit**—See *ante*, [5], [16].—An order under the Iowa statutes granting a permit to sell intoxicating liquor confers no property right, and amounts to no more than the mere privilege to sell, under certain conditions, granted in the exercise of the police power of the state —McCoy v. Clark, 491.

Rebate—See *ante*, [21], [22], [23], [24].

26. **Sales**—See *ante*. [1], [14], [15].—PURCHASE BY THIRD PERSON—In an action by a wife, under Code 1873, section 1557, for damages for the sale of intoxicating liquors to her husband, the fact that the liquor drank by the husband was bought by other persons, does not preclude a recovery.—Carrier v. Bernstein Brothers, 572.

27. SALES TO MINORS—The honest belief of defendant, justified by appearances, is not a defense to an action under Code 1873, section 1539, to recover a penalty for selling intoxicating liquor to a minor.—Fielding v La Grange, 580.

28. *Directed Verdict*—It is not error to direct a verdict for plaintiff in an action for the statutory penalty for selling liquor to a minor, where the minority of the purchaser, which was the only question in issue, was testified to by two unimpeached witnesses, and the only evidence that he was not a minor was the statements he signed when he purchased the liquor, in which he claimed he was of age.—*Idem.*

Taxation—See *ante*, [18], [19], [20].

JOINDER—See BLACKMAIL, [1]; PLEADING, [2]; PRACT. [34].

JUDGMENTS—See ASSIGNMENT; INTEREST; LIMITATION OF ACT. [3]; PRACT. [6], [9], [22], [35]; PRACT. SUP. CT. [3], [8], [14], [46].

1. **Construed**—*Effect*—A decree in a suit in which plaintiff asks, as against all defendants, a judgment of foreclosure, is good to some extent as against all the defendants, in a proceeding not regularly attacking it, but expressly ignoring or denying its existence; the entry being entitled against all the defendants, the decree reciting due and legal service on them, adjudging them in default, finding that plaintiff is entitled to foreclose as

Small figures refer to subdivisions of Index. The others to page of report.

VOL. 104 Ia—51

prayed for, and ordering the land sold, though personal judgment is given only against one, and his right of redemption
alone is cut off.—Day v. Goodwin, 374.

2. SAME—*Boundaries*— Surveyors were commissioned to locate the
corner and boundary line common to four sections, which was
the only issue raised by the pleadings. The report located, not
only the corner and lines stated, but also the quarter sections.
The court found the report correct and confirmed it as to the
line and corner in dispute, and rendered judgment establishing
the latter as shown by the report. *Held*, that such judgment
did not affect a quarter section corner in one of the four sections which had been established by the general government
survey, and recognized by all parties interested.—Muecke v.
Barrett, 413.

3. Impeachment—A recital in a decree of foreclosure that defendant appeared by attorney, who was her husband, is conclusive
as to such appearance where the only evidence to show the
recital erroneous is testimony by the husband, who is also a
party, that she did not appear or answer, and that he knew she
did not, because she told him so, and he filed the answer himself, where it is not alleged that he had no authority to do so.—
Willenburg v. Hersey, 699.

4. EVIDENCE—A contention that a party defendant in a foreclosure proceeding was not served and did not appear in the
action, although the decree rendered recites such appearance, is not established by a paragraph therein providing
that the cause be "continued as to the other defendants for
service," where there were other defendants than the party
whose appearance is denied.—*Idem*.

5. *Same*—The recitals of a decree cannot be contradicted by
extrinsic evidence which is not clear and positive.—*Idem*.

6. Lien—EXECUTION—As between lien holders, the lien of a judgment ends after ten years, and though execution may be levied
after that period, the right so to levy is a barren one.—Hansen
v. Teabout, 869

7. *Rendition*—A judgment is not rendered so as to constitute a
lien from the "time of such rendition," within the meaning
of Code, section 3801, until it is entered on the records of the
court as required by section 3784, although a form of judgment has been signed by the judge and indorsed "Filed" by
the clerk.—Callanan v. Votruba, 672.

JUDICIAL NOTICE—See PLEADING, [7].
JURISDICTION—See COUNTIES, [1]; ESTATES, [4]; EXECUTIONS, [1];
INTOX. LIQ. [22], [22]; PRACT. [28]; JUSTICE OF THE PEACE, [1].

JURORS—See CRIM. LAW, [5], [6].
JURY QUESTION—See HIGHWAYS, [4]; INTOX. LIQ. [17], [20]; PARTNER-
SHIP, [3]; PRACT. [22]; RAILWAYS, [4], [16], [17] [18], [19].
JUSTICES—See APPEAL; ATTYS, [15]; CONTR. [23], [25], [26], [27], [28], [29], [30], [31].

JUSTICE OF THE PEACE.

1. **Appeal**—*Remittitur*—Plaintiff in an action in a justice's court
   may at any time before judgment reduce his claim below the
   amount essential to the appellate jurisdiction of the district
   court, and the error of the justice in rendering judgment for a
   larger amount does not confer appellate jurisdiction upon the
   district court.—Young v. Stuart, 597.

2. **Record**—*Parol Variance*—A record of the proceedings before a
   justice of the peace, which shows an offer by the defendant,
   made in writing, to confess judgment in favor of the plaintiff
   for a certain sum, can neither be supported or contradicted by
   affidavit.—Sloss v. Bailey, 696.

3. **Tender**—A transcript of the record of a case tried before a justice of the peace, which recites an offer of judgment made by
   the defendant to the plaintiff, need not show that the plaintiff
   was in court when the offer was made, since it might be given
   to an attorney or agent acting for the plaintiff in the prosecution of the suit.—*Idem.*

LACHES—See ESTOPPEL, [2]; PRACT. [17]; REFORMATION, [1].
LAND SALES—See CONTR. [13].

LANDLORD AND TENANT—See RAILWAYS, [10].

1. **Lien**—EXEMPTION—*Burden of Proof*—Though the burden of
   proof is upon the landlord to show that property distrained was
   owned by the lessee, and used in the demised premises, under
   Code, 1873, section 2017, the one who asserts that the lien does
   not attach, by reason of the property being exempt, must
   prove such fact.—Hays v. Berry, 455.

1a. **Landlord's Lien**—EXEMPTION FROM—In Code 1873, section
   2017, reading, "a landlord shall have a lien for his rent upon
   all crops grown upon the demised premises, and upon any
   other personal property of the tenant which has been used upon
   the premises during the term, and not exempt from execution,"
   the words "not exempt from execution," refer only to "other
   personal property," and not to "crops grown upon the demised
   premises," and no part of said crops is exempt from the lien.—
   Hipsley v. Price, 282.

2. INNOCENT PURCHASERS—Want of notice on behalf of *the*
   vendee of property sold by a lessee, that it was subject to a

---

Land, and Ten. Continued

landlord's lien does not divest the lien, nor afford the purchaser protection against it.—Hays v. Berry, 455.

8. **Intervention by Landlord**—In an action by a mortgagee of chattels against a sheriff who has sold the chattels on attachment by a landlord for rent, the landlord can intervene, and assert his interest in the property, whether the attachment was valid or not.—Hipsley v. Price, 282.

4. **Removal of Improvements**—A lease for a certain term, expiring March 1, 1894, provided that the lessor, at the expiration of the lease, should pay for improvements placed on the lot, what they were reasonably worth to tear down, and for arbitration if the parties could not agree, or the lessee might remove the improvements. On February 1, 1894, the lessee attempted to agree with the lessor as to the amount to be paid, and failed. On February 10 the lessee asked for an arbitration. An attempt to arbitrate extended to April 10, when, without the lessee's fault, it failed. The lessee vacated the premises in February, and notified the lessor of such fact March 1, and removed such improvements within a reasonable time after April 10, 1894. *Held*, that the lessee was not liable for rent from March 1, 1894, to the time of his removal.—Vorse v. Des Moines Marble and M. Co., 541.

5. **Taxes**—Acts Twenty-first General Assembly, chapter 168, sections 17, 18, provide that when the owner of any lot, the assessments against which are embraced in a certificate for street improvements, shall promise in writing on the certificates that, in consideration of the right to pay in installments, he will waive any illegality, and will pay the same with interest, he shall be subject to the provisions of the act authorizing such payments in installments. *Held*, that where a lease of a lot provided that the lessee would pay all assessments for street improvements levied during the term, the lessee could not, as between him and the lessor, extend the time of payment by executing such writing.—*Idem*.

6. SAME—*Maturity*—Where the assessments were made during the last year of the lessee's term, it could not, by executing such promise, evade liability for such installments after the first.—*Idem*.

7. *Principal and Surety*—The payment by the lessor of the amount of a street paving assessment levied against the property during the term is not a condition precedent to an action by him to recover the amount thereof from the lessee, under a provision of the lease requiring the latter to pay such assessments, as the rule that a surety has no right of

action against his principal until he has paid the debt, does not apply.—*Idem*.

8.   *Same*—It is not a valid objection to the right of the lessor to maintain a suit for the amount of assessments not paid by the lessee that the lessor is not the real party in interest, because not primarily liable.—*Idem*.

LARCENY—See CRIM. LAW, [23], [23].

LAW OF CASE—See CRIM. LAW, [46]; PRACT. SUP. CT. [31], [32].

LAW AND EQUITY—See PRACT. [25], [36], [37], [38].

LEASES—See CONTR. [10], [11], [12]; FRAUD. CONV. [7]; INTOX. LIQ. [17]; MECHANIC'S LIEN, [1], [6].

LEGACY—See WILLS, [1].

LIBEL AND SLANDER—See PRACT. SUP. CT. [44].

1.   **Evidence**—Testimony that one of the witnesses for the plaintiff in an action for slander stated that the plaintiff could thank him for information concerning the slanderous words is immaterial, since it does not tend necessarily to show bias or prejudice on the part of the witness.—Trimble v. Tantlinger, 665.

2.   SAME—In an action for slander, evidence that the witness was present at a conversation between the plaintiff and defendant, but did not hear the actionable words alleged to have been spoken, is inadmissible as not amounting to a statement that the defendant did not speak the words charged.—*Idem*.

8.   **Plea and Proof**—Special damages need not be alleged nor proved in an action for slanderous words alleged to have been spoken, which are actionable *per se*.—*Idem*.

LIENS—See GENL ASSIGNMENT, [2]; JUDGMENT, [6], [7]; LAND. AND TENANT. [1], [2]; STREET R'YS. [1], [2].

LIMITATION OF ACTIONS—See ESTATES, [2], [3]; EXECUTIONS, [2].

1.   **Certiorari**—The limitation prescribed by Code, 1873, section 3224, providing that no writ of *certiorari* shall be granted after twelve months have elapsed from the time the board has, as alleged, exceeded its proper jurisdiction, does not commence to run against the writ complaining of a street paving assessment, until the assessment is made, although the objections to the assessment are based on irregularities in the preliminary proceedings.—Polk v. McCartney, 567.

2.   **Deceit**—An action for deceit in the sale of land is in tort, and barred in five years after the discovery of the fraud.—Harrison v. Palo Alto County, 883.

8.   **Judgments**—*Filing Claims*—A judgment against one who has since deceased may be enforced within ten years from the

date of its recovery, against the real estate upon which it is a lien, without filing it as a claim against the estate.—Hansen's Empire Fur Factory v. Teabout, 360.

4. *Same*—An action to subject decedent's real estate to the payment of judgments rendered before his death and to redeem from execution sales thereof because of alleged defects cannot be maintained after the expiration of ten years from the rendition of the judgment declared upon.—*Idem.*

LOTTERIES—See CONTR. [17], [18].
MALICE—See EVID. [15]; PLEAD. [4].

MECHANICS' LIEN.

1. **Assignment**—*Notice*—The assignee for value of a lease which is prior to a mechanic's lien by reason of the fact that the assignor took the same without notice of the lien is protected to the same extent the assignor would be, notwithstanding any actual knowledge such assignee may have had.—Floete v. Brown, 154.

2. **Estoppel by Fraud of Purchaser**—Where materials for improvements were furnished to one in possession of land on his false representation that he owned the land, or had an interest therein to which a lien could attach, and he afterwards acquired a life estate therein, and more materials were thereafter furnished under the same contract, a lien for all the materials attached to the life estate—*Idem.*

3. **Priorities**—*Independent buildings*—McClain's Code, section 3317, sub-division 4, provides that, where a mechanic's lien has attached for a building erected on mortgaged land, the court may order such building to be separately sold, and the purchaser may remove the same; but that if, in the discretion of the court, the buildings should not be sold, the proceeds of sale of the whole premises shall be ratably distributed between the mortgagee and the holder of the lien, and "that, in case the premises do not sell for more than sufficient to pay off the prior mortgage or other liens, the proceeds shall be applied on the prior mortgage or other liens." *Held*, that the holder of the mechanic's lien on the building has a right to priority on such building, in every case where the court shall find as a fact that such building can be removed without material injury to the security of the earlier lien holder, but where no such finding is made, the land must be sold, and the purchase price applied first in payment of the prior incumbrance.—Tower v. Moore, 345.

4. CONSTRUCTION OF STATUTE—McClain's Code, section 3817, subdivision 4, prescribing the manner in which mortgaged premises on which there is a subsequent mechanic's lien shall be subject to the payment of both liens, is merely a statement in express terms of the law with reference to priority of liens as it existed in judicial interpretation at the time the statute was passed.—*Idem.*

5. LEASE—Where a lease of a life estate was made before the statement of a mechanic's lien for materials furnished prior to the lease, was filed, and after the expiration of the time during which the statute protects such liens without statements, and the lessee had no actual notice of the mechanic's lien, the lien of the lessee is superior to the mechanic's lien.—Floete v. Brown, 154.

MINORS—See INTOX. LIQ. [17], [28].

MISJOINDER—See BLACKMAIL, [1]; PLEAD [2]; PRACT. [24].

MORTGAGES—See CONSTR. [2]; CORP. [1]; FRAUD. CONV. [1]; GENL. ASSIGN. [2]; INS. [17]; PLEDGES.

1. **Consideration**—An existing indebtedness is ample consideration, as between the debtor and creditor, for the execution of a mortgage securing its payment —Johnston & Son v Robuck, 528.

2. PARTNERSHIP—Existing indebtedness is ample consideration for the execution of a mortgage by a firm, of which the debtor is a member, securing its payment, as between the mortgagee and the members of the firm.—*Idem.*

3. **Chattel Mortgages**—CONVERSION—A chattel mortgagee who takes possession of the property before the happening of any of the contingencies which give him the right to take possession, is guilty of conversion.—*Idem.*

4. FORECLOSURE—A chattel mortgage executed to secure a debt past due, may be foreclosed *eo instante*, on delivery.—*Idem.*

5. *Private Sale*—A chattel mortgagee of a stock of goods may, if he acts in good faith and with ordinary prudence, sell the property at retail, under a provision of the mortgage authorizing to sell at private sale.—*Idem.*

6. **Creditors**—*Fraud*—A creditor whose claim is directed to be paid from the proceeds of a stock of goods, by the terms of a mortgage on the property, executed to a trustee for that purpose, is entitled to the fund as against general creditors, although a previous chattel mortgage alleged to be fraudulent had been executed in her favor, which was left unfiled for about two years, but under which she made no claim.—Miller v. Bracken, 648.

7. **Foreclosure**—OWNER OF ONE NOTE—*Protection of*—A land owner agreed that if an agent for wire fencing should furnish him a purchaser for his land at a certain price, he would purchase a fence from the agent. The purchaser was obtained, and an agreement was made for building the fence, and one of the notes for the price of the land was for the exact contract price of the fence. The notes were all secured by a mortgage on the land. *Held*, that a decree was justified, finding the agent to be the owner of the note given for the price of the fence, and entitled to the protection of said mortgage.—Cooper v. Mohler, 301.

8. INTERVENTION—The holder of one of several notes secured by the same mortgage, which is entitled to a priority over the other notes, is entitled to intervene in an action for the foreclosure of a mortgage, under Code 1873, section 2683.—*Idem.*

9. **Priority**—RECORDING—*Notice*—Where the vendee of land, on the day on which it was conveyed to her, executed a mortgage thereon to a loan company for a part of the price, and also a mortgage to her vendor for the balance, and such deed and both mortgages were filed for record on the same day; first, the mortgage to the loan company; next, the deed to the mortgagor; and last, the mortgage to her vendor, such mortgage to the loan company was entitled to priority, in the absence of notice otherwise, over that of the vendor, the holder of which was chargeable with all the knowledge the record imparted.—Higgins v. Dennis, 605.

MULCT LAW—See INTOX. LIQ. [14], [15], [16], [17], [18], [19], [20], [21], [22], [23], [24], [25].

MUNICIPAL CORPORATIONS—See CONTRACTS, [19], [20]; HIGHWAYS, [2], [3], [4], [5]; PRACT. SUP. CT. [26].

Public Improvement—HIGHWAYS—*Notice*—A public notice for bids for a street improvement is fatally defective where it fails to state when the work is to be done and the proposals acted upon, as required by Acts Twenty-third General Assembly, chapter 14, section 3, and does not specify the "extent of the work," as required by the section, except that it states that the work is to be done on certain "alleys" in a block, it appearing that the municipal authorities did not correctly understand what was included in the terms "alleys."—Polk v. McCartney 567.

MURDER—See CRIM. LAW, [10], [34], [35], [36], [37].

NEGLIGENCE—See PRACT. [21]; RAILWAYS, [11], [12], [13], [14], [15], [17], [18], [19].

NEW TRIAL—See Crim. Law, [28]; Pract. Sup. Ct. [7], [28], [40].

1. An order entered in a proceeding by an administrator to recover property alleged to belong to the estate which directs the return of a sum of money with interest, will be vacated where the administrator's petition asked for the return of a note.—In re Behren's Estate, 29.

2. **Contempt**—While a proceeding to punish for contempt is in its nature criminal, the provisions of the Code 1873 as to new trials in criminal cases do not apply, but such new trials may be granted under the statutes governing new trials in civil actions.—State of Iowa v. Stevenson, 50.

8. **Newly Discovered Evidence**—Testimony of plaintiff that he had bought books in the fall of 1890, is not such a surprise to defendant as to allow him a new trial to present newly discovered evidence contradicting such statement, where on a previous trial plaintiff had testified that he had purchased books after the spring of 1890, and counsel for the defendant had, before the trial, read depositions to that effect, and defendant had presented evidence on the trial as to the purchase of such books.—Names v. Union Ins. Co. 612.

4. **Same**—In a proceeding to punish for contempt, in violating an injunction against the maintaining of a liquor nuisance, defendant applied for a new trial for newly discovered evidence, and because that he had been advised by an attorney that such injunction had been dissolved. The alleged newly discovered evidence consisted of a package of applications for the purchase of intoxicating liquor, which had been used by an employe, who was a registered pharmacist, but whose certificate did not authorize him to do business at the place kept by defendant; and it appeared that they might have been produced on the trial with little effort. It also appeared that defendant had been informed by another attorney that the injunction was in force as against him, though not as against the building, and knew that he was carrying on such business in violation of law. *Held*, that such application was without merit, and should have been denied, and that had he acted in good faith, and upon the advice of counsel, it would constitute no defense to the contempt charged.—State of Iowa v. Stevenson, 50.

5. **Same**—A motion for a new trial on the ground of newly discovered evidence, contained affidavits of two persons, one of whom was present at the trial, that a witness for the plaintiff, who had testified to hearing defendant speak the slanderous words sued on, had stated before trial that he could

do defendant no harm nor plaintiff any good, and that he never heard defendant assail plaintiff's character or his business, and that the suit was brought for spite. The statements were all specifically denied by counter affidavit, and the witness' testimony at the trial was corroborated. *Held,* that the discretion of the trial court was not abused by the refusal of a new trial, and that the matter asserted amounted to no more than an impeachment.—Trimble v. Tantlinger, 665.

6.   DISCRETION—It is not error to deny a new trial on the ground of newly discovered evidence showing that witnesses for the successful party made statements out of court at variance with their testimony, where such testimony is cumulative — *Idem.*

NOTICE—See CONTR. [20]; DEEDS; INS. [5], [6]; INTOX. LIQ. [20]; MECHANIC'S LIEN, [1]; MTGS. [9]; MUNIC. CORP; PRACT. [13]; PRACT. SUP. CT. [34], [35], [36], [37].
NUNC PRO TUNC ORDERS—See PRACT. [26].
OBJECTIONS—See PRACT. [15]; PRACT. SUP. CT. [17], [18], [19], [28], [29], [40], [41], [45].
OBSTRUCTIONS—See HIGHWAYS, [1].

OFFICERS—See CONTR. [22], [25], [26], [27], [28], [29], [30], [31]; PRACT. [5].

Peace Officers—*Who are not*—A deputy marshal of a city of a second class is not a peace officer within the meaning of Acts Twenty-third General Assembly, chapter 43, section 6, designating those entitled to compensation from the county for services rendered in the arrest and commitment of vagrants; neither is he one within section 4109, Code 1873, which makes the marshal such an officer —Twinam v. Lucas County, 231.

ORIGINAL PACKAGE—See CONST. LAW, [2], [3], [4].
PARENT AND CHILD—See ADVANCEMENT; EVID [16].
PAROL VARIANCE—See EVIDENCE, [16], [17]; JUSTICES, [2].
PARTIES—See ADJUDICATION, [1]; INTOX. LIQ. [4]; PRACT. [22], [27], [31].
PARTITION—See PRACT [11], [28], [29].
PARTITION FENCE—See FENCES, [1], [2]

PARTNERSHIP—See MTGS [2]

1.   Banks—DUTY OF CASHIER—It is the duty of a partner in a banking business, to whom is left the active management of the business, to act in good faith, and with entire honesty, in transacting all the business of the bank, and to exercise as high a degree of care and skill as is generally exercised by business men, in the management of such business but he is not liable for honest errors in judgment, nor for the failure to take the utmost precaution possible, in making investments for the bank —Exchange Bank of Leon v. Gardner, 176.

2.   RULE APPLIED to a case where an attempt was made to incorporate a bank under Iowa law which was never so incorporated, though it was, for a time, managed according to the articles of incorporation. The bank had a large amount of idle money on which it was paying interest and one partner acting as cashier, bought Kansas City paper which proved almost wholly worthless. While some inquiries were made, more thorough ones would have disclosed the truth. The president knew or should have known that outside investments were being made, and no objection was made to the practice.—*Idem.*

8.   Evidence—The firm of B. & G. was in business at N., and several months before its failure, bought merchandise and shipped considerable quantities thereof to plaintiff, at several different places where they were sold at less than cost. A part of the goods were shipped to other addresses, although all was received by him. At one place he sold under an assumed name, and was assisted by a member of the firm. A portion of the money derived from such sales was used in purchasing the goods in controversy. The firm had a store at D. in which plaintiff took a great interest. When asked the reason of the sales, he said that trade was dull, and they were closing out their stock at M., and, when applying for a license with B. a member of the firm, to sell at auction, stated that he was in partnership with B. in selling out the goods. *Held*, that an inference of a partnership relation between plaintiff and B. and G might be drawn from such circumstances and the question should properly have been submitted to the jury.—Gensburg v. Marshall Field & Co., 599.

PAYMENTS.

1.   EXTENSION—Where the payment of an interest coupon note is extended more than thirty days in all, from time to time, pending negotiation for a new loan from the holder of the note, which is finally refused, and the holder notifies the payee that the note must be paid by the first of April, the time of extension expires with the thirty-first day in March; and under a clause, contained in the principal note, that upon a failure to pay any of said interest within thirty days after due, the holder may elect and consider the whole note due, the holder may, on April 1, if the extended note is unpaid, declare the principal note and all the interest coupon notes due, and sue thereon.—Van Vechten v. Jones, 436.

2.   *Same*—Payment of an interest coupon, which will prevent the holder from foreclosing under the provision of his mortgage giving him the right to foreclose if any interest coupon remains unpaid thirty days after maturity, is not effected by depositing the amount thereof in bank other than that at which the principal note is payable, subject to the holder's order, and instructing the bank to notify him of the deposit, and request him to forward the coupon.—*Idem*.

PEACE OFFICERS—See OFFICERS.

PERMIT—See INTOX. LIQ. **.

PHARMACISTS—See INTOX. LIQ ¹⁴.

PLATS—See DEDICATION, ¹, ², ³, ⁴; INJUNCTION, ².

PLEADING—See CRIM. LAW, ¹⁰; NEW TRIAL, ¹; PRACT. SUP. CT. ¹⁴; RAILWAYS, ²¹.

1. **Estoppel**—An estoppel which is not pleaded cannot be taken advantage of.—Sherod v. Ewell, 253.

2. SAME—If the fact that a duty required by law involves difficulty or expense would be a legal excuse for failure to meet the requirement, it must be pleaded as a matter of affirmative defense, to be available.—Kingsbury v. C., M. & St. P. R'y Co., 68.

2a. SAME—In an action to recover damages for the killing of a horse which entered the right of way at a point where the company had a right to fence, a general denial presents the issue whether the railroad had a right to fence at the point in question, and not whether it had legal excuse for failing to do so. The last is matter in estoppel which must be specially pleaded.—*Idem*.

3. **Joinder of Causes**—A complaint in an action to recover damages for an alleged unlawful arrest for failure to obey a subpoena brought against the justice who issued the subpoena and the warrant, the parties who served them, the sureties on the official bond of the justice and one who filed an affidavit in reference to which the subpoena was issued, which complaint charges in one count oppression, annoyance and extortion, and in another a conspiracy to cheat and defraud, is not, after a dismissal of the suit as to the sureties, demurrable for misjoinder of causes of action and misjoinder of parties, under Code 1873, section 2630.—Chambers v. Oehler, 278

4. **Malice**—An allegation in a petition in an action for the conversion of property levied upon, which avers that the acts of the sheriff and defendant "were done for the purpose of oppressing plaintiff, and compelling him to surrender his property without receiving compensation therefor," sufficiently charges "malice," although the word is not expressly used.—Gensburg v. Marshall Field & Co., 599.

---

5. **Motion to Strike**—*Waiver*—The remedy for the addition to a petition by amendment, of a count which is inconsistent with a count already set up in the petition is by motion to strike, and the objection is waived by answering —Keller v. Strong, 595.

6. **Plea and Proof**—The averment in a petition in an action to recover damages for the statutory penalty for illegal sales of intoxicating liquor, that the sales were made in the spring and summer of a certain year, is sufficiently definite as to time.—Carrier v. Bernstein Brothers, 572.

7. **Repetition**—*Judicial Notice*—The court will grant a motion to strike out an answer when the matter contained therein is the same in substance as the allegations in former answers to which demurrers have been sustained, although it contains a preliminary statement withdrawing all former answers and amendments. The court still takes judicial notice that the withdrawn pleadings stated matter vulnerable to demurrer.—Hoyt v. Beach, 257.

8. **Striking off**—*Discretion*—Where at the close of the evidence, defendant filed a fourth amendment to his answer, largely repeating what he had previously alleged, it was not an abuse of discretion to strike it out.—Marsh v. Chown, 556.

9. SAME—It is not error to strike out an amendment to an answer alleging want of dilligence in collecting collateral security on the part of the plaintiff, where such fact had already been sufficiently alleged.—Hartman Steel Co. v. Hoag & Son, 269.

10. SAME—It is not error to sustain a motion to strike an amend- ment to the petition which alleged matter, not in support of the cause of action, but in reply to matter alleged in defend- ant's cross petition.—Wood v. Brown, 124.

PLEA AND PROOF—See CRIM. LAW, [13]; INSURANCE, [18]; LIBEL, [1]; QUIETING TITLE, [2].

1. Evidence that plaintiff in an action to recover the value of horses and other property lost in transportation over defend- ant's road did not have time to read the shipping contract before signing it, is inadmissible under an allegation that, after the property was loaded, defendant's agent presented the contract to plaintiff, representing it to be a pass to carry him to the place of delivery and requesting him to sign it.—Faust v. C. & N. W. R'y Co., 241.

2. SAME—Under Code 1873, section 2729, which provides that a party shall not be compelled to prove more than is necessary to entitle him to the relief asked, it is only necessary, in an

PLEA AND PROOF Continued TO PRAC.

action for assault, to prove that it was unlawful, although the petition alleged that it was wanton and malicious.—Reizenstein v. Clark, 287.

8. SAME—Evidence that sales were made by the defendant's employes is admissible under the averment in a petition for damages, or for the statutory penalty prescribed for the illegal sale of liquor, that the defendant sold the liquor.—Carrier v. Bernstein Brothers, 572.

PLEDGES—See CORPOR. ⁴, ⁷.

RIGHT OF PLEDGEE OF MORTGAGE—One to whom a chattel mortgage is assigned as collateral security is not required to accept an offer by the purchaser of the mortgaged property, at a sale under a junior lien, to give security on such property.— Hartman Steel Co. v. Hoag & Son, 269,

PRACTICE—See APPEAL; BLACKMAIL, ¹; CONTR. ¹⁰, ¹¹; COSTS. ¹, ⁵, ⁶; CRIM LAW, ⁷, ⁹, ¹⁹, ²²; ESTATES, ¹, ³, ⁴, ⁶; EVID. ³, ³, ⁷, ²⁰; EXECUTION, ¹, ²; GEN'L ASSIGNMENT, ⁹, ²; INS ³, ⁴, ¹⁰; INTEREST; INTOX. LIQ ²⁴; LAND. AND TENANT. ⁹, ⁷, ⁹; LIBEL. ²; LIM. OF ACT. ⁴; NEW TRIAL, ¹, ⁵, ⁶, ⁶; PLEAD. ⁵, ³, ⁹, ¹⁰; PRACT ¹⁷; PRACT. SUP CT. ²⁰, ⁴⁰, ⁴¹; QUIETING TITLE, ²; RECEIVERS, ¹, ², ³, ⁴, ⁵, ⁶, ⁷.

1. Action--See *post*, ¹⁷—*After Appointment of Receiver*—An action may be maintained against an insolvent incorporation notwithstanding the appointment of a receiver, when it has not been enjoined by the court from the exercise of its corporate powers, and the receiver is not a necessary party to the action, and when no relief is asked against him.—Weigen v. Council Bluffs Ins. Co., 410.

2. PENALTY—*Venue*—Under Code 1873, section 1539, providing that persons who sell intoxicating liquors to intoxicated persons or habitual drunkards, shall forfeit a certain sum for each offense, to the school fund of the county, to be collected in an action brought by any citizen in the county, one-half of said amount to go to the informer, such action need not be brought in the county where the liquor was sold.—Carrier v. Bernstein Bros., 572.

8. Adjudication—*Collateral Attack*—The defendant in an action upon a promissory note brought by a receiver cannot question the appointment of the plaintiff on the ground that, as clerk of the court, he had approved his own bond, when it was adjudged sufficient at the time of his appointment.—Metropolitan N. Bk v. Commerc. S. Bk., 682.

PRAC. Continued

4. SAME—The approval by the court of a bond given by a receiver who was at the same time clerk of the court, is an adjudication in the receivership proceedings that the bond was sufficient, and cannot be collaterally attacked.—*Idem.*

5. SAME—Although a receiver has given no bond, he may be a receiver *de facto*, so that his authority to sue in such capacity cannot be questioned collaterally.—*Idem.*

6. SAME—In an action upon a promissory note in which the receiver is plaintiff, it cannot be objected that he was disqualified to accept the appointment because as clerk of the court it was necessary for him to approve his own bond as receiver, since such contention is in the nature of a collateral attack upon proceedings had and an order made in another action.—*Idem.*

7. Change of Venue—TRANSFER TO DIFFERENT COUNTY—Defendant is not entitled to a transfer of the case to the county to which he has changed his residence since the service of the notice upon him.—Kiburz v. Jacobs, 580.

Claims—See *post,* [10].

8. Collateral Attack—See *ante,* [3], [4], [5], [6]; *post,* [20]—Service appearing on the face of the record to be good, and the court having taken jurisdiction, the judgment is not void; and the extrinsic facts relied on to defeat the service can be shown only on direct attack of the judgment.—Day v. Goodwin, 374.

9. RULE APPLIED—A judgment rendered in a foreclosure action is not void, although the notice of the pendency of the foreclosure proceedings was served upon one who had previously been adjudged insane, without at the same time leaving a copy for her with her husband, with whom she resided, and who was likewise a party to the action, and served with process on the same occasion.—*Idem.*

10. Assignment—SECURED CLAIMS—*Insolvency*—Where a claim against an assigned estate is paid in part after it is filed, out of the proceeds of collaterals held by the claimant, the claim will be reduced to the extent of the payment, for the purpose of final distribution, though no objections are made to the claim as filed.—Doolittle v. Smith, 403.

11. Continuances—In an action for a partition of defendant's land, plaintiffs moved for a continuance on the ground that it could not at that time be determined whether the personalty would be sufficient to pay the debts. It appeared that, at the time of the motion, a previous order authorizing the sale of the lands, to pay the debts, was in force; but plaintiffs asserted that this order had been abandoned, and was void because no statement

Small figures refer to subdivisions of Index. The others to page of report.

PRAC. Continued

of claims was made or disposition of personalty shown at the time the order was made. There was no showing that the administrators had not filed their reports, nor that the sufficiency of personalty to pay the debts could not be then determined. *Held*, that there was no error in overruling this motion.—Cheney v. McColloch, 249.

12. **Costs**—Under Code 1873, sections 2983, 2984, making the costs of different issues taxable against the party who fails to succeed on such issue, costs are properly divided between plaintiff and defendant in an action on a contract for the sale of live stock, where plaintiff succeeds on the issues raised by the pleadings that the matters in controversy had been settled, and that the defendant accepted the stock under the contract, although as not in full performance thereof, and defendant succeeds on the issue raised by a counter-claim asking for a reduction from the amount due, on account of plaintiff's non-performance of the contract.—White v. Ledbetter, 71.

Creditors—See *post*, [17].

13. **Cross Petitions**—NOTICE—In an action to set aside a mortgage as in fraud of creditors, where the defendant mortgagee seeks by cross petition to have the mortgage foreclosed, he must serve the cross petition on the defendant mortgagor.—Cathcart v. Grieve, 830.

14. PROOF UNDER—When the defendant mortgagee, in an action to set aside a mortgage as in fraud of creditors, seeks by cross petition to have the mortgage foreclosed, and the averments of such petition are denied in the reply, there can be no foreclosure, in the absence of proof of the allegation of the cross petition.—*Idem*.

15. **Evidence**—*Timely Objection*—A motion to strike out certain evidence as irrelevant and immaterial, was correctly overruled, where no objection was lodged against such evidence until after it was fully adduced, and where it constituted a part of the history of the crime charged.—State of Iowa v. McDonough, 6.

16. **Execution Sale**—INJUNCTION—Plaintiff in an action *to restrain the sale on execution of real property* of which he is in possession, is at most only bound to show a presumptive title, where defendant has no title at all.—Moore v. Kleppish, 319.

17. **Executors and Administrators**—ACTION FOR CREDITORS—*Laches*—An action by a judgment creditor to enforce his lien against a decedent's real estate cannot be maintained independently of the administration proceedings, when the administrator has not refused to bring it, and there has been great

PRAC. Continued

delay, and it does not purport to be for the benefit of all the creditors.—Hansen's Fur Fact. v. Teabout, 860.

18. **Directed Verdict**—A verdict should not be directed for defendant in an action for personal injuries, on the ground that plaintiff was guilty of contributory negligence or that defendant was free from negligence, unless the facts are such that all reasonable men must so conclude.—McLeod v. C. & N. W. R'y Co., 139.

19. SAME—A verdict is properly directed for plaintiff in an action for a balance due on account, where plaintiff's claim is admitted by the answer and defendant's claim for damages, because of plaintiff's negligence in delaying to foreclose a chattel mortgage, assigned by plaintiff to defendants, by reason of which the collateral security was lost under a sale on a junior lien, is not sustained by evidence, but it is shown that the property covered by such mortgage was sold on a valid judgment against defendants and applied in liquidation thereof.—Hartman Steel Co. v. Hoag & Son, 269.

20. **Dismissal Without Prejudice**—An action agreed to be argued and submitted in vacation, but dismissed by the plaintiff before a hearing, is not a bar to a subsequent action for the same cause, although the defendant's answer in the first suit set up a counter-claim as set-off, where the defendant sets up the same defense in the subsequent action.—Pray v. Life Indemnity and Security Co., 114.

Injunction—See *ante*, [16].

21. **Instructions**—In an action for personal injuries, where there is a conflict in the evidence in regard to the circumstances under which the accident occurred, and there is direct evidence of proper care on the part of plaintiff, it is prejudicial error to instruct that the jury are to take into consideration the natural instinct of man to guard himself from danger and preserve himself from injury.—Salyers v. Monroe, 74.

Interest—See *post*, [34].
Intoxicating Liquors—See *post*, [34].

22. **Judgment**—*Action to Annul*—All the parties to a judgment should be made parties to a proceeding either in equity or at law, under the statute, to annul it.—Day v. Goodwin, 874.

Laches—See *ante*, [17].

23. JURY QUESTION—The finding of the jury as to competency to make a will should stand, where it cannot be properly said that the evidence is conclusive either way, especially after the trial court has declined to interfere.—In re Estate of Allison, 180.

Small figures refer to subdivisions of Index. The others to page of report,

VOL. 104 Ia—52

Prac. Continued

24. Misjoinder of Causes—Under Code 1873, section 2630, providing that "causes of action of whatever kind, where each may be prosecuted by the same kind of proceedings, provided that they be by the same party, and against the same party, in the same rights, and if suit on all may be brought and tried in that county, may be joined in the same petition," in an action for damages for the sale of intoxicating liquors, where the wife, in one count of the petition, sues as such, under section 1557, allowing her to recover actual damages and exemplary damages for injury to her person, property, and means of support, caused by sales of intoxicating liquors to her husband, whereby he was rendered intoxicated, and where in another count, she sues as a citizen of the county and an informer, under section 1539, which provided that persons who sell intoxicating liquors to intoxicated persons or habitual drunkards, shall be liable to a certain forfeit for each offense, to be collected in an action brought by any citizen in the county, one-half of said amount to go to the informer, there was a misjoinder of causes of action, since they were not in the same right, or to be brought by the same plaintiff.—Carrier v. Bernstein Brothers, 572.

Negligence—See *ante*, [21].

Notice—See *ante*, [13].

25. Nunc pro Tunc Orders—Where no rights of third parties have intervened or will be affected thereby, plaintiff is entitled to a *nunc pro tunc* order requiring a clerk to record a decree which has been prepared and signed by the judge, and given to the clerk, who filed, but failed to record it.—Day v. Goodwin, 874.

Objections—See *ante*, [15].

Officers—See *ante*, [3], [4], [5], [6].

26. Officer de Facto—That the clerk of the district court in his capacity as receiver of an insolvent bank has instituted an action to recover a debt due it, does not vacate the office of clerk and invalidate his acts in docketing the case, filing papers and making entries, thus preventing the court from acquiring jurisdiction, of the action, since he acted as clerk *de facto*, and third persons dealing with him had the right to rely upon his acts so performed as being legal.—Metropolitan National Bank v. Commercial Savings Bank, 682.

27. Parties—See *post*, [31].—In an action against an assessment insurance company on a certificate entitling the beneficiary to the amount of an assessment, it is not necessary to make the secretary a party.—Pray v. Life Indemnity & Security Co., 114.

28. Partition—See *ante*, [11].—*Priority of Title*—The fact that real property was sold upon execution sale and the plaintiff's

PRAC. Continued

dower right thereby cut off, under McClain's Code, section 3644, cannot be urged by the defendant in an action for partition when such defendant does not stand in privity with the purchaser at such sale, but claims under a hostile title.—Sherod v. Ewell, 253.

29. COLLATERAL ATTACK—An order for the sale of defendant's land, made in the absence of a statement of the claims filed or a showing as to the disposition of the personalty, if irregular, is not void.—Cheney v. McCulloch, 249.

30. Presumptions—A party will be presumed to rely upon a cause of action which may be sustained by proof, rather than upon another, to support which the evidence offered is incompetent —Keller v. Strong, 585.

31. Quieting Title—*Parties*—One in possession of land under an agreement of another to sell it to him, and to convey it to him on payment of the purchase price, is not bound by decree in suit to which he is not a party, against such other, to quiet title —Steel v. Long, 39.

32. Receivers—See *ante*, ¹, ², ³, ⁴, ⁵, ⁶—AUTHORITY TO SUE—A receiver who was directed by the court to make a settlement with reference to defendant company, and to collect the claim due the insolvent debtor by litigation, if necessary, and who was as receiver an officer of the court in which he was allowed to intervene as a plaintiff in the suit at bar, is authorized to prosecute the suit.—Metropolitan National Bank v. Commercial Savings Bank, 682.

32a. Set-off—Upon the granting of a decree directing an assessment to be ordered by a life insurance association for the payment of the plaintiff's claim, a judgment held by the defendant against the plaintiff will be allowed as a set-off against the amount realized from the assessment ordered.—Pray v. Life Indemnity and Security Co., 114.

33. Tender—Where plaintiff sued defendant for negligence in collecting a note intrusted to it, and defendant tendered a part payment it had collected, which was refused, plaintiff was entitled to the amount of the tender, without evidence, as it was an admission of the liability to that extent.—*Idem.*

34. INTEREST—Where money is tendered in part payment of an over due debt, without condition, and the tender is kept good, interest on the amount tendered ceases from the time of the tender.—*Idem.*

35. Transfer to Equity—The court did not err in transferring a cause from the law to the equity side of the calendar on its own

motion, where the petition did note state a cause of action.—
Johnston & Son v. Robuck, 528.

86.   SAME—Issues cognizable in equity may be transferred to the
equity side, under Code, section 3483, but not issues at law,
and no motion is required to have those tried separately in
the proper forum.—*Idem.*

87.   *Waiver of error in—*Going to trial does not waive the error of
the court in transferring a law case to the equity side of the
calendar.—*Idem.*

88.   Trial—LAW AND EQUITY—The ordinary rule is to hear the equitable issues first; but where a trial at law will practically settle
all matters in controversy, it ought to be first had.—Johnston
& Son v. Robuck, 528.

Venue—See *ante*, ², ⁷.

PRACTICE SUPREME COURT—See CRIM. LAW,⁴; INJUNC-
TION, ¹.

Abstracts—See *post*, ⁴⁴.

1.   AMENDMENT—An amendment to an abstract, made after the case
has been submitted on appeal, will not be considered unless
filed on permission of the court, where the party has ample
time to file it before submission, after discovering the necessity
therefor.—Watson v. Burroughs, 746.

2.   SAME—Where it was certified in the abstract that it contained
all the evidence, and appellant filed an amendment covering
alleged defects, and reaffirming such facts, and appellee also
filed an abstract setting forth some omissions and corrections,
the cause was properly before this court.—Harrison v. Palo
Alto county, 888.

3.   STRIKING—Appellee's additional abstract will not be stricken
from the files because it was not filed within the time fixed by
the rules, where it does not appear that the submission of the
cause had been delayed, or that any prejudice had been caused
by the non-compliance with the rules in that respect.—Clark
v. Ellsworth, 442.

4.   COSTS—Appellant's motion to tax the costs of the transcript on
appeal against the appellee, on the ground that his own
abstract was full, fair and complete, will be denied where his
abstract omitted to give the date of the judgment or the fact
that time was allowed for filing a bill of exceptions. and was
defective in other important particulars.—Kiburz v. Jacobs,
580.

5.   *Estoppel—*The appellee is taxable with the costs of his amendment to appellant's abstract, although the judgment is

PRAC. SUP. CT Continued

affirmed, where the abstract prepared and filed by the appellant contained everything necessary to the full understanding of the questions raised, and the amendment did not aim
to correct it or make it complete, but is an independent
abstract of all the evidence, about one-half being devoted to
questions and answers printed in full —McWhirter v. Crawford, 550.

6. **Appealable Order**—An appeal will lie from a decision which
overrules a demurrer to a petition for re-hearing in a proceeding by an administrator to obtain property alleged to belong
to the estate.—In re Behren's Estate, 29.

7. RULE APPLIED—Defendant was cited under Code 1873, section
2379, to be examined with reference to a writing in his hands
which it is claimed belonged to the estate of which petitioner
was the administrator. After the close of the term at which
the examination was held, the court made an order directing
the defendant to pay the administrator three hundred dollars. Defendant petitioned for a re-trial, on the ground that
the original petition did not ask a personal judgment against
him; that he had no notice thereof until the order was served
upon him; that the order was entered in vacation, and without
his consent; that he was misled by statements of counsel for
the petitioner into believing that no personal claim was made
against him; that he never had any money belonging to the
estate; that the writing referred to was merely a memorandum made by him as priest at the time the deceased made a
gift to the church; that the court in the examination, which
was conducted partly in German and partly in English, misunderstood the effect of the memorandum. *Held*, that the
grant of a new trial was in the sound discretion of the trial
court.—*Idem*.

8. **Assignments**—That no errors are assigned will not require the
dismissal of an appeal, although the action is at law, when the
parties treated it in the lower court, as in equity.—Harrison v.
Palo Alto County, 383.

9. **Sufficiency**—An assignment on a motion for a new trial, that
the verdict is not sustained by sufficient evidence, does not
sufficiently present the objection that notice of the injury to
the plaintiff by a defect in the street of the defendant city was
not given within six months as required by Acts Twenty-second
General Assembly, chapter 25, section 1.—Reed v. City of
Muscatine, 183.

10. **Bill of Exceptions**—*Filing*—Appellee's motion to strike from
appellant's abstract all that portion of it which must be pre-

served by a bill of exceptions will be granted where the appellant failed to prepare and submit to the judge for approval a bill of exceptions in time to reach the clerk's office for filing within the time allowed for that purpose.—Kiburz v. Jacobs, 580.

Bond—See *post*, 62, 63.

11. Certificate—See *post*, 67, 68—A question certified to the supreme court, which involves an examination of the record and the proceedings of the lower court, will not be considered, as the certificate must set out the very point to be determined.—Sloss v. Bailey, 696.

12. CLERK'S CERTIFICATE—Bringing up the evidence certified by the clerk, as provided by Code 1873, section 3184, is not sufficient for a trial *de novo*. It is the office of the judge's certificate to identify the evidence, and make it of record when filed, while the purpose of the clerk's certificate is to identify and authenticate the record.—Bauernfiend v. Jonas, 56.

13. CONSTRUCTION—On a motion to dismiss appeal, submitted on certificate, the certificate may be somewhat liberally construed to avoid dismissal.—Sarver v. C., B. & Q. R'y Co., 59.

14. Conduct Below—Where a defendant, by answer, meets issues indefinitely stated in the petition, he cannot afterwards complain that they are not properly tendered.—Grieve v. I. C. R'y Co., 659.

15. RULE APPLIED—The petition alleged that stock was damaged by delay in delivery, and by "their long confinement, * * * exposure, and lack of proper care and attention." The answer denied lack of care, and set up matter in justification of the delay. *Held*, that the answer put in issue the question of negligence in the delay and failure to exercise care.—*Idem*.

Costs—See *ante*, 4, 5; *post*, 16.
Demurrer—See *ante*, 6, 7.

16. Dismissal—*Payment for Transcript*—An appeal will not be dismissed on the ground that the clerk's fees have not been paid and cannot be waived, when he had performed all the duties required of him and certified the transcript of the record.—Harrison v. Palo Alto County, 388.

16a. A defect in preserving evidence in an equitable action is not ground for dismissing a properly perfected appeal, but it goes to the disposition of the cause on the merits.—Bauernfiend v. Jonas, 56.

Estates—See *ante*, 6, 7.

PRAC. SUP. CT. Continued

Estoppel—See *post*, [55].
Evidence—See *post*, [51].

17. **Exceptions**—*Waiver*—An exception to the erroneous admission of evidence is not waived by failure to object to the subsequent introduction of evidence of the same kind.—Metropolitan N. Bk. v. Commerc. S. Bk., 682.

18. SAME—The mere silence of a party when incompetent evidence is offered, should be treated as a waiver of the objection to the particular evidence offered only, and will not preclude him from objecting to similar testimony offered subsequently.—*Idem*.

19. RULE APPLIED—Where a question asked plaintiff by his counsel was not objected to, and defendant offered evidence in contradiction of the answer, defendant did not waive his right to object to the evidence given by another witness to the same effect, in rebuttal.—*Idem*.

21. Harmless Error—Error in overruling a motion to direct a verdict for defendant is cured so far as possible by setting aside the verdict returned and granting a new trial; and the refusal to direct will not be reviewed, on appeal.—Grieve v. I. C. R'y Co., 659.

22. SAME—Plaintiffs could not be harmed by an order requiring their petition to be made more specific, but not changing the effect of the original averments, where a demurrer was sustained to the petition as amended, because not stating a cause of action.—Sigmend v. Bebber, 431.

23. SAME—Error in striking out matter in special denial is not prejudicial where the defendant has the benefit of the latter under his general denial—Agne v. Seitsinger, 482.

24. SAME—Error in sustaining an objection to certain questions is harmless, where the answer thereto is subsequently given.—Trimble v. Tantlinger, 665.

25. SAME—An appellant cannot complain that a question asked a witness whose deposition was taken at the instance of appellee was erroneously overruled, as not a proper cross-examination, when the subject was fully inquired into by a deposition of the same witness, taken by appellant.—In re Estate of Allison, 180.

26. SAME—Admission of incompetent evidence that plaintiff in an action for loss of property during shipment did not have time to read the shipping contract before signing it, is harmless error to defendant, where the charge to the jury requires them to consider the contract as in force.—Faust v. C. & N. W. R'y Co., 241.

PRAC. SUP. CT. Continued

27. **Instructions**—In the absence of evidence, it will not be presumed to have been such as to sustain a charge which is clearly erroneous upon any imaginable state of facts.—State of Iowa v. Debolt, 105.

28. REQUESTED INSTRUCTIONS—An appellant cannot complain of the failure of the court to give a requested instruction when the facts assumed in it sufficiently depart from the record to make it partial and unfair, and the court, in a minute and correct charge, dealt with the same subject in a way that was fair to both parties.—In re Estate of Allison, 130.

29. **Joined Appeals**—Where an appeal is taken from a judgment sustaining a mortgage, and also from a subsequent order denying an injunction restraining foreclosure of such mortgage, a motion to strike out the latter appeal, as in no way connected with the main case, will be overruled, as there is nothing in the rules prohibiting printing two appeals under one cover.—Garner v. Fry, 515.

30. **Judgment**—*Construction for Appeal*—A judgment for some of the relief prayed which does not grant other relief prayed but does not expressly deny it, is a judgment against plaintiff as to such relief, so that on appeal from the judgment rendered, his right to such relief may be considered.—Floete v. Brown, 154.

31. **Law of Case**—It is proper to strike out a special denial attempting to put in issue a proposition which had been determined on an appeal, after a former trial.—Agne v. Seitsinger, 483.

32. SAME—A ruling on a prior appeal in the same cause must control on a subsequent trial, where the situation is not changed by the issues or evidence.—McFall v. Iowa Cent. R'y Co., 47

33. **New Trial**—The granting of a new trial in a proceeding instituted by an administrator to recover property alleged to belong to the estate, rests in the discretion of the court, and its decision will not be reversed on appeal, in the absence of abuse of such discretion.—In re Behren's Estate, 29.

34. **Notice**—The fact that a notice of appeal erroneously names the term or fixes the time of hearing, is immaterial.—Harrison v. Palo Alto County, 388.

35. SAME—The statute respecting notice of appeal (Code 1873, section 3178) does not require that it name the term at which the appeal will be heard; and therefore words so used, though erroneous, do not affect the validity of the notice, but are regarded as surplusage.—*Idem.*

PRAC. SUP. CT. Continued

36. *Owner of Contingent Fee*—Attorneys who agree to present a case upon appeal for a contingent fee, do not thereby become parties to the action and entitled to service of notice of appeal.—*Idem.*

37. NOTICE OF MOTION—A motion to affirm a judgment on appeal will be discharged if there is no evidence of service in the record.—Brooke v. King, 713.

38. Objection Below—An objection that plaintiff in an action for personal injuries caused by a defective street did not give notice of the accident to the city within six months as required by Acts Twenty-second General Assembly, chapter 25, section 1, cannot be first taken on appeal, on the ground that such notice is jurisdictional and may be raised at any time; as the court has jurisdiction of the general subject, and lack of the jurisdiction of the particular case cannot be first raised on appeal.—Reed v. City of Muscatine, 183

9. SAME—An objection that the levy of a landlord's attachment was invalid, because written notice thereof was not served on the attachment defendant, cannot be first presented on appeal from a judgment for plaintiff in an action to recover as mortgagee the attached property, or plaintiff's interest therein.—Hipsley v. Price, 282.

40. SAME—That one who applied for a new trial in a contempt proceeding did so by a paper entitled "motion for re-hearing and new trial," which was filed ten days after judgment, instead of by petition, cannot be first raised on appeal. - State of Iowa v. Stevenson, 50.

41. SAME—The objection that no answer was filed to an amendment to a petition cannot be raised on appeal where the case was tried in the lower court as if such answer had been filed — Fred Miller Brewing Co. v. Hansen, 307.

42. SAME—An objection by defendants in an action for malicious assault, that they were not, from the allegation of the petition, bound to anticipate a claim by plaintiff that he had been injured in a certain manner, cannot be first taken on appeal.—Reizenstein v. Clark, 289.

43. Opinion on Appeal—Where the facts are undisputed, and no questions of law are presented rendering an opinion necessary, the judgment, under Code, section 198, will be affirmed without opinion.—Clay Robinson & Co. v. Maynard Saving Bank 748.

44. Presumptions—See *ante*, ³⁷—On a trial for slander, where the jury is charged to estimate the amount of "actual injury" plaintiff would naturally sustain, the supreme court cannot

PRAC. SUP. CT. Continued

    presume, from the amount of the verdict, that exemplary damages were allowed.—Trimble v. Tantlinger, 665.

45. SAME—No inference will be drawn or presumptions indulged in in reference to the recitals in a decree, except such as support the decree.—Willenburg v. Hersey, 699

46. Relief—The relief granted on appeal will not be more favorable to a party who does not appeal than the judgment below.—McWhirter v. Crawford, 550.

47. Review—The appellate court cannot take notice of a mere remark in argument to the effect that defendant in a criminal case was forced to trial before a jury that had fixed opinions as to one of the facts essential to his conviction.—State of Iowa v. Rowe, 823.

48. CONFLICTING EVIDENCE—The finding of the district court that a so-called street was actually a street, and did not come within the term "alley" in a street paving resolution, is conclusive upon the supreme court on appeal, at law, on conflicting evidence.—Polk v. McCartney, 567.

49. *Same*—A verdict based upon conflicting testimony will not be disturbed on appeal, when it has evidence to support it.—Names v. Union Ins. Co., 612.

50. *Same*—The verdict of the jury will not be disturbed where there is evidence justifying its finding.—State of Iowa v. Shea, 724.

51. EVIDENCE—Alleged error in dismissing a petition for partition of land cannot be determined on appeal, where all the evidence offered on the trial is not in the record.—Cheney v. McColloch, 249.

52. ESTOPPEL AS TO REVIEW—A party cannot question on appeal an express statement or admission in his pleadings.—Floete v. Brown, 154.

53. FAILURE TO APPEAL—The disallowance of a claim for damages, although presented in the briefs, will not be considered, when the party injured thereby has not appealed.—Harrison v. Palo Alto County, 383.

54. *Same*—Plaintiff having asked for a *nunc pro tunc* order requiring the clerk to record a former decree, and defendant moved for leave to answer, defendant, not having appealed, cannot, on the appeal of plaintiff from the denial of the order, claim any affirmative relief as to or by reason of the motion, relative to which the lower court took no action.—Day v. Goodwin, 874.

55. FINDINGS—Special findings by a jury will not be sustained if contrary to the evidence, and when material and determinative in their character, the party found against will not be presumed to have had a fair trial.—Waterbury v. C., M. & St. P. R'y Co., 82.

56. **Presentation**—A judgment will be affirmed when the record fails to present sufficient information to enable the court to intelligently consider the assignments of error.—Odden v. Lewis, 747.

57. **Verdict**—In an action to recover the value of horses and other property burned on defendant's train, the evidence showed that, at a certain station where the train stopped, plaintiff, shipper, who by the contract was to accompany the stock, left the car and went to the caboose, but left it before the train started, to return to the stock car. He was not thereafter seen on the train. After the train started the car was found to be on fire, and the stock therein was destroyed. Plaintiff claimed to have been left at the station at which the train stopped, but his testimony was uncertain and contradictory. There were not as many carcasses of horses found in the car as plaintiff claimed to have shipped, and his reputation for truth was bad. The evidence tended to show that he set the fire. *Held*, that he was not entitled to recover.—Faust v. C. & N. W. R'y Co. 241.

58. SAME—A verdict in a criminal case is sustained by the evidence, although the proof on the part of the state is not entirely satisfactory, where it is so materially strengthened by the testimony of the defendant, given in his own behalf, as to authorize the verdict.—State of Iowa v. Hazen, 16.

59. DAMAGES—The damages awarded against a railroad company for the killing of a horse will not be adjudged excessive when the evidence as to the animal's value is conflicting, some witnesses placing it above and some below the amount for which judgment was rendered.—Riley v. C., M. & St. P. R'y Co., 235.

60. **Reserved Ruling**—Where defendant moved to strike out an answer of a witness, and the trial court reserved its ruling, and the matter was not again called to its attention, defendant cannot complain, as there was neither a ruling nor an exception.—State of Iowa v. Reilly, 18.

61. **Supersedeas**—An appellee's possession of the land in dispute, obtained by the service of a writ of possession *before* an appeal bond was filed, is not affected by a subsequent perfecting of appeal and filing of a supersedeas bond, under Code 1873, section 3186, providing that an appeal shall not stay proceedings unless a bond is filed—Hyatt v. Clever, 888.

PRAC. SUP. CT. Continued

62. COUNTIES—An appeal from a judgment against a county does
not operate as a stay of proceedings thereon without the filing
of a supersedeas bond, as Code, section 4126, providing that no
proceedings under a judgment shall be stayed by an appeal
unless the appellant executes and files a bond, makes no exceptions, and the only exemption from furnishing security is that
made by section 3475 in favor of the state.—Harrison v. Stebbins, 462.

63. SUPERSEDEAS BOND—*What Recoverable Under* — Damages for
defendant's continuing to practice his profession pending his
appeal from a decree enjoining his future practice are not
covered by the supersedeas bond conditioned for payment of
"all costs and damages that shall be adjudged against said
appellant in this appeal." Nothing but damages adjudged on
the appeal are recoverable on such bond.—Cole v. Edwards, 373.

Transcripts—See *ante,* 16.

64. Trial de Novo—See *ante* 16a—Where all the questions to be considered in a trial *de novo* in equity, by the appellate court, involve
a consideration of the evidence, and the abstract of record shows
that all the evidence is not contained therein, the decree of the
lower court must be affirmed.—Payne v. Cheaf, 749.

65. SAME·-The record as set out in the abstract contained a stipulation
that affidavits filed on a motion to dissolve a temporary injunction should be taken as the testimony of affiants. Following
it was a statement that the cause came on for trial on the evidence, "as shown by this abstract," which contained all the
evidence offered, all of which evidence was certified by the
judge and filed, and made a part of the record. Then followed
what purported to be evidence, and after it a statement that
the trial judge duly certified the same to be all the evidence
offered at the trial. The abstract then recited that it contained
all the evidence offered, but no affidavits, as such, or purporting to be testimony or depositions of affiants, appear in the
abstract. *Held,* sufficient to present the case for trial *de novo.*—
Fred Miller Brewing Co. v. Hansen, 307.

66. SAME—Where appellant's abstract does not purport to show
all the evidence, and the appellee denies that it is all in the
record, the case cannot be tried *de novo* —Watson v. Burroughs, 746.

67. JUDGE'S CERTIFICATE—The failure to file in the district court
the certificate of the judge attached to the testimony taken
before a commissioner. renders the presence of such testimony
in the abstract improper, and precludes a trial *de novo* on
appeal.—Bauernfiend v Jonas, 56.

68. SAME—A certificate by the trial judge in a case tried as in equity, that the foregoing record contains all the evidence "offered and introduced" on the trial, is insufficient to present the case for trial *de novo*. It must appear that all the evidence offered, introduced and rejected, is up.—Cheney v. McColloch, 249.

PREFERENCES—See BANKS, [1], [2], [3].

PRESCRIPTION—See HIGHWAYS, [3].

PRESUMPTIONS—See EVID [21]; PRACT. [30]; PRACT. SUP. CT. [27], [44], [45], [55]; RAILWAYS, [4], [13], [26].

PRINCIPAL AND AGENT—See ATTYS. [2]; CONTR [30]; EVID. [4],[27]; INSTR. [3]; INS [1], [2], [19], [20], [21], [22], [23], [24]; RAILWAYS, [22].

1. Authority—An agent to collect an interest coupon has no implied authority to extend the time of payment or to negotiate a new loan.—Van Vechten v. Jones, 436.

2. Implied Authority—One authorized by the owner to negotiate a sale or exchange of real estate is not thereby invested with an implied or apparent authority to make a binding contract of sale for his principal.—Homes v. Redhead., 399.

8. CORPORATION—The power conferred upon an officer of a corporation to object to a plant constructed for the corporation if he is not satisfied therewith, necessarily includes the power to accept, if he is satisfied.—Frey-Sheckler Co. v. Iowa Brick Co., 494,

PRINCIPAL AND SURETY—See LAND AND TENANT, [7], [8].

PRIORITIES—See MECHANIC'S LIENS, [3], [4], [5]; MORTG. [9]; PRACT. [28].

PRIVILEGED COMMUNICATION—See EVID. [25].

PUBLIC IMPROVEMENTS—See CONTR. [19], [20]; MUNIC. CORP.

PUBLIC OFFICERS—See CONTR. [23], [25], [26], [27], [28], [29], [30], [31].

PUBLIC POLICY— See CONTR. [22], [23], [24], [25], [29]; RAILWAYS, [3], [4].

QUIETING TITLE—See PRACT. [31].

1. Evidence—In an action to quiet title the plaintiff's chain of title showed a transfer of the title from a widow of one former grantee, and from the heirs of another former grantee, but there was nothing to show by what authority the transfers were made. *Held*, plaintiff has failed to establish his allegation of ownership.—Wood v. Brown, 124.

2. ADMISSIONS—*Plea and Proof*—An admission by defendants in an action to quiet title to land, that plaintiffs are seized of the "interest if any" owned by a specified person at his death, does not relieve plaintiff of the burden of proving title to the land, where an allegation that such person died seized of the land, was put in issue by general denial.—*Idem*.

8. RIGHTS OF CLAIMANT—*Mortgages*—Plaintiff in an action to quiet title to land cannot, where he shows no title to the land, question the right of defendants to a foreclosure of the mortgage on the land on the ground that the latter had released part of the land from the mortgage.—*Idem.*

RAILROADS.

1. Contract—PUBLIC POLICY—A railroad company cannot, under Code 2074, preventing any limitation of the liability of a common carrier, relieve itself from care of live stock by a contract providing that the cars shall be in charge of the shipper, who assumes the duty of loading and unloading, attending to and feeding the stock at his own expense and risk.—Grieve v. I. C. R'y Co., 659.

2. RULE APPLIED—Notwithstanding the invalidity of a provision of a contract for the shipment of live stock requiring the shipper to care for the same, a shipper who is furnished transportation and actually undertakes to care for his stock, cannot recover from the carrier for injuries occasioned by his neglect to exercise such care.—*Idem.*

3. SAME—Valid conditions in a shipping contract, which can be separated from those which are understood by both parties to be invalid, can be enforced.—*Idem.*

4. SAME—The fact that no notice of damage was given a railroad company, as required in a shipping contract, does not relieve the company of liability, since the condition is a limitation of the carrier's liability, and therefore void, under Code, section 2074, providing no contract shall exempt any railroad corporation engaged in transporting property from the liability of a common carrier which would exist had no contract been made or entered into—*Idem.*

Damages—See *post*, ²⁷, ²⁸.

5. Dedication and Acceptance—The fact that a railway company has left a portion of its right of way adjacent to a highway unfenced is not a dedication thereof, unless there has been an acceptance; and it is held that the facts at bar show an acceptance by travel.—Sarver v. C., B. & Q. R y Co., 59.

6. Evidence—See *post*, ¹³, ¹⁴, ¹⁵, ²³—Injury to property in transit being shown, the burden is cast upon the carrier to exculpate itself from blame.—*Idem.*

7. SAME—A shipper who has undertaken to care for his own stock while in transit, has the burden of showing that injury thereto did not result from his own negligence, and, if occasioned by failure to do what he has undertaken, then, that

---

Small figures refer to subdivisions of Index. The others to page of report.

RAIL. Continued

such failure resulted from omission on the part of the carrier to do some duty devolving upon it.—*Idem.*

8. INJURY BY TRAIN—In an action against a railway company to recover damages for the death of the plaintiff's intestate, evidence as to the value of the farm of which the deceased was a co-tenant, offered as bearing upon the question of damages, is immaterial —Dalton v. C , R. I. & P. R'y Co., 26.

9. SUFFICIENCY—A finding that horses killed on a railroad right of way entered at a point where there was no fence, will be supported by evidence that the hoof-prints of the animals indicated such to be the fact.—Kingsbury v. C., M. & St. P. R'y Co., 63.

10. Fences—See *post*, ⁵⁰—A fence built along his holding by a tenant of lands leased from a railway company is not a right of way fence, in the absence of some agreement, express or implied.— *Idem.*

Instructions—See *post*, ⁵¹, ⁵⁹.
Jury Question—See *post*, ¹⁶, ¹⁷, ¹⁸.

11. Negligence—It is negligence on the part of a railway company to allow an accumulation of ice upon the platform of its passenger station, caused by the dropping of water from the roof to remain without any effort to remove it, or cover it with some substance that would be less dangerous.—Waterbury v. C., M. & St. P. R'y Co., 32.

12. CARE OF EMPLOYE—*Presumption*—One in charge of a street car has the right to presume that one walking along the side of a track will exercise the caution which a person of ordinary prudence would exercise, and will not attempt to cross the track immediately in front of a car, until there is reasonable ground for concluding that he may do so.—Beem v. Tama & T. Electric R'y & L. Co., 568.

13. CONTRIBUTORY NEGLIGENCE — *Evidence* — Decedent was seventy-one years old. and quite deaf. A few minutes before the accident occurred, he was walking along the street, parallel to, and a short distance from, a railway track. He turned to cross the track, and was struck by the cars, and was killed. He did not look toward the approaching train, although he could have seen it for a distance of five hundred and fifty feet. The train was running at a higher rate of speed than allowed by the city. *Held*, not to warrant a finding that the decedent was free from contributory negligence.—*Idem.*

14. *Same*—Contributory negligence by a person killed by a street car is sufficiently established by evidence that he was deaf and that he could not have failed to discover the approaching

RAIL. Continued

car if he had looked in the direction from which it came, before attempting to cross the track.—*Idem.*

15. *Same*—One who in entering a railway depot, passed over a place made unsafe by an accumulation of ice, and knew of its dangerous condition, yet who soon thereafter, while watching upon the platform for the incoming train, stepped backward upon the ice without looking or taking any precaution for his safety, whereby he fell to his injury,—is guilty of contributory negligence —Waterbury v. C., M. & St. P. R'y Co , 82.

16. *Jury Question*—It is a question of fact for the jury whether the circumstances attending the death of one killed at a railway crossing are such as to overcome the presumption that the deceased, prompted by the instinct of self-preservation, exercised the care required of him, when no one witnessed the accident nor the manner in which the deceased approached and went upon the track.—Dalton v. C., R. I. & P. R'y Co., 26.

17. *Same*—An action against a railway company for injury to a brakeman through defendant's negligence in permitting its water tank to become out of repair, in consequence whereof the water was permitted to run on and over the tracks, which rendered it dangerous for brakemen to perform their duty of coupling cars, was clearly one for the jury, where there was evidence to show negligence on the part of the defendant, and that plaintiff was not guilty of negligence.—McFall v. Iowa Cent. R'y Co., 47.

18. *Same*—Employes operating a switch engine, whose duty it is to be on the lookout for employes on or near the tracks and to warn them of the approach of the engine by ringing the bell or blowing the whistle, or in some other manner, are not as a matter of law free from negligence toward an employe walking along the track in the course of his duty, where no signal of any kind is given of the approach of such engine.—McLeod v. C. & N. W. R'y Co., 189.

19. *Contributory Negligence—Jury Question*—A railway employe who is directed by his superior to walk from the rear end of the train on a particular side of the same is not as matter of law guilty of contributory negligence in walking so near the adjoining track, only six feet distant, that he is struck by a switch engine thereon, where it was the duty of the employe in charge of such engine to be on the lookout for employes on or near the tracks and warn them of the approach of the engine, and no such warning was

RAIL. Continued

given. Such employe need not look and listen as a
stranger or trespasser must.—*Idem*.

20. **Pleading**—In an action to recover damages for the killing of a
horse which entered on the right of way at a point where the
company had a right to fence, a general denial presents the
issue whether the railroad had a right to fence at the point in
question, and not whether it had legal excuse for failing to do
so. The last is matter in estoppel which must be specially
pleaded.—Kingsbury v. C., M. & St. P. R'y Co., 63.

21. **SAME**—*Instructions*—In an action to recover against a railroad
company for the killing of live stock, resulting from the failure
of said road to build a fence along a portion of its right of way,
acts of plaintiff excusing such neglect are not available under
a general denial, and under such issues, an instruction allowing a recovery if a horse was killed through neglect of defendant to fence, is proper.—*Idem*.

22. **Principal and Agent**—A telegram from the chief surgeon of a
railway company directing the sendee, a district surgeon in
another district, to go to a specified employe who had been
injured, as soon as possible, and notify the agent and local
surgeon of the company at the place when he will be there,
does not give such sendee any apparent authority to employ
another physician to assist him.—Smith v. C. & N. W. R'y co.,
147.

23. **Release**—ESTATES OF DECEDENTS—The parents of an intestate,
who was killed while employed on a railroad, settled with the
company and released all claims to damages. There were no
debts against the deceased, and his parents were his sole heirs.
Held, that the settlement and release by the parents, though
made without intervention of an administrator, was valid, and
precluded a recovery for the intestate's death by an administrator who was appointed after the settlement.—Christie v. C.,
R. I. & P. R'y Co., 707.

24. **Shipment**—DUTY OF SHIPPER IN ATTENDANCE—Mere failure of
a shipper of live stock to remain on the train as required by the
shipping contract, does not preclude him from recovering for
the loss of such live stock by the burning of the car in which it
was carried, where his contract did not require him to ride in
such car, but in the caboose.—Faust v. C. & N. W. R'y Co., 241.

25. **SAME**—*Burden of Proof*—Under such circumstances it was not
the duty of the shipper to prove that the loss was not caused by
his failure to remain on the train, nor by his failure to care for
the property while in transit. He could recover on proof that
the fire was not due to any act or negligence of his.—*Idem*.

Small figures refer to subdivisions of Index. The others to page of report.

VOL. 104 Ia—53

26. Killing Stock—The mere fact that a portion of a right of way of a railroad company adjacent to a highway is outside the cattle guard and fences, does not justify a presumption that such land was used for highway purposes.—Sarver v. C., B. & Q. R'y Co., 59.

27. DAMAGES—*Proximate Cause*—Where a horse has crossed a defective cattle guard on the right of way of a railroad, and, after crossing onto the highway, was killed, the defective cattle guard will be held to be the proximate cause of the injury, where the immediate cause of the horse being on the highway was the defective cattle guard.—Riley v. C., M. & St. P. R'y Co., 285.

28. *Same*—A railway company failing to fence a portion of its right of way adjacent to a highway, which portion has not been used for highway purposes, and which it had a right to fence, is, under Code 1873, section 1289, liable for the value, and, in case of failure to pay the actual value within thirty days after notice given, for double the value, of stock killed on such portion.—Sarver v. C., B. & Q. R'y Co., 59.

29. INSTRUCTIONS—An instruction to the jury, in an action against a railway company for the killing of a horse to find for the defendant if the animal was struck upon the highway crossing, and not within the right of way, and his death was not due to the defendant's failure to maintain a safe and sufficient cattle guard at the place where the accident occurred, is properly given when the testimony shows that the cattle guard was not out of repair, and the evidence is conflicting as to the exact point where the horse was struck.—Riley v. C., M. & St. P. R'y Co., 285.

RAPE—See CRIM. LAW, [7], [9], [12], [13], [14], [19], [20], [24], [29], [30], [31], [36], [43], [44].

RATIFICATION—See CONTR. [29], [30]; CORP. [4], [6]; REFORMATION. [6].

REAL PROPERTY—See COUNTIES, [4]; DEDICATION, [1], [3], [3], [4]; HIGHWAYS, [3]; INJUNCTION, [3], [3]; RAILWAYS, [6]; WATERS, [1], [2]

RECEIVERS—See PRACT. [1], [3], [4], [5], [6], [33].

1. When Appointed—Under McClain's Code, section 4113, which provides that a receiver may be appointed on petition of a person holding an interest in property which is in danger of being lost or impaired, a court can appoint a receiver of an insolvent corporation (all creditors, most of whom have liens, consenting, except one), which corporation was organized to build a bridge, in which the public was largely interested, under a charter granted by congress, where the property consisted of two completed and one incompleted piers and some real estate connected with the bridge, all of which would be of little value without the franchise, which would be forfeited in less than a year unless the bridge was completed.—Boston Inv. Co. v. Pacific S. L. B. Co., 811.

2. SAME—The court will not decline to appoint receivers and direct the sale of the property and franchises of a corporation organized to construct a public bridge, pending suit by a creditor to set aside a conveyance thereby, upon the intervention of an officer of the corporation, who prefers a claim for salary and advances, more than two years after the commencement of the suit, where an early sale is imperative to save the franchises from forfeiture for non-completion of the bridge. —*Idem.*

SAME—An order of sale of property in the hands of the receivers cannot be said to be in effect a foreclosure of a trust deed on the property, where it has no other effect than to bring the proceeds of the sale into court, instead of the property.— *Idem.*

4. SAME —That the sheriff is in possession, under plaintiff's execution, of the property involved in a suit to set aside a conveyance of property and franchises, does not prevent the appointment of a receiver to sell the property, pending the action, where it is in danger of being lost or destroyed. He could not avoid a forfeiture, and need not be made a party.— *Idem.*

5. SAME—It was not error for the court to order a sale of the property immediately on the appointment and qualification of the receivers and upon their application, where the property was an uncompleted bridge, which would be, when completed, a public benefit, and the franchise to build same was about to expire.—*Idem.*

6. Evidence—Findings by the court in an order appointing receivers of an insolvent bridge corporation's property, that the property is without care and abandoned and going to waste, are supported by evidence that the property has been in the hands of the sheriff for about two years and the work on the property has ceased during all that time.—*Idem*

7. SAME—An objection that no evidence was introduced to support the finding upon which an order appointing receivers was made, cannot be sustained when the pleadings show facts to sustain the findings, and the order was based upon facts admitted in open court by all the parties to the action, and made with their consent.—*Idem.*

RECORDING—See DEEDS; FRAUD.CONV. [5]; MTGS. [9].

REDEMPTION—EXECUTIONS, [1], [2].

REFORMATION—See BONA FIDE PURCHASER.

1. **Evidence**—*Laches*—A self constituted agent falsely represented that the managing member of a defendant firm had read and pronounced satisfactory a written contract of sale with plaintiff, the terms of which had previously been agreed on, and thereby induced the other member of the firm to sign it without reading the contents. The contract signed did not express the actual agreement, as it contained a clause of which the defendants were ignorant. It was not shown that plaintiffs authorized the agent to insert the clause, or to make the false representations. *Held*, that the negligence of defendant in signing the contract was not so gross as to bar them of the right of reformation of the contract on the ground of fraud and mistake.—Sutton v. Risser, 631.

2. SAME—An illiterate party, who, with the knowledge of the other party, relied upon the latter to embody their oral agreement in a written instrument, is not precluded from having the written instrument reformed to conform to their understanding, because it was read over to him before it was executed, and he mentioned certain omissions, but was assured by the other party that he had embodied everything they had agreed on.—Williams v. Hamilton, 428.

3. **Mistake**—A unilateral mistake, unaccompanied by fraud of the other party, as to the contents or legal effect of an instrument does not justify its reformation. Such mistake must be mutual to warrant reformation.—*Idem*.

4. SAME—A unilateral mistake of law, accompanied by fraud on the part of the other party, may, under some circumstances, authorize the reformation of a contract.—*Idem*.

5. **Ratification**—To preclude a party from obtaining a reformation of a written contract, on the ground that he ratified it after its execution, it must appear that he knew of and understood the contents of the instrument at the time he is claimed to have ratified it.—*Idem*.

RELEASE—See CONSTR., ²; SETTLEMENTS.

CONSIDERATION—The release of an existing indebtedness for commissions due under a mutual contract for sale of land is a new contract, and must be based on a consideration, and an oral statement by the agent that he claims no commission is not, therefore, sufficient to show release.—Metcalf v. Kent, 487.

REMITITTUR—See JUSTICES, ¹.

REMOVAL OF CAUSES.

State court's power over—A state court has no jurisdiction to sustain a motion by plaintiff to dismiss the case after defendant has filed a proper petition and bond for removal of the cause to a federal court, under United States Statute, chapter 866, sections 2, 3, providing that when such petition and bond are filed "within the time, it shall be the duty of the state court to accept the same and proceed no further" in the suit.—Chambers v. I. C. R. R. Co., 238.

REPRESENTATIONS—See ESTOPPEL, **3**.
REPUTATION—See CRIM. LAW, **12**.
RES ADJUDICATA—See ADJUDICATION, **1**.
RETAXATION—See COSTS, **1**, **3**, **5**.
REVENUE DEPARTMENT DECISION—See CONST. LAW, **4**.
RIGHT OF WAY—See RAILWAYS, **5**, **10**, **26**, **28**.
RIPARIAN RIGHTS—See WATERS, **1**, **3**.
RULING—See PRACT SUP. CT. **60**.

SALES—See CONTR. **1**, **3**, **3**, **13**; EVID **17**; FIXTURES.

1. **Acceptance** — Where a buyer refused to accept goods on account of their quality, he cannot thereafter justify such refusal by alleging a shortage which the seller offered to correct. - Sutton v. Risser, 631.

2. **Brokerage—LAND SALE COMMISSIONS**—A contract for sale of land giving the agent "exclusive right to sell" the farm described, on certain terms, and agreeing to a commission "in case the above-described property is sold during the pendency of this contract, or to person whom second party finds, or secures as a customer, after the expiration of this contract, or if second party secures a purchaser who will purchase it on the above-mentioned terms," which is indorsed "good until December 1, 1895," is a contract for exclusive right to sell, which gives a right to commission on any sale made within the time, and the question of whether or not the agent was instrumental in the sale actually made, is wholly immaterial.— Metcalf v. Kent, 487.

3. **Evidence of Shortage**—The evidence is insufficient to establish a claim of shortage, in the quantity of goods sent to a purchaser where the contract was for an exchange of land in consideration of six thousand dollars' worth of goods, shelf-worn and out of style, taken at wholesale or cost prices, since such mode of computation places a higher price upon the property than its actual value, and does not furnish any information from which that value can be determined.—*Idem.*

SALES Continued   TO   SALOON KEEPERS

4. Forfeiture—A vendor in a contract to convey land subject to
    the dower interest of his wife cannot insist upon a forfeiture
    for non-payment of the purchase price, where, before the date
    of payment he had put it out of his power to comply, on his
    part, with the terms of the contract by conveying an undivided
    one-third interest in fee to his wife.—McWhirter v. Crawford,
    550.

5. ELECTION—Where a contract for sale of real estate provided
    that if the purchaser should fail to make any payments when
    due, he should forfeit all right to the property, and also any
    money paid by him, unless the vendor·should elect other-
    wise, it was the vendor's duty to give the vendee notice,
    within a reasonable time after default, that he elected not to
    treat the contract as forfeited; and his failure so to do,
    worked a forfeiture, and barred him recovering the price.—
    Mahoney v. McCrea, 735.

6. SAME—Where a contract for sale of real estate provides that
    on the purchaser's failure to make payments when due, he
    shall forfeit all right to the property and to "any money paid
    by him," and the forfeiture occurs, a subsequent acceptance
    of part of the amount due, while it was a waiver of the for-
    feiture, gave the vendor no right to recover the balance due
    and unpaid at the time of such acceptance, after a forfeiture
    had again occurred by reason of a subsequent default.—Idem.

7. Fraud—A vendor is estopped to claim fraud in the inception of
    the contract where, with full knowledge of all the facts relied
    on to constitute the fraud, he accepted the note secured by
    mortgage as part of the purchase price and received the pay-
    ment of interest and principal.—McWhirter v. Crawford, 550.

8. SAME—A vendor's acceptance of payments on the price, long
    after the contract was made, and with full knowledge of all
    the facts, estops him from urging fraud on the vendee's part
    in procuring the contract.—Idem.

9. Warranty—Contract for sale of land which the purchaser knew
    the vendor had no patent to, though he was the owner of the
    land and entitled to patent, requires the purchaser to accept
    deed and abstract when tendered, if the abstract shows a per-
    fect title, except as to issuing of the patent; it being provided
    that he is to make payments at certain times, and that "good
    abstract and warranty deed" is to be furnished by the vendor.
    Under such circumstances the seller cannot be compelled to
    furnish patent, but the purchaser must rely on the covenant
    of warranty.—Younie, Brown & Martin v. Walrod. 475.

SALOON KEEPERS—See CRIM. LAW, ³.

SEDUCTION –See CRIM. LAW, [21], [22], [23], [44].
SELF-DEFENSE—See CRIM. LAW, [2], [34], [35], [36].

SETTLEMENTS.

Release—*Estates af Decedents*—The parents of an intestate, who was killed while employed on a railroad, settled with the company and released all claims to damages. There were no debts against the deceased, and his parents were his sole heirs. *Held*, that the settlement and release by the parents, though made without intervention of an administrator, was valid, and precluded a recovery for the intestate's death, by an administrator who was appointed after the settlement.—Christie v. C., R. I. & P. R'y Co., 707.

SET OFF--See PRACT. [22]a.
SLANDER--See PRACT. SUP. CT. [44].
SPECIAL FINDINGS—PRACT. SUP. CT. [55].
SPECIFIC PERFORMANCE—See TENDER, [1], [2].
STATE COURTS—See REMITTITUR.
STOCKHOLDERS–See CONTR. [8]; CORP [4], [8], [9], [10].

STREET RAILWAYS.

1. **Judgments**–A street "railway corporation" is not, within Code 1873, section 1309, providing that a judgment against any "railway corporation" for any injury to any person or property shall be a lien within the county where recovered, on its property, prior to the lien of any mortgage or trust deed executed since July 4, 1862, in view of the fact that there were no street railways in the state when the original act from which this section was taken was passed, and that the context apparently excludes street railways.—Fidelity Loan & Trust Co. v. Douglas, 582.

2. SAME—The fact that the franchise of a corporation denominated as a street railway company does not limit its operation to the city, but includes the territory adjacent to the city, and that it is authorized to carry freight, baggage and express matter, does not make it a commercial railway company as distinguished from a street railway company, and so bring it within the scope of Code 1873, section 1309, giving judgments for personal injuries against commercial railway corporations preference over prior mortgages, where there is nothing to indicate that it has done or intended to do any business except that usually and properly done by street railway corporations.—*Idem.*

SUPERSEDEAS—See PRACT SUP CT. [61], [62], [63]
SURETIES–See ATTYS. [15]; LAND AND TENANT, [7], [8].

Small figures refer to subdivisions of Index. The others to page of report.

SURFACE WATER—See ESTOPPEL, [1]; WATERS, [2].

TAXATION—See LAND. AND TENANT, [5], [6], [7], [8].

1. The omission by the assessor to inform the person assessed, in writing, of the valuation placed upon his property as provided by Code, section 1856, does not invalidate the assessment nor prejudice the owner, unless the valuation is excessive or property is erroneously included, and it will be presumed that the assessment was properly made.—In re Kauffman's Estate, 639.

2. SAME—Property must be assessed in the name of the owner, on January 1, previous to the time of making it under Code 1873, section 812, even though he has since died.—*Idem.*

8. EXECUTORS AND ADMINISTRATORS—An administrator may, under Code, section 831, seek redress from an excessive or erroneous assessment, before the board of equalization or on appeal to the courts—*Idem.*

TENDER—See JUSTICE, [2], [3]; PRACT. [83], [84].

1. SPECIFIC PERFORMANCE—An offer by a purchaser in his cross-petition praying the specific performance of the contract, to pay the amount found due, is sufficient, where the vendor, at the time the tender was due, was insisting that the contract was forfeited, and had put it out of his power to perform by conveying an interest in the property to another.—McWhirter v. Crawford, 550.

2. SAME—The failure of the vendor to object to the amount tendered by a purchaser at the time thereof, does not prevent him from subsequently making the objection, under Code 1873, section 2107, providing that the person to whom a tender is made must at the time, make any objections which he may have to the money tendered or he will be deemed to have waived them, as the phrase "objection to money" refers to the character or kind of money, and not to the amount.—*Idem.*

THREATS—See BLACKMAIL, [1], [2], [3], [4]; CRIM. LAW, [15], [16]; INSTR [1].
TRANSCRIPTS—See PRACT. SUP. CT. [16].
TRANSFER—See PRACT. [7], [35], [36], [37], [38].
TRESPASS—See HIGHWAYS, [1].
TRIAL DE NOVO—See PRACT. SUP. CT. [18], [20], [61], [64], [65], [66], [67].
TRUSTS—See BANKS, [1], [2], [3]; EVID. [18]; FRAUD CONV. [1]; WILLS, [3], [7].
USAGE—See ATTYS. [7].
VENUE—See CRIM. LAW, [14]; PRACT. [3], [7].
VERDICT—PRACT. [18]; PRACT. SUP. CT. [57], [58], [59].
WAIVER—GENL ASSIGNMENT, [3]; INS. [8], [9], [22], [23], [24]; PLEAD. [5]; PRACT. [37]; PRACT. SUP. CT. [17], [18], [19].

_____

WARRANTY—See COUNTIES, ³, ⁴, ⁵; EVID., ¹⁷; SALES, ⁹.

Assumpsit—In the absence of a warranty, or of fraud in inducing the conveyance, the failure of the title will not support an action against the grantee for money had and received.—Harrison v. Palo Alto County, 388.

WATERS.

1. **Accretion—NON-NAVIGABLE WATERS—***Riparian Rights*—Riparian owners of lands bordering on non-navigable lakes, which were meandered by the government surveyors in 1851 and 1852, and did not become wholly dry and fit for cultivation until 1890 and 1891, are not entitled to the bed of the lake, under the law of accretions.—Noyes v. Board of Supervisors, 174.

2. **SAME**—The rule that a riparian owner of land bordering on rivers or streams, in the absence of limitations in his title, takes to the center thread of the stream, does not apply to the case of a lake or pond.—*Idem.*

3. **DIVERSION BY GRADING**—An owner of a city lot has the right to bring his lot to grade although the flow of surface water may thereby be diverted to the lots owned by other persons.—City of Cedar Falls v. Hansen, 189.

WILLS—See INST. ⁴; PRACT. ²².

1. **ADEMPTION OF LEGACY**—A bequest of a specific amount to testator's son to be paid by deducting the same from the amount due from the son to the testator, as evidenced by notes, is specific, and is adeemed by the father's returning the notes to the son, during his lifetime.—Davis v. Close, 261.

2. **Certainty**—A bequest for a known and lawful purpose, where the power of execution is prescribed and available, should never fail for want of name or a legal classification, unless it is in obedience to a positive rule of law.—Moran v Moran, 216.

3. **RULE APPLIED**—A bequest to the pastor of a specific church, "that masses be said for me," although not a charity, creates a valid private trust.—*Idem.*

4. **CHARITIES**—A bequest of money "to be divided among the Sisters of Charity," without any limitation as to locality, state or nation, and without any provision for the exercise of discretion by the trustees, is void for uncertainty.—*Idem.*

5. **Evidence--WILL CONTEST--***Due execution*—The testimony of a proponent, to the effect that she was present when the will was executed and that the subscribing witnesses reside without the state, is admissible to show, *prima facie*, the execution of the

WILLS Continued

will and to cast the burden of proof upon the contestant, although the depositions of the subscribing witnesses are on file in the case upon other issues and though proponent took one of such depositions and all were taken by agreement.—In re Estate of Allison, 130.

6.   *Competency*—A will in favor of deceased's wife, and offered by her for probate, was contested by his father on the ground of incompetency and undue influence. It appeared that the will was executed in a town in Arkansas two days before deceased's death; that the wife was there at the time; that contestant resided in Iowa; and that deceased's only brother resided near contestant. A witness for the latter testified that she was at said town during deceased's sickness, and that she then asked the wife why she did not send for her husband's brothers, and the wife said she did not want them. The wife's cousin, who lived near contestant, was permitted to state the contents of a lost letter she received from the wife during deceased's sickness, and which she read to contestant and his daughter when received, to the effect that he was very poorly, and requesting her to take the letter to contestant and daughter, for the reason that she had no time to write to them, and to repeat a conversation with them to the effect that they desired the witness to go to Arkansas, as contestant was too old, and the daughter could not go. *Held*, that the cousin's evidence was competent and material.—*Idem.*

7.   TRUSTS—Parol evidence is inadmissible to show that, in making an absolute devise, the testator intended that the devisee should hold the property in trust for others, under Code, 1873, section 2326, requiring wills to be in writing; and this is so though the devisee acknowledges the trust in writing and defines its extent.—Moran v. Moran, 276.

8.   INTENTION—*Rule in Shelley's Case*—The rule in *Shelley's Case*, if it be in force in the state of Iowa, cannot defeat the intent of a testator as expressed by the language of the will.—Wescott v. Binford, 645.

9.   SAME—In such devise, the fact that testator is presumed to have intended a devise of all his interest in the property, and that the heirs of the devisee could not be definitely known until his death, would not create in him a larger estate than the testator intended him to have.—*Idem.*

10.   SAME—In a devise of land to one "to hold the same during the term of his natural life," and giving him the use, rents, and profits of it during such time, but providing that he should

Wills Continued

"have no power to convey or dispose of the same" for a period longer than his life, and that at his death it should descend to his heirs, the word "heirs" will not be given its technical effect, and the rule in *Shelley's Case* will not apply, as it was testator's clear intention to create a life estate only.—*Idem.*

WITNESS—See Costs, [3], [4]; Evid. [8], [9], [18], [19]; Ins. [15].

AUTHORITIES CITED

IN THE OPINIONS REPORTED IN THIS VOLUME.

A

1 Am. & Eng. Enc. Law, (Second Ed.) 260........................ 326
1 Am. & Eng. Enc. Law, (Second Ed.) 691, *et seq*................. 689
3 Am. & Eng. Enc. Law, (Second Ed.)........................... 408
3 Am. & Eng. Enc. Law, 886.................................... 663
4 Am. & Eng. Enc. Law, 674.................................... 109
5 Am. & Eng. Enc Law, 40...................................... 601
5 Am. & Eng. Enc. Law, (Second Ed.) 440........................ 664
5 Am. & Eng. Enc. Law, (Second Ed.) p. 878.................... 9
11 Am. & Eng. Enc. Law, 378................................... 109
12 Am. & Eng. Enc. Law.. 674
12 Am. & Eng. Enc. Law, 244................................... 334
13 Am. & Eng. Enc. Law, 1164.................................. 596
13 Am. & Eng. Enc. Law, 1187.................................. 595
15 Am. & Eng. Enc. Law, 758................................... ·527
16 Am. & Eng. Enc Law, 462.................................... 691
17 Am. & Eng. Enc. Law, 1154.................................. 77
20 Am. & Eng Enc. Law, 253.................................... 411
20 Am. & Eng. Enc. Law, 597...............................609, 610
22 Am & Eng. Enc. Law, 495 and note........................... 649
23 Am. & Eng. Enc. Law, p. 414................................ ·589
23 Am. & Eng. Enc. Law, 554................................... 343
25 Am. & Eng. Enc. Law, 213................................... 642
29 Am. & Eng. Enc. Law, 203................................... 134
American Cyclopædia, title "Lottery"........................... 518
Angel, Water Courses, (Sixth Ed.) secs. 108a–108s............. 192

B

2 Beach, Insurance, sec. 1203................................. 482
Beach, Modern Equity, sections 1047, 1050..................... 263
Beach, Wills. 66.. 133
1 Bishop, Criminal Procedure (Third Ed.), sec. 586............. 742
2 Bishop, Criminal Law, 181, 183.............................. 729
2 Bishop, Criminal Law, 592................................... 729
2 Bishop, Statutory Crimes, sec. 952.......................... 595
Blackstone, "Bees"... 806
Black, Judgments, sec. 106................................... 673

2 Black, Judgments, secs. 880, 981................................. 260
Brown, Jurisdiction, sec. 1 185
Brown, Jurisdiction, sec. 10 185
Bradner. Evidence, 477... 452
Bradner. Evidence. p. 499, sec. 11........ 692

C

Cooley, Constitutional Limitations, 625.. 196
Cooley, Torts, 485................... 306

E

18 Edward I (Eng.), Chancery 1 650
1 Elliott, General Practice, sec. 240........................... 185
4 Elliott, Railroads, sec. 1549 .....:....................245, 665
4 Elliott, Railroads, sec. 1552.............................. 665
1 Enc., Pleading and Practice, 968........ 404
1 Enc., Pleading and Practice, 1015 and notes.............. 374
2 Enc , Pleading and Practice, 826....... 374
4 Enc., Pleading and Practice, 766............................ 53
4 Enc., Pleading and Practice, 789........ 53

F

Freeman, Judgments (Second Ed), 249........................ 435
Freeman, Judgments (Fourth Ed.), sec. 163..... 371

G

1 Greenleaf, Evidence (Fifteenth Ed.), sec. 41.................... 255
2 Greenleaf, Evidence, sec. 123 and notes................ 520

H

Hay, Principles of Express Disposition of Real Property....... 649

J

Jones, Chattel Mortgages, sec. 44............................ 528
Jones, Chattel Mortgages, sec. 81............................ 527
Jones, Chattel Mortgages, sec. 770......................... ... 529
1 Jones, Evidence, sec. 57.. 255
3 Jones, Evidence, sec. 897....................................... 692
Jones, Mortgages, sec. 471....................................... 609
1 Jones, Mortgages, sec. 472.................................... 609
Jones, Pledges, 590, 591......................... 405
1 Jones, Real Property, sec. 601 *et seq*..... 640
1 Jones, Real Property, sec. 602 and note..................... 650
1 Jones, Real Property, sec. 606................................. 652
Jones, Real Property, secs. 880, 881............................ 388

K

4 Kent, Commentaries, 215................................ 648
4 Kent, Commentaries, *216....... 651

L

Lawson, Expert Evidence, 61, 68................ 452
Lawson, Expert Evidence, 286......................... 449
Lawson, Presumptive Evidence, Rule 66...................... 109
1 Lawson, Rights, Remedies and Practice, sec. 198.............. 451
Lawson, Rights, Remedies and Practice, sec. 3198.......... ... 133

M

1 McClain, Criminal Law, sec. 460. 9
1 McClain, Criminal Law, sec. 737............................ 107
2 McClain, Criminal Law, 9£3.................................. 729
2 McClain, Criminal Law, 968.................................. 729
McCrary, Elections, p. 209......... 196
Mechem, Agency, sec. 121...................................... 277
Mechem, Agency, sec. 168...................................... 277
Mechem, Agency, 276 152
Mechem, Agency, 714.......... 689
Mechem, Public Officers, sec. 856........ 284

N

Niblack, Benefit Soc. & Accident Ins. (Second Ed.) secs. 204, 847. 859

P

1 Parsons, Contracts, (Sixth Ed.) 489......................... ... 520
2 Parsons, Contracts, 517.. 663
1 Pomeroy, Equity Jurisprudence, secs. 554, 557.................. 263
2 Pomeroy, Equity Jurisprudence, secs. 852, 853................. 686
2 Pomeroy, Equity Jurisprudence, sec. 856............... 637
8 Pomeroy, Equity Jurisprudence, sec. 1376 ....:.... 686
Pomeroy, Specific Performance, sec. 361...................... 554

R

Rawle, Covenants, sec. 32......... 479
Rawle, Covenants, (Fifth Ed.) secs. 320, 321.................. 389
8 Redfield, Wills, 59... 222
Rogers, Expert Testimony, sec. 157................... 452
Rogers, Expert Testimony, (Second Ed) sec. 4 12

S

Schouler, Wills, sec. 587 222
Spear. Extradition, p 360........ 828
Story, Equity Jurisprudence, sec. 638 407
Story, Equity Jurisprudence, secs. 1111, 1112.................. 263
Sutherland, Damages, (Second Ed.) sec. 140.... 292
Sutherland, Statutory Construction, sec. 241.................. 585

T

1 Taylor, Landlord & Tenant, sec. 22........................... 549
3 Thompson, Corporations, sec. 4047......................... ... 399
1 Thompson, Trials, sec. 705...... 692

U

Underhill, Evidence, 291 452
Underhill, Evidence, sec. 367................................... 692

V

Van Fleet, Collateral Attack, sec. 3......... 686
2 Van Fleet, Former Adjudication, 925...................... ... 371

W

Wait, Fraudulent Conveyance, secs. 73, 75, 87 368
1 Warvelle, Vendors, 321.. 480
1 Warvelle, Vendors, 325....... 479
2 Washburn, Real Property, *272............................... . 649
Weeks, Attorneys, secs. 126, 340 452
Weeks. Attorneys. (Second Ed.) 687........... 451
2 Wharton, Criminal Law, 1341................ 729
2 Wharton, Criminal Law. sec. 1891............................ 597
Wharton, Criminal Pleading & Practice, 484.................. 345
1 Wharton, Evidence, secs. 442, 446........................... 452
2 Williams, Personal Property, 277............................. 709
Worcester's Dictionary, title "Lottery"....................... 518

CASES CITED

IN THE OPINIONS REPORTED IN THIS VOLUME.

A

Abrams v. Ervin	9 Iowa, 87.	284
Adams v Burton	48 Vt., 86	806
Adkinson v. Breeding	56 Iowa, 26	710
Adolph v. Railway Co	76 N. Y., 530	566
Albee v. Curtis	77 Iowa, 644	869
Albert v. Twohig	85 Neb., 563; 53 N. W. Rep 582.	196
Allen v. Church	101 Iowa, 116	874
Allen v. Craft	109 Ind , 476; 9 N. E. Rep. 919; 58 Am. Rep. 425	649
Allen v. Kirk	81 Iowa, 658	884
Allen v Pegram	16 Iowa, 163	889
Allen v Railway	42 Iowa, 683	411
Allen v Seaward	86 Iowa, 718	590
Allis v. Day	14 Minn , 518 (Gil 388)	451
Amory v. Francis	16 Mass , 808	407
Anderson v. Wedeking	102 Iowa, 446	142
Andre v. Railway	80 Iowa, 107	62
Andrew v Concannon	76 Iowa, 251	586
Atherton v. Dearmond	38 Iowa, 353	561
Attorney-General v. Insur'nce Co	77 N. Y., 274	686
Auxier v. Taylor	102 Iowa, 673	554

B

Babcock v. Wolf	70 Iowa, 676	676
Bacon v. Marshall	37 Iowa, 581	546
Baker v. Washington County	26 Iowa, 148	887
Baldwin v. Railway Co	63 Iowa, 210	144
Baldwin v. Tuttle	23 Iowa, 66	867
Ballinger v. Tarbell	16 Iowa, 491	811
Balm v. Nunn	63 Iowa, 641	674
Baltimore & Ohio R. Co v. State.	81 Md. 871; 32 Atl Rep. 201	694
Bank v Ash	85 Iowa, 74	251
Bank v. Baker	57 Iowa, 197	298
Bank v. Carrington	5 R. I 515	528
Bangs v. Duckenfield	18 N. Y., 595	686
Bank v. Felt	100 Iowa, 680	561
Bank v Honnold	85 Iowa, 852	285, 458
Bank v. Johnston	94 Iowa, 212	182
Bank v. Kellogg	81 Iowa, 126	357
Bank v. Lanahan	66 Md. 461; 7 Atl. Rep. 615	408
Bank v. Schloth	59 Iowa, 816	850
Barber Paving Co. v. Ullman	137 Mo. 543; 38 S. W. Rep. 458	166
Barhydt v. Bonney	55 Iowa, 717	561
Barker v. Railway Co	126 Mo. 143; 28 S. W. Rep. 866	698

Barlow v. Buckingham .... 68 Iowa, 169..................... 698
Barrett v Dean... .... 21 Iowa, 428................44, 789
Bartle v. Curtis .... 68 Iowa, 202.... 479
Bartlett v bilger............... 92 Iowa, 732................... 349
Bates v. Wilson...... 18 Colo 287; 82 Pac. Rep. 615... 260
Baxter v. Hecht .... 98 Iowa, 531..................... 519
Bearss v. Preston.............. 66 Mich. 11 529
Becker v. Waterworks Co....... 79 Iowa, 419....... 887
Beckman v. Coal Co........... 90 Iowa, 252.................. 143
Behrens v. Insurance Co........ 64 Iowa, 19.................. 412
Beindorff v Kaufman .... 41 Neb. 834; 60 N. W. Rep 101.. 680
Bender v. Been...... 78 Io+a, 288.................... 587
Benham v. Chamberlain ...... 39 Iowa, 458.................... 300
Benkert v. Jacoby............ 86 Iowa, 273..... 652
Bennett v. Parker..... 67 Iowa, 451................ 699
Berry v. Davis .... 84 Iowa, 594............... 450
Bertram v. Waterman .... 18 Iowa, 529............... 369
Blake v. Counselman.. .... 95 Iowa, 219.... 458
Blatchford v. Newberry. ... ...100 Ill 484 673
Blizzard v. Applegate.......... 61 Ind. 871................... 451
Blymire v Boistle............ 6 Watts. 182.................. 728
Bomash v. Order of Iron Hall. . 42 Minn 241; 44 N. W. Rep 12... 359
Bond v. Railway Co ....100 Ind. 301.................... 67
Boone v Mitchell .... 33 Iowa, 45..... 252
Boot v. Brewster. .... 75 Iowa, 631.................... 298
Bowman v Railway Co.........125 U. S 465; 8 Sup. Ct. Rep. 689. 469
Boyd v City of Milwaukee. .... 92 Wis 456; 66 N. W. Rep. 603.. 166
Boyd v. Collins................ 70 Iowa, 296.............. 367
Boyd v. Watson ....101 Iowa, 214 186
Boyle v Maroney .... 73 Iowa, 70................. 869
Bradshaw v. Hurst.......... 57 Iowa, 745 298
Brandt v City of Lyons .... 60 Iowa, 172............... 691
Bridgman v. Wilcut .... 4 G Greene, 563. 185
Bridgman v. City of Keokuk.... 72 Iowa, 42 643
Brockman v. City of Creston... 79 Iowa, 589................. 888
Broliar v. Marquis.............. 80 Iowa, 49............... 650
Brown v. Allen............... 85 Iowa, 306...................77, 601
Brown v. Barngrover........... 82 Iowa, 204................... 586
Brown v. Jenks .... 98 Cal. 10; 82 Pac Rep. 701..... 166
Brown v. Maryland .... 12 Wheat. 419................. 469
Brown v. Railway Co........... 88 S. W. Rep. (Ky.) 862.......... 663
Brown v. Scott .... 2 G Greene, 454............... 674
Bruner v. Wade............... 85 Iowa, 666................ 386
Bryant v. Fink............... 75 Iowa, 516 386
Buchanan v Marsh............ 17 Iowa, 494............... 868
Buchanan County Bank v Rail-
  way Co .... 62 Iowa, 494................. ... 699
Bucklew v. Railway Co......... 64 Iowa, 603................. 144
Buckwalter v Craig........... 24 Iowa, 215................... 383
Buell v. Buckingham.......... 16 Iowa, 284. 397
Burns v McNally.......... 90 Iowa, 432................. 642
Burroughs v Ellis .... 76 Iowa 649 675
Burtis v Cook .... 16 Iowa, 194............. 311
Buse v. Page.................. 82 Minn 111; 19 N. W. Rep. 736;
                                20 N. W. Rep. 95............ 356
Butler v. Railway Co.......... 87 Iowa, 206................... 694
Buzby v. Traction Co.........126 Pa. St 559; 17 Atl. Rep. 895.. 566
Byerly v. City of Anamosa..... 79 Iowa, 204.................... 113
Byers v. Rodabaugh .... 17 Iowa, 58................. ... 526

C

Cadle v. Baker................. 20 Wall , 650........ 686
Calder v. Chapman. .... 52 Pa. St , 359..... 609
Cameron v. City of Burlington.. 56 Iowa, 820 642
Campbell v. Ayres............. 6 Iowa, 839............... ...., 702
Carbon Co. v. Mills............ 78 Iowa, 460.................... 508
Carruthers v. Towne........... 86 Iowa, 818.................... 449
Carter v. City of Dubuque .... 85 Iowa, 416.................... 388
Catter v. Steyer. .... 98 Iowa, 588.................... 215
Casady v. Woodbury County.... 13 Iowa, 118.................... 663
Case v. Dwire................. 60 Iowa, 442.................... 651
Case v. Plato................. 54 Iowa, 64.................... 674
Casey v Tama County.... .... 75 Iowa, 655.................... 891
Cedar Rapids M. R. Co. v. County
  of Sac .... 46 Iowa, 243 274
Central Iowa R'y Co. v. Piersol.. 65 Iowa, 498.................. 486
Charlton v. Sloan. .... 76 Iowa, 288.................. 182
Chicago & S. W. R. Co. v. Packet
  Co.................. .... 88 Iowa, 377....... 554
Chisholm v. Forny............. 65 Iowa, 833.................... 508
Christ v. Polk County.......... 48 Iowa, 302..... 234
Chung Kee v. Davidson......... 73 Cal., 522; 15 Pac. Rep. 100.... 728
Church v Howard.............. 79 N. Y., 415.................... 692
City of Clinton v. Clinton & L.
  H Railway Co............... 37 Iowa, 61..................... 587
City of Davenport v. C , R. I. &
  P. Railway Co............... 38 Iowa, 633 698
City of McGregor v. Boyle ..... 34 Iowa, 268 487
City of New Orleans v. Ferguson 28 La. Ann 240.................. 641
Clark v. Barnes .... 72 Iowa, 568.................... 528
Clark v. City of Des Moines..... 19 Iowa, 199.................... 889
Clark v. Riddle. ....101 Iowa, 270 295
Clark v. Town of Easton.......146 Mass , 43; 14 N. E Rep. 795.. 687
Clarke v. Railway Co.......... 67 Am. Dec , 205 and note. 664
Clements v. Railway Co........ 74 Iowa 442.................... 601
Coggeshall v. City of Des Moines 78 Iowa, 235. ....164, 572
Coggin v. Railway Co .... 13 Kan. 416 663
Coglan v. Beard .... 65 Cal. 58; 2 Pac, Rep. 787.......196
Colby v. Kimball Co............ 99 Iowa, 821.................... 527
Cole v. Edwards............... 98 Iowa, 477 873
Cole v. People ....161 Ill. 16; 43 N. E. Rep. 607. ... 166
Collins v. Chantland .... 48 Iowa, 241.................... 485
Collins v. Hills .... 77 Iowa, 181.................... 474
Collins v Vandever .... 1 Iowa, 578 554
Commonwealth v. Bishman.....138 Pa St. 639; 21 Atl. Rep. 12;
  ....473, 597
Commonwealth v. Manderfield . 8 Philad. 457...... 597
Commonwealth v. Paul.........170 Pa. St. 284; 88 Atl Rep. 82... 478
Commonwealth v. S c h o l l e n-
  berger .. ..156 Pa. St. 201; 27 Atl. Rep. 30... 478
Commonwealth v Zelt ....138 Pa. St. 615; 21 Atl Rep. 7.... 478
Conger v. Lowe ....124 Ind. 368; 24 N. E. Rep. 88, 89. 649
Conrad v. Starr .... 50 Iowa, 470.................... 849
Conway v Nichols (on re-hear-
  ing)....................... — Iowa, —.. 299
Conway v. Younkin .... 28 Iowa, 295..... 641
Conwell v. Kuykendall.. .... 29 Kan 707 .. ....·....... 673
Cook v. Association .... 74 Iowa, 746 539
Cooker Co v. Olive Co......... 82 Iowa, 122 699
Cooley v. Brown .... 80 Iowa, 470.................... 871

Corbett v. Berryhill............ 29 Iowa, 157......... 479
Corbett v. Waterman........... 11 Iowa, 87...................... 731
Coriell v. Ham .... 4 G. Greene, 455........... ... 372
Corning v. Medicine Co......... 46 Mo. App. 16 528
Cothren v Connaughton........ 24 Wis. 187...... 657
Cottrell v. Piatt............. ....101 Iowa, 231..................... 291
Cowgell v. Warrington......... 66 Iowa, 666................. .. 300
Craft v. Merrill.................. 14 N. Y. 456................... 328
Crampton v. Marble Co .... 60 Vt. 291. 15 Atl. Rep. 158.. ... 601
Creswell v. Slack .... 68 Iowa, 110................... 368
Cromelin v McCauley.......... 67 Ala. 542 528
Cross v. People..... .... 18 Colo. 821; 32 Pac. Rep. 821... 595
Crowley v Railway Co .... 65 Iowa, 658.................... 144
Cuppy v. Coffman .... 82 Iowa; 214.................... 656
Curtis v. Broadwell............ 66 Iowa, 662. 350

D

Daniel v. Whartenby........... 17 Wall. 639 648
Davis v. Crandall............101 N. Y. 811; 4 N. E. Rep. 721... 262
David v Hardin County.......104 Iowa, 204.......... 295
Davis v. Kelley... . ... 14 Iowa, 523.................... 298
Davis v. Shawhan.......... .... 34 Iowa, 91.................... 367
Davis v. Shearer... .... 90 Wis. 250; 62 N. W. Rep. 1050. 686
Davis v Waterworks Co........ 54 Iowa, 59.................... 723
Dawson v. Railway Co......... 76 Mo. 514 662
Dean v. Dean..... .... 27 Vt. 746..................... 134
Deery v Hamilton............. 41 Iowa, 16................... 434
Denegre v Haun............... 13 Iowa, 240................... 369
Dennis v. Bank............... 19 Neb. 675; 28 N. W. Rep. 512. 299
Desmond v McCarthy .... 17 Iowa, 525................... 687
De Tar v Boone County........ 34 Iowa, 482.................... 387
Dickinson v. Eichorn .... 78 Iowa, 710.................... 214
Dickson v. Chorn.............. 6 Iowa, 19....... 409
Dickson v Harris....... .... 60 Iowa, 727.................... 561
Dilleber v. Insurance Co .... 69 N. Y. 256.................... 692
District Tp. of Clay v. Indepen-
   dent District of Buchanan.... 63 Iowa, 188 274
Doe v. Clark.................. 42 Iowa, 123.................... 371
Donahue v. McCosh........... 81 Iowa, 296.................... 435
Dowd v. Tucker............... 41 Conn 197................... 222
Dowell v. Railway Co.......... 62 Iowa, 629.................. ..712
Dryer v. Insurance Co......... 94 Iowa, 471.................... 357
Dudley v. Sautbine.... .... 49 Iowa, 650..... 531
Duffy v Hobson. .... 40 Cal. 240....... 403
Duncombe v. Powers. .... 75 Iowa, 185.................... 186
Dunlap v. Thomas............. 69 Iowa, 358... 519
Dunlavy v. Railway Co......... 66 Iowa, 485.................... 78
Dunn v. Zwilling.............. 94 Iowa, 233. 586
Dunton v. Woodbury.......... 84 Iowa, 74.................. 398
Durant v. Comegys............ 2 Idaho, 809; 26 Pac. Rep. 755.. 673
Dyer v. Harris................. 22 Iowa, 268..... 303

E

Easton v. Montgomery......... 90 Cal. 307; 27 Pac. Rep. 280.... 479
Edwards v. Cottrell............ 43 Iowa, 194..... 527
Eggleston v. Boardman........ 37 Mich. 14.. 451
Ela v Edwards............... 16 Gray, 91.................... 133
Emigrant Co v. Fuller......... 83 Iowa, 599.................... 702
Emmitt v. Brophy....... ...... 42 Ohio St. 82................... 260
Engleman v. State .... 2 Ind. 91..................... 210

Epley v. Ely..................... 68 Iowa, 70. 259
Eslow v. Mitchell.............. 26 Mich. 500................. .. 527
Evans v. Hunter. .... 86 Iowa, 413............... 262
Evans v. McConnell .... 99 Iowa, 326................. .. 526
Evans v. People...... .... 90 Ill. 384..... 729
Everingham v. Harris.......... 99 Iowa, 447................. 645
Everman v. Herndon..... ..... 71 Miss. 823; 15 South. Rep. 185. 403
Exhaust Ventilator Co. v. Chicago M. & St. P. Railway Co... 69 Wis. 454; 34 N. W. Rep. 509... 498

F

Fair v. Howard. .... 6 Nev., 804 528
Fairbairn v. Dana .... 68 Iowa, 281............ 590
Fairburn v. Goldsmith.......... 56 Iowa, 847............ 386
Faivre v. Gillan ... . 84 Iowa, 573............... 368
Falker v Linehan... .... 88 Iowa, 641............... 518
Farley v. Budd................. 14 Iowa, 289............... 698
Farlow v. Kemp.............. 7 Blackf, 544................. 728
Farmers Loan & Trust Co. v. City of Newton.............. 97 Iowa. 502.................... 640
Farrell v Bean............... .. 10 Md., 217. 529
Faust v Railway Co...........104 Iowa, 241............... 665
Fehler v. Gosnell. .... 85 S. W. Rep. (Ky.) 1125........ 166
Fenton v. Railway Co..... .....126 N. Y.,625; 26 N. E. Rep. 967.. 566
Ferguson v. Henry. .... 95 Iowa, 489.............. 197
Ferguson v. Miller............. 18 Am. Dec, 519............... 306
Festorazzi v St. Joseph's Catholic Church.................104 Ala., 827; 18 So Rep. 894...... 226
Field v. Schricher .. .. 14 Iowa, 119...:............... 422
Findla v. City and County of San Francisco .... 18 Cal., 534................. 888
First Congregational Church v. City of Muscatine...... ..... 2 Iowa, 61.................... 52
Fisher v. District Court......... 75 Iowa, 232.................... 52
Fisher v. Muecke.............. 82 Iowa, 547............... 417
Fitch v. Casey................. 2 G., Greene, 800.............. 479
Flagg v. Flagg............. .... 39 Neb, 229.................... 869
Fleckenstein v. Railway Co.....105 N Y., 655; 11 N. E. Rep. 951. 566
Forbes v. Appleton............. 5 Cush., 117................. 520
Ford v. Railway Co............124 N. Y, 493; 26 N. E. Rep. 1101. 146
Forward v. Insurance Co. .....142 App N. Y, 882; 87 N. E. Rep. 615......................... 412
Foster v. Clinton County........ 51 Iowa, 541............ 285
Frank v. Frank .... 71 Iowa, 646.............. 263
Freburg v. City of Davenport... 63 Iowa, 119 192
French v French............... 84 Iowa, 655...... 70
Frost v. Clark .... 82 Iowa, 298.............. 526
Fuller v. Griffith............... 91 Iowa, 632 836
Fuller v. Stebbin...... .... 49 Iowa, 376 382
Funk v. Creswell.............. 5 Iowa, 84 389
Funk v. Railway Co............ 61 Minn. 435; 68 N. W. Rep. 1099 536
Furnes v. Severtson...........102 Iowa, 322.................. 653
Furst v. Tweed .... 93 Iowa, 300............. 403

G

Galbraith v. Walker..... ..... 95 Pa. St. 481.................... 260
Garbutt v. Association .... 84 Iowa, 298................. 123
Gardner v. Lightfoot............ 71 Iowa, 577...... 512
Gassen v. Hendricks. .... 74 Cal. 444; 16 Pac. Rep. 242.... 528
Gatch v. Garretson......... .. .100 Iowa, 252.................... 526

Gere v. Insurance Co.......... 67 Iowa. 275.............. 449, 601
German Insurance Co. v. Gibe..162 Ill. 251; 44 N. E. Rep. 490.... 413
Getchell v. Allen............ 84 Iowa, 559.................... 349
Guyer v. Douglass............. 85 Iowa, 96................... . 385
Gilbank v. Stevenson......... 30 Wis. 155.................... 657
Gillet v. Mason .... 7 Johns 16.................... 306
Gilman v. McArdle............. 49 N. Y. 451; 2 N. E. Rep. 464.. 227
Gilman v. Railway Co.......... 40 Iowa, 200................... 630
Gilpin v. Gilpin.... .... 12 Colo. 504; 21 Pac. Rep. 612 .. 692
Glen v. Jeffrey............... 75 Iowa, 20................... 65
Glenn v. Statler............. 42 Iowa, 107.... ....-........429, 637
Godderis v. Executors.......... 14 Grat. 102.................. 480
Godding v. Decker............. 3 Colo. App. 198; 32 Pac. Rep.
                                  332...................... 480
Goff v. Kilts................. 15 Wend. 550........... 306
Gohegan v. Leach............. 24 Iowa, 509.... 680
Goll & Frank Co. v. Miller. ... 87 Iowa, 427................. 518
Goode v. Garret.............. 75 Iowa, 713................. 368
Goodenough v. McGrew........ 44 Iowa, 670................. 292
Goodrich v. Brown............ 68 Iowa, 247................. 300
Gould v Hurto................ 61 Iowa, 47................ 185
Graham v. Rooney .... 42 Iowa. 567................ 335
Gravel v. Clough.... .... 81 Iowa, 272 ....527, 601
Green v. Scranage............ 19 Iowa, 461................ 680
Greenleaf v. Railway Co........ 33 Iowa, 52 144
Greenwood v. Jenswold....... 69 Iowa, 53.................. 256
Grier v. Johnson............. 88 Iowa. 102............... 52
Guengerich v. Smith .... 36 Iowa, 587............. ... 553
Guenther v Dewien.:... .... 11 Iowa, 133...... 595
Guthrie v. Guthrie......... 71 Iowa, 744..... 676

H

Halley v. State................ 47 Neb. 566; 60 N. W. Rep. 962.. 473
Hall v. Tuttle .... 40 Am. Dec. 383 and note....... 673
Halsey v. Montrio ... ... 92 Va. 881; 24 S. E. Rep. 258.... 403
Hamilton v City of Shelbyville. 6 Ind. App. 538; 33 N. E. Rep·
                                  1007..................... 388
Hamilton v. Insurance Co .....137 U. S. 370; 11 Sup. Ct. Rep. 133 170
Hannah v. Hawes.............. 45 Iowa; 487................ 650, 652
Hannah v. Carrington.......... 18 Ark 85 529
Hangen v. Hachemeister ... ...114 N. Y. 566; 21 N. E. Rep. 1046. 601
Harback v. Colvin........ ..... 73 Iowa, 638................. 279
Harlin v Stevenson........... 30 Iowa, 371................ 271
Harper v. Perry.............. 28 Iowa, 57................. 512
Harris v. Brink.............. .100 Iowa, 366................ 336
Hart v. Railway Co........... 69 Iowa, 485............... 663
Hartman v. Young............. 17 Or. 150; 20 Pac Rep. 17.... .. 196
Harvey v. Tama County........ 53 Iowa, 228................ 629
Haskel v. City of Burlington.... 30 Iowa, 232............ 539
Hawkeye Insurance Co. v. Bain-
  ard........................ 73 Iowa, 180................ 630
Hayden v Hefferan..... .... 99 Mich 262; 58 N. W. Rep. 59.. 260
Hayward v. Munger........... 14 Iowa, 516............... 553
Head v. Hargrave ....105 U S. 45 451
Heitman v. Griffith..... ...... 43 Kan. 553; 23 Pac Rep. 589.... 528
Hendershott v. Ping........... 24 Iowa, 134............... 369
Henry v. Vliet.. .... 38 Neb. 130; 49 N. W. Rep. 1107. 528
Hickman v. Layne............. 47 Neb 177; 66 N. W. Rep. 298.. 694
Hick v. Swan................. 97 Iowa, 556 ....;...... 284
Hicks v. Walker... .... 2 G. Greene, 440.............. 668

Hilgers v. Quinney........ .... 51 Wis. 62; 8 N. W. Rep. 17..... 748
Hodges v. Tama County....... 91 Iowa, 578.................... 858
Hoffman v Conner........ .... 76 N. Y. 121 601
Hoge v. Hoge .... 1 Watts 216.................. 222
Holmes v. Mattoon ....111 Ill 28; 58 Am. Rep. 602...... 464
Hooker v. Axford............. 88 Mich. 454 222
Hopkins v. Grimes............ 14 Iowa, 78.................... 652
Hopkinson v Knapp Spaulding
  Co .... 92 Iowa, 328.................... 28
Hopkins v. Lewis............. 84 Iowa, 691.................. 474
Howery v. Hoover .... 97 Iowa, 581.................. 527
Hubbard v. Insurance Co....... 33 Iowa, 325.................. 412
Huff v. Farwell. .... 67 Iowa, 298. 604
Hull v. Ruggles .... 56 N. Y. 424.................. 595
Humphrey v. Havens... .. .... 9 Minn. (Gill 801) 318.......... 674
Hungate v Reynolds.......... 78 Ill. 425 529
Hunt v Hunt .... 72 N. Y. 217 185
Hunt v Insurance Co.......... 67 Iowa, 742.................. 326
Hurber v. Baugh............. 43 Iowa, 514 493
Hurd v. Neilson..............100 Iowa, 555.................. 142

I

In re Bein................. ... 42 Fed Rep, 545.... 473
In re Cook's estate .... 77 Cal, 220; 17 Pac. Rep. 938; 19
                                     Pac. Rep. 481............... 678
In re Edwards' estate.......... 58 Iowa, 431.................. 675
In re Eysaman ....118 N. Y, 62; 20 N E. Rep 613... 692
In re Harmon................. 43 Fed. Rep, 872. 478
In re Lennons .... 58 Iowa, 760.................. 519
In re Lyon's estate .... 70 Iowa, 375.................. 560
In re Miller's will..... ...... 73 Iowa, 123 560
In re Minor .... 69 Fed Rep, 285............... 478
In re Newcomb's will.......... 98 Iowa, 176 264
In re Pyle .... 82 Iowa, 146.................. 31
In re Rahrer. .. ..140 U. S., 545; 11 Sup Ct. Rep. 865 469
In re Schouler ....134 Mass, 426................. 280
Independent District v. King... 80 Iowa, 497...... 715
Insurance Co v. Bean.......... 42 Neb, 537; 60 N. W. Rep. 907.. 178
Insurance Co v. Henderson.... 38 Iowa, 450.................. 186
Insurance Co v Hesser .... 77 Iowa, 881.. 674
Iowa Union Telegraph Co. v.
  Board .... 67 Iowa, 250.... 540

J

Jackson v. Gould. .... 96 Iowa, 488.................. 880
Jackson v Vickory .... 1 Wend., 406..... 134
Jacobs v Jacobs. .... 42 Iowa, 600.................. 422
Jacobson v Miller.. .... 41 Mich. 93; 1 N. W. Rep. 1018.. 184
James v. Day. .... 37 Iowa, 164.................. 721
Jamison v Burton............. 43 Iowa, 282.................. 531
Jayne v Drorbaugh .... 63 Iowa, 711.................. 874
Jenkins v. Coal Co. .... 82 Iowa, 618 637
Jessup v Osceola County. ..... 92 Iowa, 178.......... 391
Johnson v. Railway............ 69 Miss 191; 11 So. Rep 104... 664
Jones v. Bamford ... . 21 Iowa, 217.................. 604
Jones v. Blun..... ....145 N. Y. App 888; 89 N. E. Rep.
                                     954... 686
Jordan v Circuit Court......... 69 Iowa, 180................... 53
Jordan v. Hunnell............. 96 Iowa, 834........... 710

Jordan v. Kavanaugh.......... 68 Iowa, 152.................... 691
Jordan v. Lendrum............. 55 Iowa, 488........... 384

K

Kaiser v. Seaton................ 62 Iowa, 468.................... 539
Kane v. Barstow............... 42 Kan. Sup. 465; 28 Pac. Rep.
　　　　　　　　　　　588.................... 153
Kavalair v. Machula........... 77 Iowa, 121 57
Keith v. State................... 91 Ala. 2; 8 So. Rep. 858...... .. 471
Kelley v. Mann................. 56 Iowa, 625 ....859, 710
Kelley v. Incorporated Town of
　West Bend................... .01 Iowa, 669.... 453
Kentucky v. Brooks............ 1 G. Greene, 898............... 539
Kerns v. Railway Co... .... 94 Iowa, 126................... 142
Kiene v. Gmehle............... 85 Iowa, 813.................650, 658
Kiene v. Hodge................. 90 Iowa, 212..... 349
Kimball v. Bryan.............. 56 Iowa, 682.................... 586
Kinnick v. Railway Co... ...... 69 Iowa, 665................... 663
Kitzmiller v. Van Renselaer..... 10 Ohio St. 68................ .. 257
Kleppner v. Laverty........... 70 Pa. St 73...... 649
Knapp v. Edwards .... 57 Wis 196; 15 N. W. Rep. 140.. 182
Knostman v. Davenport........ 98 Iowa, 589........... 193
Knowles v. City of Muscatine... 20 Iowa, 248.................... 62
Koon v. Tramel .... 71 Iowa, 187....... 528
Kranert v. Simon............... 65 Ill. 844..................... 527

L

Lacelles v. Georgia..... ....148 U. S. Rep. 587; 18 Sup. Ct.
　　　　　　　　　　Rep. 681.................... 328
Laidley v. Aiken..... .... 80 Iowa, 112.................... 609
Lakin v. McCormick & Bros.... 81 Iowa, 548................... 369
Lamb v. McConkey............. 76 Iowa, 47..... 435
Lanning v. Railway Co... ..... 68 Iowa, 508.................... 449
Larson v. Williams.............100 Iowa, 114.................... 380
Latham v Shipley.............. 86 Iowa, 543................... 449
Laver v. Hotaling.............115 Cal. 613; 47 Pac. Rep. 598.... 693
Laverty v. Hall's Adm'x....... 19 Iowa, 526.................... 554
Leach v. Kundson............. 97 Iowa, 643................... 526
Lee v. Percival............... 85 Iowa, 639.................... 428
Leek v. Chesley..... .... 98 Iowa, 598................... 459
Leisy v. Hardin.............135 U. S. 100; 10 Sup. Ct. Rep. 865 469
Lemert v. McKibben........... 91 Iowa, 849................... 886
Lepage v. McNamara... .... 5 Iowa, 124.................... 225
Lesure Lumber Co. v. Mutual
　Fire Insurance Co............101 Iowa, 514.................... 170
Letts-Fletcher Co. v. McMaster.. 88 Iowa, 449.................... 648
License Cases.................. 5 How. 504.................... 470
Licthenberger v. Town of Mer-
　iden........................... 91 Iowa, 48 142
Linck v. City of Litchfield...... 31 Ill. App. 104............... 260
Lindsay v Hatch............... 85 Iowa, 832 56
Lidscott v Lamart............. 46 Iowa, 312.................... 300
Lindsay v. District Court....... 75 Iowa, 509................... 374
Linton v. Crosby.............. 54 Iowa, 478.................. ... 519
Litchfield v. Hamilton County.. 40 Iowa, 66.................... 641
Littleton Savings Bank v. Osce-
　ola Land Co.................. 76 Iowa, 660................... 385
Livingston v. McDonald........ 21 Iowa, 160..... 192
Long v. Mellet........ .... 94 Iowa, 548................... 370
Long v. Railway Co........... 64 Iowa, 541.................... 699

Long v. Valleau................ 87 Iowa, 686................... 869
Loomis v. Roberts............. 57 Mich. 284; 28 N. W. Rep. 816. 828
Lorig v. City of Davenport..... 99 Iowa, 479................... 290
Lorillard v. Clyde.. ....122 N. Y. 498; 25 N. E. Rep... 917. 728
Louisville, etc, Co. v. Hedger... 9 Bush 645................... 665
Louthian v. Miller............. 85 Ind 161................... 528
Luce v. Curtis................ 77 Iowa, 847................. 850
Lufkin v. Preston............. 52 Iowa, 235................. 687
Lynch v. Rosenthal...........144 Ind. Sup. 86; 42 N. E. Rep.
                                   1103..................... 596
Lyon v Aiken................. 70 Iowa, 16................. 546
Lyon v. Lenon................106 Ind. 567; 7 N. E. Rep. 811.... 693

M

Macomber v. Peck............. 89 Iowa, 851................. 884
Malloney v. Horan............. 49 N. Y. 111................
Mandersheeid v. District Court. 69 Iowa, 240................. 53
Mann v. Corrington............ 98 Iowa, 108................. 800
Manufacturing Co. v. Sterrett.. 94 Iowa, 158................. 687
Maroney v. Maroney........... 97 Iowa, 711................. 586
Marsh v. Snyder.............. 14 Neb 237; 15 N. W. Rep. 841.. 698
Martin v. Railway Co..........108 N Y. 626; 9 N. E. Rep. 505... 698
Mason v Mason............... 72 Iowa, 457................. 561
Massie v. Mann............... 17 Iowa, 181................. 656
Mathews v. City of Cedar Rap-
  ids......................... 80 Iowa, 468................. 142
Mayer v Woodbury............ 14 Iowa, 57................. 259
Maynes v. Brockway.......... 55 Iowa, 457 698
McCandless v. Hazen. ... . 98 Iowa, 321 686
Mc' armack v. Molburg........ 43 Iowa, 561................. 429
McClain v. McClain .... 57 Iowa, 167................. 586
McClay v. City of Lincoln...... 32 Neb. 412; 49 N. W. Rep. 282. 464
McClure v. Johnson........... 56 Iowa, 620................. 358
McCormack v. Molburg...... 43 Iowa, 561................. 637
McCoy v. Railway Co.......... 44 Iowa, 424................. 663
McCullough v. Insurance Co.. .118 Mo. 606; 21 N. W. Rep. 207.. 482
McCune v. Railway Co .... 52 Iowa, 600................. 663
McDaniel v. Railway Co........ 24 Iowa, 412 663
McDonnell v. Henderson ...... 74 Iowa, 619................. 58
McFall v Railway Co.......... 96 Iowa, 723.................
McGinness v. Barton.......... 71 Iowa, 644................. 586
McGovern v. Railway Co. .....123 N. Y. 281................. 146
McGowan v. Legion of Honor.. 98 Iowa, 118................. 86
McIllhinny v. McIllhinny.......187 Ind. Sup. 411; 87 N. E. Rep.
                                   147..................... 652
McKee v. Reynolds............ 26 Iowa, 578................. 519
McKeever v. Beacom...........101 Iowa, 178................. 461
McKinney v. Herrick .... 66 Iowa, 414................. 637
McKinnon v. Gates............102 Mich. 618; 61 N. W. Rep. 74.. 692
McClain v. Paschal............ 74 Texas Sup 20; 11 S. W. Rep.
                                   837..................... 694
McLenon v Railway Co........ 69 Iowa, 320................. 699
McMannis v. Rice............. 48 Iowa, 361................. 485
McMurtie v. Riddell........... 9 Colo. 497; 18 Pac. Rep. 181... 528
Mecley v. Tomlinson.......... 79 Iowa, 885................. 885
Meech v. Lee................. 87 Mich. 274; 46 N. W. Rep. 888. 880
Meek v. Briggs .... 87 Iowa, 616................. 652
Melhop v. Ellsworth.......... 95 Iowa, 657................. 871
Mellerup v. Insurance Co....... 95 Iowa, 817................. 142
Merrils v. Goodwin .... 1 Root, 209................. 806

Meyer v. City of Dubuque ..... 49 Iowa, 193.................... 641
Meyer v. Houch...... .... 85 Iowa, 319 ......50, 141
Mickley v Tomlinson.......... 79 Iowa, 385.................... 385
Miles v. State .... 58 Ala. 390.......... 729
Miller v. Miller.................104 Iowa, 186. 519
Miller v. Seal .... 71 Iowa, 892......... 350
Miller v. Wolf .... 68 Iowa, 233.... 675
Minear v Hogg.............. 94 Iowa, 641.................... 368
Mo Pac. R'y Co. v. Vandeventer 26 Neb 223; 41 N. W. Rep. 998.. 662
Moomey v. Maas............. 22 Iowa, 340.................... 387
Moore v. Gordon.... .... 24 Iowa, 158.................... 709
Moore v. Railway Co.......... 94 Iowa, 786.................... 671
Moore v. Railway Co.......... 93 Iowa, 484.................... 142
Morris v. Merritt .... 52 Iowa, 496.................... 526
Morrow v. Weed............ 4 Iowa, 77.................... 252
Mulligan v. Railway Co........ 86 Iowa, 188.................... 245
Mudhenk v. Railway Co........ 57 Iowa, 718.................... 62
Murray v. Jones County........ 72 Iowa, 286 352
Murray v. Walker .... 83 Iowa, 202.................... 587
Murray v. Weber.............. 92 Iowa, 757.................... 671
Musch v. Burkhart .... 83 Iowa, 801.................... 706
Myers v. Davis................ 47 Iowa, 325.................... 252

N

Names v. Dwelling House Ins Co. 95 Iowa, 642... 614
Needham v. Gillett.............. 39 Mich. 574....... 711
Nelson v. Hamilton County..... 102 Iowa, 229.................... 387
New Orleans v. New York Mail
  S. S. Co...!............... 20 Wall. 392.................... 53
Newton v. Newell.............. 26 Minn. 529; 6 N. W. Rep. 346.. 196
Nix v. Goodhill. .... 95 Iowa, 282 457
Noyes v. Collins .... 92 Iowa, 566.................... 175
Noyes v. Granger.............. 51 Iowa, 227........ 374

O

Oakes v. Marquardt.... .. .... 49 Iowa, 643.................... 457
Oberholtzer v. Hazen......... . 92 Iowa, 602.................... 334
O'Brien v. Pettis......... .. 42 Iowa, 298.................... 349
Ohio & M. R. R'y Co. v. Tabor.. 98 Ky., 503; 32 S. W. Rep. 168; 36
                                S. W. Rep. 18.............. 662
Oppenheimer v. Barr . ... 71 Iowa, 525..... 691
O'Reilly v. Keim .... 34 Atl. Rep (N. J. Err. & App)
                                1073 403
Orr v. Railway Co .... 94 Iowa, 426 566
Osburn v. City of Lyons.... ....104 Iowa, 160.............. .. 572
Osgood v. Bauder .... 75 Iowa, 550 663
Osgood v Bringolf............. 32 Iowa, 265 689
Osgood v. King .... 42 Iowa, 478.................... 503
Oskaloosa College v. Fuel Co... 90 Iowa, 389.................... 186

P

Painter v. Steffen.......... .. 87 Iowa, 171. 299
Palmer v. Glover .... 73 Ind., 532..................... 260
Parker v Lewis .... 2 G. Greene, 311 669
Parker v State ....135 Ind , 584; 35 N. E. Rep 1105.. 260
Parmenter v. Fitzpatrick ......135 N. Y.. 190; 31 N. E. Rep. 1032. 601
Parsons v. Parsons .... 66 Iowa, 754.................... 12
Peacock v. Williams............ 98 N C, 324; 4 S. E Rep. 550... 722
Pelamourges v. Clark......... 9 Iowa, 1. 12

People v. Clingan.... ....,.... 5 Cal., 889 464
People v. Elliott............... 74 Mich., 264; 16 Am. St 644; 41
                N. W. Rep. 916............. 596
People v. Livingston............ 79 N Y., 290.......... 196
People v. Nelson ....133 Ill , Sup. 565; 27 N. E. Rep.
                217............................ 687
People v. Payment............. 67 N W. Rep. (Mich) 689........ 687
People v. Remington & Sons ...121 N. Y., 328; 24 N. E. Rep. 798.. 406
Perigo v. Railway Co........... 55 Iowa, 326................. 144
Perry v Mills.................. 76 Iowa, 622.............. 371
Petersilea v. Stone............119 Mass , 465 687
Phelps v. James............... 86 Iowa, 398................. 689
Phelps v. Fockler............. 61 Iowa, 340.. 529
Phillips v Carpenter.......... 79 Iowa, 600................. 359
Phillips v Gephart............ 53 Iowa, 396.... 435
Phillips v Phillips....... .... 93 Iowa, 618................. 142
Phinny v. Warren............. 52 Iowa, 332 710
Phœnix Ins Co. v. Findley...... 59 Iowa, 591.. 259
Pierson v Lane .... 60 Iowa, 60................648, 650
Pixley v. Bennett............. 11 Mass ,298............... 257
Plow Co. v. Lamp............. 80 Iowa, 723................. 715
Poole v. Seney................ 66 Iowa, 502................. 5'8
Postlewait v Howes .... 3 Iowa, 364................. 369
Powell v. Holman............. 50 Ark , 85; 6 S. W. Rep. 505.... 196
Powers v. Bowman .... 53 Iowa, 359................. 640
Pringle v Railway Co .... 64 Iowa, 616................. 144
Pursley v Hayes......... .... 22 Iowa, 11................. 686
Puttman v. Haltey. .... 24 Iowa, 425................. 512

R

Rabb v. Albright.......... 98 Iowa, 50................. 526
Rader v. Neal .... 13 W. Va , 373............. 480
Railway Co. v. Crocker......... 95 Ala., 412; 11 So. Rep. 262..... 693
Railway Co v Garteiser........ 9 Tex Civ. App., 456; 29 S. W.
                Rep. 939..................... 694
Railway Co. v. Gower.......... 1 Pickle (Tenn), 465; 3 S. W.
                Rep. 824 692
Railway Co. v. Huffman........ 32 S. W. Rep. (Tex. Civ App), 30 694
Railway Co. v. Ives............144 U. S . 417; 12 Sup Ct. Rep. 679 142
Railway Co v. John........... 9 Tex Civ. App. 342; 29 S. W.
                Rep 558..................... 694
Railway Co v. Lindley.......... 48 Iowa, 11................. 822
Railway Co. v. McRae.......... 82 Tex. Sup. Ct. Rep. 614; 18 S.
                W. Rep. 672; 27 Am. St 926.. 664
Railway Co. v. Packet Co....... 38 Iowa, 377................. 554
Railway Co. v. Piersol .... 65 Iowa, 498................
Railway Co v. Powers ....149 U. S. 45; 13 Sup. Ct. Rep. 748 142
Railway Co. v Reynolds ...... 8 Kan. 628................. 665
Railway Co v. Sherwood......132 Ind. 129; 31 N. E. Rep. 781... 246
Randall v. Packard............142 N. Y. 56; 36 N. E. Rep 823.. 451
Ramm v. Railway Co.... 94 Iowa, 300................. 142
Read v. Insurance Co...........103 Iowa, 307................170, 4;0
Reed v. Larrison.............. 77 Iowa, 399................. 250
Reiff v. Horst....... .... 55 Md 42 519
Remey v. Board .... 80 Iowa, 470................. 571
Rexroth v. Coon.............. 15 R I. 85; 23 Atl Rep. 37..... 306
Reynolds v City of Keokuk ... 72 Iowa, 372................. 78
Reynolds v. Insurance Co...... 80 Iowa, 565................. 77
Rhode v. Bank................ 52 Iowa, 375................. 859
Rhode Is v. Mass............. 12 Pet 718................... 184

Richards v. Humphreys .... 15 Pick. 188.... 263
Richardson v. Eveland. ....126 Ill Sup. Ct. Rep. 37; 18 N. E.
           Rep. 308; 1 L. R A. 203 263
Richardson v. Peterson......... 58 Iowa, 724 458
Ridgeway v Lanphear......... 99 Ind. 253.................. 651
Ripley v. Davis .... 90 Am. Dec. 262.............. 601
Ripley v. Gifford..... .... 11 Iowa, 367.................. 234
Robbins v. Magoun ....101 Iowa, 580.................. 641
Robbins v. Taxing Dist........120 U S. 489; 7 Sup. Ct Rep. 592 471
Roberts v. People............. 19 Mich. 401.............. 109
Robinson v. Erickson.......... 25 Iowa, 85................. 259
Robinson v. Bates .... 3 Metcalf (Mass) 40............ 257
Rogers v. Davis....... .... 91 Iowa. 780.................. 334
Root v. Sturdivant............. 70 Iowa, 55................. 392
Rothrock v Perkinson........ 61 Ind. 89 596
Royal Ins. Co. v. Davies ...... 40 Iowa, 469 264
Russell v. Allen ... .107 U. S. 163; 2 Sup. Ct. Rep. 327 226
Russell v. Nelson .... 32 Iowa. 215.................. 322
Rutherford v. McIvor. .... 21 Ala 750.............. 520
Ryman v. Lynch .... 76 Iowa, 587...... 526

S

Sang v. City of Duluth........ ... 58 Minn. 81; 59 N. W. Rep 878.. 388
Saville v. Chalmers .... 76 Iowa, 325................. 512
Sawrie v. Tennessee............ 82 Fed. Rep. (U.S. Cir. Ct. Tenn.).
           615.... 473
Scarbrough v. Blackman........108 Ala. 656; 18 So. Rep 735 693
Searles v. Lux.......... ... 86 Iowa, 61.................. 386
Schmidt v Deegan............. 69 Wis. 300; 34 N. W. Rep 83 .. 711
Schuck v. Hagar.............. 24 Minn 339 657
Schultz v. Catlin .... 78 Wis. 611; 47 N. W Rep. 946.. 679
Schuttloffel v Collins.........98 Iowa, 576 300
Schwartz v. Railway Co........ 30 La. Ann. 15.................. 566
Searcy v. Martin Woods Co..... 98 Iowa, 420.................. 671
Sears v. Railway Co .... 65 Iowa. 744.................. 536
Seeds v. Grand Lodge.......... 93 Iowa, 175.... 255
Seekell v. Norman .... 76 Iowa, 234.................. 386
Seibert's Appeal............. 18 Wkly Notes, Cas. 276 230
Seidenbender v. Charles .... 8 Am. Dec. 682............. ... 595
Shaffer v. McCrackin............. 90 Iowa, 576.... ....322, 586
Shane v. McNeill................ 76 Iowa. 459.................. 519
Sharon v Sharon .... 79 Cal 633; 22 Pac. Rep 36, 131. 692
Shaw v. Pratt.................. 22 Pick 808.... 490
Sheel v. City of Appleton....... 49 Wis. 125; 5 N. W. Rep. 27.... 185
Shelley v. Smith....... ..... 50 Iowa, 543 383
Shelley's Case.................. 1 Coke, 88 651
Shepard v. Railway Co.. .... 77 Iowa, 56.................. 450
Shepard v Supervisors..... ... 72 Iowa, 258 569
Sheplar v Green............... 95 Cal., 218; 81 Pac. Rep. 42..... 554
Sheriff v. Hull .... 37 Iowa, 174.................. 553
Sherman v Railway Co.........106 N. Y. 542; 13 N. E. Rep. 616.. 689
Shippen v. Hardin .... 84 N. J. Law, 79............ .. 641
Sherman v. Hastings.... 81 Iowa, 372.................. 113
Shreck v. Pierce................ 3 Iowa, 360.................. 479
Shufeldt v. Pease.............. 16 Wis , 659.................. 538
Shuster v Rader... .... 18 Colo , 329; 22 Pac Rep. 505.... 673
Sigler v. Wick................ 45 Iowa, 690.................. 739
Silcott v. McCarty .... 62 Iowa, 161.................. 640
Silva v. Hopkinson............158 Ill. Sup. 386; 41 N. E. Rep.
           1013 649

Simplot v City of Dubuque ... 49 Iowa, 630...... 886
Slemmer v. Crampton.......... 5 I Iowa, 302 650
Slone v Berlin.................. 88 Iowa, 205.................. 886
Smalley v Railway Co....... . 86 Iowa, 574 449
Smith v. Collins .... 90-Ga., 411; 17 S. E. Rep. 1018... 649
Smith v. Humphrey........... 15 Iowa, 428 651
Smith v. Mack........... .- ... 94 Iowa, 589.................. 884
Smith v. McKitterick .... 51 Iowa, 548................. 262
Smith v. Park.... .... 31 Minn., 70; 16 N. W. Rep 490.. 549
Smith v. Railway Co .... 60 Iowa, 522 450
Smith v Skow .... 97 Iowa, 640..... 206
Smith v. Smith . ... 87 Iowa 93 .... 528, 663
Smith v. State .... 54 Ark , 15 S. W. Rep. 882 ... 478
Smith v Worman.............. 19 Ohio St. 145................ 528
Solomon v McLennan... . ... 81 Iowa, 406.... 591
Soward v. Railway Co .... 88 Iowa, 886.................. 62
Spring Co v. Smith .... 90 Iowa, 835.................. 886
Spry v Williams .. .. 82 Iowa, 61.................. 859
Stafford v Fetters .... 55 Iowa, 484 428
Stahl v. Brown .... 72 Iowa, 720.................. 712
Stanton v Embrey............. 93 U. S 548; 23 L. Ed. 985..... 451
State v. Atherton .... 50 Iowa, 189 13
State v. Beabout .. ..100 Iowa, 155................... 18
State v. Birmingham........... 74 Iowa, 407. ....62, 112
State v Board of Assessors .... 46 La. 146; 15 So. Rep. 10...... 471
State v. Bowman............... 79 Iowa, 566................:. 56
State v. Brady .. ..100 Iowa, 191.................... 794
State v. Callendine .... 8 Iowa, 289.................. 345
State v. Chapman .... 1 S. D. 414; 47 N. W. Rep. 411.. 478
State v. Clarke .... 33 N H 829; 66 Am Dec. 728... 596
State v. Comstock .... 46 Iowa, 265.................. 326
State v Coonan................ 82 Iowa, 400.................. 474
State v. Cox................... 65 Mo. 29 729
State v. Cross .... 68 Iowa, 180 726
State v. Dillon .... 74 Iowa, 653................. 726
State v Donahoe .... 78 Iowa, 486................ 726
State v. Eiffert ....102 Iowa, 188............... 694
State v. Elgin .... 11 Iowa, 216................. 702
State v. Finch...... ... . 70 Iowa, 317.................. 449
State v Fowler................. 52 Iowa, 103.................. 726
State v Goetze .... 27 S. E. Rep. (W. Va.) 225....... 473
State v. Hamil .... 96 Iowa, 728.............. 10
State v. Henke................. 58 Iowa, 458.................. 255
State v. Hurd.....................101 Iowa, 891............. 23
State v Jamison.................100 Iowa, 842............... 19
State v Jamison. .... 74 Iowa, 613................. 19
State v. Jarvis................. 21 Iowa, 46. 109
State v. Jones .... 18 Iowa, 269.................. 729
State v Judge of Third Dist.... 18 La , 444 464
State v Kealy.................. 89 Iowa, 94................. 828
State v. Lewis .... 96 Iowa, 286 107
State v Malcolm............... 8 Iowa, 415.................. 109
State v Manley .... 63 Iowa, 344 ....109, 675
State v Maynes .... 61 Iowa, 120................. 449
State v McConkey....... ... 49 Iowa, 499 19
State v McDevitt.............. 69 Iowa, 549................. 12
State v McGregor .... 76 Fed. Rep., 957.............. 473
State v Mecum .... 95 Iowa, 433.................. 734
State v Miller .... 86 Iowa, 639........ 474
State v. Morphy................ 83 Iowa, 270 726

State v. Mullenhoff............ 74 Iowa, 271.................... 493
State v. Munchrath............ 78 Iowa, 268................... 734
State v. Neimeier............. 66 Iowa, 634.... 19
State v. North .... 27 Mo., 464......... 474
State v. O'Day... .... 68 Iowa, 218.................... 886
State v. Parker.............. 66 Iowa, 586............... ...345
State v. Philpot .... 97 Iowa, 365.......... 12
State v. Platt......... .... 24 N. J. Law, 108.............. 641
State v. Porter .... 34 Iowa, 181................. 726
State v. Potter. .... 28 Iowa, 554... 729
State v. Potts........ .... 78 Iowa, 659.............. 857
State v. Redman................ 17 Iowa, 329.............. 845
State v. Schmidtz.............. 65 Iowa, 556.............. 493
State v. Shapleigh............ 27 Mo. 844................. 474
State v Shelton .... 64 Iowa, 833... 12
State v. Stevens.......... ..... 80 Iowa, 391... 729
State v. Sigg .... 86 Iowa, 746............... 13
State v. Smith ....102 Iowa, 656.............. 725
State v. Smith...... .... 100 Iowa, 1................ 826
State v. Tarr....................... 28 Iowa, 897.................... 12
State v. Thompson............ 74 Iowa, 119................. 531
State v. Waite .. ..101 Iowa, 377................ 107
State v. Waltz................. 74 Iowa, 610............... 743
State v. Ward .... 75 Iowa, 641............... 531
State v. Wheelock .... 95 Iowa, 577... 475
State v. Weems .... 96 Iowa, 426................ 10
State v. Wells................. 61 Iowa, 629.................. 252
State v. Willis .... 79 Iowa, 326.............. 591
State v. Winters.............. 44 Kan Sup. Ct. Rep. 728; 25
                              Pac Rep. 287........ 471
State v. Wyatt................. 76 Iowa, 828............... 725
Steamship Co v Tugman ......106 U. S. 118; 1 Sup. Ct Rep. 58.. 239
Steel v. Long ....104 Iowa, 89 740
Stensgaard v. Smith........... 48 Minn. 11; 44 N. W. Rep. 669.. 490
Stern v. Sample............... 96 Iowa, 841.................. 699
Stevens v. Ellsworth........... 95 Iowa, 281.................. 445
Stevens v. Fisher ....144 Mass 114; 10 N. E. Rep. 803.. 262
Stevens v Hinckley... .... 43 Mo. 441...................... 836
Stephens v Railway Co......... 86 Iowa, 827................. 589
Stephens v Santee .... 49 N. Y. 85................... 673
Stewart v. Phenice .... 65 Iowa, 475.... 710
Stidger v City of Red Oak ..... 64 Iowa, 466............... 338
St. Louis R'y Co. v. Weakly..... 50 Ark. 397; 8 S. W. Rep. 134... 665
Stockwell v. Carpenter........ 27 Iowa, 119 849
Stone v. So. Carolina..........117 U. S. 431; 6 Sup. Ct Rep. 799.. 239
Stout v Folger. .... 84 Iowa, 71................. 546
Stromburg v. Lindberg.. .... 25 Minn. 513............... 529
Strong v. Lawrence............ 58 Iowa, 55 885
Suiter v. Turner.... . ... 10 Iowa, 517............... 702
Sullivan v · Carberry........... 67 Me. 531.... 549
Swearingen v. Lahner.......... 93 Iowa, 152......... 440
Sykora v. Machine Co .... 59 Minn. 130; 60 N. W. Rep. 1008. 711

T

Tackaberry v. City of Keokuk.. 82 Iowa, 155................ 640
Taylor v Adair.................. 22 Iowa, 379 303
Taylor v. Jacques...............106 Mass. 291.............. 679
Taylor v. Runyon...... .... 3 Iowa, 474.............. 673
Teague v. Fortsch...... .... 98 Iowa, 92................. 58
Tee v. Ferris................... 2 Kay & J. 357 223

Terre Haute Ry. Co. v. Sherwood.132 Ind. 129; 31 N. E. Rep. 781... 665
Thew v. Miller.................. 78 Iowa, 742.................... 601
Thompson v. Anderson......... 86 Iowa 706........ 286
Thompson v. Boyle .... 85 Pa. St 477.................... 451
Thompson v. Locke .... 65 Iowa, 429.................... 422
Thompson v. Merrill............ 58 Iowa, 419.................... 604
Tinker v. State............... 96 Ala 115; 11 So. Rep. 883..... 478
Tisdale v Insurance Co.......... 26 Iowa, 176.................. 255
Toliver v. Morgan.............. 75 Iowa, 619.................. 702
Towle v. Bradley .... 2 S. D 472; 50 N. W. Rep. 1057. 657
Tracy v Beeson .... 47 Iowa, 155.................... 882
Traer v. Whitman....... ...... 56 Iowa, 443.......... 675
Transue v. Brown............. 31 Pa St. 92.................. 134
Treadway v. Railway Co........ 40 Iowa, 526............ 689
Treat v. Stanton .... 14 Conn., 452... 723
Troup v. Morgan County.......109 Ala , 162; 19 So. Rep. 503..... 284
Trumbull v. Trumbull.........149 Mass., 200.................... 648
Trust Co. v. Maltby .... 8 Paige, 361.................... 609
Tubbs v Garrison........... .. 68 Iowa, 48.................... 449
Turk v. Funk .... 68 Mo., 18 609
Turner v. Hitchcock .... 20 Iowa, 310.................. 292
Tynan v. Paschal.............. 27 Tex., 286.................. .. 134

U

Upton v. Clinton County .... 52 Iowa, 311.................... 284
Union Pac. R'y Co v. Williams 8 Colo. App. 526; 34 Pac. Rep.
                                    781........................ 601
U S v. Dickson .... 15 Pet. 162.................... 210
U. S. v. Olney ... . 1 Deady, 461.............. 595
U. S v. One Hundred thirty two
    Packages .... 22 C C. A., 228; 76 Fed. Rep 864 471
U. S. v. Rauscher..............119 U. S. 407; 7 Sup. Ct. Rep 284. 827

V

Vadakin v. Soper........... ... 2 Am. Lead. Cas. 168 et. seq.... 723
Vail v. Anderson ... . 61 Minn 552; 64 N. W. Rep. 47.. 711
Van Horn v. Litchfield .... 70 Iowa, 12 240
Van Winter v. Henry County... 61 Iowa, 684.................... 891
Verdin v. City of St. Louis .....131 Mo. 26; 27 S. W. Rep. 447; 83
                                    S. W. Rep 480............. 166
Verry v. Railway Co........... 47 Iowa, 549... 689
Vilas v. Downer............... 21 Vt., 419 ... . 419, 451
Visek v. Doolittle .... 69 Iowa, 602..... 300
Von Schmidt v. Wedber... .... 99 Cal., 511; 32 Pac. Rep 532 ... 464

W

Walker v. Insurance Co .... 51 Kan , 725; 33 Pac Rep. 597.... 173
Wallace v. Railway Co......... 67 Iowa, 547..................... 637
Wallick v Pierce..............102 Iowa 746.................... 250
Wallis v. Mease .... 3 Bin., 546.................... 307
Walworth v. Abel.... .... 52 Pa. St 370.................... 711
Wangler v Black Hawk County. 56 Iowa, 884 640
Warburton v. Lauman .... 2 G Greene, 420 604
Ward v Railway Co .... 97 Iowa, 50.................... 288
Washington Bridge Co. v. Land
    & River Improvement Co .... 12 Wash. 272; 40 Pac. Rep. 98 .. 694
Watson v White ....152 Ill Sup. 364; 88 N. E. Rep. 902. 554
Waud v Polk County .... 88 Iowa, 617.................... 142
Way v. Railroad Co....... ..... 40 Iowa, 342 78

Webster County v. Taylor...... 19 Iowa, 117..................... 387
Weis v. Morris.................102 Iowa, 327 186
Welton v. Missouri............. 61 U. S. 275................... 473
Wendt v. Legion of Honor ..... 72 Iowa, 682.... 358
Wetherill v. Harris .... 67 Ind. 452.................... 435
Wheeler v. Wood..... ....104 Mich. 414; 62 N. W. Rep. 577. 263
White v. Levant................ 77 Me. 568; 7 Atl. Rep. 539...... 234
Whitehill v. Wilson...... ...... 3 Pen. & W. 405................ 490
Whitney v. Traynor............. 74 Wis 289; 42 N. W. Rep. 269.. 692
Whitsett v. Railway Co......... 67 Iowa, 150................... 78
Whittlesey v. Frantz .... 74 N. Y. 456.................. 686
Wickham v. Hull ....102 Iowa, 469.................. 268
Widner v. Hunt .... 4 Iowa, 355................... 252
Wilde v. Transportation Co..... 47 Iowa, 274.................. 245
Wilkinson v. Gill............... 74 N. Y. 68; 30 Am. Dec. 264..... 595
Wilkinson v. Pritchard .... 98 Iowa, 308.................. 526
Willard v. Cramer.... .... 86 Iowa, 22 256
Willemin v. Bateson............ 68 Mich. 309; 29 N. W. Rep. 734. 629
Williams v Allison...... .... . 88 Iowa, 278.................. 372
Williams v. Brown............. 28 Ohio St. 551................. 451
Williams v. Vreeland........... 29 N. J. Eq. 417 223
Winan v. Huyck..... ..... 71 Iowa, 459.................. 428
Wind v Iler.... .... 98 Iowa, 324.................. 474
Windsor v City of Des Moines..101 Iowa, 343 164
Winter v Coulthard .... 94 Iowa, 312.................. 675
Woodbury v. Maguire.......... 42 Iowa, 339.................. 881
Wright v. Schmidt.... ...... 47 Iowa, 233.................. 656
Wurtz v. Hart.................. 18 Iowa, 515.................. 408
Wygal v. Bigelow .... 42 Kan Sup. 477; 24 Am. St. Rep.
                              495; 22 Pac Rep. 612....... 529
Wymore v. Mahaska County.... 78 Iowa, 396 712

Y

Yordy v. Marshall County ..... 86 Iowa, 340............... 689
Yates v. Lansing...... ...... 5 Johns 282 184
Yellowstone Kit v. State........ 88 Ala. 196; 7 So. Rep. 338...... 595

Z

Zalesky v. Insurance Co........102 Iowa, 618.. 170
Zavitz v. Preston.......... ..... 96 Iowa, 52.............648, 650, 653
Zeigler v. Vance .. .. 3 Iowa, 528................... 678
Zuver v. Lyons................. 40 Iowa, 510................... 650

STATUTES CITED, CONSTRUED, ETC.,

IN THE OPINIONS REPORTED IN THIS VOLUME.

— — —

UNITED STATES CONSTITUTION.

Art. 1, sec. 8.................469

TWENTY-FIFTH U. S. STATUTES.

Ch 866, secs. 2, 3.............289

CONSTITUTION OF IOWA.

Art 3, sec. 28...............595

ACTS, NINTH GEN. ASSEM.

Ch 169, secs. 7, 9. ....584, 535

ACTS, SIXTEENTH GEN. ASSEM.

Ch. 100... 349
Ch. 100, sec. 13. 87
Ch 103..................... 87

ACTS, EIGHTEENTH GEN. ASSEM.

Ch 88, sec. 1................. 891
Ch. 109, sec. 3............... 641
Ch 210..................... 87
Ch 211......... 116

ACTS, TWENTIETH GEN. ASSEM.

Ch 70. 353
Ch 200..... 891

ACTS, TWENTY-FIRST GEN. ASSEM.

Ch 66, sec 8 103
Ch. 168, secs 17, 18. 548

ACTS, TWENTY SEC'ND GEN. ASSEM.

Ch. 25, sec 1.... 184

ACTS, TWENTY-THIRD GEN ASSEM

Ch 14 162
Ch 14, sec. 3 571
Ch 85 sec 7. .. ..492, 493
Ch 85, sec. 12 ....492, 493

Ch. 43 233
Ch. 48, sec. 6........282, 283, 235

ACTS TWENTY-FOURTH GEN ASSEM.

Ch 12........ 162
Ch 33. sec. 25 197
Ch. 87, sec. 1......... 852

ACTS TWENTY-FIFTH GEN. ASSEM.

Ch. 13, sec 3............. ... 232
Ch 62............ 68, 212, 294, 578
Ch 62, sec. 1...............69, 201
Ch 62, sec 2...............201, 208
Ch 62, sec 3 201
Ch. 62, sec 4............... 209
Ch. 62, sec 5... .... 207, 209
Ch. 62, sec. 6............. 207
Ch. 62, sec. 7............. 209, 295
Ch 62, sec 9....... 201, 208, 210
Ch. 62, secs. 10-15 202
Ch. 62, sec. 11............. 208
Ch 62, sec 16 202
Ch 62, sec. 17 202, 209, 210, 295, 579
Ch. 62, sec 17, par. 2........ 212
Ch 62, sec 19 579
Ch 96 186

ACTS TWENTY-SIXTH GEN ASSEM.

Ch 7.......................
Ch 7................. 3
Ch 96 468

CODE OF 1851.

Sec. 514..................... 485

REVISION OF 1860.

Art. 8, Ch 55 540
Ch 136 657
Sec 956. 887
Sec. 1818. 533
Sec. 1855. 848

Sec. 3446..................... 658
Sec. 3982................ 77

CODE OF 1878

Sec. 45. 70
Sec. 45, Sup Div 2........... 70
Sec 45, Par 11 209
Sec. 465. 165
Sec. 527. 112
Sec. 803. 641
Sec. 805. 641
Sec. 806. 641
Sec. 812. 641
Sec. 831..................... 642
Sec. 1082....... 503
Sec. 1289. 61
Sec. 1309.......534, 586, 587, 538
Sec 1487 351
Sec. 1488 351
Sec. 1490. 705
Sec. 1492.................... 705
Sec. 1539.......531, 576, 577, 578
Sec 1557... ......575, 577, 578
Sec. 1934............. .... 220, 221
Sec. 2000 300
Sec. 2017 ....285, 457
Sec. 2031................. 114
Sec. 2878.................... 260
Sec. 2080. 577
Sec. 2107.................... 558
Sec 2114 561
Sec. 2119................ 522
Sec 2122 506
Sec 2202 188
Sec. 2203......... 188
Sec 2204.................. 188
Sec 2205.......... 188
Sec. 2206............... 188
Sec 2326 220
Sec. 2367 710
Sec. 2371. 359
Sec 2372..... 359
Sec. 2379.... .... 30, 31
Sec. 2384 742
Sec. 2421................... 268
Sec. 2526.. 709
Sec 2579 282
Sec. 2603 ....378, 380
Sec. 2615.................... 380
Sec 2630..............281, 575
Sec. 2683 303
Sec 2718 344
Sec 2729...............291, 392
Sec. 2838 54
Sec 2882 367
Sec 2931. .... 656, 658
Sec 2933.................... 73
Sec 2934 73
Sec. 2942 590

Sec. 2944 590
Sec 3154.............54, 380, 589
Sec. 3155.................54, 590
Sec. 3156.................... 590
Sec. 3157................... 380
Sec 3158 380
Sec. 3178 386
Sec 3180.................... 385
Sec 3181.................... 385
Sec. 3182 385
Sec. 3184 58
Sec. 3186. ....343, 374
Sec. 3189 343
Sec. 3192 343
Sec. 3223.................... 571
Sec. 3224. 569
Sec. 3389.................... 343
Sec. 3500... 53
Sec 3576.................... 656
Sec. 3540.................... 656
Sec. 3630 235
Sec. 3689.................. 76
Sec. 3642................... 679
Sec. 3814.................... 591
Sec. 3861................ ... 3
Sec 3863.................... 12
Sec. 3871... 106
Sec. 3908................825, 826
Sec 4043.................... 595
Sec 4073 17
Sec. 4109................233, 234
Sec. 4314................325, 326
Sec. 4337.................... 20
Sec. 4345................... 20
Sec. 4349................... 344
Sec. 4352 21
Sec. 4357 21
Sec 4364 21
Sec 4444 21
Sec 4450 21
Sec. 4469.................... 53

CODE OF 1897.

Tit. 20, Ch 2 463
Sec. 198 748
Sec. 242 675
Sec. 248 675
Sec. 1169 597
Sec. 1356 640
Sec. 1554....... 104
Sec. 2074.................... 662
Sec 2075..... 537
Sec. 2355..... 706
Sec. 2427................. 103
Sec 2818................... 586
Sec. 3070................... 561
Sec 3154.................... 519
Sec. 3435................... 526
Sec. 3475.................... 463

Sec 3549 586
Sec 3769 673
Sec 3784 673
Sec 3801.... 673
Sec 3818...... 697
Sec 3954 675
Sec. 4016 457
Sec 4017.... 457
Sec 4128.... 463
Sec. 4469..... 53

Sec. 5059 729
Sec 5360................... 734

M'CLAIN'S CODE.

Sec 3113........ 256
Sec 3317...........847, 849, 350
Sec. 3317, Subd. 4 347
Sec 3644.... 256
Sec. 4331.... 871